Legislative Series

Legislative Drafter's Deskbook
A Practical Guide

By Tobias A. Dorsey

TheCapitol.Net
Alexandria, VA
2006

For over 30 years, TheCapitol.Net and its predecessor, Congressional Quarterly Executive Conferences, have been training professionals from government, military, business, and NGOs on the dynamics and operations of the legislative and executive branches and how to work with them.

Our training and publications include congressional operations, legislative and budget process, communication and advocacy, media and public relations, research, business etiquette, and more.

TheCapitol.Net is a non-partisan firm.

Our publications and courses, written and taught by current Washington insiders who are all independent subject matter experts, show how Washington works.™ Our products and services can be found on our web site at <*www.TheCapitol.Net*>.

Additional copies of the *Legislative Drafter's Deskbook* can be ordered directly from the publisher. Critical updates to the *Legislative Drafter's Deskbook* and secure online ordering are available on the *Deskbook's* web site: <*www.LegislativeDraftersDeskbook.com*>.

The Legislative Series includes the *Congressional Deskbook* by Judy Schneider and Michael Koempel, the *Congressional Directory*, and the Congressional Operations Poster.

A special version of *Legislative Drafter's Deskbook* is used as part of the course materials in a legislative drafting course offered by TheCapitol.Net. See our web site for more information: <*www.DraftingLegislation.com*>.

Citation Form—URLs

We use a standard style for all web addresses, also known as Uniform Resource Locators (URLs). URLs appear in text next to the first mention of the resource being described, and are surrounded with open and close angle brackets.

For URLs that have the standard web addressing form at the beginning of the URL of "http://www." we show only the initial "www." For example, the URL "http://.www.domainname.com" will appear in text and tables as "<*www.domainname.com*>".

For URLs that begin with anything other than "www.," such as "http://thomas.loc.gov", the URL will appear in text and tables as "<*http://thomas.loc.gov*>". For example, the URL "http://www3.domain.gov" will appear in text and tables as "<*http://www3.domain.gov*>".

Production and prepress by Zaccarine Design, Chicago, IL. *zacdesign@mac.com*

Library of Congress Control Number 2006923333

Legislative Drafter's Deskbook
Softcover: ISBN: 158733-209-4
ISBN 13: 978-1-58733-209-8
Hardbound: ISBN: 158733-015-6
ISBN 13: 978-1-58733-015-5

Acknowledgments

I happily acknowledge the many people who have helped shape this book. Pope Barrow took a chance by hiring me, breaking with the office's tendency to hire lawyers fresh out of law school. (There is a sense, in other words, in which this is all his fault.) Within the office, my primary drafting influences have been—for better or for worse—Paul Callen, Bob Cover, and Doug Bellis. Bob, Doug, Pete Goodloe, Noah Wofsy, Sherry Chriss, Lisa Daly, and Warren Burke made important contributions to the manuscript. So also did my colleague from the Senate side, Frank Burk.

For Chapter Ten, I am in the debt of Clint Brass, whose expertise in dealing with the topics covered in that chapter is surpassed only by his class and patience in dealing with me. In several of the appendices, and in a variety of places throughout the book, I have relied on other writers who have gone before, writing things—and thinking through things—better than I could myself. I am in their debt as well.

I also acknowledge Mike Cifrino in Washington, Tom Carey and John Sheldon in Maine, and George Martin, Mark Jones, Steve Dake, and Suellen Anderson in California, who have helped shape me as a lawyer; and colleagues (too many to name) at several newspapers, but especially at *The Cornell Daily Sun*, who have helped shape me as a writer. My wife Mollie has given me the support and encouragement I needed to see this project through; she is my treasure, and this book is dedicated to her.

Toby Dorsey
Silver Spring, Maryland

Acknowledgments

[illegible]

[illegible]

[illegible]

About the Author

Tobias A. Dorsey is an attorney in the Office of the Legislative Counsel of the U.S. House of Representatives. Within that office, he works primarily on issues relating to national defense, homeland security, and civil and criminal justice. He has taught at drafting seminars and is an active member of various drafting and professional associations. He serves on the governing council of the Capitol Hill Chapter of the Federal Bar Association.

Before joining the office, Mr. Dorsey was a trial and appellate lawyer in private practice. He has brought appeals to the highest state courts of Maine and California and to the Supreme Court of the United States. He has written articles, edited a legal magazine, and directed the in-house research and writing program at several law firms. He is a member of the bar in Maine, Massachusetts, and California, and a member of the bar association of the Supreme Court of the United States.

Before becoming a lawyer, Mr. Dorsey was a reporter and editor for several newspapers. He earned his bachelor's degree from Cornell University and his law degree from UCLA School of Law.

Mr. Dorsey lives in Maryland with his wife, children, and border collie.

Table of Contents

Legislative Series

Legislative Drafter's Deskbook

A Practical Guide

By Tobias A. Dorsey

Being a Drafter

Chapter 1

Drafting is not just a technical job; it requires foreseeing every possible question that may arise and eliminating every ambiguity.

This I really learned in the winter of 1935 from a great and unsung teacher. He was Middleton Beaman, legislative counsel of the House of Representatives. A tense, caustic, redheaded Yankee, he reminded me of a Vermont schoolmarm; and it was this role that he played when he and I appeared, day after day, at the executive sessions of the Ways and Means Committee. The committee's procedure was to read the bill, paragraph by paragraph. No sooner was a sentence read, however, than Mr. Beaman was on his feet asking questions: Where the bill said that employees should receive old age benefits, did it mean to include American employees stationed abroad? If the committee members said No, then Mr. Beaman, terrierlike, would ask: What about a contractor in Detroit who sent his regular crew on to a job for a few days in Windsor, Ontario? What about seamen on the Great Lakes? A cook on a ship that went from Seattle to Alaska, through Canadian waters? He insisted on answers, and the committee members generally complied.

Not always did they comply quickly. . . .

Thomas H. Eliot, "The Social Security Bill: 25 Years After," 206 *The Atlantic* 72 (August 1960)

Intellectually, the draftsman's skills are the highest in the practice of law. Judges at bottom need merely reach decisions . . .; negotiators and advocates need understand only as much of a situation as will gain a victory for their clients; counselors can be bags of wind . . . . But the documents survive, and to draw them up well requires an extraordinary understanding of everything they are supposed to accomplish. . . . Probably the greatest compliment a lawyer can receive from his profession (a compliment never publicized) is an assignment to draft a major law.

Martin Mayer, *The Lawyers* 50–51 (1966)

Being a Drafter

Chapter 1

§ 1.00 Introduction

Legislative drafting is—to the extent it is writing at all—the form of writing used for legislative measures, a category that covers original bills and resolutions as well as amendments. Ultimately, legislative drafting is the form of writing used for enacted law. The focus of this book is on legislative drafting for the Congress of the United States, but many of the principles described here apply just as well to drafting for other legislatures.

Within the profession, legislative drafting is known simply as drafting, so this book prefers that simpler term throughout. Likewise, this book uses "drafter" to mean one who drafts, "client" to mean one for whom the drafter drafts, and "draft" (as a noun) to mean the text prepared by the drafter for the client.

As forms of writing go, drafting is not freewheeling like poetry, nor showy like rhetoric, nor personal like a novel. Drafting is disciplined, rigorous, and analytical. Done well, drafting can also be creative, elegant, and clever. (Unfortunately, drafting is not always done well.)

Drafting is done by a wide variety of people with a wide variety of qualifications. Some drafters specialize in drafting, some do not. Some are full-time drafters, some not; some are in public service, some not. A drafter may or may not be a lawyer, though for some of the more advanced tasks, being a lawyer may be useful or even required.

The purpose of this book is to provide practical advice on drafting to anyone who does, or may, engage in drafting, and indirectly to provide insight into the drafting process to other interested people. For example, this book is for people who are more interested in policy than in drafting, but want to understand why drafters operate the way they do. It is also for people who are more interested in reading and interpreting the law than in drafting, but want to understand why laws are drafted the way they are. It is hoped that this book will be accessible to beginners while remaining valuable to veterans.

The traditional method of training drafters is to train them on the job; the consensus is that drafting is best learned holistically, on a case-by-case basis. For that reason this book is best used as a resource, not a course. It is a supplement to, not a substitute for, the learning that comes from experience.

The author has nearly twenty years' experience in writing and the law, first as a journalist, then as a trial and appellate lawyer, and finally as an assistant counsel in the Office of the Legislative Counsel of the United States House of Representatives. (The views expressed here are solely his own.) Based on his experiences, the author designed this book to answer the variety of questions about drafting that arise daily in the work of individuals with a professional interest in how bills, resolutions, and laws are drafted. The approach used here is pragmatic: You will find no linguistic theories or esoteric conundrums discussed here. What you will find is solid advice for everyday drafting projects.

§1.10 The Essence of Drafting

The great misconception about drafting is that it has very much to do with writing. The truth is, the actual task of writing—choosing the words and putting them into effective form—is only a small piece of the drafter's task. The draft is merely the output, not the essence, of the drafter's work.

The process of drafting is, more than anything else, a process of spotting, presenting, and resolving issues. Every drafting assignment has issues; some are policy issues, some are technical issues, but all require judgment and decision. Policy issues are for the client to resolve, but the client can't resolve an issue without first being aware of it.

And so, the most fundamental part of a drafter's job is to spot issues, present them to the client, and help the client think through them in an informed way.

Of course, the writing is important, too. Thinking and writing do, in large part, go hand in hand. But at the end of the day, if the policy is thought through properly, great writing isn't needed—and if not thought through properly, great writing won't help.

The essence of drafting is to be, as Thomas H. Eliot put it in the quotation at the beginning of this chapter, a "Vermont schoolmarm." You do not need to be tense, caustic, redheaded, or a Yankee, but you do need to foresee every doubt and difficulty and to point them out, "terrierlike," so that there is no risk that they will be overlooked.

§ 1.11 The Drafter and the Policymaker

Although some policymakers do their own drafting, the policymaking function is best kept distinct from the drafting function.

A policy is, more or less, a proposed change in the way the government operates with respect to people. Making policy requires judgments about substantive merit ("Would Policy A be good for the country?") and political consequences ("Would Policy A help me get re-elected?").

A draft is the written expression of a policy—ideally, expressed in a manner that accurately reflects the policy and effectively carries out the policy. Drafting requires judgments about substantive accuracy ("Does this draft carry out Policy A, no more and no less?") and practical consequences ("What problems or misunderstandings might arise once this is set in motion?").

The relationship between drafter and client is one of agent to principal. If the drafter is an attorney, the relationship is also one of attorney to client. The drafter performs a service for the client and has a duty to do so faithfully. A court would probably characterize the drafter (whether or not an attorney) as a fiduciary with respect to the client, standing in a special position of trust and confidence and having special, heightened obligations. It is not a two-way street: The client is probably not a fiduciary with respect to the drafter, though the client may well have a general duty of good faith and fair dealing and, depending on the particulars of the arrangement, a duty to provide compensation.

As a fiduciary, a drafter has a duty is not merely to provide an accurate and effective draft. The drafter is not a scrivener in an arm's-length transaction, but an advisor in a relationship of trust. The drafter must look out for the client's best interest and, in doing so, must be thorough and candid. In a sense, the drafter is in the "client protection business."

As a drafter, you have a duty to warn the client when a proposal is sloppy or problematic or unconstitutional. You should also be alert for things that might make the client look bad. For example, if you notice that the client's short title forms an unfortunate or embarrassing acronym, you should find a gentle way to let the client know.

You may have an interest in promoting "good government," respecting the institution of Congress, keeping existing laws tidy, and similar considerations. Indeed, some who write about drafting assert that a drafter has a duty directly to the legislature or the public, or both, to further these interests. Be careful; the assertion may go too far—the duty asserted more likely applies to a legislator than to a drafter. (But see § 9.70, "Avoiding Damage to the Statute Book.") Regardless, if a legislator has a duty to further these interests, then surely it is appropriate for a drafter, as a fiduciary, to make sure the client does not overlook them.

Having described all those duties, bear in mind that your duties are moderated by a rule of reasonableness—that is, what is reasonable under the circumstances.

§ 1.12 How Policy Can Influence Drafting

Ultimately, the drafting project belongs not to the drafter, but to the client. The client supplies the policy, and the client decides whether and how to use the draft. Accordingly, all decisions, even technical decisions, are ultimately for the client to make.

Many decisions are substantive—they will have an effect on people if enacted. The client may stick with a policy even though it is ambiguous, unworkable, or unconstitutional. Making policy is the client's responsibility.

Some decisions are not substantive. And yet, in a real sense, every decision is a policy decision. For example, many clients want a catchy short title. Many want findings with zing and flair. Some want words that are politically charged. A very few want to divert attention from substance by using a heading or title that twists or disguises the truth. Some refer to this as "spin" or "optics." By any name, this is politics, and making politics, like making policy, is the client's prerogative and the client's responsibility.

Whether the client is making policy or politics, the drafter's fundamental task is not to write, but to advise. Whatever the decision is, the drafter should help it to be fully informed. If you advise that certain words are ambiguous and possibly unconstitutional, and the client says, "so be it," nod and move on; you have done your duty.

§ 1.13 How Drafting Can Influence Policy

For a client to dabble in drafting is one thing; for a drafter to dabble in policy is something else entirely. A drafter should not initiate or recommend policy: Doing so probably violates the immediate drafter-client relationship. It also undermines your effectiveness in at least two ways.

First, as a drafter, your livelihood depends on credibility and trust. If you do not give objective advice—or even if you are perceived as one who does not give objective advice—soon enough you will not be asked for advice at all.

Second, your ability to spot and analyze issues depends on your ability to consider a draft from a clinically detached distance. If you are trying to influence a policy, you are more likely to fail, by accident or by design, to spot an issue or to bring it to the attention of the client. This holds true whether you are for the client's policy or against it.

This is not to say that, as a drafter, you cannot have strong feelings about the merits of particular policies. Of course you can, and no doubt you will.

You must, however, take pains to separate your personal feelings from your professional duties. (If you are an attorney, you probably already have experience at this; it comes with the territory.) Do not advocate a policy; do not do so directly or indirectly; do not give the appearance that you are doing so. Do not give your opinion about the merits of a policy if asked—even if pressed. There are ways to deflect the question: "I am not a policy person." "That's a policy issue for others to decide." "I have no dog in this fight." Say it with words if warranted, but say it implicitly by your demeanor at all times. When you decline to say how you feel, you are being professional. When your client can't even guess how you feel, you probably have it about right.

The fact is, every interaction you have with the client has some policy effect at some level—usually minimal, occasionally significant. The issues you choose to raise, the way you choose to raise them, and even the order in which you raise them, will prompt the client to reassess some aspect of the policy. As a drafter, you need to be aware that each statement or question inevitably has some suggestive effect. You can't eliminate this effect; the best you can do is minimize it. Educate but do not lecture; counsel but do not urge.

When you make a choice to discuss certain options with the client and not others, that choice has a policy effect. When you choose whether to draft a law freestanding or as an amendment to some other law, that choice has a policy effect. When you draft a long title, a section heading, or a subsection heading—

matters typically left to a drafter's discretion—the words you use have a policy effect. Again, these effects are usually minimal, and you should take pains to make sure they are.

The path here is narrow, but it is well-marked. One colleague said: "It's absolutely correct that a drafter should not advocate or initiate a policy. However, it's not unusual in the course of our work that we find ourselves making suggestions to help lead clients out of 'dead ends,' especially during meetings with clients from different offices who are working together to try to resolve their own differences on a bill. Sometimes, because we do approach things from an objective perspective, we are able to see common ground between competing drafts and even competing policies, and the clients appreciate it when we bring these kinds of ideas to their attention. In fact, they often expect us to do so, especially during negotiations between members of different parties or different chambers. That doesn't mean that we are advocating for these policies (at least not in the public policy sense), and it doesn't mean that we shouldn't subject the ideas that we suggest to the same analysis as the ideas brought to us by the client."

In sum, policy can and does influence drafting, and drafting can and does influence policy. That said, in the ideal drafting relationship, the drafting function is left to the drafter's discretion and the policymaking function is left to the client's discretion, with neither influencing, nor attempting to influence, the other. For the most part, this book assumes that to be the case. (But see § 10.01, "Drafters Who Are 'More Than Drafters.' ")

§ 1.20 The Drafting Process

The purpose of a drafting project is to produce a draft that has two features: first, the draft accurately reflects the client's policy, and second, the draft is legally sufficient to carry out that policy.

The legislative process being what it is, there is rarely enough time to achieve an ideal draft. In the real world, clients often have policies that are complicated or less than fully formed, and need them reduced to writing not in weeks or days but in hours or minutes—as one client put it, "in real time."

Urgency is not the only obstacle, just the most common. The policy may not be fully developed; the policy may be based on factual or legal assumptions that either are not confirmable or are not in fact correct; the client may insist on using words that are politically useful rather than words that are clear. There are many reasons why an ideal draft cannot be achieved.

In many cases all you can do is add as much value as you can under the circumstances. Learn as much about the problem, the context, and the proposed solution as you can. Review various approaches where you can. Spot as many issues as you can. Discuss them with the client as best you can. Deliver a draft that, under the circumstances, is as faithful and effective as you can make it. To the extent you have concerns about whether the draft is faithful and effective, articulate those concerns.

In microcosm, those are the steps in the drafting process. In a legislative emergency, you may cycle through those steps only once, and only fleetingly. When not in a crisis, you may cycle through those steps a dozen times or more.

§1.30 Professional Obligations

Although serving the client is your primary responsibility, it is not your only responsibility. As a drafter, you must be aware of the various legal and ethical issues that may affect your relationship with your client.

Of course, any drafter has certain other responsibilities that may override the responsibility to the client. If you are an employee, you have responsibilities to your employer. If you are a public servant, you may be subject to a code of ethics. If you are an attorney, you probably are subject to a code of professional responsibility. You almost certainly have a duty—though whether it is legal, ethical, or moral likely depends on your particular circumstances—not to assist a client in conduct you know to be criminal or fraudulent. (Generally, to be considered fraudulent, conduct must be done with a purpose to deceive, not merely a negligent misrepresentation or a failure to provide complete and accurate information.)

If nothing else, you are subject to general laws. For the most part, these matters are beyond the scope of this book. The focus here is on issues inherent in the drafting function.

§1.31 Drafting by Attorneys and by Non-Attorneys

Some general observations are in order on the differences between drafters who are attorneys and those who are not. The differences are considerable.

An attorney differs from a non-attorney in at least four important ways:

1. Legal knowledge and skills. Although law school is certainly not the only place to acquire and hone the attributes important to drafting, the fact remains that many of those attributes are taught in law school, and in few other places. In particular, an attorney is more likely than a non-attorney to excel at critical thinking and at spotting and handling legal issues. In many jurisdictions, an attorney not only must pass a rigorous bar exam, but also must engage in regular continuing legal education. On the other hand, it is sad but fair to say that for many a new lawyer, the experience of law school has wrung out the ability to write clearly. An attorney who has internalized the stuffy, puffy, convoluted style too often used in legal writing may be less likely than a non-attorney to write clearly.

2. Attorney-client privilege. When the drafter is an attorney, the communications between the client and drafter are generally protected by the attorney-client privilege. Not only is the attorney legally bound to keep these communications confidential, but tribunals are legally bound to honor that confidentiality. The attorney generally can't betray those confidences at any time to any person, and the attorney generally can't be compelled by any tribunal to do so. When the drafter is not an attorney, the client does not have this protection, and is perpetually at risk of being politically embarrassed or otherwise hurt by having sensitive communications disclosed, whether accidentally (if the drafter is not cautious), voluntarily (if the drafter is disaffected), or involuntarily (if the drafter is compelled by a tribunal to testify).

3. Professional standards. In most jurisdictions, an attorney is subject to a code of professional responsibility, designed to protect clients—and the public—from shoddy or dishonest service. The code typically requires the attorney to refrain from activities that might conflict with the client's interests, to be candid with the client, and to provide as much information and advice to the client as is reasonably possible. An attorney who fails to meet the standards is subject to discipline by an oversight board, and in most jurisdictions the board is reasonably diligent and responsive to client complaints. When the drafter is not an attorney, and therefore not subject to the code, the drafter does not have the same incentive to meet those standards, and the client does not have the option to complain to the board.

4. Malpractice. Perish the thought, but if a drafter provides service of such poor quality that the client contemplates bringing a lawsuit, the client's remedies against an attorney are more generous than against a non-attorney. A non-attorney can probably be sued only for contract damages (breach of contract), while an attorney can be sued not only for contract damages, but also for tort damages (legal malpractice). In general, this probably will result in a greater award of damages against an attorney than against a non-attorney. Also, an attorney can probably be held to a higher standard than a non-attorney, making liability easier to prove. (In addition, an attorney probably has malpractice insurance, which makes it more likely that the client can actually recover an award of damages.)

In addition to the above considerations, a drafter who is not an attorney is prohibited by law from providing the same level of service as an attorney. There is some outer boundary at which a non-attorney's drafting activities become the unauthorized practice of law.

Exactly where that boundary lies, however, is an open and vexing question. What constitutes legal information (which a non-attorney may provide), as opposed to legal advice (which only an attorney may provide)? The question is important not only to legislative drafting, but also to tax preparation, estate planning, real estate transactions, and other fields. Indeed, if any clear guidance on the question is forthcoming, it will probably come from one of those other fields.

The definition of unauthorized practice of law varies from jurisdiction to jurisdiction and in most cases is vague or even circular. One test used is whether the activity is one that has traditionally been performed by a lawyer. Other tests used are whether the activity involves the application of legal knowledge to the individual client's specific situation; whether the activity affects the individual client's legal rights; whether an attorney-client relationship exists; and whether the client believes an attorney-client relationship exists.

Taken together, these various tests seem to suggest that writing clearly and discussing factual issues do not involve the practice of law and can be performed by a non-attorney. On the other hand, discussing legal issues—providing advice to a particular client about the legal and constitutional issues in a particular draft—may well involve the practice of law. Take those suggestions, however, with a considerable grain of salt. Let it suffice to say that if you are not an attorney, tread this path with care.

In conclusion, this book does not have a solution to the quandary of whether a non-attorney should draft. Instead, it simply does what any drafter would do—spot the issue and bring it to the attention of those who must decide for themselves.

§ 1.40 Attributes Important to Drafting

At this point, there is a temptation to quote Middleton Beaman and Reed Dickerson. Beaman, the original "Vermont schoolmarm," was the first person to head the Office of the Legislative Counsel of the United States House of Representatives (a topic covered in more detail in § 2.16, "Offices of Legislative Counsel"). Dickerson worked as a drafter (for two years in Beaman's office and for many years elsewhere), taught drafting (primarily at Indiana University), and wrote several influential books on drafting.

Beaman is widely alleged to have said that a drafter must be an "intellectual eunuch." Dickerson is widely alleged to have written that a drafter must also be an "emotional oyster." Dickerson's phrase is verifiable (it appears, among other places, at page 11 of Reed Dickerson, *The Fundamentals of Legal Drafting* (2d ed., 1986)). Beaman's phrase is not, or at least not in the source usually cited; the citation given in several sources is to his testimony in 1945 before the Joint Committee on the Organization of Congress, but—alas!—the transcript of that testimony (Hearings on H. Con. Res. 18, 79th Congress, 1st Session, 413–430) does not support the story.

Regardless, drafting is certainly not for everyone. Drafting is about words and ideas, semantics, and subtle shades of meaning. It is also about organization, rules, and logic. In its own way, each draft is a form of puzzle; it should be no surprise that many drafters enjoy crossword puzzles. A colleague suggested that most drafters are—he meant this only in the most positive way—"word weenies." While that may overstate the case, it does carry the ring of truth.

As explained by one observer:

> "In the eighteenth century a Russian nobleman named Alexander Radishchev wrote a book called *Journey from St. Petersburg to Moscow*. In it he criticised bureaucracy and serfdom. Catherine the Great had him arrested, condemned to death and sent to Siberia. Having endured all that, after Catherine's death he was freed and took to drafting legislation. But a fit of melancholia soon descended on him and he committed suicide. Perhaps this should be a lesson to anyone who seeks to become a drafter.
>
> "In fact I do not know whether his melancholia was brought about by his drafting. But it might have been. There is all the difference in the world between writing a book with a passionate political motive and

writing legislation. For we all know that legislation has a very precise and narrow object. This can make the job seem to some people cabin'd, cribb'd and confined, and perhaps tending towards depression. At the same time I think it presents the draftsman with a challenge, and it is part of the reason for its fascination."

Geoffrey Bowman
"Legislation and Explanation," *The Loophole* (June 2000)

§ 1.41 Knowledge

To draft at the federal level, or at least to do so well, requires a certain amount of specialized knowledge. At the outset, you must have a mastery of American English.

You must also have a working knowledge of the substance of the Constitution and laws of the United States. This is not to suggest, of course, that you must know every clause of the Constitution and every volume of the United States Code. You must, however, understand their general structure, scope, and contents, and how to navigate and use them.

You must understand the legal and political processes that govern how laws are made. This does not require a mastery of these processes, but it does require a familiarity with them. For a straightforward summary, see Chapter Two, "Understanding How Laws Are Made." For an in-depth discussion, see the *Congressional Deskbook* by Judy Schneider and Michael Koempel (updated every two years).

You must also be familiar with the generally applicable federal management laws and other laws and procedures that govern how laws are administered by federal agencies.

Last, but by no means least, you must understand how a court—and, in particular, the Supreme Court of the United States—goes about interpreting a statute. For more on this subject, see Chapter Three, "Considering the Courts: Statutory Interpretation."

§ 1.42 Skills

Drafting requires not only specialized knowledge, but also specialized skills.

You must be a "people person," because it takes two to draft (unless, as the saying goes, you have a fool for a client). You must be able to engage your client, ask tough questions, and hear and appreciate the answers. Ultimately, you must be able to yield gracefully when the drafter-client relationship requires you to do so. You must be tactful, candid, sensible, humble, patient, and pragmatic.

You must also be an "idea person," because drafting is nothing less than the capture of ideas. You must be able to master the policy and understand its boundaries and limitations. You must be able to foresee situations that, though unlikely, might cause the policy to break down. You must be alert, flexible, creative, inquisitive, and skeptical.

And you must be a "legislative person." You must be sensitive to the client's political and parliamentary needs and concerns, and you must be able to research legal and legislative issues and find the answers quickly and effectively.

§ 1.43 The "Legislative Counsel Type"

A case study of the professional drafters of Congress, carried out in the 1950s, remains relevant today. The study found that the drafters in the Offices of Legislative Counsel of the House and Senate (for more on these offices, see § 2.16) had "almost a corporate personality":

> "Through the process of selection and training, similar personal qualities were shaped by indoctrinated attitudes into a 'legislative counsel type.' The legislative counsel and their assistants were highly articulate and in conversation readily divined what information was sought. They were imbued with an attitude of helpfulness and possessed a marked enthusiasm for their work. Awareness of the heavy responsibility devolved upon them was tempered by a widespread sense of humor. Their modesty and desire for anonymity were balanced by self-confidence, initiative, and adaptability. With a profound insight into the legislative process, they realistically appraised the various considerations they should take into account in their work. In brief, the personnel of the Office of the Legislative Counsel were the best explanation of the high regard in which it was held by the members of Congress and their staffs during the period covered."
>
> Kenneth Theodore Kofmehl
> *Professional Staffs of Congress* 187 (1962)

The "legislative counsel type" is, apparently, a fairly rare breed. Drafting offices often find that recruiting and retaining good drafters is hard to do. In

1931, Sir William Graham-Harrison, the head of the Office of Parliamentary Counsel in London, was asked whether his office could add more drafters to its staff.

He replied: "I should like to say that nothing is more difficult in the world than to get people to come to my office. It is highly specialized and extremely unpopular."

Why so unpopular? "Because it is slavery."

(As quoted in A.G. Donaldson, "The High Priests of the Mystery: A Note on Two Centuries of Parliamentary Draftsmen," in Finnie, W., et al. [ed.], *Edinburgh Essays In Public Law* 99, 112 (1991).)

§ 1.50 Resources Important to Drafting

A drafter should have the best equipment possible for producing documents. These days, that means a functional computer with a good word processing system and a reliable printer. That said, there are still times, especially in the frenzied days at the end of a Congress, when a pencil and the back of an envelope are called upon to do the trick. At all times, keep something to write with, and something to write on, close at hand.

For a useful commentary on how computers have, for better or worse, changed how drafting is done, see Appendix One. Notably, that commentary was written not by an American drafter, but by a Canadian one. It is useful not only as a commentary, but also as a reminder that drafting is more or less the same from jurisdiction to jurisdiction. The particulars may change—a British drafter does not need to know American constitutional law, for example, and an Alaskan drafter does not need to know New York law—but the task, by and large, does not. When looking for resources on drafting, do not ignore resources from elsewhere.

A drafter should have regular, reliable access to a wide variety of important documents. You need a general dictionary, a legal dictionary, and a thesaurus. It may help to have a style manual, in particular the Government Printing Office Style Manual, <*www.gpoaccess.gov/stylemanual/*>. You should have access to the text of the Constitution, <*www.gpoaccess.gov/constitution/*> (and see Appendix Eleven), and of the United States Code, <*www.gpoaccess.gov/uscode/*>. You should also have access to compilations (see § 2.70), slip laws (see § 2.62), and other update services to keep your legal library accurate and current.

Fortunately, many of these important documents are available online and at no charge. For a table of useful web sites, see Appendix Three.

Your personal library should include materials on writing, on legal writing, and on drafting. No single guide is complete or authoritative, and no single guide is best for everyone. One guide may treat a topic more fully or with more insight than another; one may simply "work" for you in a way that another does not. For a list of suggestions for further reading, including not only notable guides but also notable articles, see Appendix Two.

Understanding How Laws Are Made

Chapter 2

Laws are like sausages, it is better not to see them being made.

Attributed by some to Otto von Bismarck, by others to Mark Twain

As if from a rubbish cart, a continuously increasing and ever shapeless mass of law is from time to time shot down upon the heads of people, and out of this rubbish, and at his peril, is each man left to pick out what belongs to him.

Jeremy Bentham

I don't mind what Congress does, as long as they don't do it in the streets and frighten the horses.

Victor Hugo

Understanding How Laws Are Made

Chapter 2

§ 2.00 Introduction

This chapter and the next are not directly about drafting. They are about what happens to drafts after the drafting is done. (Or at least after the first bout of drafting—the drafting of an original measure—is done.) The draft might pass the House and Senate, be presented to the President, become law, and be published; that is what this chapter covers. It might then be interpreted by courts; that is what the next chapter covers.

Chronologically, then, these two chapters belong at the end. But the matters covered in these chapters are matters every drafter should know, or at least have at hand. They are the background against which drafting decisions are made. For that reason, they belong at the beginning. They are the foundation on which everything else rests.

To be sure, many drafters already understand how laws are made at a level as deep as, or deeper than, this chapter provides. For those drafters, this chapter might be useful only as a refresher or a reference. Perhaps, however, there is a detail or insight provided here that might yet be new.

For a series of documents that together form a working example of how a law is made, see Appendix Four.

This chapter begins with a few remarks about the structure of Congress and then covers two processes: how bills are enacted and how enactments are made public.

§2.10 Organization and Operation of Congress

The legislative power of the United States is vested by the Constitution in a bicameral legislature, consisting of the Senate and the House of Representatives.

Sooner or later, every drafter must confront the question of whether to refer to the legislature as "the Congress" or merely "Congress." There is no authoritative answer. The Constitution uses each form, with no discernible pattern, though it uses "the Congress" significantly more. Find an approach that works for you and go with it. Most drafters use both, finding that "Congress" works best for some uses and "the Congress" for others. That is more or less the approach used here.

The term "senator" is used for a member of the Senate. (The style in legislation is to capitalize the first letter of this term and others like it; that style is not followed in this book.) Senators serve six-year terms, but the terms are staggered so that about one-third of the seats in the Senate are up for election in the general congressional election held every two years.

The House has three different types of members. The term "representative" is reserved for the members from states; a representative is the only type of member allowed to vote on the floor of the House. The term "delegate" is used for the members from the District of Columbia, Guam, the United States Virgin Islands, and American Samoa. The term "resident commissioner" is used for the member from the Commonwealth of Puerto Rico. Representatives and delegates serve two-year terms, so that in the general congressional election held every two years all the House seats are up for election, save one: The resident commissioner serves a four-year term.

The terms "member of the House of Representatives," "member of Congress," and simply "member" are often used but, unless carefully defined, are ambiguous—they may or may not be read to include the delegates and the resident commissioner. This book uses the term to include the delegates and the resident commissioner.

The term "House of Congress" is sometimes used to mean a chamber of Congress. For example, one might say that a bill passed one House of Congress and was referred to the other House. Be careful when using this term, and especially so when using its shortened form, "House," so that the reader can tell whether you mean the House of Representatives only, or either of the two chambers. This book reserves "House" for the House of Representatives and uses "chamber" otherwise.

At the head of the Senate—at least on a formal basis—is the president of the Senate. As required by the Constitution (*art. I, sec. 3*), this position is filled by the Vice President of the United States. In the absence of the vice president—which is to say, most of the time—the functions are carried out by another officer, the president pro tempore, likewise required by the Constitution. Traditionally, the most senior senator (by continuous service, not by age) in the majority party serves in that capacity. The functions of the head of the Senate are more ceremonial than powerful; as a practical matter, the positions of power in the Senate are the heads of the two parties, known as the majority leader and the minority leader.

At the head of the House is the Speaker of the House of Representatives. The speaker is behind only the vice president in the presidential line of succession and, in part for that reason, is considered the highest ranking officer of the Congress, at least for formal and ceremonial purposes. The speaker is not, however, merely a ceremonial position: Unlike the head of the Senate, the head of the House is the most powerful position in the chamber. The House also has a majority leader and a minority leader.

You may be called upon to draft a measure that refers to one or more of these leadership positions. A client may, for example, want a bill to establish an advisory commission, with its members appointed by various congressional leaders. Bear in mind that the majority leader and minority leader are not chamber officers, but party officers; they are non-governmental positions within political parties, which are non-governmental associations. While they are occasionally referred to in legislation, they are not positions of equal dignity with the speaker, the president of the Senate, or the president pro tempore, and for that reason are more properly not capitalized. There may even be cases where vesting power in a party officer (as opposed to a chamber officer) is legally or constitutionally dubious. For more details about the roles of party officers, see *Congressional Deskbook*, § 7.40, "Party Leadership."

§ 2.11 Congress from Term to Term

A general congressional election is held every even-numbered year, on the "Tuesday next after the 1st Monday in November" of that year, as provided by section 25 of the Revised Statutes (2 U.S.C. 7). The term of a member of Congress elected in that election begins the following year on January 3, though the Congress may designate a later date to actually assemble (as provided by the Twentieth Amendment).

By custom, each Congress is numbered in sequence. For example, the first Congress was seated in 1789 and the 101st Congress in 1989.

Congress must assemble at least once each year (as required by Article I, Section 4). Each congressional year (not quite the same as a calendar year—from one January 3 noon to the next) is considered a separate session. The change from the first session to the second is primarily an administrative matter; it does not carry great significance for a drafter. Under the rules and precedents of each chamber, legislative business not completed in the first session automatically carries over to the second one.

The change every two years from one Congress to another, however, carries both political significance and legislative significance.

As a political matter, a change of Congress may bring a change in the officers and other positions of leadership within a chamber, and perhaps even a change in majority party.

The House is not considered a continuing body because every seat (save the resident commissioner) is up for election every two years. Accordingly, the House must reconstitute itself with each new Congress, choosing its officers and establishing its internal rules. See *Congressional Deskbook*, § 7.30, "Early Organization Meetings."

The Senate is considered a continuing body because about two-thirds of its seats carry over from Congress to Congress. Accordingly, the officers and rules of the Senate carry over from Congress to Congress much as they do from session to session. A new Congress is, however, an opportune time to revisit these matters, particularly if there has been a change in majority party.

As a legislative matter, a change of Congress wipes the slate clean. Under the rules and precedents of each chamber, legislative business not completed in the second session of a Congress expires and, to be considered in a later one, must be started anew. (This rule for legislative business does not necessarily apply to other forms of business. Impeachment proceedings, for example, carry over from one Congress to the next.)

For many drafters, a new Congress brings with it a fair number of requests for reintroduction—that is, a request to take a measure from an old Congress and update it for use in the new one. In most cases only a few technical changes are needed, such as updating any references to years (such as in a short title) or fiscal years (such as in an authorization of appropriations). Because the factual or legal context may have changed since the measure was drafted, you should also assess whether the measure still works as intended; for example, a citation to, or an amendment to, other law may no longer work properly if that other law has since changed.

Sometimes your client may want to reintroduce a measure previously introduced by someone else. Members do not typically try to steal one another's thunder, but perhaps the previous sponsor is no longer in Congress or has lost interest. In this situation, the client has access to the words on the paper but not the thinking and advice behind them. As with any project you start from scratch, educate the client about what the measure really does, figure out what the client really wants to do, and help the client accordingly.

§ 2.12 Functions of Congress

The legislative power is not the only power vested in the legislative branch. The Constitution also vests other powers in the House and Senate, some to be exercised together, some separately.

Though not "legislative" in the strict sense (that is, making enacted law), many of these powers are carried out using legislative measures. The House and Senate each fix chamber rules by simple resolution, for example; similarly, the House and Senate together manage the Capitol complex (including the Capitol itself, the congressional office buildings, and the Capitol grounds) by concurrent resolution, and together propose constitutional amendments by joint resolution. Because a drafter may be called upon to draft such a measure, a drafter needs to be aware of these other powers.

Among the Senate's sole responsibilities are providing advice and consent to treaties and nominations, trying impeachments, and choosing the vice president when no candidate receives an electoral college majority. The House, meanwhile, has sole responsibility for impeachments and for choosing the President when no candidate receives an electoral college majority.

The Senate and House are each separately responsible for establishing chamber rules, choosing chamber officers, keeping a journal, monitoring the rest of the government, and deciding whether and when to seat, punish, or expel its members.

And the Senate and House are jointly responsible for designating when and where to assemble, recess, and adjourn, managing the legislative branch, and proposing amendments to the Constitution.

This is, of course, a general survey and not an exhaustive inventory. For more information, see *Congressional Deskbook*, Chapter Seven, "Organizing Congress: Members, Leaders, and Committees."

§ 2.13 Committees

A committee is a working group of Congress for focusing attention and expertise on particular matters. Congress does most of its work, both legislative and nonlegislative, through committees. See also *Congressional Deskbook*, § 7.50, "Committees and Subcommittees."

In the early Congresses this was not the case: A committee was appointed by a chamber only on a temporary, ad hoc basis after the chamber as a whole had already agreed on a basic policy. The task of the committee was to fill in the details. (Because there were no professional drafters in those days, a committee's task then was in many ways what a drafter's task is now.)

In modern practice, a committee typically includes members from both the majority party and the minority party, with the seats allocated in some proportion to party strength in the chamber as a whole. The head of the committee is titled the "chairman" (the head of the minority party within the committee is referred to as the "ranking minority member" or, occasionally, as simply the "ranking member"). Note that the title remains "chairman," regardless of the gender of the person (and despite efforts by many to substitute "chair" or "chairperson" instead).

Each chamber can establish its own committees by simple resolution as part of its internal rules. For that reason, the number and nature of committees differ between the two chambers and, in any event, can be changed by a single vote of a single chamber. Occasionally a committee of a single chamber is established by statute, though even in that case the chamber can change or dissolve the committee by simple resolution.

Some committees, known as joint committees, are established by the two chambers together, by concurrent resolution if the joint committee is to expire at the end of the current Congress, otherwise by statute. The Joint Committee on Printing, for example, is established under section 101 of title 44, United States Code.

The jurisdiction of a committee can involve any combination of the different congressional powers. A committee's jurisdiction may, for example, relate to legislation, rulemaking, ethics, management of the legislative branch, oversight of the executive branch, and so on.

A committee that exists indefinitely is known as a standing committee. A committee that exists only temporarily is known as a special committee. At one time, the term "select committee" was used to mean only a temporary committee, but the term has come to be applied to standing committees as well. In the 109th Congress, for example, the Permanent Select Committee on Intelligence of the House and the Select Committee on Intelligence of the Senate were both standing committees.

Many committees have subcommittees, which are exactly what the term suggests—committees within committees. In most cases, a subcommittee is given a subset of the jurisdiction of the full committee and may hold hearings and markups within that jurisdiction. As with a committee, a subcommittee has a chairman and a ranking member.

A drafter is concerned primarily with legislative committees, that is, those committees that have legislative powers. Legislative committees are used to screen and amend measures. They are given jurisdiction over a particular set of subject matters and, within that jurisdiction, can hold hearings and markups. (Hearings and markups are discussed in more detail in § 2.23, "Hearings and Markups: Overview.") Typically, a legislative committee is also an oversight committee, that is, a committee with power to monitor and investigate the activities of the executive branch that fall within the committee's jurisdiction.

The jurisdictions of committees sometimes overlap, and in any case a measure may cover more than one subject matter. Sometimes more than one committee claims to have jurisdiction over a measure or some other matter; the House and the Senate have separate procedures for resolving the competing claims.

As part of their duties, legislative and oversight committees also receive outside communications—sometimes directly from the source, sometimes by referral from the chamber. For example, whenever a chamber receives a report or other communication from the executive branch, or receives a petition, memorial, or other communication from a nonfederal source, the head of the chamber refers the communication to the committee with jurisdiction over its subject matter.

In drafting, you should always use a committee's official name. Each chamber has long had a judiciary committee, for example, the official title of which has long been the Committee on the Judiciary. When referring to several committees, there is a temptation to meld the names: "the Committees on the Judiciary of the Senate and the House of Representatives," for example, or "the Committees on Armed Services and the Judiciary of the House of Representatives." Whether the modest gain in brevity is worthwhile is debatable.

It is always a fair question to ask whether the draft should name a committee at all. In many cases, a draft that names a committee might be better off naming the Congress. For example, many laws require the executive branch to submit a report. Under one approach, the report must be submitted to Congress; under another approach, the report must be submitted to specified congressional committees. The client should consider which approach is more desirable in a particular case. A report that is submitted to Congress is marked and recorded in each chamber and then referred to committees according to the subject matter. A report that is submitted to specified committees is sent directly to those committees (and only those committees); it is not marked or recorded. In some cases, the utility of having an official public log of when a report is received is useful; in other cases—particularly when the client is affiliated with a particular committee—the certainty of having a report sent to that committee (and, perhaps, not sent to other committees) is more useful.

§ 2.14 Clerks

Each chamber, as part of its full chamber staff, has clerks that are involved with measures at different stages of the legislative process. In the Senate, the clerks are under the direction of the Secretary of the Senate; in the House, the clerks are under the direction of the Clerk of the House.

In each chamber, the clerks most directly involved in legislation are the bill clerk and the enrolling clerk. Generally, the bill clerk handles measures not yet passed by the chamber, while the enrolling clerk handles those that have passed.

§ 2.15 Parliamentarians

Each chamber has an Office of the Parliamentarian under the direction of a parliamentarian. The office provides information on the rules of the chamber and advice on how those rules apply to particular cases, such as which committee has jurisdiction over a measure and whether an objection should be sustained or overruled. In doing so, the office analyzes the proceedings of the chamber and maintains and publishes a record of the precedents of the chamber.

The parliamentarian and parliamentarian's assistants are appointed on a nonpartisan basis, and the positions in the office are generally considered to be career positions.

§ 2.16 Offices of Legislative Counsel

Each chamber has an Office of the Legislative Counsel under the direction of a legislative counsel. The office provides legislative drafting services for committees and individual members, and also helps committees prepare certain other documents used in the legislative process.

As with the parliamentarian, the legislative counsel and the legislative counsel's assistants are appointed on a nonpartisan basis, and the positions in the office are generally considered to be career positions.

Though the office is available to assist committees and members, use of the office is not required. In some cases, the office is used to perform a "complete job"—brought in at the very early stages of policy development, to help the client think through the policy and reduce it to a written draft. In other cases, the office is used only to provide technical assistance with respect to a draft that was prepared elsewhere. And in some cases the office is not used at all.

Since the focus of this book is drafting federal law, perhaps a few details about the history of the offices are in order.

The idea of using professionals to draft legislation began to be taken seriously in Congress in the early part of the twentieth century. To that point, legislators had generally done their own drafting. Some scoffed at the notion that professionals could help, and some took it as a personal affront. In congressional hearings in 1913, Senator Bacon of Georgia said that the time had not come, nor was likely to come, when the Senate would need to be taught how to draft a bill. If a person so wise and sincere existed, he said, the senators should "go home, and let . . . this all-wise man perform our functions for us." 50 *Congressional Record* 2375–2380 (1913).

At the time, the most active promoter of professional drafting was a privately endowed fund at Columbia University, the Legislative Drafting Research Fund, founded by Joseph P. Chamberlain in 1911. The purpose of the fund was to promote professional drafting in the United States; the idea of professional drafting had already taken hold in the legislatures of some other countries, most notably the British Parliament, which had first employed a professional drafter (Parliamentary Counsel) in 1833 and had established an Office of Parliamentary Counsel in 1869.

In 1916, when persuasion by mere words had proven not enough to convince Congress, the fund turned to persuasion by deeds. Middleton Beaman (the "Vermont schoolmarm" we first met in Chapter One) had served on Capitol Hill as Law Librarian of the Library of Congress and had also been involved with the fund. The fund paid his way to go back to the Hill and provide any committee with any drafting help it would accept. The Committee on Ways and Means of the House of Representatives took up the offer and tried him on several revenue bills; the rest, as they say, is history. It was not long before Beaman was seen as indispensable.

After taking the fund's charity for two years, the committee decided to secure his services directly. Section 1303 of the Revenue Act of 1918 (40 Stat. 1141) provided for a "Legislative Drafting Service" under the direction of two drafters, one appointed by the head of each chamber. Through back channels, the committee saw to it that the House side got Beaman.

From the beginning, the drafters were to be appointed without regard to political affiliation and solely on the grounds of fitness to perform the duties of the office. They were directed to aid in drafting measures and amendments at the request of a committee; aid could be provided to individual members when doing so would not interfere with committee work.

Though the Legislative Drafting Service was a single office under the law, it was in practice a bifurcated office from the very beginning. Any given drafter worked for either the House or the Senate, but not both. The office was funded with a single appropriation, but with direction that it be disbursed half to the Secretary of the Senate, half to the Clerk of the House.

In 1924 the office was renamed the Office of the Legislative Counsel, as provided by section 1101 of the Revenue Act of 1924 (43 Stat. 353). In 1949 Beaman retired. And in 1970 the law was finally changed to recognize what had always been operationally the case: The office became two separate offices, one for each chamber. The House office was given a new charter, title V of the Legislative Reorganization Act of 1970 (2 U.S.C. 281 et seq.). The Senate office still operates under the original law (2 U.S.C. 271 et seq.).

The services provided by the offices have narrowed over the years. Early on, an office sometimes wrote opinions on constitutional questions, helped write committee reports, and even (on rare occasions) wrote briefs in lawsuits in which the Congress or a single chamber was involved. Those services are now performed by the Congressional Research Service, committee staff, and the Offices of Legal Counsel, respectively, and not by the Offices of Legislative Counsel.

Drafters in each office continue, as always, to draft legislative measures and other legislative documents for committees on request, and for members when doing so does not interfere with committee work. They also continue to be called upon—sometimes formally, sometimes informally—to interpret or explain a provision under consideration.

A drafter not within the House or Senate offices should not draft carelessly in the expectation that Legislative Counsel will catch and clean up any problems in a draft. The offices are rarely in a position to do so, and even when in a position to do so, the client may not be inclined to correct it. The longer a particular text is in circulation, the more crystallized it tends to become, for better or for worse. When a client has built a coalition—whether of legislators or of interest groups—around a particular set of words, it becomes politically and procedurally difficult to change those words, however problematic they may be. If you are in a position to perform a "complete job," make every effort to do so, and to do so properly.

§ 2.17 Law Revision Counsel

The Office of the Law Revision Counsel is responsible for publishing and maintaining the United States Code. The office is established within the House of Representatives and, more specifically, under the supervision of the Committee on the Judiciary of the House.

The United States Code is a more complicated document than most people, even most lawyers, realize. A drafter must have a thorough understanding of the Code and how properly to use it and refer to it. Details about the Code are provided in § 2.80, "The United States Code."

§ 2.20 The Legislative Process in Congress

The legislative process in Congress can be complex. Discussing that process in all its complexity is beyond the scope of this book. The approach here is to provide a general overview of the legislative process, with an emphasis on the parts of the process most important to drafting. (For one particularly thorough and vivid account of how the legislative process—and drafting process—played out with respect to a particular statute, see Glenn R. Schmitt, "Closing the Gap in Criminal Jurisdiction Over Civilians Accompanying the Armed Forces Abroad—A First Person Account of the Creation of the Military Extraterritorial Jurisdiction Act of 2000," 51 *Catholic University Law Review* 55 (2001).) For a thorough discussion, see *Congressional Deskbook*, Chapter Eight, "Legislating in Congress: Legislative Process."

The discussion that follows assumes that a measure originates in the House of Representatives. It is a reasonable assumption to make: The House originates about twice as many measures as the Senate, and one type of measure—a bill for raising revenue—is required by the Constitution to originate in the House. In any case, the general, fundamental processes covered by this chapter are the same for both chambers.

The discussion that follows also assumes that the measure used is a bill. It is also a reasonable assumption to make, even though the bill is only one of four measures used by the Congress. (The various measures and the differences among them are discussed in detail in Chapter Five.) The assumption is reasonable for at least two reasons.

First, the vast majority of measures are bills. Looking only at the House of Representatives in the 108th Congress, for example, there were introduced 115 joint resolutions, 532 concurrent resolutions, 875 simple resolutions—and 5,431 bills.

Second, if you understand the bill procedure, you can easily understand the other procedures. A joint resolution follows the bill procedure exactly—unless it proposes a constitutional amendment, in which case it differs only in that it requires a two-thirds (rather than a simple majority) vote of each chamber and is sent to the states rather than presented to the President. A concurrent resolution also follows the bill procedure exactly, except that it takes effect upon being passed by both chambers—it is not presented to the President. A simple resolution follows the bill procedure exactly, except that it takes effect upon being passed by its chamber of origin—it is not sent to the other chamber.

You should also bear in mind that the overview provided here assumes the bill proceeds methodically and in regular order. There are tactics in each chamber to circumvent regular order and to change or leapfrog parts of the process, and there are special rules that apply in special cases.

§ 2.21 Introducing a Bill

A bill becomes a bill when it is introduced (note that a resolution is "submitted" rather than introduced, though this is semantics). A draft not introduced is private property; a draft introduced is a public document, the property of the chamber in which it was introduced.

Only a senator can introduce a bill in the Senate, and only a member of the House can introduce a bill in the House. In an earlier era, a bill could not be introduced by anyone without the consent of the entire chamber, but by the early 1900s that practice had been abandoned.

The member who introduces a bill is known as the sponsor of the bill. Other members, to indicate their support, may add their names as cosponsors when the bill is introduced or at any later point.

A member who sponsors a bill is generally assumed to support the bill. Sometimes, however, a member may introduce a bill without wanting that assumption to be made. For example, the chairman of a committee may introduce, as a courtesy, a proposal from the executive branch or from a private party. In that situation, the face of the bill can indicate that it was introduced "by request."

A bill need not be in any special form; it may, for example, be written by hand. It must, however, bear the signature of the sponsor. (A member may cosponsor the bill without providing a signature.) In the House, a member introduces a bill simply by dropping it in a box, known as the "hopper," on the floor of the House when the House is in session. In the Senate, a senator can use a similar procedure, or the senator can rise and introduce the bill from the floor. See also *Congressional Deskbook*, § 8.20, "Drafting and Introducing Legislation."

§ 2.22 Number, Referral, and First Print

An introduced bill is examined to be sure it is in proper form and in compliance with applicable rules and, if so, the bill clerk assigns it a number, usually the next number in sequence for that Congress.

The bill is also examined to determine its subject matter, and then the presiding officer of the chamber, on the advice of the parliamentarian, refers the bill to one or more committees.

Because of the power and influence of committees, referral can have a significant effect on the fate of a bill. For that reason, the client may be keenly interested in steering the bill to a committee likely to be interested and supportive. As a drafter, you need to be aware that decisions made in the drafting process can affect the referral of a bill, and the client may ask you to tailor the draft accordingly. For example, a bill that amends title 18, United States Code, is more likely to be referred to the Committee on the Judiciary than a bill that is freestanding, even if the substantive policies contained in each bill are otherwise identical.

The number and the referral are indicated on the bill, and the bill clerk arranges for the Government Printing Office to prepare and print the bill as introduced. See also *Congressional Deskbook*, § 8.30, "Referral of Legislation to Committee."

§ 2.23 Hearings and Markups: Overview

A hearing is a proceeding at which a committee or subcommittee gathers information about a bill or any other matter within its jurisdiction. The information may include testimony, documents, exhibits, or just about anything else. Usually, a record is made and published of the information gathered at hearings. It is rare for a drafter to attend hearings, because it is rare for specific legislative language to be developed there. As a drafter, however, you should be aware that a court (as explained more fully in § 3.77) may consider what was said at hearings on a bill when deciding how to interpret the resulting law. See also *Congressional Deskbook*, § 8.40, "Committee Hearings."

A markup is a proceeding at which a committee or subcommittee considers amendments to a bill and decides whether to recommend to the parent body that the bill be passed. After considering amendments, the committee or subcommittee votes whether to recommend the bill "favorably" to the parent body. The committee or subcommittee also has the option to recommend the bill "unfavorably"—that is, that the bill not be passed. This option is rarely exercised, because if a committee does not favor a bill within its jurisdiction it can often stop it from being further considered in the chamber simply by ignoring it. (That said, there are procedures to free a bill from a hostile committee if enough support can be mustered.) A committee can also report a bill without any recommendation, though this is equally rare. See also *Congressional Deskbook*, § 8.50, "Committee Markup."

It is sometimes said that a committee or subcommittee "reported" a bill at markup, but this is not technically correct. At markup, a committee does not report the bill, but rather orders that the bill be reported.

§ 2.24 Subcommittee Action

A committee receiving a referred bill may then refer the bill to one or more of its subcommittees, and the subcommittee may hold hearings, hold a markup, and order the bill reported to the full committee.

If the subcommittee orders the bill reported with one or more amendments, a text showing the effect of those amendments is usually prepared. The form of the text varies from committee to committee and even from subcommittee to subcommittee. The form most commonly used is an amendment in the nature of a substitute—that is, a text that shows the entire bill as it would appear if all the amendments adopted were executed.

The subcommittee text is generally considered the internal work product of the committee rather than the property of the chamber. Though it is usually not kept secret, it is not formally published and, except within the committee itself, not widely distributed.

§ 2.25 Full Committee Action

When the full committee is ready to act on a bill—after receiving it directly by referral from the head of the chamber, or after a subcommittee has had an opportunity to act—the full committee may hold hearings, hold a markup, and order the bill reported to the chamber.

If the committee orders the bill reported with one or more amendments, a text showing the effect of those amendments is prepared. While a subcommittee's text is internal to the committee, the committee's text is filed with the bill clerk as part of the committee's report and becomes the property of the chamber.

Typically, the report also includes a statement explaining the bill and the reasons why the committee recommends its passage. A member with a different view about the bill may include in the report a statement to that effect. (When the meaning of particular language in the bill is in doubt, the courts often look to these statements as a source of meaning; see § 3.75, "Report Language.") In addition, a committee is required by chamber rules to include in the report certain other matters, such as an estimate of the costs that would result if the bill were enacted and, if the bill would amend a law, a document showing the effect of the amendment on the literal language of that law. See also *Congressional Deskbook*, § 8.60, "Committee Reports."

A report may also contain language (independent of the language in the bill) purporting to require, prohibit, or authorize action. This sort of language is known as "report language" and typically appears only in bills that are part of the regular cycle of authorization bills and appropriations bills. In some cases mandatory words are used ("The Secretary shall do X"); in other cases directory words are used ("The Secretary is directed to do X"); and in some cases hortatory or precatory words are used ("The Committee expects the Secretary to do X" or "The Secretary should do X"). Regardless of the precise form of the words, language of this sort is not legally binding. It is, however, taken seriously by the executive branch because of the committee's legislative and oversight powers and political influence. In that sense, report language is seen as "politically binding." The ire of a committee is not to be trifled with. After all, if the committee has the will to place a directive in report language this year, it probably has the will to place it directly into the bill (in "bill language") next year.

Once filed with the bill clerk, the committee report is considered the property of the chamber, and the bill clerk arranges for the Government Printing Office to prepare and print the report.

§ 2.26 Floor Proceedings

When the full chamber is ready to act on a bill—typically, after the committees of referral have reported the bill—the bill is placed on a list, known as a "calendar," of bills ready for floor proceedings. In many cases, the Government Printing Office is directed to prepare and print a new version of the bill, known as a "calendar print." If the bill has been reported by a committee, the calendar print shows the bill as reported by that committee; if reported by more than one committee, it shows, successively, the bill as reported by each committee.

There are several different routes by which a bill can come to a floor vote. One typical route, summarized here, is first through the Committee on Rules and then through the Committee of the Whole House on the State of the Union. This route is unique to the House.

The Committee on Rules is a standing committee with jurisdiction to determine how a bill should proceed on the floor. The committee reports special rules that apply only to one or more specified bills and that affect the ability of members to debate, to offer amendments, and to make motions and points of order with respect to those bills. If more than one version of a bill exists, the committee may specify which version is in order to be used as the base text. A special rule is in the form of a simple resolution and, once reported by the Committee on Rules, must still be passed by the House before it takes effect. See also *Congressional Deskbook*, § 8.90, "Rules Committee and Special Rules."

The Committee of the Whole House on the State of the Union, commonly known as the "Committee of the Whole," is not a standing committee. Instead, it is a temporary committee that springs into existence to consider a particular bill and vanishes when its work is done. The Committee of the Whole consists of the entire membership of the House and uses a different set of procedures for amendments and debate than does the House itself. For example, the Committee of the Whole reduces the number of members needed to constitute a quorum and limits the time allowed for debate. When it seems expedient to use these procedures, the House resolves itself into the Committee of the Whole, holds what amounts to an impromptu markup, and then orders the bill as amended reported immediately back to the full House. See also *Congressional Deskbook*, § 8.110, "Committee of the Whole: Debate."

When the full chamber is ready for a final vote on a bill, whether received from the Committee of the Whole or by some other route, the chamber holds a vote on final passage.

Upon an affirmative vote on final passage, the enrolling clerk prepares a text of the bill showing the bill as passed by the chamber. In the heading of the bill, the words "A BILL" are changed to "AN ACT," signifying not that it is an Act of Congress, but an act of one chamber. (Even so, the bill typically continues to be referred to as a bill.) If the measure is a resolution, its heading is unaffected.

The enrolling clerk arranges for the Government Printing Office to prepare and print the text and for it to be certified by the Clerk of the House or the Secretary of the Senate, as the case may be. This process is known as "engrossment," and the print shows the bill as engrossed.

The engrossed bill is then delivered, or "messaged," to the other chamber for consideration there. In delivering a bill, the chamber relinquishes jurisdiction over the bill. If an error is discovered and there is a desire to correct it, the first chamber must pass a simple resolution formally requesting the other chamber to return the bill for correction.

An article by Edward Dumbauld, "Ghosts in the Law," 14 *I.C.C. Practitioners' Journal* 625 (1947), describes an error in the engrossment process of the Urgent Deficiencies Act of 1913 that went unnoticed and was enacted into law (where it lingered for decades). The article relates that among the floor amendments adopted by the Senate was an amendment to strike two particular sentences, but in preparing the engrossment only one of those sentences was stricken. The Senate version was then agreed to by the House (after a conference) and became law. The sentence that was erroneously included was, "And in such case the notice required shall be served upon the defendants in the case and upon the attorney general of the State." (38 Stat. 220–221). The provision had been classified to 28 U.S.C. 47a and lingered until 1948, when it was repealed through the process that enacted title 28 as a positive-law title of the U.S. Code.

§ 2.30 Actions in Other Chamber

The chamber receiving the engrossed bill proceeds to consider it in much the same way as if it had been introduced there. The engrossed bill, retaining its original designation and number, is referred to the appropriate committees, and the Government Printing Office is directed to print the bill as referred.

The bill proceeds through the committee process and floor process in the second chamber in much the same manner as a bill introduced in that chamber.

Upon an affirmative vote on final passage in the second chamber, the bill is returned to the first chamber with a message stating the action taken by the second chamber.

If the bill passed the second chamber without change, it has passed both chambers in identical form and can be enrolled. If passed with amendments, a text showing the bill as passed by the second chamber is prepared, and the Government Printing Office is directed to print that text. The first chamber then proceeds to consider that text.

§ 2.31 Resolving Differences by Amendment or Conference

The two chambers may continue to exchange proposed versions until one chamber agrees to the version passed by the other; at that point, it has passed both chambers in identical form and that version can be enrolled.

The other method for resolving differences between the chambers is for one chamber to request a conference. If the other chamber agrees, a committee on conference is formed. See also *Congressional Deskbook*, § 8.280, "Conference Committees."

A committee on conference (or a "conference committee") is a temporary committee formed to negotiate the differences between the chambers and to recommend a new text that resolves those differences. Generally, a conference committee does not hold hearings or markups, but only negotiating sessions. Though formal, open negotiating sessions are held, as a practical matter most of the negotiating takes place informally and behind closed doors.

A conference committee meets as if it were a single committee but votes as if it were two separate committees, one comprised of members appointed by the House, the other comprised of members appointed by the Senate. (Members of a conference committee are referred to as "managers.") To reach a conference agreement, a majority of the managers on the part of the House must reach agreement with a majority of the managers on the part of the Senate.

When an agreement is reached, the text of the bill as recommended by the conference is prepared and filed, along with a statement explaining the differences between the House and Senate positions and the manner in which those differences were resolved.

The new text is known as the "conference report," while the statement is known as the "joint statement of managers," the "joint explanatory statement," or simply the "joint statement." The conference report and joint statement are filed in each chamber and printed by the Government Printing Office.

The joint statement is very much like a committee report. It may, for example, include report language. (For more on report language, see § 2.25, "Full Committee Action," and § 3.75, "Report Language.")

Each chamber then considers the conference report under a special procedure that permits only an up-or-down vote—no amendments may be offered. If both chambers pass the conference report, it can be enrolled.

§ 2.40 Enrollment

After a bill has passed both chambers in identical form, the enrolling clerk of the chamber in which the bill originated prepares the official text of the bill so that it can be presented to the President. This process is known as "enrollment." The clerk prepares the text and arranges for the Government Printing Office to print the bill as enrolled. An original print is made on parchment paper and signed by the presiding officer of each chamber. See also *Congressional Deskbook*, § 8.290, "Presidential Action on Enacted Measures."

§ 2.41 Last-Minute Corrections

Usually, the enrolled bill is the final form of the legislation. Occasionally, errors (or misgivings) creep into the process and are corrected if caught in time. Whether before or after the original print is signed by the presiding officers, the two chambers may pass a concurrent resolution to correct errors in the enrollment. Concurrent resolutions have even been used to recall a bill from the President and to vacate the enrollment of a bill.

In very rare cases, an error in the enrollment is discovered only after the bill has been approved by the President. In that case, the errors have become law and can be changed only by another law.

One such case came about toward the end of the session in 1986. On October 17, 1986, Congress passed H.J.Res. 738, a joint resolution making continuing appropriations for fiscal year 1987. It was presented to the President that day, signed into law the following day, and assigned Public Law No. 99-500. However, several paragraphs of text that were supposed to be in the enrolled bill were not there. To fix the problem, an odd procedure was used: H.J.Res. 738 was enrolled again (this time including the corrections), was presented to the President, and on October 30, 1986, was signed into another law, Public Law 99-591. One measure, two nearly identical laws.

As the President explained in his statement on signing the second law: "The provisions I signed into law on October 18 remain the law of the land. . . . My signing of H.J.Res. 738 today will enable the provisions previously omitted to become law as well." 100 Stat. 3341–3389. The statement does not mention that it also enabled many provisions contained in both versions to become law twice. As a matter of common sense and probable legislative intent, the two laws have been treated as one: Identical amendments required by both laws, for example, have been executed once only. One can only wonder why Congress did not pass a second law amending or repealing the first one, and can only suppose that there were pragmatic or political reasons not to do so.

§ 2.50 Executive Action

A congressional action, regardless of form—bill, resolution, order, or vote—does not have the force and effect of law unless it is first presented to the President for approval. This is the rule provided by Article I, Section 7 of the Constitution and by decisions of the Supreme Court interpreting that section, most notably *Immigration and Naturalization Service v. Chadha*, 462 U.S. 919 (1983) (holding a so-called "legislative veto" unconstitutional for violating the Presentment Clause). (See also § 5.21, The Bill—What It Means to "Make Law": The *Chadha* Decision.)

§ 2.51 Presentment to the President

After a bill is enrolled, it is delivered to the President or, more typically, some other White House official (delivery to a White House official is customarily considered to suffice). This process is known as "presentment."

Though the Constitution requires presentment, it does not require that presentment be done immediately or even swiftly. Congress may hold the enrolled bill for days or weeks. Congress holds a bill in some cases for political reasons, and in other cases as a courtesy to the President, particularly when the President is away from the capital on travel.

§ 2.52 Approval (or Disapproval)

Once a bill is presented to the President, the following applies:

> "If he approves he shall sign it, but if not he shall return it, with his Objections to that House in which it shall have originated, who shall enter the Objections at large on their Journal, and proceed to reconsider it. If after such Reconsideration two thirds of that House shall agree to pass the Bill, it shall be sent, together with the Objections, to the other House, by which it shall likewise be reconsidered, and if approved by two thirds of that House, it shall become a Law. . . . If any Bill shall not be returned by the President within ten Days (Sundays excepted) after it shall have been presented to him, the Same shall be a Law, in like Manner as if he had signed it, unless the Congress by their Adjournment prevent its Return in which Case it shall not be a Law."
>
> *(Art. I, sec. 7, cl. 2.)*

A bill becomes law on the date on which the final step required by the Constitution takes place. Thus, if it becomes law because the President signs it, it becomes law on the date of signing. If it becomes law because the President fails to return it within the ten-day period, ordinarily it becomes law on the date that ends the period. (Notice that when the President fails to return a bill timely, it either becomes a law, or fails to become a law, depending on whether

Congress adjourns before the period expires. The former is known as a "pocket approval," while the latter is known as a "pocket veto.") If a bill becomes law because both chambers override a veto, it becomes law on the date of the vote by the second chamber. See also *Congressional Deskbook*, § 8.290, "Presidential Action on Enacted Measures."

§ 2.60 Publishing the Law

An enrolled bill that becomes law is sent to the Archives of the United States, as required by section 106a of title 1, United States Code. If the bill becomes law by legislative override of an executive veto, Congress sends the bill to the Archives; if the bill becomes law by any other means (signature or pocket approval), the White House sends the bill to the Archives. See also *Congressional Deskbook*, § 8.300, "Publication of Public Laws."

§ 2.61 Public Law Number

The archivist assigns the new law a public law number (or a private law number, in the case of a private bill). The numbers run in sequence from the beginning of a Congress, and since 1957 contain a prefix that indicates the number of the Congress. For example, the eighteenth public law of the 108th Congress is Public Law 108-18. Private laws have a separate sequence; for example, there may be both a Public Law 108-18 and a Private Law 108-18. For more on private laws, see § 5.20, "The Bill."

§ 2.62 Slip Law

The first official publication of a law is in a pamphlet containing only that law. This publication is known as a slip law. Each slip law is prepared and published by the Archivist of the United States through the Office of the Federal Register.

A slip law contains the text of the new law and a host of new information: the public law number (or private law number, as the case may be), the date of approval by the President (or, if the bill became law without the approval of the President, a notation to that effect), the designation and number of the underlying bill, the volume of the Statutes at Large in which the new law will appear, a reference guide to the legislative history of the new law, and marginal notes.

The reference guide indicates whether any committee report or presidential statement was printed in connection with the legislation and, if so, provides appropriate citations. The guide also indicates the dates on which the legislation passed the House and the Senate, and provides appropriate citations to the Congressional Record.

The marginal notes—so named because they appear literally in the margins of the slip law—provide additional reference information and explanatory material. For example, whenever a provision of the act is to be classified to the United States Code, a marginal note sets forth what the United States Code citation for that provision will be. Also, whenever the text of the new act refers to another provision that already has a United States Code citation, a marginal note indicates what that Code citation is. See *Congressional Deskbook*, § 15.23a, "Public Law."

§ 2.63 Statutes at Large

The second official publication of a new law is as part of the United States Statutes at Large. The Statutes at Large is a collection of slip laws for a particular session of Congress, arranged in sequence by public law number. The Statutes at Large is published in bound volumes by the Archivist of the United States through the Office of the Federal Register, pursuant to section 112 of title 1, United States Code.

The Statutes at Large also collects and arranges in sequence several other important documents. Private laws are arranged in sequence by private law number; concurrent resolutions are arranged in sequence by date of adoption.

From 1939 through 1980, some law was made through a process known as a reorganization plan (a process no longer in use). During that period, the reorganization plans that came into effect were likewise published in the Statutes at Large. A reorganization plan was prepared, and submitted to Congress, by the President, and became law if ratified by a joint resolution. For the law relating to reorganization plans, see chapter 9 of title 5, United States Code (5 U.S.C. 901 et seq.). Many reorganization plans are recorded for posterity in the United States Code; they are listed in the tables toward the end of the Code and printed in the appendices to title 5 of the Code.

From time to time, presidential documents (such as executive orders) and other forms of congressional documents (such as simple resolutions considered to have historic significance) are published in the Statutes at Large, though this is the exception rather than the rule.

§ 2.70 Compilations

If Congress followed a system in which laws did not amend other laws, there would be no need for compilations. A statute would be published in the Statutes at Large and it would never change (though other laws might still refer to it and affect it). The Supreme Court works that way—issuing opinion after opinion, affecting (but not amending the text of) other opinions. But Congress does not work that way.

Whenever a new law amends an old one, the old law no longer reads the way it once did. You can look up the old law in the Statutes at Large, but that shows how it read as enacted, not how it reads now. When a law has never been amended, you can dust off the version in the Statutes at Large and read it just fine. But once it has been amended, the version in the Statutes at Large is like yesterday's newspaper.

A compilation, on the other hand, is a document that shows a law with every amendment later made to it correctly carried out.

For example, suppose one law provides:

> **SECTION 1. SHORT TITLE.**
>
> This Act may be cited as the "Study of Z Act".
>
> **SEC. 2. DUTY OF SECRETARY OF DEFENSE.**
>
> (a) IN GENERAL.—The Secretary of Defense shall carry out, on an annual basis, a study of Z.
>
> (b) REPORT.—Not later than March 1 of each year, the Secretary shall submit to Congress a report on the study carried out under subsection (a).

And a later law provides:

> **SECTION 1. SHORT TITLE.**
>
> This Act may be cited as the "New and Improved Study of Z Act".
>
> **SEC. 2. ATTORNEY GENERAL TO CARRY OUT STUDY.**
>
> Section 2 of the Study of Z Act is amended in each of subsections (a) and (b) by striking "Secretary" and inserting "Attorney General".

A compilation of the Study of Z Act would then provide:

> **SECTION 1. SHORT TITLE.**
>
> This Act may be cited as the "Study of Z Act".

SEC. 2. DUTY OF SECRETARY OF DEFENSE.

(a) IN GENERAL.—The Attorney General of Defense shall carry out, on an annual basis, a study of Z.

(b) REPORT.—Not later than March 1 of each year, the Attorney General shall submit to Congress a report on the study carried out under subsection (a).

Going forward, some people might casually refer to the Study of Z Act as the "New and Improved Study of Z Act," but to do so is error. The New and Improved Study of Z Act did not replace the original law; it merely amended that law. Going forward, the New and Improved Study of Z Act remains on the books, but it is inert. The law that has continuing force is the original law. In the constitutional sense, both acts are law, and should be read together (see § 3.43).

Anyone can prepare a compilation. Many committees of Congress and many executive branch agencies maintain compilations of the laws with which they are most concerned. Compilations are essential for identifying the correct text of a law at a particular moment in time. You cannot amend a law properly without first consulting a compilation of that law; in many cases you can't even cite to a law properly without first consulting a compilation of that law.

Some compilations are more exacting than others. A compilation that is absolutely faithful to the source material—showing every printed character, carrying out every amendment in a literal way, exercising no independent judgment—is a "true" compilation. If any part of the material is changed for any reason not required by law, the compilation is not a true one.

A compilation falls short of being a true compilation if, for example, it changes words, punctuation, format, or style. These changes might be made with the best of intentions; indeed, in many cases they help the reader—but they do not help the drafter.

The compilation of the Study of Z Act in the example above is a true compilation. It carries out the amendments literally, even though they appear to have been not well thought out. Notice that the section heading for section 2 still refers to the Secretary of Defense; the official referred to in subsection (a) is neither the Secretary of Defense nor the Attorney General, but the strange hybrid "Attorney General of Defense."

If you are working with a law (as a drafter, or as an interpreter) and you don't have access to a true compilation of that law, make one yourself; it's not particularly hard, though it can be time-consuming if the law has been amended many times or in complex ways. Start with the text of the original law, gather up all the later amendments, and carry out the amendments in sequence in a literal, ministerial way. If there is any doubt about how to carry out an amendment, make note of the doubt, and use your best judgment about what Congress probably intended. If you can identify a probable, but not crystal-clear, intent, you can carry it out in your compilation, so long as you know not to rely on it too heavily or expect others to do so. Remember, each act that makes an amendment is a discrete enactment with a discrete legislative intent.

The thorniest task in making a compilation is gathering up all the later amendments. How do you find them, short of going through the entire Statutes at Large page by page? Fortunately, there are indices that keep track of when one law amends another. Assuming the index you use is complete, accurate, and up to date, you can rely on it in gathering up amendments.

§2.80 The United States Code

For many laws, the third official publication of the law is as part of the United States Code. The Code is a collection of the general and permanent laws of the United States, arranged by subject matter. The Code is prepared and published by the Office of the Law Revision Counsel of the House of Representatives, under chapter 3 of title 1, United States Code.

The functions of the Law Revision Counsel are set forth in section 205(c) of H. Res. 988 of the 93d Congress (2 U.S.C. 285b), as enacted into law by Public Law 93-554.

One of the easiest ways for a drafter to look foolish—and, more importantly, to fail a client—is by failing to understand what the Code is (and is not) and how to use it properly. To understand these things, some background is in order.

The purpose of a code is to arrange important laws in a sensible, convenient, and updated way. The Statutes at Large series does not serve that purpose; its purpose is to systematically publish every law ever enacted in chronological order. That series provides an historical record, not a handbook of laws.

§ 2.81 The Revised Statutes of 1873

The U.S. Code is not the first code of laws of the United States. The first code was the Revised Statutes of the United States, which covered all laws in effect as of December 1, 1873. It was enacted into law in 1874 and was first widely published in 1875. Today, it is commonly referred to as the Revised Statutes of 1873 or simply the Revised Statutes.

To prepare the Revised Statutes, the compilers gathered together all the laws then in effect and prepared a single text that covered the substance of those laws while presenting that substance in a revised, organized, consistent manner. That single text was then enacted wholesale by a single Act of Congress, which simultaneously repealed all prior laws.

It was an impressive achievement, though one must bear in mind that federal law in 1873 was not nearly as massive and wide-ranging as today. The entire text of the Revised Statutes was printed in a single volume of 1,085 pages. It took a congressional commission about six years to complete the task.

To this day, many provisions in the Revised Statutes remain law and can be found in the Code in some form. Other than the Constitution and certain treaties, these are the oldest federal laws on the books.

Having replaced and repealed all prior laws, the Revised Statutes made all prior volumes of the Statutes at Large obsolete. In most cases, those volumes were thrown away, not being of any further legal value (though, of course, they continue to have historical and scholarly value). If you have been wondering why your local law library's collection of volumes of the Statutes at Large begins with volumes from the 1870s, now you know.

§ 2.82 The Revised Statutes of 1878

The Revised Statutes of 1873 did not come off perfectly; indeed, a great many errors were later found. Congress passed laws to make technical corrections, and then called for a revised print of the Revised Statutes. The revised print was published in 1878 in volume 18 of the Statutes at Large and was referred to then as the "second edition" of the Revised Statutes. Today, it is known as the Revised Statutes of 1878.

To prepare the second edition, compilers made a compilation: They started with the original and then carried out the later amendments. This time, however, Congress did not reenact the new text wholesale; instead, it merely passed a law authorizing that the new text be printed.

Congress later passed another law (the joint resolution of June 7, 1880; 21 Stat. 308) authorizing that a series of supplements to the second edition be compiled and printed. These were likewise not reenactments but additional prints.

§ 2.83 Positive Law and Non-Positive Law

There is a fundamental difference between the two editions of the Revised Statutes. The 1873 edition was both enacted and published; the 1878 edition was only published. One has force of law. The other is a book.

The terms used to describe this distinction are "positive law" and "non-positive law."

Positive law is the law itself; it is precisely what has been enacted, neither more nor less. To refer back to the example used in § 2.70, "Compilations," the Study of Z Act as enacted is positive law; the New and Improved Study of Z Act as enacted is also positive law.

Likewise (and this is where it starts to get tricky), the Study of Z Act in its compiled form—as modified by the New and Improved Study of Z Act—is also positive law. Positive law is not about existence on a printed page; it is about existence in the ether of law. Even if no one ever prepares a true compilation of the Study of Z Act in its updated form, that act as modified is positive law.

Non-positive law, meanwhile, is merely a representation of what the law is. It is something like a *Reader's Digest* version of the law. When you prepare a compilation of the Study of Z Act, your compilation is non-positive law—it is merely your own personal representation of what the positive law is.

For example: Suppose the Office of Law Revision Counsel prepared a series of compilations of hundreds of different laws, and took all the provisions of all of those laws and edited them and rearranged them in a particular sequence, and assigned each provision a new section number, and called the entire thing "title 42 of the United States Code," and published the entire thing in the same manner and form as it publishes a positive-law title of the Code. The result looks like a positive-law title, but it is nothing more than a repackaged series of compilations. You do not amend title 42; title 42 is not a law, but a book that contains a repackaged series of compilations of laws.

For that reason, and as discussed in more detail below, the distinction between positive law and non-positive law is an essential one for anyone who uses the Code.

§ 2.84 Origin of the Code as Non-Positive Law

Congress first set in motion what eventually became the Code in 1919, when a special committee in the House began work on the project. The Code was first published in 1926.

The full title of the Code is the "Code of the Laws of the United States of America." Most people refer to it as the United States Code, the U.S. Code, or simply the Code.

The Code was prepared in much the same manner as the Revised Statutes of 1873—the compilers gathered together all the laws then in effect and prepared a single text that covered the substance of those laws while presenting that substance in a revised, organized, and consistent manner.

But the Code was not enacted into law. Instead, Congress did something curious: It passed a law that set forth the entire new text but did not enact that text into law. The law did not repeal or amend any prior laws. It simply set forth the new text, specified that it was an attempt to restate the law, and provided that if any part of the new text was inconsistent with prior law, prior law—not the new text—would prevail.

The Code, in other words, was not positive law, but non-positive law. It was nothing more than Congress's own personal restatement of the law.

When you want to refer to or amend a provision shown in the Code, you cannot properly refer to or amend it directly; you must instead refer to or amend the source law, which remains the positive law. For example, if (to use hypothetical numbers) section 315 of the Revised Statutes had been placed in the Code as section 32 of title 42, the source law (and positive law) is section 315 of the Revised Statutes, not section 32 of title 42. Of course, you could—indeed, you generally should—provide a parenthetical citation to the Code as a convenience to the reader, who typically has more ready access to the Code than to a true compilation of section 315 of the Revised Statutes. Thus, "Section 315 of the Revised Statutes (42 U.S.C. 32)."

§ 2.85 Editorial Changes

Also, unlike the second edition of the Revised Statutes, the Code was not a true compilation of the law. Though it did not make substantive changes, it did make a great many editorial changes.

For example, if a law covered several subjects, it was broken into pieces, with some provisions placed in one title of the Code, others in other titles.

Each provision was assigned a new section number to conform to the new placement. Any reference in law to a provision's source section number was changed to refer instead to the newly assigned section number. And so on. Finally, the format of each provision was changed from its original format and style to the uniform format and style used in the Code.

In addition to the editorial changes, the Code also includes useful new information. After each section is a notation that specifies the source law from which the section is derived.

In maintaining the Code, Law Revision Counsel continues to make editorial changes of this sort. In addition, Law Revision Counsel also includes other explanatory and historical notes, making the Code a valuable tool for any drafter. But you must always bear in mind that the text is not positive law; it has been rearranged and retouched.

An extreme, but useful, example of the sort of retouching that can go on can be seen in the codification note to 33 U.S.C. 602, which comprehensively explains what has been retouched in that provision. As that codification note reveals, the text shown in 33 U.S.C. 602 in no way resembles any law ever passed by Congress; instead, the text shown is a patchwork of provisions from several different laws that collectively capture the gist of what remains relevant from those provisions today. It provides as follows:

> CODIFICATION
>
> Except for the last sentence, the first paragraph of this section was from a part of section 3 of act June 6, 1900. The omitted portion of the original text authorized the Secretary of War, in his discretion, to terminate the contract with James B. Eads and provided that the Secretary of War should take charge of the channel "in case of the termination of said contract, by virtue of the provisions hereof or by expiration of said contract."
>
> The last sentence of the first paragraph of this section was from a provision of section 1 of act June 13, 1902. Further provisions of the original text, for the purchase of lands and buildings on either side of the South Pass, were temporary merely and are omitted. The original text provided for the use of "the dredge boat Beta, or any other available government dredge."
>
> The second paragraph of this section was from section 4 of act Aug.

11, 1888. In the original text, following the words "Mississippi river," the following words appeared: "As provided for in the Act of Mar. third, eighteen hundred and seventy-five."

The words "the sum of $10,000," are substituted for "the amount appropriated in this act for such purpose." $10,000 was the amount appropriated for such purpose by section 1 of act June 13, 1902.

Act Mar. 3, 1875, ch. 134, mentioned in the original text, provided in section 4 et seq., 18 Stat. 463 to 466, for a contract with James B. Eads and others to construct jetties, etc., to maintain the channel at the South Pass.

The provisions of that act and of act Aug. 11, 1888, with regard to examinations and surveys at the South Pass, remained in force notwithstanding the termination of said contract, by a provision of act June 13, 1902.

Another way to understand the difference between the true compilation of a law and the editorial reworking of that law by Law Revision Counsel is to directly compare the true compilation to the version shown in the United States Code. The statutory charter of the Office of the Legislative Counsel is a particularly useful and telling example. That charter is section 1303 of the Revenue Act of 1918, a true compilation of which is as follows:

SEC. 1303. (a) That there is hereby created a Legislative Drafting Service under the direction of two draftsmen, one of whom shall be appointed by the President pro tempore of the Senate, and one by the Speaker of the House of Representatives, without reference to political affiliations and solely on the ground of fitness to perform the duties of the office. Each draftsman shall receive a salary of $5,000 a year, payable monthly. The draftsmen shall, subject to the approval of the President pro tempore of the Senate and the Speaker of the House of Representatives, employ and fix the compensation of such assistant draftsmen, clerks, and other employees, and purchase such furniture, office equipment, books, stationery, and other supplies, as may be necessary for the proper performance of the duties of the service and as may be appropriated for by Congress.

(b) The Drafting Service shall aid in drafting public bills and resolutions or amendments thereto on the request of any committee of either House of Congress, but the Library Committee of the Senate and the Library Committee of the House of Representatives, respectively, may determine the preference, if any, to be given to such requests of the committees of either House, respectively. The draftsmen shall, from time to time, prescribe rules and regulations for the conduct of the work of the service for the committees of each House, subject to the approval of the Library Committee of each House, respectively.

(c) For the remainder of the current fiscal year there is hereby appropriated, out of any money in the Treasury not otherwise appropriated, the sum of $25,000, or so much thereof as may be necessary, for the purpose of defraying the expenses of the establishment and maintenance of the service, including the payment of salaries herein authorized. One-half of all appropriations for the service shall be disbursed by the Secretary of the Senate and one-half by the Clerk of the House of Representatives.

(d) After this subdivision takes effect the legislative drafting service shall be known as the office of the legislative counsel, and the two draftsmen shall be known as legislative counsel. The positions of legislative counsel shall be allocated from time to time by the President pro tempore of the Senate and the Speaker of the House of Representatives, jointly, to the appropriate grade in the compensation schedules of section 13 of the Classification Act of 1923. The rate of compensation of each of the two legislative counsel shall be fixed from time to time, within the limits of such grade, by the President pro tempore of the Senate and the Speaker of the House of Representatives, respectively. The increased compensation provided for in this subdivision shall, when fixed, be in lieu of the salary specified in subdivision (a).

This single section is classified to title 2 of the Code as a series of sections within subchapter I of chapter 9 (2 U.S.C. 271 et seq.). Those sections can be found in this book, in Appendix Five. Compare the true compilation with the Code version and you will find that they have very little in common. As with the example of 33 U.S.C. 602 above, the text shown at 2 U.S.C. 271 et seq. is a patchwork of provisions from several different laws that collectively capture the gist of what remains relevant from those provisions today.

§ 2.86 General and Permanent Law

The Code does not cover all federal law. For the most part, the Code covers a law only if the law meets three criteria: that it be general, permanent, and presently in effect. (These three criteria were also the criteria used in preparing the Revised Statutes.)

A law is not general if it applies only to particular people or particular places. Private laws, for example, are not included in the Code. Likewise, laws that apply only to the District of Columbia, or only to a particular federal facility or program, are typically not included in the Code.

A law is not permanent if it applies only for a short period of time. Provisions in appropriations acts, for example, are typically not included in the Code because they typically apply only to a particular fiscal year.

A law is not presently in effect if it has been repealed or if it has expired by its terms. A law that merely amended other law—like section 2 of the New and Improved Study of Z Act in the example in § 2.70, "Compilations"—is not included in the Code.

The Code does occasionally include a law that does not fully satisfy the three criteria, but that is rare.

§ 2.87 Organization into Titles

The Code arranges provisions by subject matter under fifty different titles, placing related provisions more or less together.

The number of titles is not set by law. As originally conceived, the first six titles related to the federal government, while titles 7 through 50 related to subject matters from "Agriculture" to "War and National Defense," arranged in alphabetical order. Over the years, however, titles 10 (Army) and 34 (Navy) were consolidated into a new title 10 (Armed Forces), and title 6 (Surety Bonds) was consolidated into title 31 (Money and Finance), leaving only forty-eight titles in actual use.

When the Homeland Security Act of 2002 was enacted, Law Revision Counsel placed that material in the empty title 6 and renamed that title "Domestic Security." In 2004, Law Revision Counsel began work on a project that would create a new title 51, "National and Commercial Space Programs."

§ 2.88 Enactment of Titles into Positive Law

Law Revision Counsel is engaged in a continuing, comprehensive project to take titles of the Code that are non-positive law and enact them into positive law.

The long-term goal of the project is to achieve anew what was fleetingly achieved by the Revised Statutes of 1873: a complete statement of general and permanent law, enacted into positive law, repealing all prior law. Once achieved, that would make all prior volumes of the Statutes at Large obsolete and allow law librarians everywhere to do once again what they did circa 1874: Take all those obsolete volumes and throw them away. (Not that they would, but they could.)

Of course, it is no longer possible to fit all general and permanent law into a single volume of 1,085 pages, or to do so in six years. This is truly a long-term project: The first positive-law title was enacted in 1947, and over the next half-century about twenty more were enacted; work continues.

To enact a title into positive law, Congress passes a law containing the full text of the new title and repealing prior laws covered by the same subject. For example, Public Law 107-217 (116 Stat. 1062), enacting title 40 (Public Buildings, Property, and Works) into positive law, took effect August 21, 2002. Section 1 of the law begins: "Certain general and permanent laws of the United States, related to public buildings, property, and works, are revised, codified, and enacted as title 40, United States Code, 'Public Buildings, Property, and Works', as follows: . . . ." It then sets forth the full text of the new title, followed by a series of technical amendments and savings clauses.

When a title has been enacted into positive law, it becomes the law itself. When you want to refer to or amend a provision in that title, you amend it directly: "Section 101 of title 10, United States Code, is amended by . . . ."

A drafter needs to be able to tell at a glance whether a title of the Code is positive law or non-positive law. Unfortunately, you cannot tell from looking at the format and style of the title, because the Code uses the same format and style for positive-law titles as for non-positive-law titles.

You could memorize (or refer to) this list: As of 2002, when title 40 was enacted into positive law, the titles that were enacted into positive law were 1, 3, 4, 5, 9, 10, 11, 13, 14, 17, 18, 23, 28, 31, 32, 35, 36, 37, 38, 39, 40, 44, 46, and 49.

Or you could look in the front of any bound volume of the Code, just after the title page: You will find a page listing in two columns all the titles of the Code that had been enacted into positive law as of the date that volume was printed. The list indicates each positive-law title with an asterisk.

A third way to tell is to look at section 204 of title 1, United States Code; in the notes that follow that section there is a list of the titles enacted into positive law, together with citations to the laws by which they were enacted.

And one more way to tell is to look at the matter at the beginning of a particular title—if it is a positive-law title, this fact will be indicated immediately under the title heading, and also in a note following the title heading.

Even within a positive-law title, however, not everything shown in the title is positive law. First, each positive-law provision within the title is followed by citations to source law and other explanatory notes; these citations and notes are not part of the positive law.

Second, the title may have an appendix containing related laws or other materials; the appendices are not part of the positive law. For example, title 18 of the Code is positive law, but it has three appendices that are not positive law—one relating to unlawful possession or receipt of firearms (since repealed), one containing the Interstate Agreement on Detainers Act, and one containing the Classified Information Procedures Act.

Third, the title may also contain provisions of law that, while not codified by law into the title, have been classified by Law Revision Counsel into the title. When a non-positive-law provision is placed in a positive-law title, it is usually placed as a note following a positive-law provision to which it relates; you can easily differentiate a note from the positive-law provision by its placement and format. Typically, a non-positive provision following a positive-law provision provides an effective date or some other ancillary matter.

Sometimes, however, a non-positive provision following a positive-law provision may be an important substantive law; for example, the non-positive provisions following section 113 of title 10 (declaring that there is a Secretary of Defense) include many important laws relating to the Department of Defense that, for whatever reason, were not placed directly into title 10 by law.

For each positive-law title, the positive-law provisions within that title are presented in the Code as a true compilation. They are, unless otherwise noted, presented in their true, unedited form. Occasionally, a law attempts to amend a positive-law title in a way that cannot literally be carried out, such as when there is a typographical or clerical error in the amendatory instructions. If it seems obvious from the context what was intended, the amendment will likely be carried out to that provision as the "probable intent" of Congress, with a note following the provision indicating that fact. If it does not seem obvious what was intended, the amendment will likely not be carried out to that provision at all, with a note following the provision indicating the problem.

§ 2.89 Codification and Classification of New Laws

When Congress directly amends a positive-law title, Law Revision Counsel simply carries out the amendment in a ministerial way. An amendatory instruction in law is self-executing. Editorial decisions may be called for—such as updating the table of contents, correcting cross-references, and so on—but only Congress by law can make them. Law Revision Counsel does not carry out any editorial housekeeping with positive-law provisions.

When Congress enacts a freestanding law, on the other hand, Law Revision Counsel must decide where to place it. This process is known as "classification" (and sometimes, confusingly, as "codification") and requires a great deal of editorial judgment.

To understand the process of classification, let's refer back to the hypothetical Study of Z Act from § 2.70, "Compilations." When first enacted, the act required the Secretary of Defense to carry out a study of Z. The law could have been drafted in a way that amended title 10 of the Code or some other positive law, but it was not.

Laws relating to the duties of the Secretary of Defense are usually placed in title 10 (a positive-law title) or title 50 (a non-positive-law title). Because Congress did not directly place the substance of the Study of Z Act in title 10 by amending that title, Law Revision Counsel must decide where to classify it.

As one option, the Study of Z Act could be shown in title 10 as a note beneath a related positive-law provision. If so, Law Revision Counsel could show the entire act (both section 1 and section 2), or could drop section 1 (the short title) and show only section 2.

As another option, the Study of Z Act could be shown in title 50 as a full-fledged section rather than as a note. If so, Law Revision Counsel would probably assign section 2 of the act a new section number within title 50 and show section 1 (the short title) as a note beneath that new section.

As a third option, the Study of Z Act could be shown in title 50 as a note beneath a related non-positive-law provision. This would work much like the first option.

These are the three basic options for classifying a section: note in a positive-law title, section in a non-positive-law title, note in a non-positive-law title. When dealing with a larger act, Law Revision Counsel can break it into pieces and classify each piece separately, or keep it intact and classify it in bulk, perhaps even as an appendix to a title.

Bear in mind that, whichever option is used, Law Revision Counsel may make editorial changes to the style and text.

To continue with the example, assume Congress next enacts the New and Improved Study of Z Act. As now modified, the Study of Z Act no longer applies to the Secretary of Defense, but to the Attorney General. For that reason, Law Revision Counsel may decide to move the act from its original location in the Code to another title where functions of the Attorney General typically reside, such as title 18, title 28, or title 42.

Also, in addition to making the changes required by the New and Improved Study of Z Act, Law Revision Counsel may want to do some further editorial cleanup. The now-misleading heading of section 2 could be presented so as to refer to the Attorney General, and the bizarre reference in section 2(a) to the "Attorney General of Defense" could be presented so as to refer simply to the Attorney General.

Regardless of where or how Law Revision Counsel presents the material, however, that presentation of material is not positive law. The positive law remains the Study of Z Act, with all its flaws.

Some day the title to which the Study of Z Act has been classified might be enacted into law and the Study of Z Act repealed. From that day forward, the new title would be positive law and the Study of Z Act would be no more.

§ 2.90 Resolving Conflicts among Published Versions of Law

Sometimes there are differences between a law as published in slip law form, in the Statutes at Large, and in the United States Code. A court needs to determine which version prevails so that it can interpret the law properly and you, as a drafter, need to determine which version prevails so that you can draft properly.

The order of precedence—from most authoritative to least authoritative—is Statutes at Large, United States Code, slip law.

A slip law is least authoritative because it is merely "competent" evidence of the law, as provided by section 113 of title 1, United States Code. A slip law is prepared and printed in haste. It is useful until its contents are published in bound form in the Statutes at Large, at which point it is superseded by the version contained in the Statutes at Large.

The United States Code is "prima facie" evidence of the law in the case of a non-positive-law provision and "legal" evidence of the law in the case of a positive-law provision, as provided by section 204 of title 1, United States Code. Prima facie evidence is acceptable on its face, but can be overcome by contrary evidence. Legal evidence is substantial proof, but likewise can be overcome by contrary evidence.

The Statutes at Large is also legal evidence of the law, as provided by section 112 of title 1, United States Code. It is fair to ask, then, why the Statutes at Large is more authoritative than a positive-law part of the Code, when each is legal evidence of the law. The answer is that the Statutes at Large must prevail because it shows the law untouched by later editing. The Statutes at Large is the source material used by Law Revision Counsel to prepare the Code; any differences between the Code and the Statutes at Large are due to editorial judgment by Law Revision Counsel or, perhaps, clerical or printing errors. Editorial judgment and printing errors occurring after enactment cannot be given force of law. For example, if a law attempts to amend a positive-law title in a way that cannot literally be carried out, Law Revision Counsel may decide to carry out the amendment in a manner that reflects the "probable intent" of Congress, but that decision is not controlling. Likewise, if Law Revision Counsel omits a provision from the Code entirely, in the belief that it is obsolete, that belief is not controlling. (See *United States National Bank of Oregon v. Independent Insurance Agents*, 508 U.S. 439 (1993).) Ultimately, it is the Statutes at Large that controls.

The bottom line is that when drafting (and, incidentally, when interpreting), you are always best off using a true compilation derived from the Statutes at Large and prepared by a reliable source. For a positive-law part of the Code, you can usually rely on the Code. For a non-positive-law part of the Code, you should not rely on the Code unless you have no choice; you should always try instead to use a true compilation derived from the Statutes at Large, even if you have to prepare it yourself.

Having said that, you should also know that even the Statutes at Large is not infallible. To establish the "conclusive" evidence of the law, you must look to the enrolled bill. Under the rule in *Field v. Clark*, 143 U.S. 649 (1891), sometimes referred to as the "Marshall Field doctrine," the text of the enrolled bill, as signed by the presiding officers and presented to the President, is conclusive evidence of the text as passed by Congress. If by some chance there is a discrepancy between the Statutes at Large and the enrolled bill, the enrolled bill would control. Not long ago enrolled bills were hard to come by, but they have since become readily available over the Internet. Perhaps a case will come in which you will need to refer to an enrolled bill to determine what the law actually is; not likely, but possible, at least in theory.

Considering the Courts: Statutory Interpretation

Chapter 3

All new laws, though penned with the greatest technical skill, and passed on the fullest and most mature deliberation, are considered as more or less obscure and equivocal, until their meaning be liquidated and ascertained by a series of particular discussions and adjudications.

James Madison, *The Federalist* Number 37

The prophecies of what the courts will do in fact, and nothing more pretentious, are what I mean by the law.

Oliver Wendell Holmes Jr.

(1) Read the statute; (2) read the statute; (3) read the statute!

Justice Frankfurter's "threefold imperative to law students," as related by Henry Friendly, *Benchmarks* 202 (1967)

Considering the Courts: Statutory Interpretation

Chapter 3

§ 3.00 Introduction

As described in the Canadian case of *Regina v. Ojibway*, 8 *Criminal Law Quarterly* 137–139 (1965), a pony bearing a down pillow for a saddle was shot to put it out of its misery. The shooter was charged with killing a "small bird" in violation of the Small Birds Act, and the question on appeal was whether a pony was a "small bird" within the meaning of the act. The court held that it was.

"Statutory interpretation," the court observed, "has forced many a horse to eat birdseed for the rest of its life." For the full text of this case, see Appendix Six.

Regina v. Ojibway is a work of fiction, but a deft one—farfetched, and yet not completely absurd. Courts can and do read statutes in odd ways at times. As a drafter, you need to understand how and why that happens, so that you can draft, and advise your client, accordingly.

§ 3.01 Courts: The Most Important Audience

Some drafting projects never see the light of day, but most are intended to be read. Ultimately, the effect of a draft depends not on what you think the draft means or on what your client thinks the draft means, but on what the audience thinks the draft means.

To draft effectively, then, you need to get inside the mind of the audience and understand how the audience thinks. But who is the audience?

In drafting federal law, the most important audience (apart from the client) is the federal courts—and, in particular, the Supreme Court of the United States. Fortunately, it is not difficult to get inside the mind of the Court and understand how it thinks. The Court makes this process public in its published opinions; collectively, the process is known as statutory interpretation. (It is also known as statutory construction; the differences between the two terms are not great. For consistency's sake, this book uses "statutory interpretation" throughout.)

There are other audiences, of course. The draft will be read and interpreted by legislators, lobbyists, public officials, private individuals, industry leaders, journalists, and scholars, to name a few. In some ways these audiences are very different, but in two ways they are all alike: Each wants to know the effect of the draft, and each recognizes that the effect is ultimately determined by the courts, through judicial methods of statutory interpretation. The courts always have the last word, and the Supreme Court has the very last word: "We are not final because we are infallible, but we are infallible only because we are final." *Brown v. Allen*, 344 U.S. 443, 539 (1953) (Jackson, J., concurring). When you control how a court reads a text, you thereby control how others read that text as well.

Some who write about drafting have argued that a drafter does not need to be much concerned with statutory interpretation. Reed Dickerson, for example, argued as follows: "For the draftsman, many rules of interpretation are simply irrelevant. . . . They are irrelevant because the draftsman who tries to write a healthy instrument does not and should not pay attention to the principles that the court will apply if he fails." Reed Dickerson, *The Fundamentals of Legal Drafting* 54 (1965).

This is, to put it delicately, not the best advice. Suppose you were an appellate lawyer trying to convince a court that a statute means X. You probably would argue that the statute is clear and the plain meaning is X—but you must also be ready to argue that the statute, even if unclear, should be given the meaning X. In short, you need a fallback position. The suggestion that you should not have a fallback position in drafting is bizarre. Your job is to do all you can to give effect to the policy, not to rest on language that you think is clear.

Statutory interpretation applies at all times to all instruments, not just to those that are not, as Dickerson put it, "healthy." Indeed, it is used to determine whether an instrument is healthy in the first place. It is used to decide what a healthy instrument means, and what an unhealthy instrument means.

It is true that many principles of statutory interpretation are simply general principles about how best to read English prose. But many are not. Some are obvious, some are subtle, some are counterintuitive, some are traps for the unwary.

You can try to draft without paying attention to statutory interpretation. But rules of interpretation are like rules of the road: Drive on the right; stop on red; signal before turning; pedestrians have the right of way. If you don't know all the rules, sooner or later you will park in front of a fire hydrant or go the wrong way down a one-way street.

§ 3.02 What Kind of Judge?

Among those who write about drafting there is a curious debate about what kind of judge should be considered the primary audience. Can you safely assume that the audience is a "good-faith judge"—one who will give your words the benefit of the doubt—or should you assume that the audience is a "bad-faith judge"—one who will actively try to twist and evade your words?

This is sort of like asking whether you should be cynical or naive. It's not really a useful choice. You should be realistic.

The audience is almost certainly not a single judge. Perhaps if the Supreme Court were abolished and replaced by a single judge the question might be worth more study. But the fact is that a law is not what any one judge says it is, but what a majority of the nine justices on the Court say it is.

If it helps your process to have in mind a particular kind of judge, try the middle ground: Assume the judge is open-minded and skeptical. Do not assume the judge is sympathetic to you and your intended meaning. Thanks to you, the judge has to resolve a duel between warring lawyers—a duel that came about because your language is problematic. Do not expect the judge to cut you any slack.

Ultimately, the concern is not so much that a rogue court will invent an implausible meaning that mangles your statute. The concern is that a careful court, prodded by a persuasive attorney, or on its own initiative, will see a plausible meaning that you failed to see.

§ 3.10 Judicial Power and Legislative Supremacy

The judicial power of the United States is vested by the Constitution in the Supreme Court of the United States and any other federal courts established by law.

The task of courts is to interpret and apply the law. As Justice Marshall famously put it, "it is emphatically the province and duty of the judicial department to say what the law is." *Marbury v. Madison*, 5 U.S. 137, 177 (1803).

The judicial power can be exercised only in cases and controversies. This means that the federal courts do not have power to issue advisory opinions. This also means that federal courts do not interpret statutes as an abstract exercise; they always have a particular case before them with a particular pattern of facts.

In resolving cases and controversies, a court actually performs three separate functions. First, the court finds which facts have been proven; second, the court interprets the relevant law; and third, the court applies the law as interpreted to the facts as found.

This chapter is concerned primarily with the second function, though the second and third functions sometimes blend together. A court interprets a statute in some cases because the language is unclear, and in other cases because the language, though clear, didn't anticipate (and doesn't squarely address) a controversy of the sort before the court.

§ 3.11 The Power to Interpret

As a general matter, a court left to its own devices can interpret a statute using any technique that it likes. The court can consider the sound of a cat and the breath of a fish. Left to its own devices, a court can look to anything under the sun that it considers persuasive.

Courts have, for example, considered sources such as law review articles, history, social context, state law, and general principles of public policy. They occasionally invoke poetry or literature, such as the works of Shakespeare or Conan Doyle.

Of course, courts are not left entirely to their own devices. Most importantly, courts are bound by law to follow the Constitution and the laws of the United States.

Also, most courts are bound by custom—if not by law—to follow precedent. (Courts in a civil law system, such as the courts of Louisiana, are not.) Specifically, a court is bound to follow the precedents of courts that are higher in the judicial "chain of command." A court is not bound to follow the precedents of every higher court, but it is bound to follow the precedents of the higher courts to which appeals from its decisions are taken. Thus, each of the circuit courts is bound by the precedents of the Supreme Court, and each trial court is bound by the precedents of both the Supreme Court and one circuit court.

A court is not bound to follow the precedent of a lower court or of a court of the same level, including itself: No court is bound to follow its own precedents. As a result, the Supreme Court—having no higher court—is not bound to follow any precedents—its own or anyone else's.

That said, courts do not lightly overrule their own past decisions. This is known as the doctrine of stare decisis. "Very weighty considerations" underlie the doctrine, such as the need for laws to be clear and reliable, for disputes to be settled, and for faith in the judiciary to be maintained. See *Moragne v. States Marine Lines*, 398 U.S. 375, 403 (1970). The doctrine of stare decisis "is of fundamental importance to the rule of law." *Hilton v. South Carolina Public Railways Commission*, 502 U.S. 197, 202 (1991).

When interpreting the Constitution, the Court is somewhat flexible about overruling its past decisions, such as if the past decision is unworkable or the rationale for the decision no longer holds. In constitutional matters, what is most important to the Court is that it get the answer right (even if it takes several tries). The Constitution is not an easy document to amend, so society might be long stuck with a wrong answer if the Court did not overrule itself. See *Webster v. Reproductive Health Services*, 492 U.S. 490, 518 (1989) (plurality opinion).

A statute, on the other hand, is a relatively easy document to amend, so the Court is much less willing to overrule itself. What is most important to the Court is that once it reaches an answer, it abides by that answer. If Congress disagrees with that answer, "Congress remains free to alter what we have done." *Patterson v. McLean Credit Union*, 491 U.S. 164, 172–173 (1989).

The power to create specific techniques of statutory interpretation is seen as part of the judicial power. The Constitution does not require that specific techniques be created, but the courts, in their discretion, have seen fit to create them. Once created, a court can overrule them in much the same way as a court can overrule a statute, though—as with statutes—the courts have been reluctant to do so.

Remember, techniques of interpretation have generally not been enacted into law—a least not at the federal level. (In a fair number of states, some techniques—most notably, canons of construction—have been enacted into law.) Accordingly, techniques of interpretation reflect not the voice of the legislature but the ear of the judiciary. To the extent that applying a technique changes what the law would otherwise be, the legitimacy of the technique can be called into question.

Justice Breyer once pondered whether the Court could simply invent or adopt a new technique. "[C]an the Court simply adopt them?" he mused. "Where would it find the legal authority to do so?" He concluded that any newfangled techniques would "lack the legitimacy provided by continuous judicial use over many years." Stephen Breyer, "On the Uses of Legislative History in Interpreting Statutes," 65 *Southern California Law Review* 845, 870 (1992).

Could the Court adopt a new technique derived from continuous *drafting* use over many years? See § 3.13, relating to the *Koons* decision.

§ 3.12 Making Congress Follow the Techniques

Techniques of statutory interpretation are of great use to Congress—or so the Court claims. When courts consistently apply a set of techniques, laws are more reliable and certain, and the drafting of laws is more predictable and effective. It is of "paramount importance," the Court has stated, "that Congress be able to legislate against a background of clear interpretive rules, so that it may know the effect of the language it adopts." *Finley v. United States*, 490 U.S. 545, 556 (1989). (But see § 3.90, relating to Frank Horack.)

The Court not only supplies this background, but it presumes that Congress follows it: "It is presumable that Congress legislates with knowledge of our basic rules of statutory construction." *McNary v. Haitian Refugee Center, Inc.*, 498 U.S. 479, 496 (1991).

This is a powerful notion, but perhaps not as overbearing as at first it might seem. Courts have long presumed that everyone knows the law, and have long included Congress in that category. Thus, the Court presumes Congress is aware of existing law when it passes legislation. *South Dakota v. Yankton Sioux Tribe*, 522 U.S. 329 (1998). The Court presumes Congress is aware of how courts have interpreted a statute, *United States v. Alaska*, 521 U.S. 1 (1997), and the Court presumes Congress expects its statutes to be read in conformity with the Court's precedents, *Porter v. Nussle*, 534 U.S. 516 (2002).

In addition, the Court presumes Congress is aware of how administrative agencies have interpreted a statute. *Lorillard v. Pons*, 434 U.S. 575, 580–581 (1978). The Court even presumes that Congress is familiar with relevant scholarly writing. *Holloway v. United States*, 526 U.S. 1 (1999).

Thus, having presumed that Congress knows the results that courts reach, it is perhaps a small step to also presume that Congress knows the techniques courts use to go about reaching their results.

Whether this is a reasonable position for the Court to take is a fair question. Ironically, courts insist that Congress take into account how courts interpret statutes but by and large do not take into account how Congress drafts them: Courts are ambivalent about legislative history and almost never consult federal drafting manuals. (But see § 3.13, relating to the *Koons* decision.)

As a drafter, however, you must consider not what courts should do, but what they in fact do. Congress is on notice that the Court expects Congress to play by the Court's rules. Though not infallible, the Court has the last word.

§ 3.13 Tensions between Courts and Congress over Interpretation

Stereotypically, lawmakers think judges are mad or corrupt, and judges think lawmakers are illiterate or dense. These tensions have always been there and they will always remain. They are naturally present, and the Framers had them in mind when they separated judicial powers from legislative powers in the Constitution.

That said, tensions can be eased or they can be exacerbated. There is a generally accepted view that courts and Congress should work more closely together, or at least pay more attention to what the other is doing. See generally Robert A. Katzmann, *Courts and Congress* (1997).

Abner J. Mikva, who served not only in Congress but also as White House counsel and on the federal bench, cogently observed that courts and Congress share an "unawareness . . . of each other's game rules," and recommended that lawmakers (and drafters) pay more attention to how courts interpret statutes and, indeed, that court opinions applying principles of interpretation be distributed to drafters. Abner J. Mikva, "Reading and Writing Statutes," 28 *South Texas Law Journal* 181, 183 (1986).

This chapter is written with Mikva's recommendation in mind. Drafters should, indeed, pay more attention to how courts interpret statutes. Notably, however, that is only one part of his two-part recommendation.

Mikva also recommended that courts pay more attention to how Congress drafts laws. It seems fair to suggest that manuals specifying principles of legislative drafting be more widely consulted by courts.

In an important critique of how judges traditionally interpret statutes, Jack Stark, a longtime drafter for the Legislative Reference Bureau of the State of Wisconsin, noted that laws generally are written not by lawmakers but by drafters. Drafters generally apply a more or less universal set of conventions, such as that the word "shall" is used exclusively to require and the word "may" is used exclusively to authorize. Yet courts, Stark lamented, do not consider or apply these conventions. Jack Stark, "On Language Games and Statutory Interpretation: An Inside Narrative," 20 *Statute Law Review* 144, 150 (1999).

Perhaps that is changing. The Supreme Court in 2004 for the first time relied on the drafting manuals used by the House and Senate Offices of Legislative Counsel to interpret a statute: *Koons Buick Pontiac GMC, Inc. v. Nigh*, 543 U.S. 50 (2004). (The Court used the manuals, and other drafting guides, to determine that federal drafters conventionally give "subparagraph" a particular meaning, and applied that meaning.)

§ 3.14 Efforts by Congress to Regulate Interpretation

Congress regulates the interpretive process in many different ways, and there is no doubt that Congress has at least some power to do so. If Congress can fix rules of evidence and rules of procedure—and it is fairly well settled that it can—then Congress can probably fix rules of interpretation as well.

The simplest means by which Congress regulates meaning is by definition. Typically, a definition is in the form, "In this Act, the term 'X' means 'Y.'" Whenever a court encounters X, the court is supposed to give it the meaning Y, even if it would not normally do so. Notice, however, that definitions of this sort merely require this or that result; they do not tell the court how to interpret. They are better understood as rules of law, not interpretation.

A more nuanced means by which Congress regulates interpretation is by rule of construction. Unlike a typical definition, a rule of construction tells the court not merely what result to reach, but how to interpret. A typical rule of construction might provide, "This Act shall be construed liberally."

A good real-life example is section 103 of Public Law 94-136 (15 U.S.C. 2403), which provides, first, that it is the policy of the United States to use all practicable means and measures to stimulate a high rate of productivity growth and, second, that "the laws, rules, regulations, and policies of the United States shall be so interpreted as to give full force and effect to this policy."

Another is section 2 of the act of March 9, 1945 (popularly known as the McCarran-Ferguson Act; 15 U.S.C. 1012), which provides, "No Act of Congress shall be construed to invalidate, impair, or supersede any law enacted by any State for the purpose of regulating the business of insurance . . . unless such Act specifically relates to the business of insurance . . . ."

Still other examples are contained in chapter 1 of title 1, United States Code, which sets forth a number of rules, some of which (like definitions) dictate a result and some of which (like rules of construction) dictate a methodology. In the latter category are rules that the singular includes the plural (and vice versa), the masculine includes the feminine (but not vice versa), and the present tense includes the future tense (but not vice versa).

Some rules that are written as if they were rules of construction are, as with most definitions, better understood as rules of law. For two examples, look no further than the Constitution: The Ninth Amendment provides, "The enumeration in the Constitution, of certain rights, shall not be construed to deny or disparage others retained by the people," and the Eleventh Amendment provides, "The Judicial power of the United States shall not be construed to extend to any suit in law or equity . . . ." Though they use the word "construed," these rules require not that a methodology be followed but that a result be reached (or not be reached). Notice that in both examples you could strike "shall not be construed to" and insert "does not" without changing the meaning (and, indeed, that would probably be better drafting).

Rules of construction are often vague and rarely useful, and there are some who suggest that they unconstitutionally infringe on the judicial power. In any event, they are rarely invoked—at least the ones created by statute (the ones created by jurisprudence are invoked regularly). The example from 15 U.S.C. 2403, given above, seems never to have been applied in a published federal court decision, perhaps because courts find it vague, perhaps because courts find it unconstitutional or otherwise objectionable—or perhaps (as seems likely) because courts simply can't find it in the first place.

A more intrusive means by which Congress regulates interpretation is to tell the courts what they are required or forbidden to consider.

Here's one that seems innocent enough—section 19 of the act of June 25, 1948, which enacted title 18 of the United States Code and which is set forth in the notes at the very beginning of that Code, provides: "No inference of a legislative construction is to be drawn by reason of the chapter in Title 18, Crimes and Criminal Procedure, as set out in section 1 of this Act, in which any particular section is placed, nor by reason of the catchlines used in such title." Many of the laws that have enacted titles of the Code have similar language. Without this language, a court trying to make sense of an unclear section might try to glean meaning from the chapter in which it was placed and the catchline assigned to that chapter. But this language forbids a court from doing so. Can Congress do that? Is it constitutional?

A more interesting example is section 105(b) of the Civil Rights Act of 1991 (Public Law 102-166; 105 Stat. 1075; 42 U.S.C. 1981 note), which provides, "No statements other than the interpretive memorandum appearing at Vol. 137 Congressional Record S 15276 (daily ed. Oct. 25, 1991) shall be considered legislative history of, or relied upon in any way as legislative history in construing or applying, any provision of this Act that relates to *Wards Cove*—Business necessity/cumulation/alternative business practice." Can Congress do that? Is it constitutional?

But never mind whether that one is constitutional; what does it actually mean? Reading it casually one might think it means, "A court is required to consider this memorandum, and is forbidden to consider any other statements in the legislative record, in interpreting this Act." But on closer examination it says neither of these things. Literally, it forbids a court from relying on statements "as legislative history"—that is, by reason of its status as legislative history. It does not forbid a court from relying on statements for other reasons, such as for their inherently persuasive value. This is the sort of thing that happens when lawyers who are not drafters try to draft: The words grasp at meaning but do not grab it.

Remember, courts give weight to some statements because they are required to do so, such as the precedent of a higher court. But courts can give weight to any other statement merely because it has inherent power to persuade, such as the opinion of a sister court or lower court, or a law review article, or a line from Shakespeare. When read in a straightforward manner, that provision of the Civil Rights Act of 1991 forbids the use of a statement by reason of its status as legislative history, but does not forbid the use of a statement for any other reason—including its inherent power to persuade.

When read that way, the provision probably passes constitutional muster.

If Congress wants to disparage its own documents and tell the courts not to give them any special dignity, one would think Congress has the power to do so.

But it does beg the question of how the Court might respond if Congress tried more directly to tie the Court's hands. Suppose, for example, Congress passed a law to forbid the courts from applying a particular technique of interpretation. Would it be constitutional? The answer may vary from technique to technique. For one view, see Nicholas Quinn Rosenkranz, "Federal Rules of Statutory Interpretation," 115 *Harvard Law Review* 2085 (2002).

The Court has said the "power to determine the meaning of a statute carries with it the power to prescribe its extent and limitations as well as the method by which they shall be determined." *City of Chicago v. Morales*, 527 U.S. 41 (1999). That was in reference to the power of a state legislature, however; it does not necessarily apply to Congress.

Thus, while there are certainly boundaries, we do not yet know where they are.

§3.20 The Overriding Goal: Determine the Intent of Congress

The Supreme Court does not publish an official treatise on statutory interpretation. Instead, the Court publishes piecemeal—a little bit in this case, a little bit in that one. Over time, the lessons from these cases accumulate and become more or less settled principles.

The overriding goal of statutory interpretation is to determine and give effect to the intent of Congress. More precisely, the intent sought with respect to an act is the intent of the Congress that enacted the act, and thus needs to be determined as of enactment.

Every other consideration must yield to that overriding goal. Statutory interpretation exists "to discover and not to direct the Congressional will." *Huddleston v. United States*, 415 U.S. 814, 831 (1974).

Beyond that overriding goal, however, there is not much you can hang your hat on. "Do not expect anybody's theory of statutory interpretation, whether it is your own or somebody else's, to be an accurate statement of what courts actually do with statutes. The hard truth of the matter is that American courts have no intelligible, generally accepted, and consistently applied theory of statutory interpretation." Henry M. Hart Jr. & Albert M. Sachs, *The Legal Process: Basic Problems in the Making and Application Of Law* 1169 (1994).

And one might fairly question the overriding goal. That is, one might fairly ask why the intent of Congress should trump the words of Congress. If the words accurately express the intent, then intent is redundant; if the words don't accurately express the intent, then Congress is being sloppy or misleading.

Should sloppy or misleading behavior be tolerated—even rewarded? Regardless, doesn't due process prefer a published word to a secret thought? The Court seemed to question its own reliance on legislative intent in *Lamie v. United States Trustee*, 540 U.S. 526, 542 (2004), when it said: "If Congress enacted into law something different from what it intended, then it should amend the statute to conform to its intent. It is beyond our province to rescue Congress from its drafting errors, and to provide for what we might think is the preferred result." (internal quotation marks and ellipses omitted). Whether that is a warning to be taken seriously remains to be seen.

One might also fairly ask whether Congress can ever be said to have an intent. Congress is a collection of hundreds of people in two separate chambers, each with individual intent. When Congress passes a law, however imperfect, it is reasonable to suppose that the intent of Congress was to pass that law, but any intent of Congress beyond that seems like wishful thinking.

But, then again, one must also ask what better alternative the Court should use. If not legislative intent, then what? Should courts take it upon themselves to make policy choices? Though state courts generally have the power to do so, federal courts do not. The legislative power is vested in Congress, not in the courts.

Suppose all the animals in a zoo agree on a policy of regular feedings, but they do not agree on what "regular feedings" requires. There is no "intent of the zoo," and trying to find it would do more harm than good. The regular feedings of a lion and a lizard are not the same. What seems best is to allow the policy to be applied on a case-by-case basis, using good judgment and common sense, based on the totality of the circumstances. Courts already do this sometimes, such as when a statute provides a general standard like "reasonable" or "good faith." Should courts do this more often? Do they already have the power to do so? If not, can Congress constitutionally give courts that power? Should Congress do so? The questions do not have quick and ready answers.

Because legislative intent can be problematic, courts sometimes speak instead about a statute's "purpose." Apparently, the distinction is that legislative intent asks why the particular Congress enacted the statute, while purpose asks why a reasonable Congress would have enacted the statute. Ultimately, though, it is a distinction without much difference, and courts tend to use the terms interchangeably. See discussion in Abner J. Mikva & Eric Lane, *An Introduction to Statutory Interpretation and the Legislative Process* 6–9 (1997).

§ 3.21 Rules of Thumb, Not Rules of Law

To achieve their goal—the goal of determining and giving effect to the intent of Congress—the courts apply a variety of techniques to shed light on what Congress most likely intended.

Some techniques are called "canons" or "maxims," others "principles" or "rules," but the labels are not of much practical importance. None of the techniques are rules of law (though some are derived, at least in part, from constitutional principles); most of them are simply rules of thumb—educated guesses about whether to draw an inference about legislative intent and, if drawn, how much weight to give it.

The Court has been candid about the limited utility of its techniques. Canons of construction, the Court has said, are "simply rules of thumb which will sometimes help courts determine the meaning of legislation." *Varity Corp. v. Howe*, 516 U.S. 489, 511 (1996). One canon pointing to one result is often countered by another pointing in the opposite direction. *Chickasaw Nation v. United States*, 534 U.S. 84 (2001). The use of legislative history, meanwhile, has been described as "the equivalent of entering a crowded cocktail party and looking over the heads of the guests for one's friends." *Conroy v. Aniskoff*, 507 U.S. 511, 519 (1993) (Scalia, J., concurring, attributing the statement to Judge Harold Leventhal).

When the various techniques all point toward the same result, the case is easy—and most cases are easy cases. When some techniques point toward one result and other techniques point elsewhere, a court has some serious work to do.

In any event, the various techniques are not binding and are not applied in a slavish or mechanical fashion. They are tools, not rules. The goal is not to apply the techniques, but to determine the legislative intent, and the techniques are subordinate to that goal:

> "However well these rules may serve at times to aid in deciphering legislative intent, they long have been subordinated to the doctrine that courts will construe the details of an act in conformity with its dominant general purpose, will read text in the light of context and will interpret the text so far as the meaning of the words fairly permits so as to carry out in particular cases the generally expressed legislative policy."
>
> *Securities and Exchange Commission v. C.M. Joiner Leasing Corp.*, 320 U.S. 344, 350–351 (1943).

For a drafter, the overriding lesson is to be aware of all the different techniques that a court might apply and to make sure that, when applied to your draft, the techniques point as consistently as possible toward a single result.

§ 3.22 Three Common Theories (Intentionalism, Textualism, and Pragmatism) and Their Limitations

To understand the limitations of the Court's techniques, it may help to understand some of the theory behind them.

No principle of statutory interpretation is etched in stone. Within the Court itself, there is often disagreement over how best to apply the various principles to a particular law or to particular facts. More broadly, there is also disagreement over what the principles should be.

Three common theories about the interpretation of statutes are intentionalism, textualism, and pragmatism. These are not the only theories, but they are a representative sample. These are not, mind you, theories about how courts do interpret statutes, but theories about how courts should interpret statutes. Each theory describes not how things are, but how things ought to be.

According to intentionalism, the Court should consider legislative and historical materials to determine why Congress enacted the law, and should apply the law in the way that Congress would have wanted. According to textualism, the Court should be concerned not with what Congress wanted, but only with what Congress said; the Court should consider the text and context only, and should apply the words that Congress wrote. According to pragmatism, the Court should consider the effects on society, and should apply the law in the way that the Court believes would produce the best effects on society.

In short, these three common theories can be summarized as follows:

What Did the Lawmakers Mean? (Intentionalism)
What Does the Law Mean? (Textualism)
What Should the Lawmakers Have Meant? (Pragmatism)

As a practical matter, the Court seems to operate as if it takes something from each of these theories. Even the most ardent intentionalist or pragmatist will recognize that the Court cannot take too many liberties with the plain text; even the most dedicated textualist will acknowledge a "scrivener's error" that should not be given literal effect. And so on.

Notably, all three theories agree that the starting point is the text itself; they disagree over the extent to which matters outside the text should influence its meaning. Because a drafter generally has no control over matters outside the text, there is little a drafter can do about them but be aware that they exist—and advise the client accordingly.

It has been said, pessimistically but perhaps realistically, that courts use statutory interpretation "not as approaches to be followed consistently from one case to the next, wherever they may lead, but as techniques to support a conclusion reached for other reasons." Robert J. Martineau, "Craft and Technique, Not Canons and Grand Theories: A Neo-Realist View of Statutory Construction," 62 *George Washington Law Review* 1, 40 (1993).

You do not have to be a cynic to recognize that the techniques are not used consistently. All you need to know is that there are nine justices and they are rarely unanimous:

> "Indeed, the same judges—even very great ones—give different emphasis at different times to the two souls that dwell within their breasts. Thus Holmes, whom Frankfurter quoted as saying of legislators, 'I don't care what their intention was. I only want to know what the words mean,' wrote also that 'the general purpose is a more important aid to the meaning than any rule which grammar or formal logic may lay down,' and even that 'the meaning of a sentence is to be felt rather than to be proved.' "
>
> Henry J. Friendly, *Benchmarks* 200 (1967).

Courts do more than woodenly apply techniques; at some point they run out of useful techniques and still do not have a clear answer. At that point, the serious business begins, and the courts consider everything they can, including policy. (Whether they admit in writing to doing so is another matter.) We should not be horrified when judicial officers exercise judgment; that is, after all, why they are called judges.

§ 3.23 The Plain Meaning Rule

Typically, the first step in the Court's analysis is to determine whether the language is clear or ambiguous. If clear, one set of rules applies; if ambiguous, another set. (Note that the Court uses "ambiguity" in the broad sense, to mean lack of clarity, rather than in the narrower sense described in § 6.11.)

At one time this determination was the crux of the case. To determine whether the language was clear, the Court would look only at that language. If clear, that was the end of the inquiry; the Court did not consult any matter outside the text itself. There was a safe harbor for clear language.

As one of the major Supreme Court decisions explained:

> "It is elementary that the meaning of a statute must, in the first instance, be sought in the language in which the act is framed, and if that is plain, and if the law is within the constitutional authority of the lawmaking body which passed it, the sole function of the courts is to enforce it according to its terms . . . . Where the language is plain and admits of no more than one meaning, the duty of interpretation does not arise, and the rules which are to aid doubtful meanings need no discussion."
>
> *Caminetti v. United States*, 242 U.S. 470, 485 (1917).

This rule—"if plain, game over"—was known as the Plain Meaning Rule. But the Court no longer follows this formulation, and the term has come to be used for a different rule not nearly as pivotal.

The old Plain Meaning Rule allowed for only one exception—after all, the "duty of interpretation does not arise" when the language was plain. The exception was when the plain meaning led to an "absurd result." Perhaps the most famous use of this exception is *Church of the Holy Trinity v. United States*, 143 U.S. 457 (1892), in which the Court considered a law that made it a crime to induce a foreigner to migrate to the United States "to perform labor or service of any kind." A church induced a foreign minister to migrate to the United States to serve as its rector. The Court held that this came within the plain meaning of the law, but produced an absurd result: Given the religious heritage of the United States (about which the Court went on at great length), the claim that Congress intended to punish a house of worship for hiring a foreign pastor, priest, or rabbi "cannot be accepted as correct." 143 U.S. at 472.

The old Plain Meaning Rule that informed the *Caminetti* decision in 1917 began to break down in the 1920s and 1930s. By 1940 it was no longer being applied. In a lengthy but important passage, the Court explained the breakdown of the old Plain Meaning Rule:

> "There is, of course, no more persuasive evidence of the purpose of a statute than the words by which the legislature undertook to give expression to its wishes. Often these words are sufficient in and of themselves to determine the purpose of the legislation. In such cases we have followed their plain meaning. When that meaning has led to absurd or futile results, however, this Court has looked beyond the words to the purpose of the act. Frequently, however, even when the plain meaning did not produce absurd results but merely an unreasonable one plainly at variance with the policy of the legislation as a whole this Court has followed that purpose, rather than the literal words. When aid to construction of the meaning of words, as used in the statute, is available, there certainly can be no rule of law which forbids its use, however clear the words may appear on superficial examination. The interpretation of the meaning of statutes, as applied to justiciable controversies, is exclusively a judicial function. This duty requires one body of public servants, the judges, to construe the meaning of what another body, the legislators, has said. Obviously there is danger that the courts' conclusion as to legislative purpose will be unconsciously influenced by the judges' own views or by factors not considered by the enacting body. A lively appreciation of the danger is the best assurance of escape from its threat but hardly justifies an acceptance of a literal interpretation dogma which withholds from the courts available information for reaching a correct conclusion."
>
> *United States v. American Trucking Associations, Inc.*,
> 310 U.S. 534, 543–544 (1940)
> (internal footnotes and quotation marks omitted).

By 1940, then, the old Plain Meaning Rule was dead. To determine whether the language was clear, the Court no longer used a "superficial examination" of the "literal words," but used all information available. The safe harbor for clear language was gone.

Not only that, but the exception for an "absurd result" was no longer the only exception. The Court would decline to follow the plain meaning in any case in which the result was "unreasonable" and contrary to the legislative purpose (or, more accurately, contrary to the Court's conclusion as to the legislative purpose).

By 1981, the Plain Meaning Rule was no longer even considered a rule of law. As the Court stated in *Watt v. Alaska*, 451 U.S. 259, 266 (1981): "The starting point in every case involving construction of a statute is the language itself. But ascertainment of the meaning apparent on the face of a single statute need not end the inquiry. This is because the plain-meaning rule is rather an axiom of experience than a rule of law, and does not preclude consideration of persuasive evidence if it exists." (internal quotation marks and citations omitted).

The Court sometimes describes the modern Plain Meaning Rule as a presumption. For example, in *BedRoc Limited, LLC v. United States*, 541 U.S. 176 (2004), the Court said: "The preeminent canon of statutory interpretation requires us to presume that the legislature says in a statute what it means and means in a statute what it says there."

Under the modern Plain Meaning Rule, the Court still asks whether the language is plain, but to answer that question looks not only at the language but at everything it considers persuasive. In short, the Court carries out a hunt for other meanings that, though not obvious from the text, are plausible once all things have been considered.

Thus, the modern Plain Meaning Rule no longer has many teeth, and no longer seems to serve much purpose. The choice it poses—clear or ambiguous—assumes that every text is either black or white, when in fact most texts are different shades of gray. The point at which, say, "battleship gray" is black and "harbor fog" is white is not always obvious, and reasonable people can disagree from case to case and text to text about whether that point has been reached. For example, all nine members of the Court once agreed that the civil RICO statute had only one plain meaning, but split 5–4 over what that meaning was. See *Sedima, S.P.R.L. v. Imrex Co.*, 473 U.S. 479 (1985).

Regardless, the lesson for a drafter is that—contrary to what Dickerson asserted in scoffing at statutory interpretation—a clear text does not ensure a clear result. There is no safe harbor for a good plain draft. The Court does not look solely at the text—and so neither can you.

What seems most practical in drafting is to treat plain meaning not as a toggle switch but as a sliding scale. The more clear the draft, the more likely the Court will apply it in a straightforward manner, rather than twist it to conform to the legislative history, the views of an agency, or any other matter outside the text.

§ 3.24 The Meaning of "Plain Meaning"

The plain meaning of a statute is the "ordinary or natural meaning." *Federal Deposit Insurance Corporation v. Meyer*, 510 U.S. 471, 476 (1994). Notably, the Court uses the ordinary meaning that prevailed when the statute was enacted, not when it is being interpreted. See *BedRoc Limited, LLC v. United States*, 541 U.S. 176 (2004) (interpreting "valuable minerals" in a 1919 mining law based on which minerals were valuable in 1919).

By natural meaning, the Court means not a literal meaning but a common-sense meaning. For example, in *Roschen v. Ward*, 279 U.S. 337 (1929), a law made it unlawful to sell spectacles unless an eye specialist "be in charge of and personal attendance at" the place of sale. Read literally, the law did not require the specialist ever to examine a patient. However, the Court denounced this literal reading as a "perversion"; obviously, the Court said, an examination is not required in every case, but the specialist has a duty in every case to decide whether one is necessary. There is, the Court said, "no canon against using common sense in construing laws as saying what they obviously mean." 279 U.S. at 339.

By ordinary meaning, the Court means the meaning in an "idiomatic sense": that is, "the same way that ordinary people in common usage might speak . . . any day of the week." *General Dynamics Land Systems v. Cline*, 540 U.S. 581 (2004). In that case, the Court held that "discrimination because of age" is "naturally understood" to refer to discrimination against those who are older, and does not include discrimination against those who are younger.

Plain meaning typically can be found by consulting a general dictionary. Some justices have been known to favor prescriptive dictionaries (which indicate how words should properly be used) over descriptive dictionaries (which indicate how words are actually used). See *MCI Telecommunications Corp. v.*

AT&T Co., 512 U.S. 218, 228 n.3 (1994) (criticizing the use of a descriptive dictionary "for its portrayal of common error as proper usage").

§ 3.25 The Consequences of Plain Meaning

As discussed above, the old Plain Meaning Rule provided that the Court would determine whether meaning is plain based on the statutory text alone. Under the modern Plain Meaning Rule, the Court determines whether the meaning is plain based on all the evidence it considers persuasive.

Language does not have to be perfect to be covered by the Plain Meaning Rule. The meaning of the language must merely leave no doubt. For example, a law with punctuation errors can still have plain meaning. See *United States National Bank of Oregon v. Independent Insurance Agents of America, Inc.*, 508 U.S. 439, 463 and n.11 (1993) (despite punctuation problems, the "true meaning . . . is clear beyond question"). Likewise, a law with grammatical errors can still have plain meaning. See *Lamie v. United States Trustee*, 540 U.S. 526 (2004) (being awkward and ungrammatical "does not make it ambiguous").

Generally, a determination that the language is plain has several consequences.

First, the Court will not use certain categories of lesser evidence to change the plain meaning—though the Court may use lesser evidence to clarify and illuminate the plain meaning. Lesser evidence generally includes legislative history, headings, preambles, and other evidence not usually given much weight.

Remember, however, that the Court will use any evidence, including lesser evidence, to decide whether the meaning is plain. Indeed, the Court has said it is "error" not to do so. *Train v. Colorado Public Interest Research Group*, 426 U.S. 1, 9–10 (1976) (determining whether the meaning is plain without considering legislative history is error). Since that case, the Court has backtracked somewhat and said that legislative history need not be considered in all cases, but only in cases in which a party argues that the plain meaning of a law is demonstrably at odds with the intentions of its drafters. *United States National Bank of Oregon v. Independent Insurance Agents of America, Inc.*, 508 U.S. 439, 463 fn 11 (1993).

Second, an agency cannot interpret the language in a way that changes the plain meaning; if it tries to do so, the Court will not give that interpretation any *Chevron* deference. For more on *Chevron* deference, see § 3.62, "Agency Interpretation and *Chevron* Deference."

Third, the Court will ordinarily enforce the plain meaning "according to its terms." *Lamie v. United States Trustee*, 540 U.S. 526 (2004).

§ 3.26 When Plain Meaning Is Not Enforced

In some cases the Court will decline to apply the plain meaning and will apply another meaning instead.

The Court has emphasized that a departure from plain meaning is justified only in "rare and exceptional circumstances," *TVA v. Hill*, 437 U.S. 153, 187 fn 33 (1978), but the precise nature of those circumstances can vary.

The general principle appears to be that the plain meaning will not be followed if the plain meaning "will produce a result demonstrably at odds with the intentions of its drafters." *Griffin v. Oceanic Contractors, Inc.*, 458 U.S. 564, 571 (1982). If so, those intentions—not the plain meaning—must be controlling.

Thus, the plain meaning will not be followed if it would lead to an absurd result, or merely to an "odd result." *Public Citizen v. Department of Justice*, 491 U.S. 440, 454 (1989). Looking beyond the "naked text" for guidance is perfectly proper, the Court said, when the result it apparently decrees is "difficult to fathom," or where it "seems inconsistent with Congress' intention." 491 U.S. at 455.

In addition, the plain meaning will not be followed if it would render the statute unconstitutional, unless applying the plain meaning is "utterly unavoidable." *Branch v. Smith*, 538 U.S. 254 (2003). If a "serious doubt of constitutionality" is raised, the Court will determine whether an interpretation is "fairly possible" that avoids that doubt and, if so, will apply that interpretation instead. *Public Citizen v. Department of Justice*, 491 U.S. 440, 465–466 (1989).

And the plain meaning will not be followed if it would be contrary to the "spirit" of the statute. "It is a familiar rule that a thing may be within the letter of the statute and yet not within the statute, because not within its spirit, nor within the intention of its makers." *Church of the Holy Trinity v. United States*, 143 U.S. 457 (1892).

The *Holy Trinity* decision referred to a number of other situations that might also justify a departure from plain meaning. For example, though it is a crime to obstruct or retard a mail carrier, the crime does not apply when a sheriff arrests a mail carrier indicted for murder; though it is a crime to break out of jail, the crime does not apply when a prisoner breaks out because the jail is on fire.

Though the *Holy Trinity* decision made some very broad statements about when the Court can depart from plain meaning, the actual holding of the case is very narrow. The Court simply held that a general criminal law did not apply to a special situation not anticipated by Congress. (The other cases referred to in the decision followed the same pattern.) Had Congress considered the special situation it would (the Court concluded) have provided an express exception, so the Court corrected the oversight by providing an implied exception.

§ 3.27 When There Is No Plain Meaning

When a statute is ambiguous, all bets are off. The Court looks at everything it considers persuasive, deliberates thoroughly, and determines how best to read the statute. As always, the overriding goal is to determine and apply the legislative intent. See *United States v. Fisher*, 6 U.S. 358, 386 (1805) (when "the mind labours to discover the design of the legislature, it seizes every thing from which aid can be derived"); *Wisconsin Public Intervenor v. Mortier*, 501 U.S. 597, 611 fn 4 (1991) ("common sense suggests that inquiry benefits from reviewing additional information rather than ignoring it").

In deciding what Congress meant to do, the Court is guided by an assumption that Congress did not mean to do nothing. Unless Congress is merely restating the law—in which case the Court presumes that Congress intends not to change the law, see *Muniz v. Hoffman*, 422 U.S. 454 (1975)—the Court presumes that Congress intends its action to have real and substantial effect. See *Stone v. Immigration and Naturalization Service*, 514 U.S. 386, 397 (1995).

§ 3.30 Reading the Text of the Statute

The Court generally begins its analysis with the language of the statute. Starting with the statute has been called the "first principle" of statutory interpretation. *Mallard v. United States District Court*, 490 U.S. 296, 300 (1989).

Though the statute is the obvious starting point, many do not always start there. For that reason Justice Frankfurter once quipped, "this is a case for applying the canon of construction of the wag who said, when the legislative history is doubtful, go to the statute." *Greenwood v. United States*, 350 U.S. 366, 374 (1956).

Justice Frankfurter's droll chiding turned strangely prophetic when, just fifteen years later, his successors on the Supreme Court bench reasoned in one case as follows: "The legislative history . . . is ambiguous. . . . Because of this ambiguity it is clear that we must look primarily to the statutes themselves to find the legislative intent." *Citizens to Preserve Overton Park v. Volpe*, 401 U.S. 402, 412 fn 29 (1971). As Frankfurter would have been pleased to know, that statement has proven to be an isolated one.

The Court considers the text to be the most persuasive evidence of meaning and, as noted above, sometimes says there is a presumption that the legislature means what it says. After all, the text is the only form by which Congress, in its capacity as the constitutional legislature of the United States, directly expresses its intent. *Aldridge v. Williams*, 44 U.S. 9, 24 (1845).

§ 3.31 The Whole Act Rule

In reading the statute, the Court reads not only the word or sentence or provision that is in dispute, but the entire statute. This is known as the Whole Act Rule. As the Court has explained:

> "Statutory construction . . . is a holistic endeavor. A provision that may seem ambiguous in isolation is often clarified by the remainder of the statutory scheme—because the same terminology is used elsewhere in a context that makes its meaning clear, or because only one of the permissible meanings produces a substantive effect that is compatible with the rest of the law."
>
> *United Savings Association v. Timbers of Inwood Forest Associates*, 484 U.S. 365, 371 (1988).

Accordingly, in reading a statute, the Court is not guided by a single sentence or sentence fragment, but looks instead to "the provisions of the whole law," and also to its "object and policy," "structure," and "subject matter." *United States National Bank of Oregon v. Independent Insurance Agents of America, Inc.*, 508 U.S. 439, 455 (1993).

§ 3.32 Derive Meaning from Context

The meaning of a word should never be considered in isolation. Two giants of the law have given us two well-known similes that express this principle well.

First, in the words of Justice Holmes, "A word is not a crystal, transparent and unchanged, it is the skin of a living thought and may vary greatly in color and content according to the circumstances and the time in which it is used." *Towne v. Eisner*, 245 U.S. 418, 425 (1918).

Second, in the words of Judge Learned Hand, "Words are not pebbles in alien juxtaposition; they have only a communal existence; and not only does the meaning of each interpenetrate the other, but in all their aggregate take their purport from the setting in which they are used." *NLRB v. Federbush Co.*, 121 F.2d 954, 957 (1st Cir. 1941).

This general principle is embodied in a canon of construction known by its Latin name, *noscitur a sociis* (a thing is known by its companions). Like any other canon, it is not a rule of law but a rule of thumb, and is used to avoid giving a law "unintended breadth." *Jarecki v. G.D. Searle & Co.*, 367 U.S. 303, 307 (1961).

For example, in *Gustafson v. Alloyd Co.*, 513 U.S. 561 (1995), the Court interpreted the term "communication" in the phrase "any prospectus, notice, circular, advertisement, letter, or communication, written or by radio or television" not to mean any communication but only a communication "of wide dissemination." 513 U.S. at 575. Therefore, a "written communication" applied only to writings held out to the public at large, and not to an exchange of correspondence between two parties.

Likewise, in *Gutierrez v. Ada*, 528 U.S. 250 (2000), the Court interpreted the phrase "in any election" to apply only to an election for governor, rather than a general election, because the phrase was preceded and followed by references to gubernatorial elections.

§ 3.33 Assume Words Are Used Consistently

As part of the Whole Act Rule, the Court expects each term in the law to be used consistently. If Congress uses the same term in more than one place, the Court presumes that it has the same meaning in each place. *Ratzlaf v. United States*, 510 U.S. 135, 143 (1994). This rule is "at its most vigorous when a term is repeated within a given sentence." *Brown v. Gardner*, 513 U.S. 115, 118 (1994).

Conversely, if Congress uses one term in one place and a different term in another place, the Court presumes that each term has a distinct meaning. *Bailey v. United States*, 516 U.S. 137, 146 (1995).

Of course, these are presumptions, not requirements, and the Court has cautioned against applying them too enthusiastically. See *General Dynamics*

Land Systems v. Cline, 540 U.S. 581 (2004) ("The tendency to assume that a word which appears in two or more legal rules, and so in connection with more than one purpose, has and should have precisely the same scope in all of them, runs all through legal discussions. It has all the tenacity of original sin and must constantly be guarded against.").

§ 3.34 Assume Each Word Is Used for a Reason

As part of the Whole Act Rule, the Court expects that each clause and word in the law is included for a reason. The Court's duty is "to give effect, if possible, to every clause and word of a statute." *United States v. Menasche*, 348 U.S. 528, 538–539 (1955).

This is referred to sometimes as the "rule against surplusage," and at other times as the "rule against superfluities." A statute, the Court said, "should be construed so that effect is given to all its provisions, so that no part will be inoperative or superfluous, void or insignificant." *Hibbs v. Winn*, 542 U.S. 88 (2004).

However, this also is a presumption, not a requirement, and the Court may reject words as surplusage if inadvertently inserted or repugnant to the rest of the statute. *Chickasaw Nation v. United States*, 534 U.S. 84 (2001).

The Court has said it is "inappropriate" to apply the rule against surplusage when there are two ways to read the text—one that is plain but contains surplusage, and one that is ambiguous but free of surplusage. In such a case, the Court prefers the plain meaning, "since that approach respects the words of Congress." *Lamie v. United States Trustee*, 540 U.S. 526 (2004).

§ 3.35 Assume the Provisions Form a Coherent Whole

As another part of the Whole Act Rule, the Court expects all of the provisions of the statute to form a coherent whole.

For example, the Court presumes that when Congress uses particular language in one place and does not use that language in another place, the omission was intentional. *Keene Corp. v. United States*, 508 U.S. 200, 208 (1993).

Likewise, the Court presumes that when Congress uses a general provision in one place and a specific provision in another place, in apparent contradiction, Congress intends both to have meaning, with the specific qualifying the general. *Townsend v. Little*, 109 U.S. 504, 512 (1883). See also *State of Missouri v. Ross*, 299 U.S. 72, 76 (1936) ("special provisions prevail over general ones which, in the absence of the special provisions, would control"); *Fourco Glass Co. v. Transmirra Products Corp.*, 353 U.S. 222, 228 (1957) ("However inclusive may be the general language of a statute, it will not be held to apply to a matter specifically dealt with in another part of the same enactment . . . specific terms prevail over the general.").

§ 3.36 Purposes, Findings, Titles, and Headings

The Court places some parts of the text in the category of lesser evidence, which will not generally be used as a guide to meaning unless the law is ambiguous. In this category are purposes, findings, titles, and headings.

These parts of the text are considered lesser evidence because they are not used primarily to make law. Instead, they are used primarily as a convenience to the reader. Essentially, they are indirect evidence rather than direct evidence. That said, the Court does, on rare occasions, resort to these parts of the text to glean what it can about legislative intent.

A statement of purposes is perhaps the most useful form of lesser evidence. A statement of policy, a statement of findings, and a statement of the sense of Congress are all variations of the same idea. (See also § 4.47, "Commands That Are Not Mandatory: Hortatory, Precatory, and Directory.")

For an example of a case using a statement of purposes as a guide to meaning, see *Dole v. United Steelworkers of America*, 494 U.S. 26, 36–38 (1990) (where Congress did not mention disclosure rules in its "itemized and exhaustive" statement of purposes, that was "strong evidence" that the act did not apply to disclosure rules).

For an example of a case using findings as a guide to meaning, see *United States v. Turkette*, 452 U.S. 576, 588–590 (1981) (giving the RICO statute a broad interpretation in part because of the broad statement of findings). A preamble containing Whereas clauses is much the same as a statement of findings, and is treated in much the same way.

For an example of a case using a sense of Congress provision as a guide to meaning, see *Accardi v. Pennsylvania Railroad Co.*, 383 U.S. 225, 229 (1966) (in which the Court, interestingly enough, seemed to treat a sense of Congress as if it were actual law).

Be aware that the Court does not use the terms "title" and "heading" in the specific way that a drafter does. For example, in *Immigration and Naturalization Service v. National Center for Immigrants' Rights*, 502 U.S. 183, 189–190 (1991), the Court used what a drafter would call the heading of a clause as a guide to meaning, though the Court referred to it as the "title" of a "paragraph."

Regardless, it is fair to say that anything that a drafter might consider a title or a heading will be used by the Court as a guide to meaning when the meaning is in doubt.

This applies to long titles and short titles, as in *Caminetti v. United States*, 242 U.S. 470, 489–490 (1917). It applies also to section headings, as in *Almendarez-Torres v. United States*, 523 U.S. 224 (1998). It applies as well to chapter headings, catchlines, and any other part of the text that might be considered a title or heading in a general sense.

§ 3.37 Grammar and Punctuation

The Court generally applies ordinary rules of grammar in interpreting statutes. For example, in *United States v. Ron Pair Enterprises*, 489 U.S. 235, 241 (1989), the Court used the "grammatical structure" of a statute as a guide to meaning (concluding that the placement of commas created an independent clause). And in *Barnhart v. Thomas*, 540 U.S. 20 (2003), the Court applied the grammatical "rule of the last antecedent," according to which a limiting clause or phrase should ordinarily be read as modifying only the noun or phrase that it immediately follows. (For example, the Court said, a teenager told "you will be punished if you throw a party or engage in any other activity that damages the house" will be punished for throwing a party, whether or not the party damages the house.)

The Court also generally applies ordinary rules of punctuation in interpreting statutes. The meaning of a statute "will typically heed the commands of its punctuation." *United States National Bank of Oregon v. Independent Insurance Agents of America, Inc.*, 508 U.S. 439, 454 (1993). But if need be, the Court will "disregard the punctuation, or repunctuate," to render the true meaning of the statute. 508 U.S. at 462 (holding that certain quotation marks appeared in a statute only because of "scrivener's error").

§ 3.38 Placement in Code

An important exception to the general rule that meaning can be derived from context is that meaning is not supposed to be derived from the placement of a provision in the Code.

When a provision of an act is classified to the Code by Law Revision Counsel, the Court will "read it in the context of the entire Act, rather than in the context of the 'arrangement' selected by the codifier." *U.S. v. Welden*, 377 U.S. 95, 99 (1964).

When a provision is codified into a positive-law title, Congress typically requires—by law, in the act originally enacting that title—that no inference about a provision be drawn from the chapter in which it was placed or from the heading of that chapter. See section 19 of the act of June 25, 1948, which enacted title 18 (Crimes and Criminal Procedure) into positive law. That section is set forth in the notes at the beginning of title 18; similar requirements apply to other positive-law titles and are set forth in the notes at the beginning of those titles. It is not altogether clear whether these requirements also apply when a provision is later added to a positive-law title. Regardless, most people, and most courts, seem not to know these requirements are there.

§ 3.40 Considering Other Statutes

Having considered the text of a statute, the Court will also consider the rest of the statutory context—that is, the body of law into which the statute fits.

Generally, the Court assumes that the new law is intended to fit into the body of law to form a consistent, coherent whole. This is much the same sentiment as in the Whole Act Rule, but it is applied in a somewhat looser, less rigid way.

§ 3.41 Related Statutes

Courts do not interpret statutes in isolation, but in the context of the "corpus juris" of which they are a part. "The correct rule of interpretation is, that if divers statutes relate to the same thing, they ought all to be taken into consideration in construing any one of them." *Branch v. Smith*, 538 U.S. 254 (2003) (quoting from an 1845 Supreme Court decision). This technique is sometimes known as *in pari materia.*

Thus, if a term has a settled meaning in Statute A, and the same term is used in a related Statute B, the term will generally be read in B the same way it is read in A.

This applies, obviously, when Statute A was enacted first. Most people understand that intuitively.

But—and this may be counterintuitive—it also applies when Statute B was enacted first. That is, "if it can be gathered from a subsequent statute *in pari materia*, what meaning the legislature attached to the words of a former statute, they will amount to a legislative declaration of its meaning, and will govern the construction of the first statute." *Branch v. Smith*, 538 U.S. 254 (2003).

As the Court explained in *Food and Drug Administration v. Brown & Williamson Tobacco Corp.*, 529 U.S. 120 (2000): "At the time a statute is enacted, it may have a range of plausible meanings. Over time, however, subsequent acts can shape or focus those meanings. The classic judicial task of reconciling many laws enacted over time, and getting them to make sense in combination, necessarily assumes that the implications of a statute may be altered by the implications of a later statute." (internal quotation marks omitted).

For example, the Court added, "a specific policy embodied in a later federal statute should control our construction of the earlier statute, even though it has not been expressly amended." (internal brackets omitted).

§ 3.42 General Federal Laws

In addition to considering the immediately related statutes, the Court will also consider the broader context of general federal law. This is not limited to general definitions, though general definitions are perhaps the most important part of the broader context.

The most broadly applicable set of federal definitions is in chapter 1 of title 1, United States Code, sometimes referred to as the Dictionary Act. This chapter contains a series of definitions that apply to all federal law, unless the context indicates otherwise. If a law uses a term that is defined in the Dictionary Act, the Court will generally apply the Dictionary Act definition to that term.

For more on the Dictionary Act and how the Court interprets the phrase "unless the context indicates otherwise," see *Rowland v. California Men's Colony*, 506 U.S. 194, 199–200 (1993). In that case, the Court interpreted "context" to mean only the text of the law and related laws, and interpreted "indicates" in a very broad and flexible way. Nearly any reason, however slight, could "indicate" that the Dictionary Act definition should not apply.

Many other large organic laws contain definitions that apply to a large part of federal law. For example, section 101 of title 10, United States Code, contains a set of definitions that applies throughout that title of the Code.

§ 3.43 Earlier Versions of the Same Statute

When a statute has been amended over the years, the Court ordinarily does not care about the earlier versions. The starting point, the Court has said, is the existing statutory text "and not the predecessor statutes." *Lamie v. United States Trustee*, 540 U.S. 526 (2004). For that reason, the Court will generally look back at an earlier version only if the present version is unclear.

As an aside: This seems only partly right. When a statute is enacted as one public law and later amended by another public law, is it one law or two? There is a sense in which it is one new law—the first enactment as modified by the second enactment—and that is what the *Lamie* Court seemed to have in mind. But this "one new law" has never been enacted, as a single law, by Congress; the "one new law" is a splicing of two separate public laws, passed by two separate Congresses, each with a separate intent. So there is a sense in which the new law is really two laws—and that sense is the constitutional sense (in which a law is a measure that passes both chambers of Congress in identical form and is presented to the President), so perhaps it should not be dismissed.

For an example of a case in which the Court struggled mightily with how best to understand the statutory history, see *Koons Buick Pontiac GMC, Inc. v. Nigh*, 543 U.S. 50 (2004), in which an exasperated Justice Ginsburg, writing for the majority, said candidly: "The five separate writings this Court has produced demonstrate that [the statute] is hardly a model of the careful drafter's art." 543 U.S. 50 at fn 7 (2004).

§ 3.44 Resolving Conflicts between Statutes

Sometimes a statute does not meld seamlessly into an existing body of law. For a discussion of how the Court approaches inconsistencies and conflicts between statutes, see Chapter Nine, "Affecting and Amending Other Laws."

§ 3.50 Considering Constitutional Issues

Every Act of Congress is presumed to be constitutional. The Court does, however, consider constitutional challenges from time to time, and those challenges can color the way the Court interprets a statute in several ways.

§ 3.51 Avoiding Serious Constitutional Problems

Simply put, the Court will not interpret a statute in a way that renders it unconstitutional unless doing so is utterly unavoidable.

If a case can be decided on either statutory or constitutional grounds, the Court will—for "sound jurisprudential reasons"—decide it on the statutory ground and not reach the constitutional one. *Harris v. McRae*, 448 U.S. 297, 306–307 (1980).

Accordingly, the Court will not interpret a statute in a way that raises "serious constitutional problems." In such a case, the Court will choose some other plausible meaning that does not have the specter of constitutional difficulties hovering around it. *DeBartolo Corp. v. Florida Gulf Coast Trades Council*, 485 U.S. 568, 575 (1988). The Court will try every other plausible meaning to find one that saves the statute from being unconstitutional.

§ 3.52 When the Court Requires Clear Statements

There are certain matters that the Court treats with great delicacy. When Congress legislates in a way that may encroach on those matters, the Court requires that Congress be extremely precise. It is not enough, in these cases, for Congress to be plain; Congress must be more than plain.

When constitutional or other sensitive matters are at stake, the Court generally presumes that Congress does not intend to disturb the status quo. To overcome that presumption, Congress must state precisely its intention to do so. This is known as a "clear statement" rule. *Astoria Federal Savings & Loan Association v. Solimino*, 501 U.S. 104, 108–109 (1991).

Clear statement rules apply only when "weighty and constant" values are at stake. The purpose is to ensure that Congress "has in fact faced, and intended to bring into issue, the critical matters involved in the judicial decision." *United States v. Bass*, 404 U.S. 336, 349 (1971).

For example, a clear statement rule generally applies when a law would interfere in some way with state sovereignty, such as when it would abrogate the sovereign immunity of a state under the Eleventh Amendment (*Atascadero State Hospital v. Scanlon*, 473 U.S. 234, 243 (1985)), allow a state to be sued for damages (*Will v. Michigan*, 491 U.S. 58 (1989)), tell a state how to hire its judges (*Gregory v. Ashcroft*, 501 U.S. 452 (1991)), or impose a condition on the state's receipt of a federal grant (*South Dakota v. Dole*, 483 U.S. 203, 207 (1987)).

Similarly, the Court expects that Congress does not intend to preempt state law; the Court will not interpret a law in a way that preempts state law unless Congress makes the intent to preempt "clear and manifest." *Wisconsin Public Intervenor v. Mortier*, 501 U.S. 597, 605 (1991). Likewise, when Congress does not intend to preempt state law and provides a clear statement to that effect, the Court will apply that statement.

A clear statement rule also applies when a law would waive the sovereign immunity of the United States. *United States v. Mitchell*, 445 U.S. 535, 537 (1980).

A clear statement rule applies when Congress intends for a law to apply outside the United States (*EEOC v. Arabian American Oil Co.*, 499 U.S. 244, 248 (1991)), to apply retroactively (*Gozlon-Peretz v. United States*, 498 U.S. 395, 404 (1991)), or to apply without the possibility of judicial review or habeas review (*Demore v. Kim*, 538 U.S. 510 (2003)).

And a clear statement rule applies when a law that does not expressly apply to the President would, if applied to the President, pose a significant question regarding the President's constitutional functions. See *Franklin v. Massachusetts*, 505 U.S. 788, 800–801 (1992) (Court would require an express statement by Congress before assuming presidential actions could be reviewed for abuse of discretion under the Administrative Procedure Act); *Nixon v. Fitzgerald*, 457 U.S. 731, 748 fn 27 (1982) (Court would require an explicit statement by Congress before assuming President could be sued for damages).

Clear statement rules are like snowflakes—no two are exactly alike. One rule might require a "plain statement" of legislative intent; another might require that Congress make its intention "unmistakably clear in the language of the statute"; a third might require "express words to that effect." The basic message is the same: If you want to achieve a particular result, use words that make it unmistakably clear.

Some clear statement rules are more important than others. As the Court has explained, some clear statement rules are ordinary rules of construction, not required by the Constitution, while others are rules derived from constitutional law. *Hilton v. South Carolina Public Railways Commission*, 502 U.S. 197, 205–206 (1991). Allocating the various rules between these two categories is beyond the scope of this book.

§ 3.53 When the Court Requires Specific Findings

Another tack the Court has taken when confronted with a constitutional question is to require Congress to clearly articulate why Congress believes it has authority to act. The Court has indicated that Congress should preface a constitutionally questionable law with a formal statement of findings. If the findings are inadequate, the Court finds that the statute is unconstitutional.

For example, in *United States v. Lopez*, 514 U.S. 549 (1995), the Court struck down a prohibition on possessing a gun in a school zone, not being convinced that the activity substantially affected interstate commerce. The Court held open the possibility that the law would become constitutional if Congress revised it to include specific findings.

§ 3.60 Actions by the President and Other Executive Officers

The legislative power is vested in Congress, but the executive branch has some say in how laws are made and interpreted. The Constitution authorizes the President to make legislative proposals, and requires that a bill not become law unless it is first presented to the President. In addition, Congress can (within certain limits), and does, delegate legislative power to executive agencies.

And, of course, every branch of the federal government must, to some extent, interpret the laws. The executive branch, for example, must interpret a law so that it can carry out the law properly. "Interpreting a law enacted by Congress to implement the legislative mandate is the very essence of 'execution' of the law." *Bowsher v. Synar*, 478 U.S. 714, 733 (1986).

§ 3.61 Presidential Signing Statements

A bill can become law without the President's signature, if the President simply fails to return it within ten days after being presented with it. However, most Presidents sign most bills, and in the modern era most also provide a signing statement at the time of signing.

A signing statement is commonly used by the President to describe the likely effects of the bill, to identify constitutional concerns about the bill, and to explain how the executive branch will carry out the bill.

In addition, a signing statement is occasionally used to explain what the President believes the law means. This is sometimes referred to as "executive history," because it is more or less analogous to legislative history generated by Congress.

According to a memorandum of the Office of Legal Counsel of the Department of Justice, the use of signing statements for executive history appears to have originated (and their widespread use certainly began) in the Reagan administration, although "isolated examples can perhaps be found earlier." Walter Dellinger, Assistant Attorney General, "The Legal Significance of Presidential Signing Statements," Memorandum for Bernard N. Nussbaum, Counsel to the President (November 3, 1993).

In 1986, the memorandum relates, Attorney General Edwin Meese arranged to have signing statements published alongside legislative history in the U.S. Code Congressional and Administrative News to make sure that the President's interpretation of the bill would be recorded and available in the same manner as legislative history.

The Court apparently has never considered whether a signing statement should be given any weight. Several federal appellate courts have considered the question, however, and have given some weight to a signing statement. See *United States v. Story*, 891 F.2d 988 (2d Cir. 1989); *Berry v. Department of Justice*, 733 F.2d 1343 (9th Cir. 1984); *Clifton D. Mayhew, Inc. v. Wirtz*, 413 F.2d 658 (4th Cir. 1969). Whether the Court would follow this lead is uncertain, given that the Court is already ambivalent about using legislative history.

§ 3.62 Agency Interpretation and *Chevron* Deference

When Congress enacts a law that has more than one plausible meaning, the Court may conclude that Congress wanted the executive branch to have discretion over how best to resolve the ambiguity. If so, the Court will defer to the interpretation of the executive branch, as long as it is reasonable. This principle was first established in *Chevron U.S.A. v. Natural Resources Defense Council*, 467 U.S. 837 (1984), and therefore is known as *Chevron* deference or the *Chevron* doctrine.

When a Court defers to an agency interpretation under the *Chevron* doctrine, the Court does more than treat the interpretation with respect; the Court treats the interpretation as binding and conclusive.

Although the Court continues to refine and revise the *Chevron* doctrine, it appears that for *Chevron* deference to apply, five elements must exist.

First, the statute must be ambiguous. The Court will not defer to an agency interpretation if there is a plain meaning.

Second, Congress must have intended that the agency have discretion to interpret the statute. Evidence of intent can come from the text itself or can be implied.

Third, the agency doing the interpretation must be the agency responsible for "administering" the law. To qualify for this element, the agency must do more than frequently make use of the law; the agency must actually be responsible for carrying out the law. For example, the Department of Justice does not "administer" title 18 of the United States Code, even though that is the title relating to federal crimes and criminal procedure. (Title 18 is administered by the judicial branch, according to the Court.)

Fourth, the agency must adopt the interpretation through a formal, public process. Agency interpretations contained in policy statements, manuals, and guidelines do not qualify.

Fifth, the agency's interpretation must be reasonable. Note that the agency's interpretation is not required to be consistent with its past interpretation; an agency can adopt one interpretation and receive *Chevron* deference, and then adopt a new interpretation and receive *Chevron* deference again.

If *Chevron* deference does not apply to an agency interpretation, the Court will consider that interpretation on the same basis as it considers any other form of evidence—only to the extent that it has power to persuade.

§ 3.70 Actions by the Congress and Other Legislative Officers

In the search for legislative intent, the Court will consider a number of different types of evidence from the legislative branch. The most controversial type of evidence is legislative history, though the Court also has special rules for certain other types of evidence.

§ 3.71 Interpretation of Appropriations Acts

Most of the federal government is funded on a year-to-year basis through appropriations acts. Unlike legislation intended to make substantive law, an appropriations act is intended to allow the government to take money from the Treasury and spend it. The House and Senate each have procedures designed to keep substantive legislation separate from appropriations, although Congress with some regularity includes substantive legislation in appropriations acts.

The Court generally honors this distinction, however, and expects that

Congress does not intend to change substantive law with language in an appropriations act. The Court will permit such a change only if the intent to do so is clearly expressed. *TVA v. Hill*, 437 U.S. 153, 190 (1978); *United States v. Will*, 449 U.S. 200, 222 (1980).

A provision in an appropriations act is generally interpreted to apply for only one year—the fiscal year to which the appropriations act relates. If a provision is intended to apply beyond that year, that intent should be clearly expressed.

§ 3.72 Legislative History: Why It Is Problematic

Legislative history refers to the proceedings in Congress relating to a law before it was enacted. The legislative history includes official reports by congressional committees and official statements by members of Congress. More broadly, it also includes testimony at legislative hearings and the different versions of a bill's text as it was shaped by the legislative process.

Using legislative history as evidence of legislative intent is problematic for several reasons. A committee report is the view of only a handful of legislators of only one chamber; an individual statement is the view of only one member. And the more courts use legislative history, the more legislative history tends to be generated not to aid lawmakers but to influence judges, and that tends to subvert the entire process.

To a textualist, legislative history is so problematic that it should never be used. To others, legislative history is so problematic that, though usable, it should be taken with a considerable grain of salt. Accordingly, the Court generally turns to legislative history as a guide to meaning only when it must choose between more than one plausible meaning.

However, the Court sometimes turns to legislative history even when there is a single plain meaning, if only to confirm the plain meaning that it has already found. The Court has consistently said that legislative history can always be used as evidence of legislative intent, so long as it is not used to overturn a plain meaning. Under that reasoning, legislative history can be used to confirm or reinforce plain meaning. For a discussion of how agencies pay closer attention to legislative history than courts do, see *Congressional Deskbook*, § 10.72, "Legislative History."

Finally, in some cases the Court derives meaning not from legislative history, but from the absence of legislative history. For example, in *Koons Buick Pon-*

tiac GMC, Inc. v. Nigh, 543 U.S. 50 (2004), the Court reasoned that an apparently significant amendment to the Truth in Lending Act did not have any substantive effect, because there was "scant indication" in the legislative history that Congress meant to work a change. See also *Church of Scientology of California v. IRS*, 484 U.S. 9, 17–18 (1987) ("All in all, we think this is a case where common sense suggests, by analogy to Sir Arthur Conan Doyle's 'dog that didn't bark,' that an amendment having the effect petitioner ascribes to it would have been differently described by its sponsor, and not nearly as readily accepted by the floor manager of the bill."). The Court does not always do this, however; see *Whitfield v. United States*, 543 U.S. 209 (2005) ("Given the clarity of the text, mere silence in the legislative history cannot justify reading an overt act requirement, or a cross-reference to § 371, into § 1956(h)"); *United States v. Wells*, 519 U.S. 482, 496–497 (1997) (refusing to read a materiality element into the statute at issue based on silence in the legislative history); *Harrison v. PPG Industries, Inc.*, 446 U. S. 578, 592 (1980) (It "would be a strange canon of statutory construction that would require Congress to state in committee reports or elsewhere in its deliberations that which is obvious on the face of a statute.").

§ 3.73 Legislative History Compared with Post-Enactment Statements

There is a common misconception about why courts find legislative history useful as evidence of legislative intent. Many believe legislative history is used primarily because it reflects the views of lawmakers. Legislative history does reflect the views of some lawmakers, but that is not why legislative history is used.

Legislative history is used primarily because it was available to lawmakers and may have influenced their votes. The Court is under no delusion that the views expressed by some members in legislative history are an accurate sample of the views shared by all members. The Court does, however, recognize that the views expressed by some members can shape the views of other members and influence their votes. In short, legislative history matters not because it was said or written by lawmakers but because it was heard or read by other lawmakers.

This distinction is generally not discussed, but it appears most clearly in the Court's approach to post-enactment statements. A post-enactment statement is a statement made by a member after the enactment of a law about the member's motives and perceptions. A statement like this would be useful if the Court wanted to sample the views of members.

In fact, however, the Court almost never considers a post-enactment statement. As the Court has explained, a statement made after the fact "cannot possibly have informed the vote of the legislators who earlier enacted the law," and for that reason "there is no more basis for considering them than there is to conduct postenactment polls of the original legislators." *Pittston Coal Group v. Sebben*, 488 U.S. 105, 118–119 (1988) (post-enactment statements by key sponsors).

§ 3.74 Legislative History Compared with Subsequent Legislative History

A post-enactment statement is not the same thing as what is sometimes called "subsequent legislative history." The former term applies when lawmakers describe what their motives and understandings had been in enacting the law; the latter term applies when a committee, an individual member, or some other congressional entity describes what it understands a law to mean. You can think of a post-enactment statement as a form of first-party eyewitness testimony ("this is what we, this Congress, meant"), and of subsequent legislative history as a form of third-party interpretation ("this is what they, that Congress, meant").

Unlike a post-enactment statement, subsequent legislative history is occasionally given weight, though "subsequent legislative history will rarely override a reasonable interpretation of a statute." *Doe v. Chao*, 540 U.S. 614 (2004). But see *Seatrain Shipbuilding Corp. v. Shell Oil Co.*, 444 U.S. 572, 596 (1980) ("while the views of subsequent Congresses cannot override the unmistakable intent of the enacting one, such views are entitled to significant weight, and particularly so when the precise intent of the enacting Congress is obscure" [internal citations omitted]).

The Court is sometimes asked, in interpreting a law, to give weight to a decision by Congress not to adopt a proposed amendment to that law. The Court has repeatedly declined to do so. "Failed legislative proposals are a particularly dangerous ground on which to rest an interpretation of a prior statute," the Court has said, because the decision not to adopt the proposed amendment could mean so many different things. *United States v. Craft*, 535 U.S. 274 (2002).

Remember, too, that there is a distinction between subsequent legislative history and subsequent legislation, that is, subsequently enacted law. "Subsequent legislation declaring the intent of an earlier statute is entitled to great weight in statutory construction." *Loving v. United States*, 517 U.S. 748 (1996).

§ 3.75 Report Language

Legislative history includes the official reports generated in Congress in the course of the legislative process, such as a committee report or a joint statement of managers accompanying a conference report. (The conference report itself is not report language, but bill language, as discussed in § 2.31, "Resolving Differences by Amendment or Conference." In researching case law, however, you should be aware that court decisions often use the term "conference report" to refer to the joint statement of managers.) As with all types of legislative history, reports and joint statements are used with caution.

As between the two, the joint statement is more authoritative. Indeed, the joint statement is the most authoritative form of legislative history, because a joint statement not only is prepared by members of both chambers (who are specially appointed by the leadership of those chambers), but also must be voted on and adopted by both chambers. Thus, it is the only form of legislative history that is produced and considered by both chambers.

A committee report is inferior to a joint statement in two major ways: First, it is the product of only a single chamber; second, it is produced and considered at an earlier stage of the process. A committee report is, however, more authoritative than any form of legislative history other than a joint statement.

§ 3.76 Individual Statements

Legislative history includes statements made by members in the course of official proceedings, such as floor debate. An individual statement reflects merely the views and motives of the individual member, and the extent to which that statement may have influenced congressional intent is open to question.

An individual statement is less authoritative than a committee report, *Garcia v. United States*, 469 U.S. 70, 76 (1984), and will be disregarded if it conflicts with a joint statement or committee report. *United States v. Wrightwood Dairy Co.*, 315 U.S. 110, 125 (1942).

An individual statement will also be disregarded, even if made by a sponsor, if it conflicts with context and history. *General Dynamics Land Systems v. Cline*, 540 U.S. 581 (2004).

Accordingly, an individual statement generally carries weight only when there is no other legislative history available, such as when the statement relates to an amendment adopted on the floor. *Northeast Bancorp, Inc. v. Board of Governors*, 472 U.S. 159, 169–170 (1985).

When two or more individual statements are in conflict, the Court gives somewhat more weight to a statement made by a member in charge of the bill, such as a committee chairman, *United States v. St. Paul, Minneapolis & Manitoba Railway Co.*, 247 U.S. 310, 318 (1918), or a statement made by a sponsor of the bill, *Chrysler Corp. v. Brown*, 441 U.S. 281, 311 (1979).

The Court gives little, if any, weight to a statement made by an opponent of the bill, *Shell Oil Co. v. Iowa Department of Revenue*, 488 U.S. 19, 29 (1988).

When individual statements on the House side are in conflict with those on the Senate side, the Court gives greater weight to those from the chamber that originated the provision and to those from the chamber that produced a more definitive legislative history. *Steiner v. Mitchell*, 350 U.S. 247, 254 (1956).

§ 3.77 Hearing Testimony

Testimony at a legislative hearing does not receive any weight, with one important exception: When an executive agency actively sponsors a bill, the testimony of its officers during a legislative hearing on the bill is entitled to serious consideration. *Shapiro v. United States*, 335 U.S. 1, 12 fn 13 (1948).

Hearing testimony can also receive some weight if it can be shown that the language of the bill was revised in direct response to that testimony.

§ 3.78 Amendatory History

One might think that evidence of legislative intent could be found by comparing the version of the bill as enacted with versions of the bill at earlier stages in the legislative process.

However, the Court has held that a comparison of this sort is inconclusive, unless the change is explained elsewhere in the legislative history. *Fox v. Standard Oil Co.*, 294 U.S. 87, 96 (1935). But see *Babbitt v. Sweet Home Chapter of Communities for a Greater Oregon*, 515 U.S. 687 (1995) ("An obviously broad word that the Senate went out of its way to add to an important statutory definition is precisely the sort of provision that deserves a respectful reading."); *Doe v. Chao*, 540 U.S. 614 (2004) (rejecting a proposed interpretation because of "drafting history showing that Congress cut out the very language in the bill" that would have supported that interpretation).

§ 3.79 The Opinion of the Drafter

The last, but not least, category of legislative history is the opinion of the very person who drafted the law. In one notable case, the Court decided to give weight to a report prepared by the officer within the Department of Justice who, the Court said, "almost certainly drafted" the language at issue. The report explained the different parts of the bill. Though it was not made part of the public record, the Court reasoned that it was "likely that, at some point, the report was brought to the attention of the Congressmen considering the bill." Therefore, the Court—after first cautioning that "the ideas expressed therein should not be given great weight"—said that "it seems to us senseless to ignore entirely the views of its draftsman." *Kosak v. United States*, 465 U.S. 848, 856 (1984).

In a spirited dissent, Justice Stevens dismissed the report as "an internal Justice Department working paper" prepared fifteen years before the bill was finally enacted and dismissed the person who prepared it as "a lobbyist." He finished with a flourish that—even though it was not in a majority opinion—all drafters should take to heart:

> ". . . [W]e should be guided by the sensible statement that 'in construing a statute . . . the worst person to construe it is the person responsible for its drafting. He is very much disposed to confuse what he intended to do with the effect of the language which in fact has been employed.' *Hilder v. Dexter*, 1902. A.C. 474, 477 (Halsbury, L.C., abstaining). If the draftsman of the language in question intended it to cover such cases as this one, he failed."
>
> *Kosak v. United States*, 465 U.S. at 863–864
> (Stevens, J., dissenting).

§ 3.80 Some Topics of Special Interest to Drafters

While there are many other topics that could be discussed, the remainder of this chapter focuses on a few topics that are of special interest to drafters.

§ 3.81 Definitions and Terms of Art

Drafters make frequent use of definitions. The Court has said that when a statute includes an explicit definition, the Court will follow that definition, even if it varies from the term's ordinary meaning. *Stenberg v. Carhart*, 530 U.S.

914 (2000). That assumes, of course, that the definition clarifies matters. If it does not, the Court will look elsewhere for meaning, including other parts of the text and the common law. *Raymond B. Yates, M.D., P.C. Profit Sharing Plan v. Hendon*, 540 U.S. 1 (2004).

Drafters sometimes also make use of terms of art. A term of art is a term that has an accepted meaning in a related law, in the common law, or in a specialized field to which the law relates. If the Court finds that a term is a term of art, the Court will apply that accepted meaning. See *Gustafson v. Alloyd Co.*, 513 U.S. 561 (1995) ("prospectus" is a term of art).

For example, if Congress uses a term with a settled meaning at common law, the Court assumes Congress meant to adopt the "cluster of ideas" behind that term, and interprets the term in that light. *Beck v. Prupis*, 529 U.S. 494 (2000) (turning to the well-established common law of conspiracy to interpret the term "conspire"). To identify or interpret a term of art, the Court sometimes consults a specialized dictionary, such as a law dictionary or medical dictionary.

§ 3.82 Narrow Interpretations and Broad Interpretations

There are some policies that the Court openly favors and some that the Court openly disfavors. When a law implicates one of these policies, the Court interprets the law not in an evenhanded way, but with a thumb on the scale.

The technique is usually characterized as a "presumption." The presumption typically will not disturb a single plain meaning if there is one, but will be used to help the Court choose among plausible meanings.

Broad Interpretation. When the Court favors a policy, the Court generally interprets the law "broadly" or "liberally." For example:

The Court has said that "remedial legislation" should be interpreted broadly. *Tcherepnin v. Knight*, 389 U.S. 332, 336 (1967). But this particular presumption is so vague (what is "remedial legislation," anyway?), has come under such criticism, and is so infrequently applied, that it is unclear whether it still carries any weight as a general principle.

A statute providing benefits to a class of people should be interpreted in favor of the beneficiaries. See *King v. St. Vincent's Hosp.*, 502 U.S. 215, 220 fn 9 (1991) (benefits to members of the Armed Forces); *Montana v. Blackfeet Tribe*, 471 U.S. 759, 766 (1985) (benefits to Indians).

Federal statutes that are intended to fill a void in local law enforcement should be interpreted broadly. *Moskal v. United States*, 498 U.S. 103 (1990).

Narrow Interpretation. When the Court disfavors a policy, the Court generally interprets the law "narrowly" or "strictly." For example:

> Statutes establishing evidentiary privileges should be interpreted narrowly, because privileges impede the search for truth. *Pierce County v. Guillen*, 537 U.S. 129 (2003).
>
> Statutory procedures for removal should be interpreted strictly. *Syngenta Crop Protection, Inc. v. Henson*, 537 U.S. 28 (2002).

And perhaps the most important category of laws interpreted narrowly are laws relating to crime and criminal procedure. When interpreting these laws, the Court applies what is called the "rule of lenity." According to the rule of lenity, when there are two rational readings of a criminal statute, one harsher than the other, the Court chooses the harsher only when Congress has spoken in clear and definite language. *McNally v. United States*, 483 U.S. 350, 359–360 (1987). The Court will resolve any ambiguity in the statute in favor of the defendant. *Hughey v. United States*, 495 U.S. 411, 422 (1990). Likewise, the Court assumes that a state-of-mind requirement applies to each element of a criminal offense, unless Congress clearly indicates otherwise. *United States v. X-Citement Video, Inc.*, 513 U.S. 64, 72 (1994).

§ 3.83 Congress Does Not Mumble

The Court sometimes makes a sweeping generalization about how Congress operates and uses that generalization as a guide to meaning (or, perhaps, as a signal to Congress).

In some cases the generalization seems to be descriptive—describing how Congress does in fact operate. In other cases the generalization seems to be prescriptive—describing how the Court would like Congress to operate.

A generalization of this sort is not unlike when a teacher (a Vermont schoolmarm, perhaps?) generalizes to a student, "Students in this class do not mumble." Whether that statement is a description or a command, the student gets the message—mumbling is not tolerated.

The Court's generalizations about Congress often come across this way. "Congress does not mumble," the Court seems to be saying, tapping a ruler in its palm.

Some examples:

"Congress, we have held, does not alter the fundamental details of a regulatory scheme in vague terms or ancillary provisions—it does not, one might say, hide elephants in mouseholes." *Whitman v. American Trucking Associations, Inc.*, 531 U.S. 457, 468 (2001). Thus, Congress did not make a radical change in the law in a provision purporting to be a technical or conforming amendment—or so the Court held. *Director of Revenue of Missouri v. CoBank*, ACB, 531 U.S. 316, 323 (2001).

If "Congress had meant to set a counterintuitive limit on authority to act, it would have said more than it did." *Barnhart v. Peabody Coal Co.*, 537 U.S. 149 (2003).

"Where Congress intends to refer to ownership in other than the formal sense, it knows how to do so." *Dole Food Company v. Patrickson*, 538 U.S. 468 (2003).

"When Congress has wished to create such an addition to the law of copyright, it has done so with much more specificity." *Dastar Corp. v. Twentieth Century Fox Film Corp.*, 539 U.S. 23 (2003).

"If Congress intended the term 'demonstrates' to require that the 'burdens of production and persuasion' be met by direct evidence or some other heightened showing, it could have made that intent clear by including language to that effect." *Desert Palace v. Costa*, 539 U.S. 90 (2003).

"Congress could have conditioned the entire subsection (g)(4)(A) as applying only to 'a person entitled to recovery.' That, of course, is not what Congress wrote." *Doe v. Chao*, 540 U.S. 614 (2004).

It is hard to see how a generalization of this sort would apply in a particular case, to a particular statute. But the Court's willingness to use these generalizations reinforces the notion that the Court will look anywhere it likes in its search for meaning (§ 3.11), including its sense about how Congress does (or should) draft. And because the Court pays attention to how Congress drafts, poor drafting of one law can cause damage to the entire statute book (§ 9.70).

§ 3.84 How the Court Interprets a List

When the Court interprets a list of items, it uses two time-honored techniques as a guide to meaning. Both are canons of construction known by their Latin names.

The first technique, *noscitur a sociis* (a thing is known by its companions), was discussed above (§ 3.32). It stands for the general proposition that a word should be interpreted in context with other words. If the context is a list of items, the items should be interpreted in light of one another, that is, "words grouped in a list should be given related meaning." *Dole v. United Steelworkers of America*, 494 U.S. 26, 36 (1990).

The second technique, *ejusdem generis* (of the same kind), is simply a narrow and specialized version of the first technique. It stands for the specific proposition that when Congress ends a list of specific items with general words, "the general words are read as applying only to other items akin to those specifically enumerated." *Harrison v. PPG Industries, Inc.*, 446 U.S. 578, 588 (1980).

For example, when a law refers to "contracts of employment of seamen, railroad employees, or any other class of workers engaged in interstate commerce," the general words, "any other class of workers engaged in interstate commerce," do not mean all classes of workers engaged in interstate commerce. Instead, they mean only classes of workers like seamen and railroad employees. What classes are those? The Court's answer was "transportation workers." *Circuit City v. Adams*, 532 U.S. 105, 114–115 (2001).

The technique of *ejusdem generis* is related not only to *noscitur a sociis*, but also to the principle that Congress uses each word for a reason (discussed in § 3.34, "Assume Each Word Is Used for a Reason"). In the *Circuit City* case, if the Court had given the general words a broad meaning, that broad meaning would swallow up the other items in the list. The Court assumes that "seamen" and "railroad employees" are not idle examples but guides to meaning.

For another example of *ejusdem generis* in action, see *Washington State Department of Social & Health Services v. Guardianship Estate of Keffeler*, 537 U.S. 371 (2003). In that case, the Court considered a law that referred to "execution, levy, attachment, garnishment, or other legal process" and determined that the general words, "other legal process," should be understood to mean a process much like execution, levy, attachment, and garnishment. For that reason, the general words cover only a process that uses a "judicial or quasi-judicial mechanism."

As always, these techniques are tools, not rules. The Court will not use these techniques to overturn a plain meaning and will not apply them when the legislative intent appears to be to the contrary.

§ 3.85 The Court's Reluctance to Imply Additional Exceptions

Sometimes the Court is asked to create an implied exception to a general rule. When Congress has already created one or more express exceptions, the Court is reluctant to imply additional ones.

This technique is sometimes known as the rule against implied exceptions, but more often by its Latin name, *expressio unius est exclusio alterius* (the inclusion of one is the exclusion of others).

As with any technique, the Court will not apply this technique if legislative intent is to the contrary. Beyond that, there is some confusion about exactly when and how this technique is applied.

The Court has been known to apply this technique to a law that has only one exception. For example, in *TRW Inc. v. Andrews*, 534 U.S. 19 (2001), the Court considered a general statute of limitations that was subject to a single exception (for cases involving willful misrepresentation), and decided that Congress implicitly excluded the possibility of other exceptions, such as a discovery rule.

Likewise, in *Christensen v. Harris County*, 529 U.S. 576 (2000), the Court considered a law providing that an employee may use compensatory time unless the employer's operations would be unduly disrupted, and decided that the one basis given—undue disruptiveness—was the sole basis on which an employer could deny the use of compensatory time.

However, the Court at times has said that the technique applies only when there are "two or more" exceptions that are part of an "associated group or series," justifying the inference that the items not mentioned were excluded by deliberate choice, not inadvertence. *United States v. Vonn*, 535 U.S. 55, 65 (2002). For example, "the enunciation of two exceptions does not imply an exclusion of a third unless there is reason to think the third was at least considered." *Barnhart v. Peabody Coal Co.*, 537 U.S. 149 (2003).

§3.90 Conclusion

This chapter covers a lot of ground. The contention here is that a drafter needs to be familiar with this ground to draft effectively, and to advise clients effectively.

When a court interprets a statute, one of the questions it asks is why Congress drafted it the way it did. When you draft a statute, one of the questions you should ask is how a court will interpret it. If this chapter accomplishes nothing else, it should impress upon you that this is not an easy question to answer. What was said in 1949 by Frank Edward Horack Jr. largely remains true today:

> "If courts believe, as they say, that legislatures are presumed to know of past judicial decisions and that statutes are drafted with a knowledge of them, they must recognize that they have given legislative draftsmen poor guides for future action. To be sure, the draftsman knows that if his statute is held to be penal it will be strictly construed, while if it is considered to be remedial the interpretation will be 'liberal'; that if he uses enumeration he must face the rule of *ejusdem generis*; while if he uses words of general import the statute may be 'void for vagueness.' But he does not know when the court will determine that one set of rules is applicable and when the other. For him the rules of statutory construction are at best, meaningless; at worst, they are unseen and 'extraconstitutional obstacles' that he must avoid if possible."
>
> Frank Edward Horack Jr.
> "The Disintegration of Statutory Construction"
> 24 *Indiana Law Journal* 335, 347 (1949).

Perhaps the single most important lesson to be gleaned from this chapter is that it is not enough to use clear language in isolation: The Court does not read language in isolation. The Court interprets statutes holistically, assuming that a particular statute is a small coherent system within a body of federal law that is a large coherent system. To ensure that your draft has the effect the client wants, you need to draft not only clearly, but holistically: Your draft should work as a coherent whole and it should fit into the general body of law in a coordinated manner.

It is sometimes said that a drafter creating a statute is like an architect or engineer creating a building. Yes, but that only goes so far. A drafter is also like a mechanic, fitting a statute into a body of law like a mechanic fits a part into a machine.

This chapter should also impress upon you that the Court does not simply apply a literal reading of the text. The Court will look for meaning from any source it finds persuasive, including the many techniques it uses for guessing what Congress meant. You need to anticipate the sources and techniques the Court might apply, and draft (and advise) accordingly.

The task can be daunting; the techniques used by courts can be bewildering. You may be tempted to throw up your hands in frustration. "Loose judicial reading makes for loose legislative writing. It encourages the practice illustrated in a recent cartoon in which a senator tells his colleagues 'I admit this new bill is too complicated to understand. We'll just have to pass it to find out what it means.' " Felix Frankfurter, "Some Reflections on the Reading of Statutes," 47 *Columbia Law Review* 527, 545 (1947). Avoid that practice if you can, and do not get discouraged.

Finally, you should always bear in mind that a court interprets a statute in some cases because Congress was unclear, and in other cases because Congress didn't anticipate the question before the court. To best serve your client, you need to anticipate not only the typical controversies that might arise, but also the atypical ones. For a discussion of how to do so, see Chapter Four, "Thinking Through the Policy."

Chapter 4

Thinking Through the Policy

For days Beaman would not allow us to draft a line. He insisted instead on exploring the implications of the bill to find out exactly what we had or did not have in mind. He probed always for the extent and nature of those hiatuses that any proposed important legislation necessarily possesses.

James Landis, "The Legislative History of the Securities Act of 1933," 28 *George Washington Law Review* 29, 37 (1959)

In examining a bill . . . there is a special obligation to look for jokers that may cause difficulties in the enforcement of the law and to point these out to the sponsor if any should appear.

Harvey Walker, *The Legislative Process: Lawmaking in the United States* 340 (1940)

I am sick and tired of this damned perfectionism . . . Why can't the bill be introduced now, as it is, and put right in the House later on?

Aneurin Bevan, as quoted by Noel Hutton, "How the English Meet the Problem," in Reed Dickerson (ed.), *Professionalizing Legislative Drafting: The Federal Experience* 117 (1973)

Thinking Through the Policy

Chapter 4

§ 4.00 Introduction

Drafts can be failures for two reasons: Some are failures of communication, while others are failures of imagination.

Some who write about drafting focus only on failures of the first type. They reason that thinking and writing go hand in hand, so writing well also guides you into thinking well. That's fine as far as it goes, but it doesn't go far enough.

When there is a failure to communicate, the draft is not clear. The problem is on the page and evident to the naked eye. The failure can usually be noticed and cured by sensible editing.

When there is a failure to imagine, however, the draft is not adequate. The problem is not on the page and is invisible to the naked eye. The words look fine, but the thinking behind them is less than thorough. A failure to imagine cannot be cured by editing after the fact; it can be cured only by thinking through the policy.

The approach here is to focus on both types of failures. A draft should be comprehensive as well as clear. Failures of imagination are discussed in this chapter; failures of communication are discussed in Chapter Six.

Not to minimize the task of writing, but the task of thinking is far and away more important—and more time-consuming. One drafter decided to keep careful track of the hours spent on a particular drafting project. He logged a total of eighty hours: Only four were spent writing; fifty-eight were spent on research and eighteen on discussions. "It is," he observed, "a long and rocky road from a layman's bright idea to a matured and workable statutory provision." Harry W.

Jones, "Some Reflections on a Draftsman's Time Sheet," 35 *American Bar Association Journal* 941 (1949).

If you have been diligent in thinking through the policy, the writing is not too demanding. The actual draft is like the tip of an iceberg—it seems important because it is the part everyone sees; in fact, the true weight and force lie beneath the surface.

§ 4.10 The Perils of Ineffective Thinking

Though courts tend to call every problem with a statute a "drafting error," the problem is usually not with the writing but with the thinking: "The fact is that the difficulties of so-called interpretation arise when the legislature has had no meaning at all: when the question which is raised on the statute never occurred to it." John Chipman Gray, *The Nature and Sources of the Law* 165 (1909).

As one judge put it:

> "Now what do the courts concern themselves with most? They concern themselves most with problems that the legislature has failed to address itself to. And when the legislature has addressed itself to the problem but there is, say, awkward phrasing, or there are 2 provisions looking in opposite directions, or there are different indicators from the text and the legislative history, the question is relatively simple. The hard questions are those to which the legislature has not addressed itself."
>
> Harold Leventhal, "How the Problem Looks to the Courts," in Reed Dickerson (ed.), *Professionalizing Legislative Drafting: The Federal Experience* 30 (1973).

When the policy is not thought through properly, the result is not only more work for judges; a policy that has not been thought through effectively is simply not going to work effectively. It may respond to the problem poorly; it may not respond to the problem at all. It may have undesired side effects; it may cause confusion and controversy. It may lead to what the courts call an "absurd result."

§ 4.11 Problems of Application

Perhaps the most common result of ineffective thinking is a problem of application: The law applies to more things than the client really meant to cover, or it doesn't apply to things the client really meant to cover.

Problems of application take many forms. The law may cover the wrong people, the wrong events, or the wrong conduct. The law may cover the wrong place or the wrong time.

Sometimes the policy simply gets the facts wrong:

> A client wanted a bill that would cover the Great Lakes. For political reasons, however, he did not want to refer to them by name. He proposed to describe them as "the five largest lakes through which the international boundary line passes." That sounded good, but it didn't actually work: It applies to Lake Superior, Lake Huron, Lake Erie, and Lake Ontario, but it does not apply to Lake Michigan, which is entirely within the United States.
>
> A redistricting law in Kansas listed, for each district, the cities in that district, but some areas were not assigned to any district. *Harris v. Hanahan*, 192 Kan. 183 (1963).

Sometimes the policy makes assumptions that simply do not hold up:

> Clients routinely want a bill to apply to the states—but the United States is more than just the fifty states. What about the District of Columbia, the Commonwealth of Puerto Rico, the United States Virgin Islands, Guam, American Samoa, or any other territory or possession of the United States? And what about Indian tribes?
>
> A statute passed in 1965 imposed some rules on the qualifications for state and local "representatives." Assumptions about state and local political systems are tricky; there is a fair amount of variety from state to state. (Indeed, any assumptions about states are tricky.) In some states, judges are appointed; in others, elected by the people; in still others, appointed for a term but subject to an election to continue in office. Is an elected judge a "representative" covered by the law? See *Chisom v. Roemer*, 501 U.S. 380 (1991) (the Court's answer was "Yes").

Sometimes the policy fails to consider whether qualifiers should apply. Suppose, for example, the policy as first stated is "Thou shalt not kill." What if the killing is an accident? What if the killing is in self-defense, or in defense of someone else? What if the killing is done with the consent of the victim? These are not easy questions, but they need to be asked.

For a more complex problem of application, consider the following task, which is based on a problem suggested by William P. Statsky, *Legislative Analysis and Drafting* 24 (2d ed., 1984):

> First, draft a statute making it a crime for anyone to fail to aid someone who is drowning.
>
> Next, suppose you are in your backyard and your neighbor is in his. He doesn't like you, and he has built a barbed-wire fence along the boundary between your yard and his. In your yard you are gardening, and in his yard he is mowing his lawn while his infant grandson sits in a wading pool. You see the infant fall over, and you immediately call out to warn your neighbor, but he doesn't hear you over the din of his mower and seems annoyed by your frantic gestures. You do nothing more, and neither does he. Fortunately the baby, though momentarily drowning, rights himself.
>
> Has a crime been committed under your statute? By you? By the neighbor? Does the answer turn in part on whether the baby survives? Should it?

In many cases, a policy the client thought was easy and straightforward turns out to be anything but. Of course, a credulous drafter could simply provide what was asked for (perhaps something like, "Whoever fails to aid someone who is drowning shall be fined under title 18, United States Code, imprisoned not more than 5 years, or both"). But that would be scrivening, not drafting.

§ 4.12 Problems of Transition

A problem of transition is a special kind of problem of application: The law provides new rules for doing things but doesn't say what happens to things already being done under the old rules.

Is a transition period needed, or can the law take effect right away? Once it does take effect, does it apply to events that are already in progress?

The Endangered Species Act of 1973 requires all federal agencies to ensure that actions carried out by them do not threaten the existence of an endangered species. When Congress passed the Act, a federal dam project was underway that would, when completed, destroy the existence of the snail darter, an endangered species. Did the Act apply to existing projects like the dam? The

Act itself didn't say. See *TVA v. Hill*, 437 U.S. 153 (1978) (the Court's answer was "Yes").

Problems of transition can raise constitutional concerns. When a law tries to affect existing relationships and rights, for example, it may be an unconstitutional taking or a violation of due process.

§ 4.13 Problems of Administration

A problem of administration arises when a person who is supposed to carry out the law can't do so effectively. Perhaps the person does not have the legal authority to do so; perhaps the person does not have the means or resources to do so.

As with a problem of application, a problem of administration can be caused by bad facts, bad assumptions, or bad analysis. It can also be caused by a failure to allow for the possibility that a simple idea on paper can be a complex task to administer in practice.

Suppose a client wants a federal law limiting the amount of non-economic damages a person can be awarded when injured by medical malpractice. The limit will be $250,000, adjusted for inflation. That sounds simple on paper, but who is going to figure out the adjustment for inflation? Will a federal official figure it out for the entire country, or will a state official figure it out for each state? Or will the trial judge figure it out in each case? How exactly is the adjustment going to be figured—is it adjusted calendar year to calendar year, quarter to quarter, month to month, day to day? What information is used in calculating the adjustment—the general consumer price index, the general producer price index, a specialized index, or some other method?

Donald Hirsch related that he once drafted a bill to allow some federal workers to switch from one retirement plan to another. A worker who switched would get credit in the new plan for time served under the old plan. Because benefits were based on time served, the new plan would suffer a net loss whenever a worker switched to it: The worker would pay in to the new plan from the date of the switch, but the plan would have to pay out to the worker as if the worker had been paying in all along. The old plan, meanwhile, would receive a net gain whenever a worker switched away: It would bank the money the worker had paid in and never have to pay out.

To even out the net gains and net losses, Hirsch drafted the law to require the old plan to pay the new plan whenever a worker switched. The precise amount would depend on how much the worker would have paid into the new plan if the worker had been in the new plan all along. The bill became law.

A few days later an official called Hirsch. It's not possible, the official said, to figure out how much a worker would have paid in if the worker had been in the new plan all along. "You're kidding! How do you know?" said Hirsch. "I'm the one who has to do the calculation," replied the official, "and I just don't have the data I need, and there's no way to get it." Donald Hirsch, *Drafting Federal Law* 3 (2d ed., 1990).

§ 4.14 Problems of Enforcement

A problem of enforcement arises when people do not comply with the law. Many lawmakers fall into the trap of assuming their laws are orders to be obeyed; if the law says a person shall do X, then, by golly, that person shall do X.

It doesn't work that way. People break laws, and when they do, the question is, what happens next? If the law provides an enforcement mechanism (for example, the person shall be imprisoned), usually that is what happens next. But if the law does not, enforcement might be difficult.

Even if the law provides an enforcement mechanism, the people responsible for enforcing the law may not have the will or the resources to do so. Consider the imposition, and later repeal, of Prohibition: The task of enforcing the ban on alcohol was so taxing that it ultimately proved to be more trouble than it was worth. Albert Einstein, speaking of Prohibition, saliently observed: "Nothing is more destructive of respect for the government and the law of the land than passing laws which cannot be enforced." Always ponder whether the policy can in fact be enforced.

Even when a command is directed at a federal official, the client should consider the possibility that the command might be disobeyed.

The President signed the National Nuclear Security Administration Act into law on October 5, 1999, as part of the annual defense authorization law. The Act established within the Department of Energy a "semiautonomous" nuclear weapons agency headed by an administrator. The Secretary of Energy was allowed to set policy for the new agency and give direction to the administrator, but was forbidden to give direction to any lesser officer in the new agency.

The President and the incumbent Secretary of Energy did not embrace these changes. When the President signed the bill into law, he simultaneously announced that he would cross-appoint the secretary to serve as administrator and other incumbent officers in the department to serve in corresponding positions in the new agency. The President strongly intimated that he would not appoint a bona fide administrator unless Congress first modified the law to his liking.

In other words, Congress had required a separate new agency and the President's response was to require new business cards and letterhead. A political staredown ensued and the President did, eventually, appoint an administrator and allow the new agency to proceed.

No one—not the President, not a corporation, not a private individual—follows an order simply because it came from Congress. If Congress wants orders followed, it needs an enforcement mechanism that is credible and effective.

§ 4.15 Problems of Prediction

A problem of prediction arises when the law works in ways that the client did not have in mind.

Some problems of prediction are legal—the law might affect other law in ways not anticipated. Other problems of prediction are factual—the law might cause people to change their conduct in ways not anticipated (and not desired), either to gain the benefits or to avoid the burdens of the law.

The story is told of a law that required a train to stop at an intersection if another train was approaching, and not to start up again until the oncoming train had passed. No one realized (at first) that the law would apply not only to the first train but also to the second. Both trains would stop, and neither would start up again; the railroad system would grind to a halt.

§ 4.20 The Elements of Thinking Through the Policy

Thinking through the policy has seven elements: engaging the client, figuring out the problem and the objective, asking for details, researching the facts and law, analyzing alternatives, creating a coherent solution, and conducting a reality check.

Before you do any of that, however, you must adopt a posture of skepticism.

Look back at the quotation at the beginning of Chapter One in which Middleton Beaman is depicted asking, "terrierlike," his questions. The questions do not come from looking at words on a page; they come from taking everything with a grain of salt. Information may be wrong; assumptions may not hold; facts may shift; laws may overlap; people may disobey.

The client often comes to you with a prejudged sense of what needs to be done. Do not take that sense at face value: Respect it, but do not accept it. Clients do not always think through the policy and, when they do, they do not always do it thoroughly. In many cases a client simply starts with the recommendations of a third party. The recommendations may be sound, they may be unsound, or they may be misleading. What the client needs most from you is critical thinking and independent, frank advice. Do not surrender your judgment.

Be skeptical. Question assumptions. Imagine scenarios that might unfold and discuss them with the client. In many cases the client will have a firm sense of whether a scenario should be covered or not. Above all, use good judgment to decide when you have done enough. At some point you are not adding value so much as splitting hairs.

You have to pick your battles. Sometimes you don't have time; sometimes your client doesn't have patience. But you have a duty to your client not to be a "yes man" or a scrivener. Sometimes you need to remind the client that slowing down is an option.

§ 4.21 Engaging the Client

Thinking through the policy requires that you be intellectually engaged in the project. But that is not enough; the client must also be intellectually engaged in the project.

This may take some prodding, and you must be careful not to push the client in a particular direction (or to appear to be doing so). A drafter "leads the client, but where the client wants to go." Reed Dickerson, "How To Write a Law," 31 *Notre Dame Lawyer* 14, 16 (1955).

Engage the client right from the beginning. As Jack Stark explained:

> "Taking a request is not a meaningless or mechanical formality. That conversation may be the only one that the drafter and the requester have about the draft, and it strongly influences the latter's attitude toward the drafter and toward drafting. It is far better if, after that conversation, the requester thinks that the drafter is a competent professional who is eager to help rather than a lackadaisical scrivener. Moreover, asking enough appropriate questions induces the requester to

think about the project in sufficient detail. Otherwise, the requester probably will accomplish the necessary thinking in fits and starts, by asking for redrafts to alter or expand the draft. A drafter who is under time pressure cannot afford such inefficiency."

Jack Stark, *The Art of the Statute* 13 (1996).

Invariably, the task of drafting is made easier when you are brought in at the beginning. You have no control over when you are brought in, of course; but when you are brought in late, handed a draft already composed, and asked to "put this into form" or "check this over," the client may be reluctant to tinker with (much less to overhaul) what has already been done. This is especially the case when the draft has already been circulated to actual or prospective supporters. A change is harder to make when it needs to be cleared with many stakeholders in a large coalition.

Sometimes a client can be vexed by all the questions. James M. Landis, recalling his first experience at being on the receiving end of a drafter's questions, described it as "exasperating" and said that he and his colleagues suspected that the drafter must be complicit in "sinister Wall Street plotting" to delay the legislation. (In the end, Landis concluded, "We were wrong.") James M. Landis, "The Legislative History of the Securities Act of 1933," 28 *George Washington Law Review* 29, 37 (1959).

Each client is different, of course, and each responds differently. This is as true for the stage of engaging the client as it is for any other stage of the relationship.

Henry Thring drafted for two of the great British statesmen of the nineteenth century, Gladstone and Disraeli. Gladstone, he related, had an intimate relationship with every draft—he "understood and revised every word of a Bill and even settled the marginal notes." Disraeli, meanwhile, had an intuitive sense for politics but "cared nothing for the details of a Bill . . . once satisfied with the principle" behind it. Henry Thring, *Practical Legislation* 6 (1903). Most clients fit somewhere between these two extremes.

§ 4.22 Figuring Out the Problem and the Objective

The client has come to you because the client perceives a problem out there in the real world, and the client wants to respond to that problem with legislation.

Make sure you have a pretty good grasp of the existing state of affairs that the client wants to change and the new state of affairs that the client wants to create. The former is the problem, and the latter is the objective.

The problem and the objective are like points on a map: Things are at Point X, and the client wants them to be at Point Y. In an ideal situation, the client identifies Point X and Point Y, and you help the client plot a course between them. That course is the solution.

When a client comes to you with draft language already prepared, the client is coming to you with a solution, not a problem or an objective: Point X and Point Y have not been identified. This is not an ideal situation; indeed, it may well be the worst-case scenario. Someone else has already drawn conclusions about Point X and Point Y and how to get from one to the other. As a drafter, you need to hold each of these conclusions up to scrutiny, to see how well they really fit.

But whether you start with draft language or a clean slate, ask your clients to explain, in their own words, what the problem really is and what the objective really is.

Do not rest on abstract ideas. A particular situation has arisen that has prompted the client to act; find out what that situation is and learn as much about it as you can. Allow for the possibility that the client has not accurately perceived what the problem is; the client may be relying on information that is incomplete or simply wrong.

Once you get to the bottom of the problem, find out about the new reality the client wants to create. If you do not get to the bottom of the objective, you won't be able to tell whether a particular solution works or not.

Ask questions; listen carefully to the answers; follow up with more questions. By asking the right questions, you learn about the problem, the objective, and the range of possible solutions the client might want to consider. You also identify gaps in the client's understanding of the problem and the objective.

§ 4.23 Asking for Details

Policies come in all shapes and sizes. Some policies are broad, others are narrow; some are temporary, others are permanent. Some are sketchy, some are detailed.

Once you have figured out the problem and the objective, your work has only just begun. You need to figure out the finer points of the policy. There can be a great many.

Policymakers tend to have general ideas. They have not hashed out every detail. They have not thought through every angle. A general idea might be a great idea, but it is not, by itself, a well-developed policy. The client needs to consider not only the few big questions but also the many small ones. "You will be surprised at the number of points, both substantive and administrative, on which additional decisions of policy are necessary." James Craig Peacock, *Notes on Legislative Drafting* 22 (1961).

Get as many details from the client as you need. When you ask for details, you keep the client engaged and you make sure you and the client are on the same page.

Do not be afraid to ask dumb questions. If a word or concept, as presented to you, is less than crystal-clear, try to learn more about it. Ask the client questions that explore the specifics of the policy and chart its boundaries.

There are different ways to glean details. You can ask open-ended questions ("Who would carry this out?") or leading questions ("Do you want the attorney general to carry this out?"). Each has its place. Another effective technique is to describe a hypothetical scenario and ask whether it would be covered and, if so, how it would be handled.

Reed Dickerson offered this example:

> "To give you an idea of what is involved in developing the substantive basis for a relatively simple bill, here are some of the questions I asked a Congressman who wanted me to draft a bill emancipating Indians who could establish their general competency. I also include the answers that the discussion with him and with the Bureau of Indian Affairs ultimately developed.
>
> Q: Do you want to limit the bill to Indians of any particular age?
> A: Yes, to those 21 or above.
> Q: Who should determine the question of competency?
> A: The local naturalization court.
> Q: Should the court's jurisdiction depend on the applicant's domicile or his residence?
> A: His residence.
> Q: Who should be notified of the hearing?
> A: The head of the local governmental unit, the local welfare department, the Superintendent of the applicant's tribe, the head of its governing body, and any other persons the court considers appropriate.

Q: How much notice should be given?
A: 30 to 60 days.
Q: What factors should the court consider in determining competency?
A: The applicant's moral and mental qualifications and his ability to manage his own affairs.
Q: After a writ of competency is issued, what further steps, if any, need to be taken to assure full emancipation?
A: The Secretary of the Interior should be required to give the applicant all money and property that has been held in trust for him and to issue any necessary land patents.
Q: At what point should the applicant's tribal connection be severed?
A: When he and his tribe have fully settled all claims against each other."

Reed Dickerson, "How to Write a Law"
31 *Notre Dame Lawyer* 14 (1955).

Sooner or later you will reach a point where the client is not able to provide further details. Perhaps the client has not thought about the details, and will need to ponder them before giving you a response. The search for details sharpens the client's thinking by helping the client envision how the policy will really work, in the real world.

Sometimes the search for details reveals problems with the policy—faulty assumptions, flawed logic, constitutional difficulties, political minefields. A drafter who can catch problems quickly and discreetly will have the gratitude and respect of many clients.

At other times the client has thought about the details, but has decided not to decide. The client may not care (for example) which federal agency carries out a program, so long as the program is carried out. The client does not need to decide every detail, though the client should be made to understand that if the client does not decide them, someone else—generally, a federal agency or a federal court—will. In other words, "deciding whether to decide" and "deciding who decides" are themselves details for the client to decide. There is a substantive difference between "The appropriate Federal official shall carry out the program" and "The Federal official that the President considers appropriate shall carry out the program."

Sometimes the client turns the tables and asks you what you would do or what you think best. For most drafters, a direct answer to that sort of question is not appropriate. As discussed in Chapter One, a drafter does not recommend policy. What a drafter does is provide information and analyze options. For example, the client might ask for an annual report, and the drafter might ask whether the client wants to specify a particular due date each year. The client might turn that question around with "what do you suggest?" An appropriate answer might be as follows: "If the purpose of the report is to provide information to the congressional committees that have to perform oversight, they might prefer to get it early in the year." The key is to provide information about choices rather than recommend a particular choice. Help the client make an informed decision.

As a practical matter, a drafter does have a certain amount of leeway over details, especially when the details are essentially technical. There are only so many questions a client can tolerate. Some details are more efficiently handled by you, as a drafter, on your own.

As Henry Thring explained: "The sum of the whole matter is this, that to prepare a good Bill the draftsman must receive sufficient instructions, but they will necessarily be short, and he must exercise a very large discretion in filling up the gaps." Henry Thring, *Practical Legislation* 8 (1903). But even in that case, Thring cautioned, the drafter should still furnish the client "with information on all technical points."

§ 4.24 Researching the Facts and Law

As a drafter you are a generalist, but for each drafting project you must become a specialist in whatever the policy entails.

To do this you must research the facts and the law. "Every point of fact or law which is conceivably—and in many instances almost inconceivably—involved should be thoroughly explored before pen is put to paper on the first word of the first draft." James Craig Peacock, "Drafting a Proposed Statute," 1 *The Practical Lawyer* 19, 20 (1955).

It is not enough to know only the facts or only the law; you need to know how the facts and law relate to each other. Your bill needs to work on a legal level and on a practical level. To draft a bill on highway law, for example, you need to know highway law, "not only as highways but as law." Middleton Beaman, "Bill Drafting," 7 *Law Library Journal* 64, 69 (1914).

To a certain extent you will need to rely on the client for information: The client probably knows more about the factual aspects of the problem than you do, and may know more about the legal aspects of the problem than you do, at least at the start. The client probably has access to information and expertise as well.

To a certain extent you (and the client) might need to rely on experts. In many cases you need not only facts and law, but know-how and special expertise. In those cases, use factual experts and legal experts (or advise the client to do so). ". . . [A]ll processes involved in converting a meritorious idea into an effective statute are equally important and in each process experts must be employed." Middleton Beaman, "Bill Drafting," 7 *Law Library Journal* 64, 66 (1914).

Study the law as thoroughly as you can; this certainly applies to federal statutes and sometimes also to case law and administrative law. Explore existing law to find out what statutes are involved and where an amendment might be dovetailed. You must know not only what the text of a statute says, but how it works in practice.

How much research is enough? There is no great answer to that question. Bear in mind that if your draft ultimately comes before a court, the court will assume that Congress knows the law, every nook and cranny of it. As discussed in Chapter Three, the court will also assume that Congress knows the problem, knows the facts, knows the administrative history, knows the social history, and knows the scholarly writing on point. This is not to suggest that you need to know all these things, but it is to point out the enormousness of what is expected. Learn what you can with the time that you have.

§ 4.25 Analyzing Alternatives

There is more than one way to solve a problem. Once you have a thorough understanding of what the client wants, help identify a range of options for the client to consider, from the most drastic to the least drastic.

The client may already have a particular alternative in mind. That is fine, but set it aside for at least a moment. Make sure the client is aware of the range of alternatives and discuss the advantages and disadvantages of each alternative, so that the client can make a fully informed decision about which alternative to choose.

A solution can affect one person or many. It can be temporary or permanent, general or specific. It can address the single scenario that prompted the client to act, or it can extend to other people, events, places, times, motives, or methods.

Advise the client about constitutional issues, if there are any. In many cases the client cannot achieve the objective directly because Congress lacks the power to do so, but the client may be able to achieve something similar. Make sure the client understands the options.

In some cases the client may need to be reminded that proposing to amend the Constitution is also an option. Though very few proposed amendments manage to pass Congress and be ratified by the states, proposing a constitutional amendment seems to be a useful tactic (judging from the number of proposals).

In some cases the client may need to be reminded that proposing a "sense of" resolution is also an option. Though a resolution of this sort (whether a sense of Congress, sense of the House, or sense of the Senate) does not have any legal effect, it may also be a useful tactic.

Typically, though, proposing a constitutional amendment or a "sense of" resolution is not the best course. The solution usually involves proposing a law, and the measure of choice is a bill (although there may be reasons to choose a joint resolution instead; see § 5.50, "The Joint Resolution"). If the solution does not require a law, perhaps a concurrent resolution (see § 5.40, "The Concurrent Resolution") or a simple resolution (see § 5.30, "The Simple Resolution") would work. If the solution involves proposing a constitutional amendment, a joint resolution is needed. For more on choosing the right measure, see Chapter Five.

Some objectives can be achieved—at least in part—without any legislative measure. If the client is in a position to influence report language, for example, perhaps report language is the best solution.

Assuming the solution involves proposing a law, survey the other laws that are related and decide how best to fit the new law in with the others. Should the new law be freestanding, or should it amend some other law? Does the new law square with, or clash with, the old? If there is a clash, how does the client want it handled? For more on affecting other law, see Chapter Nine.

In identifying and discussing the range of options, you must also be sensitive to parliamentary issues and political issues.

Parliamentary issues are often matters of tactics: The client may want to influence committee referral or to avoid a point of order. You do not need to master all the chamber rules, but you should know enough about them to be able to spot and discuss them when they are relevant.

Political issues are often matters of optics: The client may want to use particular words or methods to "send a message" to supporters, opponents, or undecideds, or simply to score points in the media. A good rule of thumb is to defer always to the client's sense of politics. Do not, on your own initiative, try to spot or discuss a matter of optics; this is the client's domain.

§ 4.26 Creating a Coherent Solution

Once you have helped the client work through the alternatives and choose one to pursue, you need to create a coherent solution.

A coherent solution is one that does what the client wants. It needs to be written effectively (as discussed in Chapter Six) and organized and arranged sensibly (as discussed in Chapter Seven).

At this stage you are on the cusp of the writing process, and you need to start thinking in terms of what words and concepts to use and how to fit them all together. This stage—the task of selecting the most appropriate concepts and then fitting them together—is "unquestionably the most elusive part of drafting. The specific pieces should cover the intended areas, and they should leave no gaps: they should not duplicate each other or overlap, and they should not contradict each other." Reed Dickerson, *The Fundamentals of Legal Drafting* 59 (2d ed., 1986).

Boil down the policy into the simplest form you can. Retain only the information you need. Turn a complicated concept into a series of simple ones, if you can.

Do not reinvent the wheel without good reason. Federal law is already a vast and complex machinery. When creating a new federal crime, for example, you do not have to instruct law enforcement officers to investigate and arrest, prosecutors to prosecute, defense attorneys to defend, judges to preside, juries to decide. Those concepts and instructions, and a great many others, already exist.

What you are trying to do is tap into the existing machinery and the existing concepts as neatly as you can. Perhaps you are like a mechanic; perhaps you are like a surgeon. Regardless of the analogy, the point is that you are creating a new part to work with the old. Make it as small, simple, and compatible as you can, and give it all the connections it needs.

§ 4.27 Conducting a Reality Check

Do not forget, as Beaman once said, to "include brains among the materials used." Middleton Beaman, "Bill Drafting," 7 *Law Library Journal* 64, 69 (1914).

Simply put, things sometimes look good on paper but do not work in practice. Give the policy a reality check.

Consider, with a skeptical eye, whether the policy can be given practical and legal effect. A policy that sounds good but doesn't work can embarrass your client and cause problems down the road.

A law may be legally sufficient but nonetheless be ineffective as a practical matter; the law may be difficult to administer or enforce, or it may not adequately cover possible contingencies, or it may not provide adequate consequences for a failure to comply. In short, it may not fit reality.

A practical concern with the policy is whether it is workable. This is not a question of whether it is a good idea or a bad idea—that is a policy question for the client to decide—but whether it is a well-formed idea that responds to the problem in an attainable way.

There is no easy process for figuring out if a policy is workable. You need to hold a brainstorming session. Ponder the policy from as many angles as you can. If you had to administer it, does it provide enough guidance? If you had to comply with it, can you tell what is, and is not, allowed?

In the ordinary case, does everything seem to be in order? Does it do what is needed to meet the objective? Does it refrain from doing anything else? Does it lead to any absurd results? What sort of effect will it have on institutions? People? Society? Does it rely on assumptions that may not be valid now, or may not hold in the future?

And so much for the ordinary case. Does it still work adequately in an extraordinary, but possible, case?

The essential purpose of the reality check is to give your statute, in a very short period of time, the sort of scrutiny that a common-law rule receives over generations of cases.

The virtue of a statute is that it can make major changes to the law quickly and responsively. The virtue of common law, on the other hand, is that it has been tested over time, through the trials and errors and lessons of a great many cases, and represents a sort of received wisdom.

Common law is tested, but it is not quick and responsive. Statutes are quick and responsive, but they are not always tested. This is where you, as a drafter, come in. Simulate the common-law process. Imagine people and events and contingencies that might cause problems. Find out if the law still works; find out where the gaps, the uncertainties, and the contradictions are.

The reward is in the result. Though a statute is born untested and new, it should work as if tested and old. (Unfortunately, as Judge Dean quipped, "Laws seem to be born full-grown about as often as men are." *Waters v. Wolf*, 162 Pa. 153, 167 (1894).)

§ 4.30 Two Ways to Test Legal Rules: The Actor-Action Model and the If-Then Model

An English barrister, George Coode, was perhaps the first to suggest that laws could systematically be broken down into elements. See generally George Coode, *On Legislative Expression: or, The Language of the Written Law* (1845).

Coode classified legal rules into different types, which he identified as rights, privileges, powers, liabilities, and obligations. Though many who write about drafting still use these types, they really aren't very useful.

Coode also classified legal sentences into elements, and these elements are generally useful. The elements of a legal sentence, according to Coode, are the legal subject, the legal action, the case, and the condition.

Some of Coode's work would seem backward today, but was an important step forward in his day. For one thing, his method for composing a legal rule typically produces sentences that snake along at great length. In his time this was a serious improvement; not so anymore.

Likewise, though Coode made a distinction between a case and a condition, it seems to be a distinction without a real difference. According to Coode, a case identifies the situation in which the rule applies, while a condition identifies a condition that, if satisfied, enables the rule to apply. But, as Elmer Driedger pointed out, the same principle can be written as a case or as a condition. See Elmer A. Driedger, *A Manual of Instructions for Legislative and Legal Writing* 3 (1982). Consider:

> A treasurer, if he absconds, shall pay restitution.
> A treasurer who absconds shall pay restitution.

In the former sentence, Coode would classify "if he absconds" as a condition; in the latter sentence, Coode would classify "who absconds" as a case. The classification is semantics, not substance.

§ 4.31 The Actor-Action Model

The root idea for which George Coode deserves credit (referred to here as the Actor-Action model) is the notion that every legal rule has an actor and an action and different sorts of qualifiers. This root idea isn't the only idea that you need, but it goes a long way in helping you to think through the policy. It makes you focus on people and conduct.

The action (which Coode called the legal action) is the conduct with which the law is concerned. The actor (which Coode called the legal subject) is the person who, by taking or not taking the action, generates a legal result.

Every legal rule has an actor and an action, even if the rule fails to identify them directly. Many legal rules also have qualifiers that limit the rule in some way or other.

To test a rule with the Actor-Action model, identify the actor, the action, and the qualifiers. If you can't figure out who the actor is (or what the action is), you and the client have some more thinking to do. When a rule fails to identify the actor or the action directly, the courts may struggle to figure out what the legislature intended.

The actor could be a single identified person, such as the President of the United States; it could be a category of persons, such as units of local government; or it could be every person.

Regardless, each actor should be a legally accountable person. This category includes natural persons (human beings) and fictional extensions of natural persons that the law treats as persons (government agencies, corporations, and other legal entities). Notably, it does not include animals or plants or objects.

If the actor is not a legally accountable person, the action loses meaning and the law seems unjust or absurd. Consider a rule that a dog may not walk on the grass, or that a school bus must stop at a railroad crossing. The dog and the bus can't read, and can't conform their conduct to, the rule. Are they to be punished? What purpose would that serve? The client probably means to target the owner of the dog and the driver of the bus, but perhaps the client means to target someone else, such as the keeper of the grass or the crossing guard.

If the actor is a federal agency, the actor should also be a politically accountable person. That is, the actor should be an identifiable official rather than an unidentifiable official or an entire agency. If the official is the head of the agency, or is in an advise-and-consent position, or both, so much the better.

For example, a law that requires the Secretary of Energy to act is more precise and direct than a law that merely requires "the Department of Energy" or "an appropriate officer of the Department of Energy" to act. If there is a problem with compliance, there is no question where the buck stops.

The action could be a transitive verb (that is, one that takes a direct object) as in, "The Director shall submit a report." Alternately, the action could be an intransitive verb (one that does not take a direct object) as in, "A person shall not walk on the grass."

Whether the verb is transitive or intransitive, the action should almost always be in the active voice rather than the passive voice. The passive voice upends the structure of a sentence by placing the subject in a prepositional phrase at the end—"a report shall be submitted by the director"—or by omitting the subject entirely—"the grass shall not be walked upon."

Later, when you are actually putting pen to paper, you may find cases in which using the passive voice is appropriate. While you are thinking through the policy, however, avoid thinking in the passive voice. Thinking in the active voice forces you to focus not only on the action, but also on the actor.

§ 4.32 The If-Then Model

There is a completely different root idea that you also need in thinking through the policy, and that is the notion (referred to here as the If-Then model) that every legal rule can be expressed as a condition and a result. In other words, every legal statement can be expressed with an "if" and a "then." This is an extremely powerful and useful idea.

Here's how the If-Then model works in practice. The following sentences are in a form typically used for rules of law:

The Secretary shall do X.
The Secretary may do Y.
The Secretary shall not do Z.

The If-Then model suggests they can be written as:

If the Secretary does not do X, then [consequence 1].
If the Secretary does Y, then [consequence 2].
If the Secretary does Z, then [consequence 3].

The value of the If-Then model is that it makes you focus on consequences—when you use this model, you often realize that you and the client haven't adequately considered what the consequences should be. Notice the unconsidered consequences that appear above, when the typical sentences are translated into If-Then statements.

A consequence can be almost anything. Typically, a consequence is a burden that applies if the law is violated, though it may be a benefit that applies if the law is followed.

Among the more common sorts of consequences are damages, injunctive relief, civil penalties, criminal fines, and imprisonment. These are the types of remedies commonly ordered by courts. But as far as consequences go, these are only the beginning.

When a police officer violates a person's *Miranda* rights, the consequence is that the evidence obtained cannot be used against the person in court. When a person misses a deadline to file an appeal, the consequence might be that the right to appeal is lost. When a state does not comply with a federal program, the consequence might be that the state forfeits some or all of its federal grant money. And so on.

As Justice Holmes explained, "Legal obligations that exist but can not be enforced are ghosts that are seen in the law but that are elusive to the grasp." *The Western Maid*, 257 U.S. 419, 433 (1922). Using the If-Then model will help you grasp the ghosts.

And grasping the ghosts is essential to effective drafting. "For it is but lost labor to say 'do this, or avoid that,' unless we also declare, 'this shall be the consequence of your noncompliance.' " Sir William Blackstone, *Commentaries on the Laws Of England*, section 2.

§ 4.33 Tools for Thinking, Not Writing

The Actor-Action (§ 4.31) and If-Then (§ 4.32) models are not tools for writing; they are tools for thinking. Do not write all your legal rules as a series of If-Then statements (though this is a technique, sometimes referred to as "normalization," that has been adopted by some drafters in some jurisdictions). Do not insist on including an action, an actor, and qualifiers in every sentence. These two tools will not make your writing any better.

These tools will, however, make your thinking better. They are prisms through which you can review every legal rule you use—and that means every legal sentence you use. Try to translate the legal rule into an Actor-Action statement; then try to translate it into an If-Then statement. If you can't carry out these translations, there is a hole in your policy.

§ 4.40 The Major Types of Legal Rules

Of course, you cannot apply the Actor-Action model or the If-Then model until you translate the solution into legal rules.

Translating into legal rules is a necessary step toward writing sentences. The process of translating will help you organize the policy in your mind in a systematic and logical way. If there are basic conceptual problems with the policy, this process will help you notice them. The legal rules will not necessarily reflect or dictate the way the policy will ultimately appear when you put pen to paper, but they will help you through the process.

As the Actor-Action model suggests, you should try to visualize people doing things—things that are required (such as a director submitting a report), things that are forbidden (such as a person walking on the grass), and things that are discretionary (such as a department head pondering whether to make a grant). If you aren't sure who the actor is, or what the action is, you need further guidance from the client.

And, as the If-Then model suggests, you should consider what is supposed to happen when people do, or fail to do, the things that are required, forbidden, or discretionary.

§ 4.41 Law Is a Vast System of Legal Rules

To really understand how laws work, and thus how to draft them effectively, you need to have an understanding of the "big picture" of the system of laws. This section delves into that big picture and tries to present the important concepts in a useful way.

At its most fundamental, a law is a rule of conduct: You must do this; you must not do that. The rule of conduct often takes the form of a command to act or to refrain from acting.

At the most fundamental level, people are autonomous. In the absence of law, people can do whatever they want. They police themselves. You come onto my land and take my apples, I take them back from you (self-help), or take something else (tit-for-tat), or get others to intervene on my behalf (by force or by influence or pressure). Of course, they're not "my" land and "my" apples to begin with—not in a legal sense of recognized property rights—because at the most fundamental level there isn't any law.

Self-help can get out of hand, of course. Enter the concept of a sovereign state. States make rules of conduct for everyone to follow. Some of the rules impose burdens: If you come onto my land and take my apples, the state will make you give them back, and the state will punish you. Some of the rules confer benefits: If I do certain things, this land is "mine," and the apples on it are "mine." Some of the rules declare status, such as what it means to say that the land and apples are "mine."

At the most fundamental level, a sovereign state (like an individual) is autonomous. In the absence of higher law, it can do whatever it wants: In a monarchy, the monarch can do whatever the monarch wants; in a republic, the republic can do whatever the republic wants. Of course, many monarchies and most republics have certain self-imposed shackles, such as a constitution, that limit what they can do. There are internal checks and balances and rules, but to the outside world, the state is autonomous.

A sovereign state is not a living thing, but a legal thing. It exists to the extent people agree, by law or custom, that it exists. By what sort of law does a state exist? You might say that it is a command: "Everyone must act as if there is a sovereign state." And in a sense it is. But it is easier to think of it as a declaration: "There is a state."

Though a sovereign state can do whatever it wants, it is not a living thing, and thus it is physically capable of acting only through people. And so the ability of the state to do whatever it wants is delegated to agents, usually in narrow ways. Unlike people and sovereign states, agents are not autonomous. They cannot do, on behalf of the sovereign, whatever they want; they can do only what the sovereign enables them to do.

To work properly, a system of laws needs to be a pretty fancy piece of machinery. Most rules have other rules behind them: If I do certain things, the apples are "mine." If the apples are mine, you must not take them. If you take them, you have to give them back (and if you don't, I can set other rules in motion to make you give them back). What's more, a sheriff can arrest you; a prosecutor can prosecute you; a jury can try and convict you. And so on. Each person is covered by a set of rules—typically, rules of command.

Behind any command there may be other commands. When a command is disobeyed, some other command may apply: If you disobey the command not to take my apples, the sheriff must arrest you. (However, the sheriff must not carry out an unlawful search. If the sheriff carries out an unlawful search, the prosecutor must not use the evidence obtained from the search. If the prosecutor uses the evidence, the judge must dismiss the case. And so on.)

Not all commands have other commands behind them, however. Many commands are backed, instead, by rules of discretion. The prosecutor is not commanded to prosecute you; the prosecutor can decide whether to prosecute you or not. If the prosecutor decides to prosecute you, the march from one command to the next continues (the jury tries you). But if the prosecutor decides not to prosecute you, that is the end of the line: You get away with taking my apples. Perhaps I have other remedies—such as suing you for an order that you return the apples or pay me for them—but the remedy of having you punished is off the table.

Finally, states band together. Enter the concept of a federal government. The federal government is a sovereign state but, unlike the several states, it is not autonomous; it cannot do whatever it wants. Though every state has its own state constitution, the sovereignty of a state is inherent and exists apart from the state constitution. The sovereignty of the United States, by contrast, depends on and is conferred by the Constitution of the United States—and the powers of the federal government, though considerable, are limited to those powers granted by the Constitution.

As with state agents, federal agents are not autonomous: They can act only to the extent the Constitution or other federal law allows them to act. An act that exceeds a federal agent's authority is generally void, even if this seems to cause unfair hardship. This is known as the "*Merrill* doctrine" after the seminal case, *Federal Crop Insurance Corp. v. Merrill*, 332 U.S. 380 (1947).

In that case, a farmer wanted to take out a federal crop insurance policy on two different fields: one for summer wheat, one for winter wheat. The federal agency assured him that both the summer wheat and the winter wheat would be covered and he bought the policy in reliance on those assurances. Ultimately the winter-wheat field failed, and he sought to recover on the policy. Unfortunately for the farmer, the agency that sold him the policy was prohibited by law from insuring winter wheat. The assurances that were made to him, and his reliance on those assurances, didn't matter: The agency was barred by law from insuring winter wheat, so the farmer could not recover.

Simply put, a person who deals with a government agent is presumed to know the law just like anyone else; if the agent has been commanded not to do something, the courts cannot compel the agent to do it. Though often criticized as harsh, the *Merrill* doctrine is said to "further the interest of the citizenry as a whole in obedience to the rule of law." *Heckler v. Community Health Services, Inc.*, 467 U.S. 51 (1984).

§ 4.42 Rules of Command

As discussed in § 4.41, the most basic type of legal rule is a rule of command: You must do this, you must not do that. Many who write about drafting call the command to act a requirement and the command to refrain from acting a prohibition, but the distinction is not of great use. When a court issues a command, it is known as an injunction, whether it is an order to act or to refrain from acting. Requirements and prohibitions are two sides of the same coin.

Many important rules of command are not in statute; instead, they are established by the Constitution or by common law, and serve as background norms against which other law is enacted. For example, common-law concepts like property, criminal law, and contracts are used routinely by, but not articulated in, federal law.

Though discussed above, it bears repeating here: Do not assume that everyone will follow the law. Not everyone does, at least not all the time. Do not make this mistake, and do not let your client make this mistake. Always ponder the question: What happens when there is a violation? If the answer is not obvious, consider stating the consequence expressly.

Do not use a rule of command to establish a status or relationship. As noted above, you can command something into existence—"Everyone must act as if there is a Department of Z," for example, or more directly, "There shall be a Department of Z." But it makes more sense to consider this a stipulation to be declared: "There is a Department of Z."

§ 4.43 Rules of Discretion

A second type of legal rule is a rule of discretion: You may do this; the secretary may do that. You do not have to act, but if you do, the act has a recognized legal effect.

Many who write about drafting call this an authorization, but that term is misleading. An authorization occurs when Person A enables Person B to take binding actions on Person A's behalf. An employer authorizes an employee to sign a check on the employer's behalf; a principal authorizes an agent to enter into a contract on the principal's behalf. And, too, the federal government authorizes a federal officer to take certain actions on the government's behalf.

Not all authorizations are rules of discretion. A law can authorize the secretary to make grants just as easily with a command ("the Secretary shall make grants") as with a rule of discretion ("the Secretary may make grants"). The former is sometimes called mandatory authority, the latter discretionary authority.

Likewise—and this seems to be the trickier part—not all rules of discretion are authorizations. A rule of discretion simply provides a way for a person to avoid the burden (or perhaps to obtain the benefit) of any other rule. For that reason, it is more like a license than an authorization. Suppose, for example, there is a statute as follows:

> (a) A person who transports a border collie in interstate commerce shall be imprisoned not more than 1 year, except as provided in subsection (b).
>
> (b) A person may transport a border collie between Maine and New Hampshire.

The rule of discretion in subsection (b) is not an authorization; it does not enable a person to act on behalf of another person. It simply enables a person to avoid the burden of the general rule in subsection (a).

Notice that if there were no subsection (a), and the entire statute simply said, "A person may transport a border collie between Maine and New Hampshire," it would be an odd statute indeed. It would seem to be stating the obvious: Of course a person may transport a border collie between Maine and New Hampshire. The rule of discretion in subsection (b) can properly be understood only as an exception to the rule in subsection (a).

The point here is that every rule of discretion is best understood as an exception to some other rule—usually, a rule of command. If the other rule is stated in the law, the rule of discretion is usually clear. If the other rule is not stated in the law, the reader must look elsewhere for meaning.

To best understand a rule of discretion like "The Secretary may make grants," you need to remember that there is a general rule that a person cannot give away federal money; the gift is void and the government will take the money back. The example really means something like "If the Secretary makes grants, the general rule that a person cannot give away Federal money does not apply." This is the If-Then model in action.

Testing a rule of discretion with the If-Then model can give you a great deal of insight and help you spot problems with the rule. Rules of discretion are typically written not in If-Then form but in Actor-Action form—"The Secretary may make grants"—without identifying the underlying rule. If the underlying rule is obvious, that is fine; if it is not obvious, that is a problem.

§ 4.44 The Complex Interplay between Commands and Discretion

Suppose two different commands exist. The first one is recognized by courts as a principle of constitutional law, though it is not in statute. Let's call it the *Merrill* doctrine and imagine that it can be stated as follows:

> "If a person enters into a contract on behalf of the Federal Government, and the person is not authorized by law to do so, then the contract is void."

The second one is a statute (let's call it the Bay State Ban Act) that provides as follows:

> "Whenever a Federal officer attempts to enter into a contract with any city in Massachusetts, the officer shall pay a fine."

Now suppose a new rule of discretion (let's call it the Festivities Act) is enacted as follows:

> "The Secretary may enter into a contract with the city of Boston for Independence Day festivities."

Now suppose the secretary enters into a contract with the city of Boston for Independence Day festivities. What are the consequences? The answer depends on what sort of exception the Festivities Act creates.

Is it an exception only to the *Merrill* doctrine? If so, the contract is valid, but the secretary must still pay a fine under the Bay State Ban Act.

Is it an exception only to the Bay State Ban Act? If so, the contract is void under the *Merrill* doctrine, but the secretary need not pay a fine.

Is it an exception to both? If so, the contract is valid and the secretary need not pay a fine.

This is the sort of issue you need to anticipate and resolve when you are thinking through the policy. If you do not help the client work through it, a court will have to work through it on its own, and may not resolve it in the way the client wants.

A client who wants to cut through all the possible underlying rules might suppose the solution is to insert a phrase such as, "Notwithstanding any other provision of law, ..." Lawyers who are not drafters seem to like this phrase, but it is nearly meaningless and rarely useful. For more on this topic, see § 9.41.

Whenever you create a rule of discretion, test it with the If-Then model: Figure out what the underlying rule is to which the discretion relates, and decide whether you need to specify that rule in the law.

§ 4.45 Rules of Stipulation

The third and final type of legal rule is a stipulation: There is in the executive branch a Department of Z; the term "person" includes an individual; a person who does X commits a felony; a person who violates this section is liable in damages.

A stipulation is a declaration that something is true in law (whether or not it is true in fact). It creates a status or a relationship that the law will honor (through rules of command and discretion). Stipulations are legal shorthand, achieving indirectly (but sometimes more efficiently) what rules of command and rules of discretion achieve directly. They are helper rules that link together other rules in useful ways.

Stipulations typically are not universal. A definition, for example, is usually limited to a particular body of law: not "the term X includes Y," but "in this Act, the term X includes Y." Liability protection is usually limited to a particular category of liability: not "a company that adheres to best practices with respect to protecting private consumer information is immune from liability," but "a company that adheres to best practices with respect to protecting private consumer information is immune from liability to a consumer for a release of that information." And so on.

§ 4.46 How the Types of Rules Can Overlap

There are no hard and fast distinctions between stipulations on the one hand and rules of command or discretion on the other. Just about every rule can be written in either form. For example, "The Secretary shall do X" is a rule of command, while "The Secretary is required to do X" is a stipulation. In this example, the rule of command is shorter and more direct. But there are cases in which a stipulation is more elegant and tidy.

At this stage, however, you are not deciding how best to write the rule. You are simply deciding which concept best fits what the client wants to do, and pondering the basic questions that flow from that decision. Is the legal rule best understood as a command, a rule of discretion, or a stipulation? Who is the actor and what is the action? If a rule of command, what is the consequence of a violation? If a rule of discretion, what is the underlying rule to which the rule of discretion relates?

§ 4.47 Commands That Are Not Mandatory: Hortatory, Precatory, and Directory

Some commands are more binding than others. Courts have labels for the different grades of command: From least binding to most binding, they are hortatory, precatory, directory, and mandatory.

A hortatory command is not a true command at all, but an expression of encouragement or preference: "Congress sometimes legislates by innuendo, making declarations of policy and indicating a preference while requiring measures that, though falling short of legislating its goal, serve as a nudge in the preferred directions." *Rosado v. Wyman*, 397 U.S. 397, 413 (1970). Typically, a hortatory command uses the form "should" rather than a word of command such as "shall." A "sense of" resolution often includes a hortatory command.

A precatory command is not legally binding and enforceable, but it does declare a moral or political standard. For example, in *Pennhurst State School v. Halderman*, 451 U.S. 1 (1981), the Court held that a law stating that "Congress makes the following findings . . .: The Federal Government and the States both have an obligation to . . ." was precatory; the obligation declared in the law was a moral or aspirational one, not a legally binding and enforceable one.

The distinction of most concern to drafters is between a directory command and a mandatory one. When the consequences of violating a command are not specified and not otherwise obvious, a court must figure out the consequences. If a command is considered mandatory, the consequences of a violation are generally strict and severe. If considered directory, the consequences of a violation are generally flexible and often trivial.

For example, a command might specify as follows: "An applicant must submit an application within 30 days after the date of the enactment of this Act." Suppose a person submits an application on Day 32. The application is late, but the officer wants to consider it anyway. Is the person automatically ineligible, or can the officer bend the rule? Is the rule, in other words, mandatory or directory?

Of course, this is ultimately a question of legislative intent. A court will consider the reason for the rule in light of the purpose of the law and decide whether Congress likely wanted a strict rule or a lenient one.

Whether a rule is mandatory or directory, it is a binding rule of law and typically can be enforced in some way. Even a directory command has some effect: if nothing else, a court can usually order that the command be carried out.

Some courts have found a middle ground between a mandatory rule and a directory one: a rule that can be satisfied by "substantial compliance" or "reasonable compliance" rather than full compliance. See *Municipal Electric Utilities Association v. FPC*, 485 F.2d 967, 973 and fn 23 (D.C. Cir. 1973).

The distinction between a mandatory command and a directory one is most commonly made in the context of administrative deadlines. A deadline is usually considered directory rather than mandatory: "If a statute does not specify a consequence for noncompliance with statutory timing provisions, the federal courts will not in the ordinary course impose their own coercive sanction." *United States v. James Daniel Good Real Property*, 510 U.S. 43, 63 (1993). An agency action taken after a deadline has passed is ordinarily still valid. See *Barnhart v. Peabody Coal Co.*, 537 U.S. 149 (2003). A court may, however, order the agency to comply and hold the agency in contempt for a failure to do so. See *NRDC v. Train*, 510 F.2d 692 (D.C. Cir. 1975).

The most effective way to ensure that a command will be treated as mandatory rather than directory is not only to use words of command, but also to specify the consequence of a failure to comply. To leave out the consequence is to risk having the command be treated as directory instead.

Even if there is a specified consequence, the consequence may not be strong enough as a practical matter. Many laws require a federal officer to make a report to Congress by a statutory deadline, but not uncommonly a report is submitted late or not at all. Most people do not realize that it is a crime for a federal officer to neglect or refuse to make a report required by law. The crime (18 U.S.C. 2075) provides only a modest fine, however, and seems to be rarely, if ever, enforced.

And there is another consequence as well: When a deadline has been missed, an aggrieved party can sue under 5 U.S.C. 706(1), which provides for judicial relief in the case of "agency action unreasonably withheld or unlawfully delayed." While this is useful to a private person in many contexts, it is not particularly useful to Congress itself when trying to get the executive branch to follow a command.

Because these consequences have not caused reports to be made timely, Congress occasionally turns to other consequences to make a federal official honor a deadline. One of the more interesting consequences used was in section 3138 of the Floyd D. Spence National Defense Authorization Act for Fiscal Year 2001 (as enacted into law by Public Law 106-398; 114 Stat. 1654A-461): Congress required the Secretary of Energy to submit a certification, and specified that the secretary could not spend money on travel expenses, for himself or for anyone else within his immediate office, until the certification was submitted.

§ 4.48 Discretion That Is Not Unfettered

You might suppose that the discretion provided by a rule of discretion is unfettered, that is, not subject to being second-guessed by a court. And, indeed, when a person not within the federal government exercises discretion, that discretion is generally not reviewable by the federal courts.

The discretion of a federal agency is a bit more complex. 5 U.S.C. 701(a)(2) provides that when an action is "committed to agency discretion by law," the action is not subject to judicial review. This is, however, a "very narrow exception" to the usual rule that agency action is subject to judicial review. The exception applies only in "rare instances" where a statute is so broad that "in a given case there is no law to apply." *Citizens to Preserve Overton Park, Inc. v. Volpe*, 401 U.S. 402 (1971).

Accordingly, most exercises of discretion by a federal agency are subject to judicial review. When the client intends that a particular exercise of discretion not be subject to review, that intention should be made clear, and there are many ways of doing so.

Even when an action is committed to agency discretion by law, however, the agency has a duty to exercise discretion. Failure to exercise discretion is an abuse of discretion, and a court will compel the agency to exercise discretion. The court will not, however, interfere with or second-guess the agency's choice; the agency remains free to make any appropriate choice. *Work v. Rives*, 267 U.S. 175 (1925).

When an agency has a duty to exercise discretion, the agency must, at the very least, consider on a case-by-case basis whether or not to act. The agency cannot, for example, adopt a blanket policy of refusing to act. See *Matzke v. Block*, 732 F.2d 799 (10th Cir. 1984); *California v. Settle*, 708 F.2d 1380 (9th Cir. 1983).

§ 4.50 Considering the Constitution

A basic question to be asked of any policy is, does Congress have the power to do this?

The federal government has only limited, enumerated powers, and the powers of Congress are separate from the powers of the executive and judicial branches. That said, there are many different powers on which Congress can base a law. Perhaps the two most commonly invoked are the commerce power and the spending power.

Another question to be asked of any policy is, does this run afoul of a constitutional limitation on legislative power?

Congress might have the general power to enact a policy, but if the policy violates separation-of-powers principles, federalism principles, or individual rights, it may nonetheless be unconstitutional.

Of course, Congress can and does enact laws that the courts ultimately hold unconstitutional. The mere fact that the policy is, or may be, unconstitutional is no bar to the client's pursuing it, as long as the client can do so on an informed basis. If you have any concerns about constitutionality, explain those concerns to the client as soon as you can, so the client can take them into account.

As a drafter, it is crucial to spot and resolve constitutional issues as early in the process as you can. When there is a constitutional concern with a policy, the client may need a completely different solution than you might otherwise provide. For example, if the client has in mind a direct nationwide requirement but the commerce power does not support that requirement, the client might need instead a grant program (under the spending power) to entice states to create a network of statewide requirements. Turning up a constitutional issue can work like landing on the wrong square in a board game—it can send you back to square one. Better to discuss it with the client early in the process, before you have invested time and effort on the wrong solution.

§ 4.51 Sources of Power

The states have inherent power to enact general law, but Congress does not. The legislative power of the United States is vested in the Congress by Article I, Section 1 of the Constitution, and that power is limited to the powers enumerated in the Constitution. The enumerated powers are many but not infinite. If an act of Congress is not based on a constitutional grant of power, the law is unconstitutional and, therefore, cannot be enforced.

Congress has a large number of narrow powers and three rather broad powers.

The narrow powers include powers relating to naturalization, civil rights, patents and copyrights, elections, federal property, the military, and relations among states. Many of the narrow powers are listed in Article I, Section 8. Other powers are scattered throughout the Constitution. For example, in Article III, Section 3, Clause 2, Congress has power to declare the punishment for treason.

The broad powers are the power to tax and spend, the commerce power, and the necessary and proper power.

The General Welfare Clause (*art. I, sec. 8, cl. 1*) allows Congress to tax and spend for the general welfare. Although being able to tax and spend for the general welfare stops short of being able to regulate for the general welfare, a vast number of federal laws are based in whole or in part on this clause, including most federal taxes other than income taxes (which are founded instead on the Sixteenth Amendment) and all federal grant programs.

The Commerce Clause (*art. I, sec. 8, cl. 3*) includes three separate powers relating to interstate and foreign commerce. As described in *United States v. Lopez*, 514 U.S. 549 (1995), those powers are the power to regulate the use of the channels of commerce, the power to regulate and protect the instrumentalities of commerce, and the power to regulate activities that substantially affect commerce. Collectively, the commerce powers of Congress are very extensive, though they do have limits. In *Lopez*, for example, the Court found that possessing a gun in a school zone is not an activity that substantially affects commerce, and therefore the Commerce Clause could not sustain a law prohibiting the possession of such a gun. See also *United States v. Morrison*, 529 U.S. 598 (2000) (gender-motivated violence is not an activity that substantially affects commerce).

The Necessary and Proper Clause (*art. I, sec. 8, cl. 18*) allows Congress to enact laws that are "necessary and proper" for carrying into execution any of the powers vested in the United States. This power is broad and elastic, and it extends not only to the powers vested in Congress, but also to the powers vested in the executive or judicial branches. It is by this power, for example, that Congress establishes the various offices and agencies of the federal government.

§ 4.52 Limitations on Power

The legislative powers granted to Congress are not absolute. Under the Constitution, the powers of Congress are subject to specific limitations; they are also balanced against, and limited by, the powers of the other two branches (the executive and the judiciary), the sovereignty of the states, and the rights of the people. If an act of Congress violates one of these limitations, the law is unconstitutional, even if it is otherwise founded on a constitutional grant of power.

Many specific limitations on the powers of Congress are contained in Article I, Section 9, and others are scattered throughout the Constitution. Under Article I, Section 9, Congress may not (for example) tax exports from any state or grant a title of nobility. Likewise, under Article III, Section 3, Clause 2, Congress cannot make treason punishable by "Corruption of Blood."

Separation-of-powers concerns arise whenever Congress interferes with the powers of another branch—in most cases the executive, but in some cases the judiciary. A provision may be an unconstitutional infringement on executive powers if it (for example) burdens the President's ability to appoint or remove an executive branch official, interferes with the President's war powers, requires an executive officer to make a legislative proposal, or gives legal effect to a congressional action not presented to the President. Likewise, a provision may be an unconstitutional infringement on the judiciary if it requires a court to give an advisory opinion. In addition, whenever a law allows an official of one branch to wield power vested in another branch—such as when a member of Congress serves on (or appoints a person who serves on) a commission that wields executive power—separation of powers is a concern.

Two of the important separation-of-powers cases are *Buckley v. Valeo*, 424 U.S. 1 (1976) (a legislative officer may not appoint those who carry out executive functions), and *Bowsher v. Synar*, 478 U.S. 714 (1986) (a legislative officer may not retain removal power over those who carry out executive functions). But see also *Morrison v. Olson*, 487 U.S. 654 (1988) (Congress can by law limit the removal power), and *Mistretta v. United States*, 488 U.S. 361 (1989) (Congress can locate in the judicial branch an independent agency performing executive functions).

Note that the executive branch has very little authority to act in ways not provided by statute. (This goes back to the general rule, discussed above, that a federal agent may not act on behalf of the United States.) The Constitution does give the President some war powers (as Commander in Chief), many appointment powers, and considerable powers over foreign policy. The President's main function, however, is to "take care that the laws be faithfully executed," and the courts have consistently held that this is only an obligation and not a source of extrastatutory authority: "The duty of the President to see that the laws be executed is a duty that does not go beyond the laws." *Myers v. United States*, 272 U.S. 52, 177 (1926). See also *Kendall v. United States ex. rel. Stokes*, 37 U.S. 524 (1838); *Youngstown Sheet and Tube Co. v. Sawyer*, 343 U.S. 579 (1952).

Federalism concerns arise whenever Congress interferes with the sovereignty of the states. Of course, the states do not have much sovereignty remaining. The Tenth Amendment, which reserves to the states and to the people all powers not granted to the federal government, was once regarded as a reservoir of state sovereignty, but the Supreme Court rejected that notion in *Garcia v. San Antonio Metropolitan Transit Authority*, 469 U.S. 528 (1985). What remains of Tenth Amendment sovereignty is that Congress cannot commandeer a state's regulatory processes (*New York v. United States*, 505 U.S. 144 (1992)) or a state's executive officers (*Printz v. United States*, 521 U.S. 898 (1997)) to carry out federal objectives. Whenever a law requires states, or state officers, to administer a federal program, federalism may be a concern.

The Eleventh Amendment also preserves an aspect of state sovereignty; it protects a state from being sued without its consent in federal court, or, for that matter, in state court (*Alden v. Maine*, 527 U.S. 706 (1999)). Congress can waive that protection, however, in a law founded on the Fourteenth Amendment (*Seminole Tribe of Florida v. Florida*, 517 U.S. 44 (1996)), so long as the law contains a "clear statement" that Congress intends to do so.

Concerns about individual rights arise whenever Congress interferes with a right guaranteed by the Bill of Rights, by one of the Civil Rights Amendments, or by another provision of the Constitution, such as the Bill of Attainder Clause or the Ex Post Facto Clause. In addition, some individual rights not specified in the Constitution have been found to be inherent in the structure of the Constitution, such as the right to privacy and the right to travel.

§ 4.53 A Word of Caution

The Constitution is a long and complex document. Many of its provisions are not covered in law school in any detail. Upon graduating from law school, you can probably spot an issue relating to the Commerce Clause, the First Amendment, the Fifth Amendment, and the Fourteenth Amendment. You may be hard-pressed, however, to spot an issue relating to the Presentment Clause or the Recommendations Clause.

Many legal professionals specialize in some part of the Constitution: A prosecutor must know every nook and cranny of the Fifth Amendment, for example, while a free-speech advocate must know all the ins and outs of the First Amendment. As a drafter, your constitutional knowledge need not be deep, but it must be broad. You provide much more value to a client by spotting all the constitutional issues—the obvious ones and the obscure ones—than by discoursing about the obvious ones. When you spot an issue, whether obvious or obscure, you give the client the opportunity to seek expert advice. When you fail to spot an issue, there is no one else likely to do so; the issue will sit unnoticed until the day it causes legislative or political damage.

To give you an idea of the breadth of knowledge a drafter needs to have, consider this: From *Marbury v. Madison*, 5 U.S. 137 (1803), through *McConnell v. Federal Election Commission*, 540 U.S. 93 (2003), the Supreme Court of the United States held more than 150 different acts of Congress unconstitutional.

In most cases, the Court held that the law violated a constitutional limitation on power—most typically, the law violated a provision of the First, Fourth, Fifth, Sixth, Seventh, Eighth, Tenth, Eleventh, Thirteenth, Fourteenth, or Fifteenth Amendment. In some cases, the Court held that the law violated a constitutional separation-of-powers principle or a federalism principle—at times relying on a particular part of the Constitution, at other times relying on the inherent structure of the Constitution. In still other cases, the Court held that the law violated a provision within one of the articles of the Constitution, such as the Presentment Clause, the Export Clause, the Compensation Clause, the Appointments Clause, the Bill of Attainder Clause, the Ex Post Facto Clause, or the Jury Trial Clause.

In the remaining cases, the Court held that the law was not founded on a constitutional grant of power—the Court has held, for example, that laws could not be supported by the Commerce Clause, the Necessary and Proper Clause, the General Welfare Clause, the power to enforce the Fourteenth Amendment, the Sixteenth Amendment, the Elections Clause, the power to establish uniform bankruptcy laws, the Copyright Clause, the power to admit new states, the power to delegate, the power to borrow money, the power to regulate federal territory and property, and the various war powers.

As if that inventory of constitutional issues were not long enough, bear in mind that it is only a partial one. There are many other principles specified in the Constitution—and other principles said to be inherent in its structure—that could pose problems for a policy. They are traps for the unwary, and your job as a drafter is to keep the client from being trapped unaware. Keep a copy of the Constitution close at hand, be familiar with it, and consult it often.

§ 4.60 Parliamentary Issues

Finally, a question to be asked of any policy is whether it can be drafted to receive favorable treatment under the rules of the House and Senate.

For example, the client may want to ensure that the bill, after being introduced, is referred to a particular committee. Or the client may want to avoid a point of order that could defeat the policy on procedural grounds and prevent it from being considered on the merits. In some cases, careful drafting can ensure the result or avoid the point of order, or, at least, improve the chances of doing so.

Because the rules of the two chambers are different, and in any case can readily be revised, specific guidance here could quickly be obsolete. As a general matter, you should be familiar enough with the rules that you can warn when a policy may run afoul of them.

For links to House and Senate rules and other resources useful to drafters, see <*www.LegislativeDrafter.com*>.

§ 4.61 Budgetary Issues

As parliamentary issues go, perhaps the most important, complex, and commonly encountered relate to the budget. What follows is a brief summary of those issues, in the hope that it will not soon go out of date.

The most fundamental principle of the budget is that money cannot be drawn from the Treasury except in consequence of appropriations made by law. This is required by Article I, Section 9, Clause 7 of the Constitution; as such, an attempt to draw money from the Treasury without an appropriation by law is unconstitutional. (The *Merrill* doctrine, discussed in § 4.41, is based in part on this principle.)

In addition, the federal government cannot exercise contract or debt authority (that is, cannot legally commit to spend money or incur debt) except as provided in an appropriations act. This is required by subsection (a) of section 401 of the Congressional Budget Act of 1974 (2 U.S.C. 651).

Likewise, the federal government cannot exercise entitlement authority (that is, cannot create a program under which specific individuals have a legal right to be paid) except as provided in advance in an appropriations act. This is required by subsection (b) of section 401 of the Congressional Budget Act of 1974 (2 U.S.C. 651).

Within the legislative process, rules require a separation between bills that contain legislation and bills that contain appropriations. This is required by House rules and by Senate rules, though they differ in the particulars. The general principle, however, is the same: It violates the rules to include legislation in an appropriations bill or appropriations in a legislation bill.

Violating a budget rule does not automatically spell the end of a bill. As with any other parliamentary rule, a budget rule is enforced only to the extent someone raises a point of order. A point of order not raised has no effect, and in some cases a point of order can be waived.

For more discussion of the federal budget, see *Congressional Deskbook*, Chapter Nine, "Legislating in Congress: Federal Budget Process."

Chapter 5

Choosing the Right Measure

When a bill is hastily brought in, it generally requires mature deliberation, and many amendments in its progress through two houses, which always take up a great deal of time; whereas, when it is maturely considered, and fully concerted, before being brought in, the first draught of the bill is generally so perfect, that it requires but few amendments; and the rapidity of its progress always bears a proportion to the maturity of its first concoction.

Sir Charles Wager, in debate with Lord Baltimore, British Parliament, 1739

I'm just a bill.
Yes, I'm only a bill.
And I'm sitting here on Capitol Hill.
Well, it's a long, long journey
To the capital city.
It's a long, long wait
While I'm sitting in committee,
But I know I'll be a law some day
At least I hope and pray that I will
But today I am still just a bill.

"I'm Just a Bill," lyrics by Dave Frishberg, in Tom Yohe and George Newall, *Schoolhouse Rock!: The Official Guide* (1996)

Bills are made to pass as razors are made to sell.

Attributed to Henry Thring

Chapter 5

Choosing the Right Measure

§ 5.00 Overview

Congress is not required by the Constitution to use any particular measure. The Constitution anticipates, in Article I, Section 7, that Congress will use bills, but also anticipates that Congress may use orders, resolutions, or votes.

By custom and practice Congress has developed four different measures: the simple resolution, the concurrent resolution, the joint resolution, and the bill. They derive in part from measures used by colonial governments, which in turn were derived from measures used by Parliament in England.

Each measure has particular uses. For some uses, either of two measures will work; for other uses, only a single measure will do. Each has its place, so a drafter must be familiar with all four. See also *Congressional Deskbook*, § 8.10, "Types of Measures."

Three of these measures match up neatly with different types of congressional functions. To carry out a function of a single chamber (such as to make chamber rules), a simple resolution (§ 5.30) is used; if the function involves both chambers but does not require presentment to the President (such as to express the sense of Congress), a concurrent resolution (§ 5.40) is used; if the function involves both chambers and requires presentment to the President (such as to make law), a bill (§ 5.20) is used.

And then there is the joint resolution (§ 5.50), which is the duck-billed platypus of measures—used sometimes to do the job of a bill, other times to do the job of a concurrent resolution, and every time when the job is to propose a constitutional amendment.

Congress also uses orders and votes, but they are not considered measures because they do not involve the preparation of a formal document. For that reason, they are usually not of concern to a drafter. Orders and votes typically apply only to a single chamber and have more or less the same effect as a simple resolution, achieved with less formality. For example, the Senate typically carries out executive business (that is, acts upon nominations and treaties) by vote. An order is often put into effect by unanimous consent; if it applies on an ongoing basis it is known as a standing order.

The forms, uses, and quirks of the four measures are discussed below. For examples of the various measures, see Appendix Seven.

§5.10 Elements Common to All Measures

Terminology can vary from measure to measure. Bills and joint resolutions are "introduced," while simple and concurrent resolutions are "submitted," and bills are "passed," while simple, concurrent, and joint resolutions are "agreed to."

But all measures have many elements in common. Some of these elements are required by law, but most are required by chamber rules or merely by custom and practice.

§5.11 Designation and Number

All measures bear a designation, and once offered also bear a number. Thereafter, the measure is referred to by its designation and number. The designation and number appear prominently near the top of the bill, bold, centered, and in a large font.

The designation is an abbreviation indicating the type of measure and the chamber in which it was offered. Measures offered in the Senate begin with "S.": S. indicates a bill, S.Res. a simple resolution, S.Con.Res. a concurrent resolution, and S.J.Res. a joint resolution. Measures offered in the House begin with "H.": H.R. for a bill and H.Res., H.Con.Res., and H.J.Res. for a simple, concurrent, and joint resolution, respectively. (The designation "H.R." stands for "House of Representatives" and thus parallels the designation "S." for Senate; it does not, as is sometimes thought, stand for "House resolution.")

The set of designations in current use has been in use since about 1910 when, according to session indexes to the Congressional Record, the Senate stopped using "S.R." for joint resolutions and the Senate and House stopped using "S. C. Res." and "H. C. Res." for concurrent resolutions.

Another designation no longer in use is "S. Exec. Res.," which was once used by the Senate for a simple resolution for carrying out executive business. Though known as an "executive resolution," this was a simple resolution with a special designation, not a separate measure. The executive resolution was abandoned in 1993 and since then the Senate has carried out most executive business by vote. In the few cases in which a simple resolution is used, it bears the same designation as any other simple resolution.

One more designation no longer in use is "H.R.C.C.," which was once used by the House for a private relief bill. The designation, which may have stood for "House of Representatives, Court of Claims," was abandoned in the mid-1800s. This was a bill with a special designation, not a separate measure.

The number of a measure is assigned when the measure is offered and usually is the next number in sequence. For example, H.R. 9 is likely the ninth bill introduced in the House. Each chamber maintains four different sequences—one for each measure—so there may well be not only an H.R. 9, but also an H.Res. 9, an S.Con.Res. 9, and so on. The sequence carries over from the first session of a Congress to the second, but starts anew with a new Congress. (Occasionally, a prominent number—most typically, 1—is reserved by the presiding officer of a chamber for a particular measure with political significance.)

The numbering system has been in use in the House since about 1817 and in the Senate since about 1847. Before 1847, the Senate started the sequence anew with each new session, rather than with each new Congress. Before 1817, neither chamber used a numbering system at all.

When you prepare a measure, you should provide the designation and leave a blank space for the number ("S. Con. Res. ___").

§ 5.12 Term and Session Identifier

Each measure, once offered, bears words that identify the term and session of Congress in which it is being considered, such as:

> 109TH CONGRESS
> 2D SESSION

The words appear to the left of the designation; the word "Congress" is in all-caps form and everything else is in caps-and-small-caps form.

Note that the second session is abbreviated "2d" and not "2nd," as is sometimes supposed.

When you prepare a measure you may provide this identifier; if you do not provide one, it will undoubtedly be supplied when the measure is first printed.

§ 5.13 Chamber Identifier

Each measure, once offered, bears words that identify the chamber in which it is being considered: "IN THE HOUSE OF REPRESENTATIVES" if considered in the House, "IN THE SENATE OF THE UNITED STATES" if considered in the Senate. The words appear below the designation and number.

When you prepare a measure you may provide this identifier; if you do not provide one, it too will undoubtedly be supplied when the measure is first printed.

When preparing a measure to be offered, the chamber identifier will always match the designation—for example, a bill to be offered in the Senate always has the designation S. and the identifier "IN THE SENATE OF THE UNITED STATES." When a measure has passed one chamber and is printed so as to be considered in the other chamber, the designation does not change, but the chamber identifier does.

§ 5.14 Sponsor and Referral Information

Each measure, once offered, bears sponsor information and referral information in a single sentence in the following general form: "M_. ____ introduced the following bill; which was ______" (the blanks being appropriately filled in). This sentence appears below the chamber identifier.

Of course, the words "introduced the following bill" are changed if the measure is not a bill. The words "introduced the following joint resolution," "submitted the following concurrent resolution," and "submitted the following resolution" are used for joint, concurrent, and simple resolutions, respectively.

The blanks in "M_. ____" are appropriately filled in with the sponsor's honorific and surname. The surname appears in caps-and-small-caps form. The honorific ("Mr.," "Mrs.," or "Ms.," as the case may be) appears in normal text.

When two members share the same last name, or when two members share surnames that might easily be confused when written (such as Green and Greene) or spoken (such as Kennedy and Canady), the state is also provided—"Mr. Kennedy of Rhode Island." If that still does not put an end to the possible confusion, the first name of the member is also provided. An official list of similar names, specifying when to provide the state or first name, is maintained by the clerk of the chamber. (The list also specifies, for each female member, the honorific (Mrs. or Ms.) chosen by that member.)

If there are cosponsors, a parenthetical phrase is inserted after the sponsor's name, in the following general form: "(for [himself]/[herself] and [list])." The [list] is a list of the names of the cosponsors, usually in the order in which they became cosponsors.

If a measure is being offered by request, a parenthetical phrase is inserted after the sponsor's name: "(by request)." If there is a cosponsor, the phrase becomes "(both by request)" and appears after the parenthetical relating to the cosponsor.

The referral information, beginning with the words "which was ______," specifies the committee or committees to which the measure was referred (such as, "which was referred to the Committee on Armed Services"). In some cases a measure is not referred, and some other disposition is provided instead (such as, "which was considered and agreed to"). In the Senate, because of Senate rules, the referral information typically indicates that the measure was read twice ("which was read twice and referred to the Committee on the Judiciary").

When you prepare a measure you may indicate the sponsor; if you do not do so, it will undoubtedly be supplied when first printed. You should be wary of providing cosponsor information without the consent of that cosponsor. You should not provide referral information; that will be supplied when first printed.

When preparing a measure to be offered, you may provide a signature line in the top right corner, for use by the sponsor (who must sign the measure before introducing it). See also *Congressional Deskbook*, § 8.20, "Drafting and Introducing Legislation."

§ 5.15 Long Title

All measures bear a long title (in modern times, at least). The long title is the official name of the measure. It is sometimes referred to as the "official title," the "statutory title," or simply the "title," though drafters conventionally call it the long title. The long title appears below the sponsor and referral information.

The long title begins with the prominent words "A bill" or, in the case of a resolution, the words "Resolution," "Concurrent resolution," or "Joint resolution," as appropriate. These words appear in all-caps, bold, centered, and in a large font, though not quite as large as the font used for the designation and number. This is purely a matter of printing, however, rather than substance.

The remaining words of the long title describe the subject or effect of the measure, usually in a straightforward manner. The remaining words appear below the prominent words, and the first letter of the remainder is capitalized. (This capitalization is also purely a matter of printing rather than substance.) Because the prominent words and the remaining words are not presented as a coherent whole, many people mistakenly assume that the remainder alone is the long title.

Adding to the confusion, the remaining words are often shown twice when a measure is officially printed: first (as an aid to the reader) immediately beneath the designation and number, and then again (in its proper place) following the prominent words.

The distinction is not crucial in most cases. However, if you are in a position to draft amendments to measures, you may at some point be called upon to amend the long title of a measure. In that event, it will be useful to remember that the long title includes both the prominent words and the remaining words, rather than only the remainder. To amend the long title of a bill, your instruction would provide (for example):

> Amend the long title to read as follows: "A bill to amend title 18, United States Code, to . . ."

It would not provide:

> Amend the long title to read as follows: "To amend title 18, United States Code, to . . ."

Conversely, do not repeat the prominent words in the remainder. Do not, that is, follow the example of the Coast Guard and Maritime Transportation Act of 2004 (Public Law 108-293; 118 Stat. 1028). As printed in slip law form, the long title of that Act was "An Act An Act to authorize appropriations for the Coast Guard for fiscal year 2005, to amend various laws administered by the Coast Guard, and for other purposes." As printed in the Statutes at Large, interestingly enough, the extra "An Act" was stricken.

If describing all the subjects or effects of a measure would be tedious (or politically or strategically undesirable), there are two possible approaches: using one general description ("A bill to combat terrorism") or using one or two specific descriptions followed by the words "and for other purposes" ("Concurrent resolution expressing the sense of Congress with respect to terrorism, and for other purposes").

The typical form of a long title varies by measure, as discussed below.

When you prepare a measure, you should always provide a long title. If you do not provide one, it will not automatically be supplied.

The long title is frequently prepared by the drafter rather than the client, though of course the client may overrule the drafter. When drafting a long title, be accurate and brief.

Remember that a court, when interpreting a measure, can (and occasionally does) consider the long title as evidence of legislative intent, so you should draft, and advise your client, with that in mind.

§ 5.16 Enacting Clause or Resolving Clause

All measures bear an enacting clause or a resolving clause. An enacting clause is used for bills; a resolving clause is used for resolutions. The clause appears below the long title.

The clause traditionally appears in italic, though this is purely a matter of printing rather than substance.

The clause is the signal to the reader that what follows is what is proposed to be given effect. The matter before the clause is not given effect, while the clause and the matter that follows the clause are given effect.

The typical form of the clause varies by measure, as discussed below.

When you prepare a measure, you should always provide the appropriate enacting clause or resolving clause. If you do not provide one, or provide an inappropriate one, a proper one will not automatically be supplied.

§ 5.17 Text or "Body"

All measures have a text. The text, sometimes called the "body," is the substance of the measure, the part that is proposed to be given effect. The text appears below the enacting clause or resolving clause.

The text generally begins with a section designation, a section heading, or with the word "That," depending on the style used in the measure. The various styles are discussed in Chapter Eight.

§ 5.18 Information Provided by Legislative Counsel

When a measure is prepared by one of the Offices of Legislative Counsel, the measure may bear other information provided by the office.

A draft prepared by legislative counsel may, for example, bear in the upper right corner letters identifying the office ("H.L.C." for the House office, "S.L.C." for the Senate office). Legislative counsel may also provide filenames, bar codes, and other information, usually in a margin or corner.

This information is for the convenience of the office, the clerks, and the parliamentarian, and a draft not prepared by the office need not, and should not, attempt to replicate that information. If you violate this principle, you will look foolish, unethical, or both.

§ 5.20 The Bill

A bill is used only to make law. A bill is not the exclusive measure for making law (a joint resolution can also serve that purpose), but it is the measure most commonly used for that purpose. And because most of what Congress does is make law, the bill is far and away the most common measure.

Bills are used, for example, to make laws that describe federal programs and activities, organize federal departments and agencies, impose federal taxes, and allow federal spending. Bills are also used to make laws that amend other laws.

In addition, bills are used to provide, by law, specific relief to specific individuals. Such a bill is known as a private relief bill, or simply a private bill, and the law that results is considered a private law rather than a public law. Most private laws relate to immigration and naturalization matters, claims against the United States, special tariff treatment, and conveyances of property rights. The constitutional power of Congress to enact private bills is not expressly given but is not seriously disputed.

A bill is sometimes used on a matter for which Congress ordinarily uses a simple resolution or concurrent resolution, so that the measure will be permanent. A simple resolution or concurrent resolution generally is considered to remain binding only during the Congress in which it is agreed to, while a bill, once enacted, is generally permanent. For example, a joint committee can be established by concurrent resolution or by bill, but in the former case it expires at the end of the current Congress. (For more on joint committees, see § 2.23,

"Hearings and Markups: Overview.") Similarly, the procedures to be followed by the House in resolving a dispute over a contested House election can be established by simple resolution or by bill, but only in the latter case are the procedures permanent. See the Federal Contested Election Act (Public Law 91-138; 2 U.S.C. 381 et seq.).

To be effective, a bill must pass both chambers in identical form and be presented to the President. Once effective, a bill is an "Act of Congress." It is officially published first as a slip law, then in the Statutes at Large. If it is sufficiently general and permanent, it is also included in the United States Code.

§ 5.21 What It Means to "Make Law": The *Chadha* Decision

To say that a bill is used to make law begs the question of what it means to "make law." The Supreme Court answered that question in *Immigration and Naturalization Service v. Chadha*, 462 U.S. 919 (1983), usually referred to simply as *Chadha* and sometimes referred to as the "legislative veto case."

In the years before the *Chadha* decision, Congress had enacted a number of laws that, as applied in particular cases, could be changed by a mere resolution—either a concurrent resolution or a simple resolution, depending on the particular law. The law at issue in *Chadha* was a provision of the Immigration and Nationality Act that gave the attorney general discretion whether to deport an individual, but required the attorney general to deport the individual if either chamber passed a simple resolution to that effect. In short, an executive decision not to deport could be overriden by a resolution of a single legislative chamber—thus the term "legislative veto."

The Supreme Court reviewed Article I, Section 7 of the Constitution and read it to mean that a matter cannot become law unless it first passes both chambers and is presented to the President. A resolution that passes one or both chambers but is not presented to the President cannot become law. And law, the Court said, depends not on the form of the measure, but on whether it contains matter that is properly to be regarded as "legislative in character and effect."

In reaching this conclusion, the Court relied in part on a report by the Committee on the Judiciary of the Senate (S. Report No. 1335, 54th Congress, 2d session (1897)), which had considered the same issue and arrived at the same principle: The matter and not the form of the measure dictated whether presentment to the President was needed, and presentment was needed if the matter was "legislative in character and effect." Indeed, the Senate report indicated that Congress had followed that principle from the first days.

Though the Court did not define what "legislative in character and effect" means, it based the decision in *Chadha* primarily on the fact that the resolution "had the purpose and effect of altering the legal rights, duties, and relations of persons, including the Attorney General, Executive Branch officials and Chadha, all outside the Legislative Branch." 462 U.S. at 952.

Accordingly, a measure that has the purpose and effect of altering the legal rights, duties, and relations of persons outside the legislative branch is almost certainly one that "makes law"; it must, therefore, be presented to the President; and it must, therefore, be in the form of a bill or joint resolution rather than a simple or concurrent resolution.

One matter left unresolved by *Chadha* is whether a resolution by one or both chambers is "legislative in character and effect" if it merely directs the executive branch to provide information (such as a report or estimate) based on facts already in its possession and involving no appreciable expense. From the first Congress, the Senate and the House have had procedures in place for seeking this sort of information, some involving measures, some involving report language or other means. When a measure is used, it typically is a simple resolution (such as what is known as a "resolution of inquiry") that is not presented to the President.

The Senate report (referred to above) also considered this specific matter and concluded that an ordinary request or direction for information from the executive branch was not "legislative in character and effect" and, therefore, one or both chambers could require the executive branch to furnish information and make reports by simple or concurrent resolution. Again, the Senate report indicated that Congress had followed that specific rule from the first days.

§ 5.22 Long Title

As mentioned above, the long title of a bill begins with the words "A bill." The remainder of the long title describes the subject or effect of the bill, usually in a straightforward manner.

In a bill that proposes a public law, the long title generally uses the infinitive, such as, "A bill to authorize appropriations for ___ and to provide for ___," or, "A bill to amend the Omnibus Crime Control and Safe Streets Act of 1968 to provide grants for ___."

In a bill that proposes a private law, the long title generally names the individuals for whom relief is provided, such as, "A bill for the relief of Jane Doe" or, "A bill for the relief of Mr. and Mrs. John Q. Public."

In an appropriations bill, the form of the long title is specified by law in section 105 of title 1, United States Code. Nonetheless, the form required by that section—"An Act making appropriations (here insert the object) for the year ending September 30 (here insert the calendar year)"—is not strictly followed.

§ 5.23 Enacting Clause

The enacting clause of a bill always takes the same form, whether it originates in the Senate or in the House of Representatives. The form is provided by section 101 of title 1, United States Code, and is as follows: "Be it enacted by the Senate and House of Representatives of the United States of America in Congress assembled."

The form of the enacting clause has been the same since the first Congress in 1789; the original rules of one chamber of that first Congress provided for the enacting clause to read, "Be it enacted by the Senators and Representatives of the United States of America in Congress assembled," but that clause was almost immediately abandoned. The form of the clause was originally required by rule or by custom and practice, but has been required by statute since 1871.

To be technical about it—and that is, after all, part of a drafter's job—every bill is prepared in violation of section 101. A literal reading of section 101 requires that the enacting clause end with a period. (The final period appears within the quoted matter.) In actual practice, every bill is prepared with an enacting clause that ends with a comma, not a period.

In any case, section 101 is probably directory, not mandatory. Though the statute requires that the clause appear, and that it appear in a certain form, the statute does not specify what the consequence of a violation might be. A bill without an enacting clause, or with a variant enacting clause, is probably no less valid. For example, the Omnibus Budget Reconciliation Act of 1981 (Public Law 97-35; 95 Stat. 357) was passed without any enacting clause, but its effectiveness has never been seriously questioned.

§ 5.30 The Simple Resolution

A simple resolution is used by a single chamber to speak or act on behalf of that chamber or to address a matter internal to that chamber.

For example, a simple resolution is used to adopt or amend the rules of the chamber, to express the opinion of the chamber, to appoint a member to a committee or to an office, to expel or discipline a member, or to spend money from the chamber's contingent fund.

In the House, a simple resolution is used to impeach the President, a federal judge, or any other federal official. In the Senate, a simple resolution can be used to carry out executive business with respect to nominations and treaties.

To take effect, a simple resolution need be agreed to only by the chamber in which it was offered. It is not acted upon by the other chamber or by the President. Once effective, a simple resolution does not have the force of law, but it is binding within that chamber. (Even then, however, a simple resolution is generally considered binding only during the Congress in which it is agreed to, as discussed in § 5.20, "The Bill.")

A simple resolution is not published as a slip law or in the Statutes at Large and is not classified to the United States Code. It is printed in the Congressional Record.

§ 5.31 Long Title

The long title of a simple resolution begins with the word "Resolution" and then generally uses a gerund, such as, "Resolution electing officers of the House of Representatives" or, "Resolution expressing the sense of the Senate with respect to ___." For a simple resolution used by the Senate for executive business, the long title generally uses an infinitive, such as, "Resolution to discharge the Jane Doe nomination."

§ 5.32 Resolving Clause

The resolving clause of a simple resolution always takes the same form, whether it originates in the Senate or in the House of Representatives. The form is provided by custom and practice rather than by law, and is as follows: "Resolved" followed by a comma.

The resolving clause of a simple resolution has been the same since the first Congress in 1789.

§ 5.33 Text

A simple resolution usually does not contain multiple sections or section headings, so the text of a simple resolution usually begins with the word "That" rather than with a section number or section heading.

§ 5.40 The Concurrent Resolution

A concurrent resolution is used to speak or act on behalf of both chambers, or to address a matter internal to Congress or to the legislative branch as a whole. Typically, a concurrent resolution is used to provide procedures between the two chambers, or to express an opinion shared by both chambers.

For example, a concurrent resolution is used to set parameters for considering legislation relating to the federal budget, to express the sense of the Congress, to provide for a recess or adjournment when the consent of both chambers is required, to correct errors in a conference report or enrolled bill, to create a joint committee, or to provide for a joint session of Congress.

To take effect, a concurrent resolution must be agreed to in identical form by both chambers of Congress (in either order). It is not presented to, or acted upon by, the President.

Notably, Article I, Section 7, Clause 3 of the Constitution specifies that every "Resolution . . . to which the Concurrence of the Senate and House of Representatives may be necessary" is subject to the same process as a bill (that is, it must be presented to the President, and so on). This would appear to include every concurrent resolution, since the concurrence of each chamber is, by custom and practice, necessary for a concurrent resolution.

However, Congress has never accepted this literal interpretation. Instead, it is not the form of the measure that controls whether it must be presented to the President, but whether it is "legislative in character and effect." A resolution that proposes to make law cannot make law unless it is presented to the President. In modern practice, the only type of resolution used to propose a law is the joint resolution.

A concurrent resolution passed by only one chamber is not binding on either chamber: It does not even bind the chamber that did pass it. Though the precedents of each chamber make this principle clear, the two chambers sometimes act without regard to this principle. For example, on May 20, 1992, the Senate and the House each passed a concurrent resolution confirming the validity of the so-called congressional pay amendment to the Constitution. (Congress does not normally confirm the validity of a constitutional amendment, but because 203 years had passed from the date Congress proposed it to the date the last required state ratified it, there was some concern that a court might declare it too stale to be valid.) Oddly, however, the Senate passed S. Con. Res. 120 and the House passed H. Con. Res. 320, neither considering the concurrent resolution of the other. (Regardless, the amendment was certified as valid by the Archivist of the United States and its validity has not been seriously challenged.)

Once effective, a concurrent resolution does not have the force of law, but it is binding within and between the two chambers. As with a simple resolution, however, it is generally considered binding only during the Congress in which it is agreed to (as discussed in § 5.20, "The Bill").

A concurrent resolution is not published in slip law form, but it is printed in the Congressional Record and is officially published in the Statutes at Large, in a special part dedicated to concurrent resolutions. It is not classified to the United States Code.

The concurrent resolution as a distinct measure evolved rather late. In the early Congresses, if a resolution was legislative in character and effect it was considered a joint resolution, to be passed by both chambers and presented to the President. If it was not legislative in character and effect, it was a simple resolution, to be passed by one chamber. However, if that chamber wanted its simple resolution to apply also to the other chamber, the other chamber was asked to concur.

Though a resolution that was handled in this manner was, from the first Congress, referred to as a concurrent resolution, it was in effect a simple resolution passed separately by both chambers. Unlike the modern concurrent resolution, which is binding on neither chamber unless it is passed by both, this archaic concurrent resolution would be binding on a chamber that passed it even if the other did not, at least in theory. In practice, the resolution was commonly stated in conditional form (such as, "Resolved, That if the Senate concur, then . . ."), so if the other chamber did not concur, the resolution failed by its own terms.

In the late 1890s, the concurrent resolution began to be treated as a distinct measure in its own right—receiving a distinct resolving clause, bearing a distinct designation, and being logged in a distinct manner in the journal of each chamber.

§ 5.41 Long Title

The long title of a concurrent resolution begins with the words, "Concurrent resolution," and then generally uses the gerund form, such as, "Concurrent resolution authorizing the use of the Capitol Grounds for ___," or "Concurrent resolution expressing the sense of the Congress with respect to ___."

§ 5.42 Resolving Clause

For a concurrent resolution, the form of the resolving clause depends on the chamber in which it originated. The form is provided by custom and practice rather than by law. In the case of the Senate, the form is as follows: "Resolved by the Senate (the House of Representatives concurring)." In the case of the House, the order is reversed: "Resolved by the House of Representatives (the Senate concurring)." In either case, the resolving clause is followed by a comma.

The resolving clause has been standard since the 1890s.

§ 5.43 Text

As with a simple resolution, a concurrent resolution usually does not contain multiple sections or section headings, so the text of a concurrent resolution usually begins with the word "That" rather than with a section number or section heading.

§ 5.50 The Joint Resolution

A joint resolution has two distinct uses.

First, as with a bill, a joint resolution is used to make law. Though the style of a joint resolution is different from that of a bill, the legal effect is the same. A statute that was enacted in the form of a bill may be amended by a statute in the form of a joint resolution, and vice versa.

Traditionally, however, the use of a joint resolution to make law is reserved for making laws that are incidental, inferior, or unusual in nature. For example, a joint resolution is used to declare war, to abrogate a treaty, to provide temporary funding for the government (through what is called a continuing resolution), to approve or disapprove certain executive actions, and to change the date for the convening of Congress.

Sometimes, on a matter for which Congress ordinarily uses a concurrent resolution, Congress uses a joint resolution instead, so that the measure will be presented to the President—and will, accordingly, receive the added pomp and circumstance that apply to measures presented to the President. This is almost always done for political emphasis rather than for legal effect: The result is technically a law, but a law that is not "legislative in character and effect."

This use of a joint resolution is generally reserved for significant national occasions, such as when Congress offers support to troops engaged in conflict overseas or offers condolences, thanks, or congratulations in connection with a particularly solemn or grand event.

Second, a joint resolution is used to propose an amendment to the Constitution of the United States. This use is described in more detail in § 5.53.

To take effect when used to make law, a joint resolution proceeds in the same manner as a bill. Once effective, the joint resolution is considered an "Act of Congress" and is published in the same manner as a bill.

To take effect when used to propose a constitutional amendment, a joint resolution must be agreed to in identical form by two-thirds (not a simple majority) of both chambers of Congress (in either order). It is not presented to, or acted upon by, the President (see *Hollingsworth v. Virginia*, 3 U.S. 378 (1798)). Instead, it is sent by Congress directly to the Archivist of the United States, who submits it to the states for ratification. The constitutional amendment takes effect only after it is ratified by the legislatures of three-fourths of the states.

§ 5.51 Long Title

The long title of a joint resolution (when used to make law) begins with the words "Joint resolution" and then generally uses the gerund form, such as, "Joint resolution declaring a state of war between the United States and ___," "Joint resolution commending the members of the United States Armed Forces," or "Joint resolution disapproving the rule submitted to Congress by ___ relating to ___."

When used to propose a constitutional amendment, the same principles generally apply: "Joint resolution proposing an amendment to the Constitution of the United States relating to the right to vote."

§ 5.52 Resolving Clause

The resolving clause of a joint resolution (when used to make law) always takes the same form, whether it originates in the Senate or in the House of Representatives. The form is provided in section 102 of title 1, United States Code, and is as follows: "Resolved by the Senate and House of Representatives of the United States of America in Congress assembled."

Just as every bill is prepared in technical violation of section 101 of title 1, every joint resolution is prepared in technical violation of section 102 of that title. Section 102 requires that the resolving clause of a joint resolution end with a period, but in actual practice a comma is used.

When used to propose a constitutional amendment, the same clause is used, except that the following parenthetical phrase customarily appears after the ending comma: "(two-thirds of each House concurring therein),". Again, the inclusion of this phrase within the resolving clause appears to be a technical violation of section 102.

§ 5.53 Text When Proposing a Constitutional Amendment

The text of a joint resolution, when used to propose a constitutional amendment, generally begins as follows: "That the following article is proposed as an amendment to the Constitution of the United States:".

If Congress chooses to specify when the proposed amendment will lapse if not ratified, language is inserted before the colon as follows: ", which shall be valid to all intents and purposes as part of the Constitution when ratified by the legislatures of three-fourths of the several States within ___ years after the date of its submission for ratification."

In some cases Congress has specified the period within the text of the constitutional amendment itself, in a section at the end of the proposed amendment. See, for example, the Eighteenth, Twentieth, Twenty-first, and Twenty-second Amendments. But this unnecessarily clutters the Constitution with technical matter and, for that reason, should be avoided.

Typically, Congress provides a period for ratification of seven years, though Congress may set a different period or may set no period at all, in which case the period for ratification is a "reasonable time." Whether an amendment has been ratified within a reasonable time is a political question to be determined by Congress. *Coleman v. Miller*, 307 U.S. 433 (1939).

Chapter 6

Writing Effectively

From the Minutes of a Borough Council Meeting:

Councillor Trafford took exception to the proposed notice at the entrance to South Park: "No dogs must be brought to this Park except on a lead." He pointed out that this order would not prevent an owner from releasing his pets, or pet, from a lead when once safely inside the Park.

THE CHAIRMAN (COLONEL VINE): *What alternative wording would you propose, Councillor?*

COUNCILLOR TRAFFORD: *"Dogs are not allowed in this Park without leads."*

COUNCILLOR HOGG: *Mr. Chairman, I object. The order should be addressed to the owners, not to the dogs.*

COUNCILLOR TRAFFORD: *That is a nice point. Very well, then: "Owners of dogs are not allowed in this Park unless they keep them on leads."*

COUNCILLOR HOGG: *Mr. Chairman, I object. Strictly speaking, this would prevent me as a dog-owner from leaving my dog in the back-garden and walking with Mrs. Hogg across the Park.*

COUNCILLOR TRAFFORD: *Mr. Chairman, I suggest that our legalistic friend be asked to redraft the notice himself.*

COUNCILLOR HOGG: *Mr. Chairman, since Councillor Trafford finds it so difficult to improve on my original wording, I accept. "Nobody without his dog on a lead is allowed in this Park."*

COUNCILLOR TRAFFORD: *Mr. Chairman, I object. Strictly speaking, this notice would prevent me, as a citizen who owns no dog, from walking in the Park without first acquiring one.*

COUNCILLOR HOGG: *(with some warmth): Very simply then: "Dogs must be led in this Park."*

COUNCILLOR TRAFFORD: *Mr. Chairman, I object: this reads as if it were a general injunction to the Borough to lead their dogs into the Park.*

Councillor Hogg interposed a remark for which he was called to order; upon his withdrawing it, it was directed to be expunged from the Minutes.

THE CHAIRMAN: *I see Councillor Hogg rising quite rightly to raise another objection. May I anticipate him with another amendment: "All dogs in this Park must be kept on the lead."*

This draft was put to the vote and carried unanimously, with two abstentions.

Robert Graves and Alan Hodge,
***The Reader over Your Shoulder* 149–150 (1966)**

The minute you read something and you can't understand it, you can be sure it was written by a lawyer. . . . If it's in a few words and is plain, and understandable only one way, it was written by a non-lawyer.

Will Rogers

Think like a wise man but communicate in the language of the people.

William Butler Yeats

Anyone who has had to deal with the Copyright Act of 1909 must stand in awe of the ability of the framers to toss off a sentence that can have any number of meanings.

Henry J. Friendly, *Benchmarks* 48 (1967)

Writing Effectively

Chapter 6

§ 6.00 Introduction

Once a policy has been thought through, it is time to put pen to paper and words to the page. Your focus turns from identifying the policy to expressing it in the most effective way.

The language used for legislation is not special and mysterious; it is the same language used for anything else. For that reason, any guide about how to write well can help you draft well. Likewise, any guide specifically for legal writing applies generally to drafting.

This chapter could be spent generally on how to write well, but it would not be well spent. As a drafter, you already should have on your shelf at least two other guides on writing: one on good writing and one on good legal writing. You should not need to be told, for example, to plan before you write and to edit after you write. You already should have mastered grammar and spelling and punctuation.

As a federal drafter, you also should have on your shelf a third guide on writing: the *Government Printing Office Style Manual*, which is the style manual for most federal writing. With very few exceptions, federal drafting follows this style manual. A link to the manual is available online at <*www.LegislativeDrafter.com*>.

This chapter builds on the principles of good writing (and good legal writing) and emphasizes the techniques and approaches that are most important for drafting effectively.

The essence of effective drafting is clear writing—that is, writing the meaning of which is not in doubt. As a drafter, you should always strive to write as clearly as possible under the circumstances. Writing clearly provides two very important benefits.

First, a clear draft is an accurate draft. Take a clear draft and show it to your client. Because the draft is clear, by definition it has only one meaning; it can be read in only one possible way. After reading it, the client can only accept it as accurate or return it with an explanation of what is not yet quite right (or perhaps abandon the project).

Now take an unclear draft and show it to your client. By definition, the draft has more than one meaning; let's call them A and B. If the client accepts the draft as accurate, you cannot be certain what the acceptance means. Did the client accept the draft, thinking it meant A? Did the client accept the draft, thinking it meant B? Did the client accept the draft, recognizing that it was ambiguous (and embracing the ambiguity)? Only when you provide a clear draft can you be sure, through this sort of exchange, that you and the client have had a meeting of the minds.

Second, clear writing ensures that the draft, if enacted into law, carries out the client's policy effectively. If the law is not clear to the officer responsible for carrying it out, the officer might carry out the policy in a way the client did not intend—or might not carry it out at all. If the law is not clear to those affected by it, they might be unsure how to comply. Lawsuits might follow, and the courts might interpret the law in a way that the client did not intend—or might void it altogether.

You must be able to draft with great clarity. Until and unless the client instructs you otherwise, you should draft on that basis. And as part and parcel of being able to draft with great clarity, you must also be able to spot every way in which a draft is not clear.

Some of those who write about drafting claim that drafters have a duty not only to the client, but also to the public. They focus on the societal costs of unclear laws and exhort drafters to do their alleged civic duty to produce clear laws.

Whether such a civic duty applies to you is beside the point. (A civic duty to produce clear laws, if there is one, would seem to apply more directly to a legislator than to you.) To a drafter, the cardinal virtue of a clear draft is not that it may turn into a clear law to the benefit of society; the cardinal virtue of a clear draft is that it is necessarily an accurate draft. It fulfills your duty to your client.

In short, be clear not because you have a sense of civic duty, however virtuous and well-meaning that might be. Be clear because clarity is the way to accuracy, and being accurate is your ultimate duty.

§6.10 The Perils of Ineffective Writing

Effective writing is, in a sense, the avoidance of ineffective writing. For that reason, it is useful to review the common types of ineffective writing and their consequences.

Lack of clarity in legislative language has a range of consequences, not all of them bad. Indeed, some lack of clarity is probably unavoidable, because language by nature is flexible and shifty and law by nature is broad and general.

When a law is only slightly unclear, the lack of clarity usually works like a grant of discretion. Effectively, the courts have discretion to interpret the law one way or another, albeit within common-sense limits. Agencies, too, have that discretion, at least in the absence of clarification by the courts, under the *Chevron* doctrine (by which a court gives deference to the interpretation of an agency; see § 3.62).

When a law is somewhat unclear, the range of discretion widens and becomes political; the stakes are higher. The lack of clarity affects more people and in more profound ways. Congress has left a gap in policy to be filled by agencies and courts, and there's a good chance the agencies and courts won't fill the gaps the way Congress (or the client) had in mind. An agency interpretation is more likely to be colored by the political values held by the incumbent administration; a court is more likely to weigh the effects an interpretation would have on society.

When a law is significantly unclear, those who must read it are confused and those who must conform to it are concerned. Conflict and litigation are likely. Agency interpretations are more likely to be not only political but also unstable, perhaps even swinging from one political pole to the other when control of the White House switches. Court interpretations are more likely to be (or at least to appear to be) politically motivated. If the law is so unclear that the federal circuit courts can reasonably disagree over its meaning, the circuits may split over the meaning and (until the Supreme Court intervenes) the law will not apply across the nation in a uniform way. Ultimately, if the law is so unclear that it can be applied to people in an arbitrary or discriminatory way, a court might well find it unconstitutional.

Yet there are times when the client may want a lack of clarity. As a matter of policy, the client may want to vest a court or agency with discretion. As a matter of politics, the client may want to leave some issues fuzzy. The client makes those decisions; you make sure the decisions are informed ones.

Jeremy Bentham divided what he called the "imperfections" of statutes into two orders. Those of the first order he named ambiguity, obscurity, and overbulkiness. Imperfections of the first order were caused by imperfections of the second order, which he named unsteadiness in respect of expression, unsteadiness in respect of import, redundancy, longwindedness, entanglement, nakedness in respect of helps to intellection, and disorderliness. The hope is that Bentham would be pleased by the discussion that follows; though it does not follow him exactly, it covers the same ground.

§ 6.11 Ambiguity

A law is ambiguous if it has alternative, mutually inconsistent meanings. In short, it means either A or B, but not both. If the law says the Navy may build a shipyard in Portland, it probably refers either to the city in Oregon or to the one in Maine, but not to both. (This is the narrow meaning of ambiguity. There is also a broad meaning, under which ambiguity means any lack of clarity. Courts tend to use the term in its broad sense.)

A great many words and phrases are ambiguous, but not problematically so, because the ambiguity disappears when the word or phrase is placed in context. If the law directs the secretary to adopt an official seal and use it on appropriate occasions, it probably refers to an insignia rather than a marine mammal. If the ambiguity of a word does not disappear when the word is placed in context, you need to alter the context or alter (or define) the word.

Context can make ambiguity disappear, but it can also contribute to ambiguity. A pronoun can refer back to more than one noun ("The governor shall consult with the administrator, and he shall act"—is "he" the governor or the administrator?). A modifier placed before the first item in a series can apply to all the items in the series, or only the first one ("law enforcement agencies and organizations"—must the organizations be law enforcement organizations?); and vice versa for a modifier placed after the last item ("agencies and organizations with law enforcement missions"—must the agencies have law enforcement missions?). A chain of modifiers can apply collectively or separately ("She sells red, white, and blue caps"—does she sell three different single-color caps, or one tricolor cap?).

§ 6.12 Inconsistency

A law is inconsistent if it has simultaneous, mutually inconsistent meanings. In short, it means A and "not A" at the same time.

An inconsistency simply cannot stand, as a matter of logic or of law. One meaning or the other must yield, either partially or entirely. As a practical matter, then, reconciling inconsistency works in much the same way as resolving ambiguity.

Inconsistency is not as rare as you might think. Any time two provisions cover the same ground and do not coordinate with each other, there is some form of inconsistency.

Judge Harold Leventhal related a case in which one law had a provision that authorized the President to limit the quantity of imports; another law had a provision that authorized the Secretary of Agriculture to limit the quantity of imports. "You would have thought that somewhere someone would have referred to the relationship between" the two, he lamented, but the relationship was not described anywhere. Harold Leventhal, "How the Courts See the Problem," in Reed Dickerson (ed.), *Professionalizing Legislative Drafting: The Federal Experience* 34–35 (1973).

Context can make inconsistency disappear in the same manner as it makes ambiguity disappear.

§ 6.13 Arbitrariness

A law is arbitrary if it provides discretion without fixed standards. An arbitrary law can be unconstitutional or it can simply be a broad grant of discretion, depending on what interests are at stake.

Many laws are arbitrary: A typical federal grant program, for example, gives a federal officer nearly unfettered discretion over how to make grants, but the law is not unconstitutional because it does not affect individual rights.

However, under constitutional principles of due process, an individual cannot be deprived of life, liberty, or property without due process of law. An arbitrary law is unconstitutional if it can operate to deprive an individual of life, liberty, or property, and is so arbitrary that it leaves law enforcement officers or courts free to decide, on a case-by-case basis, what conduct is acceptable and what is not.

§ 6.14 Vagueness

A law is vague if it leaves the public uncertain as to exactly how far the law extends.

The essential difference between vagueness and ambiguity is that language is ambiguous when it has two or more possible meanings, while language is vague when it has a single meaning with an uncertain boundary. Essentially, ambiguity works like a toggle switch, while vagueness works like a dial.

While ambiguity is almost always to be avoided, vagueness is sometimes very useful. Expressions like "negligence" and "reasonable" and "good faith" are vague but not ambiguous.

Vagueness is closely related to arbitrariness, and many laws that are arbitrary are also vague. As with being arbitrary, being vague does not by itself make a law unconstitutional, but does if it violates due process. Accordingly, a law is unconstitutionally vague if it can operate to deprive an individual of life, liberty, or property, and is so vague that it leaves the public uncertain as to what conduct is acceptable and what is not.

For example, the term "domestic violence" is vague. A statute that authorizes the attorney general to make grants to prevent "domestic violence" is extremely vague—but probably not unconstitutional, because it does not operate to deprive a person of life, liberty, or property. On the other hand, a statute that makes it a crime to engage in "domestic violence" may well be unconstitutionally vague, because it can operate to deprive an individual of liberty (if punishable by imprisonment) or property (if punishable by a fine).

§ 6.15 Over-Precision

A law is precise if it specifies exactly what is covered and what is not, leaving no room for interpretation. "On October 1 of each year" is a precise date. A high degree of precision is usually desirable, but in some cases too much precision is undesirable.

Over-precision is the opposite of vagueness: too much detail rather than too little. A law is overly precise if detail is provided to a problematic degree. Over-precision has a variety of causes and effects.

One sort of over-precision arises when a provision is so narrow that it is ruthlessly inflexible. A law that requires a report to be submitted "on" October 1 of each year is nice and precise—but when October 1 falls on a weekend or holiday, the person required to submit the report might well prefer to do so a day or two before. Submitting the report early, however, would violate the law no less than submitting it late.

Consider the differences in precision given the appearances and slogans of two Forest Service characters, Woodsy Owl and Smokey Bear. Section 1 of the Act of June 22, 1974 (16 U.S.C. 580p; commonly known as the "Woodsy Owl-Smokey Bear Act of 1974") defines the two characters.

Woodsy is "a fanciful owl, who wears slacks (forest green when colored), a belt (brown when colored), and a Robin Hood style hat (forest green when colored) with a feather (red when colored), and who furthers the slogan, 'Give a Hoot, Don't Pollute.' "

Smokey, meanwhile, is simply "the name and character 'Smokey Bear' originated by the Forest Service of the United States Department of Agriculture in cooperation with the Association of State Foresters and the Advertising Council."

Smokey's definition is vague. When the Forest Service wanted in 2001 to change Smokey's slogan (from "Only You Can Prevent Forest Fires" to "Only You Can Prevent Wildfires"), it was able to do so without needing to ask Congress to change the law.

Woodsy's definition is precise, right down to hat and slogan. The Forest Service has much less flexibility with Woodsy than with Smokey. In 1995, when there was some sentiment that Woodsy needed a new appearance and new slogan, legislation (H.R. 1269 of the 104th Congress) was introduced to make Woodsy's definition less precise, but Congress did not enact it. Soon after, the Forest Service changed Woodsy's appearance—but within the statutory requirements—and changed Woodsy's primary slogan (to "Lend a Hand—Care for the Land"). Woodsy still "furthers" the Give a Hoot slogan (as the law requires), but that slogan has become a secondary slogan.

Is Woodsy's definition too precise? Is Smokey's definition too vague? Both have stood the test of time, but the questions are worth asking.

Another sort of over-precision arises when a provision includes details that are not legally useful. For example, many bills contain findings that are nothing but rhetoric, definitions that merely state the obvious, and precatory language (such as a sense of Congress provision within a bill or joint resolution) that has no binding effect. Useless details such as these are clutter. They impede the reader, create uncertainty, and in the legislative process may attract debate and controversy, all for no substantive gain.

In most cases, matter that a client proposes to include as gratuitous findings can be placed instead in supporting materials, such as a Dear Colleague letter. A definition that states the obvious, or any precatory language, can be omitted or placed in report language (if the client is in a position to influence report language). A drafter should make these alternatives known to the client.

A particularly dangerous sort of over-precision arises when a provision presents gratuitous details in a way that gives them actual, but unintended, legal significance. The problem usually arises when the client couches the problem or the solution in a particular factual context and the drafter does not help the client strip that factual context away from the core policy.

For example, a client may ask for a bill that requires the Secretary of Energy to monitor downwind radiation "whenever the Department of Energy tests a nuclear device at the Nevada Test Site." At the time of writing, the Nevada Test Site is the only site used by the Department of Energy to test nuclear devices, but that may not always be the case. Indeed, the Department of Energy is the only entity that tests nuclear devices, but that may not always be the case.

Does the client really intend for monitoring to apply only to tests by one department at one site? Or does the client intend for monitoring to apply to all tests by the United States, wherever those tests are performed? In short, is this business about the Department of Energy and the Nevada Test Site an important part of the policy, or is it just a description of current practices, masquerading as policy?

A good rule of thumb is that a new bill can assume that current statutes will hold true. If federal law provides that only the Department of Energy may test nuclear devices, and only the Nevada Test Site may be used for those tests, a new bill can probably assume that those two provisions will continue in effect.

A new bill should not, however, assume that current regulations, customs, or practices will hold true. Regulations, customs, and practices can change quickly and easily and, when they do, amending a law to respond to the change can be difficult and time-consuming. In some cases, a law addressed to current practices may be nothing more than an invitation to change current practices to get around the new law.

§ 6.16 Over-Generality and Under-Generality

A law is general if it applies not to a single unique thing but to a class of things. Because most laws regulate classes of people or classes of conduct, or both, general terms are very common and most laws use at least one. Generality is useful and, for most types of laws, necessary.

Problems can arise when a provision is too general or not general enough. For each class of ideas, there is a degree of generality that is appropriate to the policy. The challenge for you, as a drafter, is to identify and achieve that degree of generality.

A class is under-general if it is described too narrowly. A term frequently used in an under-general way is "State." Strictly speaking, the term applies only to one of the fifty states and not, for example, to the District of Columbia, the Commonwealth of Puerto Rico, Guam, American Samoa, the United States Virgin Islands, and the other territories and possessions of the United States. When the client uses the term "State," does the client mean only one of the fifty states? Or does the client have a more general meaning in mind?

A class is over-general if it is described too broadly. A term frequently used in an over-general way is "person." A client who uses the term may mean "individual"—that is, a human being only (sometimes referred to as a "natural person"). The term "person," as defined in chapter 1 of title 1, United States Code, includes not only individuals, but also legal entities such as corporations and partnerships. When the client uses the term "person," does the client mean legal persons? Or does the client have a less general meaning in mind?

§ 6.17 Overbreadth

A law is overbroad if it appears to burden certain constitutional rights, leaving the public uncertain whether those rights can be exercised freely.

Overbreadth is closely related to both vagueness and arbitrariness; however, as a matter of constitutional law, it derives not from due process principles but from certain other individual rights.

A law is unconstitutionally overbroad if, while regulating conduct that the government can constitutionally regulate, it also prohibits (or has a chilling effect on) conduct that the government cannot constitutionally regulate.

For example, the Court has recognized that laws are unconstitutionally overbroad (though not necessarily using that term) when they infringe on free speech (*Broadrick v. Oklahoma*, 413 U.S. 601 (1973)), the right to travel (*Aptheker v. Secretary of State*, 378 U.S. 500 (1964)), and the right to abortion (*Stenberg v. Carhart*, 530 U.S. 914, 938–946 (2000)). See generally *Sabri v. United States*, 541 U.S. 600 (2004).

§ 6.18 Poor Readability

A law is unreadable if it is needlessly hard to read, understand, or use. A law may be unreadable without otherwise being uncertain: A single unmistakable meaning may well be in there somewhere, but it can be arrived at only after a painful and tedious effort.

Because, in a legal sense, a law that is unreadable may still be perfectly effective, a drafter may not be too concerned with the plight of the reader. This is a mistake, and a disservice to the client.

Imagine the trouble that would follow if you wrote an entire bill in Latin. Or pig-latin. Or if you wrote a law in a cipher and provided the key to the cipher. For example, your law might provide:

> (a) Uif cjmm dpvme cf qfsgfdumz dmfbs, boe zfu vosfbebcmf.
>
> (b) To construe subsection (a), substitute each letter of that subsection with the letter that precedes it in the alphabet.

(Translation of subsection (a): "The bill could be perfectly clear, and yet unreadable.")

A law is unreadable (as that term is used here) whenever the reading is tough going. Words can be unreadable if archaic or rare. Sentences can be unreadable if long or complex. Style can be unreadable if stuffy or unfamiliar. Organization can be unreadable if counterintuitive. Typeface can be unreadable if it fails to distinguish between headings and text.

Similarly, a law is unreadable when the understanding is tough going. Citations can be unreadable if they omit useful information. Very few people know a law by its public law number; provide other handy information if available, such as the short title and a United States Code citation.

A law is unreadable on a grand scale if it does not, in fact, say what the law is. That may have an absurd, Alice-in-Wonderland ring to it, but Congress does from time to time pass a law that does not say what the law is. The problem, of course, is that when the law does not say what the law is, it is hard for anyone to be sure what the law is.

A relatively minor variety of this phenomenon is when a law takes effect only upon the occurrence of some later, unpublished event. For example, a law might make a series of amendments to another law and then specify that the amendments take effect when the secretary submits a report to this or that congressional committee. How is anyone to know whether, or when, the amendments take effect? (Besides the secretary and the committee, that is.) If the law does not have some mechanism to ensure that the submission of the report is made known, people will have a hard time figuring out what the law is. (Requiring someone to publish in the Federal Register the date on which the report was submitted is one useful approach.)

§ 6.19 Enactment by Reference

A more problematic variety of unreadability is known as enactment by reference. Enactment by reference occurs when a law refers to a document and declares that the document is enacted into law.

For example, section 1 of Public Law 106-398 (114 Stat. 1654) provides: "The provisions of H.R. 5408 of the 106th Congress, as introduced on October 6, 2000, are hereby enacted into law." Notice that Public Law 106-398 does not contain the text of H.R. 5408—it merely declares that text to be law.

Happily, the drafter of section 1 saw fit to include a section 2 that provides: "In publishing this Act in slip form and in the United States Statutes at Large . . . the Archivist of the United States shall include . . . an appendix setting forth the text of the bill referred to in section 1." And thanks to that bit of forward thinking, a person looking for the document enacted by Public Law 106-398 will find that document—all 513 pages of it—published together with the public law itself.

Whenever a document is enacted by reference, consider the advantages of having it published in the Statutes at Large so there is a permanent public record of its contents. (For other examples of laws that have been enacted by reference and published in this manner, see the notes under section 112 of title 1, United States Code.)

Sometimes there are reasons not to publish the document. For example, a common practice with the annual national defense authorization act has been to accompany the act with a classified annex, which is enacted by reference. The annex, being a classified national security document, is not made available to the general public. (For examples of laws that have enacted by reference a classified annex, see the notes under section 114 of title 10, United States Code.)

Be mindful: a reasonable argument can be made that a document incorporated by reference does not actually become law unless it is actually presented to the President with the measure that incorporates it by reference. The Presentment Clause can be given this interpretation, though it remains to be seen whether it will.

§ 6.20 The Elements of Being Clear

To a drafter, being clear has five elements: Be simple, be ordinary, be brief, be consistent, and be readable. Draft with these five elements in mind, and your drafts will be clearer.

These elements are distinct, but they are related. In most cases they work together. For example, being consistent and being brief usually help you to be simple.

They do not always work together, however; in some cases they are at odds. You can break a complex sentence into several simple sentences, but at the cost of using more words overall; you have gained simplicity but at the price of brevity. Sometimes that trade-off is worth making; other times it is not. There is no substitute for good judgment.

§ 6.21 Be Simple

Be simple. Do not make the draft any more complicated than it has to be. Boil down the information to what needs to be said, and then say it in a straightforward way.

Use simple words and simple expressions. Complex wording is harder to understand than simple wording. Short, everyday words are usually best.

Use sentences that are short, simple, and to the point. Don't try to cram lots of information into a single sentence. One idea per sentence is a good goal.

§ 6.22 Be Ordinary

Be ordinary. Stay away from unusual words. If you have to look up the word to verify its meaning, readers will have to do the same. Use words that have settled, everyday meanings. Do not be too casual, of course, and stay away from slang and idiom.

As a general rule, use ordinary sentence structure, ordinary grammar, ordinary spelling, ordinary style, and ordinary punctuation.

§ 6.23 Be Brief

Be brief. Use what is necessary to change the law, and use nothing else, except perhaps to insert citations and other aids to the reader.

Do not say the same thing twice in different ways. The first time changes the law, the second time creates doubt—was the second time to add independent meaning, was it for emphasis, or was it simply redundant?

Do not use several words if one will do. Do not use many words if a few will do. Make sure every word has a job to do. If a word is idle, cast it out.

Being brief makes your sentences short, tidy, and strong. The draft is quick and easy to read. It crackles with meaning—clear meaning. And that is what you want.

As discussed in § 3.34, a court expects each word in a law to be there for a reason. If you use a word without a reason, the court will breathe into it some reason not your own.

Be brief in all aspects of your draft, not just words. Use each sentence for a reason. Use the shortest word and the shortest sentence that does the job.

§ 6.24 Be Consistent

Be consistent. Do not use one word to mean two different things. If you use a word in one place to mean X, do not use that word in another place to mean Y.

Likewise, do not use two words to mean the same thing. If you use a word in one place to mean X, do not use a different word in another place to mean X.

As discussed in § 3.33, a court expects each word and meaning used in a law to be used consistently. If you use a word or meaning in an inconsistent way, the court will assume you meant to do so, and will create a distinction where none was intended.

Being consistent is not simply a matter of being consistent within a particular law. As discussed in § 3.41, a court reads a law in the context of other laws on related subjects. If those other laws give a certain term a specific meaning, be careful when you use that term and when you try to capture that meaning.

No matter what the subject of your law is, part of the context is chapter 1 of title 1, United States Code. That chapter contains definitions that apply generally to any act of Congress. Among the terms defined in that chapter are officer, writing, vessel, vehicle, county, company, marriage, spouse, person, individual, and child.

Be consistent in all aspects of your draft, not just words. Be consistent in how you arrange your sentences and in how you structure your sections. Be consistent in the labels you use for headings and the form of interlocked unit you use for lists. When you are consistent, the important differences are easier to spot, which helps you draft effectively and helps the reader understand.

§ 6.25 Be Readable

Be readable. Do not pass up a chance to make your draft easier to read and use. As Bentham described it, a draft that is hard to read is "naked in respect of helps to intellection." Clothe your draft; aid the reader.

If the draft is hard to read, people are less likely to read it and less likely to support it. If the draft is hard to use, people who need to use it are more likely to be frustrated and confused. In each case, it reflects badly on your client. It is less efficient and less effective.

Arrange the draft in an intuitive way. Put information where the reader expects it—the most important information up front, the least important information in back. Do the same for every provision and sentence within the draft. Provide useful references and citations. Use lists, formulas, tables, and charts wherever they might help.

A draft that is readable is an asset. It makes you look sharp to the client; it makes the client look sharp to everyone else. It makes the policy more inviting. The client can easily make sense of it; others can, too.

It does not go too far to suggest that readability helps sell the policy. It can create goodwill and credibility. In 1999, when the House and Senate were trying to restructure the nuclear weapons programs of the Department of Energy, both chambers passed proposals to establish a new nuclear weapons agency. The Senate proposal would have created an Agency for Nuclear Stewardship by adding to the Department of Energy Organization Act a single section, thirteen pages long. The new section had subsections from (a) through (w), no headings, and no table of contents—in general, it was not very readable. The House responded with a proposal that would have created a National Nuclear Security Administration by adding to the annual defense authorization bill an entire new title divided into dozens of sections, making good use of headings, and including a table of contents. Negotiators from the two chambers quickly adopted the House version as their working text and the law as enacted was derived from that version. There is no proof that the readability of the House version was an asset to the House negotiators, but it is plausible.

Perhaps the best reason of all to be readable is that being readable increases the likelihood that the law will be obeyed: "Even a dictator finds it convenient to be understood." David Hull, "Drafter's Devils," *The Loophole* (June 2000).

§6.30 Use Plain English

Words are important. Choose them wisely and use them with care. If your draft winds up in court, chances are there has been a controversy over the meaning of a single word.

Use ordinary English words. The best words to use are the ones with settled, everyday meanings. From this general principle flow other useful principles, set forth here.

Do not use Old English or Middle English expressions. In this category are words like aforesaid, hereinafter, thereof, said, and same. (Many would also put "such" in this category.) Sometimes a word from Old English or Middle English is no longer used in common parlance, except perhaps by lawyers. Most likely, the word fell from disuse for good reason: It was vague, ponderous, or useless. There is nothing magical about archaic words; generally, they have not survived because they are unfit for modern, everyday use.

Do not use "Law Latin." A few Latin terms have made it into ordinary English, like per capita. A few others have become terms of art among lawyers, like mandamus and estoppel. Unless a Latin term clearly falls into one of these categories, do not use it.

Do not use acronyms. Acronyms do have the benefit of being brief, but that is usually the only benefit. To most readers, acronyms are cryptic and ambiguous. The acronym "DOE" can stand for the Department of Energy or the Department of Education, among other things.

Stay away from words that are understood only by specialists. In this category are technical words and any other sort of insider lingo. Your draft needs to be understood by generalists, such as politicians and courts. If it takes you more words to make the meaning clear, so be it: Sacrifice brevity for clarity, simplicity, and readability.

Do not use coupled synonyms. In this category are couplets like deem and consider; authorized and directed; from and after; force and effect. Sometimes couplets exist simply because they sound important, even though they aren't. Sometimes they exist because they derive from different languages (in "goods and chattels," the former derives from Old English and the latter from Old French). In a very few cases they have become legal terms of art, and in those few cases they may be worth retaining ("metes and bounds" is one example).

§ 6.31 Beware "Plain Language"

There is a school of writing known as the Plain Language school (usually with a capital P and a capital L, as shown here). The Plain Language school endorses a range of techniques designed to create legislation that is readable and easy to use.

That sounds well and good, and indeed it is. The Plain Language school is important and relevant, and generally the approaches it advocates are useful. Some of them, however, are not.

For example, the Plain Language school advocates the use of examples in legislation. The use of examples in legislation is—how to put this delicately?—a horrible, frightening idea. Two analogies come instantly to mind. The first is the statement attributed to Napoleon that it is better to have one bad general than two good generals. The other is that when you have one clock you always know what time it is, but when you have two you never know what time it is. When a law provides a rule and also provides an example of the rule in use, it is neither brief nor simple, and unless the rule and the example are very carefully selected the law may not be consistent. This is a disaster. Adding to the misery, whenever later drafters want to amend the law—or simply to affect the law without amending it—they have to consider whether (and if so, how) to amend the example. To use an example to illustrate a rule is to concede that the rule itself is not adequately drafted.

The Plain Language school also advocates a statement of purpose. The sentiment appears to be that a statement of purpose helps a reader understand more quickly what the law is about. Being a quick read is a nice thing, but it is not the only thing. A statement of purpose can invite a judge to bend the meaning away from the meaning your client intended.

The Plain Language school is correct to argue that readability is important, but readability is just one of the five elements of an effective draft, and it is perhaps the least important of the five.

But the most vexing problem with the Plain Language school is that it claims that clarity is more important than precision.

One member of the school made the claim this way: "What is the point, after all, of being precise but unclear? The result is . . . unintelligible precision. It makes about as much sense as precise mud." Joseph Kimble, "Answering the Critics of Plain Language," 5 *Scribes Journal of Legal Writing* (1995).

The point is that being precise but unclear might be exactly what the client wanted. Your duty as a drafter is to give effect—with 100 percent faithfulness—to what the client wants. The Plain Language school seems to suggest that it is acceptable to trade faithfulness for clarity or readability. As a drafter, you cannot make that trade. You cannot sacrifice any amount of faithfulness, however slight, for any gain in clarity or readability, however great.

All of this may come across as too harsh. The quarrels here with the Plain Language school are more like quibbles; everyone agrees that plain writing is generally a virtue. The approach here is not to reject the teachings of the Plain Language school, but to take them (as with all teachings) with a grain of salt.

§6.40 Drafting an Effective Sentence

The basic unit of a draft is the same as the basic unit of any other form of writing: the sentence. Plan every sentence with care. Make every sentence pay its own way—if you don't need it, cut it.

As discussed in Chapter Four, before you put pen to paper, identify the action and the actor. If there are qualifiers, identify them too. And don't forget to identify the consequences.

Don't get too hung up on how best to arrange these various elements in a sentence. Some who write about drafting propose that the order should be qualifiers, actor, action. In some cases that works well, but in other cases it doesn't. You may want to try actor, action, qualifiers. You may want to try the actor and action in one sentence and the qualifiers in a separate sentence. Don't get too hung up on any one formula. Use your judgment; find an order that works best in your case, all things considered, and use it in that case.

Position all your words carefully. The order of words shows their relationship and guides their meaning. For that reason, keep the actor near the action. If the action has an object, keep the object near the action as well.

Use sentences of short and medium length only. Generally, a sentence should not run on for more than twenty or twenty-five words.

Each sentence should convey one major point. Avoid compound sentences and sentences with complex clauses. If one or two simple qualifiers exist, state them and then the rule. If the qualifiers are many or complex (or both), state the rule first and then the qualifiers, perhaps in one or more separate sentences.

Above all, draft each sentence in a manner that places emphasis on the thoughts and concepts that are most important.

§ 6.41 Arrange Words with Care

Arrange your words with care. Word order affects meaning; it also affects readability.

"The position of the words in a sentence is the principal means of showing their relationship. . . . The writer must, therefore, so far as possible, bring together the words, and groups of words, that are related in thought, and keep apart those that are not related." Strunk and White, *The Elements of Style* 22 (1959).

The normal English word order in the active voice is subject, verb, object. For most sentences, keep those three elements in that order, and keep them close together.

At the same time, keep modifying words as close as possible to the words they modify, so that the relationship is clear. This applies not only to adjectives and adverbs, but also to prepositional phrases. It applies to conditions, exceptions, and other qualifying language.

The word "only" is the most notorious example of how the position of a word in a sentence can change the meaning of the sentence (compare "Only I like you" with "I only like you" and "I like only you"), but there are many others.

Congress once enacted a law providing, "That no sponges taken from . . . waters shall be landed, delivered, cured or offered for sale at any port or place in the United States of a smaller size than four inches in diameter." (34 Stat. 313.) How many ports are that small?

§ 6.50 The Action

The crux of every legislative sentence is the action. This holds true whether the sentence sets forth a rule of command, a rule of discretion, or a stipulation.

§ 6.51 Active Voice

Use the active voice rather than the passive voice. With the active voice, the subject of the sentence is the one who acts ("The President submits the budget"); with the passive voice, the subject of the sentence is the one being acted upon ("The budget is submitted by the President" or simply "The budget is submitted").

There are several reasons to favor the active voice. Using the active voice forces you to name the actor, which is always useful and often essential. By naming the actor, you make known to the reader the person who is to receive the benefit or the burden of the law. The actor is put on notice (and so is the rest of the world). If the law confers discretion, you identify the person on whom it is conferred. If the law imposes a command, you identify the person on whom it is imposed.

As if that weren't reason enough, the active voice usually requires fewer words and is generally considered more readable, vivid, and interesting.

There are times when the passive voice works better, but use the passive voice only when you have good reason to do so and the actor is understood or obvious.

For example, almost all federal crimes are in the passive voice—typically, they take the form, "Whoever does X shall be fined under this title, imprisoned for a term of Y years, or both." Who does the fining and imprisoning? We know from other law that courts impose sentences and prisons carry them out. To restate the sentence in the active voice would be bizarre and less effective. It would have to read something like this: "A court shall fine under this title, or shall order a prison to imprison for a term of Y years, or both, whoever does X." The formula is awkward and places the most important information—the type of conduct being prohibited—at the end, where it is hard to find. Using the passive voice is useful in this context because it places the important information first.

§ 6.52 Present Tense

Use the present tense rather than the past tense, future tense, or any other tense. A law should speak directly to the reader at the time of reading. Since the law can be read at any time, it should be drafted in the present tense, so that it is always speaking. When you need to specify a temporal relationship between two actions, put one of them in the present tense; for the other, it may work best to use the past, the past perfect, the future, or some other tense. (Thus: "This Act applies [present tense] to civil actions filed [past tense] before the date of the enactment of this Act.")

§ 6.53 Verbs That Are Vivid and Concrete

Use verbs that are vivid and concrete rather than bland and abstract. If you can visualize a person taking the action signified by the verb, it probably works; if you can't, it probably doesn't.

To ensure that your verbs are vivid and concrete, do not "verb" a noun. You can do this in English—indeed, that last sentence just did. The results are sometimes marvelous, but usually nasty. The secretary can task the director to do something and the director can effort it, but it would be less cheeky and easier to read if the secretary required the director to do something and the director did it. As with any new word, creating a verb out of a noun can be dangerous, because the new verb may not have a settled, everyday meaning. In any case, whatever you gain in pith comes at the expense of dignity and clarity. In sum: Do not verb a noun.

Likewise, do not "noun" a verb. The secretary can give consideration, have consultations, and make decisions, but it would be more vivid and concrete if the secretary considered, consulted, and decided. Turning verbs into nouns almost always makes for a longer, duller sentence. (That said, sometimes nouning a verb, as in "The Secretary shall make a determination," enables you later to refer crisply back to the noun, as in "the determination.") But in sum: Do not noun a verb.

§ 6.54 Indicative Mood

Except when using the imperatives "shall" (§ 6.55) and "shall not" (§ 6.56), use the indicative mood. The indicative mood is the mood used to indicate—that is, to make a statement of fact. Use it for a stipulation ("This Act applies after the date of the enactment of this Act") or a condition ("If the Secretary determines X, then the Secretary may Y"). Do not use the subjunctive mood ("If the Secretary were to determine X, then the Secretary may Y").

§ 6.55 "Shall" and "May"

The convention in federal drafting is to use "shall" to require and "may" to allow. This convention is not without its problems and detractors, but it remains the convention.

More than a few English-speaking countries, having once followed this convention, have abandoned it. Simply put, "shall" is great trouble and "may" is close behind. So it is fair to question whether the convention should be abandoned in drafting federal law. Before you cast it out, though, make sure you have a better alternative to use in its place. As problematic as "shall" and "may" can be, most drafters eventually come to the conclusion that the alternatives are no better.

The crux of the problem with "shall" and "may" is that they each mean many different things (that is, they are ambiguous). Even if every drafter follows the convention—using "shall" only to command and "may" only to allow—the convention doesn't work unless courts and other readers follow suit. Courts do not always follow suit; they sometimes decide that "shall" in a particular statute really means "may," and vice versa. (See *Gutierrez de Martinez v. Lamagno*, 515 U.S. 417, 432 n.9 (1995).)

Now that the Supreme Court has recognized that drafters follow conventions, that those conventions should be followed by courts, and that those conventions can be found in drafting manuals (see *Koons Buick Pontiac GMC, Inc. v. Nigh*, 534 U.S. 50 (2004)), perhaps the Court will recognize the shall/may convention and give it teeth.

"Shall" can be used to express (among other things) a command, a prediction, or an intention. Thus, "Mary shall go to the store" can mean Mary is commanded to go to the store, Mary will go to the store, or Mary intends to go to the store. The term is rarely used in everyday English (at least in American English), though it is still used in some common questions ("Shall we dance?"). In general, "shall" is archaic and formal.

"May" can be used to express authority, capability, or possibility. Thus, "Mary may go to the store" can mean Mary is allowed to go to the store, Mary is able to go to the store, or Mary might go to the store. Like "shall," "may" also has other meanings; unlike "shall," "may" is still used in everyday English.

This is not to unduly alarm you, but it is to alarm you: The terms "may" and "shall" are problematic. Each is ambiguous, and the ambiguity cannot always be resolved easily by context. That said, the convention should be followed until a demonstrably better approach comes along—and a better approach has not yet come along.

Some propose using "must" to require, and while that seems superficially appealing—"must" is not as ambiguous nor as archaic as "shall"—most come around to the conclusion that it is not appreciably better. "Must" is not free of ambiguity: "Mary must go to the store" can mean Mary has an obligation to go to the store or Mary has a need to go to the store.

Though "shall" and "must" both carry the sense of requirement, only "shall" carries the sense of command; "must" carries the sense of obligation, which is similar, but not the same. When a host tells a guest, "You shall leave now," the host is commanding the guest to leave. When a host tells a guest, "You must leave now," the host is notifying the guest that the time to leave has arrived. In both cases the guest is required to leave, but only with "shall" is it clear that the host is the one imposing the requirement. With "must," the requirement could be imposed by the host ("You broke my vase? You must leave now") by someone else ("You have a curfew—you must leave now"), or by necessity ("You have a train to catch—you must leave now"). Try replacing "must" with "shall" in those three cases; it works only in the first one.

In short, as commands go, "must" is weaker and more ambiguous than "shall." And then there is the reality that "must" is not used in everyday English significantly more often than "shall" is. In everyday American English, most speakers use "have to" (which has its own problems). And so most drafters fall back on "shall," treating it more or less as a term of art.

As for "may," not nearly as much needs be said, because no one has come up with a particularly good alternative.

To be sure, both "shall" and "may" could be replaced by indicatives, such as "is directed to" for "shall" and "is authorized to" for "may." As with "must," these are weak, descriptive forms rather than strong, direct forms, and they take three words rather than just one.

Drafters should follow the convention: Use "shall" to command and "may" to allow. Notably, that convention has been codified into law in some parts of the Code, though not yet in all parts—titles 10 and 32 of the Code each have a section 101 providing that "shall" is used in the imperative sense and "may" is used in the permissive sense.

To bolster the convention, never use "shall" or "may" in any other sense. Use "shall" only to command, and use "may" only to allow.

Do not simply inject "shall" or "may" into a sentence and think you are done. Words are not read in isolation. The broader question is not what "shall" or "may" means in the abstract but whether the sentence as a whole, read in light of the provision as a whole and the act as a whole, is intended to be a rule of command, a rule of discretion, or something else entirely.

If the law imposes a command, for example, it should not only use "shall," but it should also specify the consequences that follow a failure to comply.

If a law uses "shall" but does not specify a consequence, a judge can do many things with it. "Shall" could be mandatory, or "shall" could be directory. "Shall" could mean "should," or "shall" could mean "may." "Shall" could be mandatory but only substantial compliance is required. There are other possibilities as well. Only by specifying the consequence can you be sure it will apply.

Finally, always be on guard when you use "shall" or "may." Consider this:

> "The individual appointed as Director shall be a citizen of the United States."

What does this mean? It could mean that an individual cannot be appointed as director unless the individual is already a citizen of the United States. It could mean that an individual, once appointed, has a duty to become a citizen. Or it could mean that citizenship is automatically conferred upon an individual when the individual is appointed.

§ 6.56 "Shall Not" and "May Not"

The question sometimes arises when to use "may not" and when to use "shall not." Truth be told, there are few cases in which it makes a difference. Each expression can be used effectively to forbid.

If there is a legal difference between the two expressions, it is a subtle one. The conventional wisdom among drafters is that, since "may" provides authority to act, "may not" denies authority to act. Likewise, since "shall" expresses a command to act, "shall not" expresses a command to refrain from acting.

The difference between denying authority to act and commanding not to act is that an act taken without authority is usually void, while an act taken in violation of a command is usually punishable. In the former case, the consequence of the violation typically falls on a third party; in the latter case, the consequence of the violation typically falls on the actor.

This is best expressed by example. Consider the following provision:

> "The Secretary may make grants, except that the Secretary—
> (1) may not make a grant to New York; and
> (2) shall not make a grant to Boston."

Now suppose the secretary makes grants to both New York and Boston. Both cities spend the money. What happens?

The secretary had no authority to make a grant to New York; the grant is probably void. New York is liable to pay back the money.

The secretary was under a command not to make a grant to Boston; the grant is not necessarily void. Perhaps Boston can keep the money. Though it probably faces an uphill battle, Boston might be able to establish that the secretary, not the grantee, is supposed to face the consequences of a violation.

Whether Boston could establish that principle will depend on many factors, including the context. Boston does not have a strong case, but it has a stronger case than New York does. Again, if there is a legal difference between the two expressions, it is a subtle one.

For most drafters—and for most judges, and most people—this distinction is too subtle to matter. Some prefer "may not," others prefer "shall not." Reasonable people seem to disagree about which one sounds stronger; to some ears, "the Secretary may not . . ." is more forbidding than "the Secretary shall not . . .," while others feel the opposite.

Develop a preference if you have one, but be flexible in every case. The distinction described above (denial of authority vs. command) might not be the only distinction. Consider this:

> "Regulations prescribed—
>
> (1) under chapter 1 shall not take effect until the date that is 30 days after the date on which those regulations are submitted to Congress; and
>
> (2) under chapter 2 may not take effect until the date that is 30 days after the date on which those regulations are submitted to Congress."

Now suppose the secretary submits both sets of regulations on the same day and specifies that each set not take effect for ninety-nine days. What happens?

A reasonable argument can be made that the regulations under chapter 1 take effect on Day 30 (despite what the secretary directed), while the regulations under chapter 2 take effect on Day 99 (as the secretary directed). The inference is certainly weak, but it is there.

In any event, the statements above probably should be in the indicative (as discussed in § 6.54)—they should state that the regulations "do not" take effect, rather than that the regulations "shall not" or "may not" take effect.

The lesson, if there is one, is to use "may not" and "shall not" with the same special care you use for "shall." Whenever you use either expression to forbid, consider whether you should also specify the consequences of a failure to comply.

§ 6.60 The Actor

The actor is the one required, forbidden, or allowed to take the action. In almost every case, your legislative sentence should identify the actor.

You can structure your sentence in a way that leaves out the actor if—and only if—the identity is obvious and the structure has other advantages. Your structure may, for example, use the passive voice (as discussed above) or the false imperative.

The false imperative is much like the passive voice, except the passive voice uses the indicative form ("the report is submitted by the Secretary") while the false imperative uses the imperative form ("the report shall include"). The false imperative is considered "false" because the command applies not to the subject of the sentence, but to an unnamed actor.

For an appropriate use of the false imperative, consider the following two sentences:

> "Not later than March 1, 2005, the Secretary shall submit to Congress a report on X. The Secretary shall include in the report the following: . . ."

The second sentence identifies the actor (the secretary), but isn't it redundant? The second sentence could instead provide as follows:

> "The report shall include the following: . . ."

This version does not identify the actor, but the actor is obvious. It uses the false imperative to be simple and brief, and is no less clear.

§ 6.61 Third Person

Use the third person, not the first person or second person. For most drafters this principle is intuitive.

Congress violates the principle every now and then, usually in a place where it is relatively harmless but still unseemly (such as in a sense of Congress or a statement of findings). For example, Congress might refer to "our Nation and our allies" instead of "the United States and its allies." The conventional wisdom among drafters is that the third person is more appropriate.

§ 6.62 Singular Rather Than Plural

Use nouns in the singular rather than the plural. This principle is embodied in chapter 1 of title 1, United States Code, which provides that the singular includes the plural.

When you always use the singular, you never have to worry about shifting between the singular and plural forms of nouns and verbs. Also, you make certain that the sentence applies to a single individual as well as to a plural class.

Plurals can create ambiguity, especially when used with "and" or "or." If a law provides that "individuals may not enter buildings A and B without appropriate security clearances," does it apply to a single individual entering a single building with a single clearance?

In the quotation at the beginning of this chapter, the chairman's final phrasing was, "All dogs in this Park must be kept on the lead." While the meaning is probably plain enough, it would have been somewhat better in the singular: "A dog in this Park must be kept on the lead."

In a very few cases the singular is awkward and unclear. For example, it may be better to say "The Secretary may make grants" than "The Secretary may make a grant," because the latter may carry the implication that the secretary may make only one grant.

§ 6.63 Articles Rather Than Indefinite Adjectives

Articles include "a," "an," and "the." Indefinite adjectives include "any," "each," "every," and "no." Generally, use an article rather than an indefinite adjective. There are, however, occasions when the extra emphasis is useful.

Articles can be tricky. In *Sprietsma v. Mercury Marine*, 537 U.S. 51 (2002), the Court found that the phrase "a law or regulation" did not include the common law. The article "a," the Court said, implies a discreteness that covers a statute or a regulation but does not cover the common law. To include the common law, the Court seemed to imply, Congress should have used the indefinite adjective "any" rather than the article "a."

If the policy is to cover all cases and using an article does not seem strong or clear enough, use each or every: "The head of a household shall list the name of each member of the household."

If the policy is to cover one and only one case, use "one": "One law enforcement officer shall serve on the task force."

§ 6.64 Avoid Pronouns

Avoid using pronouns. Pronouns can create ambiguity, particularly when the pronoun could plausibly refer back to more than one noun. Also, most pronouns are not gender-neutral. The better practice is to repeat the noun.

§ 6.65 Avoid Noun Chains

Avoid using noun chains. A noun chain is a string of nouns. Noun chains are always cumbersome and sometimes ambiguous.

An example of a noun chain is "working dog owner." Does this refer to a person who owns a working dog, or to a dog owner who works?

Noun chains can seem appealing because they seem to be short, simple, and clear. Generally, however, their only virtue is that they are short.

§ 6.70 Punctuation

Punctuation can show an orator how to read a text aloud, and it can show a reader how to understand a text. From ancient times it was used only for the former purpose; not until the 1800s did it come into common use for the latter.

Into the 1800s, bills were considered by a legislature in spoken rather than written form. The punctuation was added by the clerk responsible for creating a written record of what was agreed to. In those times, courts were reluctant to use punctuation as a guide for meaning. Now that the written form is pretty well entrenched, the pendulum has swung the other way.

In modern English prose, and in modern American legislatures, and, therefore, also in modern drafting, punctuation carries meaning. As a drafter, you have a responsibility to punctuate with care.

Consider the unpunctuated phrase, "a woman without her man is nothing." Ask a group of men to punctuate it properly and you might get, "A woman, without her man, is nothing." Ask a group of women to do so, and you might get, "A woman: Without her, man is nothing." Punctuation is important.

Some of the most famous, or infamous, cases in history have turned on punctuation. *United States v. Ron Pair Enterprises*, 489 U.S. 235 (1989), turned on the significance of a comma.

A complete guide to punctuation is beyond the scope of this book. Generally, punctuate your draft the way you would punctuate anything else in ordinary modern English. (There are a variety of style guides that cover punctuation in detail; see <*www.LegislativeDrafter.com*>.)

The focus here is on the special cases where that general rule may not apply.

§ 6.71 Use the Serial Comma

Use the serial comma. Some drafting guides urge you to omit it, and most newspapers omit it routinely, but the serial comma is needed in many cases to avoid ambiguity. Use it with enthusiasm. Even in cases where it is not strictly necessary to avoid ambiguity, it is proper.

The serial comma is the comma before the conjunction in a series of three or more items joined only with that conjunction. Here, the comma after "tigers" is the serial comma:

> lions, tigers, and bears.

In a series in which the items themselves contain internal commas, use semicolons rather than commas to separate the items. In that case, use a serial semicolon in the same manner as you would a serial comma:

> Seattle, Washington; Sacramento, California; and Austin, Texas.

§ 6.72 Include Punctuation when Amending Other Law

As discussed more fully in § 9.33, when drafting an instruction to amend other law, any punctuation that is to be included as part of the quoted matter should appear inside the quotation marks. Any punctuation not to be included as part of the quoted matter should appear outside the quotation marks.

§ 6.80 Start from Scratch if You Can

Sometimes you have the opportunity to start with language already drafted by someone else. The language may be in an existing law that you may use as a model, in a bill already introduced, or in a draft prepared by an agency or interest group. You can start with a draft prepared by someone else when there is good reason to do so, but start from scratch whenever you can.

There is a tendency to believe that language already drafted has already undergone some sort of scrutiny and therefore is more sound. Do not give in to the tendency, and do not let your client give in to the tendency either.

With language prepared elsewhere, you do not know the circumstances under which it was drafted. It may or may not have been drafted professionally; quite apart from that, it may or may not have been drafted competently. Most importantly, it may or may not have been drafted with your client's particular needs in mind.

The worst way to use language drafted elsewhere is to use it without scrutiny. You may end up borrowing phrases you don't need. Azerbaijan enacted a law based on Britain's Interpretation Act. The Azerbaijan law, as described by a British drafter, "looked like a straight copy of our Interpretation Act—including the section with the sidenote 'Application to Northern Ireland.' " Geoffrey Bowman, "Legislation and Explanation," *The Loophole* (June 2000).

You may also end up borrowing problems you don't want. Even a model that seems sound may not be all it's cracked up to be. Consider this example, from the field of workers' compensation: "Drafters of American compensation acts have repeatedly copied from the English act the words 'injuries arising out of and in the course of employment.' Apparently, it is assumed that the meaning of these words has been fixed by the English courts and is well understood. . . . [But] this phrase, instead of having a definite and fixed meaning, is one of the most prolific sources of doubt and litigation in the English act." Thomas I. Parkinson, "Legislative Drafting," 3 *Publications of the Academy of Political Science* 142, 150 (1912).

The best way to use language drafted elsewhere is as a learning tool. Reviewing the other language may tip you off to an issue that you hadn't already considered; it may point you to a constitutional problem, a related law, or a factual wrinkle. It may use an organizational scheme that seems to work.

Having said that, however, start from scratch whenever you can. Beaman's strategy was bolder than most but as effective as any:

"Mr. Beaman was always a gentleman, but he would take the draft, put it in a drawer, and say, 'Fine, now what was it that you wanted us to do?' " Edward O. Craft, as quoted in Reed Dickerson (ed.), *Professionalizing Legislative Drafting: The Federal Experience* 149 (1973).

§6.90 No Such Thing as a Perfect Draft

Legislative drafters, it has been said, "are chronic complainers." They are "always asking for more time; they are never satisfied with what they have wrought." Wilbur D. Mills, "How the Problem Looks to the Legislative Branch:

Congressional Practices That Affect Executive Responsibility," in Reed Dickerson (ed.), *Professionalizing Legislative Drafting: The Federal Experience* 19 (1973).

Always bear in mind that there is no such thing as a perfect draft. Every drafter approaches drafting from a unique perspective, and there is more than one way to draft a policy effectively. There is no single "right" or "best" draft (though, to be sure, some drafts are markedly better than others).

Though there are many rules that can be broken for good reason, one rule you should always follow is this: In each case, ponder the various techniques you can use and the various approaches you can take, and use judgment and common sense to decide what to do.

Do not draft one particular way because that way is the one way you were taught, or is the only way you can think of. There are always choices. The more alternatives you consider, the more likely it is that your draft will be effective. Techniques and approaches can come from a book, but most come from experience. Keep adding to your toolbox.

Another rule you should always follow is this: Never assume that your draft is perfect. Your perspective is just one perspective. If you think the draft is clear and the client thinks it is not, do not disagree; you need to revise your thinking—and your draft.

You must be able to look at the problem, and the draft, at arm's length and with a skeptical eye. From time to time, you will become too familiar with a subject or with a draft—you are too close to the material—and you will fail to see it fresh and new unless you make a conscious effort to do so. Even then, it helps to have a colleague review what you have written to see what fresh eyes make of it.

Whenever you are asked to review a colleague's draft, do so gladly. It will be a source of learning, and in some cases it may be a source of humor. As one drafter observed:

> "There is the more rarified kind of wry entertainment that a drafter himself can derive from spotting the blunders or inelegancies in the products of his colleagues. At a social occasion one of my children once asked one of my colleagues if I laughed much at work. The answer was, 'Only when he reads other people's Bills.' "
>
> Geoffrey Bowman, "Legislation and Explanation," *The Loophole* (June 2000).

Chapter 7

Organizing and Arranging

The Bill should be clear and should state at the very commencement the important principle of the measure and the greatest pains should be taken to separate the material from the comparatively immaterial provisions.

Henry Thring, *Practical Legislation* 8 (1902)

The most glaring example of the way bills should not be drawn are some of the hodge-podge acts of the Federal Congress which frequently intermingle substantive law, amendments, references to prior laws, repeals, savings clauses and a diversity of subjects without semblance of arrangement.

Arie Poldervaart, "Legislative Drafting in New Mexico," 28 *New Mexico Tax Bulletin* 595 (1949)

After three days of executive sessions for purposes of making policy decisions . . . an attorney from the Legislative Counsel's Office advised the committee chairman concerned that, so far as he could observe, the questions and time-consuming discussions had related to matters which did not involve the real issues that required policy decisions . . . . The attorney took a pair of scissors and cut the bill into 128 pieces and distributed them around a large conference table. With the assistance of a printing clerk he then reassembled the bill in logical order without (except for a few minor exceptions) even changing the words that were used in the introduced bill. When the committee met to consider the committee print, it was able to take up the five central policy issues and quickly dispose of the legislation.

Wilbur D. Mills, "How the Problem Looks to the Executive Branch: Congressional Practices that Affect Executive Responsibility," in Reed Dickerson (ed.), *Professionalizing Legislative Drafting: The Federal Experience* 18-19 (1973)

Organizing and Arranging

Chapter 7

§ 7.00 Introduction

The most basic rule for organization is that you should have one. A draft that is not organized is likely to be a disaster. Having an organization helps both the drafter and the reader: It helps you order your thoughts, and it helps the reader navigate and understand the draft.

Your draft should always be well-organized. You should keep the organization of the whole draft in mind when drafting the parts.

In federal law, the principal unit of organization is the section. Each section should be numbered, and each section should cover a single topic only. This is not only good sense—it is the law. Section 104 of title 1, United States Code, provides: "Each section shall be numbered, and shall contain, as nearly as may be, a single proposition of enactment."

Using a numbering system makes a law easier to use and easier to read. Referring to a section by number is clearer and more precise than referring to it by description. A section that has a number is easier to find. Laws with numbered sections are easier to navigate.

Covering one topic per section also makes a law easier to use and read. A section in drafting should work much like a paragraph in prose: It focuses the reader's attention on a single idea, fleshes out that idea, then yields to the next idea. One topic per section is simple and intuitive. One topic at a time makes a law easier for a drafter to organize and makes each topic easier for a reader to grasp.

These ideas—number each unit; one topic per unit—are so powerful and effective that they are used not only for sections, but also for smaller units within a section and "big levels" (titles, chapters, and so on) into which sections are grouped.

But these ideas tell you only what the characteristics of the principal units of your draft should be; they do not tell you how to organize and arrange those units in an effective way. To organize and arrange a bill—or a part of a bill—there are three types of problems: problems of sequence, problems of division, and problems of grouping. Handling these problems is the focus of the rest of this chapter.

When organizing and arranging, the most general principle is this: Put each provision where it can most easily be found. A reader who knows about it should be able to find it easily, and a reader who doesn't know about it should be able to stumble across it easily. The rest of this chapter discusses how to apply this general principle to your draft.

§7.10 Choosing a Sequence

Unless your bill has only one section, and a short one at that, you will have to put a series of sections into a sequence. A bill is linear; something must go first, and something must go last.

Sequencing takes place on several levels. If you group sections into titles or other big levels, you have to put the sections in a sequence within a group and the groups in a sequence within the bill. If you divide sections into subsections or still smaller units, you have to put the smaller units (at each tier) in a sequence within the section.

In almost all cases, sequence should be based on importance. Put more important topics before less important topics. Thus, put the main message first. Put rules that apply generally before rules that apply only in special cases. Put permanent provisions before temporary provisions. Put technical and housekeeping provisions at the end. If minor topics seem to have something in common, it may make sense to consolidate them into a single topic.

Putting the most important ideas first helps the reader grasp the main thrust of the bill quickly and effectively. It is what the reader needs, and it is also what the reader expects.

Readers do not like surprises; they do not like to be sandbagged or tricked. When a draft buries an important idea at the end, the reader is likely to be puzzled or annoyed.

That said, sometimes a client may insist, for optical or tactical reasons, on downplaying an important idea, so that those who oppose it might overlook it. An interesting example of this was in the drafting of the Securities Act of 1933. One of the policymakers behind that law, James M. Landis, relates that the drafter—the ever-present Middleton Beaman—opted to place important substantive material in a schedule toward the end of the bill. "I believe that it was probably due to Beaman's desire to eliminate from the draft material not essential to its main structure. I do recall his comment that, handled as a schedule, it would probably be glossed over by the committee after that committee had exhausted its patience on the bill itself. In this he proved to be right. I believe, however, that he knew as well as we that the core of the registration requirements lay in those schedules." James M. Landis, "The Legislative History of the Securities Act of 1933," 28 *George Washington Law Review* 29, 38 (1959).

Be careful. It is possible to downplay an important idea so much that a court will decide that the provision cannot possibly be given its literal meaning. "Congress would not place such an important provision in such a remote part of the law," the court might well say. (See § 3.83, "Congress Does Not Mumble.") Gamesmanship can be counterproductive in at least three ways: It can be unethical; it can offend the reader; and it can cause a court to water down the provision's effectiveness.

Readers want you to get straight to the point. Time is short; there are many other bills and laws to be read. Dallying gets in the way of the message. Do not try a reader's patience. Start with the big ideas. Capture the reader's attention.

Putting ideas in order of importance does have a general civic virtue to it, to be sure. But of more immediate concern to you is that it buys goodwill, or at least respect: It makes the draft seem more credible and the client seem more competent and serious. (See related discussion in § 6.25, "Be Readable.")

If there is a good reason to do so, sequence can be based on some other principle. There are two things to keep in mind here.

First, make sure that there is, indeed, a good reason not to base the principle on importance. Sometimes the simple fact that various parts of the bill are all of the same general importance is a good reason. Committee jurisdiction may be another reason.

Second, make sure the new principle is a logical one. It should seem intuitive and natural; the reader should not have to stop and ponder what the principle is.

There are many possible principles; use the one that works best. For example, if a bill makes a series of reforms to a process (such as how lawsuits are handled), it may make sense to arrange the provisions in chronological order (such as from service of process to judgments and appeals). If a bill covers a large number of topics of more or less the same importance, it may make sense to arrange the topics in alphabetical order. In part I of title 18, United States Code (specifying a wide variety of federal crimes), chapters 2 through 119 are in alphabetical order, from "Aircraft and Motor Vehicles" to "Wire and Electronic Communications." (The first chapter has general provisions, and a few chapters have, over the years, been inserted out of sequence.)

When the principle you use is intuitive and natural, readers can focus on whether or not the policy has merit. They are not trapped into first trying to understand what the policy is (which was the plight of one committee, as described by Wilbur Mills in the quotation at the beginning of this chapter).

The draft should flow from top to bottom. The reader should move through the draft step by step without having to look back or jump forward.

Ultimately, putting a bill into sequence is like umpiring a baseball game: When you do it properly, no one takes any notice at all.

§ 7.20 The Section

In federal drafting, the principal unit of organization is the section, in all cases but one. (For an appropriations bill, the principal unit of organization is the undesignated paragraph.)

Every measure, even an appropriations bill, has at least one section. If the measure is fairly simple, it need not have any other type of unit. Sections can, however, be subdivided into smaller units, or grouped into big levels.

Sections are numbered in a fixed manner. In general, each section has an Arabic number, beginning with section 1. The manner in which the section numbers are displayed depends on the drafting style of the bill. In general, the number of every section is displayed, but in some drafting styles (see Chapter Eight, "Using the Right Style") the number of the first section is not displayed.

While the most important principle is to cover one topic per section, another important principle is to avoid making the section too long. How long is too long? There is no hard and fast answer to that question, but there are some useful rules of thumb.

There are several different ways to measure the length of a section. It can be measured by pages. James Craig Peacock suggested that a section should not be longer than four pages, though he was referring to pages in a bound book or pamphlet, not pages in a stack. It was a virtue, he felt, for readers not to have to turn more than one page to reach a section heading (from which they could get their bearings). James Craig Peacock, *Notes on Legislative Drafting* 10–17 (1961). This is the right idea, but it's not really clear how to apply it in practice. The pagination of a bill is not the same as the pagination of the Statutes at Large, which is not the same as the pagination of the United States Code.

The length of a section can also be measured by subsections. Peacock suggested that a section should not contain more than eight subsections, that is, should not contain subsections after subsection (h). It was a virtue, he felt, not to use the designation (i) for both a subsection (in which case it represents, in lowercase form, the letter I) and a clause (in which case it represents, in lowercase form, the Roman numeral for the number 1). Likewise, subsection (l) can be confused with paragraph (1), though that is less likely now, in the word-processing age, than it was in Peacock's time, the typewriter age (when typists were routinely taught to use the letter L, in lowercase form, to represent the number 1).

The precise boundaries Peacock suggested—four pages, subsection (h)—do not need to be followed, of course. But they are useful guides, and the ideas behind them make good sense. If your section has run on for more than four pages, or if it has run on past subsection (h), take stock. Perhaps you have the makings of two or more sections, rather than just one.

§ 7.30 Subdividing a Section into Smaller Units

In federal drafting, there is a single method for subdividing a section into smaller units. All the standard drafting styles use this method.

Sections are subdivided into two or more subsections; subsections are subdivided into two or more paragraphs; and so on. The smaller units below the section are—beginning with the first tier—subsection, paragraph, subparagraph, clause, and subclause. Units below a subclause are possible, but should be avoided. When used, they are called items (and subitems).

At each tier, the smaller unit is either numbered or lettered in a fixed manner. Each subsection has a lowercase letter; each paragraph an Arabic number;

each subparagraph a capital letter; each clause a lowercase Roman number; each subclause an uppercase Roman number. The letter or number is placed in parentheses. Thus:

> Subsections use (a), (b), (c) . . .
> Paragraphs use (1), (2), (3) . . .
> Subparagraphs use (A), (B), (C) . . .
> Clauses use (i), (ii), (iii) . . .
> Subclauses use (I), (II), (III) . . .

An item typically has a doubled lowercase letter: (aa), (bb), (cc), and so on; a subitem has a tripled lowercase letter.

This single method for subdividing did not spring into use fully formed, though it has been more or less standard since the 1920s.

The early Congresses generally did not use smaller units at all. When Congress did use a smaller unit, it typically used what a modern drafter would call an undesignated paragraph (discussed below). It was very rare for Congress to subdivide to a lower tier than that.

The reluctance to use smaller units began to change after the enactment of the Revised Statutes of 1873. By the 1880s, Congress was making use—if only sporadically—of several tiers of smaller units. Congress was also designating those units, though not in the way they are designated today.

An interesting example of the early use of designated smaller units is the Civil Service Reform Act (22 Stat. 403), commonly known as the Pendleton Act, which was enacted in 1883. That Act used several tiers of smaller units. Section 2 of that Act begins, "SEC. 2. That it shall be the duty of said commissioners:". At that point it is subdivided into one tier of smaller units—what a modern drafter would consider to be paragraphs. These paragraphs are designated "FIRST" through "FIFTH." The second paragraph begins, "SECOND. And, among other things, said rules shall provide and declare, as nearly as the conditions of good administration will warrant, as follows:". At that point the paragraph is further subdivided into another tier of smaller units—what a modern drafter would consider to be subparagraphs. These subparagraphs are designated "First" through "Eighth."

By 1961, the modern method of subdividing, described here, was established enough that James Craig Peacock could describe its characteristics matter-of-factly. See James Craig Peacock, *Notes on Legislative Drafting* 12 (1961).

In 2004, the Supreme Court cited Peacock's book, as well as several other later works, in taking judicial notice that "Congress ordinarily adheres to a hierarchical scheme in subdividing statutory sections." *Koons Buick Pontiac GMC, Inc. v. Nigh*, 543 U.S. 50 (2004). Now that the Court has formally taken notice of this method and used it as a source of meaning, other courts will follow suit. All the more reason for a drafter to learn the method and not deviate from it.

You do not need to use smaller units, of course. When to use smaller units is largely a matter of judgment. One drafter might draft a bill as one section with no smaller units; another might draft it as one section with five subsections; a third might draft it as five sections. Each approach might have some merit. What is important is that when you do subdivide, or don't, you do so for good reason.

In most cases, the reason to subdivide is simply to make the text easier to read. A series of smaller units is generally less taxing to read than a single block of undivided text. As a general rule of thumb, don't string more than four or five sentences together without subdividing in some manner.

In some cases, subdividing can actually make the text more clear. Subdivisions create structure, and structure is used by courts as a guide to meaning. For example, in *Jama v. Immigration & Customs Enforcement*, 543 U.S. 335 (2004), the Court examined the relationship among several clauses and concluded, "Each clause is distinct and ends with a period, strongly suggesting that each may be understood completely without reading any further." Subdividing helps the reader understand where one idea ends and another idea begins.

Earlier it was suggested that units below a subclause should be avoided. That suggestion might not be strong enough. Units below a subclause should be avoided at all costs. Smaller units do tend to make text easier to read, but you reach a point of diminishing returns. Many drafters aspire not to use units below a paragraph, but they tend to honor that aspiration in the breach. A more attainable rule of thumb is to not use units below a subparagraph.

§ 7.31 Referring to Smaller Units

A smaller unit can often be referred to in several different ways. The long way is to name the smaller unit and each successively larger unit ("Subparagraph (C) of paragraph (2) of subsection (a) of section 101 of title I of the X Act").

You can economize by collapsing the name of a smaller unit into the name of the immediately larger unit ("Paragraph (2)(C) of section 101(a) of title I of the X Act" is one possibility), or collapsing several times at once ("Section 101(a)(2)(C) of title I of the X Act"). When doing so, the collapsed name is always the name of the largest unit involved. (See further discussion in § 9.60.)

§ 7.32 Interlocked Units

An interlocked unit occurs when text begins at one tier but is completed at a lower tier. The beginning text is not grammatically complete except when read together with the lower text. (The converse is not necessarily true—the lower text can be grammatically complete by itself, though to understand its full meaning, it must be read together with the beginning text.)

The definition used here, and the term "interlocked unit" itself, are borrowed from Jack Stark. (See generally Jack Stark, *The Art of the Statute* 53–63 (1996).) A drafter in one of the Offices of Legislative Counsel would typically use a term such as "tabulation" or "tabulated list." Tabulation means that each item is "tabbed in" from the margin. As used here, an interlocked unit generally includes a tabulated list, but it also includes the beginning text. The term also includes undesignated, flush-left text after the tabulated list.

When used properly, an interlocked unit can clarify meaning. An interlocked unit can also make text simpler, shorter, and easier to read.

In federal drafting, there are two standard types of interlocked units. In one type the beginning text ends with a colon; in the other, with a dash. (The tabulated list that follows can be called a "colon list" or a "dash list.")

The two standard types of interlocked units are shown below.

> An interlocked unit containing a colon list is drafted as follows:
>
> (1) The beginning text typically includes "the following" or "as follows."
>
> (2) The beginning text ends with a colon.
>
> (3) Each lower-tier unit—
>
> (A) is tabbed in; and
>
> (B) begins with a capital letter.
>
> (4) Each lower-tier unit ends with a period.

> In an interlocked unit containing a dash list—
>
> (1) the beginning text ends with a dash;
>
> (2) each lower-tier unit—

(A) is tabbed in; and

(B) begins with a lowercase letter;

(3) the last lower-tier unit ends with a period;

(4) the second-to-last lower-tier unit ends with a semicolon and a conjunction (almost always "and" or "or"); and

(5) the other lower-tier units, if any, each end with a semicolon.

In both examples, the main interlocked unit also contains an interlocked unit at a lower tier. When one interlocked unit nests inside another, the lower-tier unit should usually be a dash list. Do not nest a colon list within a dash list; the multiple ending periods make it grammatically odd.

There are two important things to keep in mind when creating an interlocked unit.

First, the list within the interlocked unit should use parallel structure. Parallel structure, in turn, requires that each item in the list be of the same general order of ideas. Consider the following:

> Not later than January 1 of each year, the Secretary shall submit a report on the activities carried out under this section. The report shall—
>
> (1) cover the preceding fiscal year;
>
> (2) include a description of X;
>
> (3) contain an assessment about Y; and
>
> (4) be submitted to Congress.

This example is grammatically acceptable but is counterintuitive to the reader because it is not in parallel structure. Only paragraphs (2) and (3) are of the same general order of ideas—both relate to the contents of the report. The matter contained in paragraphs (1) and (4) should probably be moved into the beginning text instead.

Second, the interlocked unit should be drafted in a way that makes clear how many items on the list must be satisfied for the rule expressed in the unit as a whole to be satisfied. The answer could be that all of them must be satisfied, that any one or more of them must be satisfied, or that one and only one of them must be satisfied.

When referring to the parts of an interlocked unit, the items in the list can be referred to in the conventional way. In the above example, "(1) cover the preceding fiscal year;" is paragraph (1). As for the beginning text, most drafters refer to it as the "matter preceding paragraph (1)" (or whatever the first item of the list may be). An amendatory instruction might properly begin, "Subsection (a) is amended in the matter preceding paragraph (1) by striking . . .".

Though the two standard types of interlocked unit are the unit containing the dash list and the unit containing the colon list, you may encounter a variant type of interlocked unit from time to time, usually in an older law. Two variants are the dash list with commas and the dash list with flush matter (so named because the matter is printed flush to the left margin) at the end.

The dash list with commas is the same as a standard dash list, except that commas are used instead of semicolons. Though considered non-standard, using commas instead of semicolons sometimes makes the text more crisp and less stilted.

The dash list with flush matter at the end is also the same as a standard dash list, except that the last item does not end in a period. Instead, the last item ends with a comma, and the text drops down to the next line, reverts back to the margin used at the beginning of the interlocked unit, and is printed flush to that margin (that is, it is not indented in the way the first word of a prose paragraph is indented). The effect looks like this:

> Whoever—
>
> (1) does X;
>
> (2) does Y; or
>
> (3) does Z,
>
> shall be imprisoned not more than 5 years, fined under title 18, United States Code, or both.

While this sort of effect can be tempting, avoid the temptation. The conventional wisdom among experienced drafters is that it usually creates more problems than it's worth.

Using flush matter at the end creates several types of organizational problems. First, how do you refer to it? Most drafters call it the "matter at the end" or the "matter following paragraph (3)" (or whatever the last item of the list may be).

Second, how do you subdivide it? In the above example, suppose that you wanted to subdivide the matter at the end like so:

Whoever—
  (1) does X;
  (2) does Y; or
  (3) does Z,
shall be—
  (?) imprisoned not more than 5 years;
  (?) fined under title 18, United States Code; or
  (?) both.

These units designated by question marks—what are they? They simply don't fit into the standard scheme of organization. They aren't smaller units within paragraph (3); that is to say, they aren't subparagraphs. They seem to be paragraphs, but they aren't parallel with paragraphs (1), (2), and (3). What sort of designations belong where the question marks are—should they be (4) through (6)? (A) through (C)? (1) through (3)? Each set of options has its own set of problems. Usually it's best to avoid this format altogether. One alternative is as follows:

(a) Whoever does W shall be—
  (1) imprisoned not more than 5 years;
  (2) fined under title 18, United States Code; or
  (3) both.
(b) For purposes of subsection (a), the term "W" means—
  (1) X;
  (2) Y; or
  (3) Z.

Using flush matter at the end can also be unclear—in some contexts, a reader can be confused into thinking that the matter at the end is merely a continuation of the last item, rather than a continuation of each item. To use an example inspired by Elliot Chabot in an online article, "The Effect of Margins on Legislative Drafting," *The Compleat Internet Researcher* (created June 8, 1997), consider the following three versions of a provision:

(c) SPECIAL GRANTS.—The Secretary of Agriculture may make the following grants:
  (1) Grants of up to two years duration—
    (A) to land-grant colleges and universities; and

(B) to State agricultural experiment stations.

(2) Grants of up to five years duration—

(A) to States; and

(B) to local governments. These grants shall be made without regard to matching funds.

(c) SPECIAL GRANTS.—The Secretary of Agriculture may make the following grants:

(1) Grants of up to two years duration—

(A) to land-grant colleges and universities; and

(B) to State agricultural experiment stations.

(2) Grants of up to five years duration—

(A) to States; and

(B) to local governments.

These grants shall be made without regard to matching funds.

(c) SPECIAL GRANTS.—The Secretary of Agriculture may make the following grants:

(1) Grants of up to two years duration—

(A) to land-grant colleges and universities; and

(B) to State agricultural experiment stations.

(2) Grants of up to five years duration—

(A) to States; and

(B) to local governments.

These grants shall be made without regard to matching funds.

These three provisions differ only in the placement of the final sentence. The final sentence is matter at the end, but at the end of what? Depending on how the margins fall on a particular printed page, the words "These grants" could appear to refer only to grants under paragraph (2)(B), or to grants under paragraph (2), or to grants under subsection (c). Generally, to use matter at the end is to rely too heavily on margins for meaning.

§ 7.33 Undesignated Units

An undesignated unit is a unit that does not have an alphabetical or numeric designation, making it difficult to refer to the unit in a narrow and specific way. Modern drafters recognize that there are few, if any, advantages to leaving a unit undesignated, and generally avoid doing so.

There are two types of undesignated units still in use: the undesignated paragraph and the undesignated item.

In an appropriations bill, the undesignated paragraph is the principal unit of organization. This type of unit typically has a heading, and it can be identified by describing the heading, such as "the matter under the heading 'OPERATION AND MAINTENANCE, MARINE CORPS.' " It can also be identified by describing the subject matter, such as "the paragraph relating to operation and maintenance, Marine Corps." These two descriptions both apply to the undesignated paragraph in the Department of Defense Appropriations Act, 2001 (Public Law 106-259; 114 Stat. 659) that provides as follows:

> OPERATION AND MAINTENANCE, MARINE CORPS
>
> For expenses, not otherwise provided for, necessary for the operation and maintenance of the Marine Corps, as authorized by law, $2,778,758,000.

In a measure other than an appropriations bill, an undesignated paragraph is used occasionally in traditional style and code style (for more on styles, see Chapter Eight, "Using the Right Style"). It is positioned and formatted in the same manner as a subsection, except that it has no designation and no heading.

For an example of an undesignated paragraph within a section, see section 659 of title 18, United States Code, which provides as follows:

> **§ 659. Interstate or foreign shipments by carrier; State prosecutions**
>
> Whoever embezzles, steals, or unlawfully takes, carries away, or conceals, or by fraud or deception obtains from any pipeline system, railroad car, wagon, motortruck, or other vehicle, or from any tank or storage facility, station, station house, platform or depot or from any steamboat, vessel, or wharf, or from any aircraft, air terminal, airport, aircraft terminal or air navigation facility with intent to convert to his own use any goods or chattels moving as or which are a part of or which constitute an interstate or foreign shipment of freight, express, or other property; or
>
> Whoever buys or receives or has in his possession any such goods or chattels, knowing the same to have been embezzled or stolen; or
>
> Whoever embezzles, steals, or unlawfully takes, carries away, or by fraud or deception obtains with intent to convert to his own use any baggage which shall have come into the possession of any common car-

rier for transportation in interstate or foreign commerce or breaks into, steals, takes, carries away, or conceals any of the contents of such baggage, or buys, receives, or has in his possession any such baggage or any article therefrom of whatever nature, knowing the same to have been embezzled or stolen; or

Whoever embezzles, steals, or unlawfully takes by any fraudulent device, scheme, or game, from any railroad car, bus, vehicle, steamboat, vessel, or aircraft operated by any common carrier moving in interstate or foreign commerce or from any passenger thereon any money, baggage, goods, or chattels, or whoever buys, receives, or has in his possession any such money, baggage, goods, or chattels, knowing the same to have been embezzled or stolen—

Shall in each case be fined under this title or imprisoned not more than ten years, or both; but if the amount or value of such money, baggage, goods or chattels does not exceed $1,000, he shall be fined under this title or imprisoned not more than one year, or both.

The offense shall be deemed to have been committed not only in the district where the violation first occurred, but also in any district in which the defendant may have taken or been in possession of the said money, baggage, goods, or chattels.

The carrying or transporting of any such money, freight, express, baggage, goods, or chattels in interstate or foreign commerce, knowing the same to have been stolen, shall constitute a separate offense and subject the offender to the penalties under this section for unlawful taking, and the offense shall be deemed to have been committed in any district into which such money, freight, express, baggage, goods, or chattels shall have been removed or into which the same shall have been brought by such offender.

To establish the interstate or foreign commerce character of any shipment in any prosecution under this section the waybill or other shipping document of such shipment shall be prima facie evidence of the place from which and to which such shipment was made. The removal of property from a pipeline system which extends interstate shall be prima facie evidence of the interstate character of the shipment of the property.

A judgment of conviction or acquittal on the merits under the laws of any State shall be a bar to any prosecution under this section for the same act or acts. Nothing contained in this section shall be construed as indicating an intent on the part of Congress to occupy the field in which provisions of this section operate to the exclusion of State laws on the same subject matter, nor shall any provision of this section be construed as invalidating any provision of State law unless such provision is inconsistent with any of the purposes of this section or any provision thereof.

For an example of an undesignated paragraph within a subsection (and indeed, within a numbered paragraph), see section 84 of title 28, United States Code, which provides as follows:

§ 84. California

California is divided into four judicial districts to be known as the Northern, Eastern, Central, and Southern Districts of California.

NORTHERN DISTRICT

(a) The Northern District comprises the counties of Alameda, Contra Costa, Del Norte, Humboldt, Lake, Marin, Mendocino, Monterey, Napa, San Benito, Santa Clara, Santa Cruz, San Francisco, San Mateo, and Sonoma.

Court for the Northern District shall be held at Eureka, Oakland, San Francisco, and San Jose.

EASTERN DISTRICT

(b) The Eastern District comprises the counties of Alpine, Amador, Butte, Calaveras, Colusa, El Dorado, Fresno, Glenn, Inyo, Kern, Kings, Lassen, Madera, Mariposa, Merced, Modoc, Mono, Nevada, Placer, Plumas, Sacramento, San Joaquin, Shasta, Sierra, Siskiyou, Solano, Stanislaus, Sutter, Tehama, Trinity, Tulare, Tuolumne, Yolo, and Yuba.

Court for the Eastern District shall be held at Fresno, Redding, and Sacramento.

CENTRAL DISTRICT

(c) The Central District comprises 3 divisions.

(1) The Eastern Division comprises the counties of Riverside and San Bernardino.

Court for the Eastern Division shall be held at a suitable site in the city of Riverside, the city of San Bernardino, or not more than 5 miles from the boundary of either such city.

(2) The Western Division comprises the counties of Los Angeles, San Luis Obispo, Santa Barbara, and Ventura.

Court for the Western Division shall be held at Los Angeles.

(3) The Southern Division comprises Orange County.

Court for the Southern Division shall be held at Santa Ana.

SOUTHERN DISTRICT

(d) The Southern District comprises the counties of Imperial and San Diego.

Court for the Southern District shall be held at San Diego.

An undesignated paragraph can be identified by describing its place in sequence: "the first undesignated paragraph," "the fifth undesignated paragraph," and so on. In modern practice, the unit would typically be drafted as a subsection or paragraph (as appropriate) rather than as an undesignated paragraph.

An undesignated item is a unit used occasionally in the lower text (that is, the list) of an interlocked unit. Though it is almost always better practice to give each element in a list its own designation, there are cases in which designations just add clutter. An undesignated item can be identified by describing the subject matter, such as "the item relating to the Under Secretary of the Air Force."

For an effective use of undesignated items, see section 5315 of title 5, United States Code, which lists the dozens of positions in Level IV of the Executive Schedule. It begins as follows:

§ 5315. Positions at level IV

Level IV of the Executive Schedule applies to the following positions, for which the annual rate of basic pay shall be the rate determined with respect to such level under chapter 11 of title 2, as adjusted by section 5318 of this title:

Deputy Administrator of General Services.

Associate Administrator of the National Aeronautics and Space Administration.

Assistant Administrators, Agency for International Development (6).

Regional Assistant Administrators, Agency for International Development (4).

Under Secretary of the Air Force.

[many more undesignated items follow]

§7.40 Grouping Sections into Big Levels

When a bill has many sections, it can be useful to group sections into big levels. Regardless of the drafting style used, the principal big level is always the title.

Titles can be subdivided into other big levels, such as parts or subtitles, and further subdivided into other big levels, such as subparts or chapters. The method for subdividing a title into other big levels, and the lettering or numbering scheme used in designating those levels, varies by drafting style (and is not always consistently followed within a drafting style, though, of course, it should be consistently followed within a single act). For each style, the most typical method for subdividing, and the lettering and numbering scheme used for designating, are as follows:

Traditional Style	**Code Style**	**Revenue Style and Modified Revenue Style**
TITLE I	TITLE 1	TITLE I
Subtitle B	Subtitle B	Subtitle B
PART 3	PART III	CHAPTER 3
Subpart D	Subpart D	Subchapter D
CHAPTER 5	CHAPTER 5	PART V
SUBCHAPTER VI	SUBCHAPTER VI	Subpart F

In addition, a group of titles can be organized into a big level called a division, though divisions usually appear only in very long, complex bills. Typically, divisions are used as an unplanned expedience, such as when several bills need to be stitched together quickly at the end of a session to form an omnibus bill; each can be assigned a division without having to undergo a systematic reformatting and renumbering. In a very few cases the use of divisions is planned, as typically happens with the annual national defense authorization act.

Not every section needs to be part of a big level. In many cases a bill with titles will have, before the first title, one or more sections that apply to the entire bill, such as a short title, table of contents, findings, or definitions. Similarly, a title may have, before the first subtitle, a short title or table of sections that applies to that title.

A big level always has a heading. The heading always contains the name and designation of the level and typically also includes descriptive words after a dash. For example, "TITLE II—RESEARCH, DEVELOPMENT, TEST, AND EVALUATION," or "Subtitle A—Army."

The sections within a title are usually numbered in the hundreds: Sections in title I are 101, 102, 103, and so on; sections in title II begin with 201. Sections preceding the first title begin with section 1.

If a title is subdivided into subtitles or other sublevels, section numbers are usually assigned in blocks so that the number of the first section of each sublevel ends with 1. For example, title III of a bill might contain a section 301 (short title), followed by a subtitle A beginning with section 311, a subtitle B beginning with section 321, and so on.

Even when titles are grouped into divisions, it is best for the designations used for sections and titles to run through the bill from lowest to highest. If Division A ends with title VI, division B should begin with title VII (or a higher designation) rather than with title I again. A bill that uses the same section number or title number twice is likely to cause confusion. When an omnibus bill is thrown together hastily at the end of a session this drafting principle (and many others) may be ignored, but that is the exception, not the rule.

In any numbering scheme, avoid the temptation to use unnecessarily large numbers. Title I of the Violent Crime Control and Law Enforcement Act of 1994 begins with section 10001 rather than 101; do not follow suit.

Do not be afraid to leave gaps in your numbering scheme, whether you are numbering sections or big levels. If you do leave gaps, try to do so under a logical principle. For example, in part I of title 18, United States Code (specifying a wide variety of federal crimes), chapters were designated using odd numbers only. When a numbering scheme for a unit (such as a section) has gaps, other units of that type can be inserted more easily and cleanly; you may not have to redesignate other units to make room and may not have to invent a nonstandard designation, such as "1074g."

§ 7.50 Using Definitions

Every ordinary word in the English language is already defined in a general dictionary. Every term of art is already defined in a specialized dictionary.

However, a definition can help make the draft simple, ordinary, brief, consistent, and readable. A definition, in other words, is a device to better arrange and organize your draft.

Use a definition to narrow meaning. If a term you want to use has several meanings and you want to be clear which meaning applies in your bill, specify what the term "means." The usual formula is, "The term 'person' means a natural person."

Use a definition to broaden meaning. If a term you want to use has one general meaning and you want the term to cover a little bit more than the general meaning, specify what the term "includes." The usual formula is, "The term 'State' includes the District of Columbia." This is sometimes known as a "partial definition" because the definition does not provide the entire meaning, but only one part of the meaning.

Those two formulas will cover almost all the definitions you ever need to draft. In rare cases it works best to use both together ("The term 'X' means Y and includes Z"), or to use some other variant, such as "does not include."

Whether you use a definition to narrow or broaden meaning, the underlying reason to use the definition is, again, to help you arrange and organize the draft. When used properly, a definition saves you from stating a complicated concept over and over; it allows you to package the concept in a simple term and use that term repeatedly. This can be called a shorthand definition because the defined term is simply a shorthand way of using a longer expression.

Do not put a substantive rule in a definition. A definition should be a stipulation, not a command or a rule of discretion. Do not say, for example, "The term 'X' means X and, if the Secretary so determines, includes Y."

Make note of terms already defined in your draft or in law. Many definitions that apply to all federal law are in chapter 1 of title 1, United States Code; the definition of "fiscal year" is in section 1102 of title 31, United States Code. Some titles of the Code have definitions that apply throughout that title.

The United States Code contains a list of all the definitions used anywhere in the Code. If you know where to look, the list is easy to find; if you don't know where to look, you likely won't find it. (Turn to the index to the Code and look under the index entry for "DEFINITIONS," in the volume that contains the entries beginning with the letter D.)

You can borrow a definition from elsewhere: "The term 'Secretary concerned' has the meaning given that term in section 101 of title 10, United States Code." Before you link your term to a term defined elsewhere, ponder what would happen to your term if the definition used elsewhere were later amended. Most likely, the later amendment would have a ripple effect on your term as well. (But see § 9.61, "Incorporating Other Laws by Reference.") Does that serve the policy? You may be better off cutting-and-pasting a definition from elsewhere than simply incorporating it by reference.

Do not define a term to mean something it does not ordinarily mean. Do not, for example, define "dog" to include "cat"—it is at best confusing and at worst unethical. Henry Thring described an 1872 law that, bizarrely, defined the term "new building" to mean "any building pulled or burnt down to or within ten feet from the surface of the adjoining ground." Henry Thring, *Practical Legislation* 3 (1902).

A definition does not have to be placed in a separate section for definitions. The general principle is that a definition should be placed where it is of most use to the reader. Terms that are used throughout the bill should generally be placed in a section of definitions; terms that are used only in one section should generally be placed in that section.

Always remember to specify the scope of the definition. The phrase "In this section" (or title, or act, or other unit) is short and sweet, but some drafters use "For the purposes of this section," or some other formula.

In a list of definitions, the convention is to include the lead-in words "The term"; thus:

> In this Act:
>
> (1) The term "canine" means dog.
>
> (2) The term "State" includes the District of Columbia.

While the words "The term" seem to be surplusage (and, being idle, should be cast out), they actually do have a job to do: They help avoid confusion about whether a term is to be capitalized. In the example above, it is clear that the defined terms are State (first letter capitalized) and canine (first letter not capitalized). Without the lead-in words, the first letter of canine would need to be capitalized, and it becomes unclear whether the defined terms are Canine and State or canine and state or something else.

Using the lead-in words also lets you more cleanly use an expression like "except that such term does not include . . . ."

In some cases it makes sense to create a shorthand definition using a parenthetical phrase after the longer expression is first used: For example, "The Secretary of Energy (in this section referred to as the 'Secretary') shall . . . ." This works best when the definition occurs in a prominent place and the bill is short. You want the reader to be able to find the definition and refer back to it easily.

Similarly, if a term has a special meaning, it may make sense to call the reader's attention to that fact with a cross-reference to the definition: For example, "For each unit of local government (as defined in section ___), the Secretary shall . . . ."

There is no consensus about whether a section of definitions should go toward the beginning of a bill or toward the end. The Offices of Legislative Counsel are split—the Senate office favors the former, the House office the latter. Both offices agree that definitions should be placed where they are of most use to the reader, but they disagree over where that is.

Perhaps the best approach is to follow the general principle for organizing and arranging: Put the most important parts at the beginning, the least important parts toward the end. If the definitions are very important to the bill, put them at the beginning; if not, put them at the end. (Above all, though, don't put them in the middle—no reader expects them there.) Ultimately, the House position seems more compelling. If a definition is so important that it belongs at the beginning, it probably is doing too much work. The major message of your bill should be presented in major substantive provisions, not in definitions.

The length of your section of definitions is a factor, too. To go at the beginning, the definitions should be important and the section should be short. A reader should not have to turn through pages of definitions to get to the main message. A section of definitions is more or less analogous to a glossary, and in any other form of writing the glossary typically goes at the end.

§ 7.60 Arranging and Drafting Commonly Used Provisions

There are a handful of provisions that tend to recur from bill to bill. Many bills have a short title, for example. Other provisions typically encountered are findings, savings clauses, severability clauses, and effective dates.

Some of these provisions (such as a short title) are typically placed at the beginning of a bill; others are typically placed at the end (such as an effective date). One possible arrangement might go something like this:

Short title
Table of contents
Statement of findings, purposes, or policy
General rules
Special rules
Temporary or transitional rules
Administrative and enforcement rules
Technical or conforming amendments
Savings clause
Severability clause
Effective date

§ 7.61 Short Title

A short title is a short, official nickname for an act. The purpose of a short title is to identify an act in a catchy way, both when it is a bill and, later, when it becomes law.

Deciding on a short title is almost purely a political function. A drafter should avoid playing a role in the process.

There are some general parameters for short titles, however, and a drafter should let the client know when a proposed short title goes outside those parameters.

The conventional form for a provision establishing a short title is as follows:

> This Act may be cited as the "Social Security Act".

Notice that the word "the" is not within the quotation marks and is not capitalized. If it were, we would have to refer to the Act as the The Social Security Act.

The short title should be short. The whole point is to make it easy to remember and refer to the bill. A short title longer than six or seven words is probably too long.

The short title should include the word "Act," unless it is a resolution (such as the War Powers Resolution). Occasionally a short title is phrased in some other manner, as with "Megan's Law" or "Authorization for Use of Military Force."

Avoid including a year, such as the Homeland Security Act of 2002. The year adds little if any value and comes at a high cost: Drafters must always remember that the words "of 2002" are part of the short title. A year may be appropriate if the bill is annual or periodical (as with an appropriations act or a major authorization act) or if the name has been used before (as with the Civil Rights Act of 1991).

Years can be misleading. There are quite a few cases in which a law with a year in the short title was not enacted until the following year; the short title is one year too early. The No Child Left Behind Act of 2001, for example, was enacted in 2002. And then there is the Atomic Energy Act of 1954, which was enacted in 1946; the short title is eight years too late. (There was an Atomic Energy Act of 1946, enacted in 1946. When Congress revised national atomic energy policy in 1954, it did not repeal the 1946 Act, and it did not make discrete amendments to the 1946 Act, either; instead, Congress rewrote the entire 1946 Act—including the short title of that Act—through an "amendment to read as follows." The curious result is a law originally enacted in 1946 that, as amended, has a short title dated 1954.)

Avoid also using a form that expressly incorporates an acronym, as with the Uniting and Strengthening America by Providing Appropriate Tools Required to Intercept and Obstruct Terrorism (USA PATRIOT ACT) Act of 2001. From a drafting point of view, it would have been better practice to give this Act two short titles:

> This Act may be cited as the "[long version]" or the "USA PATRIOT Act".

Then everyone could refer to this Act by a short title that was in fact short and sensible.

Just as a single act can have more than one short title (as above), different parts within an act can have their own short titles. An act with several titles, for example, may have an overall title and also a separate short title for each title. (The short title should still refer to an act, however. Say, "This subtitle may be cited as the 'X Act,' not "This subtitle may be cited as the 'X Subtitle.' ") Having multiple nested short titles is not a particularly good idea and should not be encouraged when drafting a bill from scratch, but if a bill that once had independent existence (and political support) is appended to another bill on the way to enactment, the separate short title may provide some value, if only political.

There are some devices that are almost, but not quite, short titles. With a true short title, the authority to use it in a citation is provided by law; the nickname is the official one. A short title is sometimes known as a statutory name.

A popular name is a short title by custom and usage rather than by law. The Administrative Procedure Act was a short title, but that Act was repealed and codified into title 5, United States Code. That part of the Code is still popularly known as the Administrative Procedure Act, but it no longer has a short title. It would be sloppy to cite to it directly as the Administrative Procedure Act, but a parenthetical phrase, such as "(popularly known as the Administrative Procedure Act)," may help inform the reader.

One of the volumes at the end of the United States Code contains a table of popular names. This table lists every short title and popular name in general use. A link to the Table of Popular Names can be found at *<www.LegislativeDrafter.com>*.

Then there are other devices that are somewhat like short titles and popular names but are considered too informal to be considered popular names. A bill may acquire a slang nickname, such as the "Nunn-Lugar bill" or the "hamburger bill," and that nickname can continue to be used informally even after the bill becomes law (and even though the bill may have an actual short title). Do not cite the law directly by this sort of nickname, but a parenthetical phrase, such as "(commonly referred to as the 'hamburger Act')," may help inform the reader.

In a few cases a drafter appears to have tried to draft a short title and failed. Subtitle A of title XVII of the Violent Crime Control and Law Enforcement Act of 1994 does not have a short title, but it does have a subtitle heading as follows: "Subtitle A—Jacob Wetterling Crimes Against Children and Sexually Violent Offender Registration Act." This is a heading, not a short title, and does not appear in the Table of Popular Names of the U.S. Code.

A short title should go at the very beginning. It is not the most important part of the bill, of course, but it is very useful information and is short enough to not get too much in the way of the most important part. Note, however, that the short title of an appropriations act is traditionally placed at the end, and there are rare cases in which a short title of an act not relating to appropriations was placed at the end—the Classified Information Procedures Act (18 U.S.C. app. 3) is one example.

§ 7.62 Authorization of Appropriations

An authorization of appropriations is among the most misunderstood provisions in federal law. The effect of an authorization of appropriations is to set a limit on the amount of money an appropriations committee can appropriate for the activity to which the authorization relates. If the client does not want to set a limit, an authorization of appropriations is generally not needed.

Typically, an authorization of appropriations sets forth the purpose, the official or agency, the amount, the fiscal year, and the restrictions (if any), but the order is not fixed.

The Constitution does not require an authorization of appropriations; it requires only an appropriation. Accordingly, an authorization of appropriations is enforced not by law but by the rules of the House and Senate, which generally provide that any member may object when an appropriations committee proposes to draw more money from the Treasury for a program than the authorization of appropriations for that program allows.

If there is no authorization of appropriations, there is no limit, and thus no meaningful ability of a member to object on that ground.

Legislation establishing an agency or authorizing the agency to carry out activities is, in and of itself, an implied authority to appropriate whatever is needed. Specific language authorizing "such sums as may be necessary" is redundant and not needed.

There are, however, some cases in which other laws make an authorization of appropriations necessary. Some laws directly prohibit the obligation of appropriated funds unless an authorization of appropriations has also been enacted for those funds. See, for example, section 313 of the Foreign Relations Authorization Act, Fiscal Years 1994 and 1995 (Public Law 103-236), which provides that "any funds appropriated for the purposes of broadcasting . . . shall not be available for obligation or expenditure . . . unless such funds are appropriated pursuant to an authorization of appropriations."

Also, some laws require an annual or periodic authorization of appropriations. See, for example, section 660 of the Department of Energy Organization Act (42 U.S.C. 7270).

For further discussion of authorizations and appropriations, see *Congressional Deskbook*, Chapter Nine, "Federal Budget Process," especially § 9.80, "Authorization and Appropriation Processes."

§ 7.63 Severability and Non-severability

To say that a law is severable is to say that if a court rules that part of a law is unconstitutional, the court should allow the remainder to continue in effect. That is, the court should sever the unconstitutional part from the constitutional part, discarding the former and saving the latter.

Severability is the default rule. A court will save the valid parts "unless it is evident that the Legislature would not have enacted" those parts independent of the invalid parts. *Immigration and Naturalization Service v. Chadha*, 462 U.S. 919, 931 (1983). A court will not be able to save the valid parts in some cases; it can save the valid parts only "if what is left is fully operative as a law." *Alaska Airlines, Inc. v. Brock*, 480 U.S. 678, 684 (1987).

Because severability is already the default rule, a bill does not need severability language. Severability language would bolster the default rule to some extent, but is almost certainly overkill.

Non-severability, by contrast, means that if one part of a statute is invalid, some or all of the valid parts must also be held invalid. See *Zobel v. Williams*, 457 U.S. 55, 65 (1982). If non-severability is what the client wants, language that specifies what is severable and what is not should be included.

§ 7.64 Applicability or Effective Date

In most cases you do not need to specify an effective date. A federal law takes effect on its date of enactment, and that is ordinarily what the client wants.

Include an effective date provision only if the act is to take effect on a different date. Specifying a later date (delayed effectiveness) is normally not a problem; specifying an earlier date (retroactive effectiveness) can cause constitutional problems, particularly if there are individual rights at stake.

The more important policy question is usually not when the act should take effect, but to what situations the act should apply—particularly to situations that are ongoing when the act takes effect.

If the act changes the rules of civil procedure, for example, do the new rules apply to lawsuits already underway, or only to lawsuits filed after the date of enactment?

Another issue sometimes worth considering is where the act should apply. A law ordinarily applies only within the territorial jurisdiction of the United States, that is, within the states and territories. In many situations, Congress has enough power under one or more clauses in the Constitution (the Necessary and Proper Clause, the Foreign Commerce Clause, and certain other clauses) to provide for a federal law to apply outside the United States. Even when the power does exist, however, the courts generally assume the law should not apply outside the United States unless Congress clearly provides that it should. The question, as always, is what the client wants.

Chapter 8

Using the Right Style

I should apologize perhaps for the style of this bill. I dislike the verbose & intricate style of the modern English statutes, and in our revised code I endeavored to restore it to the simple one of the ancient statutes, in such original bills as I drew in that work. I suppose the reformation has not been acceptable, as it has been little followed.

Thomas Jefferson, letter to Joseph C. Cabell, September 9, 1817, in Andrew A. Lipscomb (ed.), *Writings of Thomas Jefferson* 17:417-18 (1904)

The complaint is about your statute books . . . They are too plain. I have read many, many pages of them: and I found that I could understand all that I read or nearly all. That is not the sort of thing that one ought to find in any well-mannered statute book.

Sir Robert Megarry, address to the Bars of Alberta and British Columbia, 1978, as reported in 5 *Commonwealth Law Bulletin* 963 (1979)

Using the Right Style

Chapter 8

§ 8.00 Introduction

The style of a measure is its look and feel. As used here, "style" has nothing to do with the actual words used. Instead, it has everything to do with how those words are placed on the page.

A style is a combination of elements that affect the way a text is displayed. In drafting, the purpose of a style is to make the text easier to read and easier to use. Over the years, Congress has used several different styles, each intended to make the text more readable and usable. The modern Congress tends to produce bills that are very large and very complex, making them very hard to read and use. Though style alone can't make the reader's task easy, it can make it easier.

Though every drafter could use a unique personal style, there is great value in consistency. When all bills are in the same style, the reader can concentrate on the substance of the text without being distracted by the presentation.

The same principle applies to drafters. When more than one drafter works on the same bill, they can avoid haggling over style and can focus on substance. Likewise, when one drafter prepares an amendment to a bill or law drafted by someone else, the task is easier if the base text is in a common style.

For those reasons, drafters should learn the styles in use in federal drafting and draft within those styles.

Since the 1980s, the style used for almost every freestanding measure has been modified revenue style (see § 8.50). This is the style used for most purposes by the Offices of Legislative Counsel of both chambers (and, thus, is often known as "office style").

For examples of the various styles, see Appendix Eight.

§ 8.10 The Style of the Early Congresses (Style of 1789)

The original style used by Congress—that is, the style used by the early Congresses, also called the "style of 1789"—does not have much in common with modified revenue style (§ 8.50). Simply put, the early Congresses did not make many concessions to the reader. As with modified revenue style, a bill was divided into sections. And that is where the similarities end.

Some of the notable elements of this original style are the following:

Undesignated First Section. Though the first Congress generally designated the first section of a bill as "Section 1.", by 1806 this practice had fallen into disuse; a bill began with the enacting clause of the first section and proceeded right into the text of the first section. Each section that followed the first section was designated (though in abbreviated form: "Sec. 2."). The result was curious and confusing, because to a casual reader the bill appeared to begin (after some lead-in language) with section 2.

Multiple Enacting Clauses. The early Congresses generally gave each section its own enacting words, which appeared immediately after the section designation. The first section had a full enacting clause and each section after that had an abridged enacting clause—usually "And be it further enacted," though there was no standard form. The use of multiple enacting clauses persisted until 1873, when the Revised Statutes abolished the use of an enacting clause in any section other than the first.

Provisoes. The early Congresses made regular use of provisoes. A proviso was a device carried over from English practice. It appears to have come into being as a variant form of the enacting clause: Instead of enacting words such as "Be it enacted," some laws would use providing words such as "Be it provided." For example, section 9 of the first Naval Act (1 Stat. 350) begins with the hybrid words "Provided always, and be it further enacted,". The text following the providing words could either restrict or enlarge the meaning of all the preceding text of the Act. (In the case of the first Naval Act, for example, the proviso of section 9 operated to terminate the entire Act (and, in effect, abolish the navy) if the United States made peace with the pirates of Algiers.)

While an enacting clause was generally used only at the beginning of a section, a proviso was sometimes used within the text of a section, to restrict or enlarge the meaning of all the preceding text of the section.

In modern practice, do not use a proviso. Provisoes are archaic, misused, and ambiguous, and have been archaic, misused, and ambiguous for more than a century. As the Supreme Court explained in 1888: "The difficulty . . . arises from the doubt attached to the meaning of the term 'provided.' The general purpose of a proviso, as is well known, is to except the clause covered by it from the general provisions of a statute, or from some provisions of it, or to qualify the operation of the statute in some particular. But it is often used in other senses." *George Railroad and Banking Co. v. Smith*, 128 U.S. 174, 181 (1888).

No Headings. The early Congresses generally did not use headings.

No Subdivisions. The early Congresses generally did not subdivide sections into smaller units. Instead, a section was a block of text consisting of one or more sentences. The sentences tended to run on at great length, with semicolons and colons used freely and periods used sparingly. The first sentence of a section typically began (immediately after the enacting words) with the word "That." In some cases, sentences after the first also began with the word "That."

When a section included a very long list—such as in a tariff bill setting forth a list of commercial items and the tariff associated with each, or in an appropriations bill setting forth a list of budget items and the appropriation associated with each—each item would start on a new line, in effect creating what a modern drafter might call an undesignated paragraph. For an example of this approach, see the first Tariff Act (1 Stat. 24).

The style of 1789 remained the style of choice for nearly a hundred years. Though it is no longer in use today, it is the parent style of all the styles that remain in use. There are two different lines of descent: One line leads to the style used in appropriations legislation (§ 8.20), while the other line (§ 8.30) leads to all the styles used in substantive legislation.

§ 8.20 Appropriations Style

The power of the purse is likely the mightiest power that Congress possesses. That power is tightly held and closely guarded by the appropriations committees. For that reason, appropriations bills are typically drafted within the appropriations committees without direct assistance from the Offices of Legislative Counsel. New appropriations acts are needed each year, but in many cases only the dollar amounts need to be changed. Because of these institutional factors—closely guarded drafting, little need for new language—the style used for appropriations acts has been more or less frozen in time.

Appropriations style was settled by the 1840s and has changed very little since then. Appropriations acts generally used the style of the early Congresses; as of the 1790s they set forth appropriations in lists of undesignated items, and as of the 1840s they used headings to divide appropriations into categories (for example, "Legislative Branch").

In appropriations style, the act begins with an enacting clause followed by undesignated matter specifying that "the following sums are appropriated . . . namely:". What follows is a series of undesignated paragraphs. Typically, there are so many undesignated paragraphs that they are grouped into titles.

The use of undesignated paragraphs, rather than sections, as the principal unit of organization is the single most notable feature of appropriations style. While sections are used, they typically are relegated to one part of the bill.

Stylistically, these undesignated paragraphs are like coelacanths—strange creatures from an earlier era. In many respects they follow the style of the early Congresses. Though they do not each contain an enacting clause, they use complex sentences, make frequent use of provisoes, and rarely contain further subdivisions.

When sections appear in an appropriations act, they typically appear under a heading such as "Administrative Provisions." The style used in drafting these sections is traditional style, except that section headings are not used.

Another notable feature of appropriations style is the placement of the short title at the end rather than the beginning.

Many drafters consider appropriations style to be not a "real" style at all. But it is a style—one that has been methodically and consistently used since the 1800s.

Some may wonder how appropriations acts came to be drafted in such an odd style. To understand appropriations style, you need to understand a little history.

In the early Congresses, a typical appropriations act had only one section. The section declared that appropriations were made and then listed the line items and their amounts. The section was undesignated, but it was the "first section" nonetheless. Sometimes an appropriations act had more than one section, and these would be designated ("Sec. 2," and so on).

Over time, the number of line items grew long enough to be organized under headings. Then the number of headings grew long enough to be organized under titles. All the while, the line items had grown into rambling yarns laced with exceptions and provisoes. What had been the "first section" had become overstuffed. At some point, people stopped adding sections at the end of the first section and started inserting them into a separate heading within the first section instead. The undesignated paragraph had overtaken the section as the principal unit of organization.

In modern practice no one refers to the vast bulk of an appropriations bill as the "first section." Though that would be correct in an evolutionary sense, it would be incongruous, like calling a hand a fin. And, in any event, it would be confusing, because in modern practice the term "section" has been given, in appropriations bills, to other subdivisions within the bill.

As a drafter, you probably will never be called upon to draft a freestanding measure in appropriations style. There is some chance that you may be called upon to draft a measure that amends an appropriations act, or to prepare a floor or markup amendment for an appropriations bill. In that event, the best approach is to review the base act or bill and try not to depart too radically from the style it uses.

§ 8.30 Traditional Style

The original style that evolved down one path into appropriations style (§ 8.20) also evolved down a separate path into the other styles used in drafting today. The first of these styles to develop is called "traditional style" (and sometimes "old style" or "archaic style"). Many laws still on the books are in traditional style, and there are times when a new measure—most commonly, a concurrent resolution or a simple resolution—is drafted in traditional style. (See also discussion in § 8.50.)

The evolution of the original style into traditional style began in the 1870s and continued through the 1940s. It was not a smooth transition, but one that proceeded in fits and starts.

In traditional style, each section of the act begins with the designation "Sec." followed by the section number (for example, "Sec. 2."). The text of the section begins immediately afterward, on the same line.

The use of section headings is optional. If a section heading is used, it is centered on the line above the section designation.

A special rule applies to the first section of the bill. The section designation is either spelled out (thus, "Section 1." rather than "Sec. 1.") or is omitted entirely. If the section designation is omitted entirely, a section heading is not used, subsections are not used, and the text of the section begins immediately after the enacting clause, prefixed by the word "That."

When the first section is designated "Section 1.", it is referred to as "section 1"; when the first section's designation is omitted, it is referred to as the "first section."

§ 8.40 Revenue Style

Revenue style (sometimes called "tax style") was developed as a response to the increasing complexity of the income tax laws. Its purpose is to break the tangled tax code into orderly, bite-size chunks.

In revenue style, section headings are mandatory. The section heading is printed all in capital letters, is prefixed by the section designation and number (thus, "SEC. 2."), and ends with a period. For the first section of the bill, the section designation is spelled out ("SECTION 1."), as is done in traditional style.

For every subdivision, a heading is also mandatory, except for subdivisions that are within a colon list or a dash list. Within a colon list, subdivision headings are optional; within a dash list, subdivision headings are not used.

If a subdivision is further subdivided, the lower-level subdivision is dropped down to the next line and indented.

§ 8.50 Modified Revenue Style

Revenue style was so successful at managing the complexity of the tax code that it came to be used by the Offices of Legislative Counsel for almost all new drafting. Many drafters consider the rigidity of revenue style too severe, however. (In particular, the mandatory use of subdivision headings can hinder, rather than help, a reader.) For that reason, a modified version of revenue style, known as "modified revenue style" (and sometimes as "modified tax style" or "office style"), is used.

Modified revenue style is really nothing more than revenue style made somewhat flexible. Headings are still mandatory for subsections, but optional for other subdivisions.

Modified revenue style is the default style to use in modern drafting, at least for bills and joint resolutions. For concurrent resolutions and simple resolutions, traditional style is sometimes used. (For the vast majority of concurrent resolutions and simple resolutions, the distinction makes little difference. Typically, the resolution has only one section and no subsections, and the section is not numbered or designated. Given those parameters, the styles are virtually the same.)

§ 8.60 Code Style

Code style is the style used for the positive-law titles of the United States Code. It is also the style in which the non-positive-law titles of the Code are printed, though the non-positive-law titles of the Code, as discussed in § 2.83, are not of direct use to drafters.

Code style is essentially the same as traditional style, except for section headings. Section headings are mandatory in code style, and they take a different form. A section heading is set flush to the left margin and in boldface lowercase letters. The heading begins with a section symbol (§) rather than the designation "Section" or "Sec.". And the heading ends without any punctuation, rather than with a period.

§ 8.70 Variations and Mavericks

The styles described so far are not the only styles in use, but they are the only styles in widespread use. There are a fair number of acts that have been drafted in ways that can best be described as irregular. When an act seems to be drafted in a style all its own, the style is often said to be a "maverick style."

Some acts with maverick styles are the Atomic Energy Act of 1954 and the Railway Labor Act. Another body of law with a maverick style is the Federal Rules of Civil Procedure. The Constitution, too, has a style all its own, though it most closely resembles the style of the early Congresses.

In addition, in many cases a law has been drafted in a particular style, but without perfectly following all the rules for that style. Just as modified revenue style is a flexible version of revenue style, that flexibility can be exercised in different ways by different drafters. Likewise, there are different flavors of traditional style and code style. Even the Constitution's style varies from article to article and from amendment to amendment.

In some cases there are sound reasons for the variation. For example, chapter 47 of title 10, United States Code, is also known as the Uniform Code of Military Justice, and each "section" of title 10 is also an "article" of the Uniform Code of Military Justice. The section numbers do not correspond to the article numbers, and the law provides both numbers at once.

Chapter 9

Affecting and Amending Other Laws

The business of amendment or alteration of laws is a choice and tender business, neither wholly to be omitted when the necessity requires, and yet very cautiously and warily to be undertaken, though the necessity may, or at least may seem to, require it.

Sir Matthew Hale, "Considerations Touching the Amendment or Alteration of Laws," in *Hargrave's Law Tracts*, vol. I, 253 (1789)

Trinquamelle: My friend, how come you to resolve the obscurity of these various and seeming contrary passages in law?

Bridlegoose: When there are many bags on the one side and on the other, I then use my little small dice;

I have other large great dice, fair and goodly ones, which I employ . . . when the matter is more plain, clear, and liquid;

For I give out sentence in his favour unto whom hath befallen the best chance by dice.

Francois Rabelais, *Five Books of the Lives, Heroic Deeds and Sayings of Gargantua and His Son Pantagruel* (translated into English by Sir Thomas Urquhart of Cromarty and Peter Antony Motteaux), Book III, chapter 39 (1693)

To strike out what has been inserted in the statute books, for special and sinister purposes . . . would require a continuous session of several years.

Simon Sterne, *The Prevention of Defective and Slipshod Legislation* 25 (1884)

Chapter 9

Affecting and Amending Other Laws

§ 9.00 Introduction

Most policies deal with matters that have been the subject of one or more previous laws. A new measure must be carefully related to earlier laws to produce, as far as possible, a consistent body of law that will achieve the policy without producing unintended consequences.

In what way does the new policy relate to existing law? The answer will have a major effect on how you draft the bill, and you can't be sure of the answer until you have a thorough understanding of the policy and the existing law.

For one thing, you may find that the policy is already realized, in whole or in part, by existing law. Perhaps, as sometimes happens, the client did not have a full understanding of the facts and the law. (Or perhaps Congress has already changed the law in a way that fits the policy, but the change was made so recently that the client hasn't yet gotten wind of it.) If so, you can explain the true facts and law to the client and set things straight. With some tasks, that may be the end of the matter; with others, the client may want to rethink the policy or fine-tune it in a new way.

Then again, you may find that the policy can be achieved only by amending or otherwise affecting existing law. The client may need a new rule of discretion (§ 4.43), a new command (§ 4.42), or a new stipulation (§ 4.45). The client may need to change a command to a rule of discretion or vice versa. There are many possibilities. In this situation, you have some important choices to make about which law to amend (or otherwise affect) and precisely how to do so.

Finally, you may find that the policy makes use of existing law without directly changing it. The policy may simply fit itself into the existing system of laws, or it may incorporate all or part of another law by reference.

Regardless, you will have to decide how best to position the new provisions so that they will have the effect, and have the relationship with other laws, that the client wants. In deciding this, you will have to consider whether to draft a freestanding law or an amendatory law or, perhaps, a law that contains both freestanding and amendatory provisions.

Reed Dickerson explained it this way:

> "An architect wouldn't dream of remodeling a house without first taking a good look at it. As a draftsman, you must closely examine the existing law to see what to repeal, what to amend, and what to supplement. Failure to do this results in implied repeals, overlaps, and inconsistent terminology; in a word—confusion. Once I was asked to prepare a bill requiring brewers of beer to show the ingredients of their product on the label, but a check showed that there was already such a statutory requirement. The real problem was one of enforcement, not of legislation. More often there is a statute already in effect and it needs to be amended. In other cases, the legislative field is wide open. . . . The job of fitting all the pieces together is unquestionably the hardest part of drafting. The specific pieces should cover the intended area, and they shouldn't leave any gaps, they shouldn't duplicate each other or overlap, and they shouldn't contradict each other."
>
> Reed Dickerson, "How to Write a Law"
> 31 *Notre Dame Lawyer* 14 (1955).

§9.10 How Courts Reconcile Statutes

The basic rule for reading two statutes together is fairly simple. For some reason, however, people frequently get it wrong. An important drafting manual claims that when two statutes conflict, the one enacted later prevails; a notable scholar makes the same claim. But that's not right. There is no identifiable "last enacted rule" in federal law. There are states that use the concept, but it is not generally recognized at the federal level.

In federal law, the basic rule for reading two statutes together is to read them together: "The courts are not at liberty to pick and choose among congressional enactments, and when two statutes are capable of co-existence, it is the duty of the courts, absent a clearly expressed congressional intention to the contrary, to regard each as effective. When there are two acts upon the same subject, the rule is to give effect to both if possible." *Morton v. Mancari*, 417 U.S. 535, 551 (1974).

Thus, the Court gives effect to two statutes that overlap "so long as each reaches some distinct cases." *J.E.M. Ag Supply, Inc. v. Pioneer Hi-Bred International, Inc.*, 534 U.S. 124 (2001). The Court strives to give meaning to each "while preserving their sense and purpose." *Watt v. Alaska*, 451 U.S. 259, 267 (1981).

If two statutes cannot possibly be read together, the rule is that the specific statute controls the general one. The order in which they were enacted does not matter. This rule was clearly expressed many years ago: "General and specific provisions, in apparent contradiction, whether in the same or different statutes, and without regard to priority of enactment, may subsist together, the specific qualifying and supplying exceptions to the general." *Townsend v. Little*, 109 U.S. 504, 512 (1883).

The persistent but false belief that the Court follows a last enacted rule can perhaps be explained by some cases that mention the priority of enactment as if it might be important. For example, in *Smith v. Robinson*, 468 U.S. 992, 1024 (1984), the Court said that "conflicting statutes should be interpreted so as to give effect to each but to allow a later enacted, more specific statute to amend an earlier, more general statute only to the extent of the repugnancy between the two statutes." And in *Radzanower v. Touche Ross & Co.*, 426 U.S. 148, 153 (1976), the Court said that "a statute dealing with a narrow, precise, and specific subject is not submerged by a later enacted statute covering a more generalized spectrum."

If you look closely at these two statements, however, you will see that they are two halves of the same whole. One says that a later, specific statute prevails over an earlier, general one; the other says that an earlier, specific statute prevails over a later, general one. Together, they simply restate the same broad principle that *Townsend v. Little* declared in 1883.

Now and then, in more modern times, the Court gives the entire formulation. For example, in *Morton v. Mancari*, 417 U.S. 535, 550–551 (1974), the

Court said: "Where there is no clear intention otherwise, a specific statute will not be controlled or nullified by a general one, regardless of the priority of enactment."

There should be no doubt, then, that what matters for federal statutes is not which one is later but which one is more specific.

Courts will try to avoid reading the two statutes in a way that completely nullifies one of them, unless Congress clearly intends otherwise. "A statutory interpretation that renders another statute superfluous is of course to be avoided." *Dastar Corp. v. Twentieth Century Fox Film Corp.*, 539 U.S. 23 (2003).

A new law will completely nullify an old one only when the new law clearly signals that intent. *Rodriguez v. United States*, 480 U.S. 522, 524 (1987). The nullification of one law by another is sometimes called an "implied repeal" or a "repeal by implication." Repeals by implication, the Court has repeatedly said, are "not favored." See *Radzanower v. Touche Ross & Co.*, 426 U.S. 148, 153 (1976); *Morton v. Mancari*, 417 U.S. 535, 550–551 (1974).

A repeal by implication appears to be the one situation in which the order of enactment is important to interpretation. One law cannot repeal by implication a law that hasn't been enacted yet (indeed, a law almost certainly can't expressly repeal a law that hasn't been enacted yet, either—see discussion in § 9.50.

A repeal by implication will be found only where "two statutes are in irreconcilable conflict," or where "the later act covers the whole subject of the earlier one and is clearly intended as a substitute." *Branch v. Smith*, 538 U.S. 254 (2003).

§ 9.20 Repealing a Law

Drafting a provision that repeals a law is not tricky. Any plain instruction should work. A typical instruction is in the form "The X Act is repealed," or "Section Y of the Z Act is repealed."

What is important is that you clearly identify the provision being repealed. Always cite the law being repealed; do not describe it in general terms. The intention of the legislature to repeal "must be clear and manifest." *Morton v. Mancari*, 417 U.S. 535, 551 (1974).

There are some important rules with respect to repeals. Some of them are intuitive, and some of them are not. The most commonly encountered issues are reviewed here.

Repealing an amending law does not undo the amendment. That is, if Law A reads a certain way when enacted, then a different way after being amended by Law B, repealing Law B does not cause Law A to revert back to its original reading. Unlike a freestanding provision (such as Law A, in the current example), which operates continuously, an amendatory provision (such as Law B) operates once only; it springs into action upon taking effect and then is inert. Repealing Law B does not undo what Law B did. To restore Law A to its previous reading, you must directly amend Law A a second time.

For a concrete example: One of the major laws passed by Congress after the attacks of September 11, 2001, was the USA PATRIOT Act. This Act had a great many provisions, many of which amended other laws in various ways. Within a year or two after it was enacted, some in Congress were calling for its repeal. Because so many of its provisions were amendatory, however, a plain, one-sentence repeal—"The USA PATRIOT Act is repealed."—would simply not work; to undo the USA PATRIOT Act would take a draft dozens of pages long. And it would be messy: In some cases, laws amended by that Act were further amended by later acts.

As an extension of the idea that repealing an amending law does not undo the amendment, repealing a repealing law does not undo the repeal. That is, if Law A reads a certain way when enacted, then Law B repeals Law A, repealing Law B does not revive Law A. This rule is set forth in section 108 of title 1, United States Code. That section, when first enacted as part of the Revised Statutes of 1873, changed the common-law rule: At common law, the repeal of a repealing law did in fact revive the law that had been repealed. See *United States v. Philbrick*, 120 U.S. 52 (1887).

Repealing a law does not affect the underlying liabilities incurred under that law while it was in effect. For example, if Law A creates a crime, and you commit that crime, and then Law B repeals Law A, you are still accountable for that crime. This rule is set forth in section 109 of title 1, United States Code. That section also changed the common-law rule: At common law, the repeal of a law released an individual from accountability. See *Warden, Lewisburg Penitentiary v. Marrero*, 417 U.S. 653 (1974).

There are many ways that a law can stop operating without actually repealing it. Many laws that have not been repealed have simply run their course. A law might by its terms apply only for a particular period of time. Or a law might contain a one-time requirement (such as "The Secretary shall submit a report") that, once satisfied, no longer operates.

Thomas Jefferson is said to have advocated a rule under which every law would stop operating nineteen years after it was enacted, unless it was reenacted before then. The principle that motivated Jefferson was that "one generation had no right to bind another." Harvey Walker, *The Legislative Process* 353 (1940). Jefferson's proposal did not catch on, however. While Congress frequently provides for a law to stop operating, the default rule is that a law operates forever.

§ 9.30 Amending a Law

Amending a law works much like editing a document. You can manipulate the text in just about any way imaginable. You can delete existing matter, insert new matter, or rewrite an entire block of matter. You can move a block of text within the act; you can even move a block of text from one act to another. You can play around with the margins and the fonts.

The basic instructions typically used in modern drafting are reviewed here. The instructions are not necessarily exclusive; there is no rule that requires Congress to use particular instructions. Generally, though, you should not depart from the tried and true without good reason.

There are two ways to change the text of a law: by striking and inserting text, and by revising an entire block of text. The former is called the "cut-and-bite" method (§ 9.31), while the latter is called the "restatement" method (§ 9.32). Both methods have advantages and disadvantages.

§ 9.31 The Cut-and-Bite Method (Striking and Inserting)

The cut-and-bite method generally works by striking, by inserting, or by both striking and inserting. When inserting new matter at the very end of a text, the drafting convention is to use "add at the end" rather than "insert."

The basic forms are as follows:

> Section 1 is amended by striking "Secretary of Defense,".
>
> Section 2 is amended by inserting ", except as provided in subsection (b)" before the period at the end.

Section 3 is amended by striking "dog," and inserting "cat,".

Section 4 is amended by adding at the end the following new subsection:

"(d) In this section, the term 'person' means only an individual.".

The main advantage of the cut-and-bite method is that it highlights the particular changes being made to the law. The main disadvantage is that it does not show how the law will appear after being amended.

Remember that you are striking and inserting everything within the quotation marks (an entire "character string"), not just words. The character string includes punctuation marks; it also includes typeface. There should be essentially a jot-for-jot correspondence between the character string and the text. The saving grace is that your instruction will ultimately come before a human judge, not a merciless computer, and the judge will give effect to the legislative intent rather than to the literal instruction. That said, you should always draft your amendments so that if a merciless computer were to execute the instruction it would have no trouble.

Drafters generally allow for two exceptions to the jot-for-jot principle: quotation marks and space characters. As is common practice in English prose, when double quotation marks are nested within double quotation marks, the internal marks are turned into single marks instead. For example, if paragraph (6) reads:

(6) the term "dog" means a domestic canine;

and you want it to read:

(6) the term "canine" includes a domestic canine;

a proper instruction might provide:

paragraph (6) is amended by striking "the term 'dog' means" and inserting "the term 'canine' includes".

For space characters, a rule of common sense is used, notwithstanding the general principle that you should draft machine-proof character strings. For example, if you wanted to insert "only" in paragraph (6) so that it would read:

(6) the term "dog" means only a domestic canine;

you could do so as follows:

paragraph (6) is amended by inserting "only" after "means".

Notice that if a merciless machine executed that instruction, you would end up with "meansonly":

> the term "dog" meansonly a domestic canine;

After all, you didn't include a space character within your quotation marks. Fortunately, people (and nowadays many machines) are a little more flexible than that.

Always specify the location in a way that is unambiguous, and refer to a character string that is unambiguous. Sometimes text is tricky. Consider this provision:

> (a) The Secretary of Defense and the Under Secretary of Defense shall carry out a program to be known as the Special Program of the Secretary of Defense.

Now suppose you amended it as follows:

> Subsection (a) is amended by striking "Secretary of Defense" each place the term appears and inserting "President".

The result, it turns out, is this:

> The President and the Under President shall carry out a program to be known as the Special Program of the President.

The "Under President"? That amendatory instruction didn't work out so well.

One approach is to narrow the location by being descriptive:

> Subsection (a) is amended by striking "Secretary of Defense" the first and third places the term appears and inserting "President".

Notice that the drafting convention is to refer to the text as a location rather than an event—the amendment specifies the first and third *places* the term appears rather than the first and third *times* the term appears.

Another approach is to use a longer character string than you otherwise need:

> Subsection (a) is amended—
>
> (1) by striking "The Secretary of Defense" and inserting "The President"; and
>
> (2) by striking "the Secretary of Defense" and inserting "the President".

Notice that the matter stricken and the matter inserted are faithful to the capitalization of the original.

If the matter to be stricken or inserted is solely a punctuation mark, the drafting convention is to spell out the name of the punctuation mark. The sense is that it is easier on the eyes to distinguish (for example) comma and period than to distinguish "," from ".".

When striking a long block of text, you can indicate a starting point and ending point, such as:

> Section 5 is amended by striking ", except that" and all that follows through the period at the end and inserting a period.

To strike a block of text is legally the same as to repeal it. You could strike a section or a chapter or a title, but the drafting convention is to use repeal for a section or bigger unit. Likewise, you could repeal a subparagraph or a clause, but the convention is to use strike for a paragraph or smaller unit. There is no settled convention for subsections; some drafters strike them, others repeal them.

§ 9.32 The Restatement Method (Amending to Read as Follows)

The restatement method works by designating a statutory unit and providing a complete new text of that unit. The basic form is as follows:

> Paragraph (1) is amended to read as follows:
>
> "(1) the term 'State' includes the District of Columbia;".

The main advantage of the restatement method is that it shows the law as it will appear after being amended. The main disadvantage is that it hides the particular changes being made to the law; you need to compare the old and new side by side to understand exactly what is being changed.

§ 9.33 Writing Amendatory Instructions Effectively

The elements of writing effectively (as described in Chapter Six, "Writing Effectively")—be simple, be ordinary, be brief, be consistent, be readable—apply no less to writing amendments than to writing any other part of your bill.

For example, do not clutter your amendatory instructions with words you don't need. At one time it was customary to draft an instruction like so:

> Subsection (a) is amended by striking out the words "Secretary of Defense" and inserting in lieu thereof the words "Attorney General".

Do not "strike out" when you can "strike." Do not "insert in lieu thereof" when you can "insert." And do not use the words "the words." All of this has come to be recognized as surplusage.

§ 9.34 Redesignations

When you need to create an opening or close a gap in a statute, you can redesignate. Typically, you redesignate so that you can insert new matter or so that you can clean up after striking old matter.

The forms are as follows:

> Section 4 is amended—
>
> (1) by redesignating subsections (b) and (c) as subsections (c) and (d); and
>
> (2) by inserting after subsection (a) the following new subsection (b):
>
> "(b) The Secretary shall carry out subsection (a) in consultation with the Attorney General.".
>
> Section 5 is amended—
>
> (1) by striking subsection (d); and
>
> (2) by redesignating subsection (e) as subsection (d).

While redesignating can be very useful, do not redesignate without carefully considering the consequences. Many provisions of law are referred to by their designations elsewhere in law; if you redesignate the provision, you will need to track down and change all the cross-references to that provision.

And then there are many provisions of law that are referred to in regulations or other materials entirely outside the law. Imagine the trouble you would cause by redesignating chapter 11 of the Bankruptcy Code. Some things are popularly known by their statutory designations: 401(k), 501(c)(3).

§ 9.35 The Ratification Doctrine

The Supreme Court has a seemingly strange, and certainly dangerous, doctrine usually referred to as "ratification doctrine." The doctrine states that "Congress is presumed to be aware of [a] . . . judicial interpretation of a statute and to adopt that interpretation when it re-enacts a statute without change." *Lorillard v. Pons*, 434 U.S. 575 (1978).

The doctrine also applies to regulatory interpretations (especially, but not solely, Treasury interpretations of revenue laws) and even to "other" interpretations (whatever that might mean). See *Cottage Savings Assn. v. Commissioner*, 499 U.S. 554 (1991) ("Treasury regulations and interpretations long continued without substantial change, applying to unamended or substantially reenacted statutes, are deemed to have received congressional approval and have the effect of law"); *United States v. Board of Com'rs of Sheffield, Ala.*, 435 U.S. 110 (1978) ("When a Congress that re-enacts a statute voices its approval of an administrative or other interpretation thereof, Congress is treated as having adopted that interpretation, and this Court is bound thereby.").

In short: If a provision has a well-settled executive or judicial interpretation, and Congress reenacts that provision without materially changing the words, the Court may reason that the well-settled interpretation is the interpretation Congress wants. Presumably, if Congress disliked the well-settled interpretation, Congress would have done something about it while reenacting the provision.

Ratification doctrine is related to another doctrine, sometimes referred to as the "borrowed statute doctrine," which holds that when Congress borrows language from one law for use in a new law, Congress presumably knew of the existing interpretations of the old law and wanted those interpretations incorporated into the new law. See *Lorillard v. Pons*, 434 U.S. 575, 580–581 (1978).

To a drafter, ratification doctrine is problematic. What it does it mean to "reenact" a provision? The major Supreme Court cases don't seem to say. Perhaps a provision is "reenacted" when it is restated, such as when the restatement method (§ 9.32) is used to amend a provision "to read as follows." (If ratification doctrine is viewed as a special form of borrowed statute doctrine, this would seem to make some sense.) But the Court doesn't explicitly say, and there appear to be cases in which ratification doctrine has been applied to one block of text that Congress did not touch at all when using the cut-and-bite method (§ 9.31) to amend another nearby block of text.

A definitive statement of ratification doctrine is lacking, and a detailed exploration is beyond the scope of this book. Consider the issue spotted, and refer back to the lament of Frank Horack set forth in § 3.90.

§ 9.40 Affecting without Amending

You can, of course, affect a law without amending it directly. Language in one law can change the effect of language in another law. Indeed, within the same law, language in one statutory unit can change the effect of language in another statutory unit.

A provision that does not amend another law is referred to as "freestanding." It is freestanding in the sense that it stands apart from other law. It is not, however, interpreted apart from other law. As discussed in § 3.31 and § 3.35, courts read all the parts of a single law as if that law is a coherent whole, and courts also (albeit in a less strict way) read all the laws on a subject as if those laws are a coherent system.

Accordingly, at least one provision should explain how all the various provisions relate to each other, though that does not always happen.

As mentioned in § 6.12, Judge Harold Leventhal related a case in which one law had a provision that authorized the President to limit the quantity of imports; another law had a provision that authorized the Secretary of Agriculture to limit the quantity of imports. "You would have thought that somewhere someone would have referred to the relationship between" the two, he lamented, but the relationship was not described anywhere. Harold Leventhal, "How the Courts See the Problem," in Reed Dickerson (ed.), *Professionalizing Legislative Drafting: The Federal Experience* 34–35 (1973).

Some of the phrases used to explain how one provision relates to another are as follows:

Except as provided in
Subject to
Without regard to
Notwithstanding
In carrying out
In applying
By
Pursuant to
Under
In accordance with

There are many others besides. Each of these phrases has its own meaning, and thus its own particular uses, but the meanings drafters give them can be rather nuanced, and many of those meanings have not been tested in court.

One convention used by many federal drafters covers the distinctions among "by," "under," and "pursuant to." The convention goes like this: If the result is achieved by the provision itself, use "by"; if the result occurs through action required or permitted by the provision, use "under"; if the result is more remotely derived from the authority of the provision, use "pursuant to."

They are not terms of art, though drafters sometimes treat them that way. Choose among them by using a dictionary and your own sense of how they differ; that is ultimately the method a court will use in reading them.

§ 9.41 Notwithstanding Any Other Provision of Law

The phrase "notwithstanding any other provision of law" is popular with people who have not really thought through a problem. They think that it is an effective way to ensure that a new rule prevails over an old rule—but they are wrong.

Courts do not take the phrase very seriously, and for good reason: Even when Congress does use the phrase, Congress usually does not intend that all other laws are to be disregarded. When Congress says, "Notwithstanding any other provision of law, the Secretary shall ensure that X, Y, and Z happen," Congress usually does not mean that the secretary may violate criminal laws and appropriations laws and administrative procedure laws and personnel laws and a whole host of other general laws. And yet that is literally what Congress seems to have said.

A definitive statement from the Supreme Court is hard to come by, but several federal appeals courts have held that the phrase is not always to be taken literally and does not require that all otherwise applicable laws be disregarded.

For example, when Congress passed a law that required the award of timber sale contracts "notwithstanding any other provision of law," Congress meant to disregard environmental laws only; Congress did not mean to disregard other laws, such as federal contracting requirements. *Oregon Natural Resources Council v. Thomas*, 92 F.3d 792 (9th Cir. 1996).

Likewise, when Congress directed that a bridge be constructed "notwithstanding any other provision of law," Congress did not mean to disregard historic preservation laws. *D.C. Federation of Civic Associations v. Volpe*, 459 F.2d 1231 (D.C. Cir. 1971), cert. denied, 405 U.S. 1030.

On the other hand, the court will not adopt a construction that "renders meaningless" the phrase. *Schneider v. United States*, 27 F.3d 1327, 1331 (8th Cir. 1994).

In short, a court will try to give "notwithstanding any other provision of law" some meaning, but it is never clear precisely what that meaning will be. The provision might end up disregarding too many laws or too few, and might or might not disregard the ones with which your client was really concerned.

In most cases, when the client proposes to use "notwithstanding any other provision of law," try to identify the specific laws with which the client is concerned, and state that they do not apply or are to be disregarded.

The phrase usually represents sloppy or lazy thinking. There once was a proposal to state that the Department of Energy "may use project review groups notwithstanding any other provision of law." What could this possibly mean?

The drafter eventually determined that a project review group was an advisory group comprised of personnel of the department as well as personnel of one or more contractors of the department. The department already had authority to use this sort of group, so a rule of discretion ("may use project review groups") was not really what was needed.

The real problem turned out to be that a project review group qualified as an "advisory committee" under the Federal Advisory Committee Act, and that Act places burdens on advisory committees that the department did not want placed on project review groups. (Notably, however, a group that included only department personnel, and not also contractor personnel, did not qualify as an advisory committee and would not be so burdened.) The final language was precise and clear and did not cover too much or too little:

> "An officer or employee of a management and operating contractor of the Department of Energy, when serving as a member of a group reviewing or advising on matters related to any one or more management and operating contracts of the Department, shall be treated as an officer or employee of the Department for purposes of determining whether the group is an advisory committee within the meaning of section 3 of the Federal Advisory Committee Act (5 U.S.C. App.)."
>
> Section 3112 of the National Defense Authorization Act for Fiscal Year 2004 (Public Law 108-136; 117 Stat. 1743; 42 U.S.C. 7234 note).

§ 9.50 Attempting to Bind Future Congresses

Every once in a while, a client wants to tie the hands of a future Congress. That is, the client wants to create a law that cannot be trumped by later law (or at least cannot be trumped easily). Usually this is done in the name of creating some sort of general policy. There are serious questions about whether this can be done effectively, though that does not stop people from trying.

Let's start with an example. Section 3571 of title 18, United States Code, provides a table for deciding the maximum fine that can be imposed for an offense. If a crime could get you up to one year in prison, the maximum fine is X. If a crime could get you up to fifteen years in prison, the maximum fine is Y. So far, so good. But what if a new law provides a maximum fine greater or lesser than the table provides?

Section 3571 tries to answer that question in advance. According to subsection (e) of section 3571, if the new law provides a higher maximum fine than the table provides, the higher fine prevails; but if the law provides a maximum fine lower than the table provides, the table prevails—unless the new law, "by specific reference," exempts itself from the table. Subsection (e) provides as follows:

> "(e) SPECIAL RULE FOR LOWER FINE SPECIFIED IN SUBSTANTIVE PROVISION.—If a law setting forth an offense specifies no fine or a fine that is lower than the fine otherwise applicable under this section and such law, by specific reference, exempts the offense from the applicability of the fine otherwise applicable under this section, the defendant may not be fined more than the amount specified in the law setting forth the offense."

Does this work? Is this effective? Suppose Congress were to pass a new law that creates a new offense and provides that a violator "shall be imprisoned not more than 10 years but may not be fined." The new law makes no specific reference to section 3571. If section 3571 prevails, then the person can be fined as provided in the table, even though the new law specified that the person not be fined at all.

Many courts—and, it seems, the Department of Justice—have generally assumed that section 3571 prevails, but the few courts that have squarely considered the question have decided otherwise. During one fifteen-year period, a handful of offenses in title 18, United States Code, provided for a term of imprisonment or a fine (without expressly providing for both). The period ran from 1987 (when section 3571 took effect) to 2002 (when the offenses were changed to allow imprisonment, fine, or both). Only one of these, section 401 (setting forth the power of a court to punish for contempt), generated significant case law with respect to section 3571. All four circuits to consider the question decided that section 401's either-or language prevailed over section 3571's formula. See *United States v. Versaglio*, 85 F.3d 943, 945–947 (2d Cir. 1996) (and cases cited).

Those decisions turned on a nuanced reading of section 3571 (and a related law, section 3551) and the notion that if Congress had meant to change section 401's either-or language it would have done so directly. Whether a court would reach the same result if faced not with an earlier-enacted law but a later-enacted one is an open question, but (as discussed in § 9.10) priority of enactment generally does not count for much when interpreting statutes—and when it does count for something, it generally favors the later-enacted law.

No doubt a court would first try to resolve the question solely as a matter of statutory interpretation. It would embark on a general search for legislative intent and apply customary techniques, such as the notion that a specific statute usually controls a general one.

But there is also a constitutional aspect to the question. Can one Congress, by law, set up an obstacle that if not avoided would impair or invalidate a later law?

There is little doubt that Congress can create an obstacle by constitutional amendment, though amending the Constitution is not easy. And there is little doubt that Congress can create an obstacle by chamber rules, though a chamber rule affects only pending legislation, not enacted law, and can be avoided or waived.

As an issue of constitutional power, the question of whether Congress can tell itself how to draft laws seems related to the question of whether Congress can tell the courts how to interpret them (a topic discussed in Chapter Three). When Congress tries to bind itself, it typically does so by creating what amounts to a congressional, rather than judicial, "clear statement" rule: One law trumps any contrary law unless there is a clear statement that the contrary law is exempt from being trumped.

(An interesting variation on this theme appeared in section 8 of H.R. 3514, as introduced in the 109th Congress. That section referred to a bill not yet enacted and attempted to preemptively repeal a section of that bill should it be enacted. It provided: "Effective on the date of enactment of the Safe, Accountable, Flexible, Efficient Transportation Equity Act: A Legacy for Users, section 1942 of such Act is repealed." Yes, note that the short title of the bill not yet enacted is miserably long and awkward. More importantly, however, ponder whether section 8 would actually work. The answer is by no means clear.)

Section 3571 of title 18, United States Code, is perhaps the most commonly encountered congressional clear statement rule. For other rules of this sort, see subsection (k) of section 2304 of title 10, United States Code (providing that a law cannot require the government to award a contract to a specific person unless the law "specifically" refers to, and exempts itself from, that subsection); section 6 of the Religious Freedom Restoration Act of 1993 (42 U.S.C. 2000bb-3) (providing that a law cannot substantially burden a person's exercise of religion without compelling reason unless the law "explicitly" refers to, and exempts itself from, that Act).

There are some who suggest that rules of this sort unconstitutionally infringe upon the legislative power. See Laurence H. Tribe, *American Constitutional Law* sections 2–3 note 1 (3d ed. 2000) (concluding that attempts by one Congress to bind another raise serious constitutional questions); but see Nicholas Quinn Rosenkranz, "Federal Rules of Statutory Interpretation," 115 *Harvard Law Review* 2085 (2002) (questioning Tribe's conclusion).

Tribe's point seems well taken. After all, if a law complies with Article I, Section 7 of the Constitution, it is an act of Congress and the supreme law of the land; how can an obstacle created by a mere law make it a nullity?

The idea that one legislature cannot bind a future legislature goes back to Sir William Blackstone and, further still, to Cicero. In his *Commentaries on the Laws of England*, Blackstone cited Cicero for the proposition that "Acts of parliament derogatory from the power of subsequent parliaments bind not. . . . Because the legislature, being in truth the sovereign power, is always of equal, always of absolute authority: it acknowledges no superior upon earth, which the prior legislature must have been, if its ordinances could bind the present parliament."

The Court has given a nod to this idea from time to time, but not in a case squarely addressing the question. For example, in *Reichelderfer v. Quinn*, 287 U.S. 315, 318 (1932), the Court was asked to decide whether park land dedicated by law to public use could be rededicated by law to another use. The

Court said it could: "the will of a particular Congress . . . does not impose itself upon those to follow in succeeding years." See also *Newton v. Commissioners*, 100 U.S. 548, 559 (1880), in which the Court was asked to decide whether a law granting a license could be revoked. The Court said it could: "Every succeeding legislature possesses the same jurisdiction and power . . . as its predecessors. The latter have the same power of repeal and modification which the former had of enactment, neither more nor less. All occupy, in this respect, a footing of perfect equality. This must necessarily be so in the nature of things. It is vital to the public welfare that each one should be able at all times to do whatever the varying circumstances and present exigencies touching the subject involved may require. A different result would be fraught with evil."

In 2005, in *Lockhart v. United States*, 546 U.S. ____ (2005), the Court could have squarely addressed the question, but declined to do so. In a concurring opinion, however, Justice Scalia chided the Court for passing up the opportunity to declare, once and for all, that one Congress cannot bind a later one with an express reference requirement. The concurring opinion is well worth reading; it independently covers the ground that this section covers, while drawing similar conclusions. Scalia's closing point is also well worth emphasizing: "In any event, I think it does no favor to the Members of Congress, and to those who assist in drafting their legislation, to keep secret the fact that such express-reference provisions are ineffective."

Perhaps the best guess is that a court will not automatically give determinative weight to a congressional clear statement attempting to bind a future Congress, but will take the clear statement into account in some way. That doesn't provide much in the way of useful guidance, but that is about all there is to go on.

Consider, for example, section 101 of title 1, United States Code, the law setting forth the form of an enacting clause of a bill. If read literally, this section is an attempt to bind future Congresses. But as discussed in § 5.23, this section is probably directory rather than mandatory; it does not command what is required but describes what is desired. If push came to shove, a court would probably find that a congressional clear statement rule is, likewise, directory rather than mandatory (see § 4.47, "Commands That Are Not Mandatory: Hortatory, Precatory, and Directory").

§ 9.51 Attempting to Authorize Future Congresses

Sometimes the client does not want to bind a future Congress, but instead wants to authorize a future Congress. For example, the client may ask for a draft that would prevent the President from carrying out a test of a nuclear weapon "unless Congress otherwise provides."

This sort of language—attempting to authorize a future Congress—could mean either of two things, and each one is problematic.

First, the client could mean that the ban can be overturned by some congressional device short of a law, such as a concurrent resolution. If that is the intended meaning, it violates the *Chadha* doctrine (discussed in § 5.21) and is unconstitutional. Congress can make law only by means of a bill or joint resolution that passes both chambers and is presented to the President.

Alternately, the client could mean that the ban can be overturned by another law—in effect, the ban applies "unless Congress otherwise provides in an Act enacted after this Act." This is not unconstitutional, but it is meaningless. Congress does not need permission to "otherwise provide" in a later law; it has inherent authority to do so under the Constitution. It is surplusage.

If the client has strong political reasons for including this sort of surplusage, there is probably no great harm in leaving it in (though it is, from a drafting perspective, unseemly). But if it must stay in the draft, better to make it read like an obvious case of surplusage than a potential violation of the *Chadha* doctrine.

§ 9.60 Referring to Other Law

The general principle when referring to other law is to provide useful information to the reader. In practice, federal drafters follow several drafting conventions, and you should too, unless there are compelling reasons not to do so in a particular case.

For referring to a provision that has been enacted into a positive-law title of the United States Code (§ 2.83 et seq.), the form is as follows:

> section 101 of title 10, United States Code

If the provision making the reference is itself within a positive-law title, drop the ", United States Code":

> section 101 of title 10

If the provision making the reference is within the same positive-law title (one section of title 10 referring to another section of title 10), use "section 101" only, unless in a particular context "section 101 of this title" is needed for clarity.

For referring to a provision that has not been enacted into a positive-law title of the Code (§ 2.83 et seq.), the primary reference should be to the short title of the act, with other finding aids provided for the convenience of the reader. The form is as follows:

> section 3112 of the National Defense Authorization Act for Fiscal Year 2004 (Public Law 108-136; 117 Stat. 1743; 42 U.S.C. 7234 note)

If there is no short title, use the public law number as the primary reference. If there is no public law number (because the act was enacted before the public law numbering system went into effect), use the enactment date. In either case, include the long title if useful:

> the Act of June 7, 1924
> Public Law 86-787
> the Act entitled "An Act to provide for the construction of the Cheney division, Wichita Federal reclamation project, Kansas, and for other purposes" (Public Law 86-787)

A citation to the Statutes at Large should be included if the citation would do more good than harm. Bear in mind that if the provision has been amended at some point after being enacted, the version of the statute shown in the Statutes at Large is no longer the current version of the statute, so a citation to the Statutes at Large could be misleading.

When referring to an act classified to the Code as non-positive law, never use the Code citation as the primary reference. The non-positive-law parts of the Code, as discussed in § 2.84, are not source law. Do always include a Code citation (if there is one), but do so as a secondary reference, not as the primary one.

When referring to sections and smaller units, the designations can be run together. The following citations all refer to the same unit:

> paragraph (1) of subsection (c) of section 2
> paragraph (1) of section 2(c)
> subsection (c)(1) of section 2
> section 2(c)(1)

Note that whenever designations are run together, the whole unit is referred to by the senior designation: section 2(c)(1), not paragraph 2(c)(1).

Generally, the elements of writing effectively will lead you to use the most compact, run-together form of citation (here, section 2(c)(1)). However, this can quickly lead to ambiguity if you refer to a provision more than once.

When you refer to "section 2(c)(1)," for example, and later refer to "that section," does the later reference mean section 2, or paragraph (1)?

For that reason, when you want to refer to a provision more than once, use a form that allows you to do so unambiguously. For example, on first reference say "paragraph (1) of section 2(c)" (rather than "section 2(c)(1)") if on second reference you want to be able to say "that paragraph."

§ 9.61 Incorporating Other Laws by Reference

Though in many cases one law refers to another simply to clarify the relationship between the two, in some cases one law refers to another to borrow and use the substance of the other law. This device is known as "incorporation by reference" (and sometimes as "referential legislation"), and it can be problematic.

A typical example is a definition—for example, suppose the New Act provides in part: "In this Act, the term 'armed forces' has the meaning given such term in section 101 of title 10, United States Code."

This definition can be problematic if the target provision (in the example, section 101 of title 10, United States Code) is later amended. Does the pointer provision (in the example, the New Act) automatically adjust so that it points at the target as amended? Or does it point at the old version of the target, in effect pointing at a ghost?

The conventional wisdom among drafters is that the pointer provision automatically adjusts. When you amend the target, you do not have to also amend all the laws that point to that target to clarify that they point to the revised target. That would seem to be a pretty silly exercise, and indeed it would be.

The conventional wisdom among drafters is based on common sense and the elements of effective writing. And yet there is some case law that suggests that Congress needs to update every pointer—or at least any pointer that is a "specific" reference rather than a "general" one.

There has not been a Supreme Court case on this topic since 1938, when the Court identified as a "wellsettled canon" the following:

> " 'Where one statute adopts the particular provisions of another by a specific and descriptive reference to the statute or provisions adopted, the effect is the same as though the statute or provisions adopted had been incorporated bodily into the adopting statute. . . . Such adoption takes the statute as it exists at the time of adoption and does not include subsequent additions or modifications by the statute so taken unless it does so by express intent.' [citation.] The weight of authority holds this rule respecting two separate acts applicable where, as here, one section of a statute refers to another section which alone is amended."
>
> *Hassett v. Welch*, 303 U.S. 303 (1938).

This language is dicta; while the Court noted this "wellsettled canon" supported the position of the respondents, the Court ultimately decided the case against the respondents.

The *Hassett* case was based in part on a general statutory construction treatise and in part on another Supreme Court case decided precisely 100 years earlier, *Kendall v. United States*, 37 U.S. 524 (1838). In *Kendall*, the Court observed:

> "It was not an uncommon course of legislation in the States at an early day to adopt, by reference, British statutes, and this has been the course of legislation by Congress in many instances where State practice and State process has been adopted. And such adoption has always been considered as referring to the law existing at the time of adoption, and no subsequent legislation has ever been supposed to affect it. And such must necessarily be the effect and operation of such adoption. No other rule would furnish any certainty as to what was the law, and would be adopting prospectively, all changes that might be made in the law. And this has been the light in which this Court has viewed such legislation. In the case of Cathcart v. Robinson, 5 Peters 280, the Court, in speaking of the adoption of certain English statutes said, by adopting them, they become our own as entirely as if they had been enacted by the legislature. We are then to construe this third section of the act of 27th of February, 1801, as if the eleventh section of the Act of 13th of February, 1801, had been incorporated at full length . . . ."

The rule described in *Kendall* and in the statutory construction treatise appears to be designed to protect one legislature from being stuck with changes made by another legislature; it is aimed at an early practice in which Congress would incorporate an English statute or one state would incorporate the statute of another state. The rule makes sense (and may well be constitutionally necessary) in that context, but does not make sense when one legislature incorporates its own statutes.

However, the Supreme Court has not, since the troublesome dicta in *Hassett*, taken an opportunity to indicate whether the conventional wisdom among drafters is safe.

In the absence of guidance from the Court, several appellate courts have struggled to make sense of *Hassett* and *Kendall*, not appearing to recognize that the language in *Hassett* is dicta and the language in *Kendall* appears to be concerned only with cases in which Congress incorporates foreign law.

A third Supreme Court case of note is *Panama Railroad Company v. Johnson*, 264 U.S. 375 (1924), which provided in pertinent part as follows:

> "Criticism is made of the statute because it does not set forth the new rules but merely adopts them by a generic reference. But the criticism is without merit. . . . This is a recognized mode of incorporating one statute or system of statutes into another, and serves to bring into the latter all that is fairly covered by the reference."

In this passage, the Court seemingly draws a distinction between a statute that incorporates another by "specific reference" and a statute that incorporates another by "general reference" (or "generic reference"). This is a distinction not clearly spelled out in *Panama Railroad*, but one that was clearly made in statutory construction treatises derived from state laws.

Under that distinction, a "specific reference" to another statute incorporates the substance of that statute as in effect when (and only when) the specific reference was enacted, while a "general reference" to another body of law incorporates the substance of that body of law as in effect whenever the general reference is applied, and thus incorporates any changes made over time.

The general reference in the statute at issue in *Panama Railroad* was as follows: "all statutes of the United States modifying or extending the common-law right or remedy in cases of personal injury to railway employees shall apply; and . . . all statutes of the United States conferring or regulating the right of action for death in the case of railway employees shall be applicable."

A notable federal court of appeals decision trying to make sense of, and apply, the distinction is *Director, Office of Workers' Compensation Programs, United States Department of Labor v. Peabody Coal Co.*, 554 F.2d 310 (7th Cir. 1977). That case analyzed the three Supreme Court cases described above, as well as the relevant statutory construction treatise.

The Seventh Circuit concluded that there are two types of incorporation provisions, one type that refers specifically to a specific statute and one type that refers to a general body of law. The former type incorporates the specific provision as in effect on date of enactment only; the latter type incorporates the general body of law as amended from time to time.

Having drawn that distinction, the court then had to decide how to categorize the provisions in the case before it; they were specific references to specific provisions, almost certainly of the former type. But the court declared that "facially specific references can and sometimes do operate as general legislative references," and decided to treat the specific references as general references (thus incorporating later amendments).

In short, the conventional wisdom among drafters—that a reference to another statute automatically adjusts when the other statute is amended—is probably worth following, though it may not be quite as safe as one would like. The Offices of Legislative Counsel of both the House and Senate follow the conventional wisdom, and most other federal drafters appear to do so as well. From time to time a drafter (or, more likely, a client) will want to insert a phrase after a reference to ensure that it will automatically adjust; the phrase typically takes the form:

> section 101 of title 10, United States Code, as such section may be amended from time to time

or simply:

> section 101 of title 10, United States Code, as amended

A phrase of this sort is almost certainly worthless clutter (more accurately, it is certainly clutter, almost certainly worthless). There is good reason to believe that if the issue were squarely presented to the Court, it would recognize that *Hassett* was dicta, *Kendall* was concerned with incorporating foreign statutes, and the distinction in *Panama Railroad* is not sensible, not workable, and in any event not what Congress generally intends. A drafter should, however, be aware that the conventional wisdom, though wise and conventional, is not quite as safe as one would like. (Even so, to avoid damage to the statute book (see § 9.70), it is better to leave out the worthless clutter.)

§ 9.70 Avoiding Damage to the Statute Book

You can affect other laws even when you don't mean to do so. Once a draft becomes a law, it becomes part of the context against which all other laws are interpreted. (See generally Chapter Three, "Considering the Courts: Statutory Interpretation.")

If you aren't disciplined and responsible, you can cause damage to that context, and that damage can cause problems for you, for other drafters, and ultimately for the system of federal laws as a whole.

When the courts interpret one law, they consider how Congress has drafted other laws. The courts take note of differences and generally assume that differences are meant to have significance. When Congress sends mixed signals over time, principles that were settled can become unsettled.

Suppose your client wants the provisions of the bill to be severable. Should you include a severability clause? (See discussion in § 7.63.) You plainly don't need one; the courts will presume the provisions are severable if your draft says nothing. But perhaps the client, "out of an abundance of caution," is tempted to include one anyway. The client might reason that including one is "harmless," and could possibly help.

The problem is that including a severability clause when one is plainly not needed is not harmless. It throws into question all the other laws that do not have a severability clause. If enough drafters include "harmless" severability language enough times, the courts might abandon the presumption of severability. After all, Congress does not mumble (§ 3.83), and Congress uses each word for a reason (§ 3.34). If the courts were to abandon the presumption, the severability of every law on the books would be thrown into doubt, and every future law would need to specify whether it is severable or risk being incomplete.

A provision that seems harmless almost certainly causes harm—not immediate harm, but harm nonetheless. When an antibiotic is used too often, it becomes less effective; when an aerosol is used too often, the ozone layer is damaged; when a boy cries "wolf" too many times, he loses credibility; and when Congress uses a severability clause when one isn't needed, Congress erodes the presumption that one isn't needed.

In short, there is no such thing as a "harmless" provision. Every provision has some effect on the statute book—ordinarily on the immediate act of which it is a part, occasionally on the background against which courts interpret statutes. In deciding whether to include the provision in your draft, the issue is not whether the provision is harmless but whether it is helpful, and most "harmless" provisions fail that test. If a provision does not affirmatively add value, it should not be used.

Avoiding damage to the statute book is about more than severability clauses, of course. It is about understanding the principle that your draft has not only immediate, direct effects, but also long-term, systemic effects. Many clients readily grasp this principle, and find it sensible, once you bring it to their attention. And when you internalize this principle yourself, congratulations—you are well on your way to being an effective drafter.

Chapter 10

Working in, and Working with, the Executive Branch

By Clinton T. Brass

For it cannot be overlooked that, in Washington, at least, the extent to which the spade work in the actual drafting of important legislation has been shifted all the way back to the agency level, is a major phenomenon of present day government.

James Craig Peacock, *Notes on Legislative Drafting* 2 (1961)

OMB performs legislative coordination and clearance functions to (a) assist the President in developing a position on legislation, (b) make known the Administration's position on legislation for the guidance of the agencies and information of Congress, (c) assure appropriate consideration of the views of all affected agencies, and (d) assist the President with respect to action on enrolled bills.

U.S. Office of Management and Budget,
***Circular No. A-19*, Revised Sept. 20, 1979**

At the OMB level, interagency consultation, negotiation and clearance is frequently necessary. The objective is to have an Administration "position" rather than have Congress be faced with multiple views coming from multiple agencies.

Ronald C. Moe, "Central Legislative Clearance," in U.S. Congress, Senate Committee on Governmental Affairs, *Office of Management and Budget: Evolving Roles and Future Issues* 170 (1986)

Administrative departments, even though not hostile to bills initiated by other departments, quite often present amendments to these bills without clearing them with the initiating departments or through the clearance machinery established by the President. . . . At times, however, tactics of this kind are resorted to to get through pet ideas which standing alone would have little chance of passage.

Edwin E. Witte, "The Preparation of Proposed Legislative Measures by Administrative Departments," in U.S. President's Committee on Administrative Management, *Studies on Administrative Management in the Government of the United States*, No. V, 57 (1937)

Chapter 10

Working in, and Working with, the Executive Branch*

§ 10.00 Introduction

If you are a drafter within the executive branch, this chapter is for you. It explains the process through which the executive branch makes official decisions about legislative proposals.

But if you are a drafter not within the executive branch, this chapter is also for you, because that process matters to you as well. Why? The President and the executive branch agencies can wield strong influence on the legislative process, and members of Congress often look to the President and the agencies for information and perspective on legislative matters. (See also *Congressional Deskbook*, § 3.30, "Executive-Branch Pressure.")

How will an agency, or the President, react to the proposal? How will members of Congress react to the proposal, given how the agency or the President is reacting? In short, many people in the executive branch will have opinions— and those opinions could affect how the proposal is received.

Your client should try to be aware of the opinions that have been voiced in the past, and should try to anticipate the ones that could be voiced in the future.

Your client should also be aware of how those opinions are formally communicated and deliberated among agencies within the executive branch. That

---

**By Clinton T. Brass. These views are those of the author and do not necessarily represent the views of the Congressional Research Service or the Library of Congress.*

process, known as legislative coordination and clearance, is the focus of much of this chapter. (The internal process used by an agency to develop legislative proposals, though also important, can differ from agency to agency and is beyond the scope of this chapter.)

The entity of the executive branch responsible for legislative coordination and clearance (and thus also the focus of much of this chapter) is the Office of Management and Budget, a staff agency to the President. The office is commonly known as OMB, and this chapter prefers that shorter term throughout. (OMB is described in more detail in § 10.20.)

As a drafter, the more you know about the agencies and the likely opinions (some institutional, some political) each one might voice, the more you can help your client. That knowledge can be useful as you start a project, consider the courts (Chapter Three), and think through the policy (Chapter Four).

§ 10.01 Drafters Who Are "More Than Drafters"

This book began with the assumption (in Chapter One) that a drafter is responsible for carrying out drafting functions and not for carrying out policymaking functions. However, if you are a drafter in the executive branch, that assumption probably does not hold. A drafter in an executive branch agency often assumes a role of "more than drafter," with at least some responsibility for making or advising on policy, creating strategy, or both.

If your only role is to be a drafter, you are not responsible for helping to craft policy or strategy. Those responsibilities are for your client (in this case, your client is a government employee or officer).

More often, however, a drafter in an executive branch agency assumes a role of "more than drafter." You may be expected to do more than drafting functions, depending on your job responsibilities and the client's expectations. You may even be "the client" or a representative of the client. In this situation, you may be called upon to shape policy or to craft legislative strategy. That is, you may be asked not only to draft the proposal, but also to help develop strategies for shepherding the proposal through your home agency and among other agencies. As you might imagine, there are many possible strategies. Some of the factors you might consider are discussed in this chapter's final section (§ 10.50, "Choosing Strategies for Developing Proposals").

§ 10.02 Drafters Who Draft Regulations

In many situations, the executive branch has authority to make rules. An agency typically has authority to make rules that interpret the laws for which the agency is responsible, and rules that govern how the agency goes about its business. In some cases, an agency has authority to make rules that are legally binding on others—that is, the rules have "force of law."

Agency rulemaking is a vast and complex topic and is beyond the scope of this book. Generally, it is governed by subchapter II of chapter 5 of title 5, United States Code, commonly known as the Administrative Procedure Act. The term "rule" is the generic term used in that law to mean "an agency statement of general or particular applicability and future effect designed to implement, interpret, or prescribe law or policy or describing the organization, procedure, or practice requirements of an agency" (5 U.S.C. § 551). It includes "regulations," "guidelines," and other similar documents, regardless of label (and, indeed, not all agencies use the same labels).

Many drafters in the executive branch are responsible not only for drafting proposed laws, but also for drafting proposed rules. (Others are responsible only for drafting proposed rules.) The art and science of drafting regulations are in some ways similar to the art and science of drafting laws, and in other ways different. These similarities and differences are beyond the scope of this book. However, many of the principles in this book for drafting proposed laws also apply to drafting proposed rules. Regardless, you should know that the role of the Office of Management and Budget (§ 10.20) in overseeing and reviewing the making of rules is different from its role in coordinating and clearing proposed legislation. Specifically, OMB's approach for "regulatory review" is governed in large part by Executive Order 12866 (5 U.S.C. § 601 note). For the text of that document, see Appendix 9.30. (See also *Congressional Deskbook*, § 10.40, "Congress and the Executive: Regulation.")

§ 10.10 The Role of the President in Legislation

The executive power of the United States is vested by the Constitution in a single President (specifically, a "President of the United States of America"). Many observers argue that this executive power includes some functions that are more accurately called duties, as well as other functions that are true powers. Other observers might not agree. These arguments about constitutional law can be contentious and are not within the scope of this chapter (but see § 4.52). Regardless, through the President's various functions, the President can try to, and often does, influence Congress.

For example, under Article II, Section 3, the President "shall from time to time give to the Congress Information of the State of the Union, and recommend to their Consideration such Measures as he shall judge necessary and expedient." The latter half of this provision is known as the Recommendations Clause. (The former half of this provision is the basis for the traditional "State of the Union" address each year.) Presidents have used the Recommendations Clause not only as a basis for making legislative proposals to Congress, but also as a basis for declining to make a legislative proposal even when Congress calls for the executive branch to make one. This tension between the branches appears frequently. See also Article II, Section 2 of the Constitution, which provides that the President "may require the Opinion, in writing, of the principal Officer in each of the executive Departments, upon any Subject relating to the Duties of their respective Offices."

Another relevant clause, which also appears in Article II, Section 3 of the Constitution, provides that the President "shall take Care that the Laws be faithfully executed." This provision is known as the Take Care Clause. Some laws require agencies to submit proposals to the President before submitting them to Congress. However, the question of to what extent Congress can restrict the President's control over the inner workings of the executive branch also has sometimes been contentious, and Congress has often acted to give agencies and federal employees some independence from the President. (See § 10.44, "Agencies with Legislative 'Bypass' Authority.")

Finally, a measure passed by Congress cannot become law until it is first presented to the President for his approval or disapproval. (See §§ 2.50–2.52; see also § 5.21, "What It Means to 'Make Law': The *Chadha* Decision.")

§ 10.11 Agencies and Tensions within the Executive Branch

An agency, whether created by Congress (by law) or the President (by executive order or administrative action, as authorized by law), is usually vested with authority to execute certain laws. To do so, the agency employs government employees, and those employees are on the front lines of interpreting and implementing laws. They also must abide by decisions from the courts. In many cases, the agency may have played a role in drafting a law in the first place. Because agencies have day-to-day experience with the legal, political, and operational aspects of the laws, they potentially have a great deal of expertise and wisdom to offer. Thus, many actors in the political system value the knowledge and wisdom that agency personnel can provide in the legislative process.

It is not surprising that a fair proportion of the legislation that is considered in the legislative process tends to have been drafted or influenced at some point by executive branch employees, including both career civil servants and political appointees. As one observer said, "Indeed the executive branch of the Government is no longer even expected to confine itself to the mere making of recommendations or proposals. It is practically expected to implement them in the form of already drafted bills." James Craig Peacock, *Notes on Legislative Drafting* 3 (1961).

At the same time, every agency has its own point of view and culture. Sometimes agencies disagree with one another. This can be problematic when agencies "own" different pieces of a policy problem or "share ownership" of a piece of a policy problem. In those situations, a President frequently finds it beneficial to have agencies discuss and resolve these disparate points of view in a formal way, under supervision of OMB, and outside the view of Congress and the public.

Many of these conversations take place under the so-called "*Circular A-19* process." This process is discussed at length in § 10.40, "Legislative Coordination and Clearance (*Circular No. A-19*)," later in this chapter. However, in summary, the process generally involves an agency either taking initiative or being given responsibility to draft a legislative proposal, or commenting upon a legislative proposal. Upon completion of the draft legislative proposal and any accompanying materials (transmittal letters and section-by-section analyses), the agency then sends that draft and materials to OMB. OMB circulates the draft legislative proposal among agencies it deems should receive it (including appropriate staff within the Executive Office of the President), receives their comments, and presents the comments back to the originating (or "lead") agency. The lead agency then works with OMB and other agencies to "clear" the proposal by working out any problems and getting a decision whether to submit the legislative proposal to Congress. (For related discussion, see also *Congressional Deskbook*, § 10.20, "Congress and the Executive: Legislation.")

From the perspective of the President, one potential benefit of resolving interagency disagreements is that the executive branch speaks with one voice, and has only one position, when interacting with Congress. Members of Congress have at times seen this as a benefit as well, but certainly not always. For example, on occasion, some observers see a President as focused on stifling dissent within the executive branch in order to achieve policy objectives. Furthermore, having such a formal discussion can be a way to make sure all appropriate voices are heard—at least, within the executive branch. However, OMB and sometimes the White House decide who those "appropriate" voices will be and sometimes exclude agencies from the process, either by mistake or on purpose.

In sum, a formal process can, at times, be used to synthesize an overall solution that is satisfactory to every agency involved. Other times, one or more agencies "lose" the battle of ideas and get only some or none of what they would like. These formal discussions can be used to help the presidential administration to speak with one voice, and thereby exercise political control of the executive branch, when communicating views about legislation to Congress. In the process, these formal discussions also frequently drive decision-making within the executive branch about policy.

§ 10.12 Ways in Which Agencies Interact with Congress

Agencies interact with Congress in many ways. This chapter discusses one of those ways in detail: the legislative coordination and clearance of legislative proposals (§ 10.40). However, you should also know about the others.

The executive branch does more than prepare and submit drafts of proposed legislation, of course. Agencies also prepare other supporting materials (for example, letters and reports) that relate to proposed legislation, and agency personnel often give testimony relating to proposed legislation. Generally, whenever an executive branch actor takes a position on proposed legislation (other than in discussions solely within the executive branch), that activity is subject to legislative coordination and clearance.

While the development of legislative proposals by the executive branch is a process that originates within the executive branch itself, another process, usually called "executive branch comment on legislation," originates within the legislative branch. At the discretion of actors within the legislative branch, and especially its committees, a legislative branch actor contacts an executive agency to solicit information and policy preferences on legislation. This can be done formally (with a letter or email to an agency official) or informally (by telephone or in person). When responding, agencies do not always clear their responses with OMB under the *Circular A-19* process, sometimes—but not always—to the consternation of OMB. Clearly, it would be infeasible for an agency to clear every telephone call with OMB, but this can be a gray area under the *A-19* process.

Agencies also interact with Congress in myriad other ways that are not discussed in this chapter, but are discussed more comprehensively in the *Congressional Deskbook*. These include: general pressures from the President throughout the legislative process (*Congressional Deskbook*, § 3.30); presidential action on enacted measures (*Congressional Deskbook*, § 8.290); presidential submissions and actions in the budget process (*Congressional Deskbook*, Chapter Nine); and a variety of special procedures and considerations involving the President, including oversight, investigation, and confirmation (*Congressional Deskbook*, Chapter Ten).

One document prepared within the executive branch, known as a Statement of Administration Policy (SAP), deserves special mention because of its prominence in the legislative process. The purpose of a SAP (usually pronounced "sap") is to communicate to Congress the coordinated views of the President and agencies regarding a piece of legislation. A SAP is a prominent way for the executive branch to tell Congress that the President supports, has concerns about, or might veto legislation. Frequently, the support, concern, or opposition applies only to one or more parts of a bill and not necessarily to the entire bill. However, a SAP typically does not provide a detailed, proposed "fix" for contents that the President has concerns about or opposes. Instead, the executive branch usually follows up with letters and personal contacts to discuss the specifics with Congress. As appropriate, a SAP can also include the executive branch's estimate, or "scoring," carried out by the Office of Management and Budget (§ 10.20), of a bill's cost for purposes of "pay-as-you-go" (PAYGO) calculations (see *Congressional Deskbook*, Chapter Nine, for discussion). A list of SAPs for each session of Congress, in electronic pdf format, is available at the following web site: *<www.whitehouse.gov/omb/legislative/sap/index.html>*.

SAPs are prepared within the Office of Management and Budget (§ 10.20), in coordination with the agency or agencies principally concerned and the

White House. Generally, a SAP is prepared for each appropriations bill, for most major bills that are not appropriations bills, and even for some bills seen as minor or non-controversial. The OMB roles and responsibilities for SAPs are discussed further in § 10.22 under the heading "Legislative coordination and clearance." For an example of a SAP, see Appendix Four. (For further discussion and examples of SAPs, see *Congressional Deskbook*, §§ 5.180, 10.20, 15.08, and 15.13.)

§ 10.13 Who Is Your Client?

If you work in a federal executive branch agency, the question of who your client is can be a controversial topic. There are a number of views on the subject. Most broadly, a career federal employee might consider the client to be the citizens of the United States, and serve the interests of those citizens, consistent with the Constitution and laws of the United States as interpreted by the employee. A political appointee might consider the client to be a higher-ranking political appointee (or, ultimately, the President), and serve the interests of the appointee or of the President, consistent with the Constitution and laws of the United States as interpreted by the appointee or by the President. However, even the President is constrained by the Constitution to "take Care that the Laws be faithfully executed" (*art. II, sec. 3*), as they are made by Congress. As you might imagine, this situation can get messy and the stakes can become high if a career employee disagrees with a political appointee, or an employee or appointee disagrees with the President, about how to interpret a statutory provision or the Constitution.

More narrowly, who your client is can depend on where you work, what your duties and qualifications are, and the person to whom you report. However, if you work in an executive branch agency, it is important to remember that your client is often the position in which Congress, by law, has vested authority to implement a given law. Many laws vest this authority in the head of an agency, not in the President or in a White House official. Thus, for purposes of developing legislative proposals, depending on your individual circumstances, your primary client will often be the head of your agency, not the President or a White House official. If you have questions about any of these issues, you should seek appropriate guidance.

§ 10.20 Overview of the Office of Management and Budget (OMB)

The President has an entire agency at his disposal to assist him on legislative matters: the Office of Management and Budget. This office is commonly known by its acronym, OMB. The history, major functions, and organizational units of OMB are described here. Whether you are working on a legislative proposal or on any other matter that involves OMB, it can be useful to have insight into these topics. (See also *Congressional Deskbook*, § 5.180, "Office of Management and Budget.")

§ 10.21 OMB's Organizational Units

OMB is a staff agency to the President located within the Executive Office of the President (EOP). With approximately 500 workers (over 90 percent of whom are career civil service employees), OMB is by far the largest agency within the EOP. The agency was established by the Budget and Accounting Act, 1921 (42 Stat. 20), under which it was called the Bureau of the Budget and located within the Department of the Treasury. Even though the Bureau of the Budget was located within a department, the bureau functioned under the direct supervision of the President. The bureau was redesignated the Office of Management and Budget with Reorganization Plan No. 2 of 1970 (84 Stat. 2085; reprinted both at 5 U.S.C. App. and at 31 U.S.C. 501 note). Since 1982, OMB has operated under chapter 5 of title 31, United States Code (31 U.S.C. 501 et seq.). OMB's current organization chart, complete with identification of the agency's politically appointed leadership, is available at OMB's web site: *<www.whitehouse.gov/omb/omb_org_chart.pdf>*.

Led by a director, deputy director, and deputy director for management (all appointed by the President with Senate confirmation), OMB is organized into three groups of offices. The first group is composed of resource management offices (also called RMOs), which are organized according to policy areas and agencies. For example, the National Security Programs resource management office oversees agencies including the Department of Defense, the Department of State, and the Agency for International Development. Staff within the resource management offices are known as "program examiners" and are responsible for integrating several perspectives in their work with agencies, including management perspectives, budgetary perspectives, and policy perspectives. The resource management offices are also frequently involved in the legislative coordination and clearance process, described later in this chapter (§ 10.40).

The offices in the second group are collectively called the "statutory offices," because each was established by statute instead of by administrative action. These offices include the Office of Federal Procurement Policy (OFPP, established in 1974; 31 U.S.C. § 506), the Office of Information and Regulatory Affairs (OIRA, established in 1980; 31 U.S.C. § 505), the Office of Federal Financial Management (OFFM, established in 1990; 31 U.S.C. § 504), and the Office of Electronic Government (usually called the E-Gov Office, established in 2002; 31 U.S.C. § 507). As is evident from their names, the statutory offices focus on specific management functions rather than exclusively on specific agencies. A staff member of a statutory office is usually called a "policy analyst," and each policy analyst works closely with agencies and with resource management offices.

The third group is composed of agency-wide support offices, some of which are usually closely involved in the legislative process. The Legislative Reference Division (LRD) and Budget Review Division (BRD) both monitor legislation (non-appropriations and appropriations, respectively) in cooperation with the resource management offices. The Legislative Reference Division administers the overall process of interagency review of agency draft bills, congressional testimony, and correspondence.

The Budget Review Division also coordinates the preparation of the President's annual budget submission, including the preparation of proposed appropriations legislation (what has been called the *Budget Appendix*). A third support office, the Legislative Affairs Office (OMB/LA), plays a key role in directly interacting with the White House and with Congress during the legislative process for both appropriations and non-appropriations legislation. The other support offices are General Counsel, Economic Policy, Communications, and Administration.

§ 10.22 OMB's Major Functions

OMB has described its mission in this way:

> "OMB's predominant mission is to assist the President in overseeing the preparation of the Federal budget and to supervise its administration in Executive Branch agencies. In helping to formulate the Pres-

> ident's spending plans, OMB evaluates the effectiveness of agency programs, policies, and procedures, assesses competing funding demands among agencies, and sets funding priorities. OMB ensures that agency reports, rules, testimony, and proposed legislation are consistent with the President's Budget and with Administration policies. In addition, OMB oversees and coordinates the Administration's procurement, financial management, information, and regulatory policies. In each of these areas, OMB's role is to help improve administrative management, to develop better performance measures and coordinating mechanisms, and to reduce any unnecessary burdens on the public."
>
> *<www.whitehouse.gov/omb/organization/role.html>*

In undertaking these activities, OMB's influence is felt throughout the executive branch and throughout the federal government generally. Indeed, OMB's actions and statements have at times been controversial, and a large literature about OMB has developed. (A full discussion is beyond the scope of this book.)

Most observers include among OMB's major functions the following: budget formulation and execution, legislative coordination and clearance, regulatory and information policy, and management of the executive branch.

Budget Formulation and Execution. Budget formulation relates to the President's function (formerly under the Budget and Accounting Act, 1921; now under section 1105 of title 31, United States Code) to submit, on an annual basis, a proposed budget for congressional consideration. Each year, OMB sends detailed guidance to agencies in its *Circular No. A-11* (described in more detail in § 10.31, as it relates to the legislative process). Agencies respond by submitting detailed budget requests to OMB, which are then reviewed by the relevant resource management offices and statutory offices. After final decisions are made by the White House, OMB submits the President's budget to Congress on behalf of the President. For each appropriations bill, once Congress completes action on the bill (and it becomes law), OMB concentrates on budget execution, which involves, among other things, apportionment of appropriated funds to prevent agencies from exhausting funds before the end of the fiscal year. See *Congressional Deskbook*, §§ 9.120–9.160.

Legislative Coordination and Clearance. This function, as it pertains to OMB's *Circular No. A-19*, is described in detail later in the chapter (§ 10.40).

OMB organizations also play key roles in another legislative activity, producing Statements of Administration Policy, or SAPs (described in § 10.12). SAPs are prepared for appropriations legislation and non-appropriations legislation. OMB's Legislative Reference Division prepares SAPs for most major non-appropriations bills scheduled for House or Senate floor action in the coming week, including those to be considered by the Committee on Rules of the House (see § 2.26). In addition, SAPs are sometimes prepared for "non-controversial" bills considered in the House under suspension of the rules. (See also *Congressional Deskbook*, § 8.80, "House Floor: Methods of Consideration.") A SAP is prepared in coordination with other parts of OMB, the agency or agencies principally concerned, and other Executive Office of the President organizations and individuals. For appropriations legislation, OMB's Budget Review Division is responsible for preparing SAPs. While the Legislative Reference Division and Budget Review Division are responsible for coordinating and clearing SAPs through OMB and agencies, OMB's Legislative Affairs Office is responsible for clearing SAPs through the OMB director and the White House's West Wing.

Regulatory and Information Policy. Regulatory and information policy includes reviewing, under Executive Order 12866 (5 U.S.C. 601 note), the rules and cost-benefit analyses proposed by agencies. The Office of Information and Regulatory Affairs usually works together with the relevant resource management offices in this process. The Office of Information and Regulatory Affairs also oversees executive branch statistical policy, paperwork reduction, and (in cooperation with the E-Gov Office) information technology investment and security.

Management of the Executive Branch. OMB's management function is broad and includes overall responsibility for the functions of the statutory offices as well as for human resources management in the executive branch. The resource management offices and the statutory offices often work together on these issues. OMB also is responsible for clearing proposed executive orders and many presidential proclamations.

§10.30 Relationship between Legislative Proposals and Budget Submissions

It has been only in the last century that the President formally and systematically enforced a legislative coordination and clearance process on executive branch agencies. What follows is a brief sketch of the historical development of OMB's role in legislative coordination and clearance, which, in many ways, grew out of OMB's budgetary duties.

As noted previously (§ 10.21), OMB's precursor agency, the Bureau of the Budget, was established by the Budget and Accounting Act, 1921. Before 1921, the federal budget process was considerably less centralized, in spite of occasional efforts by some presidents to dictate or cajole otherwise. In the nineteenth century, for example, agency budget requests were compiled by the Treasury Department into a "Book of Estimates" that was sent to several congressional committees, often with little or no participation by the President or his advisors.

Nevertheless, as Louis Fisher has suggested, it would be wrong to say that "nothing existed before [1921], that all was void and darkness." Louis Fisher, "Budget, Management, and Personnel," in Harold C. Relyea (ed.), *The Executive Office of the President* 100 (1996). Several presidents at different times had sought to wield more centralized influence on budgetary matters in the executive branch, both with and without success. However, the financial impact upon the federal government of several developments in the late nineteenth century, culminating in World War I at the beginning of the twentieth century, helped drive centralized budgetary power to the President.

With the Budget and Accounting Act, 1921, the President was made responsible for transmitting a proposed budget to Congress with "estimates of the expenditures and appropriations necessary in his judgment for the support of the Government for the ensuing fiscal year" (see section 201(a) of that act). The budget was to be prepared by the new Bureau of the Budget. Notably, with section 206 of that act, Congress prohibited any officer or employee of an agency from submitting to Congress or to a congressional committee an "estimate or request for an appropriation," a "request for an increase in an item of any such estimate or request," or a "recommendation as to how the revenue needs of the Government should be met," unless such things were requested by either chamber of Congress. In other words, an "end-run" (§ 10.50) around the President was not allowed in the budget process, unless Congress requested or legislated otherwise. (Congress has subsequently made some exceptions to this prohibition, as discussed in § 10.44.)

According to one account, the bureau then issued a "circular" containing guidance and instructions for agencies (*Circular No. 49*, issued December 19, 1921) that established a clearance process for certain legislative proposals originating in agencies or referred to them by Congress. Among other things, the circular stated that "all requests for recommendations for legislation, the effect of which would be to create a charge upon the public treasury or commit the Government to obligations which would later require appropriations to meet them, should be first submitted to the President before being presented to Congress." Quoted in Norman M. Pearson, "The Budget Bureau: From Routine Business to General Staff," 3 *Public Administration Review* 138 (1943).

Later, "[a] plan for central clearance of other types of bills originating in administrative departments was initiated by [President Franklin D. Roosevelt] in December 1934," providing that "no proposal for legislation was to be submitted by any administrative department to the Congress until it had been cleared through the Bureau of the Budget or the National Emergency Council." Edwin E. Witte, "The Preparation of Proposed Legislative Measures by Administrative Departments," in U.S. President's Committee on Administrative Management, *Studies on Administrative Management in the Government of the United States*, No. V, 53 (1937). That plan was revised in 1935 (*Budget Circular No. 336*) to require that agencies submit legislative proposals, reports, and recommendations to the Bureau of the Budget for central clearance. In addition, *Budget Circular No. 336* required an officer or employee, before testifying to congressional committees on legislation, to "ascertain from the Bureau of the Budget . . . whether such legislation is or is not in accord with the program of the President, and he shall so inform the committee."

OMB continues to strongly emphasize to the other entities of the executive branch its central role in preparing the budget (including proposed appropriations language) and clearing all budget justification materials before they are transmitted to Congress. For example, OMB reminds agencies that officers and employees are prohibited by law from submitting to Congress or a committee of Congress "an appropriations estimate or request, a request for an increase in that estimate or request, or a recommendation on meeting the financial needs of the Government" unless requested by either chamber of Congress. Office of Management and Budget, *Circular No. A-11*, Sec. 22.2 (2005), quoting 31 U.S.C. § 1108(e). Furthermore, OMB instructs officers and employees when testifying before any congressional committee or communicating with members of Congress that they are to "give frank and complete answers to all questions" but "avoid volunteering personal opinions that reflect positions inconsistent with the President's program or appropriation request." (As experience has shown, witnesses have not always navigated successfully between these directions.)

OMB now operates its legislative coordination and clearance activity under another circular, *Circular No. A-19* (revised September 20, 1979). See § 10.40.

§ 10.31 The Annual Cycle *(Circular No. A-11)*

The federal budget process is a long one. The federal government's fiscal year is three months ahead of the calendar year; fiscal year 2009, for example, begins October 1, 2008. The executive branch's planning for a fiscal year begins twelve to eighteen months before the fiscal year begins; the planning period is called the "budget season."

OMB *Circular No. A-11* is a well-known document to agency budget officers. The circular sets forth how an agency is to execute its budget; also, and of more relevance to a drafter, it sets forth how an agency is to prepare its budget request and submit that request (and supporting materials) to OMB. The circular is revised on an annual basis. The most recent version of the circular is available at this web address: *<www.whitehouse.gov/omb/circulars/index.html>*.

OMB typically issues *Circular No. A-11* in the summer (summer 2007, that is, in the case of fiscal year 2009). Even so, a summer issuance is sometimes viewed as not timely for agency needs (especially if the circular has changed significantly from the previous year's edition), because many agencies begin to make decisions on their wants and needs months before, in the spring (spring 2007, in the case of fiscal year 2009). Within OMB, the budget season typically begins in September (September 2007, in the case of fiscal year 2009), so that the President can arrive at a final budget proposal in time to submit it to Congress by February (February 2008, in the case of fiscal year 2009), as the law contemplates.

The annual budget cycle can potentially have many implications for developing legislative proposals, but three of them stand out.

First, an agency is required by *Circular No. A-19* to submit annually to OMB its "proposed legislative program" for the next session of Congress (described in more detail in § 10.41). The agency's deadline under *Circular No. A-19* to submit this program, which consists of a listing of legislative proposals and other detailed information, is the same as the agency's deadline under *Circular No. A-11* for submitting to OMB its annual budget request.

Second, an agency is required by *Circular No. A-11* to submit new or revised appropriations language to OMB (and potentially also general provisions) for inclusion with the President's budget proposal. When the President releases the proposed budget, this language is contained in the *Budget Appendix* volume. This process is usually not difficult for many agencies, because appropriations language for many agencies does not change significantly from year to year. However, when an agency or the administration wants to submit legislative proposals to Congress along with the budget (for example, proposed policy changes), an agency may need to draft appropriations or other legislation. The structure (section numbers) and content of *Circular No. A-11* sometimes change from year to year, but OMB's guidance on appropriations language can be found in the circular by looking in its table of contents or index. Typically, the process involves marking up language enacted as part of the agency's current year's appropriations act, which is provided by OMB to the agency on revised galleys, to indicate needed changes. If regular appropriations have not been enacted for the current year, OMB provides agencies with special instructions.

Third, Congress required under the Congressional Budget Act of 1974 (section 607 of Public Law 93-344, now codified as 31 U.S.C. § 1110) that executive branch requests for the enactment of legislation authorizing the enactment of new budget authority to continue a program or activity for a fiscal year must be submitted to Congress before May 16 of the year preceding the year in which the fiscal year begins. For example, if an authorization expired on September 30, 2008, draft legislation to extend the authorization should have been transmitted to Congress by May 15, 2007. Specifically, *Circular No. A-19*'s Attachment B provides detailed instructions from OMB on how to prepare these legislative proposals, including reference in Attachment B's section 3.b.(1) to "criteria for long-range projections" in *Circular No. A-11*.

§ 10.40 Legislative Coordination and Clearance *(Circular No. A-19)*

Legislative coordination and clearance is operated by OMB under *Circular No. A-19*. *Circular No. A-19* is generally considered to be clearly written and relatively easy to comprehend, but it is detailed. If a person is involved in legislative coordination and clearance under the circular, there is no substitute for reading and understanding the circular itself. *Circular No. A-19* is included in Appendix Nine.

Circular No. A-19 was last revised in 1979, and its processes have evolved into a mature state among OMB and the agencies that participate in legislative coordination and clearance. (Not all agencies are required to participate, as discussed in § 10.44.) One difference now, when compared with the past, is the advent of electronic mail. The use of email has simultaneously made the *A-19* process more convenient (expedited delivery) and sometimes more difficult (inadvertent attachment of the wrong version of a draft and general acceleration of the process).

Circular No. A-19 is available online at this web address: <*www.whitehouse.gov/omb/circulars/index.html*>. Notably, the circular not only covers the coordination and clearance of legislative proposals for submission by an agency to Congress; it also covers the coordination and clearance of other legislative communications made by an agency to Congress (or to any other entity outside the executive branch). In addition, it covers the coordination and clearance of recommendations made by an agency to the White House as to whether the President should approve or disapprove an enrolled bill (a bill that has passed both houses of Congress and has been presented to the President for action). (See also §§ 2.40–2.52.)

This chapter discusses the first of these three items, coordination and clearance of agency proposed legislation for submission to Congress (sections 7–9 of the circular). However, the same process applies when agencies send communications to Congress (or outside the executive branch) regarding pending legislation. The circular calls for a different process (section 10) when agencies send their views to OMB on enrolled bills. The circular also provides detailed guidance on how agencies must annually submit their legislative programs to OMB (section 6), which is discussed in § 10.41.

Sections 1–3 of the circular relate to its purpose, revision, and background.

Section 4 of the circular discusses the circular's coverage, which is briefly discussed in § 10.44. Section 5 of the circular lists a set of key definitions that are worth examining closely, for terms including advice, agency, proposed legislation, pending bill, report, enrolled bill, and views letter.

In particular, the term "proposed legislation" is defined in the circular in a broad sense, to cover not only what a drafter (and this book) would call a "draft" (that is, a proposed legislative measure); it also covers any supporting document to a draft bill, including transmittal letters to the Speaker of the House of Representatives and President of the Senate, section-by-section analyses, and other justification materials. (See the circular's section 5.e.) Accordingly, this chapter uses the term in that broad sense.

§ 10.41 Submission of Legislative Program by Agency

OMB requires each agency (except those not covered by *Circular No. A-19*) to submit, on an annual basis, a legislative program. This process is outlined in section 6 of *Circular No. A-19*.

The purposes of this process are to "help agencies coordinate their legislative program with the preparation of their annual budget submissions to OMB," "to give agencies an opportunity to recommend specific proposals for Presidential endorsement," and "to aid OMB and other staff of the Executive Office of the President in developing the President's legislative program, budget, and annual and special messages" (section 6.b.). In its proposed legislative program, the agency is required to include, among other things, a list of all items of legislation that the agency contemplates proposing to Congress (or supporting, if the legislation is already pending) and proposals that are under active consideration by the agency but that are not yet ready for inclusion in the program (section 6.e.). The circular's Attachment A describes in detail how to prepare a legislative program.

The agency is required to submit this proposed legislative program to OMB "at the same time as it initially submits its annual budget request as required by OMB *Circular No. A-11*" (section 6.c.). Notably, "items that are not included in an agency's legislative program and have significant upward budget impact will not be considered after the budget is prepared unless they result from circumstances not foreseeable at the time of final budget decisions" (section 6.c.(2)). Therefore, it behooves a person who is developing a legislative proposal to make an appropriate work plan with the client to identify ahead of time what items should be included in an agency's legislative program. Legislative programs are not subject to interagency clearance (section 6.f.).

§ 10.42 Submission of Proposed Legislation by Agency

The process to be used by an agency to submit proposed legislation to OMB is provided in section 7 of *Circular No. A-19*. This process typically includes coordinating by telephone and email with a legislative analyst in OMB's Legislative Reference Division, to ensure the analyst knows that the proposed legislation will be coming.

In the circular, OMB is careful to instruct each agency to avoid committing itself to provide testimony on a pending bill, to submit a report, or to submit proposed legislation to Congress on a time schedule that does not allow for "orderly" coordination and clearance. OMB urges the agency to "make every effort" to allow five full working days for clearance (section 7.c.(4)). On occasion, it can become very difficult to follow that guidance in the fast-paced environment on Capitol Hill. Agencies have been known to submit proposed testimony for clearance fewer than twenty-four hours before the testimony is to be given.

Each submission is required to identify where in the agency's proposed legislative program the proposed legislation was listed, to provide a section-by-section analysis of the proposed legislation, to include transmittal letters to the Speaker of the House and President of the Senate, to specify the budgetary and personnel impacts of the proposed legislation, to identify the other agencies that have an interest in the proposal, to discuss the agency's consultations, if any, with other agencies in developing the proposal, and to provide certain other information (section 7.f.).

Notably, however, OMB strongly encourages agencies to consult with one another ahead of time to reach interagency agreement on proposed legislation, particularly "in cases of overlapping interest" (section 9).

Participants in the coordination and clearance process should be aware of section 3 of Executive Order 12988 (28 U.S.C. § 519 note), which instructs agencies to "make every reasonable effort" to use a number of techniques, when preparing and reviewing a draft of legislation (and, also, when preparing and reviewing a draft regulation or other rule), in order to "not unduly burden the Federal court system." In particular, the executive order calls upon agencies to "eliminate drafting errors and ambiguity," write proposed legislation and regulations "to minimize litigation," and "provide a clear legal standard for affected conduct rather than a general standard . . . ." Many of those principles are similar to, and worth reviewing as complements to, those discussed in this book. (For the text of this executive order, see Appendix Nine.)

§ 10.43 Coordination and Clearance of Proposed Legislation by OMB

When OMB receives proposed legislation from an agency, it is assigned to a legislative analyst in the Legislative Reference Division, and that analyst identifies the other agencies, and the individuals within the Executive Office of the President, having an interest in the proposed legislation. The analyst then sends an email memorandum and corresponding attachments to those agencies and individuals, notifying them of the proposed legislation and specifying a deadline by which to respond to the analyst. In many cases, the analyst has the power to extend the deadline, if requested.

The Legislative Reference Division then works closely with other relevant offices within OMB (for example, the resource management office that oversees the relevant policy area) and with the Executive Office of the President, as well as with selected agencies, to come to a consensus, if possible, on the proposed legislation. OMB might, for example, ask for more information from the submitting agency or call an interagency meeting to exchange views and resolve differences of opinion. During this process, a submission from the Department of Justice regarding constitutional concerns is usually given special weight.

When the coordination process is complete, the analyst formally transmits to the submitting agency OMB's "advice" as to whether the proposed legislation is cleared and, if so, what the agency may say with respect to the proposed legislation. The "advice" typically assigns the proposed legislation into one of three categories, depending on its relationship to the President's own legislative priorities: the proposed legislation might be "in accord" with the program of the President; it might be "consistent" with the program of the President; or there might be "no objection" to the proposed legislation from the standpoint of the program of the President. (See Attachment C of the circular.) If an agency submits to Congress proposed legislation that has not been cleared by OMB, the event can be cited by OMB as a "violation," with potential repercussions for responsible agency staff.

§ 10.44 Agencies with Legislative "Bypass" Authority

Some agencies are not required to submit proposed legislation to OMB for coordination and clearance. Some agencies are exempt from the requirement by law; others are exempt by convention. In either case, these agencies may send proposed legislation directly to Congress without sending it first to OMB. However, agencies with this authority sometimes go through the *A-19* process regardless of this "bypass" authority, in order to curry favor with the administration, resolve potential disagreements, or benefit from the views of other agencies.

OMB's *Circular No. A-19* does not identify these agencies, but OMB typically groups these agencies into three categories.

The first category consists of agencies that are considered by OMB to have bypass authority based on statute. Examples of these agencies include the Consumer Product Safety Commission and the Merit Systems Protection Board.

The second category consists of agencies that are considered by OMB to have "conditional" bypass authority based on statute. Conditional bypass authority allows an agency to bypass the *A-19* process if the proposed legislation includes a statement indicating that the proposed legislation does not necessarily represent the view of the President. Examples of these agencies include the Securities and Exchange Commission and the Federal Reserve Board of Governors.

The third category consists of agencies that are considered by OMB to have "customary" or "informal" bypass authority, indicating that the bypass is informally allowed even though it is not in statute. Examples of these agencies include the United States Postal Service and the Federal Communications Commission.

§ 10.50 Choosing Strategies for Developing Proposals

What strategy should you choose for developing a legislative proposal? A great deal rides on that decision. The strategy you choose for developing a proposal will likely affect the form it ultimately takes, the substance it ultimately contains, and the reception it ultimately generates (not only within your agency, but also in other agencies, OMB, and Congress). All of these considerations, in turn, could strongly influence whether the proposal will find success. For example, before submitting draft legislation to OMB, should you informally circulate your draft proposal among other agencies? Should you meet with them in person to discuss? With whom, and how extensively?

Depending on your client's goals, the strategy you should choose for developing a legislative proposal will depend on your particular circumstances. Therefore, you should discuss these questions early in the process with your client. As many drafters in the executive branch have learned, there are different strategies for the process of developing legislative proposals that present corresponding risks and opportunities for the client.

For example, getting buy-in from other agencies before submission to OMB, under the *A-19* process, might provide benefits. Doing so might help you and your client think through the policy, speed things along during the *A-19* process, and prevent other agencies from misunderstanding your client's intent (perhaps preventing your client's draft proposal from being derailed in the *A-19* process). Also, if your client anticipates encountering a skeptical reception from OMB, support from other agencies might be helpful.

On the other hand, if your client anticipates opposition from another agency, perhaps it would be best to avoid sharing the draft proposal and giving the other agency extra time to marshal arguments against it. It is important to be mindful of all of these risks and opportunities, to the extent you become aware of them during your research and drafting work, because your client may not think of them.

Other phenomena that have been known to occur are called the "end-run" and "forum-shopping." If a client is close to the President or a presidential advisor, it is not unheard of for the client to approach the President or presidential advisor informally with the legislative proposal or, more likely, with an oral summary of what it is and why it should be pursued. If the client secures support from the President (that is, does an end-run around anticipated opposition in an agency, the executive branch, or OMB), the client may be successful in overcoming any opposition in an agency or the OMB *A-19* process, because the issue has already been "decided."

Variations on this process can occur by doing an end-run around a supervisor, a political appointee, a policy council, an agency head, another agency, OMB, and so on, by forum-shopping and looking for the most receptive ears for your draft legislative proposal. For example, OMB is a powerful agency, but agency political appointees have been known to successfully end-run OMB on occasion. Needless to say, forum-shopping and doing end-runs can also have repercussions. If you have questions about any of these issues, you should seek appropriate guidance.

As illustrated by the Edwin Witte quotation at the beginning of this chapter, actors within the executive branch have been known for decades to sometimes avoid official coordination and clearance processes when formulating legislative proposals. It is the client's responsibility to decide the process by which drafting will occur, so long as you, in your role as drafter or "more than drafter," are not called upon to do things that conflict with your professional, legal, and ethical obligations (§ 1.30).

You should be mindful that Congress has provided federal employees the right under 5 U.S.C. § 7211 to petition and furnish information to Congress; you should also be mindful of the restriction under 18 U.S.C. § 1913 against the use of appropriated funds to lobby Congress. Finally, you should also be aware that Congress typically includes a provision in annual appropriations acts (for example, Transportation-Treasury appropriations bill general provisions) that prohibits payment of the salary of any officer or employee of the federal government who prohibits or attempts to prohibit any other officer or employee of the federal government from having direct oral or written communications with any member, committee, or subcommittee of Congress.

The President, and the President's immediate staff, can become annoyed when an agency works outside "formal" channels, and doing so can have repercussions. You and your client need to be mindful of these issues, but they are beyond the scope of this book. If you have questions about these issues, you should seek appropriate guidance.

Appendices

(Continued on page 296)

Appendix One: The Impact of Information Technology on Drafting

App. 1.00 Introduction

The article that follows is, as mentioned in Chapter One (specifically, in §1.50), included here for two reasons. First, it is a useful commentary about how the use of computers has changed, for better or worse, how drafting is done. Second, it is a reminder that drafting is more or less the same from jurisdiction to jurisdiction, and that when looking for resources on drafting, you should not ignore resources from elsewhere.

Special thanks are given to the author, Don Macpherson, who granted permission to have the article reprinted here, subject to an annotation and a disclaimer. The annotation is as follows: "This article is based on a paper presented in Montego Bay on July 13, 2003, at the 2nd Annual Caribbean Legislative Drafting Forum, sponsored by the University of the West Indies Faculty of Law." The disclaimer is as follows: "The views expressed in this article are those of the author and should not be ascribed to either the Legislation Section or the Department of Justice of Canada."

Special thanks are also given to the Commonwealth Association of Legislative Counsel (CALC) and to its then-President, Duncan Berry, who likewise granted permission to have the article reprinted here.

The article originally appeared in the March 2005 edition of *The Loophole*, the journal of CALC. It is reprinted here without modification.

App. 1.10 Instant Bills: The Impact of Information Technology (IT) on Legislative Drafting in Canada

Instant Bills: The impact of information technology (IT) on legislative drafting in Canada[1]

Don Macpherson[2]

Introduction

In every legislative drafting office in Canada (even if not in every legislative counsel's office) is the ubiquitous purveyor of the information revolution – the digital computer. Ralston and Reilly's *Encyclopaedia of Computer Science* defines the digital computer as "a machine that will accept data and information presented to it in the required form, carry out arithmetic and logical operations on this raw material and then supply the required results in acceptable form." Surely it is the answer to the prayers of legislative counsel driven by deadlines!

In addition to its attractiveness as a word processor, the digital computer offers writers of laws a consolidated compendium of their work – in the form of a database of statutes and regulations. Moreover, the linking of digital computers into networks allows legislative counsel to communicate with each other on-line and provides access to legal and legislative databases for their day-to-day work. The advent of the Internet allows legislative counsel to envisage the time when their legislative texts will be accessible to, and perhaps even understandable by, everyone. It even has the potential to facilitate, one day, the interactive development of legislative texts in cyberspace by legislative counsel, policy-makers, stakeholders and groups of citizens.

The lure of this powerful technology is irresistible. In seizing it however, legislative counsel have irreversibly changed the parameters of their job, the organization of their work and even the product of their labours. I will describe in this paper how information technology has become embedded in the Bill-drafting process in Canada and how it has changed the legislative counsel's job and the way he or she does it. I will examine some of the positive and negative impacts of information technology on legislative counsel, drafting and the language of statutes. Finally, I will draw some conclusions based on our experience in Canada. My objective is not to promote the Canadian model for export to other jurisdictions. Rather, it is to cause drafters in legislative drafting offices around the world to reflect on how they are coping with the rapid pace of change brought about by information technology and how they might best approach the inevitable restructuring of their business in response to it.

Part 1: A change in pace: Legislative drafting from Driedger to Macpherson

The rapid pace of change

Information technology has undeniably made the legislative counsel's life more hectic in a number of respects:

- the seemingly endless series of drafts to be prepared before tabling a Bill, and escalating numbers of motions to amend to be prepared thereafter,

---

1 This paper is based on a paper presented in Montego Bay on 13 July 2003 at the 2nd Annual Caribbean Legislative Drafting Forum, sponsored by the University of the West Indies Faculty of Law.

2 Legislative Counsel of the Legislation Section, Department of Justice, Canada. The views expressed in this paper are those of the author and should not be ascribed to either the Legislation Section or the Department of Justice Canada.

App. 1.10 Instant Bills: The Impact of Information Technology (IT) on Legislative Drafting in Canada (continued)

- unrelenting pressures to develop and perfect the underlying policy of a Bill at the same time as it is being drafted,
- numerous intervenors, both inside and outside the drafting office, whose comments legislative counsel must solicit, digest and act on,
- the necessity to master many different computer software programs,
- a daily barrage of e-mails and telephone messages, and
- the expectation by clients in government departments, by ministers and by the general public that legislative solutions to their problems be drafted for introduction into Parliament instantly.

The pace of drafting in Driedger's day

How different was the lot of the legislative drafter even 25 years ago when the technology was the typewriter (or perhaps a dictaphone) and legislative counsel had secretaries to do the typing. In the Preface to the 1976 edition of his book *The Composition of Legislation*, [3] Elmer Driedger, the doyen of Canadian drafting, provides a description of the process for drafting Bills then in place in the Department of Justice. Drafting did not begin until the sponsors of the Bill had decided on their policy.[4] This was because of the inevitable delay that would result, according to Driedger, if legislative counsel took instructions before the policy work was complete.[5] After carrying out the necessary legal research and familiarizing himself with the background for the legislative proposal (through several meetings with the sponsors of the Bill or several weeks of meetings, if necessary), the drafter then prepared a legislative plan. Only at this point was he ready to prepare a first draft of the proposed Bill, working by himself. Driedger underlined the solitary nature of the legislative counsel's work and the importance of his individual responsibility for the outcome.

> He cannot work with other people looking over his shoulder and offering comments. And no satisfactory draft can be prepared by a group of draftsmen acting as a drafting committee; they will all have different ideas about how the work should be done, there will be endless discussions over trivialities, and the final product will be at best only a compromise. Drafts can be discussed, criticized and tested in a discussion group, but the responsibility for setting up the draft or making any changes must devolve upon one person.

The drafter then revised the first draft in repeated meetings with the sponsors, until it was approved by their deputy minister or minister.

How long did the process take? For a short, ordinary Bill that had taken approximately 6 months from its inception in the sponsoring Department until Cabinet approval of the policy and drafting instructions, Driedger estimated the drafting time to be 36 working days. The draftsman only took

---

3 *The Composition of Legislation: Legislative Forms and Precedents*, Elmer A. Driedger, 2 edn, Minister of Supply and Services, 1976, pp. xv to xxiv.

4 Ibid. at p. xvi. Driedger says that "A draftsman must receive a reasonably complete proposal before he can start his work, and the sponsors must therefore first settle the policy they want implemented."

5 Ibid. at p. xviii. Driedger cites an example of a Bill that the client wanted in 3 weeks that took an experienced draftsman 18 months to prepare because the department had not decided or even considered many major questions of policy.

App. 1.10 Instant Bills: The Impact of Information Technology (IT) on Legislative Drafting in Canada (continued)

7 days of that time however to complete 3 drafts. Most of the time was taken by departmental officials to consider the drafts. Driedger said that there was a certain irreductable amount of work required to draft a Bill and was not optimistic that the time required to do it could be reduced.

> This period [*of one month normally required to prepare a particular Bill*] could be reduced, without sacrificing quality by according the Bill top priority and by working at it evenings and weekends, which might bring the preparation period down to (say) three weeks. But the time cannot then be further reduced without sacrificing quality; as the time is cut down, the quality deteriorates, so that ultimately the point is reached where no Bill fit for introduction can be produced.[6]

The pace of drafting in Ontario

In a paper delivered at last year's Conference of the Canadian Institute for the Administration of Justice in Ottawa, Don Revell, the Chief Legislative Counsel for the Government of Ontario, compared Driedger's estimate of the time required to draft a short Bill with the speed of drafting in his office. He estimated that legislative counsel in Ontario produce a "short Bill" (including drafting, translation, editing and client review) at the rate of 1 to 2 pages a day. The rate of production of a "long Bill" is 2 to 4 pages a day.[7] This change in the speed of drafting in just 25 years is phenomenal. In the 36 days that it took to prepare a short, normal Bill in Driedger's day, the Ontario Legislative Counsel office can today prepare a Bill that is 100 pages in length.

The change in the method of doing the work is no less remarkable. One aspect highlighted by Mr. Revell is the amount of collaboration and consultation required when drafting Bills today. He lamented the loss of the legislative counsel's "splendid isolation". While 25 years ago the drafter had minimal contact with anyone other than clients and committees, today legislative counsel in Ontario have regular involvement with, and demands placed on them by, the Premier's office, the Cabinet Office, the Office of the Deputy Attorney General's Office (in particular its Constitutional Law Branch), the Government House Leader's Office and the Clerk's office. In short, the Ontario drafter no longer works alone, and there is always someone looking over his or her shoulder.

***A new standard—the* Anti-terrorism Act**

The events of 11 September 2001 set a new standard for the drafting of legislation at the federal level in Canada. The *Anti-terrorism Act* is a complex piece of legislation that defines terrorist activity, creates new terrorist offences, identifies terrorist entities, provides new tools for law enforcement and security agencies to investigate and prevent terrorist activities, seize terrorist property and track and prevent terrorist financing. The Act also contains provisions protecting official secrets and the integrity of the registration system for charities. This 186-page Bill was drafted in the Legislation Section of the Department of Justice in just three weeks.

The preparation of the Bill was a government-wide initiative involving a series of integrated teams of policy experts, lawyers and legislative counsel, led by Justice Canada. The first drafting team

6 Ibid. at p. xix.

7 "Drafting in a changing world", paper delivered at the Conference of the Canadian Institute for the Administration of Justice in Ottawa, *Drafting to Communicate the Law: the State of the Art*, 12-13 September 2002.

App. 1.10 Instant Bills: The Impact of Information Technology (IT) on Legislative Drafting in Canada (continued)

began work on the Bill in the last week of September. The following week, five additional teams of legislative counsel (one English and one French drafter for each team) were assigned to various components of the Bill. The teams worked concurrently to produce a draft Bill, which was assembled, together with the consequential and coordinating amendments, by additional teams of legislative counsel.[8] The draft Bill was edited, reviewed for bijural and bilingual consistency, and approved by senior officials and Cabinet, and was then tabled in the House of Commons on 15 October 2001—only 3 weeks after the drafting began and just over a month after the tragic events of 11 September.

The drafting rooms enabled the six teams to develop draft text for their parts of the Bill in both official languages, to consult outside experts by telephone and e-mail and to conduct legal research as a group. The computers in the drafting rooms provided access to legal databases on the Internet and on the Department's intranet, a network linking the computers of all Justice lawyers. Policy and legal advisers joined and left each team, according to the expertise required as the legislative counsel progressed through each of their parts of the Bill; client experts interested in several parts of the Bill rotated from room to room as the drafting process unfolded. Copies of draft legislation were printed and distributed to clients as each team passed various project milestones; clients repeatedly returned with new policy ideas and revisions.

Throughout the project, participants were faced with numerous constraints, including completely new and emerging government priorities, short time frames, and inter-departmental tensions. The success of this exercise won the Department of Justice the prestigious Head of the Public Service Award. But it set a new standard for legislative counsel to meet when faced with other high-priority, urgent legislative assignments (regardless of their complexity) – the "instant Bill".

For legislative drafting at the federal level in Canada, the *Anti-terrorism Act* rang the death knell of the Driedger era, where policy development and drafting were separate functions and the drafter worked alone, with control over, and individual responsibility for, his text. The *Antiterrorism Act* confirmed the emergence of a new era – the era of the "drafting team." In this new era, policy and legislation are developed together, over a collapsed time-period, by a horizontal inter-departmental team, composed of policy advisors, legal counsel and legislative counsel. The legislative counsel are responsible for the co-ordination and management of the drafting phase of the exercise. But the end-product of this process – the instant Bill – is the collective responsibility of the drafting team. These changes in the pace and methods of work of the drafter are caused by and mediated by information technology.

However, the new standard comes to us at a cost. The instant Bill has generated unrealistic expectations of the drafting process among federal departments and agencies. If a complex and lengthy Bill like the *Anti-terrorism Act* can be drafted in three weeks, why can't Department X's Bill be drafted in two weeks? What clients fail to realize is that the *Anti-terrorism Act* was an exceptional situation. The production of the Bill within such tight time limits was made possible

[8] In all, 18 drafters worked on the Bill. In addition, several teams from the Regulations Section were assigned to draft the subordinate legislation. This work was supported by legislative editors, jurilinguists, and the informatics group.

App. 1.10 Instant Bills: The Impact of Information Technology (IT) on Legislative Drafting in Canada (continued)

by dedicating almost all of the resources of the Legislation Section to it and by temporarily setting aside other government legislative priorities. Even the Cabinet approval process was adjusted so as to ensure quick introduction of the Bill. The instant Bill is costly in terms of the resources required to support the legislative counsel[9] and the effect of overtime and stresses on their health. For the leisurely pace of drafting that Driedger described, the instant Bill has substituted a new norm—drafting under pressure.

Part 2: An IT tour of Justice Canada's legislative drafting offices

The IT home page of the Legislative Services Branch

The Legislative Services Branch has created a new Home Page on the Department of Justice intranet. It has a picture of a woman's fingers typing on a computer keyboard and the scales of justice as a backdrop. It is hard to tell, but I think she's typing "ALT P" because that is the function that opens the style sheet for drafting Bills in Wordperfect 5.1 for DOS, the program that has replaced the pen as the drafting tool for legislative counsel in the Branch. Our legislative counsel are not only comfortable with this program; we would be unable to draft without it.

This was the program that the most technologically savvy of our legislative counsel used, in the mid-eighties,[10] to drag the Legislation Section kicking and screaming into the information age.[11] They created a series of styles[12] that allow Bills to be formatted consistently. They also developed a series of macros[13] tailored to our needs that automatically perform a number of tedious tasks and allow us to print bilingual Bills for clients that look like Bills that are tabled in Parliament. In our experience, Wordperfect 5.1 has proven superior to Microsoft Word (which was adopted as the Departmental standard in the late eighties) as a tool for legislative drafting, principally because it does not require the use of the mouse.

Wordperfect 5.1 is difficult to support however and has become obsolete. Legislative counsel in our office are now in the midst of training on the use of a new "authoring-tool" tool, which will enable us to draft Bills in the fall of 2003 in XML. This program will eliminate the conversion

---

9 See below at pages 12 to 15.

10 The Legislation Section was using computers even before Wordperfect – an IBM mainframe system. However the inputting was done by the drafters' secretaries.

11 Ed Hicks, our Informatics Coordinator related an anecdote to me concerning the protests of the then Director of the Section, the late Hilton McIntosh, to the introduction of computers in the Section. Hilton's retort, on being prodded to try out a few computers, was that lawyers would never use computers to draft legislation – typing was for secretaries! In the late 1980s, in response to budgetary cut-backs across government, most of the secretaries in the Legislation Section were assigned other duties, and all the drafters were equipped with computers.

12 The list of styles includes styles for formatting the opening headings for Bills, the enacting formula, marginal notes, subsections, paragraphs, headings, Part numbers, explanatory notes, schedules, etc.

13 There are macros for running headers on each page of the Bill (identifying the drafters, the name of the Bill and indicating that it is secret), renumbering the sections of the Bill and internal cross-references, creating a table of provisions and presenting the French and English versions in 2 columns on each page. There is also a "motion-maker macro" which sets up motions in the form and styles used by Parliament.

App. 1.10 Instant Bills: The Impact of Information Technology (IT) on Legislative Drafting in Canada (continued)

time formerly required to print Bills from Wordperfect 5.1, as well as the errors caused by conversion. By separating format from content, XML will allow the government's printer and Parliament to print Bills in their own formats directly from the text drafted by the Legislation Section. Eventually users will be able to search our XML legislative database using point in time searches.

IT also offers legislative counsel a number of electronic research tools for use in their day-to day work. The most important of these is the FolioViews database of consolidated Canadian statutes and regulations, maintained by the Legislative Services Branch Database Management Unit. FolioViews, with its flexible searching capacity, has proved indispensable in finding precedents, locating statutes for the purpose of making consequential amendments or repeals in a particular Bill and promoting greater uniformity of legal terminology and precedents across the statute book.

We also have access through the Department of Justice intranet to the Legislation Section's deskbook and drafting notes, as well as to legal research tools and opinions produced by other groups in the Department. Legislative counsel have desktop access to on-line dictionaries and to Canadian and foreign jurisprudence through commercial services. The Internet provides access to Bills and reports on their status via the website of the Parliament of Canada (www.parl.gc.ca). Other Internet websites offer access to Bills and legislation from the provinces and foreign jurisdictions.

The offices of the Legislation Section

Let me briefly describe our office environment. All legislative counsel have computers in their offices equipped with the above informatics tools and all draft by computer. The combined effects of information technology and government cut-backs in Canada over the last 25 years has meant the continual reduction of the size of lawyers' offices.[14] The computer is the main feature of our increasingly "paperless offices" and the surrounding modular furniture is ergonomically designed to accommodate people working at the computer for most of the day. The offices are set up to allow for co-drafting – the contemporaneous drafting of text in French and in English by 2 legislative counsel on 2 computers.[15]

Most legislative counsel choose to draft in the drafting rooms. Drafting rooms are board rooms, with space for 2 legislative counsel and from 4 to 8 clients, equipped with 4 flat-panel LCD

[14] The palatial spaces occupied by drafters and their secretaries in Driedger's time have shrunk so that drafter's offices in St. Andrew's Tower today are smaller than the anterooms occupied by drafter's secretaries years ago. There are two reasons for this. First, the offices must comply with Treasury Board regulations. Second, when the Legislation Section moved into St. Andrew's Tower, the drafters agreed to reduce the size of their offices so that more space could be made available for drafting rooms, which at that time were exclusively used by drafters in the Section.

[15] The *Official Languages Act*, passed in 1969, specifically provided for the legal equality of the French and English versions of Canadian laws. In response to a report by the Commissioner of Official Languages in 1975, the Department of Justice undertook to develop original versions of legislation in each official language. Rather than translating the French version of Bills from the original draft (the English version) the Department assigned a French and English drafter to each Bill. The two drafters co-draft both versions from instructions received in both official languages.

App. 1.10 Instant Bills: The Impact of Information Technology (IT) on Legislative Drafting in Canada (continued)

computer screens (one with keyboard for each of the 2 legislative counsel and 2 display screens for clients – one for the English text of the draft Bill and the other for the French text). Each room has a speaker telephone, e-mail and Internet access and is close to a high-speed printer. The drafting room is the legislative counsel's court room and the crucible for producing the instant Bill.

Some legislative counsel prefer to draft the initial draft of a Bill together in the absence of instructing officers and to draft in teams with instructing officers in the drafting rooms only when the first draft is complete. Others prefer to do all their work in teams in the drafting rooms. This is sometimes the only option if the Bill is urgent. The Legislative Services Branch currently has eleven fully equipped drafting rooms, which are usually all in continuous use when Parliament is in session.

I might note, before closing the Branch IT Home Page, that several legislative counsel engage in "telework" from time to time, drafting on computers in their homes and communicating with co-drafters (of the other language version) by telephone and e-mail. One drafter in the Section does most of his work at home, communicates with colleagues by e-mail and transfers drafts back and forth by secure fax.

Part 3: Speeding up the drafting: the impact of IT on the process and organization of the work

The impact of IT on our economy, business and society is immense. According to one author, the reduction of transaction time brought about by IT is causing a seminal shift in the way we structure our business processes.[16] The fact that immediate information transactions are possible creates public expectations that information, whatever its nature, will be immediately available when required. We live and work in a society that demands that information be ready "just in time", a culture where nobody waits.

The main impact of IT on the drafting process is to reduce the amount of time available to do the work. IT permits the compression of the time frame required to transform policy into a Bill. However, the ability to produce Bills quickly is a speed trap for legislative counsel. It creates unreasonable expectations of the drafting process by clients and generates the demand for legislative counsel to produce instant Bills in every case.

The demand to create legislation in a hurry is not a new phenomenon.[17] Even in Driedger's time, society looked to the law for solutions to intractable social and economic problems. Politicians made electoral promises (and ministers made legislative commitments) to prepare Bills to address those problems. Officials proposed legislative solutions to Cabinet, which approved drafting instructions for a Bill. Then the officials arrived at the legislative counsel's door with the

---

[16] See *Computer Law*, George S. Takach, Toronto, Irwin Law, 1998, at p. 38-40

[17] See note 4 above. Driedger, indicates that his drafters often drafted under pressure and were pushed to do the work in a hurry.

App. 1.10 Instant Bills: The Impact of Information Technology (IT) on Legislative Drafting in Canada (continued)

conviction that the matter was one of highest priority to the government and that a Bill was urgently required.

What is a new phenomenon in Canada is that instructing officers arrive at the legislative counsel's door with no drafting instructions approved by Cabinet and only very diffuse ideas about legislative solutions to their problem. They have the same convictions as to the Bill's priority and urgency, and often also have a very clear idea as to the date in the current session on which their minister wants the Bill introduced in Parliament.

Fortunately, the drafter is no longer alone. We have IT. IT allows us to conscript help in the form of an inter-disciplinary team of persons who contribute to the preparation of a Bill in the area of their expertise and who fulfil their various functions contemporaneously, in the same limited period of time that is available to the drafter. IT permits the work to be done in concert by many contributors and permits the drafting to be allocated to several teams of legislative counsel. IT supports instantaneous communications among all contributors and permits the disassembling of the work and reassembling of the drafts of several teams of legislative counsel into a final product – the instant Bill. Finally, IT allows the Bill to be printed instantly in the form required by Parliament.

Merging policy development and drafting

One of the ways to reduce the amount of time required to transform an idea into government policy and the policy into a draft Bill fit for introduction into Parliament is to merge the policy development and drafting processes. This approach is becoming quite common in Canada as more and more Bills are drafted by drafting teams in drafting rooms.

In this environment, the legislative counsel become participants in the development and refinement of the policy underlying a Bill. And the instructing officers (policy and legal advisors) participate in drafting the Bill. Although the legislative counsel have the keyboard, "drafting by committee" (as Driedger called it) in the drafting room reduces legislative counsel's control over their draft. The onus is on counsel in the drafting room to maintain discipline and, above all, to maintain the legal and linguistic integrity of the draft Bill. Work in the drafting room is often exhausting, and can at times be quite intense. Issues requiring further policy or legal work by instructing officers or further study by the legislative counsel are often tabled. Once proposals for resolving them are developed, the issues are returned to the drafting room for discussion and drafting.

Traditionally, policy development and drafting have been entirely separate exercises, the former tightly controlled by Cabinet and the latter by the Chief Legislative Counsel. Both have traditionally been carried out under the close supervision of the Government House Leader and the Privy Council Office. In recent years, central agency controls have been loosened to allow the merger of the policy and drafting processes, particularly for urgent Bills.

Consider the time savings from merging the two functions for a short, ordinary Bill. Normally according to Driedger, after the initial policy development, the work would require 36 working

App. 1.10 Instant Bills: The Impact of Information Technology (IT) on Legislative Drafting in Canada (continued)

days, 7 for the legislative counsel. Merging the policy development and drafting offers an immediate saving of at least 7 days, although additional time would be required of the legislative counsel because they are drawn into the policy development.

In our experience in drafting the *Anti-terrorism Act*, the time saved can be even greater. Merging the two processes blurs the line between the policy product and the legislative product. For all intents and purposes the Bill becomes the objective. Ancillary policy documents, if necessary, are developed as a function of drafting the Bill. In the drafting room, the team of policy advisors, legal advisors and legislative counsel are collectively responsible for delivering the Bill to the sponsoring minister. The draft Bill is on everyone's computer screen and is developed as a group enterprise. This sharing of responsibility between the legislative counsel and instructing officers creates a kind of synergy[18] that propels the work forward, on a common timetable, towards a common objective—a legislative proposal for introduction into Parliament.

Dividing the work among legislative counsel

The greatest gain in efficiency in drafting Bills comes from distributing the work to more people. IT makes this possible and not only allows the work to be parcelled out among different teams of legislative counsel but also permits the involvement of many specialists on particular aspects of a Bill. IT allows instantaneous communications among participants during the drafting phase, and enables the various components of the Bill to be reassembled into a final product when the project is complete.

In our Legislative Services Branch, management has successfully capitalized on efficiencies gained through the division of labour, by assigning a single Bill to more than one team of legislative counsel. Even in the mid 1990s, the Chief Legislative Counsel assigned large Bills and Bills comprising several distinct subject-areas[19] to more than one team of legislative counsel. The practice has subsequently proven useful for urgent Bills and for meeting unusual or unforeseen demands on drafting resources.

Not all drafting assignments can be split among different teams of course. Some Bills, for example budget implementation Bills, are naturally broken down into a number of discrete components that are not intertwined in law or policy. The components of amending Bills that target a number of distinct statutes can also be assigned to different drafting teams without risk of loss of continuity in the Bill. After all, a consistent drafting style is not necessary in a Bill the components of which will eventually be housed in different places in the statute book, each with the statute it amends.

On the other hand, a Bill establishing a new program or a regulatory scheme is not easy to split. As a single integrated piece of legislation, this type of Bill must be coherent from beginning to

[18] The creative group dynamic in the drafting room is most unlike the frustrating exercise in group drafting cited by Driedger. See above at page 3.

[19] The policy of the Privy Council Office during this period to combine smaller Bills with similar subject-matter into a single large Bill also had the effect of incorporating the work of different teams of drafters into one Bill.

App. 1.10 Instant Bills: The Impact of Information Technology (IT) on Legislative Drafting in Canada (continued)

end. Even if the Bill's subject-matter logically breaks down into discrete compartments, the amount of time and effort required to achieve legal and linguistic uniformity when the components of the Bill are reassembled may defeat the efficiency gains from splitting it.

Drafting support services

Branch management has also increased the efficiency of the drafting process by retaining the services of specialists to support legislative counsel. Support services, like the services of legislative editors,[20] have been available to drafters of federal legislation in Canada since Driedger's time. With the advent of co-drafting in the mid 1970s, the services of several French jurilinguists were also retained to support the quality of the French version of legislation. This service has since expanded[21] to include the comparison of the two language versions of Bills to ensure consistency.

In response to a Cabinet decision, the Department of Justice made a commitment in the late 1990s to ensure that federal legislation accurately reflects the private law concepts of Canada's two legal systems, the civil law and the common law. This requires a review of the corpus of Canadian legislation and the preparation of a series of harmonization Bills to incorporate both civil and common law concepts into the French and English versions of Canadian legislation. The Bijuralism and Drafting Support Services Group, recently established in our Branch to carry out this function, also reviews Bills drafted by our office before they are tabled to determine if they raise any bijuralism concerns. If they do, the Group provides advice to legislative counsel on how to resolve the issue.

Some of the legal work formerly done by legislative counsel in the Legislation Section has been assigned to a special Advisory and Development Services Group, recently established as part of the Legislative Services Branch. This Group conducts in-house training of legislative counsel, undertakes pilot projects, conducts research on plain language drafting and provides advice on issues related to statutory interpretation.[22]

IT is not the source of efficiency gains through management's use of specialists to supplement the work done by legislative counsel. After all, use of legislative editors by legislative counsel predated the information revolution. And the engagement of jurilinguists and experts in comparative law would have been desirable in any event to support the equality of the two language versions and two legal systems in Canada. However, without IT, these specialized inputs would have been very costly (in terms of delays to tabling Bills in Parliament) compared to the value added to Bills. IT turned the cost-benefit calculation in favour of enhancing the quality of

20 Editors' work includes correcting, simplifying, formatting, ensuring consistency of language use and adding historic references and notes to Bills.

21 Jurilinguistic services are now provided by a specialized unit in the Branch, composed of 7 French jurilinguists and 2 English linguists.

22 Specialist positions were created in the Legislation Section in the mid '90's to provide opinions on statutory interpretation and matters of Parliamentary procedure. Only the latter function remains with the Section.

App. 1.10 Instant Bills: The Impact of Information Technology (IT) on Legislative Drafting in Canada (continued)

Bills, by allowing the work of jurilinguists and bijuralists to be done contemporaneously with the drafting.

IT also facilitates review of draft Bills by a far greater number of persons. As in Ontario,[23] routine consultations on the text of draft Bills are required with more and more people before they are introduced into Parliament – for example, with legal and policy experts in the government and with people working for central agencies. It is also common for ministers to ask Cabinet's permission to consult stakeholders, or even the public, on a draft Bill before it is tabled. This permits technical improvements to be made to the Bill and, in the case of stakeholder or public consultations, enables a minister to tailor the Bill to external realities. While IT may have ended the legislative counsel's "splendid isolation" and deprived them of definitive control over draft legislation, the extended consultation and review process often results in corrections and improvements being made to Bills.

Impact on legislative counsel and the organization of drafting services

The changes brought about by the information revolution are, for legislative counsel going through them, reminiscent of the transformations brought about by the industrial revolution. Like nineteenth century artisans displaced from their workshops by the factory owners exploiting efficiencies gained by a process of division of labour and specialization of functions in the production of goods,[24] legislative counsel have been driven from their offices and into the drafting rooms. There they work in teams, under the watchful eye of management, on one component of Bill production, the drafting. This component, along with others added down the line (drafts of other drafting teams, editing, jurilinguistic and bijural review) is assembled, in the final stages of the process, into a Bill that is then marketed to the public by Ministers and communications specialists.

The skill sets required by legislative counsel today have changed. Informatics skills, for example, are now essential to the job. The ability to participate in policy development, particularly legal policy development, is also required. So are project management skills and team leadership skills. After all, it is the legislative counsel who must ensure that the contributions of all participants in the Bill production process are integrated into the text of the Bill and that it is prepared for tabling according to the agreed timetable.

There may also be changes in the organization of the drafting office, or to the institution that houses it. For example, our Legislative Services Branch has just gone through a major reorganization. Of interest is the priority placed on management of the various services that are now part of the Bill production process. The reorganization produced a new management class responsible for the coordination and organization of the Bill production process, the coordination

23 See above.

24 Some of senior legislative counsel in the Canadian Department of Justice remember the age of the artisan, when legislative counsel took instructions from Deputy Ministers and Ministers and controlled the production of Bills. The database of information required to prepare a Bill was all in their heads, or at their fingertips in the printed copies of Bills they had themselves drafted.

App. 1.10 Instant Bills: The Impact of Information Technology (IT) on Legislative Drafting in Canada (continued)

of the work of the legislative counsel and of drafting support services, and Branch communications with the Department of Justice and other client departments.

The shifting of responsibility from the individual counsel to the drafting team, the development and expansion of drafting support services and the establishment of a new layer of management has changed the role of the legislative counsel. Not only must legislative counsel provide team leadership in the drafting room, integrate the work of all participants in the Bill production process and keep managers abreast of the progress on and problems with particular files, they must also ensure the legal and linguistic quality and integrity of the Bill and, above all, produce it on time.

Part 4: Impacts of IT on the language of legislation

According to David Howes, the Internet challenges our perception of the law and even the language of legislation.[25] The positivist idea of law as a unilateral command, so convincingly conveyed by print, does not really come across in digital text. Digital text is fluid and interactive, rather than unilateral, like print. Howes notes that on the Internet all types of information are equal; whereas one of the main messages conveyed by legislation is its authority.

Governments have grappled with this inconsistency when launching their electronic databases of statutes and regulations on the Internet by denying the authority of the electronic version. The Canadian government, for example, has a disclaimer on its Internet site indicating that electronic statutes and regulations are maintained for convenience of reference and that only the print versions are official.[26] This, according to Howes, is an inadequate response to the change in the relationship between legislator and subject and to the inevitable change in the dialogue on law and legislation that takes place between them.

Improving readability – the plain language movement

There is some evidence that IT is having an impact on legal discourse in our society. The Internet is democratizing the law, by providing public access to it, much like the printing press

[25] "Understanding the Code of Codes: On the Prospects for Legislation in the Digital Age", paper delivered by David Howes at the Conference of the Canadian Institute for the Administration of Justice in Ottawa, *Drafting to Communicate the Law: the State of the Art*, 12-13, September, 2002.

[26] The notice on the Department of Justice web site reads as follows: "The legislative material on this site has been prepared for convenience of reference only and does not yet have official sanction. For all purposes of interpreting and applying the law, users should consult:

- the Acts as passed by Parliament, which are published in the "Assented to" Acts service, Part III of the Canada Gazette and the annual Statutes of Canada, and
- the regulations, as registered by the Clerk of the Privy Council and published in Part II of the Canada Gazette.

The above-mentioned publications are available in most public libraries."

The electronic version will have official status when Part 5 of chapter 5 of the Statutes of Canada 2000 is brought into force.

App. 1.10 Instant Bills: The Impact of Information Technology (IT) on Legislative Drafting in Canada (continued)

democratized the Vulgate Bible. Law and legislation have become subject to unprecedented public interest in the media and there is unprecedented public demand for legal information. Democratic governments in the developed world have responded by posting electronic versions of their Bills, statutes and regulations on the Internet. Many have officially adopted plain language policies that promote the modernization of the layout of statutes and regulations and writing them in plain language.

Under the banner of "readability", the access to the law movement has called into question some long-settled drafting conventions respecting the layout of the official (printed) version of legislation. Based on work done in other jurisdictions,[27] our Branch plain language project is currently examining improvements to the readability of legislation through graphic design. They are proposing radical changes to the layout of the "official" printed versions of Canadian statutes to improve their readability, including the use of more white space and user-friendly typefaces. The project is also proposing changes to marginal notes and headings and the inclusion of reader aids[28] to make it easier for readers to "navigate" their way around a statute.

Taking its lead from the community-based plain language movement in Canada, the project is also promoting techniques to change the way Bills are drafted so that they can be more easily understood. Many prescriptions of the plain language movement, like those promoting logical organization of ideas in a statute, shorter sentences and greater use of paragraphing, are based on recognized principles for good writing and easily fit within the traditions established by Driedger. Lowering readability levels to the point where even complicated statutes can be understood by the man in the street does not fit so easily with Driedger's philosophy.[29] This objective would bring about a change in the nature of the legal discourse in which legislators and citizens have historically engaged in Canada. Many legislative counsel would question whether such an objective is proper or attainable. Nonetheless, plain language is the policy of the Legislative Services Branch and it is making inroads in the Legislation Section. Legislative counsel, with the support of legislative editors and jurilinguists, are making efforts, subject to time constraints, to simplify, shorten and clarify draft legislation in order to make it accessible to as wide a readership as possible.

Unfortunately the speeding up of the drafting process leaves very little time for legislative counsel to do the rewriting, reorganization and testing necessary to write Bills in plain language or ensure that they are understandable by their intended audiences. Ironically, information technology has

---

27 For examples, see the layout of recent legislation in Australia and New Zealand, both of which have reformatted their legislation to improve its readability.

28 In its rewrite of the *Employment Insurance Act*, our plain language project proposes the addition of reader's guides at the beginning of statutes and parts, examples demonstrating how a provision operates and notes containing cross-references to other relevant sections and regulations.

29 Op. cit. n. 2 at p. xxiii. "A reader who has no knowledge or the subject-matter of a statute cannot be expected to understand it; nor can a draftsman be expected to write it so that he will. .... some statutes are, indeed, frightfully complicated, but it is not the draftsman who made them so. Laws must sometimes be enacted to deal with very complex situations, and obviously no one can understand the statute unless he understands those situations."

App. 1.10 Instant Bills: The Impact of Information Technology (IT) on Legislative Drafting in Canada (continued)

generated a demand (through the Internet) for plain language texts, but the use of IT in support of legislation drafting has created conditions in which there is not enough time to produce them.

The quality of legislation

What is the impact of the remarkable changes of the last 25 years in the speed of drafting, the drafting process and the role of the legislative counsel on the product of our work? Has the quality of Bills been reduced? In some respects, I think it has. A Bill, like the *Anti-terrorism Act*, that is drafted by several teams of legislative counsel under enormous time pressure cannot possibly have the coherence of a text developed in the fullness of time, under the guiding discipline of a single legal mind. Despite the efforts of the legislative editors, stylistic discrepancies are inherent in texts drafted as separate parts of the same Bill by different teams of legislative counsel.

Does legislation developed in haste contain more errors? There has been considerable inflation in the number of motions that are tabled by the government before Parliamentary committees in recent years.[30] But on closer examination, it can be seen that most were made to effect policy changes, not to fix errors. What the inflation in the number of motions reflects is not a higher error rate, but the fact that policy development continues after Bills are introduced. Where motions are made to correct drafting errors, these corrections are usually the result of last-minute policy changes before the tabling of the Bill. As for errors in statute book, there is no evidence of an increase since the advent of IT. The frequency and volume of corrections made by the Miscellaneous Statute Law Amendments Act has in fact remained quite stable since the inception of this program to correct errors and anomalies in federal statutes in 1975.[31]

In some respects, the quality of Bills has improved since Driedger's day. In the day-to-day drafting of legislation for example, IT operates as a powerful tool for promoting uniformity of language usage, both within statutes and throughout the statute book. Although we have not developed the kind of automated checkers that are in use in the Office of Parliamentary Counsel in Australia,[32] the legislative counsel and legislative editors in our Branch work tirelessly to achieve uniformity of legislative expression. The goal is so much easier to reach when drafting by computer because of the capacity of the computer to perform searches within a draft Bill, and within the statute book. The latter search capacity offers access to a range of precedents used by legislative counsel to solve similar legislative problems in other contexts. The legislative

30 The total number of motions tabled before Parliamentary Committees over the last 12 years are approximately 500 per year from 1992 to 1995, 650 per year from 1996 to 1999 and 900 per year from 2000 to 2003 (assuming trends for the first half of 2003 continue for the second half).

31 There have been 11 *Miscellaneous Statute Law Amendments Acts* since 1975, 5 during the period from 1977 to 1987 (comprising 383 pages of legislation) and 6 during the period 1991 to 2001 (comprising 353 pages of legislation).

32 See "The Australian Approach in the New Drafting Environment", a paper delivered by Hilary Penfold at the Conference of the Canadian Institute for the Administration of Justice in Ottawa, *Drafting to Communicate the Law: the State of the Art*, September 12-13, 2002.

App. 1.10 Instant Bills: The Impact of Information Technology (IT) on Legislative Drafting in Canada (continued)

counsel's normal penchant to use and adjust precedents to fit novel situations, has the happy side-effect of promoting the more uniform use of language in Canadian statutes over time.[33]

The increase in the number of participants involved in the production of Bills today also produces substantive legal and policy improvements in Bills that were not possible in Driedger's day. In particular, the expansion of the number of participants who review draft Bills before they are tabled (especially legal and policy specialists) reduces the risk of legal and policy problems. Moreover, consultations held with stakeholders and other groups who stand to be affected by a Bill often results in very important changes to the Bill to tailor its implementation and administration to practical realities. The process guarantees a better quality of legislation.

Conclusion

The changes that the computer has wrought in the world of legislative drafting in just 25 years are almost unbelievable. In Canada, the results from using IT in support of legislative drafting are overwhelmingly positive. Bills are ready sooner. The drafting is as good as, or better than ever. And, most importantly, we have a searchable electronic database that provides immediate access to Canada's Bills, statutes and regulations for legislative counsel, clients in government and the public.

Legislative counsel can endlessly debate the positive and negative impacts of information technology on their work, on their organizations, and even on the quality of the Bills they write. But one thing is beyond debate. We must embrace information technology and adapt to the inevitable changes of our times. Those who resist or are unable to adapt to the new information technology will be left behind. The laws of the 21st century will be drafted by computer. And the pen will join the hammer and chisel in the legislative counsel's waste bin.

[33] The search for uniformity and standardization of legislative precedents across the statute book is a worthwhile objective. However, transplanting precedent from one context to another is a complex business. There is often a need for substantial adjustment to the new statutory environment and verification of whether all necessary supporting provisions attached to the precedent in its original context have also been transplanted.

Appendix Two: Suggestions for Further Reading

App. 2.00 Introduction

Of interest to drafters are a wide variety of written materials. This appendix strives to be thorough, but is by no means exhaustive.

App. 2.10 Books

Administrative Conference of the United States, Office of the Chairman, *Drafting Federal Grant Statutes*. Washington, DC: U.S. Government Printing Office, 1990.

Bakshi, P.M., *An Introduction to Legislative Drafting*. Bombay: N.M. Tripathi,1972.

Butt, Peter, and Richard Castle, *Modern Legal Drafting: A Guide to Using Clearer Language*. Cambridge, U.K.: Cambridge University Press, 2001.

Coode, George, *Legislative Expression: Or, the Language of the Written Law*. Philadelphia: T. & J.W. Johnson, 1848.

Crabbe, V.C.R.A.C., *Legislative Drafting*. London: Cavendish, 1993.

Dickerson, Reed, *Legislative Drafting*. Boston: Little, Brown, and Co., 1954.

Dickerson, Reed, *The Fundamentals of Legal Drafting*. Boston: Little, Brown, and Co., 1965.

Dickerson, Reed, *Materials on Legal Drafting*. St. Paul, MN: West Publishing Co., 1981.

Dickerson, Reed, ed., *Professsionalizing Legislative Drafting: The Federal Experience*. Chicago: American Bar Association, 1973.

Driedger, Elmer A., *The Composition of Legislation*. 2d ed. Ottawa: Department of Justice of Canada, 1976.

Eskridge, William N., et al., *Legislation and Statutory Interpretation*. New York: Foundation Press, 2000.

Filson, Lawrence E., *The Legislative Drafter's Desk Reference*. Washington, DC: Congressional Quarterly, 1992.

Freund, Ernst, *Standards of American Legislation*. Chicago: University of Chicago Press, 1917.

Goldstein, Tom, and Jethro K. Lieberman, *The Lawyer's Guide to Writing Well.* 2d ed. Berkeley, CA: University of California Press, 2002.

Hart, Henry M., Jr., and Albert M. Sacks, *The Legal Process: Basic Problems in the Making and Application of Law*, prepared for publication from the 1958 tentative edition by, and containing an introductory essay by, William N. Eskridge, Jr. and Philip P. Frickey. Westbury, NY: Foundation Press, 1994.

Hetzel, Otto J., et al., *Legislative Law and Process: Cases and Materials.* 2d ed. Charlottesville, VA: The Michie Co., 1993.

Hirsch, Donald, *Drafting Federal Law.* 2d ed. Washington, DC: U.S. Government Printing Office, 1989.

Ilbert, Sir Courtenay, *The Mechanics of Law Making.* New York: Columbia University Press, 1914.

Jones, Chester Llloyd, *Statute Law Making in the United States.* Boston: Boston Book Co., 1912.

Katzmann, Robert A., *Courts and Congress.* Washington, DC: Brookings Institution Press/Governance Institute, 1997.

Martineau, Robert J., *Drafting Legislation and Rules in Plain English.* St. Paul, MN: West Publishing Co., 1991.

Mellinkoff, David, *The Language of the Law.* Boston: Little, Brown, and Co., 1963.

Mellinkoff, David, *Legal Writing: Sense and Nonsense.* St. Paul, MN: West Publishing Co., 1982.

Mikva, Abner J., and Eric Lane, *An Introduction to Statutory Interpretation and the Legislative Process.* New York: Aspen Law & Business, 1997.

Office of the Legislative Counsel, U.S. House of Representatives, *House Legislative Counsel's Manual on Drafting Style.* Washington, DC: U.S. Government Printing Office, 1995.

Peacock, James C., *Notes on Legislative Drafting.* Washington, DC: National Republic Publishing Co., 1961.

Popkin, William D., *Materials on Legislation.* 4th ed. New York: Foundation Press, 2005.

Redish, Janice C., *How to Write Regulations (and Other Legal Documents) in Plain English.* Washington, DC: American Institutes for Research, 1981.

Russell, Sir Alison, *Legislative Drafting and Forms.* London: Butterworths, 1938.

Smock, Raymond W., ed., *Landmark Documents on the U.S. Congress.* Washington, DC: Congressional Quarterly, 1999.

Stark, Jack, *The Art of the Statute.* Littleton, CO: Fred B. Rothman & Co., 1996.

Statsky, William P., *Legislative Analysis and Drafting*. 2d ed. St. Paul, MN: West Publishing Co., 1984.

Sterne, Simon, *The Prevention of Defective and Slipshod Legislation*. Philadelphia: G.S. Harris & Sons, 1884.

Strunk, William Jr., and E.B. White, *The Elements of Style*. 3d ed. New York: Macmillan Publishing Co., 1979.

Thorne, Samuel E., ed., *A Discourse upon the Exposicion & Understandinge of Statutes, with Sir Thomas Egerton's Additions*. Clark, NJ: The Lawbook Exchange, 2003.

Thornton, G.C., *Legislative Drafting*. 3d ed. London: Butterworths, 1987.

Thring, Lord Henry, *Practical Legislation: The Composition and Language of Acts of Parliament and Business Documents*. Boston: Little, Brown, and Co., 1902.

United States General Accounting Office, Office of the General Counsel, *Principles of Federal Appropriations Law*. 3d ed. Washington, DC: U.S. Government Printing Office, 2004.

United States Government Printing Office, *Bill Style Manual*. revised ed. Washington, DC: U.S. Government Printing Office, 1955.

Walker, Harvey, *The Legislative Process: Lawmaking in the United States* (New York: Ronald Press Co., 1948).

Weihofen, Henry, *Legal Writing Style*. 2d ed. St. Paul, MN: West Publishing Co., 1980.

Wydick, Richard C., *Plain English for Lawyers*. 4th ed. Durham, NC: Carolina Academic Press, 1998.

Yakubu, John Ademola, *Legislative Drafting Process*. Ibadan, Nigeria: Demyaxs Law Books, 2003.

App. 2.20 Journals and Periodicals

Clarity, the journal of the organization Clarity, an international association promoting plain legal language.

Harvard Journal on Legislation, published by students of Harvard Law School.

Journal of Legislation and Public Policy, published by students of New York University School of Law.

The Legislative Lawyer, the newsletter of the National Conference of State Legislatures, Legal Services Staff Section.

The Loophole, the journal of the Commonwealth Association of Legislative Counsel.

The Scribes Journal of Legal Writing, the journal of Scribes, the American society of writers on legal subjects.

Statute Law Review, the journal of the Statute Law Society.

App. 2.30 Articles

Allen, Layman E., and C. Rudy Engholm, "Normalized Legal Drafting and the Query Method," 29 *Journal of Legal Education* 380 (1977).

Allen, Layman E., and C. Rudy Engholm, "The Need for Clear Structure in 'Plain Language' Legal Drafting," 13 *University of Michigan Journal of Law Reform* 455 (1979).

Beaman, Middleton, "Bill Drafting," 7 *Law Library Journal* 64 (1915).

Bellis, M. Douglass, "Drafting in the U.S. Congress," 22 *Statute Law Review* 38 (2001).

Bellis, M. Douglass, "A View from the House of Representatives," 85 *Georgetown Law Journal* 2209 (1997).

Benson, Robert W., "Up a Statute with Gun and Camera: Isolating Linguistic and Logical Structures in the Analysis of Legislative Language," 8 *Seton Hall Legislative Journal* 279 (1984).

Berry, Duncan, "Legislative Drafting: Could Our Statutes Be Simpler?" 8 *Statute Law Review* 92 (1987).

Blackwell, Thomas F., "Finally Adding Method to Madness: Applying Principles of Object-Oriented Analysis and Design to Legislative Drafting," 3 *Journal of Legislation and Public Policy* 227 (2000).

Brossard, E.E., "Punctuation of Statutes," 24 *Oregon Law Review* 157 (1945).

Cavers, David F., "The Simplification of Government Regulations," 8 *Federal Bar Journal* 339 (1947).

Conard, Alfred F., "New Ways to Write Laws," 56 *Yale Law Journal* 458 (1947).

Costello, George A., "Average Voting Members and Other 'Benign Fictions': The Relative Reliability of Committee Reports, Floor Debates, and Other Sources of Legislative History," 1990 *Duke Law Journal* 39 (1990).

Crabbe, V.C., "The Legislative Sentence," 10 *Statute Law Review* 79 (1989).

Cranston, Ross F., "Reform Through Legislation: The Dimension of Legislative Technique," 73 *Northwestern University Law Review* 873 (1978).

Dickerson, F. Reed, "How to Write a Law," 31 *Notre Dame Lawyer* 15 (1955).

Dickerson, Reed, "Legal Drafting: Writing As Thinking, Or, Talk-Back From Your Draft and How to Exploit It," 29 *Journal of Legal Education* 373 (1978).

Dickerson, Reed, "The Diseases of Legislative Language," 1 *Harvard Journal on Legislation* 5 (1964).

Donaldson, A.G., "The High Priests of the Mystery: A Note on Two Centuries of Parliamentary Draftsmen," in Finnie, W., et al., ed., *Edinburgh Essays in Public Law* 99 (Edinburgh: Edinburgh University Press, 1991).

Driedger, E. A., "Legislative Drafting," 27 *Canadian Bar Review* 291 (1949).

Elhauge, Einer, "Preference-Estimating Statutory Default Rules," 102 *Columbia Law Review* 2027 (2002).

Elliott, David C., "Innovative Legislative Drafting," 73 *Michigan Bar Journal* 40 (1994).

Engholm, Rudy, "Logic and Laws: Relief from Statutory Obfuscation," 9 *University of Michigan Journal of Law Reform* 322 (1975).

Frankfurter, Felix, "Some Reflections on the Reading of Statutes," 47 *Columbia Law Review* 527 (1947).

Ginsburg, Ruth Bader, and Peter W. Huber, "The Intercircuit Committee," 100 *Harvard Law Review* 1417 (1986).

Graham, R.N., "In Defence of Maxims," 22 *Statute Law Review* 45 (2001).

Gray, Grayfred B., "Reducing Unintended Ambiguity in Statutes: An Introduction to Normalization of Statutory Drafting," 54 *Tennessee Law Review* 433 (1986).

Herman, Shael, "The 'Equity of the Statute' and Ratio Scripta: Legislative Interpretation Among Legislative Agnostics and True Believers," 69 *Tulane Law Review* 535 (1994).

Hoffman, Craig, "Parse the Sentence First: Curbing the Urge to Resort to the Dictionary When Interpreting Legal Texts," 6 *Journal of Legislation and Public Policy* 401 (2003).

Horack, Frank E., Jr., "Congressional Silence: A Tool of Judicial Supremacy," 25 *Texas Law Review* 247 (1946).

Horack, Frank E., Jr., "The Disintegration of Statutory Construction," 24 *Indiana Law Journal* 335 (1949).

Horack, Frank E., Jr., "In the Name of Legislative Intention," 38 *West Virginia Law Quarterly* 119 (1931).

Jones, Harry W., "Some Reflections on a Draftsman's Time Sheet," 35 *American Bar Association Journal* 941 (1949).

Jones, Harry W., "Bill-Drafting Services in Congress and the State Legislatures," 65 *Harvard Law Review* 441 (1952).

Kimble, Joseph, "Answering the Critics of Plain Language," 1994–1995 *The Scribes Journal of Legal Writing* 51 (1994).

Kiracofe, Adam W., "The Codified Canons of Statutory Construction: A Response and Proposal to Nicholas Rosenkranz' Federal Rules of Statutory Interpretation," 84 *Boston University Law Review* 571 (2004).

Landis, James M., "The Legislative History of the Securities Act of 1933," 28 *George Washington Law Review* 29 (1959).

Lee, Frederick P., "The Office of the Legislative Counsel," 29 *Columbia Law Review* 381 (1929).

Linde, Hans A., "Due Process of Lawmaking," 55 *Nebraska Law Review* 197 (1975).

Lovgren, A. Craig, "The Place of the Case in Legislative Sentences," 7 *Statute Law Review* 23 (1986).

Marcello, David A., "The Ethics and Politics of Legislative Drafting," 70 *Tulane Law Review* 2437 (1996).

Martineau, Robert J., "Craft and Technique, Not Canons and Grand Theories: A Neo-Realist View of Statutory Construction," 62 *George Washington Law Review* 1 (1993).

Menard, Albert R., Jr., "Legislative Bill Drafting," 26 *Rocky Mountain Law Review* 368 (1954).

Mikva, Abner J., "Reading and Writing Statutes," 48 *University of Pittsburgh Law Review* 627 (1987).

Nourse, Victoria F., and Jane S. Schachter, "The Politics of Legislative Drafting: A Congressional Case Study," 77 *New York University Law Review* 575 (2002).

O'Connor, Gary E., "Restatement (First) of Statutory Interpretation," 7 *New York University Journal of Legislation and Public Policy* 333 (2004).

Parkinson, Thomas I., "Legislative Contribution to Progress," *American Bar Association Journal* 95.

Payne, Jery, "The Drafting Critique," 27 *The Legislative Lawyer* 2 (2003).

Peacock, James Craig, "Drafting a Proposed Statute," *The Practical Lawyer* 19 (1961).

Poldervaart, Arie, "Legislative Drafting in New Mexico," 28 *New Mexico Tax Bulletin* 593 (1949).

Poldervaart, Arie, "Legislation By Reference: A Statutory Jungle," 38 *Iowa Law Review* 705 (1952).

Radin, Max, "Statutory Interpretation," 43 *Harvard Law Review* 863 (1929).

Read, Horace Emerson, "Is Referential Legislation Worth While?" 25 *Minnesota Law Review* 261 (1940).

Romero, Alan R., "Interpretive Directions In Statutes," 31 *Harvard Journal on Legislation* 211 (1994).

Rosenkranz, Nicholas Quinn, "Federal Rules of Statutory Interpretation," 115 *Harvard Law Review* 2085 (2002).

Schachter, Jane S., "The Confounding Common Law Originalism in Recent Supreme Court Statutory Interpretation: Implications for the Legislative History Debate and Beyond," 51 *Stanford Law Review* 1 (1998).

Stark, Jack, "Plain Language and Accurate Language," 27 *The Legislative Lawyer* 1 (2003).

Stark, Jack, "Shall or Must?" 26 *The Legislative Lawyer* 5 (2002).

Stark, Jack, "A Tool-Box Approach to 'Shall,' " 11 *The Legislative Lawyer* 1 (1997).

Stark, Jack, "On Language Games and Statutory Interpretation: An Inside Narrative," 20 *Statute Law Review* 144 (1999).

Stark, Jack, "Should the Main Goal of Statutory Drafting Be Accuracy or Clarity?" 15 *Statute Law Review* 1 (1994).

Stark, Jack, "Reader Expectation Theory and Legislative Drafting," 17 *Statute Law Review* 210 (1996).

Stark, Jack, "Legislative Sentences," 16 *Statute Law Review* 187 (1995).

Strokoff, Sandra, "How Our Laws Are Made: A Ghost Writer's View," 59 *The Philadelphia Lawyer* (1996).

Sutton, Dale E., "Use of 'Shall' in Statutes," 4 *John Marshall Law Quarterly* 204 (1938).

Turnbull, I.M.L., "Clear Legislative Drafting: New Approaches in Australia," 11 *Statute Law Review* 161 (1990).

Appendix Three: Useful Web Sites

App. 3.00 Introduction

Of interest to drafters are many web sites. This appendix strives to be thorough, but is by no means exhaustive.

App. 3.10 Federal Drafting Offices and Related Sites

U.S. House of Representatives, *<www.house.gov>*

U.S. Senate, *<www.senate.gov>*

Office of the Legislative Counsel, U.S. House of Representatives, *<http://legcoun.house.gov>*

Office of the Legislative Counsel, U.S. Senate, *<http://slc.senate.gov>*

Office of the Law Revision Counsel, *<http://uscode.house.gov/lawrevisioncounsel.shtml>*

THOMAS, *<http://thomas.loc.gov>*

Government Printing Office (GPOAccess), *<www.gpoaccess.gov/>*

Law Library of Congress, *<www.loc.gov/law/public/law.html>*

Law Library of Congress, Guide to Law Online: Compilations, *<www.loc.gov/law/guide/compilations.html>*

"How Our Laws Are Made: A Ghost Writer's View," by Sandra Strokoff, *<http://legcoun.house.gov/ghost.html>*

TheCapitol.Net, "Non-partisan training and publications that show how Washington works," *<www.thecapitol.net/>*

App. 3.20 State and Local Drafting Offices and Related Sites

Alabama: Legislative Reference Service, *<www.lrs.state.al.us>*

Alaska: Legislative Publications, *<http://w3.legis.state.ak.us/infodocs/infodocs.htm>*

American Samoa: Office of the Legislative Counsel, *<www.samoanet.com/asg/asglb97.html>*

Arizona: State Legislature, *<www.azleg.state.az.us>*

Arkansas: Bureau of Legislative Research, <*www.arkleg.state.ar.us/*>

California: Office of Legislative Counsel, <*www.legislativecounsel.ca.gov*>

Colorado: Office of Legislative Legal Services,
<*www.state.co.us/gov_dir/leg_dir/olls/olls1.htm*>

Connecticut: Legislative Commissioners' Office, <*www.cga.ct.gov/lco/*>

Delaware: Legislative Council,
<*www.state.de.us/gic/phonelist/department/01-08-00/directory.shtml*>

District of Columbia: Council of the District of Columbia, General Counsel,
<*www.dccouncil.washington.dc.us/*>

Florida: Legislature, <*www.leg.state.fl.us/Welcome/index.cfm*>

Georgia: Legislative Counsel,
<*www.legis.state.ga.us/legis/2001_02/senate/facts.htm#legcounsel*>

Guam: Legislature, <*www.guamlegislature.com/*>

Hawaii: Legislative Reference Bureau, <*www.hawaii.gov/lrb/*>

Idaho: Legislative Services Office, <*www.legislature.idaho.gov/lso/lso.htm*>

Illinois: Legislative Reference Bureau, <*www.ilga.gov/commission/lrb_home.html*>

Indiana: General Assembly, <*www.in.gov/legislative/index.html*>

Iowa: Legislative Service Bureau,
<*www2.legis.state.ia.us/GA/76GA/LSB/LegHandbook/NonLegAgencies/LSB.html*>

Kansas: Legislative Research Department,
<*http://skyways.lib.ks.us/ksleg/KLRD/klrd.html*>

Kentucky: Legislative Research Commission,
<*www.lrc.state.ky.us/Org_Adm/lrc/aboutlrc.htm*>

Louisiana: House Legislative Services,
<*http://house.legis.state.la.us/H-Staff//hls.htm*>

Maine: Office of Policy and Legal Analysis,
<*www.state.me.us/legis/opla/opla1.htm*>

Maryland: Department of Legislative Services, <*http://dls.state.md.us/*>

Massachusetts: General Court, <*www.mass.gov/legis/*>

Michigan: Legislative Service Bureau, <*http://council.legislature.mi.gov/lsb.html*>

Minnesota: House Research Department,
<*www.house.leg.state.mn.us/hrd/hrd.htm*>

Mississippi: Legislature, <*www.ls.state.ms.us/*>

Missouri: Joint Committee on Legislative Research,
<*www.moga.state.mo.us/legres/legreshome.htm*>

Montana: Legislative Council, <*http://leg.state.mt.us/css/committees/administration/2003_2004/leg_council/default.asp*>

Nebraska: Revisor of Statutes, <*www.unicam.state.ne.us/offices/revisors.htm*>

Nevada: Legislative Counsel Bureau, <*www.leg.state.nv.us/General/drafting.cfm*>

New Hampshire: General Court, <*http://gencourt.state.nh.us/ie/*>

New Jersey: Office of Legislative Services, <*www.njleg.state.nj.us/legislativepub/ols.asp*>

New Mexico: Legislative Council Service, <*http://legis.state.nm.us/lcs/legisagencies.asp#lcs*>

New York: State Assembly, <*http://assembly.state.ny.us/*>

North Carolina: General Assembly, <*www.ncleg.net/homePage.pl*>

North Dakota: Legislative Council, <*www.legis.nd.gov/council*>

Ohio: Legislative Service Commission, <*www.lsc.state.oh.us/about.html*>

Oklahoma: House of Representatives, Legal Division, <*www.lsb.state.ok.us/house/leg_page.htm*>

Oregon: Legislative Counsel, <*www.lc.state.or.us/*>

Pennsylvania: Legislative Reference Bureau, <*www.dgs.state.pa.us/dgs/lib/dgs/pa_manual/section3/legislative_reference_bureau.pdf*>

Puerto Rico: Government, <*http://welcome.topuertorico.org/government.shtml*>

Rhode Island: General Assembly, <*www.rilin.state.ri.us/*>

South Carolina: Legislative Council, <*www.scstatehouse.net/man03/LegCouncil03.pdf*>

South Dakota: Legislative Research Council, <*http://legis.state.sd.us/index.aspx*>

Tennessee: General Assembly, <*www.legislature.state.tn.us/*>

Texas: Legislative Council, <*www.tlc.state.tx.us/*>

Utah: Office of Legislative Research and General Counsel, <*www.le.state.ut.us/lrgc/lrgc.htm*>

Vermont: Legislative Council, <*www.leg.state.vt.us/legdir/staff.cfm*>

Virgin Islands: Legislature, <*www.senate.gov.vi/*>

Virginia: Code Commission, <*http://legis.state.va.us/codecomm/codehome.htm*>

Washington: Office of the Code Reviser, <*www1.leg.wa.gov/CodeReviser/*>

West Virginia: Legislative Services Division, <*www.legis.state.wv.us/Joint/Bill_Drafting/bill_draft.cfm*>

Wisconsin: Legislative Reference Bureau,
<*www.legis.state.wi.us/lrb/Legal/index.htm*>

Wyoming: Legislative Service Office,
<*http://legisweb.state.wy.us/leginfo/lso/lso.htm*>

App. 3.30 Foreign and Multinational Drafting Offices and Related Sites

Australia (Federal): Office of Parliamentary Counsel,
<*www.opc.gov.au/index.htm*>

Australia (Capital Territory): Parliamentary Counsel's Office,
<*www.pco.act.gov.au/*>

Australia (New South Wales): Parliamentary Counsel's Office,
<*www.pco.nsw.gov.au/*>

Australia (Queensland): Office of the Parliamentary Counsel,
<*www.legislation.qld.gov.au/ABOUT.htm*>

Australia (South Australia): Office of the Parliamentary Counsel,
<*www.justice.sa.gov.au/agency_show.asp?id=26*>

Australia (Tasmania): Office of Parliamentary Counsel,
<*www.dpac.tas.gov.au/divisions/opc/*>

Australia (Victoria): Office of the Chief Parliamentary Counsel,
<*www.ocpc.vic.gov.au/domino/web_notes/ocpcweb.nsf*>

Australia (Western Australia): Parliamentary Counsel,
<*www.justice.wa.gov.au/portal/server.pt/gateway/PTARGS_0_2_323_201_0_43/http;/justicecontent.extranet.justice.wa.gov.au/displayPage.aspx/The+Department/The+Department/Parliamentary+20Counsel/structureID=77181095/resourceID=2137831*>

Canada (Federal): Department of Justice, <*http://canada.justice.gc.ca/*>

Canada (Newfoundland and Labrador): Legislative Counsel,
<*www.justice.gov.nl.ca/just/legislative_counsel.htm*>

Canada (Northwest Territories): Department of Justice, Legislation Division,
<*www.justice.gov.nt.ca/legislation/legislation.htm*>

Canada (Nova Scotia): Office of the Legislative Counsel,
<*www.gov.ns.ca/legislature/legc/*>

Canada (Nunavut): Department of Justice, Legislation Division,
<*www.gov.nu.ca/english/legislation.html*>

Canada (Saskatchewan): Law Clerk and Parliamentary Counsel,
<*www.legassembly.sk.ca/legcounsel/*>

Canada (Yukon): Department of Justice, Legislative Counsel Office, *<www.justice.gov.yk.ca/prog/ls/lco/index.html>*

India: Ministry of Law and Justice, Legislative Department, *<http://lawmin.nic.in/Legis.htm>*

New Zealand: Parliamentary Counsel Office, *<www.pco.parliament.govt.nz/>*

United Kingdom: Parliamentary Counsel Office, *<www.parliamentary-counsel.gov.uk/>*

App. 3.40 Manuals and Guides

Alaska Manual of Legislative Drafting, *<http://w3.legis.state.ak.us/infodocs/draft_manual/DMWeb/Drafting%20Manual%202003.pdf>*

Arizona Legislative Bill Drafting Manual, *<www.azleg.state.az.us/alisPDFs/council/bdmwog2006.pdf>*

Colorado Legislative Drafting Manual, *<www.state.co.us/gov_dir/leg_dir/olls/HTML/legislative_drafting_manual.htm>*

Hawaii Legislative Drafting Manual, *<www.hawaii.gov/lrb/rpts96/dftman.pdf>*

Indiana Bill Drafting Manual, *<www.in.gov/legislative/session/manual/chap02/index.html#draftingrules>*

Maine Legislative Drafting Manual, *<http://janus.state.me.us/legis/ros/manual/Draftman2004.pdf>*

Massachusetts Legislative Drafting and Legal Manual, *<www.mass.gov/legis/drafting.htm>*

Oregon Bill Drafting Manual, *<www.lc.state.or.us/draftman.htm>*

South Dakota Drafting Manual, *<http://legis.state.sd.us/general/DraftingManual.pdf>*

Washington Bill Drafting Guide, *<http://slc.leg.wa.gov/BillDraftingGuide/RCWBDG.htm>*

App. 3.50 Non-Governmental Organizations

American Law Institute, *<www.ali.org/>*

Canadian Institute for the Administration of Justice: Serving Legal Drafters, *<www.ciaj-icaj.ca/english/legaldrafters/servinglegaldrafters.html>*

Clarity (International), *<www.clarity-international.net/>*

Commonwealth Association of Legislative Counsel (CALC), <*www.opc.gov.au/calc/*>

Communication Research Institute of Australia, <*www.communication.org.au/*>

Council of the European Union: Legislative Drafting, <*http://europa.eu.int/eur-lex/en/about/techleg/*>

International Law Institute: Legislative Drafting, <*www.ili.org/ld/manuals.htm*>

Legislative Drafting Research Fund at Columbia Law School, <*www.law.columbia.edu/center_program/leg_drafting*>

National Conference of Commissioners on Uniform State Laws, <*www.nccusl.org*>

National Conference of State Legislatures, Legal Services Staff Section, <*www.ncsl.org/programs/legman/legalsrv/lssshome.htm*>

Plain English Campaign (UK), <*www.plainenglish.co.uk/*>

Plain Language Association International (PLAIN), <*http://plainlanguagenetwork.org/*>

Plain Language Commission (UK), <*www.clearest.co.uk/*>

PlainLanguage.gov, <*www.plainlanguage.gov/*>

Scribes, <*www.scribes.org/*>

Seton Hall Law School Legislative Bureau, <*http://law.shu.edu/journals/legbureau/*>

Sir William Dale Centre for Legislative Studies, Institute of Advanced Legal Studies (IALS), University of London, <*http://ials.sas.ac.uk/research/dale/cls.htm*>

TheCapitol.Net, "Drafting Effective Federal Legislation and Amendments," <*www.thecapitol.net/PublicPrograms/legisdrafting.html*>

App. 3.60 Other Online Resources

The Legislative Lawyer, <*www.ncsl.org/programs/legman/legalsrv/lssshome.htm*>

The Loophole, <*www.opc.gov.au/calc/papers.htm*>

Statutory Construction Zone, <*www.statconblog.blogspot.com/*>

Appendix Four: The Legislative Process— A Working Example

App. 4.00 Introduction

The material that follows is included here to provide a working example of the legislative process in Congress, a topic covered by Chapter Two.

Special thanks are given to the authors, Michael L. Koempel and Judy Schneider, and to TheCapitol.Net, for making the material available.

The material originally appeared as Chapter Fifteen of the *Congressional Deskbook*. It is reprinted here in a different format and with some technical changes, but otherwise without modification.

App. 4.10 Key Legislative Documents Depicting the History of Financial Services Modernization Legislation in the 106th Congress

Throughout this book, we have presented the legislative process by describing its often esoteric procedures and the documents that are generated at each stage. In this section, our goal is to bring life to the process by describing the progression of a specific piece of legislation—financial services modernization—as it moved through various procedural stages in 1999, the first session of the 106th Congress.

On each following page, the reader will find cover pages and selections from the principal, formal documents generated during the consideration of the financial services legislation. The reader will also find on each of these pages an explanation of the purpose of the representative document in the legislative process and the information that can be gleaned from it. As mentioned throughout this book, many of the documents generated in the legislative process are available from THOMAS, GPO Access, and the House and Senate web sites.

Recall that comprehensive legislation is rarely introduced, considered, and enacted within one session of Congress. It is the product of years of hearings, negotiation, and political timing. For example, the hearings that were held by the House Banking and Financial Services Committee in February 1999, and by the House Commerce Committee's Subcommittee on Finance and Hazardous Materials in April 1999, were the last in a series of hearings on the financial services industry and its regulation by the federal and state governments that had begun years before.

Therefore, to get a full appreciation of the history of this particular legislation, it would be useful to go back at least several Congresses, read the hearings, examine the earlier legislation introduced and perhaps considered, and review statements and any debate that appeared in the *Congressional Record*. There is always a history to a legislative issue, and many members of Congress have participated in at least part of that history before one Congress is able to align policy, politics, and procedure to enact legislation that the president signs into law.

In the 107th Congress, the Banking and Financial Services Committee was renamed the Financial Services Committee, and the Commerce Committee was renamed the Energy and Commerce Committee. In addition, the Financial

This section is from the Congressional Deskbook, *by Judy Schneider and Michael Koempel, <www.CongressionalDeskbook.com>.*

Services Committee was given jurisdiction over the "business of insurance" and "securities and exchanges," jurisdictional authority that had generally resided in the Commerce Committee. An important cause of the name change and jurisdictional realignment was the enactment of the financial services modernization legislation.

A January 30, 2001, memorandum of understanding that was printed in the *Congressional Record* supplemented the jurisdictional changes to explain certain aspects of insurance and securities issues that would remain in the Energy and Commerce Committee. In the 109th Congress, the Speaker announced that the memorandum of understanding would be modified by deleting a paragraph. The announcement was printed in the *Congressional Record* on January 4, 2005. The paragraph deleted read:

> While it is agreed that the jurisdiction of the Committee on Financial Services over securities and exchanges includes anti-fraud authorities under the securities laws, the Committee on Energy and Commerce will retain jurisdiction only over the issue of setting accounting standards by the Financial Accounting Standards Board.

It is important to know as well that financial services reform as an issue has been considered, in various forms, almost from the time that the Glass-Steagall Act of 1933, the New Deal foundation of twentieth-century financial services regulation, was originally enacted. Major financial services legislation—covering banking, insurance, securities, and related financial services—was subsequently enacted in 1934, 1940, 1945, 1956, 1974, 1977, 1978, 1989, 1991, and 1994. Other major laws preceded Glass-Steagall and numerous other changes were reflected in amendments and minor legislation over the years. Likewise, oversight continues, and changes to the financial services modernization law can be tucked into new legislation on related subjects or be considered in separate legislation. The government affairs professional, scholar, or anyone working in a subject area needs to develop a good knowledge of the legislative and regulatory history of that subject area.

App. 4.11 Bill as Introduced in the House

H.R. 10 was introduced by Mr. Leach, chair of the House Committee on Banking and Financial Services, on January 6, 1999, the first day of the 106th Congress. Upon introduction there were eleven original cosponsors. The measure was referred to the Committee on Banking and Financial Services *(primary committee)*, and in addition to the Committee on Commerce for consideration of provisions within its jurisdiction. Those provisions were not spelled out in the referral language. The Speaker was granted authority to impose time limitations on the referral.

H.R. 10 is designated as *A Bill* at this stage of the process. The *official title* is the language immediately following the bill designation. The *enacting clause*, "*Be it enacted by the Senate and House of Representatives of the United States of America in Congress assembled,*" provides force of law to the measure, if enacted. Section 1(a) identifies the *short (popular) title*; a short title is how most people refer to a measure as it makes its way through the legislative process. *(See App. 4.11a.)*

This section is from the Congressional Deskbook, *by Judy Schneider and Michael Koempel, <www.CongressionalDeskbook.com>.*

App. 4.11a

Bill as Introduced in the House

1 Measure number

2 Sponsor and original cosponsors

3 Primary committee referral and sequential referral

4 Official title

5 Enacting clause

6 Short (popular) title

106TH CONGRESS
1ST SESSION

1 **H. R. 10**

To enhance competition in the financial services industry by providing a prudential framework for the affiliation of banks, securities firms, and other financial service providers, and for other purposes.

IN THE HOUSE OF REPRESENTATIVES

JANUARY 6, 1999

2 Mr. LEACH (for himself, Mr. McCOLLUM, Mrs. ROUKEMA, Mr. BAKER, Mr. LAZIO, Mr. BACHUS, Mr. CASTLE, Mr. KING, Mr. NEY, Mr. COOK, Mr. LATOURETTE, and Mrs. KELLY) introduced the following bill; which was 3 referred to the Committee on Banking and Financial Services, and in addition to the Committee on Commerce, for a period to be subsequently determined by the Speaker, in each case for consideration of such provisions as fall within the jurisdiction of the committee concerned

---

A BILL

4 To enhance competition in the financial services industry by providing a prudential framework for the affiliation of banks, securities firms, and other financial service providers, and for other purposes.

5 *Be it enacted by the Senate and House of Representatives of the United States of America in Congress assembled,*

2

SECTION 1. SHORT TITLE; PURPOSES; TABLE OF CONTENTS.

6 (a) SHORT TITLE.—This Act may be cited as the "Financial Services Act of 1999".

This section is from the Congressional Deskbook, *by Judy Schneider and Michael Koempel, <www.CongressionalDeskbook.com>.*

App. 4.12 Bill as Reported

The Committee on Banking and Financial Services reported H.R. 10 from committee to the House on March 23, 1999, by a vote of 51 to 8. The vote to report followed two markup sessions held on March 10 and 11. The language on the cover of the reported measure following the phrase "March 23, 1999" indicates that the committee reported a full-text substitute to H.R. 10, *an amendment in the nature of a substitute. (See App. 4.12a, notes 3, 4.)*

The accompanying committee report was H. Rept. 106-74, the 74th House report filed in the 106th Congress. It was filed in three parts. When more than one committee reports a measure, the report number remains the same for all committees. Each committee version is identified as Part I, Part II, and so forth. (Arabic numbers are gaining popularity for numbering parts, but Roman numerals are traditional.) For H.R. 10, the Banking Committee filed both Parts I and II *(see explanation at App. 4.14)*. The measure was placed on the *Union Calendar* and was the 105th measure placed on the calendar. *(See App. 4.12a, note 1.)*

H.R. 10 was *sequentially* referred to the Committee on Commerce until May 14, 1999. On May 13, the Commerce Committee received an extension until June 11, and, on June 11, it received another extension until June 15. On June 15, the Committee on Commerce reported H.R. 10 from committee to the House with *an amendment in the nature of a substitute*. Within the document (the bill as reported by the two committees), the Commerce Committee amendment followed the Banking Committee amendment. The Banking Committee amendment was printed in italicized type, and the Commerce Committee amendment, in boldface Roman type. *(Compare excerpts at notes 9 and 10 in App. 4.12a.)*

On June 15, Mr. Maloney, a member of the Banking and Financial Services Committee, was also added as a cosponsor on the legislation. Members can be added as cosponsors until the measure is reported by all committees that received a referral. *(See App. 4.12a, note 6.)*

This section is from the Congressional Deskbook, *by Judy Schneider and Michael Koempel, <www.CongressionalDeskbook.com>.*

App. 4.12a

Bill as Reported

1 Calendar number

2 Committee report in three parts

3 Reported from primary committee

4 Form in which amendment was reported (amendment in the nature of a substitute)

5 Sequential referral

6 Additional cosponsor

1 **Union Calendar No. 105**

106TH CONGRESS
1ST SESSION

H. R. 10

2 **[Report No. 106–74, Parts I, II, and III]**

To enhance competition in the financial services industry by providing a prudential framework for the affiliation of banks, securities firms, and other financial service providers, and for other purposes.

IN THE HOUSE OF REPRESENTATIVES

JANUARY 6, 1999

Mr. LEACH (for himself, Mr. MCCOLLUM, Mrs. ROUKEMA, Mr. BAKER, Mr. LAZIO, Mr. BACHUS, Mr. CASTLE, Mr. KING, Mr. NEY, Mr. COOK, Mr. LATOURETTE, and Mrs. KELLY) introduced the following bill; which was referred to the Committee on Banking and Financial Services, and in addition to the Committee on Commerce, for a period to be subsequently determined by the Speaker, in each case for consideration of such provisions as fall within the jurisdiction of the committee concerned

MARCH 23, 1999

3 Reported from the Committee on Banking and Financial Services with an amendment

4 [Strike out all after the enacting clause and insert the part printed in italic]

MARCH 23, 1999

5 Referral to the Committee on Commerce extended for a period ending not later than May 14, 1999

MAY 13, 1999

Referral to the Committee on Commerce extended for a period ending not later than June 11, 1999

JUNE 11, 1999

Referral to the Committee on Commerce extended for a period ending not later than June 15, 1999

JUNE 15, 1999

6 Additional sponsor: Mr. MALONEY of Connecticut

(Continued on page 334)

This section is from the Congressional Deskbook, *by Judy Schneider and Michael Koempel, <www.CongressionalDeskbook.com>.*

App. 4.12a (continued)

Bill as Reported

❼ Reported from Commerce Committee

❽ Form in which amendment was reported (amendment in the nature of a substitute)

❾ Banking Committee amendment

2

JUNE 15, 1999

❼ Reported from the Committee on Commerce with an amendment, committed to the Committee of the Whole House on the State of the Union, and ordered to be printed

❽ [Strike out all after the enacting clause and insert the part printed in boldface roman]

[For text of introduced bill, see copy of bill as introduced on January 6, 1999]

A BILL

To enhance competition in the financial services industry by providing a prudential framework for the affiliation of banks, securities firms, and other financial service providers, and for other purposes.

Be it enacted by the Senate and House of Representatives of the United States of America in Congress assembled,

❾ ***SECTION 1. SHORT TITLE; PURPOSES; TABLE OF CONTENTS.***

(a) SHORT TITLE.—This Act may be cited as the "Financial Services Act of 1999".

(b) PURPOSES.—The purposes of this Act are as follows:

(1) To enhance competition in the financial services industry, in order to foster innovation and efficiency.

(2) To ensure the continued safety and soundness of depository institutions.

(Continued on page 335)

This section is from the Congressional Deskbook, by Judy Schneider and Michael Koempel, <www.CongressionalDeskbook.com>.

App. 4.12a (continued)

Bill as Reported

375

of a Federal savings association to a national bank or a State bank after the date of the enactment of the Financial Services Act of 1999 may retain the term 'Federal' in the name of such institution if such depository institution remains an insured depository institution.

"(2) DEFINITIONS.—For purposes of this subsection, the terms 'depository institution', 'insured depository institution', 'national bank', and 'State bank' have the same meanings as in section 3 of the Federal Deposit Insurance Act.".

⑩ Commerce Committee amendment

⑩ **SECTION 1. SHORT TITLE; PURPOSES; TABLE OF CONTENTS.**

(a) SHORT TITLE.—This Act may be cited as the "Financial Services Act of 1999".

(b) PURPOSES.—The purposes of this Act are as follows:

(1) To enhance competition in the financial services industry, in order to foster innovation and efficiency.

(2) To ensure the continued safety and soundness of depository institutions.

(3) To provide necessary and appropriate protections for investors and en-

App. 4.13 Banking and Financial Services Committee Report

Both the Banking Committee and the Commerce Committee reported H.R. 10. Part 1 of H. Rept. 106-74 was filed in the House by the primary committee, the Committee on Banking and Financial Services. When that panel reported H.R. 10 on March 23, 1999, the committee chose to retain H.R. 10 as the legislative vehicle and to report an *amendment in the nature of a substitute.* The committee could have chosen to introduce the amended language as a new, or *clean bill.*

Supplemental, additional, and dissenting views were also filed. They are included in the body of the report. Minority committee members usually request the inclusion of supplemental, additional, and dissenting views in a committee report. Although the request is traditionally made by minority-party members, all committee members are entitled to file such views. To be included, supplemental, additional, and dissenting views must be filed within two days of a committee vote to report. The cover page of the report must indicate when such views are included.

This section is from the Congressional Deskbook, *by Judy Schneider and Michael Koempel, <www.CongressionalDeskbook.com>.*

App. 4.13a

Banking and Financial Services Committee Report

❶ Committee report and part number

106TH CONGRESS, 1st Session } HOUSE OF REPRESENTATIVES ❶ { REPT. 106–74, Part 1

FINANCIAL SERVICES ACT OF 1999

MARCH 23, 1999.—Ordered to be printed

❷ Reporting committee

❷ Mr. LEACH, from the Committee on Banking and Financial Services, submitted the following

REPORT

together with

❸ Other views

❸ SUPPLEMENTAL, ADDITIONAL AND DISSENTING VIEWS

[To accompany H.R. 10]

The Committee on Banking and Financial Services, to whom was referred the bill (H.R. 10) to enhance competition in the financial services industry by providing a prudential framework for the affiliation of banks, securities firms, and other financial service providers, and for other purposes, having considered the same, report favorably thereon with an amendment and recommend that the bill as amended do pass.

The amendment is as follows:

❹ Banking Committee amendment

❹ Strike out all after the enacting clause and insert in lieu thereof the following:

SECTION 1. SHORT TITLE; PURPOSES; TABLE OF CONTENTS.

(a) SHORT TITLE.—This Act may be cited as the "Financial Services Act of 1999".

(b) PURPOSES.—The purposes of this Act are as follows:

★69–006

App. 4.14 Banking and Financial Services Committee Supplementary Report

The Committee on Banking and Financial Services filed in the House a supplementary report containing a cost estimate from the Congressional Budget Office. According to House rules, such an estimate must be included in a committee report. The committee filed a supplementary report to comply with this requirement. The supplementary report also contains an errata correction to Part 1 of the report. The report retains the same number, but is designated Part 2.

This section is from the Congressional Deskbook, *by Judy Schneider and Michael Koempel, <www.CongressionalDeskbook.com>.*

App. 4.14a

Banking and Financial Services Committee Supplementary Report

❶ Committee report and part number

❷ Reporting committee

❸ Supplementary report

❹ Purpose of supplementary report

106TH CONGRESS, *1st Session* } HOUSE OF REPRESENTATIVES ❶ { REPT. 106–74, Part 2

FINANCIAL SERVICES ACT OF 1999

JUNE 10, 1999.—Ordered to be printed

❷ Mr. LEACH, from the Committee on Banking and Financial Services, submitted the following

❸ SUPPLEMENTARY REPORT

[To accompany H.R. 10]

❹ This supplemental report shows the cost estimate of the Congressional Budget Office with respect to the bill (H.R. 10), as reported, which was not included in part 1 of the report submitted by the Committee on Banking and Financial Services on March 23, 1999 (H. Rept. 106–74, pt. 1).

This supplemental report is submitted in accordance with clause 3(a)(2) of rule XIII of the Rules of the House of Representatives.

This supplemental report also contains an errata correction to page 2 of part 1 of the report.

U.S CONGRESS,
CONGRESSIONAL BUDGET OFFICE,
Washington, DC, June 10, 1999.

Hon. JAMES A. LEACH,
Chairman, Committee on Banking and Financial Services, House of Representatives, Washington, DC.

DEAR MR. CHAIRMAN: The Congressional Budget Office has prepared the enclosed costs estimate and mandate statements for H.R. 10, the Financial Services Act of 1999. One enclosure includes the estimate of federal costs and the estimate of the impact of the legislation on state, local, and tribal governments. The estimated impact of mandates on the private sector is discussed in a separate enclosure.

If you wish further details on these estimates, we will be pleased to provide them. The CBO staff contacts are Robert S. Seiler (for costs to the Federal Home Loan Banks); Mary Maginniss (for other federal costs); Carolyn Lynch (for federal revenues); Susan Seig (for

57–234

App. 4.15 Commerce Committee Report

Here is the report filed in the House by the House Committee on Commerce, which received a sequential referral of H.R. 10. The report was filed by Mr. Bliley, the chair of the Committee on Commerce, on June 15, 1999, the day the measure was reported with an *amendment in the nature of a substitute*. The report is designated Part 3 of H. Rept. 106-74. Additional views were also filed and included in the body of the report.

This section is from the Congressional Deskbook, *by Judy Schneider and Michael Koempel, <www.CongressionalDeskbook.com>.*

App. 4.15a

Commerce Committee Report

❶ Committee report and part number

❷ Reporting committee

❸ Additional views

106TH CONGRESS *1st Session*	HOUSE OF REPRESENTATIVES ❶	REPT. 106–74 Part 3

FINANCIAL SERVICES ACT OF 1999

JUNE 15, 1999.—Committed to the Committee of the Whole House on the State of the Union and ordered to be printed

❷ Mr. BLILEY, from the Committee on Commerce, submitted the following

R E P O R T

together with

❸ ADDITIONAL VIEWS

[To accompany H.R. 10]

The Committee on Commerce, to whom was referred the bill (H.R. 10) to enhance competition in the financial services industry by providing a prudential framework for the affiliation of banks, securities firms, and other financial service providers, and for other purposes, having considered the same, report favorably thereon with an amendment and recommend that the bill as amended do pass.

CONTENTS

57–325

(Continued on page 342)

App. 4.15a (continued)

Commerce Committee Report

❹ Commerce Committee amendment

2

AMENDMENT

The amendment is as follows:

❹ Strike out all after the enacting clause and insert in lieu thereof the following:

SECTION 1. SHORT TITLE; PURPOSES; TABLE OF CONTENTS.

(a) SHORT TITLE.—This Act may be cited as the "Financial Services Act of 1999".

(b) PURPOSES.—The purposes of this Act are as follows:

(1) To enhance competition in the financial services industry, in order to foster innovation and efficiency.

(2) To ensure the continued safety and soundness of depository institutions.

(3) To provide necessary and appropriate protections for investors and ensure fair and honest markets in the delivery of financial services.

(4) To avoid duplicative, potentially conflicting, and overly burdensome regulatory requirements through the creation of a regulatory framework for financial holding companies that respects the divergent requirements of each of the component businesses of the holding company, and that is based upon principles of strong functional regulation and enhanced regulatory coordination.

(5) To reduce and, to the maximum extent practicable, to eliminate the legal barriers preventing affiliation among depository institutions, securities firms, insurance companies, and other financial service providers and to provide a prudential framework for achieving that result.

(6) To enhance the availability of financial services to citizens of all economic circumstances and in all geographic areas.

(7) To enhance the competitiveness of United States financial service providers internationally.

(8) To ensure compliance by depository institutions with the provisions of the Community Reinvestment Act of 1977 and enhance the ability of depository institutions to meet the capital and credit needs of all citizens and communities, including underserved communities and populations.

(c) TABLE OF CONTENTS.—The table of contents for this Act is as follows:

This section is from the Congressional Deskbook, *by Judy Schneider and Michael Koempel, <www.CongressionalDeskbook.com>.*

App. 4.16 Special Rule from the Rules Committee

On June 30, 1999, the House Rules Committee reported from committee to the House H. Res. 235, a *special rule* providing for consideration of H.R. 10. The special rule was placed on the *House Calendar* as the eighty-first item. The special rule was reported by Mr. Sessions, a Rules Committee majority member, who was selected to manage the special rule on the floor. The special rule was accompanied by H. Rept. 106-214.

A special rule itself is considered in the House under the *one-hour rule*. Mr. Sessions yielded half of his one hour to a minority member of the Rules Committee *for purposes of debate only*. The two floor managers then parceled out short blocks of time to their colleagues to speak on the rule.

The special rule on H.R. 10 provided ninety minutes of general debate time on the bill, equally divided and controlled by the chairs and ranking minority members of the two committees that reported the legislation, Banking and Financial Services, and Commerce. The special rule also provided for consideration of a new version of H.R. 10, included in the Rules Committee report (H. Rept. 106-214) and cited as "Rules Committee Print dated June 24, 1999." The special rule referred to the Rules Committee report for a list of amendments made in order and the time allocated for each amendment.

This section is from the Congressional Deskbook, *by Judy Schneider and Michael Koempel, <www.CongressionalDeskbook.com>.*

App. 4.16a

Special Rule from the Rules Committee

IV

(1) Calendar number

(2) Resolution number

(3) Committee report number

(4) Majority manager of special rule

(5) Special rule for the consideration of H.R. 10

(1) **House Calendar No. 81**

106TH CONGRESS
1ST SESSION

(2) **H. RES. 235**

(3) **[Report No. 106–214]**

Providing for consideration of the bill (H.R. 10) to enhance competition in the financial services industry by providing a prudential framework for the affiliation of banks, securities firms, and other financial service providers, and for other purposes.

IN THE HOUSE OF REPRESENTATIVES

JUNE 30, 1999

(4) Mr. SESSIONS, from the Committee on Rules, reported the following resolution; which was referred to the House Calendar and ordered to be printed

---

RESOLUTION

(5) Providing for consideration of the bill (H.R. 10) to enhance competition in the financial services industry by providing a prudential framework for the affiliation of banks, securities firms, and other financial service providers, and for other purposes.

Resolved, That at any time after the adoption of this resolution the Speaker may, pursuant to clause 2(b) of rule XVIII, declare the House resolved into the Committee of the Whole House on the state of the Union for consideration of the bill (H.R. 10) to enhance competition in the

(Continued on page 346)

This section is from the Congressional Deskbook, *by Judy Schneider and Michael Koempel, <www.CongressionalDeskbook.com>.*

App. 4.16a (continued)

Special Rule from the Rules Committee

❻ General debate

❼ Alternate version of H.R. 10

❽ Amendment process

2

financial services industry by providing a prudential framework for the affiliation of banks, securities firms, and other financial service providers, and for other purposes. The first reading of the bill shall be dispensed with. All points of order against consideration of the bill are ❻ waived. General debate shall be confined to the bill and shall not exceed 90 minutes, with 45 minutes equally divided and controlled by the chairman and ranking minority member of the Committee on Banking and Financial Services and 45 minutes equally divided and controlled by the chairman and ranking minority member of the Committee on Commerce. After general debate the bill shall be considered for amendment under the five-minute rule. ❼ In lieu of the amendments now printed in the bill, it shall be in order to consider as an original bill for the purpose of amendment under the five-minute rule an amendment in the nature of a substitute consisting of the text of the ❽ Rules Committee Print dated June 24, 1999. That amendment in the nature of a substitute shall be considered as read. All points of order against that amendment in the nature of a substitute are waived. No amendment to that amendment in the nature of a substitute shall be in order except those printed in the report of the Committee on Rules accompanying this resolution. Each amendment may be offered only in the order printed in

(Continued on page 347)

This section is from the Congressional Deskbook, *by Judy Schneider and Michael Koempel, <www.CongressionalDeskbook.com>.*

App. 4.16a (continued)

Special Rule from the Rules Committee

3

the report, may be offered only by a Member designated in the report, shall be considered as read, shall be debatable for the time specified in the report equally divided and controlled by the proponent and an opponent, shall not be subject to amendment, and shall not be subject to a demand for division of the question in the House or in the Committee of the Whole. All points of order against the amendments printed in the report are waived.

9 Cluster voting

(9) The Chairman of the Committee of the Whole may: (1) postpone until a time during further consideration in the Committee of the Whole a request for a recorded vote on any amendment; and (2) reduce to five minutes the minimum time for electronic voting on any postponed question that follows another electronic vote without intervening business, provided that the minimum time for electronic voting on the first in any series of questions shall be 15 minutes.

10 House action

(10) At the conclusion of consideration of the bill for amendment the Committee shall rise and report the bill to the House with such amendments as may have been adopted. Any Member may demand a separate vote in the House on any amendment adopted in the Committee of the Whole to the bill or to the amendment in the nature of a substitute made in order as original text. The previous question shall be considered as ordered on the bill and amendments thereto to final passage without intervening motion except one motion to recommit with or without instructions.

This section is from the Congressional Deskbook, *by Judy Schneider and Michael Koempel, <www.CongressionalDeskbook.com>.*

App. 4.17 Rules Committee Report

Accompanying H. Res. 235 was H. Rept. 106-214, a report from the Committee on Rules. The special rule was reported from the Rules Committee by a recorded vote of 9 to 3, and the report filed in the House June 30, 1999, by Mr. Sessions. The report summarized the provisions of the special rule, provided information on all votes taken in the Rules Committee, and, most importantly, designated which amendments would be allowed to be offered on the floor and how much time would be allocated for each amendment. Eleven amendments were made in order under the special rule. Each amendment's sponsor was identified, the amendment was summarized, and the amount of time allocated for each amendment was noted. The full text of each amendment was also included in the Rules Committee report.

App. 4.17a

Rules Committee Report

❶ Committee report number

❷ Purpose of special rule

❸ Provisions of special rule

106TH CONGRESS 1st Session } HOUSE OF REPRESENTATIVES { ❶ REPORT 106–214

❷ PROVIDING FOR THE CONSIDERATION OF H.R. 10, FINANCIAL SERVICES ACT OF 1999

JUNE 30, 1999.—Referred to the House Calendar and ordered to be printed

Mr. SESSIONS, from the Committee on Rules, submitted the following

REPORT

[To accompany H. Res. 235]

The Committee on Rules, having had under consideration House Resolution 235, by a record vote of 9 to 3, report the same to the House with the recommendation that the resolution be adopted.

❸ SUMMARY OF PROVISIONS OF RESOLUTION

The resolution provides for the consideration of H.R. 10, the "Financial Services Act of 1999," under a structured rule. The rule provides 90 minutes of general debate: 45 minutes divided equally between the chairman and ranking minority member of the Committee on Commerce.

The rule waives all points of order against consideration of the bill. The rule makes in order the amendment in the nature of a substitute consisting of the text of the Rules Committee Print dated June 24, 1999, as original text for the purpose of amendment. The rule waives all points of order against the amendment in the nature a substitute.

The rule provides that no amendment to the amendment in the nature of a substitute shall be in order except those printed in this report, which may be offered in the order printed in this report, may be offered only by a Member designated in this report, shall be considered as read, shall be debatable for the time specified in this report equally divided and controlled by the proponent and an opponent, shall not be subject to amendment, and shall not be subject to a demand for a division of the question. The rule waives all points of order against the amendments printed in this report.

The rule allows the chairman of the Committee of the Whole to postpone recorded votes and reduce voting time to five minutes on any postponed question, provided voting time on the first in any se-

69–008

App. 4.18 Statement of Administration Policy (House)

On July 1, 1999, the Office of Management and Budget issued a Statement of Administration Policy on H.R. 10, the House bill. The statement announced the president's support for the legislation and opposition to selected amendments to be offered to it.

App. 4.18a

Statement of Administration Policy (House)

EXECUTIVE OFFICE OF THE PRESIDENT
OFFICE OF MANAGEMENT AND BUDGET
WASHINGTON, D.C. 20503

STATEMENT OF ADMINISTRATION POLICY
(THIS STATEMENT HAS BEEN COORDINATED BY OMB WITH THE CONCERNED AGENCIES.)

July 1, 1999
(House)

H.R. 10 - Financial Services Act of 1999
(Leach (R) IA and 12 co-sponsors)

The Administration supports H.R. 10, the Financial Services Act of 1999. The Administration has been a strong proponent of financial modernization legislation that would best serve the interests of consumers, business, and communities, while protecting the safety and soundness of the financial system. H.R. 10 would:

- allow affiliations among banks, securities firms, and insurance companies, thereby increasing the competitiveness of the U.S. financial services sector and giving consumers greater choice and lower prices;
- preserve the relevance of the Community Reinvestment Act by requiring that banks have and maintain a satisfactory CRA record as a condition for their affiliates or subsidiaries engaging in new financial activities;
- uphold a bipartisan compromise allowing financial services firms to conduct financial activities in the structure -- subsidiaries or affiliates of banks -- that best serves their customers, in a way that is best for safety and soundness;
- generally provide for the continued separation of banking and commerce.

The President has stated the importance of adopting protections to ensure the privacy of consumers' financial records. The amendment to be considered by the House would improve the bill by including new privacy protections, although it does not address all of the issues involved. The Administration will continue to pursue additional protections.

The Administration strongly opposes the medical privacy provisions of the bill. Unfortunately, those provisions would preempt important existing protections and do not reflect the extensive legislative work that has already been done on this complex issue. The Administration thus urges striking the medical privacy provisions and will pursue medical privacy in other fora.

The Administration strongly opposes the Barr-Paul-Campbell Amendment, which would seriously erode our ability to fight financial criminals and the drug cartels. The amendment would effectively eliminate suspicious activity reporting by financial institutions -- one of our

(Continued on page 351)

This section is from the Congressional Deskbook, *by Judy Schneider and Michael Koempel, <www.CongressionalDeskbook.com>.*

App. 4.18a (continued)

Statement of Administration Policy (House)

most important tools in fighting money laundering and fraud. The amendment would mark a significant retreat in our fight against narcotraffickers. The Administration strongly opposes the bill's Federal Home Loan Bank System provisions, particularly a provision that would allow each Home Loan Bank to cut its capital requirement in half and thereby effectively increase the System's taxpayer subsidy without any commensurate return in public benefits. In addition, the Administration believes that the System must focus more on lending to community banks and less on arbitrage activities and short-term lending that do not advance its public purpose. The Administration opposes granting the Federal Housing Finance Board independent litigating authority, which would be inconsistent with the Attorney General's authority to coordinate and conduct litigation on behalf of the United States.

The Administration strongly objects to the refusal to allow House consideration of Representative Lee's anti-redlining amendment, which would help deter violations of the Fair Housing Act. The Administration strongly supports the amendment.

The Administration is concerned that the bill would unduly restrict banks' authority to sell insurance, thereby diminishing competition and reducing choice for consumers.

Because of its commitment to maintaining a separation of banking and commerce, the Administration continues to favor a clear prohibition on existing unitary thrift holding companies selling their subsidiary thrifts to non-financial firms. Allowing such sales could lead to substantial non-financial ownership of insured depository institutions.

The Administration opposes section 154 because it could be seen as undermining principles of normal trade relations and national treatment, which could weaken efforts to negotiate further market access liberalization and expose U.S. firms to additional restrictions abroad.

App. 4.19 Legislation as Passed the House

Pursuant to the provisions of the special rule that had been adopted, the legislation was considered in the Committee of the Whole. Of the eleven amendments made in order under H. Res. 235 (the special rule), five were agreed to by voice vote, four were agreed to by recorded vote, and two failed by recorded vote. The measure passed the House on a 343 to 86 vote.

The measure was now designated as *An Act*, which is how the reader knows that the legislation has passed one chamber. This document is also now referred to as the *House engrossed bill.*

App. 4.19a

Legislation as Passed the House

❶ No longer *A Bill* but *An Act* (engrossed measure)

106TH CONGRESS
1ST SESSION

H. R. 10

❶ **AN ACT**

To enhance competition in the financial services industry by providing a prudential framework for the affiliation of banks, securities firms, and other financial service providers, and for other purposes.

Be it enacted by the Senate and House of Representatives of the United States of America in Congress assembled,

(Continued on page 353)

This section is from the Congressional Deskbook, *by Judy Schneider and Michael Koempel, <www.CongressionalDeskbook.com>.*

App. 4.19a (continued)

Legislation as Passed the House

2

SECTION 1. SHORT TITLE; PURPOSES; TABLE OF CONTENTS.

(a) SHORT TITLE.—This Act may be cited as the "Financial Services Act of 1999".

(b) PURPOSES.—The purposes of this Act are as follows:

(1) To enhance competition in the financial services industry, in order to foster innovation and efficiency.

(2) To ensure the continued safety and soundness of depository institutions.

(3) To provide necessary and appropriate protections for investors and ensure fair and honest markets in the delivery of financial services.

(4) To avoid duplicative, potentially conflicting, and overly burdensome regulatory requirements through the creation of a regulatory framework for financial holding companies that respects the divergent requirements of each of the component businesses of the holding company, and that is based upon principles of strong functional regulation and enhanced regulatory coordination.

(5) To reduce and, to the maximum extent practicable, to eliminate the legal barriers preventing affiliation among depository institutions, securities firms, insurance companies, and other financial serv-

•HR 10 EH

App. 4.110 Legislation as Received in the Senate

H.R. 10 was received by the Senate on July 12, 1999. It was not referred to a Senate committee, although that could have happened. It was *placed directly on the calendar*, in part because a companion Senate measure had already been considered by a Senate committee.

App. 4.110a

Legislation as Received in the Senate

(1) Calendar number

(2) House-passed measure received by Senate

II

(1) Calendar No. 204

106TH CONGRESS
1ST SESSION

H. R. 10

---

(2) IN THE SENATE OF THE UNITED STATES

JULY 12, 1999

Received; read twice and placed on the Calendar

AN ACT

To enhance competition in the financial services industry by providing a prudential framework for the affiliation of banks, securities firms, and other financial service providers, and for other purposes.

Be it enacted by the Senate and House of Representatives of the United States of America in Congress assembled,

(Continued on page 355)

This section is from the Congressional Deskbook, *by Judy Schneider and Michael Koempel,* <*www.CongressionalDeskbook.com*>.

App. 4.110a (continued)

Legislation as Received in the Senate

2

SECTION 1. SHORT TITLE; PURPOSES; TABLE OF CONTENTS.

(a) SHORT TITLE.—This Act may be cited as the "Financial Services Act of 1999".

(b) PURPOSES.—The purposes of this Act are as follows:

(1) To enhance competition in the financial services industry, in order to foster innovation and efficiency.

(2) To ensure the continued safety and soundness of depository institutions.

(3) To provide necessary and appropriate protections for investors and ensure fair and honest markets in the delivery of financial services.

(4) To avoid duplicative, potentially conflicting, and overly burdensome regulatory requirements through the creation of a regulatory framework for financial holding companies that respects the divergent requirements of each of the component businesses of the holding company, and that is based upon principles of strong functional regulation and enhanced regulatory coordination.

(5) To reduce and, to the maximum extent practicable, to eliminate the legal barriers preventing affiliation among depository institutions, securities firms, insurance companies, and other financial serv-

HR 10 PCS

App. 4.111 Legislation as Introduced in the Senate

S. 900 is an *original bill*, which means that it was not introduced and referred to the Senate Committee on Banking, Housing, and Urban Affairs, but rather was drafted in the committee and then reported to the Senate. The chair of the committee, Mr. Gramm, reported the measure on April 28, 1999. A committee report, S. Rept. 106-44, was also filed in the Senate. The measure was placed on the Senate calendar as the ninety-fourth item.

This section is from the Congressional Deskbook, *by Judy Schneider and Michael Koempel, <www.CongressionalDeskbook.com>.*

App. 4.111a

Legislation as Introduced in the Senate

(1) Calendar number

(2) Committee report number

(3) Original bill reported from committee

(4) Official title

(5) Enacting clause

(6) Short (popular) title

II

(1) **Calendar No. 94**

106TH CONGRESS
1ST SESSION

S. 900

(2) **[Report No. 106–44]**

To enhance competition in the financial services industry by providing a prudential framework for the affiliation of banks, securities firms, insurance companies, and other financial service providers, and for other purposes.

IN THE SENATE OF THE UNITED STATES

APRIL 28, 1999

(3) Mr. GRAMM, from the Committee on Banking, Housing, and Urban Affairs, reported the following original bill, which was read twice and placed on the calendar

---

A BILL

(4) To enhance competition in the financial services industry by providing a prudential framework for the affiliation of banks, securities firms, insurance companies, and other financial service providers, and for other purposes.

(5) *Be it enacted by the Senate and House of Representatives of the United States of America in Congress assembled,*

SECTION 1. SHORT TITLE; TABLE OF CONTENTS.

(6) (a) SHORT TITLE.—This Act may be cited as the "Financial Services Modernization Act of 1999".

This section is from the Congressional Deskbook, *by Judy Schneider and Michael Koempel, <www.CongressionalDeskbook.com>.*

App. 4.112 Senate Committee Report

The Committee on Banking, Housing, and Urban Affairs reported S. 900 to the Senate, by an 11 to 9 vote. A committee report was filed in the Senate on April 28, 1999, and numbered S. Rept. 106-44, the forty-fourth Senate committee report filed in the 106th Congress. *Additional views* were also filed and included in the body of the report. The calendar number is repeated on the cover page of the Senate report. A section entitled *introduction* and another entitled *history of legislation* summarized the Senate Banking Committee's actions on the legislation.

This section is from the Congressional Deskbook, *by Judy Schneider and Michael Koempel,* <*www.CongressionalDeskbook.com*>.

App. 4.112a

Senate Committee Report

1 Calendar number

2 Committee report number

3 Reporting committee

4 Measure reported

5 Additional views

1 **Calendar No. 94**

106TH CONGRESS 1st Session	SENATE	2 REPORT 106–44

FINANCIAL SERVICES MODERNIZATION ACT OF 1999

REPORT

OF THE

3 COMMITTEE ON BANKING, HOUSING, AND URBAN AFFAIRS UNITED STATES SENATE

TO ACCOMPANY

4 S. 900

together with

5 ADDITIONAL VIEWS

APRIL 28, 1999.—Ordered to be printed

U.S. GOVERNMENT PRINTING OFFICE
69–010 WASHINGTON : 1999

This section is from the Congressional Deskbook, *by Judy Schneider and Michael Koempel, <www.CongressionalDeskbook.com>.*

App. 4.113 Statement of Administration Policy (Senate)

On May 3, 1999, the Office of Management and Budget issued a Statement of Administration Policy on S. 900, the Senate bill, announcing the administration's opposition to S. 900. The statement indicated that the president would veto the Senate measure in its current form.

This section is from the Congressional Deskbook, *by Judy Schneider and Michael Koempel, <www.CongressionalDeskbook.com>.*

App. 4.113a

Statement of Administration Policy (Senate)

EXECUTIVE OFFICE OF THE PRESIDENT
OFFICE OF MANAGEMENT AND BUDGET
WASHINGTON, D.C. 20503

STATEMENT OF ADMINISTRATION POLICY

(THIS STATEMENT HAS BEEN COORDINATED BY OMB WITH THE CONCERNED AGENCIES.)

May 3, 1999
(Senate)

S. 900 - Financial Services Modernization Act of 1999
(Gramm (R) TX)

The Administration strongly opposes S. 900, which would revise laws governing the financial services industry. This Administration has been a strong proponent of financial modernization legislation that would best serve the interests of consumers, businesses, and communities, while protecting the safety and soundness of our financial system. Consequently, it supports the bill's repeal of the Glass-Steagall Act's prohibition on banks affiliating with securities firms and of the Bank Holding Company Act's prohibitions on insurance underwriting. Nevertheless, because of crucial flaws in the bill, the President has stated that, if the bill were presented to him in its current form, he would veto it.

In its current form, the bill would undermine the effectiveness of the Community Reinvestment Act (CRA), a law that has helped to build homes and create jobs by encouraging banks to serve creditworthy borrowers throughout the communities they serve. The bill fails to require that banks seeking to conduct new financial activities achieve and maintain a satisfactory CRA record. In addition, the bill's "safe harbor" provision would amend current law to effectively shield financial institutions from public comment on banking applications that they file with Federal regulators. The CRA exemption for banks with less than $100 million in assets would repeal CRA for approximately 4,000 banks and thrifts that banking agency rules already exempt from CRA paperwork reporting burdens. In all, these limitations constitute an assault upon CRA and are unacceptable.

The bill would unjustifiably deny financial services firms holding 99 percent of national bank assets the choice of conducting new financial activities through subsidiaries, forcing them to conduct those activities exclusively through bank holding company affiliates. Thus the bill largely prohibits a structure with proven advantages for safety and soundness, effectively denying many financial services firms the freedom to organize themselves in the way that best serves their customers.

The bill would also inadequately inform and protect consumers under the new system of financial products it authorizes. If Congress is to authorize large, complex organizations to offer a wide range of financial products, then consumers should be guaranteed appropriate disclosures and other protections.

The bill would dramatically expand the ability of depository institutions and nonfinancial firms to affiliate. The Administration has serious concerns about mixing banking and commercial activity under any circumstances, and these concerns are heightened by the financial crises affecting other countries over the past few years.

The Administration also opposes the bill's piecemeal modification of the Federal Home Loan Bank System. The Administration believes that the System must focus more on lending to community banks and less on arbitrage activities and short-term lending that do not advance its public purpose. The Administration opposes any changes to the System that do not include these crucial reforms.

In addition, the Administration opposes granting the Federal Housing Finance Board independent litigation authority. Such authority would be inconsistent with the Attorney General's authority to coordinate and conduct litigation on behalf of the United States.

Pay-As-You-Go Scoring

S. 900 would affect direct spending and receipts. Therefore, it is subject to the pay-as-you-go requirement of the Omnibus Budget Reconciliation Act of 1990. OMB's pay-as-you-go scoring of this bill is under development.

App. 4.114 Legislation as Passed the Senate

The legislation was considered in the Senate by agreeing to a *motion to proceed to consideration*. Numerous amendments were offered and disposed of, either by being agreed to, rejected, withdrawn, or tabled. The measure passed the Senate by a vote of 54 to 44, on May 6, 1999.

The legislation is now designated as *An Act*, which is how the reader knows that the legislation has passed one chamber. This document is referred to as the *Senate engrossed bill*.

App. 4.114a

Legislation as Passed the Senate

106TH CONGRESS
1ST SESSION

S. 900

❶ No longer *A Bill* but *An Act* (engrossed measure)

❶ AN ACT

To enhance competition in the financial services industry by providing a prudential framework for the affiliation of banks, securities firms, insurance companies, and other financial service providers, and for other purposes.

Be it enacted by the Senate and House of Representatives of the United States of America in Congress assembled,

SECTION 1. SHORT TITLE; TABLE OF CONTENTS.

(a) SHORT TITLE.—This Act may be cited as the "Financial Services Modernization Act of 1999".

This section is from the Congressional Deskbook, *by Judy Schneider and Michael Koempel, <www.CongressionalDeskbook.com>.*

App. 4.115 Legislation Received in the House from the Senate

On July 20, 1999, the Senate bill, S. 900, was transmitted to the House, which considered it and amended it with its own version. This is evident from the language "strike out all after the enacting clause and insert."

The House and Senate took their first step toward reconciling differences—selecting one bill number, S. 900, to use as the legislative vehicle for further action.

App. 4.115a

Legislation Received in the House from the Senate

In the House of Representatives, U. S.,

July 20, 1999.

Resolved, That the bill from the Senate (S. 900) entitled "An Act to enhance competition in the financial services industry by providing a prudential framework for the affiliation of banks, securities firms, insurance companies, and other financial service providers, and for other purposes", do pass with the following

AMENDMENTS:

❶ House amendment to Senate bill (text of H.R. 10)

❶ Strike out all after the enacting clause and insert:

SECTION 1. SHORT TITLE; PURPOSES; TABLE OF CONTENTS.

(a) SHORT TITLE.—This Act may be cited as the "Financial Services Act of 1999".

(b) PURPOSES.—The purposes of this Act are as follows:

(1) To enhance competition in the financial services industry, in order to foster innovation and efficiency.

(2) To ensure the continued safety and soundness of depository institutions.

This section is from the Congressional Deskbook, *by Judy Schneider and Michael Koempel, <www.CongressionalDeskbook.com>.*

App. 4.116 Side-by-Side Comparative Print

Before convening a conference committee, it is customary for respective committee staff to prepare a side-by-side comparative print of the two versions of the measure to be reconciled in conference. This document enables conferees to see the differences between the two versions of a measure. A side-by-side often includes a fourth column—current law.

App. 4.116a

Side-by-Side Comparative Print

COMPARISON OF

S. 900, FINANCIAL SERVICES MODERNIZATION ACT OF 1999

AND

H.R. 10, FINANCIAL SERVICES ACT OF 1999

September 1, 1999

COMPARISON OF H.R. 10 AND S. 900

September 1, 1999

	H.R. 10	S. 900
1. Title	"Financial Services Act of 1999" (p.1)	"Financial Services Modernization Act of 1999" (p.1)
2. Statement of purpose	Purposes of this Act are: (1) to enhance competition in the financial services industry, in order to foster innovation and efficiency; (2) to ensure the continued safety and soundness of depository institutions; (3) to provide necessary and appropriate protections for investors and ensure fair and honest markets in the delivery of financial services; (4) to avoid duplicative, potentially conflicting, and overly burdensome regulatory requirements through creation of a regulatory framework for financial holding companies that respects the divergent requirements of each of the component businesses of the holding company, and that is based upon principles of strong functional regulation and enhanced regulatory coordination; (5) to reduce and, to the maximum extent practicable, to eliminate the legal barriers preventing affiliation among depository institutions, securities firms, insurance companies, and other financial service providers and to provide a prudential framework for achieving that result; (6) to enhance the availability of financial services to citizens of all economic circumstances and in all geographic areas; (7) to enhance the competitiveness of US financial services providers internationally; and, (8) to ensure compliance by depository institutions with the provisions of the CRA of	No provision.

-1-

This section is from the Congressional Deskbook, *by Judy Schneider and Michael Koempel, <www.CongressionalDeskbook.com>.*

App. 4.117 Conference Chair's Letter to Conferees

Informal documents relevant to a measure's consideration in conference are often produced, such as letters to conference committee members and leadership memoranda. In this case, Representative Leach, the House Banking and Financial Services Committee chair and the chair of the conference, provided to all conferees a set of ground rules related to consideration of the measure in the conference. Senate conferees were appointed on July 23, 1999. House conferees were named on July 30, 1999. The appointment of conferees is reported in the *Congressional Record.*

App. 4.117a

Conference Chair's Letter to Conferees

JAMES A. LEACH, IOWA, CHAIRMAN

BILL McCOLLUM, FLORIDA
MARGE ROUKEMA, NEW JERSEY
DOUG BEREUTER, NEBRASKA
RICHARD H. BAKER, LOUISIANA
RICK LAZIO, NEW YORK
SPENCER BACHUS, III, ALABAMA
MICHAEL CASTLE, DELAWARE
PETER KING, NEW YORK
TOM CAMPBELL, CALIFORNIA
EDWARD ROYCE, CALIFORNIA
FRANK D. LUCAS, OKLAHOMA
JACK METCALF, WASHINGTON
ROBERT NEY, OHIO
BOB BARR, GEORGIA
SUE W. KELLY, NEW YORK
RON PAUL, TEXAS
DAVE WELDON, FLORIDA
JIM RYUN, KANSAS
MERRILL COOK, UTAH
BOB RILEY, ALABAMA
RICK HILL, MONTANA
STEVEN LaTOURETTE, OHIO
DONALD A. MANZULLO, ILLINOIS
WALTER B. JONES, Jr., NORTH CAROLINA
PAUL RYAN, WISCONSIN
DOUG OSE, CALIFORNIA
JOHN E. SWEENEY, NEW YORK
JUDY BIGGERT, ILLINOIS
LEE TERRY, NEBRASKA
MARK GREEN, WISCONSIN
PAT TOOMEY, PENNSYLVANIA

U.S. HOUSE OF REPRESENTATIVES
COMMITTEE ON BANKING AND FINANCIAL SERVICES
ONE HUNDRED SIXTH CONGRESS
2129 RAYBURN HOUSE OFFICE BUILDING
WASHINGTON, DC 20515–6050

JOHN J. LaFALCE, NEW YORK
BRUCE F. VENTO, MINNESOTA
BARNEY FRANK, MASSACHUSETTS
PAUL E. KANJORSKI, PENNSYLVANIA
MAXINE WATERS, CALIFORNIA
CAROLYN B. MALONEY, NEW YORK
LUIS V. GUTIERREZ, ILLINOIS
NYDIA M. VELÁZQUEZ, NEW YORK
MELVIN WATT, NORTH CAROLINA
GARY ACKERMAN, NEW YORK
KEN BENTSEN, TEXAS
JAMES H. MALONEY, CONNECTICUT
DARLENE HOOLEY, OREGON
JULIA CARSON, INDIANA
ROBERT A. WEYGAND, RHODE ISLAND
BRAD SHERMAN, CALIFORNIA
MAX SANDLIN, TEXAS
GREGORY MEEKS, NEW YORK
BARBARA LEE, CALIFORNIA
VIRGIL H. GOODE, Jr., VIRGINIA
FRANK MASCARA, PENNSYLVANIA
JAY R. INSLEE, WASHINGTON
JAN SCHAKOWSKY, ILLINOIS
DENNIS MOORE, KANSAS
CHARLES A. GONZALEZ, TEXAS
STEPHANIE TUBBS JONES, OHIO
MICHAEL E. CAPUANO, MASSACHUSETTS

BERNARD SANDERS, VERMONT

(202) 225–7502

October 13, 1999

** CONFERENCE COMMITTEE **

To: House/Senate Conferees on S. 900
From: James A. Leach, Chairman

All conferences are unique, with rules less stringently observed than in other legislative contexts. The principal rule of conferences is that a majority of conferees in each body must sign the conference report before it can be considered by the full House and Senate.

In this conference, it is my intention to proceed title-by-title through the mark, alternating recognition to the extent practicable between House and Senate Members and Republicans and Democrats for purposes of offering amendments. As Members understand, in conference committees, each body has a single vote, but it will be my intention to assume that any amendment offered by a Member of the conference represents his or her body's position unless another Member of that body requests a vote of that body to determine whether that is in fact the case.

On the House side we have a particularly complex conference arrangement. Conferees will only be able to vote on and offer amendments to those provisions on which they are designated as conferees.

While precedents are mixed, it will be my intention to proceed on the basis that if an amendment is offered by a Member, it may only be amended by Members within the body of the offeror until it is formally presented to the other side, at which point it may be amended by that side. The original offeror, however, may accept suggestions from any member of the Conference and at his or her discretion modify an amendment before it is passed to the opposite side.

I have consulted with the parliamentarian, and while no firm rules apply in this area, the precedent is that each body determines how to proceed in the voting process. This means that on the House side, proxy voting will not be permitted, while in the Senate, it will be.

The first amendment to be offered at the mark-up may be a manager's amendment making certain technical and other revisions to the Chairmen's mark. Any Member who has a proposed technical amendment or other issue that fits a manager's amendment should contact the staffs of one of the relevant chairmen or ranking members.

App. 4.118 Conference Committee Amendment Proposed

Each conference committee conducts its work differently. Some conferences proceed through the engrossed measure *section-by-section;* others consider *full-text substitutes.* The document excerpted in App. 4.118a, and the text of the substitute, provided a summary of a *chairmen's mark*, a full-text substitute considered by the conferees.

App. 4.118a

Conference Committee Amendment Proposed

Financial Services Modernization Act

Summary of Provisions of Chairmen's Mark

TITLE I - FACILITATING AFFILIATION AMONG BANKS, SECURITIES FIRMS, AND INSURANCE COMPANIES

- Repeals the restrictions on banks affiliating with securities firms contained in sections 20 and 32 of the Glass-Steagall Act.
- Creates a new "financial holding company" under section 4 of the Bank Holding Company Act. Such holding company can engage in a statutorily provided list of financial activities, including insurance and securities underwriting and merchant banking activities. The financial holding company may also engage in developing activities and activities which the Federal Reserve Board, subject to a Treasury coordinating process, determines are financial in nature or incidental to such financial activities. Complementary activities are also authorized. The nonfinancial activities of firms predominantly engaged in financial activities are grandfathered (subject to a 15% limitation) for at least 10 years, but no more than 15 years. Such financial holding companies must be well capitalized, well managed, and have at least a satisfactory CRA rating.
- Provides for state regulation of insurance, subject to certain specified state preemption standards.
- Provides that a bank holding company organized as a mutual holding company will be regulated on terms and subject to limitations, comparable to any other bank holding company.
- Liberalizes the restrictions governing nonbank banks.
- Provides for a study of the use of subordinated debt to protect financial system and deposit funds from "too big to fail" institutions and a study on the effect of financial modernization on the accessibility of small business and farm loans.
- Streamlines bank holding company supervisions by clarifying the regulatory roles of the Federal Reserve as the umbrella holding company supervisor and the state and Federal nonbank financial functional regulators.

This section is from the Congressional Deskbook, *by Judy Schneider and Michael Koempel, <www.CongressionalDeskbook.com>.*

App. 4.119 Conference Report

The conference report, H. Rept. 106-434, was filed in the House on November 2, 1999, by Mr. Leach, the chair of the conference committee. The measure was now officially called the Gramm-Leach-Bliley Act, after the three chairs of the committees that considered the legislation.

App. 4.119a

Conference Report

106TH CONGRESS *1st Session*	HOUSE OF REPRESENTATIVES	REPORT 106–434

GRAMM-LEACH-BLILEY ACT

NOVEMBER 2, 1999.—Ordered to be printed

Mr. LEACH, from the committee of conference, submitted the following

CONFERENCE REPORT

[To accompany S. 900]

The committee of conference on the disagreeing votes of the two Houses on the amendments of the House to the bill (S. 900), to enhance competition in the financial services industry by providing a prudential framework for the affiliation of banks, securities firms, insurance companies, and other financial service providers, and for other purposes, having met, after full and free conference, have agreed to recommend and do recommend to their respective Houses as follows:

That the Senate recede from its disagreement to the amendment of the House to the text of the bill and agree to the same with an amendment as follows:

In lieu of the matter proposed to be inserted by the House amendment, insert the following:

SECTION 1. SHORT TITLE; TABLE OF CONTENTS.

(a) SHORT TITLE.—This Act may be cited as the "Gramm-Leach-Bliley Act".

(b) TABLE OF CONTENTS.—The table of contents for this Act is as follows:

60–398

This section is from the Congressional Deskbook, *by Judy Schneider and Michael Koempel, <www.CongressionalDeskbook.com>.*

App. 4.120 Joint Explanatory Statement

A second conference document is appended to the conference report and is called the *joint explanatory statement*. This document explains in lay terms what was in the House text and the Senate text of the measure in conference and what is the agreement recommended by the committee on conference. A majority of conferees from each chamber must sign not only the conference report but also the joint explanatory statement.

This section is from the Congressional Deskbook, *by Judy Schneider and Michael Koempel, <www.CongressionalDeskbook.com>.*

App. 4.120a

Joint Explanatory Statement

JOINT EXPLANATORY STATEMENT OF THE COMMITTEE OF CONFERENCE

The Managers on the part of the House and the Senate at the conference on the disagreeing votes of the two Houses on the amendments of the House to the bill (S. 900), to enhance competition in the financial services industry by providing a prudential framework for the affiliation of banks, securities firms, insurance companies, and other financial service providers, and for other purposes, submit the following joint statement to the House and the Senate in explanation of the effect of the action agreed upon by the managers and recommended in the accompanying conference report:

The House amendment to the text of the bill struck all of the Senate bill after the enacting clause and inserted a substitute text.

The Senate recedes from its disagreement to the amendment of the House with an amendment that is a substitute for the Senate bill and the House amendment. The differences between the Senate bill, the House amendment, and the substitute agreed to in conference are noted below, except for clerical corrections, conforming changes made necessary by agreements reached by the conferees, and minor drafting and clerical changes.

TITLE I—FACILITATING AFFILIATIONS AMONG BANKS, SECURITIES FIRMS, AND INSURANCE COMPANIES

The legislation approved by the Conference Managers eliminates many Federal and State law barriers to affiliations among banks and securities firms, insurance companies, and other financial service providers. The House and Senate bills established an identical statutory framework (except for minor drafting differences) pursuant to which full affiliations can occur between banks and securities firms, insurance companies, and other financial companies. The Conferees adopted this framework. Furthermore, the legislation provides financial organizations with flexibility in structuring these new financial affiliations through a holding company structure, or a financial subsidiary (with certain prudential limitations on activities and appropriate safeguards). Reflected in the legislation is the determination made by both Houses to preserve the role of the Board of Governors of the Federal Reserve System (the "Federal Reserve Board" or the "Board") as the umbrella supervisor for holding companies, but to incorporate a system of functional regulation designed to utilize the strengths of the various Federal and State financial supervisors. Incorporating provisions found in both the House and Senate bills, the legislation establishes a mechanism for coordination between the Federal Reserve Board and the Secretary of the Treasury ("the Secretary") regarding the approval of new financial activities for both holding companies and national bank financial subsidiaries. The legislation

(151)

App. 14.121 Special Rule from the Rules Committee for Consideration of the Conference Report

Conference reports are *privileged* in the House and as such do not require a special rule for consideration. However, special rules are often sought for conference reports if *waivers* of existing rules are needed. H. Res. 355 was a special rule providing for the consideration of the conference report on S. 900. The special rule provided that the conference report be considered as read, and waived all points of order against the report and its consideration by the House. The special rule was reported on November 2, 1999.

This section is from the Congressional Deskbook, *by Judy Schneider and Michael Koempel, <www.CongressionalDeskbook.com>.*

App. 4.121a

Special Rule from the Rules Committee for Consideration of the Conference Report

(1) Calendar number

(2) Resolution number

(3) Committee report number

(4) Majority manager of special rule

(5) Special rule waiving points of order against the conference report (S. 900)

(1) **House Calendar No. 147**

106TH CONGRESS
1ST SESSION

(2) **H. RES. 355**

(3) **[Report No. 106–440]**

Waiving points of order against the conference report to accompany the bill (S. 900) to enhance competition in the financial services industry by providing a prudential framework for the affiliation of banks, securities firms, insurance companies, and other financial service providers, and for other purposes.

IN THE HOUSE OF REPRESENTATIVES

NOVEMBER 2, 1999

(4) Mr. SESSIONS, from the Committee on Rules, reported the following resolution; which was referred to the House Calendar and ordered to be printed

---

RESOLUTION

(5) Waiving points of order against the conference report to accompany the bill (S. 900) to enhance competition in the financial services industry by providing a prudential framework for the affiliation of banks, securities firms, insurance companies, and other financial service providers, and for other purposes.

Resolved, That upon adoption of this resolution it shall be in order to consider the conference report to accompany the bill (S. 900) to enhance competition in the

(Continued on page 372)

This section is from the Congressional Deskbook, *by Judy Schneider and Michael Koempel, <www.CongressionalDeskbook.com>.*

App. 4.121a (continued)

Special Rule from the Rules Committee for Consideration of the Conference Report

2

financial services industry by providing a prudential framework for the affiliation of banks, securities firms, insurance companies, and other financial service providers, and for other purposes. All points of order against the conference report and against its consideration are waived. The conference report shall be considered as read.

This section is from the Congressional Deskbook, *by Judy Schneider and Michael Koempel, <www.CongressionalDeskbook.com>.*

App. 4.122 Enrolled Measure

The conference report was agreed to by the Senate by a 90 to 8 vote on November 4, 1999. The House also agreed to the conference report on November 4, 1999, by a vote of 362 to 57. The measure was then cleared for the White House. It was printed on parchment paper and presented to the president on November 9, 1999.

App. 4.122a

Enrolled Measure

One Hundred Sixth Congress
of the
United States of America

AT THE FIRST SESSION

Begun and held at the City of Washington on Wednesday, the sixth day of January, one thousand nine hundred and ninety-nine

An Act

To enhance competition in the financial services industry by providing a prudential framework for the affiliation of banks, securities firms, insurance companies, and other financial service providers, and for other purposes.

Be it enacted by the Senate and House of Representatives of the United States of America in Congress assembled,

SECTION 1. SHORT TITLE; TABLE OF CONTENTS.

(a) SHORT TITLE.—This Act may be cited as the "Gramm-Leach-Bliley Act".

(b) TABLE OF CONTENTS.—The table of contents for this Act is as follows:

This section is from the Congressional Deskbook, *by Judy Schneider and Michael Koempel, <www.CongressionalDeskbook.com>.*

App. 4.123 Public Law

The president signed the Gramm-Leach-Bliley Act on November 12, 1999. The adoption of the *short title* was part of the conference committee agreement. It now was Public Law 106-102, 113 Stat. 1338.

App. 4.123a

Public Law

113 STAT. 1338 PUBLIC LAW 106–102—NOV. 12, 1999

Public Law 106–102
106th Congress

An Act

Nov. 12, 1999
[S. 900]

To enhance competition in the financial services industry by providing a prudential framework for the affiliation of banks, securities firms, insurance companies, and other financial service providers, and for other purposes.

Be it enacted by the Senate and House of Representatives of the United States of America in Congress assembled,

Gramm-Leach-Bliley Act.
Inter-governmental relations.
12 USC 1811 note.

SECTION 1. SHORT TITLE; TABLE OF CONTENTS.

(a) SHORT TITLE.—This Act may be cited as the "Gramm-Leach-Bliley Act".

(b) TABLE OF CONTENTS.—The table of contents for this Act is as follows:

This section is from the Congressional Deskbook, *by Judy Schneider and Michael Koempel, <www.CongressionalDeskbook.com>.*

Appendix Five: Positive Law and Non-Positive Law

App. 5.00 Introduction

A distinction that is crucial for drafters, and one that should be crucial for others who work with federal law, is the distinction between positive law and non-positive law. This topic is covered in detail in Chapter Two (specifically, § 2.83).

The materials that follow are included here for several reasons. First, they show the distinction between positive law and non-positive law. Second, they reprint particular laws the substance of which are of particular interest to drafters. Third, they provide an example of the drafting style known as Code style, a topic covered in detail in Chapter Eight (specifically, § 8.60).

App. 5.10 List of Titles of the United States Code

The *United States Code* is available online for free at several web sites, including:

- Office of the Law Revision Counsel, <*uscode.house.gov*>
- Cornell's Legal Information Institute, at <*law.cornell.edu/uscode/*>

USC Titles

*Title 1	General Provisions
Title 2	The Congress
*Title 3	The President
*Title 4	Flag and Seal, Seat of Government, and the States
*Title 5	Government Organization and Employees; and Appendix
Title 6	Domestic Security
Title 7	Agriculture
Title 8	Aliens and Nationality
*Title 9	Arbitration
*Title 10	Armed Forces
*Title 11	Bankruptcy; and Appendix
Title 12	Banks and Banking
*Title 13	Census
*Title 14	Coast Guard
Title 15	Commerce and Trade
Title 16	Conservation
*Title 17	Copyrights
*Title 18	Crimes and Criminal Procedure; and Appendix
Title 19	Customs Duties
Title 20	Education
Title 21	Food and Drugs
Title 22	Foreign Relations and Intercourse
*Title 23	Highways
Title 24	Hospitals and Asylums

*This title has been enacted as positive law. However, any Appendix to this title has not been enacted as part of the title. See <*uscode.house.gov*> for current list.

USC Titles (continued)

Title 25	Indians
Title 26	Internal Revenue Code
Title 27	Intoxicating Liquors
*Title 28	Judiciary and Judicial Procedure; and Appendix
Title 29	Labor
Title 30	Mineral Lands and Mining
*Title 31	Money and Finance
*Title 32	National Guard
Title 33	Navigation and Navigable Waters
Title 34	Navy (Repealed)
*Title 35	Patents
*Title 36	Patriotic and National Observances, Ceremonies, and Organizations
*Title 37	Pay and Allowances of the Uniformed Services
*Title 38	Veterans' Benefits
*Title 39	Postal Service
*Title 40	Public Buildings, Property, and Works
*Title 41	Public Contracts
Title 42	The Public Health and Welfare
Title 43	Public Lands
*Title 44	Public Printing and Documents
Title 45	Railroads
*Title 46	Shipping
Title 47	Telecommunications
Title 48	Territories and Insular Possessions
*Title 49	Transportation
Title 50	War and National Defense; and Appendix
*Title 51	National and Commercial Space Programs
Title 52	Voting and Elections
Title 53	[Reserved]
*Title 54	National Park Service and Related Programs

*This title has been enacted as positive law. However, any Appendix to this title has not been enacted as part of the title. See <*uscode.house.gov*> for current list.

App. 5.20 The Code as Positive Law: Title 1

TITLE 1—GENERAL PROVISIONS

CHAPTER 1—RULES OF CONSTRUCTION

§ 1. Words denoting number, gender, and so forth

In determining the meaning of any Act of Congress, unless the context indicates otherwise—

words importing the singular include and apply to several persons, parties, or things;

words importing the plural include the singular;

words importing the masculine gender include the feminine as well;

words used in the present tense include the future as well as the present;

the words "insane" and "insane person" and "lunatic" shall include every idiot, lunatic, insane person, and person non compos mentis;

the words "person" and "whoever" include corporations, companies, associations, firms, partnerships, societies, and joint stock companies, as well as individuals;

"officer" includes any person authorized by law to perform the duties of the office;

"signature" or "subscription" includes a mark when the person making the same intended it as such;

"oath" includes affirmation, and "sworn" includes affirmed;

"writing" includes printing and typewriting and reproductions of visual symbols by photographing, multigraphing, mimeographing, manifolding, or otherwise.

§ 2. "County" as including "parish", and so forth

The word "county" includes a parish, or any other equivalent subdivision of a State or Territory of the United States.

§ 3. "Vessel" as including all means of water transportation

The word "vessel" includes every description of watercraft or other artificial contrivance used, or capable of being used, as a means of transportation on water.

§ 4. "Vehicle" as including all means of land transportation

The word "vehicle" includes every description of carriage or other artificial contrivance used, or capable of being used, as a means of transportation on land.

§ 5. "Company" or "association" as including successors and assigns

The word "company" or "association", when used in reference to a corporation, shall be deemed to embrace the words "successors

App. 5.20 The Code as Positive Law: Title 1 (continued)

and assigns of such company or association", in like manner as if these last-named words, or words of similar import, were expressed.

§ 6. Limitation of term "products of American fisheries"

Wherever, in the statutes of the United States or in the rulings, regulations, or interpretations of various administrative bureaus and agencies of the United States there appears or may appear the term "products of American fisheries" said term shall not include fresh or frozen fish fillets, fresh or frozen fish steaks, or fresh or frozen slices of fish substantially free of bone (including any of the foregoing divided into sections), produced in a foreign country or its territorial waters, in whole or in part with the use of the labor of persons who are not residents of the United States.

§ 7. Definition of "marriage" and "spouse"

In determining the meaning of any Act of Congress, or of any ruling, regulation, or interpretation of the various administrative bureaus and agencies of the United States, the word "marriage" means only a legal union between one man and one woman as husband and wife, and the word "spouse" refers only to a person of the opposite sex who is a husband or a wife.

§ 8. "Person", "human being", "child", and "individual" as including born-alive infant

(a) In determining the meaning of any Act of Congress, or of any ruling, regulation, or interpretation of the various administrative bureaus and agencies of the United States, the words "person", "human being", "child", and "individual", shall include every infant member of the species homo sapiens who is born alive at any stage of development.

(b) As used in this section, the term "born alive", with respect to a member of the species homo sapiens, means the complete expulsion or extraction from his or her mother of that member, at any stage of development, who after such expulsion or extraction breathes or has a beating heart, pulsation of the umbilical cord, or definite movement of voluntary muscles, regardless of whether the umbilical cord has been cut, and regardless of whether the expulsion or extraction occurs as a result of natural or induced labor, cesarean section, or induced abortion.

(c) Nothing in this section shall be construed to affirm, deny, expand, or contract any legal status or legal right applicable to any member of the species homo sapiens at any point prior to being "born alive" as defined in this section.

CHAPTER 2—ACTS AND RESOLUTIONS; FORMALITIES OF ENACTMENT; REPEALS; SEALING OF INSTRUMENTS

§ 101. Enacting clause

The enacting clause of all Acts of Congress shall be in the following form: "Be it enacted by the Senate and House of Representatives of the United States of America in Congress assembled."

App. 5.20 The Code as Positive Law: Title 1 (continued)

§ 102. Resolving clause

The resolving clause of all joint resolutions shall be in the following form: "Resolved by the Senate and House of Representatives of the United States of America in Congress assembled."

§ 103. Enacting or resolving words after first section

No enacting or resolving words shall be used in any section of an Act or resolution of Congress except in the first.

§ 104. Numbering of sections; single proposition

Each section shall be numbered, and shall contain, as nearly as may be, a single proposition of enactment.

§ 105. Title of appropriation Acts

The style and title of all Acts making appropriations for the support of Government shall be as follows: "An Act making appropriations (here insert the object) for the year ending September 30 (here insert the calendar year)."

§ 106. Printing bills and joint resolutions

Every bill or joint resolution in each House of Congress shall, when such bill or resolution passes either House, be printed, and such printed copy shall be called the engrossed bill or resolution as the case may be. Said engrossed bill or resolution shall be signed by the Clerk of the House or the Secretary of the Senate, and shall be sent to the other House, and in that form shall be dealt with by that House and its officers, and, if passed, returned signed by said Clerk or Secretary. When such bill, or joint resolution shall have passed both Houses, it shall be printed and shall then be called the enrolled bill, or joint resolution, as the case may be, and shall be signed by the presiding officers of both Houses and sent to the President of the United States. During the last six days of a session such engrossing and enrolling of bills and joint resolutions may be done otherwise than as above prescribed, upon the order of Congress by concurrent resolution.

§ 106a. Promulgation of laws

Whenever a bill, order, resolution, or vote of the Senate and House of Representatives, having been approved by the President, or not having been returned by him with his objections, becomes a law or takes effect, it shall forthwith be received by the Archivist of the United States from the President; and whenever a bill, order, resolution, or vote is returned by the President with his objections, and, on being reconsidered, is agreed to be passed, and is approved by two-thirds of both Houses of Congress, and thereby becomes a law or takes effect, it shall be received by the Archivist of the United States from the President of the Senate, or Speaker of the House of Representatives in whichsoever House it shall last have been so approved, and he shall carefully preserve the originals.

§ 106b. Amendments to Constitution

Whenever official notice is received at the National Archives and Records Administration that any amendment proposed to the

App. 5.20 The Code as Positive Law: Title 1 (continued)

Constitution of the United States has been adopted, according to the provisions of the Constitution, the Archivist of the United States shall forthwith cause the amendment to be published, with his certificate, specifying the States by which the same may have been adopted, and that the same has become valid, to all intents and purposes, as a part of the Constitution of the United States.

§ 107. Parchment or paper for printing enrolled bills or resolutions

Enrolled bills and resolutions of either House of Congress shall be printed on parchment or paper of suitable quality as shall be determined by the Joint Committee on Printing.

§ 108. Repeal of repealing act

Whenever an Act is repealed, which repealed a former Act, such former Act shall not thereby be revived, unless it shall be expressly so provided.

§ 109. Repeal of statutes as affecting existing liabilities

The repeal of any statute shall not have the effect to release or extinguish any penalty, forfeiture, or liability incurred under such statute, unless the repealing Act shall so expressly provide, and such statute shall be treated as still remaining in force for the purpose of sustaining any proper action or prosecution for the enforcement of such penalty, forfeiture, or liability. The expiration of a temporary statute shall not have the effect to release or extinguish any penalty, forfeiture, or liability incurred under such statute, unless the temporary statute shall so expressly provide, and such statute shall be treated as still remaining in force for the purpose of sustaining any proper action or prosecution for the enforcement of such penalty, forfeiture, or liability.

§ 110. Saving clause of Revised Statutes

All acts of limitation, whether applicable to civil causes and proceedings, or to the prosecution of offenses, or for the recovery of penalties or forfeitures, embraced in the Revised Statutes and covered by the repeal contained therein, shall not be affected thereby, but all suits, proceedings, or prosecutions, whether civil or criminal, for causes arising, or acts done or committed prior to said repeal, may be commenced and prosecuted within the same time as if said repeal had not been made.

§ 111. Repeals as evidence of prior effectiveness

No inference shall be raised by the enactment of the Act of March 3, 1933 (ch. 202, 47 Stat. 1431), that the sections of the Revised Statutes repealed by such Act were in force or effect at the time of such enactment: Provided, however, That any rights or liabilities existing under such repealed sections shall not be affected by their repeal.

§ 112. Statutes at Large; contents; admissibility in evidence

The Archivist of the United States shall cause to be compiled, edited, indexed, and published, the United States Statutes at Large, which shall contain all the laws and concurrent resolutions

App. 5.20 The Code as Positive Law: Title 1 (continued)

enacted during each regular session of Congress; all proclamations by the President in the numbered series issued since the date of the adjournment of the regular session of Congress next preceding; and also any amendments to the Constitution of the United States proposed or ratified pursuant to article V thereof since that date, together with the certificate of the Archivist of the United States issued in compliance with the provision contained in section 106b of this title. In the event of an extra session of Congress, the Archivist of the United States shall cause all the laws and concurrent resolutions enacted during said extra session to be consolidated with, and published as part of, the contents of the volume for the next regular session. The United States Statutes at Large shall be legal evidence of laws, concurrent resolutions, treaties, international agreements other than treaties, proclamations by the President, and proposed or ratified amendments to the Constitution of the United States therein contained, in all the courts of the United States, the several States, and the Territories and insular possessions of the United States.

§ 112a. United States Treaties and Other International Agreements; contents; admissibility in evidence

(a) The Secretary of State shall cause to be compiled, edited, indexed, and published, beginning as of January 1, 1950, a compilation entitled "United States Treaties and Other International Agreements," which shall contain all treaties to which the United States is a party that have been proclaimed during each calendar year, and all international agreements other than treaties to which the United States is a party that have been signed, proclaimed, or with reference to which any other final formality has been executed, during each calendar year. The said United States Treaties and Other International Agreements shall be legal evidence of the treaties, international agreements other than treaties, and proclamations by the President of such treaties and agreements, therein contained, in all the courts of the United States, the several States, and the Territories and insular possessions of the United States.

(b) The Secretary of State may determine that publication of certain categories of agreements is not required, if the following criteria are met:

(1) such agreements are not treaties which have been brought into force for the United States after having received Senate advice and consent pursuant to section 2(2) of Article II of the Constitution of the United States;

(2) the public interest in such agreements is insufficient to justify their publication, because (A) as of the date of enactment of the Foreign Relations Authorization Act, Fiscal Years 1994 and 1995, the agreements are no longer in force, (B) the agreements do not create private rights or duties, or establish standards intended to govern government action in the treatment of private individuals; (C) in view of the limited or specialized nature of the public interest in such agreements, such interest can adequately be satisfied by an alternative means; or (D) the public disclosure of the text of the agreement would, in the opinion of the President, be prejudicial to the national security of the United States; and

App. 5.20 The Code as Positive Law: Title 1 (continued)

(3) copies of such agreements (other than those in paragraph (2)(D)), including certified copies where necessary for litigation or similar purposes, will be made available by the Department of State upon request.

(c) Any determination pursuant to subsection (b) shall be published in the Federal Register.

§ 112b. United States international agreements; transmission to Congress

(a) The Secretary of State shall transmit to the Congress the text of any international agreement (including the text of any oral international agreement, which agreement shall be reduced to writing), other than a treaty, to which the United States is a party as soon as practicable after such agreement has entered into force with respect to the United States but in no event later than sixty days thereafter. However, any such agreement the immediate public disclosure of which would, in the opinion of the President, be prejudicial to the national security of the United States shall not be so transmitted to the Congress but shall be transmitted to the Committee on Foreign Relations of the Senate and the Committee on Foreign Affairs of the House of Representatives under an appropriate injunction of secrecy to be removed only upon due notice from the President. Any department or agency of the United States Government which enters into any international agreement on behalf of the United States shall transmit to the Department of State the text of such agreement not later than twenty days after such agreement has been signed.

(b) Not later than March 1, 1979, and at yearly intervals thereafter, the President shall, under his own signature, transmit to the Speaker of the House of Representatives and the chairman of the Committee on Foreign Relations of the Senate a report with respect to each international agreement which, during the preceding year, was transmitted to the Congress after the expiration of the 60-day period referred to in the first sentence of subsection (a), describing fully and completely the reasons for the late transmittal.

(c) Notwithstanding any other provision of law, an international agreement may not be signed or otherwise concluded on behalf of the United States without prior consultation with the Secretary of State. Such consultation may encompass a class of agreements rather than a particular agreement.

(d) The Secretary of State shall determine for and within the executive branch whether an arrangement constitutes an international agreement within the meaning of this section.

(e) The President shall, through the Secretary of State, promulgate such rules and regulations as may be necessary to carry out this section.

§ 113. "Little and Brown's" edition of laws and treaties; slip laws; Treaties and Other International Acts Series; admissibility in evidence

The edition of the laws and treaties of the United States, published by Little and Brown, and the publications in slip or pamphlet form of the laws of the United States issued under the authority of the Archivist of the United States, and the Treaties and

App. 5.20 The Code as Positive Law: Title 1 (continued)

Other International Acts Series issued under the authority of the Secretary of State shall be competent evidence of the several public and private Acts of Congress, and of the treaties, international agreements other than treaties, and proclamations by the President of such treaties and international agreements other than treaties, as the case may be, therein contained, in all the courts of law and equity and of maritime jurisdiction, and in all the tribunals and public offices of the United States, and of the several States, without any further proof or authentication thereof.

§ 114. Sealing of instruments

In all cases where a seal is necessary by law to any commission, process, or other instrument provided for by the laws of Congress, it shall be lawful to affix the proper seal by making an impression therewith directly on the paper to which such seal is necessary; which shall be as valid as if made on wax or other adhesive substance.

CHAPTER 3—CODE OF LAWS OF UNITED STATES AND SUPPLEMENTS; DISTRICT OF COLUMBIA CODE AND SUPPLEMENTS

§ 201. Publication and distribution of Code of Laws of United States and Supplements and District of Columbia Code and Supplements

In order to avoid duplication and waste—

(a) PUBLISHING IN SLIP OR PAMPHLET FORM OR IN STATUTES AT LARGE.—Publication in slip or pamphlet form or in the Statutes at Large of any of the volumes or publications enumerated in sections 202 and 203 of this title, shall, in event of enactment, be dispensed with whenever the Committee on the Judiciary of the House of Representatives so directs the Archivist of the United States;

(b) CURTAILING NUMBER OF COPIES PUBLISHED.—Curtailment of the number provided by law to be printed and distributed of the volumes or publications enumerated in sections 202 and 203 of this title may be directed by such committee, except that the Public Printer shall print such numbers as are necessary for depository library distribution and for sale; and

(c) DISPENSING WITH PUBLICATION OF MORE THAN ONE SUPPLEMENT FOR EACH CONGRESS.—Such committee may direct that the printing and distribution of any supplement to the Code of Laws of the United States or to the Code of the District of Columbia be dispensed with entirely, except that there shall be printed and distributed for each Congress at least one supplement to each such code, containing the legislation of such Congress.

§ 202. Preparation and publication of Codes and Supplements

There shall be prepared and published under the supervision of the Committee on the Judiciary of the House of Representatives—

App. 5.20 The Code as Positive Law: Title 1 (continued)

(1) CUMULATIVE SUPPLEMENTS TO CODE OF LAWS OF UNITED STATES FOR EACH SESSION OF CONGRESS.—A supplement for each session of the Congress to the then current edition of the Code of Laws of the United States, cumulatively embracing the legislation of the then current supplement, and correcting errors in such edition and supplement;

(2) CUMULATIVE SUPPLEMENT TO DISTRICT OF COLUMBIA CODE FOR EACH SESSION OF CONGRESS.—A supplement for each session of the Congress to the then current edition of the Code of the District of Columbia, cumulatively embracing the legislation of the then current supplement, and correcting errors in such edition and supplement;

(3) NEW EDITIONS OF CODES AND SUPPLEMENTS.—New editions of the Code of Laws of the United States and of the Code of the District of Columbia, correcting errors and incorporating the then current supplement. In the case of each code new editions shall not be published oftener than once in each five years. Copies of each such edition shall be distributed in the same manner as provided in the case of supplements to the code of which it is a new edition. Supplements published after any new edition shall not contain the legislation of supplements published before such new edition.

§ 203. District of Columbia Code; preparation and publication; cumulative supplements

The Committee on the Judiciary of the House of Representatives is authorized to print bills to codify, revise, and reenact the general and permanent laws relating to the District of Columbia and cumulative supplements thereto, similar in style, respectively, to the Code of Laws of the United States, and supplements thereto, and to so continue until final enactment thereof in both Houses of the Congress of the United States.

§ 204. Codes and Supplements as evidence of the laws of United States and District of Columbia; citation of Codes and Supplements

In all courts, tribunals, and public offices of the United States, at home or abroad, of the District of Columbia, and of each State, Territory, or insular possession of the United States—

(a) UNITED STATES CODE.—The matter set forth in the edition of the Code of Laws of the United States current at any time shall, together with the then current supplement, if any, establish prima facie the laws of the United States, general and permanent in their nature, in force on the day preceding the commencement of the session following the last session the legislation of which is included: Provided, however, That whenever titles of such Code shall have been enacted into positive law the text thereof shall be legal evidence of the laws therein contained, in all the courts of the United States, the several States, and the Territories and insular possessions of the United States.

(b) DISTRICT OF COLUMBIA CODE.—The matter set forth in the edition of the Code of the District of Columbia current at any time shall, together with the then current supplement, if

App. 5.20 The Code as Positive Law: Title 1 (continued)

any, establish prima facie the laws, general and permanent in their nature, relating to or in force in the District of Columbia on the day preceding the commencement of the session following the last session the legislation of which is included, except such laws as are of application in the District of Columbia by reason of being laws of the United States general and permanent in their nature.

(c) DISTRICT OF COLUMBIA CODE; CITATION.—The Code of the District of Columbia may be cited as "D.C. Code".

(d) SUPPLEMENTS TO CODES; CITATION.—Supplements to the Code of Laws of the United States and to the Code of the District of Columbia may be cited, respectively, as "U.S.C., Sup. ", and "D.C. Code, Sup. ", the blank in each case being filled with Roman figures denoting the number of the supplement.

(e) NEW EDITION OF CODES; CITATION.—New editions of each of such codes may be cited, respectively, as "U.S.C., ed.", and "D.C. Code, ed.", the blank in each case being filled with figures denoting the last year the legislation of which is included in whole or in part.

§ 205. Codes and Supplement; where printed; form and style; ancillaries

The publications provided for in sections 202, 203 of this title shall be printed at the Government Printing Office and shall be in such form and style and with such ancillaries as may be prescribed by the Committee on the Judiciary of the House of Representatives. The Librarian of Congress is directed to cooperate with such committee in the preparation of such ancillaries. Such publications shall be furnished with such thumb insets and other devices to distinguish parts, with such facilities for the insertion of additional matter, and with such explanatory and advertising slips, and shall be printed on such paper and bound in such material, as may be prescribed by such committee.

§ 206. Bills and resolutions of Committee on the Judiciary of House of Representatives; form and style; ancillaries; curtailment of copies

All bills and resolutions relating to the revision of the laws referred to or reported by the Committee on the Judiciary of the House of Representatives shall be printed in such form and style, and with such ancillaries, as such committee may prescribe as being economical and suitable, to so continue until final enactment thereof in both Houses of Congress; and such committee may also curtail the number of copies of such bills to be printed in the various parliamentary stages in the House of Representatives.

§ 207. Copies of acts and resolutions in slip form; additional number printed for Committee on the Judiciary of House of Representatives

The Public Printer is directed to print, in addition to the number provided by existing law, and, as soon as printed, to distribute in such manner as the Committee on the Judiciary of the House

App. 5.20 The Code as Positive Law: Title 1 (continued)

of Representatives shall determine, twenty copies in slip form of each public Act and joint resolution.

§ 208. Delegation of function of Committee on the Judiciary to other agencies; printing, and so forth, under direction of Joint Committee on Printing

The functions vested by sections 201, 202, 204–207 of this title in the Committee on the Judiciary of the House of Representatives may from time to time be vested in such other agency as the Congress may by concurrent resolution provide: Provided, That the printing, binding, and distribution of the volumes and publications enumerated in sections 202, 203 of this title shall be done under the direction of the Joint Committee on Printing.

§ 209. Copies of Supplements to Code of Laws of United States and of District of Columbia Code and Supplements; conclusive evidence of original

Copies of the Code of Laws relating to the District of Columbia and copies of the supplements provided for by sections 202 and 203 of this title printed at the Government Printing Office and bearing its imprint, shall be conclusive evidence of the original of such code and supplements in the custody of the Administrator of General Services.

§ 210. Distribution of Supplements to Code of Laws of United States and of District of Columbia Code and Supplements; slip and pamphlet copies

Copies of the Code of Laws relating to the District of Columbia, and of the supplements provided for by sections 202, 203 of this title shall be distributed by the Superintendent of Documents in the same manner as bound volumes of the Statutes at Large: Provided, That no slip or pamphlet copies of the Code of Laws relating to the District of Columbia, and of the supplements provided for by sections 202, 203 of this title need be printed or distributed.

§ 211. Copies to Members of Congress

In addition to quotas provided for by section 210 of this title there shall be printed, published, and distributed of the Code of Laws relating to the District of Columbia with tables, index, and other ancillaries, suitably bound and with thumb inserts and other convenient devices to distinguish the parts, and of the supplements to both codes as provided for by sections 202, 203 of this title, ten copies of each for each Member of the Senate and House of Representatives of the Congress in which the original authorized publication is made, for his use and distribution, and in addition for the Committee on the Judiciary of the House of Representatives and the Committee on the Judiciary of the Senate a number of bound copies of each equal to ten times the number of members of such committees, and one bound copy of each for the use of each committee of the Senate and House of Representatives.

§ 212. Additional distribution at each new Congress

In addition the Superintendent of Documents shall, at the beginning of the first session of each Congress, supply to each Sen-

App. 5.20 The Code as Positive Law: Title 1 (continued)

ator and Representative in such Congress, who may in writing apply for the same, one copy each of the Code of Laws of the United States, the Code of Laws relating to the District of Columbia, and the latest supplement to each code: Provided, That such applicant shall certify in his written application for the same that the volume or volumes for which he applies is intended for his personal use exclusively: And provided further, That no Senator or Representative during his term of service shall receive under this section more than one copy each of the volumes enumerated herein.

§ 213. Appropriation for preparing and editing supplements

For preparation and editing an annual appropriation of $6,500 is authorized to carry out the purposes of sections 202 and 203 of this title.

App. 5.30 The Code as Non-Positive Law: Chapter 9 of Title 2

TITLE 2—THE CONGRESS

CHAPTER 9—OFFICE OF LEGISLATIVE COUNSEL

SUBCHAPTER I—SENATE

§ 271. Establishment

There shall be in the Senate an office to be known as the Office of the Legislative Counsel, and to be under the direction of the Legislative Counsel of the Senate.

§ 272. Legislative Counsel

The Legislative Counsel shall be appointed by the President pro tempore of the Senate, without reference to political affiliations and solely on the ground of fitness to perform the duties of the office.

§ 273. Compensation

The Legislative Counsel of the Senate shall be paid at an annual rate of compensation of $40,000.

§ 274. Staff; office equipment and supplies

The Legislative Counsel shall, subject to the approval of the President pro tempore of the Senate, employ and fix the compensation of such Assistant Counsel, clerks, and other employees, and purchase such furniture, office equipment, books, stationery, and other supplies, as may be necessary for the proper performance of the duties of the Office and as may be appropriated for by Congress.

§ 275. Functions

The Office of the Legislative Counsel shall aid in drafting public bills and resolutions or amendments thereto on the request of any committee of the Senate but the Committee on Rules and Administration of the Senate may determine the preference, if any, to be given to such requests of the committees. The Legislative Counsel shall, from time to time, prescribe rules and regulations for the conduct of the work of the Office for the committees, subject to the approval of such Committee on Rules and Administration.

§ 276. Disbursement of appropriations

All appropriations for the Office of the Legislative Counsel shall be disbursed by the Secretary of the Senate.

§ 276a. Expenditures

With the approval of the President Pro Tempore of the Senate, the Legislative Counsel of the Senate may make such expenditures

App. 5.30 The Code as Non-Positive Law: Chapter 9 of Title 2 (continued)

as may be necessary or appropriate for the functioning of the Office of the Legislative Counsel of the Senate.

§ 276b. Travel and related expenses

Funds expended by the Legislative Counsel of the Senate for travel and related expenses shall be subject to the same regulations and limitations (insofar as they are applicable) as those which the Senate Committee on Rules and Administration prescribes for application to travel and related expenses for which payment is authorized to be made from the contingent fund of the Senate.

SUBCHAPTER II—HOUSE OF REPRESENTATIVES

PART I—PURPOSE, POLICY, AND FUNCTION

§ 281. Establishment

There is established in the House of Representatives an office to be known as the Office of the Legislative Counsel, referred to hereinafter in this subchapter as the "Office".

§ 281a. Purpose and policy

The purpose of the Office shall be to advise and assist the House of Representatives, and its committees and Members, in the achievement of a clear, faithful, and coherent expression of legislative policies. The Office shall maintain impartiality as to issues of legislative policy to be determined by the House of Representatives, and shall not advocate the adoption or rejection of any legislation except when duly requested by the Speaker or a committee to comment on a proposal directly affecting the functions of the Office. The Office shall maintain the attorney-client relationship with respect to all communications between it and any Member or committee of the House.

§ 281b. Functions

The functions of the Office shall be as follows:

(1) Upon request of the managers on the part of the House at any conference on the disagreeing votes of the two Houses, to advise and assist the managers on the part of the House in the course of the conference, and to assist the committee of conference in the preparation of the conference report and any accompanying explanatory statement.

(2) Upon request of any committee of the House, or any joint committee having authority to report legislation to the House, to advise and assist the committee in the consideration of any legislation before it, and to assist the committee in the preparation of drafts of any such legislation, amendments thereto, and reports thereon.

(3) Upon request of any Member having control of time during the consideration of any legislation by the House, to have in attendance on the floor of the House not more than two members of the staff of the Office (and, in his discretion, the Legislative Counsel) to advise and assist such Member and, to the extent feasible, any other Member, in the course of such consideration.

App. 5.30 The Code as Non-Positive Law: Chapter 9 of Title 2 (continued)

(4) Upon request of any Member, subject to such reasonable restrictions as the Legislative Counsel may impose with the approval of the Speaker on the proportion of the resources of the Office which may be devoted to the requests of any one Member, to prepare drafts of legislation and to furnish drafting advice with respect to drafts of legislation prepared by others.

(5) At the direction of the Speaker, to perform on behalf of the House of Representatives any legal services which are within the capabilities of the Office and the performance of which would not be inconsistent with the provisions of section 281a of this title or the preceding provisions of this section.

PART II—ADMINISTRATION

§ 282. Legislative Counsel

The management, supervision, and administration of the Office are vested in the Legislative Counsel, who shall be appointed by the Speaker of the House of Representatives without regard to political affiliation and solely on the basis of fitness to perform the duties of the position. Any person so appointed shall serve at the pleasure of the Speaker.

§ 282a. Staff; Deputy Legislative Counsel; delegation of functions

(a) With the approval of the Speaker, or in accordance with policies and procedures approved by the Speaker, the Legislative Counsel shall appoint such attorneys and other employees as may be necessary for the prompt and efficient performance of the functions of the Office. Any such appointment shall be made without regard to political affiliation and solely on the basis of fitness to perform the duties of the position. Any person so appointed may be removed by the Legislative Counsel with the approval of the Speaker, or in accordance with policies and procedures approved by the Speaker.

(b)(1) One of the attorneys appointed under subsection (a) of this section shall be designated by the Legislative Counsel as Deputy Legislative Counsel. During the absence or disability of the Legislative Counsel, or when the office is vacant, the Deputy Legislative Counsel shall perform the functions of the Legislative Counsel.

(2) The Legislative Counsel may delegate to the Deputy Legislative Counsel and to other employees appointed under subsection (a) of this section such of his functions as he considers necessary or appropriate.

§ 282b. Compensation

(a) The Legislative Counsel shall be paid at a per annum gross rate equal to the rate of basic pay, as in effect from time to time, for level III of the Executive Schedule of section 5314 of title 5.

(b) Members of the staff of the Office other than the Legislative Counsel shall be paid at per annum gross rates fixed by the Legislative Counsel with the approval of the Speaker or in accordance with policies approved by the Speaker, but not in excess of the rate of basic pay for one pay level above the maximum pay level for em-

App. 5.30 The Code as Non-Positive Law: Chapter 9 of Title 2 (continued)

ployees of the House of Representatives provided under clause 6(c) of Rule XI of the Rules of the House of Representatives.

§ 282c. Expenditures

In accordance with policies and procedures approved by the Speaker, the Legislative Counsel may make such expenditures as may be necessary or appropriate for the functioning of the Office.

§ 282d. Official mail matter

The Legislative Counsel may send the official mail matter of the Office as franked mail under section 3210 of title 39.

§ 282e. Authorization of appropriations

There are authorized to be appropriated, for the fiscal year ending June 30, 1971, and for each fiscal year thereafter, such sums as may be necessary to carry out this subchapter and to increase the efficiency of the Office and the quality of the services which it provides.

Appendix Six: Concerning Birds and Ponies, Poultry and Rabbits

App. 6.00 Introduction

The materials that follow are curious amusements—one fictional, one factual. They are included here as a reminder that a drafter should have a sense of humor. The former equates birds with ponies; the second equates poultry with rabbits.

The author of this book first encountered *Regina v. Ojibway* while a student in Professor Ken Karst's constitutional law class at UCLA School of Law. As described in Chapter Three (specifically, § 3.00), it is a work of fiction, but a deft one. Courts can and do read statutes in odd ways at times.

Special thanks are given to Canada Law Book for permission to reprint *Regina v. Ojibway* here.

Special thanks are also given to the co-author, Hart Pomerantz, who indicated in correspondence that *Regina v. Ojibway* was written while in law school in Toronto in 1965.

The other matter included here is not a fictional article, but a real bill—one that very nearly became law. Donald Hirsch referred to it as the "rabbit bill" in section 2.7.2 of his book, *Drafting Federal Law* (2d ed. 1989). For a lively and thorough discussion of the rabbit bill, that book is unsurpassable.

The rabbit bill was twice passed by Congress and twice vetoed by the President. The purpose was to require the Department of Agriculture to inspect domesticated rabbits slaughtered for human food. Hirsch called the rabbit bill "surely one of the most peculiar bills ever vetoed (twice) by an American president," and that seems fair enough.

Purely as a drafting matter, the rabbit bill is an abomination. Under reasonable circumstances, a drafter would never draft a bill in this way. But Hirsch theorized—and, again, it seems fair enough—that the drafter was not an amateur, but a skilled drafter working under quick and dirty conditions: "In short," Hirsch wrote, "a bill that is a legal and technical nightmare, and a reproach to the craft, turns out to be the only kind of bill that, given our imagined constraints," would do what was needed. Donald Hirsch, *Drafting Federal Law* 19 (2d ed. 1989).

Did the drafter of the rabbit bill have *Regina v. Ojibway* in mind when deeming that poultry means rabbits and feathers means pelts? Who knows? One can only hope, for the drafter's sake, that a sense of humor was involved, for it is under those quick and dirty conditions that a sense of humor is most needed.

App. 6.10 *Regina v. Ojibway*

Regina v. Ojibway was written by H. Pomerantz and S. Breslin and published in 8 *Criminal Law Quarterly* 137 by Canada Law Book Inc. (1-800-263-3269, <*www.canadalawbook.ca*>). It is reprinted here with the permission of Canada Law Book Inc.

In the Supreme Court: *Regina v. Ojibway*
August, 1965

BLUE, J. This is an appeal by the Crown by way of a stated case from a decision of the magistrate acquitting the accused of a charge under the Small Birds Act, R.S.O., 1960, c. 724, s. 2. The facts are not in dispute. Fred Ojibway, an Indian, was riding his pony through Queen's Park on January 2, 1965. Being impoverished, and having been forced to pledge his saddle, he substituted a downy pillow in lieu of the said saddle. On this particular day the accused's misfortune was further heightened by the circumstance of his pony breaking its foreleg. In accord with Indian custom, the accused then shot the pony to relieve it of its awkwardness. The accused was then charged with having breached the Small Birds Act, s. 2 of which states: "2. Anyone maiming, injuring or killing small birds is guilty of an offence and subject to a fine not in excess of two hundred dollars." The learned magistrate acquitted the accused holding, in fact, that he had killed his horse and not a small bird. With respect, I cannot agree.

In light of the definition section my course is quite clear. Section 1 defines "bird" as "a two-legged animal covered with feathers." There can be no doubt that this case is covered by this section.

Counsel for the accused made several ingenious arguments to which, in fairness, I must address myself. He submitted that the evidence of the expert clearly concluded that the animal in question was a pony and not a bird, but this is not the issue. We are not interested in whether the animal in question is a bird or not in fact, but whether it is one in law. Statutory interpretation has forced many a horse to eat birdseed for the rest of its life.

Counsel also contended that the neighing noise emitted by the animal could not possibly be produced by a bird. With respect, the sounds emitted by an animal are irrelevant to its nature, for a bird is no less a bird because it is silent.

Counsel for the accused also argued that since there was evidence to show accused had ridden the animal, this pointed to the fact that it could not be a bird but was actually a pony. Obviously, this avoids the issue. The issue is not whether the animal was ridden or not, but whether it was shot or not, for to ride a pony or a bird is of no offence at all. I believe counsel now sees his mistake.

Counsel contends that the iron shoes found on the animal decisively disqualify it from being a bird. I must inform counsel, however, that how an animal dresses is of no consequence to this court.

Counsel relied on the decision in *Re Chicadee*, where he contends that in similar circumstances the accused was acquitted. However, this is a horse of a different colour. A close reading of that case indicates that the animal in question there was not a small bird, but, in fact, a midget of a much larger species. Therefore, that case is inapplicable to our facts.

Counsel finally submits that the word "small" in the title Small Birds Act refers not to "Birds" but to "Act," making it The Small Act relating to Birds. With respect, counsel did not do his homework very well, for the Large Birds Act, R.S.O. 1960, c. 725 is just as small. If pressed, I need only refer to the Small Loans Act, R.S.O. 1960, c. 727 which is twice as large as the Large Birds Act.

It remains then to state my reason for judgment which, simply, is as follows: Different things may take on the same meaning for different purposes. For the purpose of the Small Birds Act, all two-legged, feather-covered animals are birds. This, of course, does not imply that only two-legged animals qualify, for the legislative intent is to make two legs merely the minimum requirement. The statute therefore contemplated multi-legged animals with feathers as well. Counsel submits that having regard to the purpose of the statute only small animals "naturally covered" with feathers could have been contemplated. However, had this been the intention of the legislature, I am certain that the phrase "naturally covered" would have been expressly inserted just as "Long" was inserted in the Longshoreman's Act.

Therefore, a horse with feathers on its back must be deemed for the purposes of this Act to be a bird, and a fortiori, a pony with feathers on its back is a small bird.

Counsel posed the following rhetorical question: If the pillow had been removed prior to the shooting, would the animal still be a bird? To this let me answer rhetorically: Is a bird any less of a bird without its feathers?

Appeal allowed.

App. 6.20 The "Rabbit Bill"

95th Congress, 1st Session **House Document No. 95-261**

VETO OF H.R. 2521

MESSAGE

FROM

THE PRESIDENT OF THE UNITED STATES

VETOING

H.R. 2521, AN ACT TO PROVIDE FOR THE MANDATORY INSPECTION OF DOMESTICATED RABBITS SLAUGHTERED FOR HUMAN FOOD, AND FOR OTHER PURPOSES

NOVEMBER 11, 1977.—Message and accompanying act ordered to be printed as a House document

U.S. GOVERNMENT PRINTING OFFICE
29 011 **WASHINGTON : 1977**

App. 6.20 The "Rabbit Bill" (continued)

To the House of Representatives:

I am returning, without my approval, H.R. 2521, an Act "To provide for the mandatory inspection of domesticated rabbits slaughtered for human food and for other purposes."

This Act would establish a new mandatory federal inspection program for domesticated rabbits and rabbit products processed for human consumption. The program would be similar to that already applicable to poultry products, and would apply to imported rabbit meat as well as rabbit meat processed in the United States.

In my view, the costs to the general taxpayer associated with H.R. 2521 cannot be justified on several grounds:

—A voluntary inspection program operated by the Department of Agriculture, but paid for by the processors of rabbit meat, is already available to processors wishing to enjoy the marketing benefits of federal wholesomeness certification and grading. Moreover, rabbit meat marketed in the United States (including imports) is subject to inspection by the Food and Drug Administration to ensure sanitation and wholesomeness. Neither the Agriculture Department nor the Food and Drug Administration has been able to substantiate a significant health problem with rabbit meat in this country.

—Existing federal inspection programs are intended to apply to meats consumed by large numbers of Americans. Rabbit is essentially a specialty food purchased by a relatively small number of consumers. I believe that it would be inequitable to require all taxpayers to support extension of federal inspection of specialty meats to include rabbits. While the initial federal cost is small, once in the law, the subsidy may grow increasingly over the years. Moreover, signing this bill would provide an incentive for federal payments for the inspection of other exotic or specialty foods.

—Requirements for on-site inspection of foreign processing facilities by Department of Agriculture employees would strain relations with the People's Republic of China, a major exporter of domesticated rabbit meat to the United States. Extensive Food and Drug Administration inspection of Chinese imports have uncovered no health problems.

The primary beneficiaries of this special interest legislation would be a few large processors of rabbit meat which would no longer be required to reimburse the Federal Government for inspection services required to market their product as USDA inspected and graded. A significant source of competition from the People's Republic of China also would be severely restricted or eliminated with little or no improvement in consumer health protection.

Accordingly, I do not believe that approval of H.R. 2521 would be in the best interest of the American people.

JIMMY CARTER.

THE WHITE HOUSE, *November 9, 1977.*

(1)

H.D. 261

App. 6.20 The "Rabbit Bill" (continued)

H.R. 2521

NINETY-FIFTH CONGRESS OF THE UNITED STATES OF AMERICA

AT THE FIRST SESSION

Begun and held at the city of Washington on Tuesday, the fourth day of January, one thousand nine hundred and seventy-seven

AN ACT To provide for the mandatory inspection of domesticated rabbits slaughtered for human food, and for other purposes

Be it enacted by the Senate and House of Representatives of the United States of America in Congress assembled, That, except as provided in section 2 of this Act all the penalties, terms, and other provisions in the Poultry Products Inspection Act (71 Stat. 441; 21 U.S.C. 451-470) are hereby made applicable (1) to domesticated rabbits, the carcasses of such rabbits, and parts and products thereof, and to the establishments in which domesticated rabbits are slaughtered or in which the carcasses, or parts or products thereof, are processed, (2) to all persons who slaughter domesticated rabbits or prepare or handle the carcasses of such rabbits or parts or products thereof, and (3) to all other persons who perform any act relating to domesticated rabbits or other carcasses of such rabbits or parts or products thereof, and who would be subject to such provisions if such acts related to poultry or the carcasses of poultry, or parts or products thereof; and such provisions shall apply in the same manner and to the same extent as such provisions apply with respect to poultry and the carcasses of poultry, and parts and products thereof, and to persons who perform acts relating to poultry, the carcasses of poultry, or parts or products thereof.

SEC. 2. (a) The provisions in paragraph (a)(2) of section 15, section 24(a), and section 29 of the Poultry Products Inspection Act shall not apply with respect to domesticated rabbits or the carcasses of such rabbits, or parts or products thereof. The two-year period specified in paragraph (c)(1) of section 5 of such Act and the periods contemplated by paragraph (c)(4) of such section shall commence upon the effective date hereof, with respect to domesticated rabbits and the carcasses of such rabbits, and parts and products thereof; and in applying the volume provisions in paragraphs (c)(3) and (c)(4) of section 15 of such Act, the volume restrictions applicable to poultry shall apply to domesticated rabbits.

(b) For purposes of this Act—

(1) wherever the term "poultry" is used in the Poultry Products Inspection Act, such term shall be deemed to refer to domesticated rabbits;

(2) wherever the term "poultry product" is used in the Poultry Products Inspection Act, such term shall be deemed to refer to domesticated rabbit products;

H.D. 261

App. 6.20 The "Rabbit Bill" (continued)

(3) the reference to "domesticated bird" in section 4(e) of the Poultry Products Inspection Act, shall be deemed to refer to domesticated rabbit; and

(4) the reference to "feathers" in section 9(a)(4) shall be deemed to be "pelt".

SEC. 3. This Act shall become effective on October 1, 1978.

SEC. 4. The provisions hereof shall not in any way affect the application of the Poultry Products Inspection Act in relation to poultry, poultry carcasses, and parts and products thereof.

THOMAS P. O'NEILL, Jr.,
Speaker of the House of Representatives.
JAMES O. EASTLAND,
President of the Senate.

I certify that this act originated in the House of Representatives.

EDMUND L. HENSHAW, Jr.,
Clerk.

H.D. 261

Appendix Seven: The Federal Legislative Measures—Some Examples

App. 7.00 Introduction

The material that follows is included here to provide working examples of the various federal legislative measures, a topic covered in detail in Chapter Five.

App. 7.10 A Bill

I

109TH CONGRESS
1ST SESSION

H. R. 706

To amend title 28, United States Code, to provide for an additional place of holding court in the District of Colorado.

IN THE HOUSE OF REPRESENTATIVES

FEBRUARY 9, 2005

Mr. HEFLEY (for himself, Mr. TANCREDO, Mr. BEAUPREZ, Mr. UDALL of Colorado, Mr. SALAZAR, Mrs. MUSGRAVE, and Ms. DEGETTE) introduced the following bill; which was referred to the Committee on the Judiciary

---

A BILL

To amend title 28, United States Code, to provide for an additional place of holding court in the District of Colorado.

Be it enacted by the Senate and House of Representatives of the United States of America in Congress assembled,

SECTION 1. ADDITIONAL PLACE OF HOLDING COURT IN THE DISTRICT OF COLORADO.

Section 85 of title 28, United States Code, is amended by inserting "Colorado Springs," after "Boulder,".

○

App. 7.20 A Private Bill

V

109TH CONGRESS
1ST SESSION

H. R. 2645

For the relief of Web's Construction Company, Incorporated.

IN THE HOUSE OF REPRESENTATIVES

MAY 25, 2005

Mr. WYNN introduced the following bill; which was referred to the Committee on the Judiciary

---

A BILL

For the relief of Web's Construction Company, Incorporated.

Be it enacted by the Senate and House of Representatives of the United States of America in Congress assembled,

SECTION 1. PAYMENT FOR CONSTRUCTION WORK.

The Secretary of the Treasury shall pay, out of any money in the Treasury not otherwise appropriated, to Web's Construction Company, Incorporated, a company incorporated in the State of Maryland, $262,500, plus a reasonable rate of interest (as determined by the Secretary) for the period beginning February 1, 1990, and ending on the date of such payment, for construction work performed for the benefit of the Corps of Engineers in connection with Contract No. DACA31–88–C–0316. Pay-

App. 7.20 A Private Bill (continued)

2

ment of the sum shall be in full satisfaction of any claim of Web's Construction Company, Incorporated, against the United States in connection with the construction work.

SEC. 2. LIMITATION ON ATTORNEY FEES.

It shall be unlawful for an amount exceeding 10 percent of the amount paid pursuant to section 1 to be paid to, or received by, any agent or attorney for any service rendered in connection with the claim described in section 1. Any person who violates this section shall be guilty of an infraction, and shall be subject to a fine in the amount provided in title 18, United States Code.

○

App. 7.30 A Simple Resolution

III

108TH CONGRESS
1ST SESSION

S. RES. 277

Tendering the sincere thanks of the Senate to the staffs of the Offices of the Legislative Counsel of the Senate and the House of Representatives for their dedication and service to the legislative process.

IN THE SENATE OF THE UNITED STATES

NOVEMBER 25, 2003

Mr. FRIST (for himself, Mr. GRASSLEY, Mr. HATCH, Mr. BREAUX, Mr. BAUCUS, and Mr. NICKLES) submitted the following resolution; which was considered and agreed to

---

RESOLUTION

Tendering the sincere thanks of the Senate to the staffs of the Offices of the Legislative Counsel of the Senate and the House of Representatives for their dedication and service to the legislative process.

Whereas the Offices of the Legislative Counsel of the Senate and the House of Representatives have demonstrated great expertise, dedication, professionalism, and integrity in faithfully discharging the duties and responsibilities of their positions;

Whereas legislative drafting is a lengthy, arduous, and demanding process requiring a keen intellect, thorough knowledge, stern constitution, and remarkable patience;

App. 7.30 A Simple Resolution (continued)

2

Whereas the staff of the Senate and House Offices of the Legislative Counsel, in particular, Ruth Ann Ernst, John Goetcheus, Peter Goodloe, Edward G. Grossman, Pierre Poisson, and James G. Scott, have performed above and beyond the call of duty in drafting the Medicare Prescription Drug, Improvement, and Modernization Act of 2003; and

Whereas the Senate and House Offices of the Legislative Counsel have met the legislative drafting needs of the Senate and the House of Representatives with unfailing professionalism, exceptional skill, undying dedication, and, above all, patience and good humor as the Medicare Prescription Drug, Improvement, and Modernization Act of 2003 passed through the legislative process: Now, therefore, be it

Resolved, That the sincere thanks of the Senate are hereby tendered to the staff of both the Office of the Legislative Counsel of the Senate and the Office of the Legislative Counsel of the House of Representatives for their outstanding work and dedication to the United States Congress and the people of the United States of America.

○

App. 7.40 A Concurrent Resolution

109TH CONGRESS
1ST SESSION

S. CON. RES. 1

CONCURRENT RESOLUTION

Resolved by the Senate (the House of Representatives concurring), That the two Houses of Congress shall meet in the Hall of the House of Representatives on Thursday, the sixth day of January 2005, at 1 o'clock post meridian, pursuant to the requirements of the Constitution and laws relating to the election of President and Vice President of the United States, and the President of the Senate shall be their Presiding Officer; that two tellers shall be previously appointed by the President of the Senate on the part of the Senate and two by the Speaker on the part of the House of Representatives, to whom shall be handed, as they are opened by the President of the Senate, all the certificates and papers purporting to be certificates of the electoral votes, which certificates and papers shall be opened, presented, and acted upon in the alphabetical order of the States, beginning with the letter "A"; and said tellers, having then read the same in the presence and hearing of the two Houses, shall make a list of the votes as they shall appear from the said certificates; and

App. 7.40 A Concurrent Resolution (continued)

2

the votes having been ascertained and counted in the manner and according to the rules by law provided, the result of the same shall be delivered to the President of the Senate, who shall thereupon announce the state of the vote, which announcement shall be deemed a sufficient declaration of the persons, if any, elected President and Vice President of the United States, and, together with a list of the votes, be entered on the Journals of the two Houses.

Passed the Senate January 4, 2005.

Attest:

Secretary.

App. 7.50 A Joint Resolution

IA

109TH CONGRESS
1ST SESSION

H. J. RES. 27

Withdrawing the approval of the United States from the Agreement establishing the World Trade Organization.

IN THE HOUSE OF REPRESENTATIVES

MARCH 2, 2005

Mr. SANDERS (for himself and Mr. PAUL) introduced the following joint resolution; which was referred to the Committee on Ways and Means

---

JOINT RESOLUTION

Withdrawing the approval of the United States from the Agreement establishing the World Trade Organization.

Resolved by the Senate and House of Representatives of the United States of America in Congress assembled, That the Congress withdraws its approval, provided under section 101(a) of the Uruguay Round Agreements Act, of the WTO Agreement as defined in section 2(9) of that Act.

○

App. 7.60 A Joint Resolution Proposing a Constitutional Amendment

IA

109TH CONGRESS
1ST SESSION

H. J. RES. 10

Proposing an amendment to the Constitution of the United States authorizing the Congress to prohibit the physical desecration of the flag of the United States.

IN THE HOUSE OF REPRESENTATIVES

JANUARY 25, 2005

Mr. CUNNINGHAM (for himself, Mr. MURTHA, Mr. BARTLETT of Maryland, Mr. BASS, Mr. BOEHLERT, Mr. BUYER, Mr. CROWLEY, Mr. DAVIS of Tennessee, Mr. DOOLITTLE, Mr. FERGUSON, Mr. GARRETT of New Jersey, Mr. GOODE, Mr. HEFLEY, Mr. HOLDEN, Mr. ISSA, Mrs. JOHNSON of Connecticut, Mr. KENNEDY of Minnesota, Mr. KING of Iowa, Mr. McINTYRE, Mr. MENENDEZ, Mr. PITTS, Mr. RAMSTAD, Mr. ROGERS of Michigan, Mr. SIMMONS, Mr. SMITH of Texas, Mr. TANCREDO, Mr. TAYLOR of North Carolina, Mr. TAYLOR of Mississippi, Mr. WAMP, Mr. WICKER, Mr. WILSON of South Carolina, Mr. McCAUL of Texas, Mrs. JO ANN DAVIS of Virginia, Mr. HUNTER, Mrs. CUBIN, Mr. KNOLLENBERG, Mr. MOLLOHAN, Mr. MCHUGH, Mr. WOLF, Mr. OTTER, Mr. ROYCE, Mr. GREEN of Wisconsin, Mrs. McCARTHY, Mr. GIBBONS, Mr. HASTINGS of Washington, Mr. McGOVERN, Mr. TERRY, and Mr. BRADLEY of New Hampshire) introduced the following resolution; which was referred to the Committee on the Judiciary

---

JOINT RESOLUTION

Proposing an amendment to the Constitution of the United States authorizing the Congress to prohibit the physical desecration of the flag of the United States.

Resolved by the Senate and House of Representatives of the United States of America in Congress assembled (two-thirds of each House concurring therein), That the fol-

App. 7.60 A Joint Resolution Proposing a Constitutional Amendment (continued)

2

lowing article is proposed as an amendment to the Constitution of the United States, which shall be valid to all intents and purposes as part of the Constitution when ratified by the legislatures of three-fourths of the several States within seven years after the date of its submission for ratification:

"ARTICLE —

"The Congress shall have power to prohibit the physical desecration of the flag of the United States.".

Appendix Eight: The Federal Drafting Styles—Some Examples

App. 8.00 Introduction

The material that follows is included here to provide working examples of the various federal drafting styles, a topic covered in detail in Chapter Eight.

The inclusion here of an example is in no way an endorsement of the drafting; the examples are not necessarily "models" of good drafting.

In App. 8.10, the style of 1789, note in particular the use of enacting words in each section, the use of "that" to begin each section, and the absence of designated subdivisions.

In App. 8.20, appropriations style, note in particular the use of undesignated subdivisions rather than sections, except for section 101 at the end. Note also the many provisoes, and the placement of the short title at the end.

In App. 8.30, traditional style, note the manner in which the section headings appear above the section designations. Note also the absence of subdivision headings and the device of "running in" a lower-tier subdivision into an upper-tier subdivision—thus, in section 215, subsection (a) has text, but subsections (b), (c), and (d) run right into a paragraph (1) without intervening text (and without dropping down to the next line and indenting the margin).

In App. 8.40, revenue style, note the enthusiastic use of subdivision headings and the absence of the "running in" device—each subdivision begins on a new line with a distinct margin. Also, note that the form of the section heading differs from traditional style.

In App. 8.50, modified revenue style, note that headings are used for subsections and paragraphs, but not for lower-tier subdivisions.

In App. 8.60, code style, note that the body of the provision has the same form as traditional style, but the heading has a distinct form.

App. 8.10 The Style of 1789

24 FIRST CONGRESS. Sess. I. Ch. 2. 1789.

By whom the oaths or affirmations shall be administered in the several States.

appointed before the first day of August next, and who shall then be in office, shall, within one month thereafter, take the same oath or affirmation, except where they shall have taken it before; which may be administered by any person authorized by the law of the State, in which such office shall be holden, to administer oaths. And the members of the several State legislatures, and all executive and judicial officers of the several States, who shall be chosen or appointed after the said first day of August, shall, before they proceed to execute the duties of their respective offices, take the foregoing oath or affirmation, which shall be administered by the person or persons, who by the law of the State shall be authorized to administer the oath of office; and the person or persons so administering the oath hereby required to be taken, shall cause a record or certificate thereof to be made, in the same manner, as, by the law of the State, he or they shall be directed to record or certify the oath of office.

To all officers of the U. States appointed, or to be appointed, before they act.

Sec. 4. *And be it further enacted,* That all officers appointed, or hereafter to be appointed under the authority of the United States, shall, before they act in their respective offices, take the same oath or affirmation, which shall be administered by the person or persons who shall be authorized by law to administer to such officers their respective oaths of office; and such officers shall incur the same penalties in case of failure, as shall be imposed by law in case of failure in taking their respective oaths of office.

Oath of secretary of the Senate and clerk of the House of Representatives.

Sec. 5. *And be it further enacted,* That the secretary of the Senate, and the clerk of the House of Representatives for the time being, shall, at the time of taking the oath or affirmation aforesaid, each take an oath or affirmation in the words following, to wit: "I, A. B. secretary of the Senate, or clerk of the House of Representatives (as the case may be) of the United States of America, do solemnly swear or affirm, that I will truly and faithfully discharge the duties of my said office, to the best of my knowledge and abilities."

Approved, June 1, 1789.

Statute I.

July 4, 1789.

[Repealed.]

Chap. II.—*An Act for laying a Duty on Goods, Wares, and Merchandises imported into the United States.*(*a*)

Sec. 1. Whereas it is necessary for the support of government, for the discharge of the debts of the United States, and the encouragement and protection of manufactures, that duties be laid on goods, wares and merchandises imported: (*b*)

Act of August 10, 1790, ch. 38, sec. 1 and 2.

Be it enacted by the Senate and House of Representatives of the United States of America in Congress assembled, That from and after the first day of August next ensuing, the several duties hereinafter mentioned shall be laid on the following goods, wares and merchandises imported into the United States from any foreign port or place, that is to say:

(*a*) Duty Acts. Act of July 4, 1789, chap. 2; act of August 4, 1790, chap. 35; act of June 5, 1794, chap. 51; act of January 29, 1795, chap. 17; act of March 3, 1797, chap. 10; act of May 13, 1800, chap. 66; act of March 27, 1804, chap. 57; act of June 7, 1794, chap. 54; act of January 29, 1795, chap. 17; act of March 27, 1804, chap. 46; act of July 8, 1797, chap. 15; act of May 7, 1800, chap. 43; act of March 27, 1804, chap. 57; act of July 1, 1812, chap. 112; act of February 25, 1813, chap. 30; act of August 2, 1813, chap. 38; act of April 27, 1816, chap. 107; act of January 14, 1817, chap. 3; act of April 20, 1818, chap. 105; act of April 20, 1818, chap. 93; act of May 21, 1824, chap. 136; act of May 19, 1828, chap. 55; act of May 24, 1828, chap. 102; act of May 28, 1830, chap. 147; act of July 14, 1832, chap. 227; act of March 2, 1833, chap. 62; act of September 11, 1841, chap. 24; act of August 30, 1842, chap. 270.

(*b*) The powers of Congress to levy and collect taxes, duties, exposts and excises, is co-extensive with the United States. Loughborough *v.* Blake, 5 Wheat. 317; 4 Cond. Rep. 660.

App. 8.10 The Style of 1789 (continued)

FIRST CONGRESS. Sess. I. Ch. 2. 1789. 25

Specific duties on certain enumerated articles.

On all distilled spirits of Jamaica proof, imported from any kingdom or country whatsoever, per gallon, ten cents.
On all other distilled spirits, per gallon, eight cents.
On molasses, per gallon, two and a half cents.
On Madeira wine, per gallon, eighteen cents.
On all other wines, per gallon, ten cents.
On every gallon of beer, ale or porter in casks, five cents.
On all cider, beer, ale or porter in bottles, per dozen, twenty cents.
On malt, per bushel, ten cents.
On brown sugars, per pound, one cent.
On loaf sugars, per pound, three cents.
On all other sugars, per pound, one and a half cents.
On coffee, per pound, two and a half cents.
On cocoa, per pound, one cent.
On all candles of tallow, per pound, two cents.
On all candles of wax or spermaceti, per pound, six cents.
On cheese, per pound, four cents.
On soap, per pound, two cents.
On boots, per pair, fifty cents.
On all shoes, slippers or goloshoes made of leather, per pair, seven cents.
On all shoes or slippers made of silk or stuff, per pair, ten cents.
On cables, for every one hundred and twelve pounds, seventy-five cents.
On tarred cordage, for every one hundred and twelve pounds, seventy-five cents.
On untarred ditto, and yarn, for every one hundred and twelve pounds, ninety cents.
On twine or packthread, for every one hundred and twelve pounds, two hundred cents.
On all steel unwrought, for every one hundred and twelve pounds, fifty-six cents.
On all nails and spikes, per pound, one cent.
On salt, per bushel, six cents.
On manufactured tobacco, per pound, six cents.
On snuff, per pound, ten cents.
On indigo, per pound, sixteen cents.
On wool and cotton cards, per dozen, fifty cents.
On coal, per bushel, two cents.
On pickled fish, per barrel, seventy-five cents.
On dried fish, per quintal, fifty cents.

On teas imported from India or China.

On all teas imported from China or India, in ships built in the United States, and belonging to a citizen or citizens thereof, or in ships or vessels built in foreign countries, and on the sixteenth day of May last wholly the property of a citizen or citizens of the United States, and so continuing until the time of importation, as follows:
On bohea tea, per pound, six cents.
On all souchong, or other black teas, per pound, ten cents.
On all hyson teas, per pound, twenty cents.
On all other green teas, per pound, twelve cents.

On teas imported from Europe.

On all teas imported from Europe in ships or vessels built in the United States, and belonging wholly to a citizen or citizens thereof, or in ships or vessels built in foreign countries, and on the sixteenth day of May last wholly the property of a citizen or citizens of the United States, and so continuing until the time of importation, as follows:
On bohea tea, per pound, eight cents.
On all souchong, and other black teas, per pound, thirteen cents.
On all hyson teas, per pound, twenty-six cents.
On all other green teas, per pound, sixteen cents.

Vol. I.—4 C

App. 8.10 The Style of 1789 (continued)

On all teas imported, in any other manner than as above mentioned, as follows:—
On bohea tea, per pound, fifteen cents.
On all souchong, or other black teas, per pound, twenty-two cents.
On all hyson teas, per pound, forty-five cents.
On all other green teas, per pound, twenty-seven cents.

On all other goods imported from India or China, 12½ per centum ad valorem.

On all goods, wares and merchandises, other than teas, imported from China or India, in ships not built in the United States, and not wholly the property of a citizen or citizens thereof, nor in vessels built in foreign countries, and on the sixteenth day of May last wholly the property of a citizen or citizens of the United States, and so continuing until the time of importation, twelve and a half per centum ad valorem.

On other enumerated articles, 10 per centum ad valorem.

On all looking-glasses, window and other glass (except black quart bottles),
On all China, stone and earthern ware,
On gunpowder,
On all paints ground in oil,
On shoe and knee buckles,
On gold and silver lace, and
On gold and silver leaf,
} Ten per centum ad valorem.

On other enumerated articles, 7½ per ct. ad valorem.

On all blank books,
On all writing, printing or wrapping paper, paper-hangings and pasteboard,
On all cabinet wares,
On all buttons,
On all saddles,
On all gloves of leather,
On all hats of beaver, fur, wool, or mixture of either,
On all millinery ready made,
On all castings of iron, and upon slit and rolled iron,
On all leather tanned or tawed, and all manufacture of leather, except such as shall be otherwise rated,
On canes, walking sticks and whips,
On clothing ready made,
On all brushes,
On gold, silver, and plated ware, and on jewelry and paste work,
On anchors, and on all wrought, tin, and pewter ware,
} Seven and a half per centum ad valorem.

On playing cards, per pack, ten cents.
On every coach, chariot or other four wheel carriage, and on every chaise, solo, or other two wheel carriage, or parts thereof, } fifteen per centum ad valorem.

On all other goods, except certain articles, 5 per cent. on the value at the time and place of importation.

On all other goods, wares and merchandise, five per centum on the value thereof at the time and place of importation, except as follows: saltpetre, tin in pigs, tin plates, lead, old pewter, brass, iron and brass wire, copper in plates,(a) wool, cotton, dyeing woods and dyeing drugs, raw hides, beaver, and all other furs, and deer skins.

Duty on hemp and cotton imported after the 1st Dec. 1790.

Sec. 2. *And be it further enacted by the authority aforesaid*, That from and after the first day of December, which shall be in the year one thousand seven hundred and ninety, there shall be laid a duty on every one hundred and twelve pounds, weight of hemp imported as aforesaid, of sixty cents; and on cotton per pound, three cents.

Drawback allowed for the duties on goods exported within 12 months.

Sec. 3. *And be it [further] enacted by the authority aforesaid*, That all the duties paid, or secured to be paid upon any of the goods, wares and merchandises as aforesaid, except on distilled spirits, other than brandy and geneva, shall be returned or discharged upon such of the said goods,

(a) Round copper in bars, and copper plates turned up at the edges, are not subject to duty under this act, or under the act of August 10, 1790, and the act of May 2, 1792; by which "copper in plates, and copper in pigs and bars," is exempted from duty. United States v. Kidd & Watson, 4 Cranch, 1; 2 Cond. Rep. 1.

App. 8.10 The Style of 1789 (continued)

wares, or merchandises, as shall within twelve months after payment made, or security given, be exported to any country without the limits of the United States, as settled by the late treaty of peace; except one per centum on the amount of the said duties, in consideration of the expense which shall have accrued by the entry and safe-keeping thereof.

Except one per cent.

Sec. 4. *And be it [further] enacted by the authority aforesaid,* That there shall be allowed and paid on every quintal of dried, and on every barrel of pickled fish, of the fisheries of the United States, and on every barrel of salted provision of the United States, exported to any country without the limits thereof, in lieu of a drawback of the duties imposed on the importation of the salt employed and expended therein, viz:

Allowance in lieu of a draw-back on dried and pickled fish and salted provisions exported.

On every quintal of dried fish, five cents.

On every barrel of pickled fish, five cents.

On every barrel of salted provision, five cents.

Sec. 5. *And be it further enacted by the authority aforesaid,* That a discount of ten per cent. on all the duties imposed by this act, shall be allowed on such goods, wares and merchandises, as shall be imported in vessels built in the United States, and which shall be wholly the property of a citizen or citizens thereof, or in vessels built in foreign countries, and on the sixteenth day of May last, wholly the property of a citizen or citizens of the United States, and so continuing until the time of importation.

Discount on duties for goods imported in vessels of citizens.

Sec. 6. *And be it further enacted by the authority aforesaid,* That this act shall continue and be in force until the first day of June, which shall be in the year of our Lord one thousand seven hundred and ninety-six, and from thence until the end of the next succeeding session of Congress which shall be held thereafter, and no longer.

Continuance of the act.

Approved, July 4, 1789.

Statute I.

Chap. III.—*An Act imposing Duties on Tonnage.*(a)

July 20, 1789.

Section 1. ***Be it enacted by the Senate and House of Representatives of the United States of America in Congress assembled,*** That the following duties shall be, and are hereby imposed on all ships or vessels entered in the United States, that is to say:

Repealed by act of July 20, 1790, chap. 30.

On all ships or vessels built within the said States, and belonging wholly to a citizen or citizens thereof; or not built within the said States, but on the twenty-ninth day of May, one thousand seven hundred and eighty-nine, belonging, and during the time such ships or vessels shall continue to belong wholly to a citizen or citizens thereof, at the rate of six cents per ton. On all ships or vessels hereafter built in the United States, belonging wholly, or in part, to subjects of foreign powers, at the rate of thirty cents per ton. On all other ships or vessels, at the rate of fifty cents per ton.

Six cents per ton on vessels built in U. S., or belonging to citizens. On vessels hereafter built in the U. S., belonging to foreigners, 30 cts. per ton. On all others, 50 cts. per ton.

Sec. 2. *Provided always, and be it enacted,* That no ship or vessel built within the aforesaid States, and belonging to a citizen or citizens thereof, shall, whilst employed in the coasting trade, or in the fisheries, pay tonnage more than once in any year.

Vessels built in the U. S., in the coasting trade, to pay tonnage but once a year.

Sec. 3. *And be it further enacted,* That every ship or vessel employed in the transportation of any of the produce or manufactures of the United States, coastwise within the said States, except such ship or

50 cts. a ton on foreign vessels engaged in the coasting trade.

(a) General acts relating to tonnage duties: Act of July 20, 1789, chap. 3; act of September 16, 1789, chap. 15; act of July 20, 1790, chap. 30; act of May 1, 1802; act of March 3, 1815, chap. 76; April 27. 1816, chap. 107; April 27, 1816, chap. 110; January 14, 1817, chap. 3; act of March 1, 1817, chap. 31; act of March 3, 1817, chap. 50; act of March 3, 1819, chap. 74; act of January 7, 1824, chap. 4.

App. 8.20 Appropriations Style

Public Law 109–62
109th Congress

An Act

Sept. 8, 2005
[H.R. 3673]

Making further emergency supplemental appropriations to meet immediate needs arising from the consequences of Hurricane Katrina, for the fiscal year ending September 30, 2005, and for other purposes.

Second Emergency Supplemental Appropriations Act to Meet Immediate Needs Arising From the Consequences of Hurricane Katrina, 2005.

Be it enacted by the Senate and House of Representatives of the United States of America in Congress assembled, That the following sums are appropriated, out of any money in the Treasury not otherwise appropriated, for the fiscal year ending September 30, 2005, namely:

DEPARTMENT OF DEFENSE—MILITARY

OPERATION AND MAINTENANCE

OPERATION AND MAINTENANCE, DEFENSE-WIDE

(INCLUDING TRANSFERS OF FUNDS)

Expiration date.

For an additional amount for "Operation and Maintenance, Defense-Wide", $1,400,000,000 for emergency hurricane expenses, to support costs of evacuation, emergency repairs, deployment of personnel, and other costs resulting from immediate relief efforts, to remain available until September 30, 2006: *Provided*, That the Secretary of Defense may transfer these funds to appropriations for military personnel, operation and maintenance, procurement, family housing, Defense Health Program, and working capital funds: *Provided further*, That not to exceed $6,000,000 may be transferred to "Armed Forces Retirement Home" for emergency hurricane expenses: *Provided further*, That funds transferred shall be merged with and be available for the same purposes and for the same time period as the appropriation or fund to which transferred: *Provided further*, That this transfer authority is in addition to any other transfer authority available to the Department of Defense: *Provided further*, That upon a determination that all or part of the funds transferred from this appropriation are not necessary for the purposes provided herein, such amounts may be transferred back to this appropriation: *Provided further*, That the Secretary of Defense shall, not more than 5 days after making transfers from this appropriation, notify the Committees on Appropriations in writing of any such transfer: *Provided further*, That the amounts provided herein are designated as an emergency requirement pursuant to section 402 of H. Con. Res. 95 (109th Congress).

Deadline.
Notification.

App. 8.20 Appropriations Style (continued)

PUBLIC LAW 109–62—SEPT. 8, 2005 119 STAT. 1991

DEPARTMENT OF DEFENSE—CIVIL

DEPARTMENT OF THE ARMY

CORPS OF ENGINEERS—CIVIL

OPERATION AND MAINTENANCE

For an additional amount for "Operation and Maintenance" for emergency expenses for repair of storm damage to authorized projects in the Gulf states affected by Hurricane Katrina, $200,000,000, to remain available until expended: *Provided*, That the Chief of Engineers, acting through the Assistant Secretary of the Army for Civil Works, shall provide, at a minimum, a weekly report to the Committees on Appropriations detailing the allocation and obligation of these funds, beginning not later than September 15, 2005: *Provided further*, That the amount provided herein is designated as an emergency requirement pursuant to section 402 of H. Con. Res. 95 (109th Congress).

Reports. Deadline.

FLOOD CONTROL AND COASTAL EMERGENCIES

For an additional amount for "Flood Control and Coastal Emergencies", as authorized by section 5 of the Flood Control Act of August 16, 1941 (33 U.S.C. 701), for emergency expenses for repair of damage to flood control and hurricane shore protection projects in the Gulf states caused by Hurricane Katrina, $200,000,000, to remain available until expended: *Provided*, That the Chief of Engineers, acting through the Assistant Secretary of the Army for Civil Works, shall provide, at a minimum, a weekly report to the Committees on Appropriations detailing the allocation and obligation of these funds, beginning not later than September 15, 2005: *Provided further*, That the amount provided herein is designated as an emergency requirement pursuant to section 402 of H. Con. Res. 95 (109th Congress).

Reports. Deadline.

DEPARTMENT OF HOMELAND SECURITY

EMERGENCY PREPAREDNESS AND RESPONSE

DISASTER RELIEF

(INCLUDING TRANSFERS OF FUNDS)

For an additional amount for "Disaster Relief", $50,000,000,000, to remain available until expended: *Provided*, That up to $100,000,000 may be transferred to and merged with "Emergency Preparedness and Response, Public Health Programs" for the National Disaster Medical System to support medical care as authorized by the Public Health Security and Bioterrorism Preparedness and Response Act of 2002 (42 U.S.C. 300hh–11): *Provided further*, That $15,000,000 shall be transferred to and merged with "Departmental Management and Operations, Office of Inspector General" for necessary expenses of the Office of Inspector General for audits and investigations as authorized by law for Hurricane Katrina response and recovery activities: *Provided further*, That the Secretary of Homeland Security shall provide, at a minimum, a weekly report to the Committees on Appropriations detailing the allocation and obligation of these funds,

Reports. Deadline.

App. 8.20 Appropriations Style (continued)

beginning not later than September 15, 2005: *Provided further*, That the amounts provided herein are designated as an emergency requirement pursuant to section 402 of H. Con. Res. 95 (109th Congress).

GENERAL PROVISION

SEC. 101. For procurements of property or services determined by the head of an executive agency to be used in support of Hurricane Katrina rescue and relief operations—

(1) the emergency procurement authority in subsection 32A(c) of the Office of Federal Procurement Policy Act (41 U.S.C. 428a(c)) may be used; and

(2) the amount specified in subsections (c), (d), and (f) of section 32 of the Office of Federal Procurement Policy Act (41 U.S.C. 428) shall be $250,000.

This Act may be cited as the "Second Emergency Supplemental Appropriations Act to Meet Immediate Needs Arising From the Consequences of Hurricane Katrina, 2005".

Approved September 8, 2005.

LEGISLATIVE HISTORY—H.R. 3673:

CONGRESSIONAL RECORD, Vol. 151 (2005):
Sept. 8, considered and passed House and Senate.

○

App. 8.30 Traditional Style

PUBLIC LAW 106–65—OCT. 5, 1999 113 STAT. 955

SEC. 3204. ORGANIZATION OF DEPARTMENT OF ENERGY COUNTER-INTELLIGENCE AND INTELLIGENCE PROGRAMS AND ACTIVITIES.

(a) ESTABLISHMENT OF OFFICES.—The Department of Energy Organization Act (42 U.S.C. 7101 et seq.) is amended by inserting after section 213, as added by section 3203(a), the following new sections:

"ESTABLISHMENT OF SECURITY, COUNTERINTELLIGENCE, AND INTELLIGENCE POLICIES

"SEC. 214. The Secretary shall be responsible for developing and promulgating the security, counterintelligence, and intelligence policies of the Department. The Secretary may use the immediate staff of the Secretary to assist in developing and promulgating those policies. 42 USC 7144a.

"OFFICE OF COUNTERINTELLIGENCE

"SEC. 215. (a) There is within the Department an Office of Counterintelligence. 42 USC 7144b.

"(b)(1) The head of the Office shall be the Director of the Office of Counterintelligence, which shall be a position in the Senior Executive Service. The Director of the Office shall report directly to the Secretary.

"(2) The Secretary shall select the Director of the Office from among individuals who have substantial expertise in matters relating to counterintelligence.

"(3) The Director of the Federal Bureau of Investigation may detail, on a reimbursable basis, any employee of the Bureau to the Department for service as Director of the Office. The service of an employee of the Bureau as Director of the Office shall not result in any loss of status, right, or privilege by the employee within the Bureau.

"(c)(1) The Director of the Office shall be responsible for establishing policy for counterintelligence programs and activities at Department facilities in order to reduce the threat of disclosure or loss of classified and other sensitive information at such facilities.

"(2) The Director of the Office shall be responsible for establishing policy for the personnel assurance programs of the Department.

"(3) The Director shall inform the Secretary, the Director of Central Intelligence, and the Director of the Federal Bureau of Investigation on a regular basis, and upon specific request by any such official, regarding the status and effectiveness of the counterintelligence programs and activities at Department facilities.

"(d)(1) Not later than March 1 each year, the Director of the Office shall submit a report on the status and effectiveness of the counterintelligence programs and activities at each Department facility during the preceding year. Each such report shall be submitted to the following: Reports. Deadline.

"(A) The Secretary.

"(B) The Director of Central Intelligence.

"(C) The Director of the Federal Bureau of Investigation.

"(D) The Committee on Armed Services and the Permanent Select Committee on Intelligence of the House of Representatives.

App. 8.30 Traditional Style (continued)

113 STAT. 956 PUBLIC LAW 106–65—OCT. 5, 1999

"(E) The Committee on Armed Services and the Select Committee on Intelligence of the Senate.

"(2) Each such report shall include for the year covered by the report the following:

"(A) A description of the status and effectiveness of the counterintelligence programs and activities at Department facilities.

"(B) A description of any violation of law or other requirement relating to intelligence, counterintelligence, or security at such facilities, including—

"(i) the number of violations that were investigated; and

"(ii) the number of violations that remain unresolved.

"(C) A description of the number of foreign visitors to Department facilities, including the locations of the visits of such visitors.

"(D) The adequacy of the Department's procedures and policies for protecting national security information, making such recommendations to Congress as may be appropriate.

"(E) A determination of whether each Department of Energy national laboratory is in full compliance with all departmental security requirements and, in the case of any such laboratory that is not, what measures are being taken to bring that laboratory into compliance.

Deadline. "(3) Not less than 30 days before the date that the report required by paragraph (1) is submitted, the director of each Department of Energy national laboratory shall certify in writing to the Director of the Office whether that laboratory is in full compliance with all departmental security requirements and, if not, what measures are being taken to bring that laboratory into compliance and a schedule for implementing those measures.

"(4) Each report under this subsection as submitted to the committees referred to in subparagraphs (D) and (E) of paragraph (1) shall be submitted in unclassified form, but may include a classified annex.

"OFFICE OF INTELLIGENCE

42 USC 7144c. "SEC. 216. (a) There is within the Department an Office of Intelligence.

"(b)(1) The head of the Office shall be the Director of the Office of Intelligence, which shall be a position in the Senior Executive Service. The Director of the Office shall report directly to the Secretary.

"(2) The Secretary shall select the Director of the Office from among individuals who have substantial expertise in matters relating to foreign intelligence.

"(c) Subject to the authority, direction, and control of the Secretary, the Director of the Office shall perform such duties and exercise such powers as the Secretary may prescribe.".

(b) CLERICAL AMENDMENT.—The table of contents at the beginning of the Department of Energy Organization Act is amended by inserting after the item relating to section 213, as added by section 3203(b), the following new items:

"214. Establishment of security, counterintelligence, and intelligence policies.
"215. Office of Counterintelligence.
"216. Office of Intelligence.".

App. 8.40 Revenue Style

118 STAT. 1438 PUBLIC LAW 108–357—OCT. 22, 2004

imposed a tax of 0.1 cent per gallon on any liquid other than gasoline (as defined in section 4083)—

"(A) sold by any person to an owner, lessee, or other operator of a diesel-powered train for use as a fuel in such train, or

"(B) used by any person as a fuel in a diesel-powered train unless there was a taxable sale of such fuel under subparagraph (A).

No tax shall be imposed by this paragraph on the sale or use of any liquid if tax was imposed on such liquid under section 4081.".

(B) Subsection (f) of section 4082 is amended by striking "section 4041(a)(1)" and inserting "subsections (a)(1) and (d)(3) of section 4041".

(C) Subparagraph (B) of section 6421(f)(3) is amended to read as follows:

"(B) so much of the rate specified in section 4081(a)(2)(A) as does not exceed the rate applicable under section 4041(a)(1)(C)(ii).".

(D) Subparagraph (B) of section 6427(l)(3) is amended to read as follows:

"(B) so much of the rate specified in section 4081(a)(2)(A) as does not exceed the rate applicable under section 4041(a)(1)(C)(ii).".

(b) FUEL USED ON INLAND WATERWAYS.—Subparagraph (C) of section 4042(b)(2) is amended to read as follows:

"(C) The deficit reduction rate is—

"(i) 3.3 cents per gallon after December 31, 2004, and before July 1, 2005,

"(ii) 2.3 cents per gallon after June 30, 2005, and before January 1, 2007, and

"(iii) 0 after December 31, 2006.".

26 USC 4041 note.

(c) EFFECTIVE DATE.—The amendments made by this section shall take effect on January 1, 2005.

SEC. 242. MODIFICATION OF APPLICATION OF INCOME FORECAST METHOD OF DEPRECIATION.

(a) IN GENERAL.—Section 167(g) (relating to depreciation under income forecast method) is amended by adding at the end the following new paragraph:

"(7) TREATMENT OF PARTICIPATIONS AND RESIDUALS.—

"(A) IN GENERAL.—For purposes of determining the depreciation deduction allowable with respect to a property under this subsection, the taxpayer may include participations and residuals with respect to such property in the adjusted basis of such property for the taxable year in which the property is placed in service, but only to the extent that such participations and residuals relate to income estimated (for purposes of this subsection) to be earned in connection with the property before the close of the 10th taxable year referred to in paragraph (1)(A).

"(B) PARTICIPATIONS AND RESIDUALS.—For purposes of this paragraph, the term 'participations and residuals' means, with respect to any property, costs the amount of which by contract varies with the amount of income earned in connection with such property.

App. 8.40 Revenue Style (continued)

PUBLIC LAW 108–357—OCT. 22, 2004 118 STAT. 1439

"(C) SPECIAL RULES RELATING TO RECOMPUTATION YEARS.—If the adjusted basis of any property is determined under this paragraph, paragraph (4) shall be applied by substituting 'for each taxable year in such period' for 'for such period'.

"(D) OTHER SPECIAL RULES.—

"(i) PARTICIPATIONS AND RESIDUALS.—Notwithstanding subparagraph (A), the taxpayer may exclude participations and residuals from the adjusted basis of such property and deduct such participations and residuals in the taxable year that such participations and residuals are paid.

"(ii) COORDINATION WITH OTHER RULES.—Deductions computed in accordance with this paragraph shall be allowable notwithstanding paragraph (1)(B), section 263, 263A, 404, 419, or 461(h).

"(E) AUTHORITY TO MAKE ADJUSTMENTS.—The Secretary shall prescribe appropriate adjustments to the basis of property and to the look-back method for the additional amounts allowable as a deduction solely by reason of this paragraph.".

(b) DETERMINATION OF INCOME.—Section 167(g)(5) (relating to special rules) is amended by redesignating subparagraphs (E) and (F) as subparagraphs (F) and (G), respectively, and inserting after subparagraph (D) the following new subparagraph:

"(E) TREATMENT OF DISTRIBUTION COSTS.—For purposes of this subsection, the income with respect to any property shall be the taxpayer's gross income from such property.".

(c) EFFECTIVE DATE.—The amendments made by this section shall apply to property placed in service after the date of the enactment of this Act. 26 USC 167 note.

SEC. 243. IMPROVEMENTS RELATED TO REAL ESTATE INVESTMENT TRUSTS.

(a) EXPANSION OF STRAIGHT DEBT SAFE HARBOR.—Section 856 (defining real estate investment trust) is amended—

(1) in subsection (c) by striking paragraph (7), and

(2) by adding at the end the following new subsection:

"(m) SAFE HARBOR IN APPLYING SUBSECTION (c)(4).—

"(1) IN GENERAL.—In applying subclause (III) of subsection (c)(4)(B)(iii), except as otherwise determined by the Secretary in regulations, the following shall not be considered securities held by the trust:

"(A) Straight debt securities of an issuer which meet the requirements of paragraph (2).

"(B) Any loan to an individual or an estate.

"(C) Any section 467 rental agreement (as defined in section 467(d)), other than with a person described in subsection (d)(2)(B).

"(D) Any obligation to pay rents from real property (as defined in subsection (d)(1)).

"(E) Any security issued by a State or any political subdivision thereof, the District of Columbia, a foreign government or any political subdivision thereof, or the Commonwealth of Puerto Rico, but only if the determination of any payment received or accrued under such security does not depend in whole or in part on the profits of

App. 8.50 Modified Revenue Style

PUBLIC LAW 106–65—OCT. 5, 1999 113 STAT. 915

Subtitle A—National Security Programs Authorizations

SEC. 3101. WEAPONS ACTIVITIES.

(a) IN GENERAL.—Funds are hereby authorized to be appropriated to the Department of Energy for fiscal year 2000 for weapons activities in carrying out programs necessary for national security in the amount of $4,489,995,000, to be allocated as follows:

(1) STOCKPILE STEWARDSHIP.—Funds are hereby authorized to be appropriated to the Department of Energy for fiscal year 2000 for stockpile stewardship in carrying out weapons activities necessary for national security programs in the amount of $2,252,300,000, to be allocated as follows:

(A) For core stockpile stewardship, $1,743,500,000, to be allocated as follows:

(i) For operation and maintenance, $1,610,355,000.

(ii) For plant projects (including maintenance, restoration, planning, construction, acquisition, modification of facilities, and the continuation of projects authorized in prior years, and land acquisition related thereto), $133,145,000, to be allocated as follows:

Project 00–D–103, terascale simulation facility, Lawrence Livermore National Laboratory, Livermore, California, $8,000,000.

App. 8.50 Modified Revenue Style (continued)

113 STAT. 916 PUBLIC LAW 106–65—OCT. 5, 1999

Project 00–D–105, strategic computing complex, Los Alamos National Laboratory, Los Alamos, New Mexico, $26,000,000.

Project 00–D–107, joint computational engineering laboratory, Sandia National Laboratories, Albuquerque, New Mexico, $1,800,000.

Project 99–D–102, rehabilitation of maintenance facility, Lawrence Livermore National Laboratory, Livermore, California, $3,900,000.

Project 99–D–103, isotope sciences facilities, Lawrence Livermore National Laboratory, Livermore, California, $2,000,000.

Project 99–D–104, protection of real property (roof reconstruction, Phase II), Lawrence Livermore National Laboratory, Livermore, California, $2,400,000.

Project 99–D–105, central health physics calibration facility, Los Alamos National Laboratory, Los Alamos, New Mexico, $1,000,000.

Project 99–D–106, model validation and system certification test center, Sandia National Laboratories, Albuquerque, New Mexico, $6,500,000.

Project 99–D–108, renovate existing roadways, Nevada Test Site, Nevada, $7,005,000.

Project 97–D–102, dual-axis radiographic hydrotest facility, Los Alamos National Laboratory, Los Alamos, New Mexico, $61,000,000.

Project 96–D–102, stockpile stewardship facilities revitalization, Phase VI, various locations, $2,640,000.

Project 96–D–104, processing and environmental technology laboratory, Sandia National Laboratories, Albuquerque, New Mexico, $10,900,000.

(B) For inertial fusion, $475,700,000, to be allocated as follows:

(i) For operation and maintenance, $227,600,000.

(ii) For the following plant project (including maintenance, restoration, planning, construction, acquisition, and modification of facilities, and land acquisition related thereto), $248,100,000, to be allocated as follows:

Project 96–D–111, national ignition facility, Lawrence Livermore National Laboratory, Livermore, California, $248,100,000.

(C) For technology partnership and education, $33,100,000, of which $14,500,000 shall be allocated for technology partnership and $18,600,000 shall be allocated for education.

(2) STOCKPILE MANAGEMENT.—Funds are hereby authorized to be appropriated to the Department of Energy for fiscal year 2000 for stockpile management in carrying out weapons activities necessary for national security programs in the amount of $2,023,300,000, to be allocated as follows:

(A) For operation and maintenance, $1,864,621,000.

App. 8.60 Code Style

PUBLIC LAW 108–277—JULY 22, 2004 118 STAT. 865

Public Law 108–277
108th Congress

An Act

To amend title 18, United States Code, to exempt qualified current and former law enforcement officers from State laws prohibiting the carrying of concealed handguns.

July 22, 2004
[H.R. 218]

Be it enacted by the Senate and House of Representatives of the United States of America in Congress assembled,

Law Enforcement Officers Safety Act of 2004. 18 USC 921 note.

SECTION 1. SHORT TITLE.

This Act may be cited as the "Law Enforcement Officers Safety Act of 2004".

SEC. 2. EXEMPTION OF QUALIFIED LAW ENFORCEMENT OFFICERS FROM STATE LAWS PROHIBITING THE CARRYING OF CONCEALED FIREARMS.

(a) IN GENERAL.—Chapter 44 of title 18, United States Code, is amended by inserting after section 926A the following:

"§ 926B. Carrying of concealed firearms by qualified law enforcement officers

"(a) Notwithstanding any other provision of the law of any State or any political subdivision thereof, an individual who is a qualified law enforcement officer and who is carrying the identification required by subsection (d) may carry a concealed firearm that has been shipped or transported in interstate or foreign commerce, subject to subsection (b).

"(b) This section shall not be construed to supersede or limit the laws of any State that—

"(1) permit private persons or entities to prohibit or restrict the possession of concealed firearms on their property; or

"(2) prohibit or restrict the possession of firearms on any State or local government property, installation, building, base, or park.

"(c) As used in this section, the term 'qualified law enforcement officer' means an employee of a governmental agency who—

"(1) is authorized by law to engage in or supervise the prevention, detection, investigation, or prosecution of, or the incarceration of any person for, any violation of law, and has statutory powers of arrest;

"(2) is authorized by the agency to carry a firearm;

"(3) is not the subject of any disciplinary action by the agency;

"(4) meets standards, if any, established by the agency which require the employee to regularly qualify in the use of a firearm;

App. 8.60 Code Style (continued)

118 STAT. 866 PUBLIC LAW 108–277—JULY 22, 2004

"(5) is not under the influence of alcohol or another intoxicating or hallucinatory drug or substance; and

"(6) is not prohibited by Federal law from receiving a firearm.

"(d) The identification required by this subsection is the photographic identification issued by the governmental agency for which the individual is employed as a law enforcement officer.

"(e) As used in this section, the term 'firearm' does not include—

"(1) any machinegun (as defined in section 5845 of the National Firearms Act);

"(2) any firearm silencer (as defined in section 921 of this title); and

"(3) any destructive device (as defined in section 921 of this title).".

(b) CLERICAL AMENDMENT.—The table of sections for such chapter is amended by inserting after the item relating to section 926A the following:

"926B. Carrying of concealed firearms by qualified law enforcement officers.".

SEC. 3. EXEMPTION OF QUALIFIED RETIRED LAW ENFORCEMENT OFFICERS FROM STATE LAWS PROHIBITING THE CARRYING OF CONCEALED FIREARMS.

(a) IN GENERAL.—Chapter 44 of title 18, United States Code, is further amended by inserting after section 926B the following:

"§ 926C. Carrying of concealed firearms by qualified retired law enforcement officers

"(a) Notwithstanding any other provision of the law of any State or any political subdivision thereof, an individual who is a qualified retired law enforcement officer and who is carrying the identification required by subsection (d) may carry a concealed firearm that has been shipped or transported in interstate or foreign commerce, subject to subsection (b).

"(b) This section shall not be construed to supersede or limit the laws of any State that—

"(1) permit private persons or entities to prohibit or restrict the possession of concealed firearms on their property; or

"(2) prohibit or restrict the possession of firearms on any State or local government property, installation, building, base, or park.

"(c) As used in this section, the term 'qualified retired law enforcement officer' means an individual who—

"(1) retired in good standing from service with a public agency as a law enforcement officer, other than for reasons of mental instability;

"(2) before such retirement, was authorized by law to engage in or supervise the prevention, detection, investigation, or prosecution of, or the incarceration of any person for, any violation of law, and had statutory powers of arrest;

"(3)(A) before such retirement, was regularly employed as a law enforcement officer for an aggregate of 15 years or more; or

"(B) retired from service with such agency, after completing any applicable probationary period of such service, due to a service-connected disability, as determined by such agency;

"(4) has a nonforfeitable right to benefits under the retirement plan of the agency;

App. 8.60 Code Style (continued)

PUBLIC LAW 108–277—JULY 22, 2004 118 STAT. 867

"(5) during the most recent 12-month period, has met, at the expense of the individual, the State's standards for training and qualification for active law enforcement officers to carry firearms;

"(6) is not under the influence of alcohol or another intoxicating or hallucinatory drug or substance; and

"(7) is not prohibited by Federal law from receiving a firearm.

"(d) The identification required by this subsection is—

"(1) a photographic identification issued by the agency from which the individual retired from service as a law enforcement officer that indicates that the individual has, not less recently than one year before the date the individual is carrying the concealed firearm, been tested or otherwise found by the agency to meet the standards established by the agency for training and qualification for active law enforcement officers to carry a firearm of the same type as the concealed firearm; or

"(2)(A) a photographic identification issued by the agency from which the individual retired from service as a law enforcement officer; and

"(B) a certification issued by the State in which the individual resides that indicates that the individual has, not less recently than one year before the date the individual is carrying the concealed firearm, been tested or otherwise found by the State to meet the standards established by the State for training and qualification for active law enforcement officers to carry a firearm of the same type as the concealed firearm.

"(e) As used in this section, the term 'firearm' does not include—

"(1) any machinegun (as defined in section 5845 of the National Firearms Act);

"(2) any firearm silencer (as defined in section 921 of this title); and

"(3) a destructive device (as defined in section 921 of this title).".

(b) CLERICAL AMENDMENT.—The table of sections for such chapter is further amended by inserting after the item relating to section 926B the following:

"926C. Carrying of concealed firearms by qualified retired law enforcement officers.".

Approved July 22, 2004.

LEGISLATIVE HISTORY—H.R. 218 (S. 253):

HOUSE REPORTS: No. 108–560 (Comm. on the Judiciary).
SENATE REPORTS: No. 108–29 accompanying S. 253 (Comm. on the Judiciary).
CONGRESSIONAL RECORD, Vol. 150 (2004):
June 23, considered and passed House.
July 7, considered and passed Senate.

○

App. 8.00 [illegible] Style (continued)

Appendix Nine: Executive Branch Materials

App. 9.00 Introduction

The material that follows is included here as a reference for drafters who are working in, or working with, the executive branch, a topic covered by Chapter Ten.

Not included in this appendix is a Statement of Administration Policy (described in § 10.12). For an example of a Statement of Administration Policy, see Appendix Four.

App. 9.10 OMB Circular No. A-19

OMB Circular No. A-19

Revised
September 20, 1979

TABLE OF CONTENTS

8. Clearance of agency proposed legislation and reports
   a. OMB action on agency submissions
   b. Forms of OMB advice
   c. Agency action on receipt of advice from OMB
   d. Agency action where prior clearance has not been effected
   e. Reclearance requirements

9. Interagency consultation

10. Enrolled bills
   a. Initial OMB action
   b. Agency action
   c. Preparation of enrolled bill letters
   d. Subsequent OMB action

11. Agency legislative liaison officers

12. Communications to OMB

Attachments:

A. Instructions Relating to the Preparation of Agency Legislative Programs

B. Instructions for the Preparation and Submission to Congress of Legislative Proposals Authorizing the Enactment of Additional Appropriations or Providing New Budget Authority Outside of Appropriation Acts

C. Basic Forms of OMB Advice

September 20, 1979

CIRCULAR NO. A-19
Revised
Transmittal Memorandum No. 1

TO THE HEADS OF EXECUTIVE
DEPARTMENTS AND ESTABLISHMENTS

SUBJECT: Revision of Circular No. A-19, Revised, Dated July 31, 1972: Legislative Coordination and Clearance

This transmits a revision of Circular No. A-19, Revised, dated July 1972: Legislative Coordination and Clearance.

The attached revision updates the Circular generally and makes explicit several long-standing practices. It does not change the basic aspects of the legislative coordination and clearance requirements and process.

The principal changes are as follows:

1. The Circular has been extensively restructured and a table of contents has been added to facilitate its reference use.
2. Requirements to identify the effect of legislation on personnel needs have been made explicit (sections 6e(5), 7f(1)(c), 7f(2), and 1Oc(4)(f)).
3. Requirements are set forth with respect to section 607 of the Congressional Budqet Act of 1974 dealing with year-ahead requests for authorizing the enactment of new budget authority (section 7e and Attachment B).
4. Additions have been made to the list of statutory and other requirements and Administration policies that should be taken into account (section 7h).
5. Forms of clearance advice given by OMB are set forth and explained (section 8(b) and Attachment C).
6. Previous Attachments B, C, and D have been deleted.

Attachments

CIRCULAR NO. A-19
Revised

TO THE HEADS OF EXECUTIVE DEPARTMENTS AND ESTABLISHMENTS

SUBJECT: Legislative coordination and clearance

1. **Purpose.** This Circular outlines procedures for the coordination and clearance by the Office of Management and Budget (OMB) of agency recommendations on proposed, pending, and enrolled legislation. It also includes instructions on the timing and preparation of agency legislative programs.

2. **Rescission.** This revision supersedes and rescinds Circular No. A-19, Revised, dated July 31, 1972.

3. **Background.** OMB performs legislative coordination and clearance functions to (a) assist the President in developing a position on legislation, (b) make known the Administration's position on legislation for the guidance of the agencies and information of Congress, (c) assure appropriate consideration of the views of all affected agencies, and (d) assist the President with respect to action on enrolled bills.

4. **Coverage.** All executive branch agencies (as defined in section 5b) are subject to the provisions of this Circular, except those agencies that are specifically required by law to transmit their legislative proposals, reports, or testimony to the Congress without prior clearance. OMB will, however, honor requests from such agencies for advice on the relationship of particular legislation, reports, or testimony to the program of the President. The municipal government of the District of Columbia is covered to the extent that legislation involves the relationship between it and the Federal Government. Agencies of the legislative and judicial branches are not covered by this Circular.

5. **Definitions.** For the purpose of this Circular, the following definitions apply:

a. **Advice.** Information transmitted to an agency by OMB stating the relationship of particular legislation and reports thereon to the program of the President or stating the views of OMB as a staff agency for the President with respect to such legislation and reports.

b. **Agency.** Any executive department or independent commission, board, bureau, office, agency, Government-owned or controlled corporation, or other establishment of the Government, including any regulatory commission or board and also the municipal government of the District of Columbia.

c. **Proposed legislation*.** A draft bill or any supporting document (e.g., Speaker letter, section-by-section analysis, statement of purpose and justification, etc.) that an agency wishes to present to Congress for its consideration. Also, any proposal for or endorsement of Federal legislation included in an agency's annual or special report or in other written form which an agency proposes to transmit to Congress, or to any Member or committee, officer or employee of Congress, or staff of any committee or Member, or to make available to any study group, commission, or the public.

d. **Pending bill.** Any bill or resolution that has been introduced in Congress or any amendment to a bill or resolution while in committee or when proposed for House or Senate floor consideration during debate. Also, any proposal placed before the conferees on a bill that has passed both Houses.

e. **Report** (including testimony).* Any written expression of official views prepared by an agency on a pending bill for (1) transmittal to any committee, Member, officer or employee of Congress, or staff of any committee or Member, or (2) presentation as testimony before a congressional committee. Also, any comment or recommendation on pending legislation included in an agency's annual or special report that an agency proposes to transmit to Congress, or any Member or committee, or to make available to any study group, commission, or the public.

f. **Enrolled bill.** A bill or resolution passed by both Houses of Congress and presented to the President for action.

g. **Views letter.** An agency's written comments provided at the request of OMB on a pending bill or on another agency's proposed legislation, report, or testimony.

6. **Agency legislative programs.**

a. Submission to OMB. Each agency shall prepare and submit to OMB annually its proposed legislative program for the next session of Congress. If an agency has no legislative program, it should submit a statement to this effect.

---

* The terms "proposed legislation" and "report" do not include materials submitted in justification of appropriation requests or proposals for reorganization plans.

b. Purposes of legislative program submission. The essential purposes for requiring agencies to submit annual legislative programs are: (1) to assist agency planning for legislative objectives; (2) to help agencies coordinate their legislative program with the preparation of their annual budget submissions to OMB; (3) to give agencies an opportunity to recommend specific proposals for Presidential endorsement; and (4) to aid OMB and other staff of the Executive Office of the President in developing the President's legislative program, budget, and annual and special messages.

c. Timing of submission to OMB. (1) Each agency shall submit its proposed legislative program to OMB at the same time as it initially submits its annual budget request as required by OMB Circular No. A-11. Timely submission is essential if the programs are to serve the purposes set forth in section 6b.

(2) Items that are not included in an agency's legislative program and have significant upward budget impact will not be considered after the budget is prepared unless they result from circumstances not foreseeable at the time of final budget decisions.

d. Number of copies. Each agency shall furnish 25 copies of its proposed legislative program to OMB. These copies will be distributed by OMB within the Executive Office of the President.

e. Program content. Each agency shall prepare its legislative program in accordance with the instructions in Attachment A. Agency submissions shall include:

(1) All items of legislation that an agency contemplates proposing to Congress (or actively supporting, if already pending legislation) during the coming session, including proposals to extend expiring laws or repeal provisions of existing laws. These items should be based on policy-level decisions within the agency and should take into account the President's known legislative, budgetary, and other relevant policies. Agencies' proposed legislative programs should identify those items of sufficient importance to be included in the President's legislative program.

(2) A separate list of legislative proposals under active consideration in the agency that are not yet ready for inclusion in its proposed legislative program. For each item in this list, the agency should indicate when it expects to reach a policy-level decision and, specifically, whether it expects to propose the item in time for its consideration for inclusion in the annual budget under preparation.

(3) A separate list of all laws or provisions of law affecting an agency that will expire between the date the program is submitted to OMB and the end of the two following calendar years, whether or not the agency plans to propose their extension.

(4) All items in the submissions that are proposed, or expected to be proposed, for inclusion in the annual budget shall be accompanied by a tabulation showing amounts of budget authority and outlays or other measure of budgetary impact for the budget year and for each of the four succeeding fiscal years. See section 201(a)(5),(6), and (12) of the Budget and Accounting Act, 1921, as amended (31 U.S.C. 11(a)(12)). Criteria in OMB Circular No. A-11 shall be used in preparing these tabulations.

(5) All items covered by section 6e(4) above shall also be accompanied by estimates of work-years of employment and of personnel required to carry out the proposal in the budget year and four succeeding fiscal years.

f. Relationship to advice. Submission of a legislative program to OMB does not constitute a request for advice on individual legislative proposals. Such requests should be made in the manner prescribed in section 7 of this Circular.

7. **Submission of agency proposed legislation and reports.**

a. Submission to OMB. Before an agency transmits proposed legislation or a report (including testimony) outside the Executive branch, it shall submit the proposed legislation or report or testimony to OMB for coordination and clearance.

b. Agency scheduling of submissions. Agencies should not commit themselves to testify on pending bills or to submit reports or proposed legislation to Congress on a time schedule that does not allow orderly coordination and clearance. To facilitate congressional action on Administration proposals and to forestall hasty, last-minute clearance requests, agencies should plan their submissions to OMB on a time schedule that will permit orderly coordination and clearance. Particular care should be given to ensuring that draft legislation to carry out Presidential legislative recommendations is submitted promptly to OMB to allow sufficient time for analysis and review.

c. Timing of agency submissions.

(1) Agencies should submit proposed legislation, reports, and testimony to OMB well in advance of the desired date of transmittal to Congress.

(2) Agencies should include in their submissions to OMB of proposed reports and testimony a copy of any committee request for such reports and testimony, if the request calls for special information or includes specific questions to be covered in the reports or testimony.

(3) Depending on the complexity and significance of the subject matter, the policy issues involved, and the number of agencies affected, an adequate period for clearance by OMB may range from several days to a number of months. Agencies shall consult with OMB staff as to necessary periods for clearance, particularly in cases of major or complex legislation.

(4) On occasion, very short periods for clearances may be unavoidable because of congressional time schedules or other factors. Nevertheless, agencies should make every effort to give OMB a minimum of five full working days for clearance of proposed reports or testimony.

(5) Agencies shall state in their transmittal letters to OMB any information on congressional schedules or other special circumstances that may require expedited clearance.

d. Number of copies. Agencies should furnish to OMB 10 copies of proposed legislation and supporting materials and six copies of draft reports or testimony. If wide circulation or expedited action is required, the originating agency shall consult informally in advance with OMB staff on the number of copies to be supplied. Similarly, agencies should furnish to OMB six copies of their views letters on other agencies' proposed legislation, reports, or testimony.

e. Submission of legislation authorizing the enactment of new budget authority.

Section 607 of P.L. 93-344, the Congressional Budget Act of 1974, requires year-ahead requests for authorizing the enactment of new budget authority, as follows:

> "Notwithstanding any other provision of law, any request for the enactment of legislation authorizing the enactment of new budget authority to continue a program or activity for a fiscal year (beginning with the fiscal year commencing October 1, 1976) shall be submitted to the Congress not later than May 15 of the year preceding the year in which such fiscal year begins. In the case of a request for the enactment of legislation authorizing the enactment of new budget authority for a new program or activity which is to continue for more than one fiscal year, such request shall be submitted for at least the first 2 fiscal years."

Attachment B sets forth instructions, necessitated by section 607 of P.L. 93-344, for the preparation and submission to Congress of legislative proposals authorizing additional appropriations or providing new budget authority outside of appropriation acts.

f. Items to be included in agency submissions.

(1) Agencies should identify proposed legislation submitted to OMB by using the number assigned to the proposal in the agency's legislative program submission; e.g., Agriculture, 96-12 (see Attachment A). Each legislative proposal shall include a draft transmittal letter to the Speaker of the House and the President of the Senate as well as background information and justification, including where applicable:

(a) a section-by-section analysis of the provisions of the proposed legislation;

(b) comparison with existing law presented in "Ramseyer" or "Cordon" rule form by underscoring proposed additions to existing law and bracketing the text of proposed deletions (This need be done only when it would facilitate understanding of the proposed legislation.);

(c) budgetary and personnel impacts as described in sections 6e(4) and (5), including a statement of the relationship of these estimates to those previously incorporated in the President's budgetary program. (Public

Law 89-554, 5 U.S.C. 2953, requires in certain cases that agencies, in proposing legislation and in submitting reports favoring legislation, provide estimates of expenditures and personnel that would be needed. Public Law 91-510, sections 252(a) (2 U.S.C. 190j) and 252(b) imposes similar requirements on congressional committees.);

(d) comparison with previous agency proposals or related bills introduced in the Congress;

(e) an identification of other agencies that have an interest in the proposal;

(f) an indication of any consultation with other agencies in the development of the proposal; and

(g) information required by statute or by Administration policies, as, for example, that noted in section 7h below.

(2) Similarly, in their letters to OMB requesting advice on reports or testimony, agencies should identify related bills and set forth any relevant comments not included in the report or testimony itself. As indicated in section 7f(1)(c), certain reports or testimony favoring legislation are required by law to include budget and personnel estimates. Where such estimates are not included in other reports or in testimony favoring or opposing legislation, agencies should provide in their letters to OMB a statement of budgetary and personnel impacts as described in sections 6e(4) and (5), including a statement of the relationship of these estimates to those previously incorporated in the President's budgetary program.

(3) In cases where legislation carries out a Presidential recommendation, agencies should include in the proposed report or the letter transmitting proposed legislation a statement identifying the recommendation and indicating the degree to which the legislation concerned will carry it out.

g. Views letters. In views letters to OMB, an agency should indicate whether it supports, opposes, or has no objection to all or part of a pending bill or of another agency's proposed legislation, report, or testimony and should state the reasons for its position. If an agency proposes changes to a pending bill or to another agency's submission, its views letter should recommend, insofar as practicable, specific substitute language.

h. Certain statutory and other requirements and Administration policies. Agencies shall carefully consider and take into account certain requirements of existing statutes and Executive orders and Administration policies and directives that are of general applicability. Agency reports and proposed legislation shall, to the maximum extent possible, contain or be accompanied by appropriate recommendations, statements, or provisions to give effect to such requirements, including but not limited to:

(1) Civil rights
(2) Environmental impact
(3) Economic impact
(4) Federal budgetary impact and personnel requirements
(5) Federal and non-federal paperwork requirements
(6) State and local government impact
(7) Urban and community impact

i. Drafting service. Agencies need not submit for clearance bills that they prepare as a drafting service for a congressional committee or a Member of Congress, provided that they state in their transmittal letters that the drafting service does not constitute a commitment with respect to the position of the Administration or the agency. Agencies shall advise OMB of these drafting service requests while the requests are being complied with, and supply a copy of the request, if in writing. A copy of each such draft bill and the accompanying letter should be furnished to OMB at the time of transmittal, together with an explanatory statement of what the bill would accomplish if that is not contained in the transmittal letter.

j. Use of "no comment" reports. Agencies should submit no comment reports only when they have no interest in the pending legislation or nothing to contribute by way of informed comment. Agencies should submit such reports for clearance, unless a different procedure is informally arranged with OMB. In either event, they should furnish OMB with one copy of each such report at the time it is transmitted to Congress.

8. **Clearance of agency proposed legislation and reports.**

a. OMB action on agency submissions.

(1) OMB will undertake the necessary coordination with other interested agencies of an agency's proposed legislation or report. If congressional committees have not requested reports from all of the interested agencies, OMB will request other agency views within specified time limits. OMB will consult with the President, when appropriate, and undertake such staff work for him as may be necessary in cooperation with other Presidential staff. OMB may request the originating agency to provide additional information or may call interagency meetings to exchange views, resolve differences of opinion, or clarify the facts.

(2) When coordination is completed, OMB will transmit advice to the appropriate agencies, either in writing or by telephone. In transmitting advice, OMB may indicate considerations that agencies should or may wish to take into account before submitting proposed legislation or reports to Congress.

b. Forms of OMB advice. The exact forms of OMB advice will vary to suit the particular case. The basic forms of advice that are commonly used are set forth and explained in Attachment C.

c. Agency action on receipt of advice from OMB.

(1) Agencies shall incorporate the advice received from OMB in their reports and in their letters transmitting proposed legislation to Congress. Advice on testimony is usually not included in the testimony as delivered unless it would be likely to have a significant effect on a committee's consideration of particular legislation or would not otherwise be available to a committee through a written report.

(2) In the case of reports, receipt of advice contrary to views expressed does not require an agency to change its views. In such cases, however, the agency will review its position. If it decides to modify its views, the agency shall consult with OMB to determine what change, if any, in advice previously received is appropriate. If, after the review, the views of the agency are not modified, it shall incorporate in its report the full advice it received.

(3) In the case of proposed legislation, the originating agency shall not submit to Congress any proposal that OMB has advised is in conflict with the program of the President or has asked the agency to reconsider as a result of the coordination process. In such cases, OMB will inform the agency of the reasons for its action.

(4) Agencies are expected to transmit reports and proposed legislation to Congress promptly after receiving OMB clearance. Should circumstances arise that make prompt transmittal inadvisable, the agency shall immediately notify OMB. Similarly, in the case of cleared testimony, the agency shall immediately notify OMB if its testimony has been cancelled or rescheduled.

(5) Agencies should observe the instructions in House and Senate rules to forward proposed legislation or various reports required by law to the Speaker of the House and the President of the Senate. Reports that have been requested by committee chairmen on bills and resolutions pending before their committees should be transmitted directly to the requesting committees.

(6) Agencies shall furnish to OMB two copies of all proposed legislation, transmittal letters and accompanying materials, and reports (including testimony) in the form actually transmitted to the Congress. If reports or testimony cover more than one bill, agencies shall furnish two copies for each bill.

d. Agency action where prior clearance has not been effected.

(1) Agencies shall not submit to Congress proposed legislation that has not been coordinated and cleared within the Executive branch in accordance with this Circular.

(2) If congressional time schedules do not allow an agency to send its proposed report to OMB in time for the normal clearance and advice, the agency shall consult informally with OMB as to the advice to be included in the proposed report. OMB may advise the agency to state in its report that time has not permitted securing advice from OMB as to the relationship of the proposed legislation to the program of the President. Agencies shall send to OMB six copies of such reports at the same time that they are transmitted to Congress. Where appropriate, OMB will subsequently furnish advice on the report, which the agency shall transmit promptly to Congress.

(3) In cases where an agency has not submitted a report for clearance and its views on pending legislation are to be expressed in the form of oral, unwritten testimony, OMB will undertake such coordination and give such advice as the circumstances permit. In presenting oral testimony, the agency should indicate what advice, if any, has been received from OMB. If no advice has been obtained, the agency should so indicate.

e. Reclearance requirements. The advice received from OMB generally applies to all sessions of each Congress, but it does not carry over from one Congress to the next. Generally, agencies do not need to seek reclearance of reports on which they have already received advice before making the same reports on identical bills introduced in the same Congress, unless considerable time has elapsed or changed conditions indicate that the need for reclearance is appropriate or should be rechecked. Prior to transmitting such reports, however, agencies shall consult informally with appropriate OMB staff to determine whether reclearance is necessary. In cases where reclearance does not take place, agencies shall include in the subsequent report appropriate reference to the advice received on the original report. They shall also send one copy of any subsequent report to OMB at the same time that it is transmitted to Congress. The transmittal letter to OMB should identify the related report that was previously cleared.

9. **Interagency Consultation.** In carrying out their legislative functions, agencies are encouraged to consult with each other in order that all relevant interests and points of view may be considered and accommodated, where appropriate, in the formulation of their positions. Such consultation is particularly important in cases of overlapping interest, and intensive efforts should be made to reach interagency agreement before proposed legislation or reports are sent to OMB. In order that the President may have the individual views of the responsible heads of the agencies, however, proposed legislation or reports so coordinated shall be sent to OMB by the individual agencies involved, with appropriate reference to the interagency consultation that has taken place.

10. **Enrolled Bills.** Under the Constitution, the President has 10 days (including holidays but excluding Sundays) to act on enrolled bills after they are presented to him. To assure that the President has the maximum possible time for consideration of enrolled bills, agencies shall give them top priority.

a. Initial OMB action. OMB will obtain facsimiles of enrolled bills from the Government Printing Office and immediately forward one facsimile to each interested agency, requesting the agency's views and its recommendation for Presidential action.

b. Agency action. Each agency receiving such a request shall immediately prepare a letter presenting its views and deliver it in duplicate to OMB not later than two days (including holidays but excluding Sundays) after receipt of the facsimile. OMB may set different deadlines as dictated by circumstances. Agencies shall deliver these letters by special messenger to OMB.

c. Preparation of enrolled bill letters.

(1) Agencies' letters on enrolled bills are transmitted to the President and should be written so as to assist the President in reaching a decision. Each letter should, therefore, be complete in itself and should not, as a general rule, incorporate earlier reports by reference.

(2) Agencies' letters on enrolled bills are privileged communications, and agencies shall be guided accordingly in determining their content.

(3) Because of the definitive nature of Presidential action on enrolled bills, agency letters shall be signed by a Presidential appointee.

(4) Agencies' letters shall contain:

(a) an analysis of the significant features of the bill including changes from existing law. OMB staff will advise the agencies on which one should write the detailed analysis of the bill where more than one agency is substantially affected;

(b) a comparison of the bill with the Administration proposals, if any, on the same subject;

(c) comments, criticisms, analyses of benefits and shortcomings, or special considerations that will assist the President in reaching a decision;

(d) identification of any factors that make it necessary or desirable for the President to act by a particular date;

(e) an estimate of the first-year and recurring costs or savings and the relationship of the estimates to those previously incorporated in the President's budgetary program;

(f) an estimate of the additional number of personnel required to implement the bill; and

(g) a specific recommendation for approval or disapproval by the President.

(5) Agencies recommending disapproval shall submit with their letters a proposed veto message or memorandum of disapproval, in quadruplicate, prepared on legal-size paper and double-spaced. Such messages or memoranda should be finished products in form and substance that can be used by the President without further revision.

(6) Agencies may wish to recommend issuance of a signing statement by the President. Agencies so recommending shall submit with their letters a draft of such statement, in the same form and quantity as required for a proposed veto message. In some cases, OMB may request an agency to prepare a draft signing statement.

(7) Agencies' letters on private bills shall cite, where appropriate, precedents that support the action they recommend or that need to be distinguished from the action recommended.

d. Subsequent OMB action. OMB will transmit agencies' letters to the President, together with a covering memorandum, not later than the fifth day following receipt of the enrolled bill at the White House.

11. **Agency legislative liaison officers.** To assist in effecting interagency coordination, each agency shall furnish OMB with the name of a liaison officer who has been designated by the agency to handle the coordination of legislative matters under this Circular. From time to time, OMB will send agencies lists of the liaison officers so designated. Agencies should promptly notify OMB of any change in their liaison officers.

12. **Communications to OMB.**

a. Written agency communications to OMB transmitting proposed legislation, proposed reports, views letters on other agencies' proposed legislation or reports, and letters on enrolled bills should be addressed to:

Director, Office of Management and Budget
Attention: Assistant Director for Legislative Reference

The envelope containing such communications should be addressed:

Legislative Reference Division
Office of Management and Budget
Room 7203, New Executive Office Building

unless a different arrangement is made with an appropriate OMB staff member.

b. Questions on status of proposed legislation, reports, testimony, or enrolled bills should be directed to appropriate OMB staff or to the Legislative Information Center (telephone 395-3230).

DIRECTOR

Attachments

ATTACHMENT A
Circular No. A-19
Revised

INSTRUCTIONS RELATING TO THE PREPARATION OF AGENCY LEGISLATIVE PROGRAMS

1. Agencies' proposed legislative programs should be divided into two parts:

PART I—PRESIDENT'S PROGRAM PROPOSALS

Those items that the agency believes are of sufficient importance to be included in the President's legislative program and given specific endorsement by him in one of the regular annual messages, such as the budget message, or in a special message.

PART II—ALL OTHER PROPOSALS

2. Within each Part, agencies should list the items in order of relative priority. Each item of proposed legislation should be given a separate number for purposes of ready identification, using a numbering system which identifies the Congress; e.g., Agriculture, 96-12.

3. With respect to each item, agencies should provide the following information:

   a. A brief description of the proposal, its objectives, and its relationship to existing programs. Agencies should include greater detail on the specific provisions of proposals included in Part I or where the subject matter of the proposal contains new policies or programs or raises complex issues;

   b. Pertinent comments as to timing and readiness of draft legislation;

   c. Pertinent references to bills and reports concerning the subject of the proposal in current or recent sessions of Congress;

   d. An estimate for each of the first five fiscal years of (1) any budget authority and outlays that would be required, (2) any savings in budget authority and outlays, (3) any changes in budget receipts, and (4) work years of employment and numbers of personnel. These estimates should be prepared in accordance with the instructions in OMB Circular No. A-ll.

4. The lists of (a) legislative proposals still under consideration in an agency and (b) expiring laws (see section 6 of the Circular) should be presented separately from Parts I and II. The following special instructions apply to them:

   a. Items still under consideration should be listed in approximate order of priority and each briefly described in terms of subject matter and status.

   b. Each expiring law should be described in terms of (1) the subject, (2) the citation, (3) the date of expiration, (4) the agency's views as to whether the law should be extended or permitted to expire, and (5) other pertinent information. If an agency recommends extension, the proposal should also be included in Part I or Part II, as appropriate.

5. The legislative program submission should be prepared on letter-size paper. General conformance to the format of the attached exhibit will greatly facilitate the use of these programs.

EXHIBIT FOR ATTACHMENT A
Circular No. A-19
Revised

DEPARTMENT OF GOVERNMENT

PROPOSED LEGISLATIVE PROGRAM FOR THE ______ SESSION OF THE ______ CONGRESS

(Items in each Part are listed in order of priority)

PART I—PRESIDENT'S PROGRAM PROPOSALS

96-3 Amend the provisions of the 1902 Reclamation Act regarding acreage limitation, residency, leasing, excess land sales, the use of Class 1 Equivalency, contracts and contracting procedures, and certain administrative procedures. This proposal would modify and update the acreage limitation provisions of Federal Reclamation law to reflect and accommodate modern agricultural practices, but at the same time retain the basic concept of the Reclamation program—providing opportunities for family farms.

The Department has recommended that legislation amending the law reflect the following: Eligibility to receive project water would be limited to adults—18 years of age or older; Residency as provided in the Reclamation Act of 1902, and defined as a maximum distance of 50 miles from the land, would be reimposed on both lessors and lessees of project lands, with specific guidelines for phasing in the requirement; the acreage entitlement for which project water would be available would be increased to 320 acres owned per adult individual, with an additional allowance of 160 acres leased, or the entire 480 acres could be leased (family corporations and multiple ownerships could hold up to 960 acres without regard to the number of people in the arrangement); Class 1 equivalency would be authorized for general use for projects with a frost-free growing season of 180-days or less and would be applied on a project-by-project basis; contracts with districts containing provisions for exemption from acreage limitation provisions upon payout of construction charges would be approved; Sale of excess land by the owner to immediate family members, long-time tenants, employees, or adjoining neighbors would be permitted; Charitable and religious organizations holding project lands on January 1, 1978, would be exempt from acreage limitations.

Cost: The estimated cost to the government of administering this proposal would be comparable to the estimated cost of implementing the compliance program under regulations which are being promulgated at this time. The estimated cost of the compliance program for the 5-year period after the final rules are published (not including EIS costs prior to the final rules) is:

	FY 1980	FY 1981	FY 1982	FY 1983	FY 1984
(millions)	2.4	2.4	2.0	2.0	2.0

Personnel requirements: Estimated personnel requirements are:

	FY 1980	FY 1981	FY 1982	FY 1983	FY 1984
(work-years)	76	76	64	64	64
(personnel)	85	85	70	70	70

PART II—ALL OTHER PROPOSALS

96-14 Amend Federal Power Commission Act of 1920. This proposal would amend the Federal Power Commission Act of 1920 to provide that a license will be issued only after the Secretary administering affected public lands makes a determination that the license will not interfere or be inconsistent with the purposes for which such lands are reserved. The Federal Power Commission has interpreted Section 4(e) to require only consideration of the affected Secretary's recommendations.

The proposal would also amend the act to provide for extinguishment of withdrawals created by the Federal Energy Regulatory Commission (FERC) applications if the FERC has not responded to the applicant within 6 months or as of date of denial or expiration, surrender, revocation, or termination of the license. Most applications do not result in FPC licenses; yet the land is withdrawn. The administrative process of removing the withdrawals is cumbersome and time consuming and constrains the land managing agency from fully managing these lands for their resource values or from using these lands in exchanges. Revocation of the FERC withdrawal within a specified time period would be consistent with the provisions of Title II of the Federal Lands Policy and Management Act relating to withdrawals.

No additional appropriations or outlays would be required.

ATTACHMENT B
Circular No. A-19
Revised

INSTRUCTIONS FOR THE PREPARATION AND SUBMISSION TO CONGRESS OF LEGISLATIVE PROPOSALS AUTHORIZING THE ENACTMENT OF ADDITIONAL APPROPRIATIONS OR PROVIDING NEW BUDGET AUTHORITY OUTSIDE OF APPROPRIATION ACTS

1. **Legislative proposals providing authorizations to continue programs or activities.**

Under section 607 of P.L. 93-344, the Congressional Budget Act of 1974, legislative proposals to extend authorizations scheduled to expire at the end of a given fiscal year should be transmitted to Congress by May 15 of the fiscal year preceding that fiscal year. (For example, if an authorization expired on September 30, 1979, draft legislation to extend the authorization should have been transmitted to Congress by May 15, 1978.) If such proposals were not transmitted or were not enacted, new or revised proposals with language covering the budget year (i.e., the upcoming fiscal year) should be included in the same bill as proposals for the budget year plus one and subsequent years.

More specifically:

a. Proposals for agencies and programs that are customarily authorized on an annual basis (e.g., NASA, NSF, State, Justice, Peace Corps, military procurement and construction) should cover, in the same bill, proposed language for the budget year plus one and resubmittals or revisions of previously proposed authorizations for the budget year. Subsequent years should also be included if agencies deem it desirable and feasible.

b. Other legislative proposals to extend authorizations for the enactment of new budget authority expiring at the end of the budget year should cover, in the same bill, the budget year plus one and such subsequent years as is customary or deemed desirable for the particular program or activity involved.

c. Any proposals that provide for authorizations for the budget year or the current fiscal year should be submitted to Congress immediately after OMB clearance.

2. **Legislative proposals providing authorizations for new programs or activities.**

a. Proposals authorizing enactment of budget authority for a new program or activity should include at least two fiscal years, unless such new program or activity is proposed to be effective for only one fiscal year and to terminate at the end of that year.

b. Proposals that provide for authorizations to begin in the budget year plus one should, to the extent feasible, be prepared for submission to Congress no later than May 15 of the current fiscal year.

3. **General instructions for legislation authorizing the enactment of new budget authority.**

a. In keeping with the intent of section 401 of P.L. 93-344, proposals including contract authority or borrowing authority should provide that such authority is to be effective only to such extent or in such amounts as are provided in appropriation acts. Backdoor financing provisions may be proposed only when the exceptions set forth in section 401(d) of P.L. 93-344 apply.

b. As a general rule, bills submitted to Congress authorizing new budget authority for the current fiscal year or budget year will contain specific dollar amounts for those years. These amounts should be those approved for the Budget. For subsequent years, the bills should include "such sums as may be necessary" authorizations unless the agency and OMB agree that special circumstances warrant inclusion of specific amounts.

(1) Where specific amounts are included for years beyond the budget year, those amounts should be consistent with the five-year projections of budget authority printed in the Budget pursuant to P.L. 93-344. Such amounts will be based on the criteria provided for long-range projections in OMB Circular No. A-11.

(2) Authorizing legislation covering principally salaries and administrative expenses which heretofore has been enacted without specific dollar amounts may continue to be proposed for "such sums as may be necessary" for all fiscal years, including the current and budget fiscal years.

c. Agencies should draft their authorizing bills to incorporate the highest feasible level of aggregation for new budget authority.

4. **Required materials.**

a. **Budget year authorization extensions.** Proposed legislation authorizing the continuation of existing programs in the budget year should have been submitted to Congress not later than May 15 of the fiscal year preceding the current fiscal year. In cases where Congress did not enact budget year authorizations, new or revised authorizations should be submitted to Congress at the earliest possible date after the budget is published.

Accordingly, each agency will submit to OMB **no later than December 15** of each year 10 copies of drafts of proposed authorizing legislation to extend programs and activities that are authorized through the current fiscal year, but for which it will be necessary to propose new or revised authorizations for the budget year and subsequent years.

Since the specific amounts of the authorizations to be included cannot be determined until after decisions are made in connection with the budget, the draft bills are submitted to OMB should contain blank spaces for these amounts. When the budget decisions are final, OMB and the agencies will agree on the figures to be inserted.

b. **Authorization extensions for the budget year plus one.** Proposed legislation authorizing the continuation of existing programs in the budget year plus one must be submitted to Congress not later than May 15 of the current fiscal year. To meet this deadline, sufficient time must be provided for the legislative coordination and clearance process.

Accordingly, each agency will submit to OMB as early as possible but **no later than February 28** of each year 10 copies of legislative proposals for programs and activities that are authorized through the budget year, but for which an authorization request is necessary for the budget year plus one and subsequent years.

These draft legislative proposals should include "such sums as may be necessary" authorizations, unless the agency and OMB agree that special circumstances warrant inclusion of specific amounts. These figures should be the amounts agreed on as a result of the budget review and should be consistent with the five-year projections included in the Budget.

c. **Authorizations of new programs or activities.** In cases where decisions have been made during the budget review calling for authorizing legislation for new programs or activities proposed to begin in the budget year plus one, draft bills reflecting those decisions should be submitted to OMB no later than February 28 of each year, as in paragraph 4b of this Attachment.

ATTACHMENT C
Circular No. A-19
Revised

BASIC FORMS OF OMB ADVICE

The basic forms of advice and their implications are set forth below:

1. **"In accord (not in accord) with the program of the President."** When an agency or a committee of Congress is advised that enactment of a bill would be in accord with the program of the President, the advice means that the bill is of sufficient importance for the President to give it his personal and public support. That identification of the legislative proposal with the President is made in a variety of ways; e.g., by inclusion in one of his regular messages (State of the Union, Economic, Budget), a special message, speech, press conference, letter, or leadership meeting.

"Not in accord" advice indicates that a bill is so contrary to the President's legislative proposals or other policies or is otherwise so objectionable that should it be enacted in its current form, a veto would be considered. It is not, however, necessarily a commitment to veto.

2. **"Consistent with"** advice is used where the relationship of a legislative proposal to the Administration's objectives is direct and the Administration's expressed support is desirable, but the item does not warrant personal identification with, or support by, the President. "Not consistent with" advice signals to Congress that there are major objections to a bill, but does not indicate as clearly as "not in accord" advice that a veto would be considered if it were enacted.

3. **"No objection from the standpoint of the Administration's program."** Advice that there is no objection to a bill from the standpoint of the Administration's program is given on the large number of agency draft bills that deal with matters primarily of agency concern and do not bear a direct or immediate relationship to the President's program or the Administration's objectives. In effect, such advice indicates to Congress that OMB knows of no reason why the President would not approve the bill if Congress should enact it.

Advice to an agency that there is no objection from the standpoint of the Administration's program to its submission of a report (or testimony) on a bill to a committee of Congress does not indicate any commitment as to ultimate Presidential approval or disapproval of the bill if it is enacted. Nevertheless, such "no objection" clearance does set up certain presumptions. If all agencies' views are favorable, the presumption is that no major objection to the bill is known and that the agencies affected will recommend Presidential approval if it becomes enrolled. If all agencies' views are adverse, the presumption is that the agencies may wish to recommend a veto if the bill becomes enrolled.

Infrequently, "no objection" clearance is given to agency reports expressing divergent views on the same bill. When this is done, it normally means that there is no objection to the bill if Congress acts favorably after considering the adverse views. Occasionally, it means that the Administration's position is being reserved pending resolution of the agencies' differences, and this reservation may be explicitly stated. The interested agencies are advised of each other's differing views in these cases.

4. **Qualified advice.** In some cases the advice given is qualified. For example, the advice may be that there would be no objection to enactment of the bill from the standpoint of the Administration's program, or that the bill would be consistent with the Administration's objectives, if it were revised in specified respects.

App. 9.20 OMB Circular No. A-11

OMB *Circular No. A-11*, "Preparation, Submission, and Execution of the Budget," is updated annually and is available on the White House web site: <*www.whitehouse.gov/omb/circulars/a11/current_year/a11_toc.html*>

App. 9.30 Executive Order 12866

(5 U.S.C. § 601 note)

federal register

Monday
October 4, 1993

Part VIII

The President

Executive Order 12866—Regulatory Planning and Review

App. 9.30 Executive Order 12866 (continued)

Federal Register
Vol. 58, No. 190
Monday, October 4, 1993

Presidential Documents

Title 3—

The President

Executive Order 12866 of September 30, 1993

Regulatory Planning and Review

The American people deserve a regulatory system that works for them, not against them: a regulatory system that protects and improves their health, safety, environment, and well-being and improves the performance of the economy without imposing unacceptable or unreasonable costs on society; regulatory policies that recognize that the private sector and private markets are the best engine for economic growth; regulatory approaches that respect the role of State, local, and tribal governments; and regulations that are effective, consistent, sensible, and understandable. We do not have such a regulatory system today.

With this Executive order, the Federal Government begins a program to reform and make more efficient the regulatory process. The objectives of this Executive order are to enhance planning and coordination with respect to both new and existing regulations; to reaffirm the primacy of Federal agencies in the regulatory decision-making process; to restore the integrity and legitimacy of regulatory review and oversight; and to make the process more accessible and open to the public. In pursuing these objectives, the regulatory process shall be conducted so as to meet applicable statutory requirements and with due regard to the discretion that has been entrusted to the Federal agencies.

Accordingly, by the authority vested in me as President by the Constitution and the laws of the United States of America, it is hereby ordered as follows:

Section 1. *Statement of Regulatory Philosophy and Principles.*

(a) *The Regulatory Philosophy.* Federal agencies should promulgate only such regulations as are required by law, are necessary to interpret the law, or are made necessary by compelling public need, such as material failures of private markets to protect or improve the health and safety of the public, the environment, or the well-being of the American people. In deciding whether and how to regulate, agencies should assess all costs and benefits of available regulatory alternatives, including the alternative of not regulating. Costs and benefits shall be understood to include both quantifiable measures (to the fullest extent that these can be usefully estimated) and qualitative measures of costs and benefits that are difficult to quantify, but nevertheless essential to consider. Further, in choosing among alternative regulatory approaches, agencies should select those approaches that maximize net benefits (including potential economic, environmental, public health and safety, and other advantages; distributive impacts; and equity), unless a statute requires another regulatory approach.

(b) *The Principles of Regulation.* To ensure that the agencies' regulatory programs are consistent with the philosophy set forth above, agencies should adhere to the following principles, to the extent permitted by law and where applicable:

(1) Each agency shall identify the problem that it intends to address (including, where applicable, the failures of private markets or public institutions that warrant new agency action) as well as assess the significance of that problem.

(2) Each agency shall examine whether existing regulations (or other law) have created, or contributed to, the problem that a new regulation is

App. 9.30 Executive Order 12866 (continued)

Federal Register / Vol. 58, No. 190 / Monday, October 4, 1993 / Presidential Documents

intended to correct and whether those regulations (or other law) should be modified to achieve the intended goal of regulation more effectively.

(3) Each agency shall identify and assess available alternatives to direct regulation, including providing economic incentives to encourage the desired behavior, such as user fees or marketable permits, or providing information upon which choices can be made by the public.

(4) In setting regulatory priorities, each agency shall consider, to the extent reasonable, the degree and nature of the risks posed by various substances or activities within its jurisdiction.

(5) When an agency determines that a regulation is the best available method of achieving the regulatory objective, it shall design its regulations in the most cost-effective manner to achieve the regulatory objective. In doing so, each agency shall consider incentives for innovation, consistency, predictability, the costs of enforcement and compliance (to the government, regulated entities, and the public), flexibility, distributive impacts, and equity.

(6) Each agency shall assess both the costs and the benefits of the intended regulation and, recognizing that some costs and benefits are difficult to quantify, propose or adopt a regulation only upon a reasoned determination that the benefits of the intended regulation justify its costs.

(7) Each agency shall base its decisions on the best reasonably obtainable scientific, technical, economic, and other information concerning the need for, and consequences of, the intended regulation.

(8) Each agency shall identify and assess alternative forms of regulation and shall, to the extent feasible, specify performance objectives, rather than specifying the behavior or manner of compliance that regulated entities must adopt.

(9) Wherever feasible, agencies shall seek views of appropriate State, local, and tribal officials before imposing regulatory requirements that might significantly or uniquely affect those governmental entities. Each agency shall assess the effects of Federal regulations on State, local, and tribal governments, including specifically the availability of resources to carry out those mandates, and seek to minimize those burdens that uniquely or significantly affect such governmental entities, consistent with achieving regulatory objectives. In addition, as appropriate, agencies shall seek to harmonize Federal regulatory actions with related State, local, and tribal regulatory and other governmental functions.

(10) Each agency shall avoid regulations that are inconsistent, incompatible, or duplicative with its other regulations or those of other Federal agencies.

(11) Each agency shall tailor its regulations to impose the least burden on society, including individuals, businesses of differing sizes, and other entities (including small communities and governmental entities), consistent with obtaining the regulatory objectives, taking into account, among other things, and to the extent practicable, the costs of cumulative regulations.

(12) Each agency shall draft its regulations to be simple and easy to understand, with the goal of minimizing the potential for uncertainty and litigation arising from such uncertainty.

Sec. 2. *Organization.* An efficient regulatory planning and review process is vital to ensure that the Federal Government's regulatory system best serves the American people.

(a) *The Agencies.* Because Federal agencies are the repositories of significant substantive expertise and experience, they are responsible for developing regulations and assuring that the regulations are consistent with applicable law, the President's priorities, and the principles set forth in this Executive order.

App. 9.30 Executive Order 12866 (continued)

Federal Register / Vol. 58, No. 190 / Monday, October 4, 1993 / Presidential Documents

(b) *The Office of Management and Budget.* Coordinated review of agency rulemaking is necessary to ensure that regulations are consistent with applicable law, the President's priorities, and the principles set forth in this Executive order, and that decisions made by one agency do not conflict with the policies or actions taken or planned by another agency. The Office of Management and Budget (OMB) shall carry out that review function. Within OMB, the Office of Information and Regulatory Affairs (OIRA) is the repository of expertise concerning regulatory issues, including methodologies and procedures that affect more than one agency, this Executive order, and the President's regulatory policies. To the extent permitted by law, OMB shall provide guidance to agencies and assist the President, the Vice President, and other regulatory policy advisors to the President in regulatory planning and shall be the entity that reviews individual regulations, as provided by this Executive order.

(c) *The Vice President.* The Vice President is the principal advisor to the President on, and shall coordinate the development and presentation of recommendations concerning, regulatory policy, planning, and review, as set forth in this Executive order. In fulfilling their responsibilities under this Executive order, the President and the Vice President shall be assisted by the regulatory policy advisors within the Executive Office of the President and by such agency officials and personnel as the President and the Vice President may, from time to time, consult.

Sec. 3. *Definitions.* For purposes of this Executive order: (a) "Advisors" refers to such regulatory policy advisors to the President as the President and Vice President may from time to time consult, including, among others: (1) the Director of OMB; (2) the Chair (or another member) of the Council of Economic Advisers; (3) the Assistant to the President for Economic Policy; (4) the Assistant to the President for Domestic Policy; (5) the Assistant to the President for National Security Affairs; (6) the Assistant to the President for Science and Technology; (7) the Assistant to the President for Intergovernmental Affairs; (8) the Assistant to the President and Staff Secretary; (9) the Assistant to the President and Chief of Staff to the Vice President; (10) the Assistant to the President and Counsel to the President; (11) the Deputy Assistant to the President and Director of the White House Office on Environmental Policy; and (12) the Administrator of OIRA, who also shall coordinate communications relating to this Executive order among the agencies, OMB, the other Advisors, and the Office of the Vice President.

(b) "Agency," unless otherwise indicated, means any authority of the United States that is an "agency" under 44 U.S.C. 3502(1), other than those considered to be independent regulatory agencies, as defined in 44 U.S.C. 3502(10).

(c) "Director" means the Director of OMB.

(d) "Regulation" or "rule" means an agency statement of general applicability and future effect, which the agency intends to have the force and effect of law, that is designed to implement, interpret, or prescribe law or policy or to describe the procedure or practice requirements of an agency. It does not, however, include:

(1) Regulations or rules issued in accordance with the formal rulemaking provisions of 5 U.S.C. 556, 557;

(2) Regulations or rules that pertain to a military or foreign affairs function of the United States, other than procurement regulations and regulations involving the import or export of non-defense articles and services;

(3) Regulations or rules that are limited to agency organization, management, or personnel matters; or

(4) Any other category of regulations exempted by the Administrator of OIRA.

(e) "Regulatory action" means any substantive action by an agency (normally published in the **Federal Register**) that promulgates or is expected to lead to the promulgation of a final rule or regulation, including notices

App. 9.30 Executive Order 12866 (continued)

Federal Register/Vol. 58, No. 190/Monday, October 4, 1993/Presidential Documents

of inquiry, advance notices of proposed rulemaking, and notices of proposed rulemaking.

(f) "Significant regulatory action" means any regulatory action that is likely to result in a rule that may:

(1) Have an annual effect on the economy of $100 million or more or adversely affect in a material way the economy, a sector of the economy, productivity, competition, jobs, the environment, public health or safety, or State, local, or tribal governments or communities;

(2) Create a serious inconsistency or otherwise interfere with an action taken or planned by another agency;

(3) Materially alter the budgetary impact of entitlements, grants, user fees, or loan programs or the rights and obligations of recipients thereof; or

(4) Raise novel legal or policy issues arising out of legal mandates, the President's priorities, or the principles set forth in this Executive order.

Sec. 4. *Planning Mechanism.* In order to have an effective regulatory program, to provide for coordination of regulations, to maximize consultation and the resolution of potential conflicts at an early stage, to involve the public and its State, local, and tribal officials in regulatory planning, and to ensure that new or revised regulations promote the President's priorities and the principles set forth in this Executive order, these procedures shall be followed, to the extent permitted by law:

(a) *Agencies' Policy Meeting.* Early in each year's planning cycle, the Vice President shall convene a meeting of the Advisors and the heads of agencies to seek a common understanding of priorities and to coordinate regulatory efforts to be accomplished in the upcoming year.

(b) *Unified Regulatory Agenda.* For purposes of this subsection, the term "agency" or "agencies" shall also include those considered to be independent regulatory agencies, as defined in 44 U.S.C. 3502(10). Each agency shall prepare an agenda of all regulations under development or review, at a time and in a manner specified by the Administrator of OIRA. The description of each regulatory action shall contain, at a minimum, a regulation identifier number, a brief summary of the action, the legal authority for the action, any legal deadline for the action, and the name and telephone number of a knowledgeable agency official. Agencies may incorporate the information required under 5 U.S.C. 602 and 41 U.S.C. 402 into these agendas.

(c) *The Regulatory Plan.* For purposes of this subsection, the term "agency" or "agencies" shall also include those considered to be independent regulatory agencies, as defined in 44 U.S.C. 3502(10). (1) As part of the Unified Regulatory Agenda, beginning in 1994, each agency shall prepare a Regulatory Plan (Plan) of the most important significant regulatory actions that the agency reasonably expects to issue in proposed or final form in that fiscal year or thereafter. The Plan shall be approved personally by the agency head and shall contain at a minimum:

(A) A statement of the agency's regulatory objectives and priorities and how they relate to the President's priorities;

(B) A summary of each planned significant regulatory action including, to the extent possible, alternatives to be considered and preliminary estimates of the anticipated costs and benefits;

(C) A summary of the legal basis for each such action, including whether any aspect of the action is required by statute or court order;

(D) A statement of the need for each such action and, if applicable, how the action will reduce risks to public health, safety, or the environment, as well as how the magnitude of the risk addressed by the action relates to other risks within the jurisdiction of the agency;

(E) The agency's schedule for action, including a statement of any applicable statutory or judicial deadlines; and

App. 9.30 Executive Order 12866 (continued)

Federal Register / Vol. 58, No. 190 / Monday, October 4, 1993 / Presidential Documents

(F) The name, address, and telephone number of a person the public may contact for additional information about the planned regulatory action.

(2) Each agency shall forward its Plan to OIRA by June 1st of each year.

(3) Within 10 calendar days after OIRA has received an agency's Plan, OIRA shall circulate it to other affected agencies, the Advisors, and the Vice President.

(4) An agency head who believes that a planned regulatory action of another agency may conflict with its own policy or action taken or planned shall promptly notify, in writing, the Administrator of OIRA, who shall forward that communication to the issuing agency, the Advisors, and the Vice President.

(5) If the Administrator of OIRA believes that a planned regulatory action of an agency may be inconsistent with the President's priorities or the principles set forth in this Executive order or may be in conflict with any policy or action taken or planned by another agency, the Administrator of OIRA shall promptly notify, in writing, the affected agencies, the Advisors, and the Vice President.

(6) The Vice President, with the Advisors' assistance, may consult with the heads of agencies with respect to their Plans and, in appropriate instances, request further consideration or inter-agency coordination.

(7) The Plans developed by the issuing agency shall be published annually in the October publication of the Unified Regulatory Agenda. This publication shall be made available to the Congress; State, local, and tribal governments; and the public. Any views on any aspect of any agency Plan, including whether any planned regulatory action might conflict with any other planned or existing regulation, impose any unintended consequences on the public, or confer any unclaimed benefits on the public, should be directed to the issuing agency, with a copy to OIRA.

(d) *Regulatory Working Group.* Within 30 days of the date of this Executive order, the Administrator of OIRA shall convene a Regulatory Working Group ("Working Group"), which shall consist of representatives of the heads of each agency that the Administrator determines to have significant domestic regulatory responsibility, the Advisors, and the Vice President. The Administrator of OIRA shall chair the Working Group and shall periodically advise the Vice President on the activities of the Working Group. The Working Group shall serve as a forum to assist agencies in identifying and analyzing important regulatory issues (including, among others (1) the development of innovative regulatory techniques, (2) the methods, efficacy, and utility of comparative risk assessment in regulatory decision-making, and (3) the development of short forms and other streamlined regulatory approaches for small businesses and other entities). The Working Group shall meet at least quarterly and may meet as a whole or in subgroups of agencies with an interest in particular issues or subject areas. To inform its discussions, the Working Group may commission analytical studies and reports by OIRA, the Administrative Conference of the United States, or any other agency.

(e) *Conferences.* The Administrator of OIRA shall meet quarterly with representatives of State, local, and tribal governments to identify both existing and proposed regulations that may uniquely or significantly affect those governmental entities. The Administrator of OIRA shall also convene, from time to time, conferences with representatives of businesses, nongovernmental organizations, and the public to discuss regulatory issues of common concern.

Sec. 5. *Existing Regulations.* In order to reduce the regulatory burden on the American people, their families, their communities, their State, local, and tribal governments, and their industries; to determine whether regulations promulgated by the executive branch of the Federal Government have become unjustified or unnecessary as a result of changed circumstances; to confirm that regulations are both compatible with each other and not

App. 9.30 Executive Order 12866 (continued)

Federal Register/Vol. 58, No. 190/Monday, October 4, 1993/Presidential Documents

duplicative or inappropriately burdensome in the aggregate; to ensure that all regulations are consistent with the President's priorities and the principles set forth in this Executive order, within applicable law; and to otherwise improve the effectiveness of existing regulations: (a) Within 90 days of the date of this Executive order, each agency shall submit to OIRA a program, consistent with its resources and regulatory priorities, under which the agency will periodically review its existing significant regulations to determine whether any such regulations should be modified or eliminated so as to make the agency's regulatory program more effective in achieving the regulatory objectives, less burdensome, or in greater alignment with the President's priorities and the principles set forth in this Executive order. Any significant regulations selected for review shall be included in the agency's annual Plan. The agency shall also identify any legislative mandates that require the agency to promulgate or continue to impose regulations that the agency believes are unnecessary or outdated by reason of changed circumstances.

(b) The Administrator of OIRA shall work with the Regulatory Working Group and other interested entities to pursue the objectives of this section. State, local, and tribal governments are specifically encouraged to assist in the identification of regulations that impose significant or unique burdens on those governmental entities and that appear to have outlived their justification or be otherwise inconsistent with the public interest.

(c) The Vice President, in consultation with the Advisors, may identify for review by the appropriate agency or agencies other existing regulations of an agency or groups of regulations of more than one agency that affect a particular group, industry, or sector of the economy, or may identify legislative mandates that may be appropriate for reconsideration by the Congress.

Sec. 6. *Centralized Review of Regulations.* The guidelines set forth below shall apply to all regulatory actions, for both new and existing regulations, by agencies other than those agencies specifically exempted by the Administrator of OIRA:

(a) *Agency Responsibilities.* (1) Each agency shall (consistent with its own rules, regulations, or procedures) provide the public with meaningful participation in the regulatory process. In particular, before issuing a notice of proposed rulemaking, each agency should, where appropriate, seek the involvement of those who are intended to benefit from and those expected to be burdened by any regulation (including, specifically, State, local, and tribal officials). In addition, each agency should afford the public a meaningful opportunity to comment on any proposed regulation, which in most cases should include a comment period of not less than 60 days. Each agency also is directed to explore and, where appropriate, use consensual mechanisms for developing regulations, including negotiated rulemaking.

(2) Within 60 days of the date of this Executive order, each agency head shall designate a Regulatory Policy Officer who shall report to the agency head. The Regulatory Policy Officer shall be involved at each stage of the regulatory process to foster the development of effective, innovative, and least burdensome regulations and to further the principles set forth in this Executive order.

(3) In addition to adhering to its own rules and procedures and to the requirements of the Administrative Procedure Act, the Regulatory Flexibility Act, the Paperwork Reduction Act, and other applicable law, each agency shall develop its regulatory actions in a timely fashion and adhere to the following procedures with respect to a regulatory action:

(A) Each agency shall provide OIRA, at such times and in the manner specified by the Administrator of OIRA, with a list of its planned regulatory actions, indicating those which the agency believes are significant regulatory actions within the meaning of this Executive order. Absent a material change in the development of the planned regulatory action, those not designated as significant will not be subject to review under this section unless, within 10 working days of receipt

App. 9.30 Executive Order 12866 (continued)

Federal Register / Vol. 58, No. 190 / Monday, October 4, 1993 / Presidential Documents

of the list, the Administrator of OIRA notifies the agency that OIRA has determined that a planned regulation is a significant regulatory action within the meaning of this Executive order. The Administrator of OIRA may waive review of any planned regulatory action designated by the agency as significant, in which case the agency need not further comply with subsection (a)(3)(B) or subsection (a)(3)(C) of this section.

(B) For each matter identified as, or determined by the Administrator of OIRA to be, a significant regulatory action, the issuing agency shall provide to OIRA:

(i) The text of the draft regulatory action, together with a reasonably detailed description of the need for the regulatory action and an explanation of how the regulatory action will meet that need; and

(ii) An assessment of the potential costs and benefits of the regulatory action, including an explanation of the manner in which the regulatory action is consistent with a statutory mandate and, to the extent permitted by law, promotes the President's priorities and avoids undue interference with State, local, and tribal governments in the exercise of their governmental functions.

(C) For those matters identified as, or determined by the Administrator of OIRA to be, a significant regulatory action within the scope of section 3(f)(1), the agency shall also provide to OIRA the following additional information developed as part of the agency's decision-making process (unless prohibited by law):

(i) An assessment, including the underlying analysis, of benefits anticipated from the regulatory action (such as, but not limited to, the promotion of the efficient functioning of the economy and private markets, the enhancement of health and safety, the protection of the natural environment, and the elimination or reduction of discrimination or bias) together with, to the extent feasible, a quantification of those benefits;

(ii) An assessment, including the underlying analysis, of costs anticipated from the regulatory action (such as, but not limited to, the direct cost both to the government in administering the regulation and to businesses and others in complying with the regulation, and any adverse effects on the efficient functioning of the economy, private markets (including productivity, employment, and competitiveness), health, safety, and the natural environment), together with, to the extent feasible, a quantification of those costs; and

(iii) An assessment, including the underlying analysis, of costs and benefits of potentially effective and reasonably feasible alternatives to the planned regulation, identified by the agencies or the public (including improving the current regulation and reasonably viable nonregulatory actions), and an explanation why the planned regulatory action is preferable to the identified potential alternatives.

(D) In emergency situations or when an agency is obligated by law to act more quickly than normal review procedures allow, the agency shall notify OIRA as soon as possible and, to the extent practicable, comply with subsections (a)(3)(B) and (C) of this section. For those regulatory actions that are governed by a statutory or court-imposed deadline, the agency shall, to the extent practicable, schedule rulemaking proceedings so as to permit sufficient time for OIRA to conduct its review, as set forth below in subsection (b)(2) through (4) of this section.

(E) After the regulatory action has been published in the **Federal Register** or otherwise issued to the public, the agency shall:

(i) Make available to the public the information set forth in subsections (a)(3)(B) and (C);

(ii) Identify for the public, in a complete, clear, and simple manner, the substantive changes between the draft submitted to OIRA for review and the action subsequently announced; and

App. 9.30 Executive Order 12866 (continued)

Federal Register / Vol. 58, No. 190 / Monday, October 4, 1993 / Presidential Documents

(iii) Identify for the public those changes in the regulatory action that were made at the suggestion or recommendation of OIRA.

(F) All information provided to the public by the agency shall be in plain, understandable language.

(b) *OIRA Responsibilities.* The Administrator of OIRA shall provide meaningful guidance and oversight so that each agency's regulatory actions are consistent with applicable law, the President's priorities, and the principles set forth in this Executive order and do not conflict with the policies or actions of another agency. OIRA shall, to the extent permitted by law, adhere to the following guidelines:

(1) OIRA may review only actions identified by the agency or by OIRA as significant regulatory actions under subsection (a)(3)(A) of this section.

(2) OIRA shall waive review or notify the agency in writing of the results of its review within the following time periods:

(A) For any notices of inquiry, advance notices of proposed rulemaking, or other preliminary regulatory actions prior to a Notice of Proposed Rulemaking, within 10 working days after the date of submission of the draft action to OIRA;

(B) For all other regulatory actions, within 90 calendar days after the date of submission of the information set forth in subsections (a)(3)(B) and (C) of this section, unless OIRA has previously reviewed this information and, since that review, there has been no material change in the facts and circumstances upon which the regulatory action is based, in which case, OIRA shall complete its review within 45 days; and

(C) The review process may be extended (1) once by no more than 30 calendar days upon the written approval of the Director and (2) at the request of the agency head.

(3) For each regulatory action that the Administrator of OIRA returns to an agency for further consideration of some or all of its provisions, the Administrator of OIRA shall provide the issuing agency a written explanation for such return, setting forth the pertinent provision of this Executive order on which OIRA is relying. If the agency head disagrees with some or all of the bases for the return, the agency head shall so inform the Administrator of OIRA in writing.

(4) Except as otherwise provided by law or required by a Court, in order to ensure greater openness, accessibility, and accountability in the regulatory review process, OIRA shall be governed by the following disclosure requirements:

(A) Only the Administrator of OIRA (or a particular designee) shall receive oral communications initiated by persons not employed by the executive branch of the Federal Government regarding the substance of a regulatory action under OIRA review;

(B) All substantive communications between OIRA personnel and persons not employed by the executive branch of the Federal Government regarding a regulatory action under review shall be governed by the following guidelines: (i) A representative from the issuing agency shall be invited to any meeting between OIRA personnel and such person(s);

(ii) OIRA shall forward to the issuing agency, within 10 working days of receipt of the communication(s), all written communications, regardless of format, between OIRA personnel and any person who is not employed by the executive branch of the Federal Government, and the dates and names of individuals involved in all substantive oral communications (including meetings to which an agency representative was invited, but did not attend, and telephone conversations between OIRA personnel and any such persons); and

(iii) OIRA shall publicly disclose relevant information about such communication(s), as set forth below in subsection (b)(4)(C) of this section.

App. 9.30 Executive Order 12866 (continued)

Federal Register/Vol. 58, No. 190/Monday, October 4, 1993/Presidential Documents

(C) OIRA shall maintain a publicly available log that shall contain, at a minimum, the following information pertinent to regulatory actions under review:

(i) The status of all regulatory actions, including if (and if so, when and by whom) Vice Presidential and Presidential consideration was requested;

(ii) A notation of all written communications forwarded to an issuing agency under subsection (b)(4)(B)(ii) of this section; and

(iii) The dates and names of individuals involved in all substantive oral communications, including meetings and telephone conversations, between OIRA personnel and any person not employed by the executive branch of the Federal Government, and the subject matter discussed during such communications.

(D) After the regulatory action has been published in the **Federal Register** or otherwise issued to the public, or after the agency has announced its decision not to publish or issue the regulatory action, OIRA shall make available to the public all documents exchanged between OIRA and the agency during the review by OIRA under this section.

(5) All information provided to the public by OIRA shall be in plain, understandable language.

Sec. 7. *Resolution of Conflicts.* To the extent permitted by law, disagreements or conflicts between or among agency heads or between OMB and any agency that cannot be resolved by the Administrator of OIRA shall be resolved by the President, or by the Vice President acting at the request of the President, with the relevant agency head (and, as appropriate, other interested government officials). Vice Presidential and Presidential consideration of such disagreements may be initiated only by the Director, by the head of the issuing agency, or by the head of an agency that has a significant interest in the regulatory action at issue. Such review will not be undertaken at the request of other persons, entities, or their agents.

Resolution of such conflicts shall be informed by recommendations developed by the Vice President, after consultation with the Advisors (and other executive branch officials or personnel whose responsibilities to the President include the subject matter at issue). The development of these recommendations shall be concluded within 60 days after review has been requested.

During the Vice Presidential and Presidential review period, communications with any person not employed by the Federal Government relating to the substance of the regulatory action under review and directed to the Advisors or their staffs or to the staff of the Vice President shall be in writing and shall be forwarded by the recipient to the affected agency(ies) for inclusion in the public docket(s). When the communication is not in writing, such Advisors or staff members shall inform the outside party that the matter is under review and that any comments should be submitted in writing.

At the end of this review process, the President, or the Vice President acting at the request of the President, shall notify the affected agency and the Administrator of OIRA of the President's decision with respect to the matter.

Sec. 8. *Publication.* Except to the extent required by law, an agency shall not publish in the **Federal Register** or otherwise issue to the public any regulatory action that is subject to review under section 6 of this Executive order until (1) the Administrator of OIRA notifies the agency that OIRA has waived its review of the action or has completed its review without any requests for further consideration, or (2) the applicable time period in section 6(b)(2) expires without OIRA having notified the agency that it is returning the regulatory action for further consideration under section 6(b)(3), whichever occurs first. If the terms of the preceding sentence have not been satisfied and an agency wants to publish or otherwise issue a

App. 9.30 Executive Order 12866 (continued)

Federal Register/Vol. 58, No. 190/Monday, October 4, 1993/Presidential Documents

regulatory action, the head of that agency may request Presidential consideration through the Vice President, as provided under section 7 of this order. Upon receipt of this request, the Vice President shall notify OIRA and the Advisors. The guidelines and time period set forth in section 7 shall apply to the publication of regulatory actions for which Presidential consideration has been sought.

Sec. 9. *Agency Authority.* Nothing in this order shall be construed as displacing the agencies' authority or responsibilities, as authorized by law.

Sec. 10. *Judicial Review.* Nothing in this Executive order shall affect any otherwise available judicial review of agency action. This Executive order is intended only to improve the internal management of the Federal Government and does not create any right or benefit, substantive or procedural, enforceable at law or equity by a party against the United States, its agencies or instrumentalities, its officers or employees, or any other person.

Sec. 11. *Revocations.* Executive Orders Nos. 12291 and 12498; all amendments to those Executive orders; all guidelines issued under those orders; and any exemptions from those orders heretofore granted for any category of rule are revoked.

THE WHITE HOUSE,
September 30, 1993.

[FR citation 58 FR 51735]

App. 9.40 Executive Order 12988

(28 U.S.C. § 519 note)

federal register

Wednesday
February 7, 1996

Part V

The President

Executive Order 12988—Civil Justice Reform

4727

App. 9.40 Executive Order 12988 (continued)

4729

Federal Register
Vol. 61, No. 26
Wednesday, February 7, 1996

Presidential Documents

Title 3—

The President

Executive Order 12988 of February 5, 1996

Civil Justice Reform

By the authority vested in me as President by the Constitution and the laws of the United States of America, including section 301 of title 3, United States Code, and in order to improve access to justice for all persons who wish to avail themselves of court and administrative adjudicatory tribunals to resolve disputes, to facilitate the just and efficient resolution of civil claims involving the United States Government, to encourage the filing of only meritorious civil claims, to improve legislative and regulatory drafting to reduce needless litigation, to promote fair and prompt adjudication before administrative tribunals, and to provide a model for similar reforms of litigation practices in the private sector and in various states, it is hereby ordered as follows:

Section 1. *Guidelines to Promote Just and Efficient Government Civil Litigation.* To promote the just and efficient resolution of civil claims, those Federal agencies and litigation counsel that conduct or otherwise participate in civil litigation on behalf of the United States Government in Federal court shall respect and adhere to the following guidelines during the conduct of such litigation:

(a) *Pre-filing Notice of a Complaint.* No litigation counsel shall file a complaint initiating civil litigation without first making a reasonable effort to notify all disputants about the nature of the dispute and to attempt to achieve a settlement, or confirming that the referring agency that previously handled the dispute has made a reasonable effort to notify the disputants and to achieve a settlement or has used its conciliation processes.

(b) *Settlement Conferences.* As soon as practicable after ascertaining the nature of a dispute in litigation, and throughout the litigation, litigation counsel shall evaluate settlement possibilities and make reasonable efforts to settle the litigation. Such efforts shall include offering to participate in a settlement conference or moving the court for a conference pursuant to Rule 16 of the Federal Rules of Civil Procedure in an attempt to resolve the dispute without additional civil litigation.

(c) *Alternative Methods of Resolving the Dispute in Litigation.* Litigation counsel shall make reasonable attempts to resolve a dispute expeditiously and properly before proceeding to trial.

(1) Whenever feasible, claims should be resolved through informal discussions, negotiations, and settlements rather than through utilization of any formal court proceeding. Where the benefits of Alternative Dispute Resolution ("ADR") may be derived, and after consultation with the agency referring the matter, litigation counsel should suggest the use of an appropriate ADR technique to the parties.

(2) It is appropriate to use ADR techniques or processes to resolve claims of or against the United States or its agencies, after litigation counsel determines that the use of a particular technique is warranted in the context of a particular claim or claims, and that such use will materially contribute to the prompt, fair, and efficient resolution of the claims.

(3) To facilitate broader and effective use of informal and formal ADR methods, litigation counsel should be trained in ADR techniques.

App. 9.40 Executive Order 12988 (continued)

4730 Federal Register / Vol. 61, No. 26 / Wednesday, February 7, 1996 / Presidential Documents

(d) *Discovery.* To the extent practical, litigation counsel shall make every reasonable effort to streamline and expedite discovery in cases under counsel's supervision and control.

(1) *Review of Proposed Document Requests.* Each agency within the executive branch shall establish a coordinated procedure for the conduct and review of document discovery undertaken in litigation directly by that agency when that agency is litigation counsel. The procedure shall include, but is not necessarily limited to, review by a senior lawyer prior to service or filing of the request in litigation to determine that the request is not cumulative or duplicative, unreasonable, oppressive, unduly burdensome or expensive, taking into account the requirements of the litigation, the amount in controversy, the importance of the issues at stake in the litigation, and whether the documents can be obtained from some other source that is more convenient, less burdensome, or less expensive.

(2) *Discovery Motions.* Before petitioning a court to resolve a discovery motion or petitioning a court to impose sanctions for discovery abuses, litigation counsel shall attempt to resolve the dispute with opposing counsel. If litigation counsel makes a discovery motion concerning the dispute, he or she shall represent in that motion that any attempt at resolution was unsuccessful or impracticable under the circumstances.

(e) *Sanctions.* Litigation counsel shall take steps to seek sanctions against opposing counsel and opposing parties where appropriate.

(1) Litigation counsel shall evaluate filings made by opposing parties and, where appropriate, shall petition the court to impose sanctions against those responsible for abusive practices.

(2) Prior to filing a motion for sanctions, litigation counsel shall submit the motion for review to the sanctions officer, or his or her designee, within the litigation counsel's agency. Such officer or designee shall be a senior supervising attorney within the agency, and shall be licensed to practice law before a State court, courts of the District of Columbia, or courts of any territory or Commonwealth of the United States. The sanctions officer or designee shall also review motions for sanctions that are filed against litigation counsel, the United States, its agencies, or its officers.

(f) *Improved Use of Litigation Resources.* Litigation counsel shall employ efficient case management techniques and shall make reasonable efforts to expedite civil litigation in cases under that counsel's supervision and control. This includes but is not limited to:

(1) making reasonable efforts to negotiate with other parties about, and stipulate to, facts that are not in dispute;

(2) reviewing and revising pleadings and other filings to ensure that they are accurate and that they reflect a narrowing of issues, if any, that has resulted from discovery;

(3) requesting early trial dates where practicable;

(4) moving for summary judgment in every case where the movant would be likely to prevail, or where the motion is likely to narrow the issues to be tried; and

(5) reviewing and revising pleadings and other filings to ensure that unmeritorious threshold defenses and jurisdictional arguments, resulting in unnecessary delay, are not raised.

Sec. 2. *Government Pro Bono and Volunteer Service.* All Federal agencies should develop appropriate programs to encourage and facilitate pro bono legal and other volunteer service by government employees to be performed on their own time, including attorneys, as permitted by statute, regulation, or other rule or guideline.

Sec. 3. *Principles to Enact Legislation and Promulgate Regulations Which Do Not Unduly Burden the Federal Court System.*

App. 9.40 Executive Order 12988 (continued)

(a) *General Duty to Review Legislation and Regulations.* Within current budgetary constraints and existing executive branch coordination mechanisms and procedures established in OMB Circular A-19 and Executive Order No. 12866, each agency promulgating new regulations, reviewing existing regulations, developing legislative proposals concerning regulations, and developing new legislation shall adhere to the following requirements:

(1) The agency's proposed legislation and regulations shall be reviewed by the agency to eliminate drafting errors and ambiguity;

(2) The agency's proposed legislation and regulations shall be written to minimize litigation; and

(3) The agency's proposed legislation and regulations shall provide a clear legal standard for affected conduct rather than a general standard, and shall promote simplification and burden reduction.

(b) *Specific Issues for Review.* In conducting the reviews required by subsection (a), each agency formulating proposed legislation and regulations shall make every reasonable effort to ensure:

(1) that the legislation, as appropriate—

(A) specifies whether all causes of action arising under the law are subject to statutes of limitations;

(B) specifies in clear language the preemptive effect, if any, to be given to the law;

(C) specifies in clear language the effect on existing Federal law, if any, including all provisions repealed, circumscribed, displaced, impaired, or modified;

(D) provides a clear legal standard for affected conduct;

(E) specifies whether private arbitration and other forms of private dispute resolution are appropriate under enforcement and relief provisions; subject to constitutional requirements;

(F) specifies whether the provisions of the law are severable if one or more of them is found to be unconstitutional;

(G) specifies in clear language the retroactive effect, if any, to be given to the law;

(H) specifies in clear language the applicable burdens of proof;

(I) specifies in clear language whether it grants private parties a right to sue and, if so, the relief available and the conditions and terms for authorized awards of attorney's fees, if any;

(J) specifies whether State courts have jurisdiction under the law and, if so, whether and under what conditions an action would be removable to Federal court;

(K) specifies whether administrative proceedings are to be required before parties may file suit in court and, if so, describes those proceedings and requires the exhaustion of administrative remedies;

(L) sets forth the standards governing the assertion of personal jurisdiction, if any;

(M) defines key statutory terms, either explicitly or by reference to other statutes that explicitly define those terms;

(N) specifies whether the legislation applies to the Federal Government or its agencies;

(O) specifies whether the legislation applies to States, territories, the District of Columbia, and the Commonwealths of Puerto Rico and of the Northern Mariana Islands;

(P) specifies what remedies are available such as money damages, civil penalties, injunctive relief, and attorney's fees; and

App. 9.40 Executive Order 12988 (continued)

4732 Federal Register / Vol. 61, No. 26 / Wednesday, February 7, 1996 / Presidential Documents

(Q) addresses other important issues affecting clarity and general draftsmanship of legislation set forth by the Attorney General, with the concurrence of the Director of the Office of Management and Budget ("OMB") and after consultation with affected agencies, that are determined to be in accordance with the purposes of this order.

(2) that the regulation, as appropriate—

(A) specifies in clear language the preemptive effect, if any, to be given to the regulation;

(B) specifies in clear language the effect on existing Federal law or regulation, if any, including all provisions repealed, circumscribed, displaced, impaired, or modified;

(C) provides a clear legal standard for affected conduct rather than a general standard, while promoting simplification and burden reduction;

(D) specifies in clear language the retroactive effect, if any, to be given to the regulation;

(E) specifies whether administrative proceedings are to be required before parties may file suit in court and, if so, describes those proceedings and requires the exhaustion of administrative remedies;

(F) defines key terms, either explicitly or by reference to other regulations or statutes that explicitly define those items; and

(G) addresses other important issues affecting clarity and general draftsmanship of regulations set forth by the Attorney General, with the concurrence of the Director of OMB and after consultation with affected agencies, that are determined to be in accordance with the purposes of this order.

(c) *Agency Review.* The agencies shall review such draft legislation or regulation to determine that either the draft legislation or regulation meets the applicable standards provided in subsections (a) and (b) of this section, or it is unreasonable to require the particular piece of draft legislation or regulation to meet one or more of those standards.

Sec. 4. *Principles to Promote Just and Efficient Administrative Adjudications.*

(a) *Implementation of Administrative Conference Recommendations.* In order to promote just and efficient resolution of disputes, an agency that adjudicates administrative claims shall, to the extent reasonable and practicable, and when not in conflict with other sections of this order, implement the recommendations of the Administrative Conference of the United States, entitled "Case Management as a Tool for Improving Agency Adjudication," as contained in 1 C.F.R. 305.86-7 (1991).

(b) *Improvements in Administrative Adjudication.* All Federal agencies should review their administrative adjudicatory processes and develop specific procedures to reduce delay in decision-making, to facilitate self-representation where appropriate, to expand non-lawyer counseling and representation where appropriate, and to invest maximum discretion in fact-finding officers to encourage appropriate settlement of claims as early as possible.

(c) *Bias.* All Federal agencies should review their administrative adjudicatory processes to identify any type of bias on the part of the decision-makers that results in an injustice to persons who appear before administrative adjudicatory tribunals; regularly train all fact-finders, administrative law judges, and other decision-makers to eliminate such bias; and establish appropriate mechanisms to receive and resolve complaints of such bias from persons who appear before administrative adjudicatory tribunals.

(d) *Public Education.* All Federal agencies should develop effective and simple methods, including the use of electronic technology, to educate the public about its claims/benefits policies and procedures.

Sec. 5. *Coordination by the Department of Justice.*

(a) The Attorney General shall coordinate efforts by Federal agencies to implement sections 1, 2 and 4 of this order.

App. 9.40 Executive Order 12988 (continued)

Federal Register / Vol. 61, No. 26 / Wednesday, February 7, 1996 / Presidential Documents 4733

(b) To implement the principles and purposes announced by this order, the Attorney General is authorized to issue guidelines implementing sections 1 and 4 of this order for the Department of Justice. Such guidelines shall serve as models for internal guidelines that may be issued by other agencies pursuant to this order.

Sec. 6. *Definitions.* For purposes of this order:

(a) The term "agency" shall be defined as that term is defined in section 105 of title 5, United States Code.

(b) The term "litigation counsel" shall be defined as the trial counsel or the office in which such trial counsel is employed, such as the United States Attorney's Office for the district in which the litigation is pending or a litigating division of the Department of Justice. Special Assistant United States Attorneys are included within this definition. Those agencies authorized by law to represent themselves in court without assistance from the Department of Justice are also included in this definition, as are private counsel hired by any Federal agency to conduct litigation on behalf of the agency or the United States.

Sec. 7. *No Private Rights Created.* This order is intended only to improve the internal management of the executive branch in resolving disputes, conducting litigation in a reasonable and just manner, and reviewing legislation and regulations. This order shall not be construed as creating any right or benefit, substantive or procedural, enforceable at law or in equity by a party against the United States, its agencies, its officers, or any other person. This order shall not be construed to create any right to judicial review involving the compliance or noncompliance of the United States, its agencies, its officers, or any other person with this order. Nothing in this order shall be construed to obligate the United States to accept a particular settlement or resolution of a dispute, to alter its standards for accepting settlements, to forego seeking a consent decree or other relief, or to alter any existing delegation of settlement or litigating authority.

Sec. 8. *Scope.*

(a) *No Applicability to Criminal Matters or Proceedings in Foreign Courts.* This order is applicable to civil matters only. It is not intended to affect criminal matters, including enforcement of criminal fines or judgments of criminal forfeiture. This order does not apply to litigation brought by or against the United States in foreign courts or tribunals.

(b) *Application of Notice Provision.* Notice pursuant to subsection (a) of section 1 is not required (1) in any action to seize or forfeit assets subject to forfeiture or in any action to seize property; (2) in any bankruptcy, insolvency, conservatorship, receivership, or liquidation proceeding; (3) when the assets that are the subject of the action or that would satisfy the judgment are subject to flight, dissipation, or destruction; (4) when the defendant is subject to flight; (5) when, as determined by litigation counsel, exigent circumstances make providing such notice impracticable or such notice would otherwise defeat the purpose of the litigation, such as in actions seeking temporary restraining orders or preliminary injunctive relief; or (6) in those limited classes of cases where the Attorney General determines that providing such notice would defeat the purpose of the litigation.

(c) *Additional Guidance as to Scope.* The Attorney General shall have the authority to issue further guidance as to the scope of this order, except section 3, consistent with the purposes of this order.

Sec. 9. *Conflicts with Other Rules.* Nothing in this order shall be construed to require litigation counsel or any agency to act in a manner contrary to the Federal Rules of Civil Procedure, Tax Court Rules of Practice and Procedure, State or Federal law, other applicable rules of practice or procedure, or court order.

Sec. 10. *Privileged Information.* Nothing in this order shall compel or authorize the disclosure of privileged information, sensitive law enforcement infor-

App. 9.40 Executive Order 12988 (continued)

4734 Federal Register / Vol. 61, No. 26 / Wednesday, February 7, 1996 / Presidential Documents

mation, information affecting national security, or information the disclosure of which is prohibited by law.

Sec. 11. *Effective Date.* This order shall become effective 90 days after the date of signature. This order shall not apply to litigation commenced prior to the effective date.

Sec. 12. *Revocation.* Executive Order No. 12778 is hereby revoked.

THE WHITE HOUSE,
February 5, 1996.

[FR Doc. 96-2755
Filed 2-6-96; 8:45 am]
Billing code 3195-01-P

Appendix Ten: A Drafting Practicum

App. 10.00 Introduction

The material that follows is included here as an example of a typical drafting exercise. It includes a letter from the client, an initial draft transmitted by the client, and a discussion draft prepared by the drafter.

The letter, the initial draft, and the discussion draft are each problematic, and each can fairly be critiqued. Notably, the discussion draft is an improvement over the initial draft, but it is not the "right answer" or a "model" solution—nor can it be, given the difficulties posed by the letter and the initial draft. The drafter has sought to clarify the policy that has been provided and to frame the issues that have not been resolved. Likely, the drafter has failed in capturing the client's intent, but has succeeded in capturing the client's attention.

This material can be used effectively in a training workshop in a variety of ways. A thorough approach would be to have a participant first critique the letter, then critique the initial draft, then prepare a discussion draft, and, finally, compare and contrast that draft with the discussion draft included here.

App. 10.10 Sample Letter to Drafter

To: The Drafter
From: The Boss

Health care costs are a big problem. I'm not so sure we can solve the problem in one fell swoop. So I want a bill that will solve a part of the problem. I want to focus on limiting liability for health care provided in an emergency on a Good Samaritan basis. I have already received one draft from a first-responder association and it is attached. They say their draft should do the trick. Use it if it is useful, but give me a clean draft. The bill I need would conform to the following specifications:

(1) In a lawsuit of this type, there needs to be a cap on non-economic damages of $250,000, adjusted for inflation.

(2) Lawsuits of this type should be resolved swiftly. I want a statute of limitations of three years. It can be tolled for fraud or for minors but not for any other reason. Appeals have to be filed within 30 days.

(3) Dishonest contingent-fee lawyers are not allowed in a lawsuit of this type. By that I mean an attorney convicted of a felony or misdemeanor involving dishonesty.

Concentrate on getting (1) right. If you have time, try your hand at (2) or (3), or both.

Thanks,
The Boss

PS—Of course these specifications should apply not only to lawsuits but to arbitration proceedings and settlements as well.

PPS—As always, I need this yesterday.

App. 10.20 Initial Draft

[INITIAL DRAFT]

SECTION 1. SHORT TITLE.

This bill may be cited as "The Quality Urgent Assisted Care Act."

SEC. 2. DEFINITIONS.

In this Act—

(1) ALTERNATIVE DISPUTE RESOLUTION SYSTEM; ADR.—The term "alternative dispute resolution system" or "ADR" means a system that provides for the resolution of urgent care lawsuits in a manner other than through a civil action brought in a State or Federal court;

(2) URGENT CARE LAWSUIT.—The term "urgent care lawsuit" means any dispute in which an urgent care liability claim concerning the provision of health care goods or services or any medical product affecting interstate commerce is asserted; and

(3) URGENT CARE LIABILITY CLAIM.—The term "urgent care liability claim" means the following:

(A) A demand by any person, whether or not pursuant to ADR, based upon health care, regardless of the theory of liability on which the claim is based, or the number of plaintiffs, de-

App. 10.20 Initial Draft (continued)

2

fendants, or other parties, or the number of causes of action.

(B) However, the term does not include services or products not provided on an urgent Good Samaritan basis.

(C) The Secretary shall prescribe regulations to implement this section.

(4) STATE.—The term "State" means the District of Columbia, the Commonwealth of Puerto Rico, and any other territory or possession of, or under the jurisdiction of, the United States, or any political subdivision thereof.

SEC. 3. FINDINGS AND PURPOSE.

(a) FINDINGS.—Congress finds that—

(1) An emergency room doctor is reluctant to provide emergency care because he or she is afraid of open-ended liability.

(2) First responders have raised issues about whether it is fair to impose liability for emergency care rendered with no expectation of payment.

(3) Insurance companies throughout America are having trouble turning an honest profit.

(b) EFFECT ON INTERSTATE COMMERCE.—Doctors, first responders, and insurance companies are industries affecting interstate commerce and the health care liability

App. 10.20 Initial Draft (continued)

3

litigation systems existing throughout the United States are activities that affect interstate commerce.

(c) PURPOSES.—The purpose of this Act is to assure that the liability system of each State is fair with respect to emergency Good Samaritan care.

SEC. 4A. ENCOURAGING SPEEDY RESOLUTION OF CLAIMS.

The time to bring, file, commence, or otherwise initiate an urgent care lawsuit (hereafter "the time") should be—

(1) 3 years after the date of manifestation of injury, or

(2) after the claimant discovers, or through the use of reasonable diligence should have discovered the injury,

whichever occurs first. In no event shall the time exceed 3 years after the date of manifestation of injury. Provided, however, that the period in subsection (1) may be tolled upon proof of fraud. In addition, a State shall insure that an appeal shall be filed within 30 days and heard within 180 days.

SEC. 4B. EXCEPTION.

Notwithstanding any other provision of law, section 4A, hereinabove, does not apply if the party is a minor.

App. 10.20 Initial Draft (continued)

4

SEC. 5. COMPENSATING PATIENTS.

(a) Economic Damages.—In any lawsuit based on urgent care, there is no limit on the amount of economic damages a patient may recover.

(b) Noneconomic Damages.—Economic damages may not exceed $250,000.

(c) Adustment for inflation.—The limits in this section are hereby increased annually for inflation.

SEC. 6. MAXIMIZING PATIENT RECOVERY.

(a) Court Supervision of Share of Damages Actually Paid to Claimants.—In any urgent care lawsuit, the court shall supervise the arrangements for payment of damages to protect against conflicts of interest that may have the effect of reducing the amount of damages awarded that are actually paid to claimants.

(b) Contingent Fees.—A contingent-fee attorney who commits a felony or misdemeanor involving dishonesty cannot be retained to bring an urgent care lawsuit.

SEC. 7. EFFECTIVE DATE; APPLICABILITY.

The requirements of this Act shall—

(1) take effect upon enactment; and

(2) apply to every State.

SEC. 8. AUTHORIZATION OF APPROPRIATIONS.

There are authorized to be appropriated such sums as may be necessary to carry out this section.

App. 10.30 Discussion Draft

[DISCUSSION DRAFT]

A BILL

To limit liability for health care provided in an emergency on a Good Samaritan basis, and for other purposes.

Be it enacted by the Senate and House of Representatives of the United States of America in Congress assembled,

SECTION 1. SHORT TITLE.

This Act may be cited as the "______________ Act".

SEC. 2. CASES COVERED.

This Act applies to a case in which—

(1) a provider provides urgent care to a patient;

(2) by reason of that urgent care, the patient is injured or dies; and

(3) by reason of that injury or death, the provider is, under State law, liable in damages to the patient or to any other person.

SEC. 3. STATUTE OF LIMITATIONS.

(a) IN GENERAL.—A civil action based on liability described in section 2 shall be brought within 3 years, except as provided in subsection (b).

App. 10.30 Discussion Draft (continued)

2

(b) TOLLING.—The statute of limitations provided by subsection (a) is tolled by either of the following:

(1) Fraud.

(2) The minority of the person to whom the provider is liable.

SEC. 4. LIMITATION ON NONECONOMIC DAMAGES.

(a) NONECONOMIC DAMAGES.—A provider liable as described in section 2 to a person by reason of an injury or death is not liable to that person by reason of that injury or death for more than $250,000 in noneconomic damages.

(b) ADUSTMENT FOR INFLATION.—The dollar amount in subsection (a) applies to a judgment entered in calendar year 2006 or earlier. For calendar years after 2006, the dollar amount that applies is determined according to the adjustments in the Consumer Price Index between January 1, 2006, and January 1 of the calendar year concerned.

SEC. 5. DEADLINE FOR FILING APPEALS.

In a civil action based on liability described in section 2, a party otherwise entitled to file an appeal must file that appeal within 30 days or the appeal is barred.

App. 10.30 Discussion Draft (continued)

3

SEC. 6. LIMITATION ON ENFORCEABILITY OF CONTINGENT-FEE AGREEMENTS.

An attorney convicted of a felony, or convicted of a misdemeanor involving dishonesty, may not enforce a contingent-fee agreement against a client, to the extent the services rendered under that agreement relate to liability described in section 2.

SEC. 7. APPLICABILITY.

This Act applies to liability incurred after the date of the enactment of this Act.

SEC. 8. DEFINITIONS.

In this Act:

(1) The term "provider" means ____________________.

(2) The term "urgent care" means health care goods or services provided on an emergency basis without expectation of payment.

(3) The term "State" includes the District of Columbia, the Commonwealth of Puerto Rico, and any other territory or possession of the United States.

Appendix Eleven: The Constitution of the United States

App. 11.00 Introduction

The material that follows is included here because, as discussed in Chapter Four (specifically, in § 4.60), a working knowledge of the Constitution of the United States is essential to thinking through the policy.

App. 11.10 The Constitution of the United States

108TH CONGRESS 1st Session | HOUSE OF REPRESENTATIVES | DOCUMENT No. 108–95

THE CONSTITUTION OF THE UNITED STATES OF AMERICA

As Amended

Unratified Amendments

Analytical Index

PRESENTED BY MR. NEY

June 20, 2003 • Ordered to be printed

UNITED STATES
GOVERNMENT PRINTING OFFICE
WASHINGTON: 2003

For sale by the Superintendent of Documents, U.S. Government Printing Office
Internet: bookstore.gpo.gov Phone: toll free (866) 512-1800; DC area (202) 512-1800
Fax: (202) 512-2250 Mail: Stop SSOP, Washington, DC 20402-001
ISBN 0-16-051424-X

App. 11.10 The Constitution of the United States (continued)

House Doc. 108–95

The printing of the revised version of The Constitution of the United States of America As Amended (Document Size) is hereby ordered pursuant to H. Con. Res. 139 as passed on June 20, 2003, 108th Congress, 1st Session. This document was compiled at the direction of Chairman Robert Ney of the Joint Committee on Printing, and printed by the U.S. Government Printing Office.

(II)

App. 11.10 The Constitution of the United States (continued)

CONTENTS

(III)

App. 11.10 The Constitution of the United States (continued)

"Scene at the Signing of the Constitution of the United States"
By Howard Chandler Christy.
Provided by the Architect of the Capitol.

App. 11.10 The Constitution of the United States (continued)

HISTORICAL NOTE

The Delegates who convened at the Federal Convention on May 25, 1787, quickly rejected the idea of revising the Articles of Confederation and agreed to construct a new framework for a national government. Throughout the summer months at the Convention in Philadelphia, delegates from 12 States debated the proper form such a government should take, but few questioned the need to establish a more vigorous government to preside over the union of States. The 39 delegates who signed the Constitution on September 17, 1787, expected the new charter to provide a permanent guarantee of the political liberties achieved in the Revolution.

Prior to the adoption of the Federal Constitution, an Articles of Confederation, drafted by the Continental Congress and approved by 13 States, provided for a union of the former British colonies. Even before Maryland became the last State to accede to the Articles in 1781, a number of Americans, particularly those involved in the prosecution of the Revolutionary War, recognized the inadequacies of the Articles as a national government. In the 1780s these nationally-minded Americans became increasingly disturbed by the Articles' failure to provide the central government with authority to raise revenue, regulate commerce, or enforce treaties.

Despite repeated proposals that the Continental Congress revise the Articles, the movement for a new national government began outside the Congress. Representatives of Maryland and Virginia, meeting at Mt. Vernon to discuss trade problems between the two States, agreed to invite delegates from all States to discuss commercial affairs at a meeting in Annapolis, Maryland, in September 1786. Although delegates from only five States reached the Annapolis Convention, that group issued a call for a meeting of all States to discuss necessary revisions of the Articles of Confederation. Responding to this call and the endorsement of the Continental Congress, every State except Rhode Island selected delegates for the meeting in the State House at Philadelphia.

The document printed here was the product of nearly 4 months of deliberations in the Federal Convention at Philadelphia. The challenging task before the delegates was to create a republican form of government that could encompass the 13 States and accommodate the anticipated expansion to the West. The distribution of authority between legislative, executive, and judicial branches was a boldly original attempt to create an energetic central government at the same time that the sovereignty of the people was preserved.

The longest debate of the Convention centered on the proper form of representation and election for the Congress. The division between small States that wished to perpetuate the equal representation of States in the Continental Congress and the large States

(V)

App. 11.10 The Constitution of the United States (continued)

VI

that proposed representation proportional to population threatened to bring the Convention proceedings to a halt. Over several weeks the delegates developed a complicated compromise that provided for equal representation of the States in a Senate elected by State legislature and proportional representation in a popularly-elected House of Representatives.

The conflict between large and small States disappeared in the early years of the republic. More lasting was the division between slave and free States that had been a disturbing undercurrent in the Convention debates. The Convention's strained attempt to avoid using the word slavery in the articles granting recognition and protection to that institution scarcely hid the regional divisions that would remain unresolved under the terms of union agreed to in 1787.

The debates in the State ratification conventions of 1787 and 1788 made clear the need to provide amendments to the basic framework drafted in Philadelphia. Beginning with Massachusetts, a number of State conventions ratified the Constitution with the request that a bill of rights be added to protect certain liberties at the core of English and American political traditions. The First Congress approved a set of amendments which became the Bill of Rights when ratified by the States in 1791. The continuing process of amendment, clearly described in the note of the following text, has enabled the Constitution to accommodate changing conditions in American society at the same time that the Founders' basic outline of national government remains intact.

App. 11.10 The Constitution of the United States (continued)

CONSTITUTION OF THE UNITED STATES [1]

WE THE PEOPLE of the United States, in Order to form a more perfect Union, establish Justice, insure domestic Tranquility, provide for the common defence, promote the general Welfare, and secure the Blessings of Liberty to ourselves and our Posterity, do ordain and establish this Constitution for the United States of America.

ARTICLE I.

SECTION 1. All legislative Powers herein granted shall be vested in a Congress of the United States, which shall consist of a Senate and House of Representatives.

[1] This text of the Constitution follows the engrossed copy signed by Gen. Washington and the deputies from 12 States. The small superior figures preceding the paragraphs designate clauses, and were not in the original and have no reference to footnotes.

The Constitution was adopted by a convention of the States on September 17, 1787, and was subsequently ratified by the several States, on the following dates: Delaware, December 7, 1787; Pennsylvania, December 12, 1787; New Jersey, December 18, 1787; Georgia, January 2, 1788; Connecticut, January 9, 1788; Massachusetts, February 6, 1788; Maryland, April 28, 1788; South Carolina, May 23, 1788; New Hampshire, June 21, 1788.

Ratification was completed on June 21, 1788.

The Constitution was subsequently ratified by Virginia, June 25, 1788; New York, July 26, 1788; North Carolina, November 21, 1789; Rhode Island, May 29, 1790; and Vermont, January 10, 1791.

In May 1785, a committee of Congress made a report recommending an alteration in the Articles of Confederation, but no action was taken on it, and it was left to the State Legislatures to proceed in the matter. In January 1786, the Legislature of Virginia passed a resolution providing for the appointment of five commissioners, who, or any three of them, should meet such commissioners as might be appointed in the other States of the Union, at a time and place to be agreed upon, to take into consideration the trade of the United States; to consider how far a uniform system in their commercial regulations may be necessary to their common interest and their permanent harmony; and to report to the several States such an act, relative to this great object, as, when ratified by them, will enable the United States in Congress effectually to provide for the same. The Virginia commissioners, after some correspondence, fixed the first Monday in September as the time, and the city of Annapolis as the place for the meeting, but only four other States were represented, viz: Delaware, New York, New Jersey, and Pennsylvania; the commissioners appointed by Massachusetts, New Hampshire, North Carolina, and Rhode Island failed to attend. Under the circumstances of so partial a representation, the commissioners present agreed upon a report, (drawn by Mr. Hamilton, of New York) expressing their unanimous conviction that it might essentially tend to advance the interests of the Union if the States by which they were respectively delegated would concur, and use their endeavors to procure the concurrence of the other States, in the appointment of commissioners to meet at Philadelphia on the Second Monday of May following, to take into consideration the situation of the United States; to devise such further provisions as should appear to them necessary to render the Constitution of the Federal Government adequate to the exigencies of the Union; and to report such an act for that purpose to the United States in Congress assembled as, when agreed to by them and afterwards confirmed by the Legislatures of every State, would effectually provide for the same.

Congress, on the 21st of February, 1787, adopted a resolution in favor of a convention, and the Legislatures of those States which had not already done so (with the exception of Rhode Island) promptly appointed delegates. On the 25th of May, seven States having convened, George Washington, of Virginia, was unanimously elected President, and the consideration of the proposed constitution was commenced. On the 17th of September, 1787, the Constitution as engrossed and agreed upon was signed by all the members present, except Mr. Gerry of Massachusetts, and Messrs. Mason and Randolph, of Virginia. The president of the convention transmitted it to Congress, with a resolution stating how the proposed Federal Government should

Continued

(1)

App. 11.10 The Constitution of the United States (continued)

SECTION. 2. [1] The House of Representatives shall be composed of Members chosen every second Year by the People of the several States, and the Electors in each State shall have the Qualifications requisite for Electors of the most numerous Branch of the State Legislature.

[2] No Person shall be a Representative who shall not have attained to the Age of twenty five Years, and been seven Years a Citizen of the United States, and who shall not, when elected, be an Inhabitant of that State in which he shall be chosen.

[3] Representatives and direct Taxes shall be apportioned among the several States which may be included within this Union, according to their respective Numbers, which shall be determined by adding to the whole Number of free Persons, including those bound to Service for a Term of Years, and excluding Indians not taxed, three fifths of all other Persons.[2] The actual Enumeration shall be made within three Years after the first Meeting of the Congress of the United States, and within every subsequent Term of ten Years, in such Manner as they shall by Law direct. The Number of Representatives shall not exceed one for every thirty Thousand, but each State shall have at Least one Representative; and until such enumeration shall be made, the State of New Hampshire shall be entitled to chuse three, Massachusetts eight, Rhode-Island and providence Plantations one, Connecticut five, New-York six, New Jersey four, Pennsylvania eight, Delaware one, Maryland six, Virginia ten, North Carolina five, South Carolina five, and Georgia three.

[4] When vacancies happen in the Representation from any State, the Executive Authority thereof shall issue Writs of Election to fill such Vacancies.

[5] The House of Representatives shall chuse their Speaker and other Officers; and shall have the sole Power of Impeachment.

SECTION. 3. [1] The Senate of the United States shall be composed of two Senators from each State, chosen by the Legislature thereof.[3] for six Years; and each Senator shall have one Vote.

[2] Immediately after they shall be assembled in Consequence of the first Election, they shall be divided as equally as may be into three Classes. The Seats of the Senators of the first Class shall be vacated at the Expiration of the second Year, of the second Class at the Expiration of the fourth Year, and of the third Class at the Expiration of the sixth Year, so that one third may be chosen every

---

be put in operation, and an explanatory letter. Congress, on the 28th of September, 1787, directed the Constitution so framed, with the resolutions and letter concerning the same, to "be transmitted to the several Legislatures in order to be submitted to a convention of delegates chosen in each State by the people thereof, in conformity to the resolves of the convention."

On the 4th of March, 1789, the day which had been fixed for commencing the operations of Government under the new Constitution, it had been ratified by the conventions chosen in each State to consider it, as follows: Delaware, December 7, 1787; Pennsylvania, December 12, 1787; New Jersey, December 18, 1787; Georgia, January 2, 1788; Connecticut, January 9, 1788; Massachusetts, February 6, 1788; Maryland, April 28, 1788; South Carolina, May 23, 1788; New Hampshire, June 21, 1788; Virginia, June 25, 1788; and New York, July 26, 1788.

The President informed Congress, on the 28th of January, 1790, that North Carolina had ratified the Constitution November 21, 1789; and he informed Congress on the 1st of June, 1790, that Rhode Island had ratified the Constitution May 29, 1790. Vermont, in convention, ratified the Constitution January 10, 1791, and was, by an act of Congress approved February 18, 1791, "received and admitted into this Union as a new and entire member of the United States."

[2] The part of this clause relating to the mode of apportionment of representatives among the several States has been affected by section 2 of amendment XIV, and as to taxes on incomes without apportionment by amendment XVI.

[3] This clause has been affected by clause 1 of amendment XVII.

App. 11.10 The Constitution of the United States (continued)

second Year; and if Vacancies happen by Resignation or otherwise, during the Recess of the Legislature of any State, the Executive thereof may make temporary Appointments until the next Meeting of the Legislature, which shall then fill such Vacancies.[4]

[3] No Person shall be a Senator who shall not have attained to the Age of thirty Years, and been nine Years a Citizen of the United States, and who shall not, when elected, be an Inhabitant of that State for which he shall be chosen.

[4] The Vice President of the United States shall be President of the Senate, but shall have no Vote, unless they be equally divided.

[5] The Senate shall chuse their other Officers, and also a President pro tempore, in the Absence of the Vice President, or when he shall exercise the Office of President of the United States.

[6] The Senate shall have the sole Power to try all Impeachments. When sitting for that Purpose, they shall be on Oath or Affirmation. When the President of the United States is tried, the Chief Justice shall preside: And no Person shall be convicted without the Concurrence of two thirds of the Members present.

[7] Judgment in Cases of Impeachment shall not extend further than to removal from Office, and disqualification to hold and enjoy any Office of honor, Trust or Profit under the United States: but the Party convicted shall nevertheless be liable and subject to Indictment, Trial, Judgment and Punishment, according to Law.

SECTION. 4. [1] The Times, Places and Manner of holding Elections for Senators and Representatives, shall be prescribed in each State by the Legislature thereof; but the Congress may at any time by Law make or alter such Regulations, except as to the Places of chusing Senators.

[2] The Congress shall assemble at least once in every Year and such Meeting shall be on the first Monday in December,[5] unless they shall by Law appoint a different Day.

SECTION. 5. [1] Each House shall be the Judge of the Elections, Returns and Qualifications of its own Members, and a Majority of each shall constitute a Quorum to do Business; but a smaller Number may adjourn from day to day, and may be authorized to compel the Attendance of absent Members, in such Manner, and under such Penalties as each House may provide.

[2] Each House may determine the Rules of its Proceedings, punish its Members for disorderly Behavior, and, with the Concurrence of two thirds, expel a Member.

[3] Each House shall keep a Journal of its Proceedings, and from time to time publish the same, excepting such Parts as may in their Judgment require Secrecy; and the Yeas and Nays of the Members of either House on any question shall, at the Desire of one fifth of those Present, be entered on the Journal.

[4] Neither House, during the Session of Congress, shall, without the Consent of the other, adjourn for more than three days, nor to any other Place than that in which the two Houses shall be sitting.

SECTION. 6. [1] The Senators and Representatives shall receive a Compensation for their Services, to be ascertained by Law, and

[4] This clause has been affected by clause 2 of amendment XVIII.
[5] This clause has been affected by amendment XX.

App. 11.10 The Constitution of the United States (continued)

paid out of the Treasury of the United States.[6] They shall in all Cases, except Treason, Felony and Breach of the Peace, be privileged from Arrest during their Attendance at the Session of their respective Houses, and in going to and returning from the same; and for any Speech or Debate in either House, they shall not be questioned in any other Place.

[2] No Senator or Representative shall, during the Time for which he was elected, be appointed to any civil Office under the Authority of the United States, which shall have been created, or the Emoluments whereof shall have been encreased during such time; and no Person holding any Office under the United States, shall be a Member of either House during his Continuance in Office.

SECTION. 7. [1] All Bills for raising Revenue shall originate in the House of Representatives; but the Senate may propose or concur with Amendments as on other Bills.

[2] Every Bill which shall have passed the House of Representatives and the Senate, shall, before it become a Law, be presented to the President of the United States; If he approve he shall sign it, but if not he shall return it, with his Objections to that House in which it shall have originated, who shall enter the Objections at large on their Journal, and proceed to reconsider it. If after such Reconsideration two thirds of that House shall agree to pass the Bill, it shall be sent, together with the Objections, to the other House, by which it shall likewise be reconsidered, and if approved by two thirds of that House, it shall become a Law. But in all such Cases the Votes of both Houses shall be determined by Yeas and Nays, and the Names of the Persons voting for and against the Bill shall be entered on the Journal of each House respectively. If any Bill shall not be returned by the President within ten Days (Sundays excepted) after it shall have been presented to him, the Same shall be a Law, in like Manner as if he had signed it, unless the Congress by their Adjournment prevent its Return, in which Case it shall not be a Law.

[3] Every Order, Resolution, or Vote to which the Concurrence of the Senate and House of Representatives may be necessary (except on a question of Adjournment) shall be presented to the President of the United States; and before the Same shall take Effect, shall be approved by him, or being disapproved by him, shall be repassed by two thirds of the Senate and House of Representatives, according to the Rules and Limitations prescribed in the Case of a Bill.

SECTION. 8. [1] The Congress shall have Power To lay and collect Taxes, Duties, Imposts and Excises, to pay the Debts and provide for the common Defence and general Welfare of the United States; but all Duties, Imposts and Excises shall be uniform throughout the United States;

[2] To borrow Money on the credit of the United States;

[3] To regulate Commerce with foreign Nations, and among the several States, and with the Indian Tribes;

[4] To establish a uniform Rule of Naturalization, and uniform Laws on the subject of Bankruptcies throughout the United States;

[5] To coin Money, regulate the Value thereof, and of foreign Coin, and fix the Standard of Weights and Measures;

[6] This clause has been affected by amendment XXVII.

App. 11.10 The Constitution of the United States (continued)

[6]To provide for the Punishment of counterfeiting the Securities and current Coin of the United States;

[7]To establish Post Offices and post Roads;

[8]To promote the Progress of Science and useful Arts, by securing for limited Times to Authors and Inventors the exclusive Right to their respective Writings and Discoveries;

[9]To constitute Tribunals inferior to the supreme Court;

[10]To define and punish Piracies and Felonies committed on the high Seas, and Offences against the Law of Nations;

[11]To declare War, grant Letters of Marque and Reprisal, and make Rules concerning Captures on Land and Water;

[12]To raise and support Armies, but no Appropriation of Money to that Use shall be for a longer Term than two Years;

[13]To provide and maintain a Navy;

[14]To make Rules for the Government and Regulation of the land and naval Forces;

[15]To provide for calling forth the Militia to execute the Laws of the Union, suppress Insurrections and repel Invasions;

[16]To provide for organizing, arming, and disciplining, the Militia, and for governing such Part of them as may be employed in the Service of the United States, reserving to the States respectively, the Appointment of the Officers, and the Authority of training the Militia according to the discipline prescribed by Congress;

[17]To exercise exclusive Legislation in all Cases whatsoever, over such District (not exceeding ten Miles square) as may, by Cession of particular States, and the Acceptance of Congress, become the Seat of the Government of the United States, and to exercise like Authority over all Places purchased by the Consent of the Legislature of the State in which the Same shall be, for the Erection of Forts, Magazines, Arsenals, dock-Yards, and other needful buildings;—And

[18]To make all Laws which shall be necessary and proper for carrying into Execution the foregoing Powers, and all other Powers vested by this Constitution in the Government of the United States, or in any Department or Officer thereof.

SECTION. 9. [1]The Migration or Importation of such Persons as any of the States now existing shall think proper to admit, shall not be prohibited by the Congress prior to the Year one thousand eight hundred and eight, but a Tax or duty may be imposed on such Importation, not exceeding ten dollars for each Person.

[2]The Privilege of the Writ of Habeas Corpus shall not be suspended, unless when in Cases of Rebellion or Invasion the public Safety may require it.

[3]No Bill of Attainder or ex post facto Law shall be passed.

[4]No Capitation, or other direct, Tax shall be laid, unless in Proportion to the Census or Enumeration herein before directed to be taken.[7]

[5]No Tax or Duty shall be laid on Articles exported from any State.

[6]No Preference shall be given by any Regulation of Commerce or Revenue to the Ports of one State over those of another: nor shall

[7]This clause has been affected by amendment XVI.

App. 11.10 The Constitution of the United States (continued)

Vessels bound to, or from, one State, be obliged to enter, clear, or pay Duties in another.

[7] No Money shall be drawn from the Treasury, but in Consequence of Appropriations made by Law; and a regular Statement and Account of the Receipts and Expenditures of all public Money shall be published from time to time.

[8] No Title of Nobility shall be granted by the United States: And no Person holding any Office of Profit or Trust under them, shall, without the Consent of the Congress, accept of any present, Emolument, Office, or Title, of any kind whatever, from any King, Prince, or foreign State.

SECTION. 10. [1] No State shall enter into any Treaty, Alliance, or Confederation; grant Letters of Marque and Reprisal; coin Money; emit Bills of Credit; make any Thing but gold and silver Coin a Tender in Payment of Debts; pass any Bill of Attainder, ex post facto Law, or Law impairing the Obligation of Contracts, or grant any Title of Nobility.

[2] No State shall, without the Consent of the Congress, lay any Imposts or Duties on Imports or Exports, except what may be absolutely necessary for executing its inspection Laws: and the net Produce of all Duties and Imposts, laid by any State on Imports or Exports, shall be for the Use of the Treasury of the United States; and all such Laws shall be subject to the Revision and Control of the Congress.

[3] No State shall, without the Consent of Congress, lay any Duty of Tonnage, keep Troops, or Ships of War in time of Peace, enter into any Agreement or Compact with another State, or with a foreign Power, or engage in War, unless actually invaded, or in such imminent Danger as will not admit of delay.

ARTICLE. II.

SECTION. 1. [1] The executive Power shall be vested in a President of the United States of America. He shall hold his Office during the Term of four Years, and, together with the Vice President, chosen for the same Term, be elected, as follows

[2] Each State shall appoint, in such Manner as the Legislature thereof may direct, a Number of Electors, equal to the whole Number of Senators and Representatives to which the State may be entitled in the Congress: but no Senator or Representative, or Person holding an Office of Trust or Profit under the United States, shall be appointed an Elector.

[3] The Electors shall meet in their respective States, and vote by Ballot for two Persons, of whom one at least shall not be an Inhabitant of the same State with themselves. And they shall make a List of all the Persons voted for, and of the Number of Votes for each; which List they shall sign and certify, and transmit sealed to the Seat of the Government of the United States, directed to the President of the Senate. The President of the Senate shall, in the Presence of the Senate and House of Representatives, open to all the Certificates, and the Votes shall then be counted. The Person having the greatest Number of Votes shall be the President, if such Number be a Majority of the whole Number of Electors appointed; and if there be more than one who have such Majority, and have an equal Number of Votes, then the House of Representatives shall

App. 11.10 The Constitution of the United States (continued)

immediately chuse by Ballot one of them for President; and if no Person have a Majority, then from the five highest on the List the said House shall in like Manner chuse the President. But in chusing the President, the Votes shall be taken by States, the Representation from each State having one Vote; A quorum for this Purpose shall consist of a Member or Members from two thirds of the States, and a Majority of all the States shall be necessary to a Choice. In every Case, after the Choice of the President, the Person having the greatest Number of Votes of the Electors shall be the Vice President. But if there should remain two or more who have equal Votes, the Senate shall chuse from them by Ballot the Vice President.[8]

4 The Congress may determine the Time of chusing the Electors, and the Day on which they shall give their Votes; which Day shall be the same throughout the United States.

5 No Person except a natural born Citizen, or a Citizen of the United States, at the time of the Adoption of this Constitution, shall be eligible to the Office of President; neither shall any Person be eligible to that Office who shall not have attained to the Age of thirty five Years, and been fourteen Years a Resident within the United States.

6 In Case of the Removal of the President from Office, or of his Death, Resignation, or Inability to discharge the Powers and Duties of the said Office,[9] the Same shall devolve on the Vice President, and the Congress may by Law provide for the Case of Removal, Death, Resignation or Inability, both of the President and Vice President, declaring what Officer shall then act as President, and such Officer shall act accordingly, until the Disability be removed, or a President shall be elected.

7 The President shall, at stated Times, receive for his Services, a Compensation, which shall neither be encreased nor diminished during the Period for which he shall have been elected, and he shall not receive within that Period any other Emolument from the United States, or any of them.

8 Before he enter on the Execution of his Office, he shall take the following Oath or Affirmation:—"I do solemnly swear (or affirm) that I will faithfully execute the Office of President of the United States, and will to the best of my Ability, preserve, protect and defend the Constitution of the United States."

SECTION. 2. 1 The President shall be Commander in Chief of the Army and Navy of the United States, and of the Militia of the several States, when called into the actual Service of the United States; he may require the Opinion, in writing, of the principal Officer in each of the executive Departments, upon any Subject relating to the Duties of their respective Offices, and he shall have Power to grant Reprieves and Pardons for Offences against the United States, except in Cases of Impeachment.

2 He shall have Power, by and with the Advice and Consent of the Senate, to make Treaties, provided two thirds of the Senators present concur; and he shall nominate, and by and with the Advice and Consent of the Senate, shall appoint Ambassadors, other pub-

[8] This clause has been superseded by amendment XII.
[9] This clause has been affected by amendment XXV.

App. 11.10 The Constitution of the United States (continued)

lic Ministers and Consuls, Judges of the supreme Court, and all other Officers of the United States, whose Appointments are not herein otherwise provided for, and which shall be established by Law: but the Congress may by Law vest the Appointment of such inferior Officers, as they think proper, in the President alone, in the Courts of Law, or in the Heads of Departments.

[3] The President shall have Power to fill up all Vacancies that may happen during the Recess of the Senate, by granting Commissions which shall expire at the End of their next Session.

SECTION. 3. He shall from time to time give to the Congress Information of the State of the Union, and recommend to their Consideration such Measures as he shall judge necessary and expedient; he may, on extraordinary Occasions, convene both Houses, or either of them, and in Case of Disagreement between them, with Respect to the Time of Adjournment, he may adjourn them to such Time as he shall think proper; he shall receive Ambassadors and other public Ministers; he shall take Care that the Laws be faithfully executed, and shall Commission all the Officers of the United States.

SECTION. 4. The President, Vice President and all civil Officers of the United States, shall be removed from Office on Impeachment for, and Conviction of, Treason, Bribery, or other high Crimes and Misdemeanors.

ARTICLE. III.

SECTION. 1. The judicial Power of the United States, shall be vested in one supreme Court, and in such inferior Courts as the Congress may from time to time ordain and establish. The Judges, both of the supreme and inferior Courts, shall hold their Offices during good Behaviour, and shall, at stated Times, receive for their Services, a Compensation, which shall not be diminished during their Continuance in Office.

SECTION. 2. [1] The judicial Power shall extend to all Cases, in Law and Equity, arising under this Constitution, the Laws of the United States, and Treaties made, or which shall be made, under their Authority;—to all Cases affecting Ambassadors, other public Ministers and Consuls;—to all Cases of admiralty and maritime Jurisdiction;—to Controversies to which the United States will be a party;—to Controversies between two or more States;—between a State and Citizens of another State;[10]—between Citizens of different States,—between Citizens of the same State claiming Lands under Grants of different States, and between a State, or the Citizens thereof, and foreign States, Citizens or Subjects.

[2] In all Cases affecting Ambassadors, other public Ministers and Consuls, and those in which a State shall be Party, the supreme Court shall have original Jurisdiction. In all the other Cases before mentioned, the supreme Court shall have appellate Jurisdiction, both as to Law and Fact, with such Exceptions, and under such Regulations as the Congress shall make.

[3] The Trial of all Crimes, except in Cases of Impeachment, shall be by Jury; and such Trial shall be held in the State where the said Crimes shall have been committed; but when not committed

[10] This clause has been affected by amendment XI.

App. 11.10 The Constitution of the United States (continued)

within any State, the Trial shall be at such Place or Places as the Congress may by Law have directed.

SECTION. 3. [1]Treason against the United States, shall consist only in levying War against them, or in adhering to their Enemies, giving them Aid and Comfort. No Person shall be convicted of Treason unless on the Testimony of two Witnesses to the same overt Act, or on Confession in open Court.

[2]The Congress shall have Power to declare the Punishment of Treason, but no Attainder of Treason shall work Corruption of Blood, or Forfeiture except during the Life of the Person attainted.

ARTICLE. IV.

SECTION. 1. Full Faith and Credit shall be given in each State to the public Acts, Records, and judicial Proceedings of every other State. And the Congress may by general Laws prescribe the Manner in which such Acts, Records and Proceedings shall be proved, and the Effect thereof.

SECTION. 2. [1]The Citizens of each State shall be entitled to all Privileges and Immunities of Citizens in the several States.

[2]A Person charged in any State with Treason, Felony, or other Crime, who shall flee from Justice, and be found in another State, shall on Demand of the executive Authority of the State from which he fled, be delivered up, to be removed to the State having Jurisdiction of the Crime.

[3]No Person held to Service or Labour in one State, under the Laws thereof, escaping into another, shall, in Consequence of any Law or Regulation therein, be discharged from such Service or Labour, but shall be delivered up on Claim of the Party to whom such Service or Labour may be due.[11]

SECTION. 3. [1]New States may be admitted by the Congress into this Union; but no new State shall be formed or erected within the Jurisdiction of any other State; nor any State be formed by the Junction of two or more States, or Parts of States, without the Consent of the Legislatures of the States concerned as well as of the Congress.

[2]The Congress shall have Power to dispose of and make all needful Rules and Regulations respecting the Territory or other Property belonging to the United States; and nothing in this Constitution shall be so construed as to Prejudice any Claims of the United States, or of any particular State.

SECTION. 4. The United States shall guarantee to every State in this Union a Republican Form of Government, and shall protect each of them against Invasion; and on Application of the Legislature, or of the Executive (when the Legislature cannot be convened) against domestic Violence.

ARTICLE. V.

The Congress, whenever two thirds of both Houses shall deem it necessary, shall propose Amendments to this Constitution, or, on the Application of the Legislatures of two thirds of the several States, shall call a Convention for proposing Amendments, which,

[11]This clause has been affected by amendment XIII.

App. 11.10 The Constitution of the United States (continued)

10 CONSTITUTION OF THE UNITED STATES

in either Case, shall be valid to all Intents and Purposes, as Part of this Constitution, when ratified by the Legislatures of three fourths of the several States, or by Conventions in three fourths thereof, as the one or the other Mode of Ratification may be proposed by the Congress; Provided that no Amendment which may be made prior to the Year One thousand eight hundred and eight shall in any Manner affect the first and fourth Clauses in the Ninth Section of the first Article; and that no State, without its Consent, shall be deprived of its equal Suffrage in the Senate.

ARTICLE. VI.

[1] All Debts contracted and Engagements entered into, before the Adoption of this Constitution, shall be as valid against the United States under this Constitution, as under the Confederation.

[2] This Constitution, and the Laws of the United States which shall be made in Pursuance thereof; and all Treaties made, or which shall be made, under the Authority of the United States, shall be the supreme Law of the Land; and the Judges in every State shall be bound thereby, any Thing in the Constitution or Laws of any State to the Contrary notwithstanding.

[3] The Senators and Representatives before mentioned, and the Members of the several State Legislatures, and all executive and judicial Officers, both of the United States and of the several States, shall be bound by Oath or Affirmation, to support this Constitution; but no religious Test shall ever be required as a Qualification to any Office or public Trust under the United States.

ARTICLE. VII.

The Ratification of the Conventions of nine States, shall be sufficient for the Establishment of this Constitution between the States so ratifying the Same.

DONE in Convention by the Unanimous Consent of the States present the Seventeenth Day of September in the Year of our Lord one thousand seven hundred and Eighty seven and of the Independence of the United States of America the Twelfth IN WITNESS whereof We have hereunto subscribed our Names,

G°. WASHINGTON—*Presid*ᵗ.
and deputy from Virginia

App. 11.10 The Constitution of the United States (continued)

[Signed also by the deputies of twelve States.]

Delaware

GEO: READ
GUNNING BEDFORD JUN
JOHN DICKINSON
RICHARD BASSETT
JACO: BROOM

Maryland

JAMES McHENRY
DAN OF ST THOS JENIFER
DANL. CARROLL.

Virginia

JOHN BLAIR—
JAMES MADISON JR.

North Carolina

WM BLOUNT
RICHD. DOBBS SPAIGHT.
HU WILLIAMSON

South Carolina

J. RUTLEDGE
CHARLES COTESWORTH PINCKNEY
CHARLES PINCKNEY
PIERCE BUTLER.

Georgia

WILLIAM FEW
ABR BALDWIN

New Hampshire

JOHN LANGDON
NICHOLAS GILMAN

Massachsetts

NATHANIEL GORHAM
RUFUS KING

Connecticut

WM. SAML. JOHNSON
ROGER SHERMAN

New York

ALEXANDER HAMILTON

New Jersey

WIL: LIVINGSTON
DAVID BREARLEY.
WM. PATERSON.
JONA: DAYTON

Pennsylvania

B FRANKLIN
THOMAS MIFFLIN
ROBT MORRIS
GEO. CLYMER
THOS. FITZSIMONS
JARED INGERSOLL
JAMES WILSON.
GOUV MORRIS

Attest: WILLIAM JACKSON *Secretary*

App. 11.10 The Constitution of the United States (continued)

ARTICLES IN ADDITION TO, AND AMENDMENT OF, THE CONSTITUTION OF THE UNITED STATES OF AMERICA, PROPOSED BY CONGRESS, AND RATIFIED BY THE LEGISLATURES OF THE SEVERAL STATES, PURSUANT TO THE FIFTH ARTICLE OF THE ORIGINAL CONSTITUTION [12]

ARTICLE [I.] [13]

Congress shall make no law respecting an establishment of religion, or prohibiting the free exercise thereof; or abridging the freedom of speech, or of the press; of the right of the people peaceably to assemble, and to petition the Government for a redress of grievances.

ARTICLE [II.]

A well regulated Militia, being necessary to the security of a free State, the right of the people to keep and bear Arms, shall not be infringed.

ARTICLE [III.]

No Soldier shall, in time of peace be quartered in any house, without the consent of the Owner, nor in time of war, but in a manner to be prescribed by law.

ARTICLE [IV.]

The right of the people to be secure in their persons, houses, papers, and effects, against unreasonable searches and seizures, shall not be violated, and no Warrants shall issue, but upon probable cause, supported by Oath or affirmation, and particularly describing the place to be searched, and the persons or things to be seized.

ARTICLE [V.]

No person shall be held to answer for a capital, or otherwise infamous crime, unless on a presentment or indictment of a Grand Jury, except in cases arising in the land or naval forces, or in the

[12] The first ten amendments of the Constitution of the United States (and two others, one of which failed of ratification and the other which later became the 27th amendment) were proposed to the legislatures of the several States by the First Congress on September 25, 1789. The first ten amendments were ratified by the following States, and the notifications of ratification by the Governors thereof were successively communicated by the President to Congress: New Jersey, November 20, 1789; Maryland, December 19, 1789; North Carolina, December 22, 1789; South Carolina, January 19, 1790; New Hampshire, January 25, 1790; Delaware, January 28, 1790; New York, February 24, 1790; Pennsylvania, March 10, 1790; Rhode Island, June 7, 1790; Vermont, November 3, 1791; and Virginia, December 15, 1791.

Ratification was completed on December 15, 1791.

The amendments were subsequently ratified by the legislatures of Massachusetts, March 2, 1939; Georgia, March 18, 1939; and Connecticut, April 19, 1939.

[13] Only the 13th, 14th, 15th, and 16th articles of amendment had numbers assigned to them at the time of ratification.

(13)

App. 11.10 The Constitution of the United States (continued)

Militia, when in actual service in time of War or public danger; nor shall any person be subject for the same offence to be twice put in jeopardy of life or limb; nor shall be compelled in any criminal case to be a witness against himself, nor be deprived of life, liberty, or property, without due process of law; nor shall private property be taken for public use, without just compensation.

ARTICLE [VI.]

In all criminal prosecutions, the accused shall enjoy the right to a speedy and public trial, by an impartial jury of the State and district wherein the crime shall have been committed, which district shall have been previously ascertained by law, and to be informed of the nature and cause of the accusation; to be confronted with the witnesses against him; to have compulsory process for obtaining witnesses in his favor, and to have the Assistance of Counsel for his defense.

ARTICLE [VII.]

In Suits at common law, where the value in controversy shall exceed twenty dollars, the right of trial by jury shall be preserved, and no fact tried by a jury, shall be otherwise re-examined in any Court of the United States, than according to the rules of the common law.

ARTICLE [VIII.]

Excessive bail shall not be required, nor excessive fines imposed, nor cruel and unusual punishments inflicted.

ARTICLE [IX.]

The enumeration in the Constitution, of certain rights, shall not be construed to deny or disparage others retained by the people.

ARTICLE [X.]

The powers not delegated to the United States by the Constitution, nor prohibited by it to the States, are reserved to the States respectively, or to the people.

[ARTICLE XI.]

The Judicial power of the United States shall not be construed to extend to any suit in law or equity, commenced or prosecuted against one of the United States by Citizens of another State, or by Citizens or Subjects of any Foreign State.

PROPOSAL AND RATIFICATION

The eleventh amendment to the Constitution of the United States was proposed to the legislatures of the several States by the Third Congress, on the 4th of March 1794; and was declared in a message from the President to Congress, dated the 8th of January, 1798, to have been ratified by the legislatures of three-fourths of the States. The dates of ratification were: New York, March 27, 1794; Rhode Island, March 31, 1794; Connecticut, May 8, 1794, New Hampshire, June 16, 1794; Massachusetts, June 26, 1794; Vermont, between October 9, 1794 and November 9, 1794; Virginia, November 18, 1794; Georgia, November 29, 1794; Kentucky, December 7,

App. 11.10 The Constitution of the United States (continued)

1794; Maryland, December 26, 1794; Delaware, January 23, 1795; North Carolina, February 7, 1795.

Ratification was completed on February 7, 1795.

The amendment was subsequently ratified by South Carolina on December 4, 1797. New Jersey and Pennsylvania did not take action on the amendment.

[ARTICLE XII.]

The Electors shall meet in their respective states, and vote by ballot for President and Vice-President, one of whom, at least, shall not be an inhabitant of the same state with themselves; they shall name in their ballots the person voted for as President, and in distinct ballots the person voted for as Vice-President, and they shall make distinct lists of all persons voted for as President, and of all persons voted for as Vice-President, and of the number of votes for each, which lists they shall sign and certify, and transmit sealed to the seat of the government of the United States, directed to the President of the Senate;—The President of the Senate shall, in the presence of the Senate and House of Representatives, open all the certificates and the votes shall then be counted;—The person having the greatest number of votes for President, shall be the President, if such number be a majority of the whole number of Electors appointed; and if no person have such majority, then from the persons having the highest numbers not exceeding three on the list of those voted for as President, the House of Representatives shall choose immediately, by ballot, the President. But in choosing the President, the votes shall be taken by states, the representation from each state having one vote; a quorum for this purpose shall consist of a member or members from two-thirds of the states, and a majority of all the states shall be necessary to a choice. And if the House of Representatives shall not choose a President whenever the right of choice shall devolve upon them, before the fourth day of March next following, then the Vice-President shall act as President, as in the case of the death or other constitutional disability of the President.[14]—The person having the greatest number of votes as Vice-President, shall be the Vice-President, if such number be a majority of the whole number of Electors appointed, and if no person have a majority, then from the two highest numbers on the list, the Senate shall choose the Vice-President; a quorum for the purpose shall consist of two-thirds of the whole number of Senators, and a majority of the whole number shall be necessary to a choice. But no person constitutionally ineligible to the office of President shall be eligible to that of Vice-President of the United States.

PROPOSAL AND RATIFICATION

The twelfth amendment to the Constitution of the United States was proposed to the legislatures of the several States by the Eighth Congress, on the 9th of December, 1803, in lieu of the original third paragraph of the first section of the second article; and was declared in a proclamation of the Secretary of State, dated the 25th of September, 1804, to have been ratified by the legislatures of 13 of the 17 States. The dates of ratification were: North Carolina, December 21, 1803; Maryland, December 24, 1803; Kentucky, December 27, 1803; Ohio, December 30, 1803; Pennsylvania, January 5, 1804; Vermont, January 30, 1804; Virginia, February 3, 1804; New York, February 10, 1804; New Jersey, February 22, 1804; Rhode Island, March

[14] This sentence has been superseded by section 3 of amendment XX.

App. 11.10 The Constitution of the United States (continued)

12, 1804; South Carolina, May 15, 1804; Georgia, May 19, 1804; New Hampshire, June 15, 1804.

Ratification was completed on June 15, 1804.

The amendment was subsequently ratified by Tennessee, July 27, 1804.

The amendment was rejected by Delaware, January 18, 1804; Massachusetts, February 3, 1804; Connecticut, at its session begun May 10, 1804.

ARTICLE XIII.

SECTION 1. Neither slavery nor involuntary servitude, except as a punishment for crime whereof the party shall have been duly convicted, shall exist within the United States, or any place subject to their jurisdiction.

SECTION 2. Congress shall have power to enforce this article by appropriate legislation.

PROPOSAL AND RATIFICATION

The thirteenth amendment to the Constitution of the United States was proposed to the legislatures of the several States by the Thirty-eighth Congress, on the 31st day of January, 1865, and was declared, in a proclamation of the Secretary of State, dated the 18th of December, 1865, to have been ratified by the legislatures of twenty-seven of the thirty-six States. The dates of ratification were: Illinois, February 1, 1865; Rhode Island, February 2, 1865; Michigan, February 2, 1865; Maryland, February 3, 1865; New York, February 3, 1865; Pennsylvania, February 3, 1865; West Virginia, February 3, 1865; Missouri, February 6, 1865; Maine, February 7, 1865; Kansas, February 7, 1865; Massachusetts, February 7, 1865; Virginia, February 9, 1865; Ohio, February 10, 1865; Indiana, February 13, 1865; Nevada, February 16, 1865; Louisiana, February 17, 1865; Minnesota, February 23, 1865; Wisconsin, February 24, 1865; Vermont, March 9, 1865; Tennessee, April 7, 1865; Arkansas, April 14, 1865; Connecticut, May 4, 1865; New Hampshire, July 1, 1865; South Carolina, November 13, 1865; Alabama, December 2, 1865; North Carolina, December 4, 1865; Georgia, December 6, 1865.

Ratification was completed on December 6, 1865.

The amendment was subsequently ratified by Oregon, December 8, 1865; California, December 19, 1865; Florida, December 28, 1865 (Florida again ratified on June 9, 1868, upon its adoption of a new constitution); Iowa, January 15, 1866; New Jersey, January 23, 1866 (after having rejected the amendment on March 16, 1865); Texas, February 18, 1870; Delaware, February 12, 1901 (after having rejected the amendment on February 8, 1865); Kentucky, March 18, 1976 (after having rejected it on February 24, 1865).

The amendment was rejected (and not subsequently ratified) by Mississippi, December 4, 1865.

ARTICLE XIV.

SECTION 1. All persons born or naturalized in the United States, and subject to the jurisdiction thereof, are citizens of the United States and of the State wherein they reside. No State shall make or enforce any law which shall abridge the privileges or immunities of citizens of the United States; nor shall any State deprive any person of life, liberty, or property, without due process of law; nor deny to any person within its jurisdiction the equal protection of the laws.

SECTION 2. Representatives shall be apportioned among the several States according to their respective numbers, counting the whole number of persons in each State, excluding Indians not taxed. But when the right to vote at any election for the choice of electors for President and Vice President of the United States, Representatives in Congress, the Executive and Judicial officers of a State, or the members of the Legislature thereof, is denied to any of the male inhabitants of such State, being twenty-one years of

App. 11.10 The Constitution of the United States (continued)

age,[15] and citizens of the United States, or in any way abridged, except for participation in rebellion, or other crime, the basis of representation therein shall be reduced in the proportion which the number of such male citizens shall bear to the whole number of male citizens twenty-one years of age in such State.

SECTION 3. No person shall be a Senator or Representative in Congress, or elector of President and Vice President, or hold any office, civil or military, under the United States, or under any State, who, having previously taken an oath, as a member of Congress, or as an officer of the United States, or as a member of any State legislature, or as an executive or judicial officer of any State, to support the Constitution of the United States, shall have engaged in insurrection or rebellion against the same, or given aid or comfort to the enemies thereof. But Congress may by a vote of two-thirds of each House, remove such disability.

SECTION 4. The validity of the public debt of the United States, authorized by law, including debts incurred for payment of pensions and bounties for services in suppressing insurrection or rebellion, shall not be questioned. But neither the United States nor any State shall assume or pay any debt or obligation incurred in aid of insurrection or rebellion against the United States, or any claim for the loss or emancipation of any slave; but all such debts, obligations and claims shall be held illegal and void.

SECTION 5. The Congress shall have power to enforce, by appropriate legislation, the provisions of this article.

PROPOSAL AND RATIFICATION

The fourteenth amendment to the Constitution of the United States was proposed to the legislatures of the several States by the Thirty-ninth Congress, on the 13th of June, 1866. It was declared, in a certificate of the Secretary of State dated July 28, 1868 to have been ratified by the legislatures of 28 of the 37 States. The dates of ratification were: Connecticut, June 25, 1866; New Hampshire, July 6, 1866; Tennessee, July 19, 1866; New Jersey, September 11, 1866 (subsequently the legislature rescinded its ratification, and on March 24, 1868, readopted its resolution of rescission over the Governor's veto, and on Nov. 12, 1980, expressed support for the amendment); Oregon, September 19, 1866 (and rescinded its ratification on October 15, 1868); Vermont, October 30, 1866; Ohio, January 4, 1867 (and rescinded its ratification on January 15, 1868); New York, January 10, 1867; Kansas, January 11, 1867; Illinois, January 15, 1867; West Virginia, January 16, 1867; Michigan, January 16, 1867; Minnesota, January 16, 1867; Maine, January 19, 1867; Nevada, January 22, 1867; Indiana, January 23, 1867; Missouri, January 25, 1867; Rhode Island, February 7, 1867; Wisconsin, February 7, 1867; Pennsylvania, February 12, 1867; Massachusetts, March 20, 1867; Nebraska, June 15, 1867; Iowa, March 16, 1868; Arkansas, April 6, 1868; Florida, June 9, 1868; North Carolina, July 4 1868 (after having rejected it on December 14, 1866); Louisiana, July 9, 1868 (after having rejected it on February 6, 1867); South Carolina, July 9, 1868 (after having rejected it on December 20, 1866).

Ratification was completed on July 9, 1868.

The amendment was subsequently ratified by Alabama, July 13, 1868; Georgia, July 21, 1868 (after having rejected it on November 9, 1866); Virginia, October 8, 1869 (after having rejected it on January 9, 1867); Mississippi, January 17, 1870; Texas, February 18, 1870 (after having rejected it on October 27, 1866); Delaware, February 12, 1901 (after having rejected it on February 8, 1867); Maryland April 4, 1959 (after having rejected it on March 23, 1867); California, May 6 1959; Kentucky, March 18, 1976 (after having rejected it on January 8, 1867).

[15] See amendment XIX and section 1 of amendment XXVI.

App. 11.10 The Constitution of the United States (continued)

ARTICLE XV.

SECTION 1. The right of citizens of the United States to vote shall not be denied or abridged by the United States or by any State on account of race, color, or previous condition of servitude.

SECTION 2. The Congress shall have power to enforce this article by appropriate legislation.

PROPOSAL AND RATIFICATION

The fifteenth amendment to the Constitution of the United States was proposed to the legislatures of the several States by the Fortieth Congress, on the 26th of February, 1869, and was declared, in a proclamation of the Secretary of State, dated March 30, 1870, to have been ratified by the legislatures of twenty-nine of the thirty-seven States. The dates of ratification were: Nevada, March 1, 1869; West Virginia, March 3, 1869; Illinois, March 5, 1869; Louisiana, March 5, 1869; North Carolina, March 5, 1869; Michigan, March 8, 1869; Wisconsin, March 9, 1869; Maine, March 11, 1869; Massachusetts, March 12, 1869; Arkansas, March 15, 1869; South Carolina, March 15, 1869; Pennsylvania, March 25, 1869; New York, April 14, 1869 (and the legislature of the same State passed a resolution January 5, 1870, to withdraw its consent to it, which action it rescinded on March 30, 1970); Indiana, May 14, 1869; Connecticut, May 19, 1869; Florida, June 14, 1869; New Hampshire, July 1, 1869; Virginia, October 8, 1869; Vermont, October 20, 1869; Missouri, January 7, 1870; Minnesota, January 13, 1870; Mississippi, January 17, 1870; Rhode Island, January 18, 1870; Kansas, January 19, 1870; Ohio, January 27, 1870 (after having rejected it on April 30, 1869); Georgia, February 2, 1870; Iowa, February 3, 1870.

Ratification was completed on February 3, 1870, unless the withdrawal of ratification by New York was effective; in which event ratification was completed on February 17, 1870, when Nebraska ratified.

The amendment was subsequently ratified by Texas, February 18, 1870; New Jersey, February 15, 1871 (after having rejected it on February 7, 1870); Delaware, February 12, 1901 (after having rejected it on March 18, 1869); Oregon, February 24, 1959; California, April 3, 1962 (after having rejected it on January 28, 1870); Kentucky, March 18, 1976 (after having rejected it on March 12, 1869).

The amendment was approved by the Governor of Maryland, May 7, 1973; Maryland having previously rejected it on February 26, 1870.

The amendment was rejected (and not subsequently ratified) by Tennessee, November 16, 1869.

ARTICLE XVI.

The Congress shall have power to lay and collect taxes on incomes, from whatever source derived, without apportionment among the several States, and without regard to any census or enumeration.

PROPOSAL AND RATIFICATION

The sixteenth amendment to the Constitution of the United States was proposed to the legislatures of the several States by the Sixty-first Congress on the 12th of July, 1909, and was declared, in a proclamation of the Secretary of State, dated the 25th of February, 1913, to have been ratified by 36 of the 48 States. The dates of ratification were: Alabama, August 10, 1909; Kentucky, February 8, 1910; South Carolina, February 19, 1910; Illinois, March 1, 1910; Mississippi, March 7, 1910; Oklahoma, March 10, 1910; Maryland, April 8, 1910; Georgia, August 3, 1910; Texas, August 16, 1910; Ohio, January 19, 1911; Idaho, January 20, 1911; Oregon, January 23, 1911; Washington, January 26, 1911; Montana, January 30, 1911; Indiana, January 30, 1911; California, January 31, 1911; Nevada, January 31, 1911; South Dakota, February 3, 1911; Nebraska, February 9, 1911; North Carolina, February 11, 1911; Colorado, February 15, 1911; North Dakota, February 17, 1911; Kansas, February 18, 1911; Michigan, February 23, 1911; Iowa, February 24, 1911; Missouri, March 16, 1911; Maine, March 31, 1911; Tennessee, April 7, 1911; Arkansas, April 22, 1911 (after having rejected it earlier); Wisconsin, May 26, 1911; New York, July 12, 1911; Arizona, April 6, 1912; Minnesota, June 11, 1912; Louisiana, June 28, 1912; West Virginia, January 31, 1913; New Mexico, February 3, 1913.

Ratification was completed on February 3, 1913.

App. 11.10 The Constitution of the United States (continued)

The amendment was subsequently ratified by Massachusetts, March 4, 1913; New Hampshire, March 7, 1913 (after having rejected it on March 2, 1911).

The amendment was rejected (and not subsequently ratified) by Connecticut, Rhode Island, and Utah.

[ARTICLE XVII.]

The Senate of the United States shall be composed of two Senators from each State, elected by the people thereof, for six years; and each Senator shall have one vote. The electors in each State shall have the qualifications requisite for electors of the most numerous branch of the State legislatures.

When vacancies happen in the representation of any State in the Senate, the executive authority of such State shall issue writs of election to fill such vacancies: *Provided*, That the legislature of any State may empower the executive thereof to make temporary appointments until the people fill the vacancies by election as the legislature may direct.

This amendment shall not be so construed as to affect the election or term of any Senator chosen before it becomes valid as part of the Constitution.

PROPOSAL AND RATIFICATION

The seventeenth amendment to the Constitution of the United States was proposed to the legislatures of the several States by the Sixty-second Congress on the 13th of May, 1912, and was declared, in a proclamation of the Secretary of State, dated the 31st of May, 1913, to have been ratified by the legislatures of 36 of the 48 States. The dates of ratification were: Massachusetts, May 22, 1912; Arizona, June 3, 1912; Minnesota, June 10, 1912; New York, January 15, 1913; Kansas, January 17, 1913; Oregon, January 23, 1913; North Carolina, January 25, 1913; California, January 28, 1913; Michigan, January 28, 1913; Iowa, January 30, 1913; Montana, January 30, 1913; Idaho, January 31, 1913; West Virginia, February 4, 1913; Colorado, February 5, 1913; Nevada, February 6, 1913; Texas, February 7, 1913; Washington, February 7, 1913; Wyoming, February 8, 1913; Arkansas, February 11, 1913; Maine, February 11, 1913; Illinois, February 13, 1913; North Dakota, February 14, 1913; Wisconsin, February 18, 1913; Indiana, February 19, 1913; New Hampshire, February 19, 1913; Vermont, February 19, 1913; South Dakota, February 19, 1913; Oklahoma, February 24, 1913; Ohio, February 25, 1913; Missouri, March 7, 1913; New Mexico, March 13, 1913; Nebraska, March 14, 1913; New Jersey, March 17, 1913; Tennessee, April 1, 1913; Pennsylvania, April 2, 1913; Connecticut, April 8, 1913.

Ratification was completed on April 8, 1913.

The amendment was subsequently ratified by Louisiana, June 11, 1914.

The amendment was rejected by Utah (and not subsequently ratified) on February 26, 1913.

ARTICLE [XVIII].[16]

SECTION 1. After one year from the ratification of this article the manufacture, sale, or transportation of intoxicating liquors within, the importation thereof into, or the exportation thereof from the United States and all territory subject to the jurisdiction thereof for beverage purposes is hereby prohibited.

SEC. 2. The Congress and the several States shall have concurrent power to enforce this article by appropriate legislation.

SEC. 3. This article shall be inoperative unless it shall have been ratified as an amendment to the Constitution by the legislatures of the several States, as provided in the Constitution, within seven

[16] Repealed by section 1 of amendment XXI.

App. 11.10 The Constitution of the United States (continued)

years from the date of the submission hereof to the States by the Congress.

PROPOSAL AND RATIFICATION

The eighteenth amendment to the Constitution of the United States was proposed to the legislatures of the several States by the Sixty-fifth Congress, on the 18th of December, 1917, and was declared, in a proclamation of the Secretary of State, dated the 29th of January, 1919, to have been ratified by the legislatures of 36 of the 48 States. The dates of ratification were: Mississippi, January 8, 1918; Virginia, January 11, 1918; Kentucky, January 14, 1918; North Dakota, January 25, 1918; South Carolina, January 29, 1918; Maryland, February 13, 1918; Montana, February 19, 1918; Texas, March 4, 1918; Delaware, March 18, 1918; South Dakota, March 20, 1918; Massachusetts, April 2, 1918; Arizona, May 24, 1918; Georgia, June 26, 1918; Louisiana, August 3, 1918; Florida, December 3, 1918; Michigan, January 2, 1919; Ohio, January 7, 1919; Oklahoma, January 7, 1919; Idaho, January 8, 1919; Maine, January 8, 1919; West Virginia, January 9, 1919; California, January 13, 1919; Tennessee, January 13, 1919; Washington, January 13, 1919; Arkansas, January 14, 1919; Kansas, January 14, 1919; Alabama, January 15, 1919; Colorado, January 15, 1919; Iowa, January 15, 1919; New Hampshire, January 15, 1919; Oregon, January 15, 1919; Nebraska, January 16, 1919; North Carolina, January 16, 1919; Utah, January 16, 1919; Missouri, January 16, 1919; Wyoming, January 16, 1919.

Ratification was completed on January 16, 1919. See *Dillon v. Gloss*, 256 U.S. 368, 376 (1921).

The amendment was subsequently ratified by Minnesota on January 17, 1919; Wisconsin, January 17, 1919; New Mexico, January 20, 1919; Nevada, January 21, 1919; New York, January 29, 1919; Vermont, January 29, 1919; Pennsylvania, February 25, 1919; Connecticut, May 6, 1919; and New Jersey, March 9, 1922.

The amendment was rejected (and not subsequently ratified) by Rhode Island.

ARTICLE [XIX].

The right of citizens of the United States to vote shall not be denied or abridged by the United States or by any State on account of sex.

Congress shall have power to enforce this article by appropriate legislation.

PROPOSAL AND RATIFICATION

The nineteenth amendment to the Constitution of the United States was proposed to the legislatures of the several States by the Sixty-sixth Congress, on the 4th of June, 1919, and was declared, in a proclamation of the Secretary of State, dated the 26th of August, 1920, to have been ratified by the legislatures of 36 of the 48 States. The dates of ratification were: Illinois, June 10, 1919 (and that State readopted its resolution of ratification June 17, 1919); Michigan, June 10, 1919; Wisconsin, June 10, 1919; Kansas, June 16, 1919; New York, June 16, 1919; Ohio, June 16, 1919; Pennsylvania, June 24, 1919; Massachusetts, June 25, 1919; Texas, June 28, 1919; Iowa, July 2, 1919; Missouri, July 3, 1919; Arkansas, July 28, 1919; Montana, August 2, 1919; Nebraska, August 2, 1919; Minnesota, September 8, 1919; New Hampshire, September 10, 1919; Utah, October 2, 1919; California, November 1, 1919; Maine, November 5, 1919; North Dakota, December 1, 1919; South Dakota, December 4, 1919; Colorado, December 15, 1919; Kentucky, January 6, 1920; Rhode Island, January 6, 1920; Oregon, January 13, 1920; Indiana, January 16, 1920; Wyoming, January 27, 1920; Nevada, February 7, 1920; New Jersey, February 9, 1920; Idaho, February 11, 1920; Arizona, February 12, 1920; New Mexico, February 21, 1920; Oklahoma, February 28, 1920; West Virginia, March 10, 1920; Washington, March 22, 1920; Tennessee, August 18, 1920.

Ratification was completed on August 18, 1920.

The amendment was subsequently ratified by Connecticut on September 14, 1920 (and that State reaffirmed on September 21, 1920); Vermont, February 8, 1921; Delaware, March 6, 1923 (after having rejected in on June 2, 1920); Maryland, March 29, 1941 (after having rejected it on February 24, 1920, ratification certified on February 25, 1958); Virginia, February 21, 1952 (after having rejected it on February 12, 1920); Alabama, September 8, 1953 (after having rejected it on September 22, 1919); Florida, May 13, 1969; South Carolina, July 1, 1969 (after having rejected it on January 28, 1920, ratification certified on August 22, 1973); Georgia, February

App. 11.10 The Constitution of the United States (continued)

20, 1970 (after having rejected it on July 24, 1919); Louisiana, June 11, 1970 (after having rejected it on July 1, 1920); North Carolina, May 6, 1971; Mississippi, March 22, 1984 (after having rejected it on March 29, 1920).

ARTICLE [XX.]

SECTION 1. The terms of the President and Vice President shall end at noon on the 20th day of January, and the terms of Senators and Representatives at noon on the 3d day of January, of the years in which such terms would have ended if this article had not been ratified; and the terms of their successors shall then begin.

SEC. 2. The Congress shall assemble at least once in every year, and such meeting shall begin at noon on the 3d day of January, unless they shall by law appoint a different day.

SEC. 3. If, at the time fixed for the beginning of the term of the President, the President elect shall have died, the Vice President elect shall become President. If a President shall not have been chosen before the time fixed for the beginning of his term, or if the President elect shall have failed to qualify, then the Vice President elect shall act as President until a President shall have qualified; and the Congress may by law provide for the case wherein neither a President elect nor a Vice President elect shall have qualified, declaring who shall then act as President, or the manner in which one who is to act shall be selected, and such person shall act accordingly until a President or Vice President shall have qualified.

SEC. 4. The Congress may by law provide for the case of the death of any of the persons from whom the House of Representatives may choose a President whenever the right of choice shall have devolved upon them, and for the case of the death of any of the persons from whom the Senate may choose a Vice President whenever the right of choice shall have devolved upon them.

SEC. 5. Sections 1 and 2 shall take effect on the 15th day of October following the ratification of this article.

SEC. 6. This article shall be inoperative unless it shall have been ratified as an amendment to the Constitution by the legislatures of three-fourths of the several States within seven years from the date of its submission.

PROPOSAL AND RATIFICATION

The twentieth amendment to the Constitution was proposed to the legislatures of the several states by the Seventy-Second Congress, on the 2d day of March, 1932, and was declared, in a proclamation by the Secretary of State, dated on the 6th day of February, 1933, to have been ratified by the legislatures of 36 of the 48 States. The dates of ratification were: Virginia, March 4, 1932; New York, March 11, 1932; Mississippi, March 16, 1932; Arkansas, March 17, 1932; Kentucky, March 17, 1932; New Jersey, March 21, 1932; South Carolina, March 25, 1932; Michigan, March 31, 1932; Maine, April 1, 1932; Rhode Island, April 14, 1932; Illinois, April 21, 1932; Louisiana, June 22, 1932; West Virginia, July 30, 1932; Pennsylvania, August 11, 1932; Indiana, August 15, 1932; Texas, September 7, 1932; Alabama, September 13, 1932; California, January 4, 1933; North Carolina, January 5, 1933; North Dakota, January 9, 1933; Minnesota, January 12, 1933; Arizona, January 13, 1933, Montana, January 13, 1933; Nebraska, January 13, 1933; Oklahoma, January 13, 1933; Kansas, January 16, 1933; Oregon, January 16, 1933; Delaware, January 19, 1933; Washington, January 19, 1933; Wyoming, January 19, 1933; Iowa, January 20, 1933, South Dakota, January 20, 1933; Tennessee, January 20, 1933; Idaho, January 21, 1933; New Mexico, January 21, 1933; Georgia, January 23, 1933; Missouri, January 23, 1933; Ohio, January 23, 1933; Utah, January 23, 1933.

Ratification was completed on January 23, 1933.

App. 11.10 The Constitution of the United States (continued)

The amendment was subsequently ratified by Massachusetts on January 24, 1933; Wisconsin, January 24, 1933; Colorado, January 24, 1933; Nevada, January 26, 1933; Connecticut, January 27, 1933; New Hampshire, January 31, 1933; Vermont, February 2, 1933; Maryland, March 24, 1933; Florida, April 26, 1933.

ARTICLE [XXI.]

SECTION 1. The eighteenth article of amendment to the Constitution of the United States is hereby repealed.

SECTION 2. The transportation or importation into any State, Territory, or possession of the United States for delivery or use therein of intoxicating liquors, in violation of the laws thereof, is hereby prohibited.

SECTION 3. This article shall be inoperative unless it shall have been ratified as an amendment to the Constitution by conventions in the several States, as provided in the Constitution, within seven years from the date of the submission hereof to the States by the Congress.

PROPOSAL AND RATIFICATION

The twenty-first amendment to the Constitution was proposed to the several states by the Seventy-Second Congress, on the 20th day of February, 1933, and was declared, in a proclamation by the Secretary of State, dated on the 5th day of December, 1933, to have been ratified by 36 of the 48 States. The dates of ratification were: Michigan, April 10, 1933; Wisconsin, April 25, 1933; Rhode Island, May 8, 1933; Wyoming, May 25, 1933; New Jersey, June 1, 1933; Delaware, June 24, 1933; Indiana, June 26, 1933; Massachusetts, June 26, 1933; New York, June 27, 1933; Illinois, July 10, 1933; Iowa, July 10, 1933; Connecticut, July 11, 1933; New Hampshire, July 11, 1933; California, July 24, 1933; West Virginia, July 25, 1933; Arkansas, August 1, 1933; Oregon, August 7, 1933; Alabama, August 8, 1933; Tennessee, August 11, 1933; Missouri, August 29, 1933; Arizona, September 5, 1933; Nevada, September 5, 1933; Vermont, September 23, 1933; Colorado, September 26, 1933; Washington, October 3, 1933; Minnesota, October 10, 1933; Idaho, October 17, 1933, Maryland, October 18, 1933; Virginia, October 25, 1933; New Mexico, November 2, 1933; Florida, November 14, 1933; Texas, November 24, 1933; Kentucky, November 27, 1933; Ohio, December 5, 1933; Pennsylvania, December 5, 1933; Utah, December 5, 1933.

Ratification was completed on December 5, 1933.

The amendment was subsequently ratified by Maine, on December 6, 1933, and by Montana, on August 6, 1934.

The amendment was rejected (and not subsequently ratified) by South Carolina, on December 4, 1933.

ARTICLE [XXII.]

SECTION 1. No person shall be elected to the office of the President more than twice, and no person who has held the office of President, or acted as President, for more than two years of a term of which some other person was elected President shall be elected to the office of the President more than once. But this Article shall not apply to any person holding the office of President when this Article was proposed by the Congress, and shall not prevent any person who may be holding the office of President, or acting as President, during the term within which this Article becomes operative from holding the office of President or acting as President during the remainder of such term.

SEC. 2. This article shall be inoperative unless it shall have been ratified as an amendment to the Constitution by the legislatures of three-fourths of the several States within seven years from the date of its submission to the States by the Congress.

App. 11.10 The Constitution of the United States (continued)

PROPOSAL AND RATIFICATION

This amendment was proposed to the legislatures of the several States by the Eightieth Congress on Mar. 21, 1947 by House Joint Res. No. 27, and was declared by the Administrator of General Services, on Mar. 1, 1951, to have been ratified by the legislatures of 36 of the 48 States. The dates of ratification were: Maine, March 31, 1947; Michigan, March 31, 1947; Iowa, April 1, 1947; Kansas, April 1, 1947; New Hampshire, April 1, 1947; Delaware, April 2, 1947; Illinois, April 3, 1947; Oregon, April 3, 1947; Colorado, April 12, 1947; California, April 15, 1947; New Jersey, April 15, 1947; Vermont, April 15, 1947; Ohio, April 16, 1947; Wisconsin, April 16, 1947; Pennsylvania, April 29, 1947; Connecticut, May 21, 1947; Missouri, May 22, 1947; Nebraska, May 23, 1947; Virginia, January 28, 1948; Mississippi, February 12, 1948; New York, March 9, 1948; South Dakota, January 21, 1949; North Dakota, February 25, 1949; Louisiana, May 17, 1950; Montana, January 25, 1951; Indiana, January 29, 1951; Idaho, January 30, 1951; New Mexico, February 12, 1951; Wyoming, February 12, 1951; Arkansas, February 15, 1951; Georgia, February 17, 1951; Tennessee, February 20, 1951; Texas, February 22, 1951; Nevada, February 26, 1951; Utah, February 26, 1951; Minnesota, February 27, 1951.

Ratification was completed on February 27, 1951.

The amendment was subsequently ratified by North Carolina on February 28, 1951; South Carolina, March 13, 1951; Maryland, March 14, 1951; Florida, April 16, 1951; Alabama, May 4, 1951.

The amendment was rejected (and not subsequently ratified) by Oklahoma in June 1947, and Massachusetts on June 9, 1949.

CERTIFICATION OF VALIDITY

Publication of the certifying statement of the Administrator of General Services that the amendment had become valid was made on Mar. 1, 1951, F.R. Doc. 51–2940, 16 F.R. 2019.

ARTICLE [XXIII.]

SECTION 1. The District constituting the seat of Government of the United States shall appoint in such manner as the Congress may direct:

A number of electors of President and Vice President equal to the whole number of Senators and Representatives in Congress to which the District would be entitled if it were a State, but in no event more than the least populous State; they shall be in addition to those appointed by the States, but they shall be considered, for the purposes of the election of President and Vice President, to be electors appointed by a State; and they shall meet in the District and perform such duties as provided by the twelfth article of amendment.

SEC. 2. The Congress shall have power to enforce this article by appropriate legislation.

PROPOSAL AND RATIFICATION

This amendment was proposed by the Eighty-sixth Congress on June 17, 1960 and was declared by the Administrator of General Services on Apr. 3, 1961, to have been ratified by 38 of the 50 States. The dates of ratification were: Hawaii, June 23, 1960 (and that State made a technical correction to its resolution on June 30, 1960); Massachusetts, August 22, 1960; New Jersey, December 19, 1960; New York, January 17, 1961; California, January 19, 1961; Oregon, January 27, 1961; Maryland, January 30, 1961; Idaho, January 31, 1961; Maine, January 31, 1961; Minnesota, January 31, 1961; New Mexico, February 1, 1961; Nevada, February 2, 1961; Montana, February 6, 1961; South Dakota, February 6, 1961; Colorado, February 8, 1961; Washington, February 9, 1961; West Virginia, February 9, 1961; Alaska, February 10, 1961; Wyoming, February 13, 1961; Delaware, February 20, 1961; Utah, February 21, 1961; Wisconsin, February 21, 1961; Pennsylvania, February 28, 1961; Indiana, March 3, 1961; North Dakota, March 3, 1961; Tennessee, March 6, 1961; Michigan, March 8, 1961; Connecticut, March 9, 1961; Arizona, March 10, 1961; Illinois, March 14, 1961; Nebraska, March 15, 1961; Vermont, March 15, 1961;

App. 11.10 The Constitution of the United States (continued)

Iowa, March 16, 1961; Missouri, March 20, 1961; Oklahoma, March 21, 1961; Rhode Island, March 22, 1961; Kansas, March 29, 1961; Ohio, March 29, 1961.

Ratification was completed on March 29, 1961.

The amendment was subsequently ratified by New Hampshire on March 30, 1961 (when that State annulled and then repeated its ratification of March 29, 1961).

The amendment was rejected (and not subsequently ratified) by Arkansas on January 24, 1961.

CERTIFICATION OF VALIDITY

Publication of the certifying statement of the Administrator of General Services that the amendment had become valid was made on Apr. 3, 1961, F.R. Doc. 61–3017, 26 F.R. 2808.

ARTICLE [XXIV.]

SECTION 1. The right of citizens of the United States to vote in any primary or other election for President or Vice President, for electors for President or Vice President, or for Senator or Representative in Congress, shall not be denied or abridged by the United States or any State by reason of failure to pay any poll tax or other tax.

SEC. 2. The Congress shall have power to enforce this article by appropriate legislation.

PROPOSAL AND RATIFICATION

This amendment was proposed by the Eighty-seventh Congress by Senate Joint Resolution No. 29, which was approved by the Senate on March 27, 1962, and by the House of Representatives on Aug. 27, 1962. It was declared by the Administrator of General Services on Feb. 4, 1964, to have been ratified by the legislatures of 38 of the 50 States.

This amendment was ratified by the following States:

Illinois, November 14, 1962; New Jersey, December 3, 1962; Oregon, January 25, 1963; Montana, January 28, 1963; West Virginia, February 1, 1963; New York, February 4, 1963; Maryland, February 6, 1963; California, February 7, 1963; Alaska, February 11, 1963; Rhode Island, February 14, 1963; Indiana, February 19, 1963; Utah, February 20, 1963; Michigan, February 20, 1963; Colorado, February 21, 1963; Ohio, February 27, 1963; Minnesota, February 27, 1963; New Mexico, March 5, 1963; Hawaii, March 6, 1963; North Dakota, March 7, 1963; Idaho, March 8, 1963; Washington, March 14, 1963; Vermont, March 15, 1963; Nevada, March 19, 1963; Connecticut, March 20, 1963; Tennessee, March 21, 1963; Pennsylvania, March 25, 1963; Wisconsin, March 26, 1963; Kansas, March 28, 1963; Massachusetts, March 28, 1963; Nebraska, April 4, 1963; Florida, April 18, 1963; Iowa, April 24, 1963; Delaware, May 1, 1963; Missouri, May 13, 1963; New Hampshire, June 12, 1963; Kentucky, June 27, 1963; Maine, January 16, 1964; South Dakota, January 23, 1964; Virginia, February 25, 1977.

Ratification was completed on January 23, 1964.

The amendment was subsequently ratified by North Carolina on May 3, 1989.

The amendment was rejected by Mississippi (and not subsequently ratified) on December 20, 1962.

CERTIFICATION OF VALIDITY

Publication of the certifying statement of the Administrator of General Services that the amendment had become valid was made on Feb. 5, 1964, F.R. Doc. 64–1229, 29 F.R. 1715.

ARTICLE [XXV.]

SECTION 1. In case of the removal of the President from office or of his death or resignation, the Vice President shall become President.

SEC. 2. Whenever there is a vacancy in the office of the Vice President, the President shall nominate a Vice President who shall

App. 11.10 The Constitution of the United States (continued)

take office upon confirmation by a majority vote of both Houses of Congress.

SEC. 3. Whenever the President transmits to the President pro tempore of the Senate and the Speaker of the House of Representatives his written declaration that he is unable to discharge the powers and duties of his office, and until he transmits to them a written declaration to the contrary, such powers and duties shall be discharged by the Vice President as Acting President.

SEC. 4. Whenever the Vice President and a majority of either the principal officers of the executive departments or of such other body as Congress may by law provide, transmit to the President pro tempore of the Senate and the Speaker of the House of Representatives their written declaration that the President is unable to discharge the powers and duties of his office, the Vice President shall immediately assume the powers and duties of the office as Acting President.

Thereafter, when the President transmits to the President pro tempore of the Senate and the Speaker of the House of Representatives his written declaration that no inability exists, he shall resume the powers and duties of his office unless the Vice President and a majority of either the principal officers of the executive department[17] or of such other body as Congress may by law provide, transmit within four days to the President pro tempore of the Senate and the Speaker of the House of Representatives their written declaration that the President is unable to discharge the powers and duties of his office. Thereupon Congress shall decide the issue, assembling within forty-eight hours for that purpose if not in session. If the Congress, within twenty-one days after receipt of the latter written declaration, or, if Congress is not in session, within twenty-one days after Congress is required to assemble, determines by two-thirds vote of both Houses that the President is unable to discharge the powers and duties of his office, the Vice President shall continue to discharge the same as Acting President; otherwise, the President shall resume the powers and duties of his office.

PROPOSAL AND RATIFICATION

This amendment was proposed by the Eighty-ninth Congress by Senate Joint Resolution No. 1, which was approved by the Senate on Feb. 19, 1965, and by the House of Representatives, in amended form, on Apr. 13, 1965. The House of Representatives agreed to a Conference Report on June 30, 1965, and the Senate agreed to the Conference Report on July 6, 1965. It was declared by the Administrator of General Services, on Feb. 23, 1967, to have been ratified by the legislatures of 39 of the 50 States.

This amendment was ratified by the following States:

Nebraska, July 12, 1965; Wisconsin, July 13, 1965; Oklahoma, July 15, 1965; Massachusetts, August 9, 1965; Pennsylvania, August 18, 1965; Kentucky, September 15, 1965; Arizona, September 22, 1965; Michigan, October 5, 1965; Indiana, October 20, 1965; California, October 21, 1965; Arkansas, November 4, 1965; New Jersey, November 29, 1965; Delaware, December 7, 1965; Utah, January 17, 1966; West Virginia, January 20, 1966; Maine, January 24, 1966; Rhode Island, January 28, 1966; Colorado, February 3, 1966; New Mexico, February 3, 1966; Kansas, February 8, 1966; Vermont, February 10, 1966; Alaska, February 18, 1966; Idaho, March 2, 1966; Hawaii, March 3, 1966; Virginia, March 8, 1966; Mississippi, March 10, 1966; New York, March 14, 1966; Maryland, March 23, 1966; Missouri, March 30, 1966; New Hampshire, June 13, 1966; Louisiana, July 5, 1966; Tennessee, Janu-

[17] So in original. Probably should be "departments".

App. 11.10 The Constitution of the United States (continued)

ary 12, 1967; Wyoming, January 25, 1967; Washington, January 26, 1967; Iowa, January 26, 1967; Oregon, February 2, 1967; Minnesota, February 10, 1967; Nevada, February 10, 1967.

Ratification was completed on February 10, 1967.

The amendment was subsequently ratified by Connecticut, February 14, 1967; Montana, February 15, 1967; South Dakota, March 6, 1967; Ohio, March 7, 1967; Alabama, March 14, 1967; North Carolina, March 22, 1967; Illinois, March 22, 1967; Texas, April 25, 1967; Florida, May 25, 1967.

CERTIFICATION OF VALIDITY

Publication of the certifying statement of the Administrator of General Services that the amendment had become valid was made on Feb. 25, 1967, F.R. Doc. 67–2208, 32 F.R. 3287.

ARTICLE [XXVI.]

SECTION 1. The right of citizens of the United States, who are eighteen years of age or older, to vote shall not be denied or abridged by the United States or by any State on account of age.

SEC. 2. The Congress shall have power to enforce this article by appropriate legislation.

PROPOSAL AND RATIFICATION

This amendment was proposed by the Ninety-second Congress by Senate Joint Resolution No. 7, which was approved by the Senate on Mar. 10, 1971, and by the House of Representatives on Mar. 23, 1971. It was declared by the Administrator of General Services on July 5, 1971, to have been ratified by the legislature of 39 of the 50 States.

This amendment was ratified by the following States: Connecticut, March 23, 1971; Delaware, March 23, 1971; Minnesota, March 23, 1971; Tennessee, March 23, 1971; Washington, March 23, 1971; Hawaii, March 24, 1971; Massachusetts, March 24, 1971; Montana, March 29, 1971; Arkansas, March 30, 1971; Idaho, March 30, 1971; Iowa, March 30, 1971; Nebraska, April 2, 1971; New Jersey, April 3, 1971; Kansas, April 7, 1971; Michigan, April 7, 1971; Alaska, April 8, 1971; Maryland, April 8, 1971; Indiana, April 8, 1971; Maine, April 9, 1971; Vermont, April 16, 1971; Louisiana, April 17, 1971; California, April 19, 1971; Colorado, April 27, 1971; Pennsylvania, April 27, 1971; Texas, April 27, 1971; South Carolina, April 28, 1971; West Virginia, April 28, 1971; New Hampshire, May 13, 1971; Arizona, May 14, 1971; Rhode Island, May 27, 1971; New York, June 2, 1971; Oregon, June 4, 1971; Missouri, June 14, 1971; Wisconsin, June 22, 1971; Illinois, June 29, 1971; Alabama, June 30, 1971; Ohio, June 30, 1971; North Carolina, July 1, 1971; Oklahoma, July 1, 1971.

Ratification was completed on July 1, 1971.

The amendment was subsequently ratified by Virginia, July 8, 1971; Wyoming, July 8, 1971; Georgia, October 4, 1971.

CERTIFICATION OF VALIDITY

Publication of the certifying statement of the Administrator of General Services that the amendment had become valid was made on July 7, 1971, F.R. Doc. 71–9691, 36 F.R. 12725.

ARTICLE [XXVII.]

No law, varying the compensation for the services of the Senators and Representatives, shall take effect, until an election of Representatives shall have intervened.

PROPOSAL AND RATIFICATION

This amendment, being the second of twelve articles proposed by the First Congress on Sept. 25, 1789, was declared by the Archivist of the United States on May 18, 1992, to have been ratified by the legislatures of 40 of the 50 States.

This amendment was ratified by the following States: Maryland, December 19, 1789; North Carolina, December 22, 1789; South Carolina, January 19, 1790; Dela-

App. 11.10 The Constitution of the United States (continued)

ware, January 28, 1790; Vermont, November 3, 1791; Virginia, December 15, 1791; Ohio, May 6, 1873; Wyoming, March 6, 1978; Maine, April 27, 1983; Colorado, April 22, 1984; South Dakota, February 21, 1985; New Hampshire, March 7, 1985; Arizona, April 3, 1985; Tennessee, May 23, 1985; Oklahoma, July 10, 1985; New Mexico, February 14, 1986; Indiana, February 24, 1986; Utah, February 25, 1986; Arkansas, March 6, 1987; Montana March 17, 1987; Connecticut, May 13, 1987; Wisconsin, July 15, 1987; Georgia, February 2, 1988; West Virginia, March 10, 1988; Louisiana, July 7, 1988; Iowa, February 9, 1989; Idaho, March 23, 1989; Nevada, April 26, 1989; Alaska, May 6, 1989; Oregon, May 19, 1989; Minnesota, May 22, 1989; Texas, May 25, 1989; Kansas, April 5, 1990; Florida, May 31, 1990; North Dakota, March 25, 1991; Alabama, May 5, 1992; Missouri, May 5, 1992; Michigan, May 7, 1992; New Jersey, May 7, 1992.

Ratification was completed on May 7, 1992.

The amendment was subsequently ratified by Illinois on May 12, 1992.

CERTIFICATION OF VALIDITY

Publication of the certifying statement of the Archivist of the United States that the amendment had become valid was made on May 18, 1992, F.R. Doc. 92–11951, 57 F.R. 21187.

[EDITORIAL NOTE: There is some conflict as to the exact dates of ratification of the amendments by the several States. In some cases, the resolutions of ratification were signed by the officers of the legislatures on dates subsequent to that on which the second house had acted. In other cases, the Governors of several of the States "approved" the resolutions (on a subsequent date), although action by the Governor is not contemplated by article V, which required ratification by the legislatures (or conventions) only. In a number of cases, the journals of the State legislatures are not available. The dates set out in this document are based upon the best information available.]

App. 11.10 The Constitution of the United States (continued)

PROPOSED AMENDMENTS TO THE CONSTITUTION NOT RATIFIED BY THE STATES

During the course of our history, in addition to the 27 amendments that have been ratified by the required three-fourths of the States, six other amendments have been submitted to the States but have not been ratified by them.

Beginning with the proposed Eighteenth Amendment, Congress has customarily included a provision requiring ratification within seven years from the time of the submission to the States. The Supreme Court in *Coleman* v. *Miller,* 307 U.S. 433 (1939), declared that the question of the reasonableness of the time within which a sufficient number of States must act is a political question to be determined by the Congress.

In 1789, twelve proposed articles of amendment were submitted to the States. Of these, Articles III–XII were ratified and became the first ten amendments to the Constitution, popularly known as the Bill of Rights. In 1992, proposed Article II was ratified and became the 27th amendment to the Constitution. Proposed Article I which was not ratified is as follows:

"ARTICLE THE FIRST

"After the first enumeration required by the first article of the Constitution, there shall be one Representative for every thirty thousand, until the number shall amount to one hundred, after which the proportion shall be so regulated by Congress, that there shall be not less than one-hundred Representatives, nor less than one Representative for every forty thousand persons, until the number of Representatives shall amount to two hundred; after which the proportion shall be so regulated by Congress, that there shall not be less than two hundred Representatives, nor more than one Representative for every fifty thousand persons."

Thereafter, in the 2d session of the Eleventh Congress, the Congress proposed the following article of amendment to the Constitution relating to acceptance by citizens of the United States of titles of nobility from any foreign government.

The proposed amendment, which was not ratified by three-fourths of the States, is as follows:

Resolved by the Senate and House of Representatives of the United States of America in Congress assembled, two thirds of both houses concurring, That the following section be submitted to the legislatures of the several states, which, when ratified by the legislatures of three fourths of the states, shall be valid and binding, as a part of the constitution of the United States.

If any citizen of the United States shall accept, claim, receive or retain any title of nobility or honour, or shall, without the consent of Congress, accept and retain any present, pension, office or emolument of any kind whatever, from any emperor, king, prince or foreign power, such person shall cease to be a citizen of the United States, and shall be incapable of holding any office of trust or profit under them, or either of them.

The following amendment to the Constitution relating to slavery was proposed by the 2d session of the Thirty-sixth Congress on

(29)

App. 11.10 The Constitution of the United States (continued)

30 CONSTITUTION OF THE UNITED STATES

March 2, 1861, when it passed the Senate, having previously passed the House on February 28, 1861. It is interesting to note in this connection that this is the only proposed (and not ratified) amendment to the Constitution to have been signed by the President. The President's signature is considered unnecessary because of the constitutional provision that on the concurrence of two-thirds of both Houses of Congress the proposal shall be submitted to the States for ratification.

Resolved by the Senate and House of Representatives of the United States of America in Congress assembled, That the following article be proposed to the Legislatures of the several States as an amendment to the Constitution of the United States, which, when ratified by three-fourths of said Legislatures, shall be valid, to all intents and purposes, as part of the said Constitution, viz:

"ARTICLE THIRTEEN

"No amendment shall be made to the Constitution which will authorize or give to Congress the power to abolish or interfere, within any State, with the domestic institutions thereof, including that of persons held to labor or service by the laws of said State."

A child labor amendment was proposed by the 1st session of the Sixty-eighth Congress on June 2, 1926, when it passed the Senate, having previously passed the House on April 26, 1926. The proposed amendment, which has been ratified by 28 States, to date, is as follows:

JOINT RESOLUTION PROPOSING AN AMENDMENT TO THE CONSTITUTION OF THE UNITED STATES

Resolved by the Senate and House of Representatives of the United States of America in Congress assembled (two-thirds of each House concurring therein), That the following article is proposed as an amendment to the Constitution of the United States, which, when ratified by the legislatures of three-fourths of the several States, shall be valid to all intends and purposes as a part of the Constitution:

"ARTICLE—.

"SECTION 1. The Congress shall have power to limit, regulate, and prohibit the labor of persons under eighteen years of age.

"SECTION 2. The power of the several States is unimpaired by this article except that the operation of State laws shall be suspended to the extent necessary to give effect to legislation enacted by the Congress."

An amendment relative to equal rights for men and women was proposed by the 2d session of the Ninety-second Congress on March 22, 1972, when it passed the Senate, having previously passed the House on October 12, 1971. The seven-year deadline for ratification of the proposed amendment was extended to June 30, 1982, by the 2d session of the Ninety-fifth Congress. The proposed amendment, which was not ratified by three-fourths of the States by June 30, 1982, is as follows:

JOINT RESOLUTION PROPOSING AN AMENDMENT TO THE CONSTITUTION OF THE UNITED STATES RELATIVE TO EQUAL RIGHTS FOR MEN AND WOMEN

Resolved by the Senate and House of Representatives of the United States of America in Congress assembled (two-thirds of each House concurring therein), That the following article is proposed as an amendment to the Constitution of the United States, which shall be valid to all intents and purposes as part of the Constitution when ratified by the legislatures of three-fourths of the several States within seven years from the date of its submission by the Congress:

App. 11.10 The Constitution of the United States (continued)

"ARTICLE—

"SECTION 1. Equality of rights under the law shall not be denied or abridged by the United States or by any State on account of sex.

"SEC. 2. The Congress shall have the power to enforce, by appropriate legislation, the provisions of this article.

"SEC. 3. This amendment shall take effect two years after the date of ratification."

An amendment relative to voting rights for the District of Columbia was proposed by the 2d session of the Ninety-fifth Congress on August 22, 1978, when it passed the Senate, having previously passed the House on March 2, 1978. The proposed amendment, which was not ratified by three-fourths of the States within the specified seven-year period, is as follows:

JOINT RESOLUTION PROPOSING AN AMENDMENT TO THE CONSTITUTION TO PROVIDE FOR REPRESENTATION OF THE DISTRICT OF COLUMBIA IN THE CONGRESS.

Resolved by the Senate and House of Representatives of the United States of America in Congress assembled (two-thirds of each House concurring therein), That the following article is proposed as an amendment to the Constitution of the United States, which shall be valid to all intents and purposes as part of the Constitution when ratified by the legislatures of three-fourths of the several States within seven years from the date of its submission by the Congress:

"ARTICLE—

"SECTION 1. For purposes of representation in the Congress, election of the President and Vice President, and article V of this Constitution, the District constituting the seat of government of the United States shall be treated as though it were a State.

"SEC. 2. The exercise of the rights and powers conferred under this article shall be by the people of the District constituting the seat of government, and as shall be provided by the Congress.

"SEC. 3. The twenty-third article of amendment to the Constitution of the United States is hereby repealed.

"SEC. 4. This article shall be inoperative, unless it shall have been ratified as an amendment to the Constitution by the legislatures of three-fourths of the several States within seven years from the date of its submission."

App. 11.10 The Constitution of the United States (continued)

INDEX TO THE CONSTITUTION AND AMENDMENTS

[1] Article of original Constitution or of amendment.

(33)

App. 11.10 The Constitution of the United States (continued)

INDEX TO THE CONSTITUTION AND AMENDMENTS—Continued

App. 11.10 The Constitution of the United States (continued)

INDEX TO THE CONSTITUTION AND AMENDMENTS—Continued

App. 11.10 The Constitution of the United States (continued)

INDEX TO THE CONSTITUTION AND AMENDMENTS—Continued

App. 11.10 The Constitution of the United States (continued)

INDEX TO THE CONSTITUTION AND AMENDMENTS—Continued

App. 11.10 The Constitution of the United States (continued)

INDEX TO THE CONSTITUTION AND AMENDMENTS—Continued

App. 11.10 The Constitution of the United States (continued)

INDEX TO THE CONSTITUTION AND AMENDMENTS—Continued

App. 11.10 The Constitution of the United States (continued)

INDEX TO THE CONSTITUTION AND AMENDMENTS—Continued

App. 11.10 The Constitution of the United States (continued)

INDEX TO THE CONSTITUTION AND AMENDMENTS—Continued

App. 11.10 The Constitution of the United States (continued)

INDEX TO THE CONSTITUTION AND AMENDMENTS—Continued

App. 11.10 The Constitution of the United States (continued)

INDEX TO THE CONSTITUTION AND AMENDMENTS—Continued

App. 11.10 The Constitution of the United States (continued)

INDEX TO THE CONSTITUTION AND AMENDMENTS—Continued

App. 11.10 The Constitution of the United States (continued)

INDEX TO THE CONSTITUTION AND AMENDMENTS—Continued

App. 11.10 The Constitution of the United States (continued)

INDEX TO THE CONSTITUTION AND AMENDMENTS—Continued

App. 11.10 The Constitution of the United States (continued)

INDEX TO THE CONSTITUTION AND AMENDMENTS—Continued

App. 11.10 The Constitution of the United States (continued)

INDEX TO THE CONSTITUTION AND AMENDMENTS—Continued

App. 11.10 The Constitution of the United States (continued)

INDEX TO THE CONSTITUTION AND AMENDMENTS—Continued

App. 11.10 The Constitution of the United States (continued)

INDEX TO THE CONSTITUTION AND AMENDMENTS—Continued

App. 11.10 The Constitution of the United States (continued)

INDEX TO THE CONSTITUTION AND AMENDMENTS—Continued

App. 11.10 The Constitution of the United States (continued)

INDEX TO THE CONSTITUTION AND AMENDMENTS—Continued

App. 11.10 The Constitution of the United States (continued)

INDEX TO THE CONSTITUTION AND AMENDMENTS—Continued

App. 11.10 The Constitution of the United States (continued)

INDEX TO THE CONSTITUTION AND AMENDMENTS—Continued

App. 11.10 The Constitution of the United States (continued)

INDEX TO THE CONSTITUTION AND AMENDMENTS—Continued

App. 11.10 The Constitution of the United States (continued)

INDEX TO THE CONSTITUTION AND AMENDMENTS—Continued

App. 11.10 The Constitution of the United States (continued)

INDEX TO THE CONSTITUTION AND AMENDMENTS—Continued

App. 11.10 The Constitution of the United States (continued)

INDEX TO THE CONSTITUTION AND AMENDMENTS—Continued

App. 11.10 The Constitution of the United States (continued)

INDEX TO THE CONSTITUTION AND AMENDMENTS—Continued

App. 11.10 The Constitution of the United States (continued)

INDEX TO THE CONSTITUTION AND AMENDMENTS—Continued

App. 11.10 The Constitution of the United States (continued)

CONSTITUTION OF THE UNITED STATES 61

INDEX TO THE CONSTITUTION AND AMENDMENTS—Continued

App. 11.10 The Constitution of the United States (continued)

INDEX TO THE CONSTITUTION AND AMENDMENTS—Continued

App. 11.10 The Constitution of the United States (continued)

INDEX TO THE CONSTITUTION AND AMENDMENTS—Continued

App. 11.10 The Constitution of the United States (continued)

INDEX TO THE CONSTITUTION AND AMENDMENTS—Continued

App. 11.10 The Constitution of the United States (continued)

INDEX TO THE CONSTITUTION AND AMENDMENTS—Continued

App. 11.10 The Constitution of the United States (continued)

INDEX TO THE CONSTITUTION AND AMENDMENTS—Continued

App. 11.10 The Constitution of the United States (continued)

INDEX TO THE CONSTITUTION AND AMENDMENTS—Continued

App. 11.10 The Constitution of the United States (continued)

INDEX TO THE CONSTITUTION AND AMENDMENTS—Continued

App. 11.10 The Constitution of the United States (continued)

INDEX TO THE CONSTITUTION AND AMENDMENTS—Continued

App. 11.10 The Constitution of the United States (continued)

INDEX TO THE CONSTITUTION AND AMENDMENTS—Continued

App. 11.10 The Constitution of the United States (continued)

INDEX TO THE CONSTITUTION AND AMENDMENTS—Continued

App. 11.10 The Constitution of the United States (continued)

INDEX TO THE CONSTITUTION AND AMENDMENTS—Continued

App. 11.10 The Constitution of the United States (continued)

INDEX TO THE CONSTITUTION AND AMENDMENTS—Continued

App. 11.10 The Constitution of the United States (continued)

INDEX TO THE CONSTITUTION AND AMENDMENTS—Continued

App. 11.10 The Constitution of the United States (continued)

INDEX TO THE CONSTITUTION AND AMENDMENTS—Continued

App. 11.10 The Constitution of the United States (continued)

INDEX TO THE CONSTITUTION AND AMENDMENTS—Continued

App. 11.10 The Constitution of the United States (continued)

INDEX TO THE CONSTITUTION AND AMENDMENTS—Continued

App. 11.10 The Constitution of the United States (continued)

INDEX TO THE CONSTITUTION AND AMENDMENTS—Continued

App. 11.10 The Constitution of the United States (continued)

INDEX TO THE CONSTITUTION AND AMENDMENTS—Continued

○

Table of Cases

Case	Section
Accardi v. Pennsylvania Railroad Co., 383 U.S. 225 (1966)	3.36
Alaska Airlines, Inc. v. Brock, 480 U.S. 678 (1987)	7.63
Alden v. Maine, 527 U.S. 706 (1999)	4.52
Aldridge v. Williams, 44 U.S. 9 (1845)	3.30
Almendarez-Torres v. United States, 523 U.S. 224 (1998)	3.36
Aptheker v. Secretary of State, 378 U.S. 500 (1964)	6.17
Astoria Federal Savings & Loan Association v. Solimino, 501 U.S. 104 (1991)	3.52
Atascadero State Hospital v. Scanlon, 473 U.S. 234 (1985)	3.52
Babbitt v. Sweet Home Chapter of Communities for a Greater Oregon, 515 U.S. 687 (1995)	3.78
Bailey v. United States, 516 U.S. 137, 146 (1995)	3.33
Barnhart v. Peabody Coal Co., 537 U.S. 149 (2003)	3.83; 3.85; 4.47
Barnhart v. Thomas, 540 U.S. 20 (2003)	3.37
Beck v. Prupis, 529 U.S. 494 (2000)	3.81
BedRoc Limited, LLC v. United States, 541 U.S. 176 (2004)	3.23; 3.24
Berry v. Department of Justice, 733 F.2d 1343 (9th Cir. 1984)	3.61
Bowsher v. Synar, 478 U.S. 714 (1986)	3.60; 4.52
Branch v. Smith, 538 U.S. 254 (2003)	3.26; 3.41; 9.10
Broadrick v. Oklahoma, 413 U.S. 601 (1973)	6.17
Brown v. Allen, 344 U.S. 443 (1953)	3.01
Brown v. Gardner, 513 U.S. 115 (1994)	3.33
Buckley v. Valeo, 424 U.S. 1 (1976)	4.52
California v. Settle, 708 F.2d 1380 (9th Cir. 1983)	4.48

Case	**Section**
Caminetti v. United States, 242 U.S. 470 (1917)	3.23; 3.36
Cathcart v. Robinson, 5 Peters 280	9.61
Chevron U.S.A. v. Natural Resources Defense Council, 467 U.S. 837 (1984)	3.62
Chickasaw Nation v. United States, 534 U.S. 84 (2001)	3.21; 3.34
Chisom v. Roemer, 501 U.S. 380 (1991)	4.11
Christensen v. Harris County, 529 U.S. 576 (2000)	3.85
Chrysler Corp. v. Brown, 441 U.S. 281 (1979)	3.76
Church of Scientology of California v. IRS, 484 U.S. 9 (1987)	3.72
Church of the Holy Trinity v. United States, 143 U.S. 457 (1892)	3.23; 3.26
Circuit City v. Adams, 532 U.S. 105 (2001)	3.85
Citizens to Preserve Overton Park v. Volpe, 401 U.S. 402 (1971)	3.30; 4.48
City of Chicago v. Morales, 527 U.S. 41 (1999)	3.14
Clifton D. Mayhew, Inc. v. Wirtz, 413 F.2d 658 (4th Cir. 1969)	3.61
Coleman v. Miller, 307 U.S. 433 (1939)	5.53
Conroy v. Aniskoff, 507 U.S. 511 (1993)	3.21
Cottage Savings Assn. v. Commissioner, 499 U.S. 554 (1991)	9.35
D.C. Federation of Civic Associations v. Volpe, 459 F.2d 1231 (D.C. Cir. 1971)	9.41
Dastar Corp. v. Twentieth Century Fox Film Corp., 539 U.S. 23 (2003)	3.83; 9.10
DeBartolo Corp. v. Florida Gulf Coast Trades Council, 485 U.S. 568 (1988)	3.51
Demore v. Kim, 538 U.S. 510 (2003)	3.52
Desert Palace v. Costa, 539 U.S. 90 (2003)	3.83
Director of Revenue of Missouri v. CoBank, ACB, 531 U.S. 316 (2001)	3.83
Director, Office of Workers' Compensation Programs, United States Department of Labor v. Peabody Coal Co., 554 F.2d 310 (7th Cir. 1977)	9.61

Case	Section
Doe v. Chao, 540 U.S. 614 (2004)	3.74; 3.78; 3.83
Dole Food Company v. Patrickson, 538 U.S. 468 (2003)	3.83
Dole v. United Steelworkers of America, 494 U.S. 26 (1990)	3.36; 3.84
EEOC v. Arabian American Oil Co., 499 U.S. 244 (1991)	3.52
Federal Crop Insurance Corp. v. Merrill, 332 U.S. 380 (1947)	4.41
Federal Deposit Insurance Corporation v. Meyer, 510 U.S. 471 (1994)	3.24
Field v. Clark, 143 U.S. 649 (1891)	2.90
Finley v. United States, 490 U.S. 545 (1989)	3.12
Food and Drug Administration v. Brown & Williamson Tobacco Corp., 529 U.S. 120 (2000)	3.41
Fourco Glass Co. v. Transmirra Products Corp., 353 U.S. 222 (1957)	3.35
Fox v. Standard Oil Co., 294 U.S. 87 (1935)	3.78
Franklin v. Massachusetts, 505 U.S. 788 (1992)	3.52
Garcia v. San Antonio Metropolitan Transit Authority, 469 U.S. 528 (1985)	4.52
Garcia v. United States, 469 U.S. 70 (1984)	3.76
General Dynamics Land Systems v. Cline, 540 U.S. 581 (2004)	3.24; 3.33; 3.76
George Railroad and Banking Co. v. Smith, 128 U.S. 174 (1888)	8.10
Gozlon-Peretz v. United States, 498 U.S. 395 (1991)	3.52
Greenwood v. United States, 350 U.S. 366 (1956)	3.30
Gregory v. Ashcroft, 501 U.S. 452 (1991)	3.52
Griffin v. Oceanic Contractors, Inc., 458 U.S. 564 (1982)	3.26
Gustafson v. Alloyd Co., 513 U.S. 561 (1995)	3.32; 3.81
Gutierrez de Martinez v. Lamagno, 515 U.S. 417 (1995)	6.55
Gutierrez v. Ada, 528 U.S. 250 (2000)	3.32
Harris v. Hanahan, 192 Kan. 183 (1963)	4.11

Case	Section
Harris v. McRae, 448 U.S. 297 (1980)	3.51
Harrison v. PPG Industries, Inc., 446 U. S. 578 (1980)	3.72; 3.84
Hassett v. Welch, 303 U.S. 303 (1938)	9.61
Heckler v. Community Health Services, Inc., 467 U.S. 51 (1984)	4.41
Hibbs v. Winn, 542 U.S. 88 (2004)	3.34
Hilder v. Dexter, 1902. A.C. 474	3.79
Hilton v. South Carolina Public Railways Commission, 502 U.S. 197 (1991)	3.11; 3.52
Hollingsworth v. Virginia, 3 U.S. 378 (1798)	5.50
Holloway v. United States, 526 U.S. 1 (1999)	3.12
Huddleston v. United States, 415 U.S. 814 (1974)	3.20
Hughey v. United States, 495 U.S. 411 (1990)	3.82
Immigration and Naturalization Service v. Chadha, 462 U.S. 919 (1983)	2.50; 5.21; 7.63
Immigration and Naturalization Service v. National Center for Immigrants' Rights, 502 U.S. 183 (1991)	3.36
J.E.M. Ag Supply, Inc. v. Pioneer Hi-Bred International, Inc., 534 U.S. 124 (2001)	9.10
Jama v. Immigration & Customs Enforcement, 543 U.S. 335 (2004)	7.30
Jarecki v. G.D. Searle & Co., 367 U.S. 303 (1961)	3.32
Keene Corp. v. United States, 508 U.S. 200 (1993)	3.35
Kendall v. United States ex. rel. Stokes, 37 U.S. 524 (1838)	4.52
Kendall v. United States, 37 U.S. 524 (1838)	9.61
King v. St. Vincent's Hosp., 502 U.S. 215 (1991)	3.82
Koons Buick Pontiac GMC, Inc. v. Nigh, 534 U.S. 50 (2004)	3.13; 3.43; 3.72; 7.30
Kosak v. United States, 465 U.S. 848 (1984)	3.79
Lamie v. United States Trustee, 540 U.S. 526 (2004)	3.20; 3.25; 3.34; 3.43
Lockhart v. United States, 546 U.S. ____ (2005)	9.50

Case	Section
Panama Railroad Company v. Johnson, 264 U.S. 375 (1924)	9.61
Patterson v. McLean Credit Union, 491 U.S. 164 (1989)	3.11
Pennhurst State School v. Halderman, 451 U.S. 1 (1981)	4.47
Pierce County v. Guillen, 537 U.S. 129 (2003)	3.82
Pittston Coal Group v. Sebben, 488 U.S. 105 (1988)	3.73
Porter v. Nussle, 534 U.S. 516 (2002)	3.12
Printz v. United States, 521 U.S. 898 (1997)	4.52
Public Citizen v. Department of Justice, 491 U.S. 440 (1989)	3.26
Radzanower v. Touche Ross & Co., 426 U.S. 148 (1976)	9.10
Ratzlaf v. United States, 510 U.S. 135 (1994)	3.33
Raymond B. Yates, M.D., P.C. Profit Sharing Plan v. Hendon, 540 U.S. 1 (2004)	3.81
Reichelderfer v. Quinn, 287 U.S. 315 (1932)	9.50
Rodriguez v. United States, 480 U.S. 522 (1987)	9.10
Rosado v. Wyman, 397 U.S. 397 (1970)	4.47
Roschen v. Ward, 279 U.S. 337 (1929)	3.24
Rowland v. California Men's Colony, 506 U.S. 194 (1993)	3.42
Sabri v. United States, 541 U.S. 600 (2004)	6.17
Schneider v. United States, 27 F.3d 1327 (8th Cir. 1994)	9.41
Seatrain Shipbuilding Corp. v. Shell Oil Co., 444 U.S. 572 (1980)	3.74
Securities and Exchange Commission v. C.M. Joiner Leasing Corp., 320 U.S. 344 (1943)	3.21
Sedima, S.P.R.L. v. Imrex Co., 473 U.S. 479 (1985)	3.23
Seminole Tribe of Florida v. Florida, 517 U.S. 44 (1996)	4.52
Shapiro v. United States, 335 U.S. 1 (1948)	3.77
Shell Oil Co. v. Iowa Department of Revenue, 488 U.S. 19 (1988)	3.76
Smith v. Robinson, 468 U.S. 992 (1984)	9.10
South Dakota v. Dole, 483 U.S. 203 (1987)	3.52
South Dakota v. Yankton Sioux Tribe, 522 U.S. 329 (1998)	3.12

Case	Section
Sprietsma v. Mercury Marine, 537 U.S. 51 (2002)	6.63
State of Missouri v. Ross, 299 U.S. 72 (1936)	3.35
Steiner v. Mitchell, 350 U.S. 247 (1956)	3.76
Stenberg v. Carhart, 530 U.S. 914 (2000)	3.81; 6.17
Stone v. Immigration and Naturalization Service, 514 U.S. 386 (1995)	3.27
Syngenta Crop Protection, Inc. v. Henson, 537 U.S. 28 (2002)	3.82
Tcherepnin v. Knight, 389 U.S. 332 (1967)	3.82
Towne v. Eisner, 245 U.S. 418 (1918)	3.32
Townsend v. Little, 109 U.S. 504, 512 (1883)	3.35; 9.10
Train v. Colorado Public Interest Research Group, 426 U.S. 1 (1976)	3.25
TRW Inc. v. Andrews, 534 U.S. 19 (2001)	3.85
TVA v. Hill, 437 U.S. 153 (1978)	3.26; 3.71; 4.12
U.S. v. Welden, 377 U.S. 95 (1964)	3.38
United Savings Association v. Timbers of Inwood Forest Associates, 484 U.S. 365 (1988)	3.31
United States National Bank of Oregon v. Independent Insurance Agents, 508 U.S. 439 (1993)	2.90; 3.25; 3.31; 3.37
United States v. Alaska, 521 U.S. 1 (1997)	3.12
United States v. American Trucking Associations, Inc., 310 U.S. 534 (1940)	3.23
United States v. Bass, 404 U.S. 336 (1971)	3.52
United States v. Board of Com'rs of Sheffield, Ala., 435 U.S. 110 (1978)	9.35
United States v. Craft, 535 U.S. 274 (2002)	3.74
United States v. Fisher, 6 U.S. 358 (1805)	3.27
United States v. James Daniel Good Real Property, 510 U.S. 43 (1993)	4.47
United States v. Lopez, 514 U.S. 549 (1995)	3.53; 4.51

Case	Section
United States v. Menasche, 348 U.S. 528 (1955)	3.34
United States v. Morrison, 529 U.S. 598 (2000)	4.51
United States v. Philbrick, 120 U.S. 52 (1887)	9.20
United States v. Ron Pair Enterprises, 489 U.S. 235 (1989)	3.37; 6.70
United States v. St. Paul, Minneapolis & Manitoba Railway Co., 247 U.S. 310 (1918)	3.76
United States v. Story, 891 F.2d 988 (2d Cir. 1989)	3.61
United States v. Turkette, 452 U.S. 576 (1981)	3.36
United States v. Versaglio, 85 F.3d 943 (2d Cir. 1996)	9.50
United States v. Vonn, 535 U.S. 55 (2002)	3.85
United States v. Wells, 519 U.S. 482 (1997)	3.72
United States v. Will, 449 U.S. 200 (1980)	3.71
United States v. Wrightwood Dairy Co., 315 U.S. 110 (1942)	3.76
United States v. X-Citement Video, Inc., 513 U.S. 64 (1994)	3.82
Varity Corp. v. Howe, 516 U.S. 489 (1996)	3.21
Warden, Lewisburg Penitentiary v. Marrero, 417 U.S. 653 (1974)	9.20
Washington State Department of Social & Health Services v. Guardianship Estate of Keffeler, 537 U.S. 371 (2003)	3.84
Waters v. Wolf, 162 Pa. 153 (1894)	4.27
Watt v. Alaska, 451 U.S. 259 (1981)	3.23; 9.10
Webster v. Reproductive Health Services, 492 U.S. 490 (1989)	3.11
Whitfield v. United States, 543 U.S. 209 (2005)	3.72
Whitman v. American Trucking Associations, Inc., 531 U.S. 457 (2001)	3.83
Will v. Michigan, 491 U.S. 58 (1989)	3.52
Wisconsin Public Intervenor v. Mortier, 501 U.S. 597, 605 (1991)	3.27; 3.52
Work v. Rives, 267 U.S. 175 (1925)	4.48
Youngstown Sheet and Tube Co. v. Sawyer, 343 U.S. 579 (1952)	4.52
Zobel v. Williams, 457 U.S. 55 (1982)	7.63

Table of Constitutional Provisions

Amendment (continued)	Section
Ninth Amendment	3.14
Tenth Amendment	4.52; 4.53
Eleventh Amendment	3.14; 3.52; 4.52; 4.53
Thirteenth Amendment	4.53
Fourteenth Amendment	4.52; 4.53
Fifteenth Amendment	4.53
Sixteenth Amendment	4.51; 4.53
Eighteenth Amendment	5.53
Twentieth Amendment	2.11; 5.53
Twenty-first Amendment	5.53
Twenty-second Amendment	5.53
Bill of Rights	4.52
Civil Rights Amendments	4.52

Clause	Section
Appointments Clause	4.53
Bill of Attainder Clause	4.52; 4.53
Commerce Clause	4.51
Commerce Clause	4.53
Compensation Clause	4.53
Copyright Clause	4.53
Elections Clause	4.53
Ex Post Facto Clause	4.52; 4.53
Export Clause	4.53
Foreign Commerce Clause	7.64
General Welfare Clause	4.51; 4.53
Jury Trial Clause	4.53
Necessary and Proper Clause	4.51; 4.53; 7.64
Presentment Clause	2.50; 4.53
Recommendations Clause	4.53; 10.10
Take Care Clause	10.10

Table of Acts

Act by Popular Name (continued)	**Section**
Floyd D. Spence National Defense Authorization Act for Fiscal Year 2001	4.47
Foreign Relations Authorization Act, Fiscal Years 1994 and 1995	7.62
Homeland Security Act of 2002	2.87; 7.61
Immigration and Nationality Act	5.21
Legislative Reorganization Act of 1970	2.16
McCarran-Ferguson Act	3.14
Military Extraterritorial Jurisdiction Act of 2000	2.20
National Defense Authorization Act	6.19
National Defense Authorization Act for Fiscal Year 2004	9.41; 9.60
National Nuclear Security Administration Act	4.14
Naval Act	8.10
No Child Left Behind Act of 2001	7.61
Omnibus Budget Reconciliation Act of 1981	5.23
Omnibus Crime Control and Safe Streets Act of 1968	5.22
Pendleton Act	7.30
Railway Labor Act	8.70
Religious Freedom Restoration Act of 1993	9.50
Revenue Act of 1918	2.16; 2.85
Revenue Act of 1924	2.16
Securities Act of 1933	4.21; 7.10
Tariff Act	8.10
Truth in Lending Act	3.72
Uniform Code of Military Justice	8.70
Uniting and Strengthening America by Providing Appropriate Tools Required to Intercept and Obstruct Terrorism (USA PATRIOT ACT) Act of 2001	7.61
Urgent Deficiencies Act of 1913	2.26
USA PATRIOT Act	7.61; 9.20
Violent Crime Control and Law Enforcement Act of 1994	7.40; 7.61
Woodsy Owl-Smokey Bear Act of 1974	6.15

Table of Statutes at Large

Statute	Section
1 Stat. 24	8.10
1 Stat. 350	8.10
18 Stat. 463–466	2.85
21 Stat. 308	2.82
22 Stat. 403	7.30
34 Stat. 313	6.41
38 Stat. 220–221	2.26
40 Stat. 1141	2.16
42 Stat. 20	10.21
43 Stat. 353	2.16
84 Stat. 2085	10.21
95 Stat. 357	5.23
100 Stat. 3341–3389	2.40
105 Stat. 1075	3.14
114 Stat. 659	7.33
114 Stat. 1654	6.19
114 Stat. 1654A-461	4.47
116 Stat. 1062	2.88
117 Stat. 1743	9.41; 9.60
118 Stat. 1028	5.15

Table of Public Laws

Public Law	Section
Public Law 86-787	9.60
Public Law 91-138	5.20
Public Law 93-344	10.31
Public Law 93-554	2.80
Public Law 94-136	3.14
Public Law 97-35	5.23
Public Law 99-500	2.41
Public Law 99-591	2.41
Public Law 102-166	3.14
Public Law 103-236	7.62
Public Law 106-259	7.33
Public Law 106-398	4.47; 6.19
Public Law 107-217	2.88
Public Law 108-18	2.61
Public Law 108-136	9.41; 9.60
Public Law 108-293	5.15

Table of U.S. Code Sections

U.S. Code Section	Section
1 U.S.C. § 101	5.23; 9.50
1 U.S.C. § 102	5.52
1 U.S.C. § 104	7.00
1 U.S.C. § 105	5.22
1 U.S.C. § 106a	2.60
1 U.S.C. § 108	9.20
1 U.S.C. § 109	9.20
1 U.S.C. § 112	2.63; 6.19
1 U.S.C. § 113	2.90
1 U.S.C. § 204	2.88; 2.90
1 U.S.C. ch. 1	3.14; 3.42; 6.16; 6.24; 6.62; 7.50
2 U.S.C. § 7	2.11
2 U.S.C. § 271 et seq.	2.16; 2.85
2 U.S.C. § 281 et seq.	2.16
2 U.S.C. § 285b	2.80
2 U.S.C. § 381 et seq.	5.20
5 U.S.C.	7.61
5 U.S.C. § 551	10.02
5 U.S.C. § 601 note	10.02; 10.22
5 U.S.C. § 706(1)	4.47
5 U.S.C. § 7211	10.50
5 U.S.C. § 901 et seq.	2.63
5 U.S.C. § 5315	7.33
5 U.S.C. App.	9.41; 10.21
5 U.S.C. ch. 5, subch. II	10.02
10 U.S.C. § 101	3.42; 6.55; 7.50; 9.60; 9.61
10 U.S.C. § 114	6.19
10 U.S.C. § 2304(k)	9.50
10 U.S.C. ch. 47	8.70

U.S. Code Section (continued)	**Section**
15 U.S.C. § 1012	3.14
15 U.S.C. § 2403	3.14
16 U.S.C. § 580p	6.15
18 U.S.C.	3.14; 3.62; 4.11; 9.50
18 U.S.C. § 659	7.33
18 U.S.C. § 1913	10.50
18 U.S.C. § 2075	4.47
18 U.S.C. § 3571	9.50
18 U.S.C. app. 3	7.61
18 U.S.C. Part I	7.10; 7.40
28 U.S.C. § 47a	2.26
28 U.S.C. § 84	7.33
28 U.S.C. § 519 note	10.42
31 U.S.C. § 501 et seq.	10.21
31 U.S.C. § 501 note	10.21
31 U.S.C. § 504	10.21
31 U.S.C. § 505	10.21
31 U.S.C. § 506	10.21
31 U.S.C. § 507	10.21
31 U.S.C. § 1102	7.50
31 U.S.C. § 1105	10.22
31 U.S.C. § 1108(e)	10.30
31 U.S.C. § 1110	10.31
32 U.S.C. § 101	6.55
33 U.S.C. § 602	2.85
42 U.S.C. § 32	2.84
42 U.S.C. § 1981 note	3.14
42 U.S.C. § 2000bb-3	9.50
42 U.S.C. § 7234 note	9.41; 9.60
42 U.S.C. § 7270	7.62
44 U.S.C. § 101	2.13

Index

In this index, the term "im," which stands for "introductory matter," is used to refer to the matter (typically, quotations) preceding the first section of a chapter; for example, "1im" refers to the matter in Chapter 1 preceding 1.00.

www.ingramcontent.com/pod-product-compliance
Lightning Source LLC
Chambersburg PA
CBHW081416220926
51613CB00011B/260